PLUNKETT'S INTERNET OF THINGS (IoT) & DATA ANALYTICS INDUSTRY ALMANAC 2022

The only comprehensive guide to the IoT, data analytics and M2M industry

Jack W. Plunkett

Published by:
Plunkett Research®, Ltd., Houston, Texas
www.plunkettresearch.com

PLUNKETT'S INTERNET OF THINGS (IoT) & DATA ANALYTICS INDUSTRY ALMANAC 2022

Editor and Publisher:
Jack W. Plunkett

Executive Editor and Database Manager:
Martha Burgher Plunkett

Senior Editor and Researchers:
Michael Cappelli
Isaac Snider

Editors, Researchers and Assistants:
Annie Paynter
Gina Sprenkel

Information Technology Manager:
Rebeca Tijiboy

Special Thanks to:
Cisco Systems
Hewlett Packard Enterprise
International Data Corporation (IDC)
International Telecommunications Union (ITU)
Internetworldstats.com
U.S. Census Bureau
U.S. Federal Communications Commission (FCC)
U.S. National Science Foundation

Plunkett Research®, Ltd.
P. O. Drawer 541737, Houston, Texas 77254 USA
Phone: 713.932.0000 Fax: 713.932.7080
www.plunkettresearch.com

Plunkett Research®, Ltd.
P. O. Drawer 541737
Houston, Texas 77254-1737
Phone: 713.932.0000, Fax: 713.932.7080 www.plunkettresearch.com

ISBN13 # 978-1-62831-594-3 (eBook Edition # 978-1-62831-942-2)

Limited Warranty and Terms of Use:

Users' publications in static electronic format containing any portion of the content of this book (and/or the content of any related Plunkett Research, Ltd. online service to which you are granted access, hereinafter collectively referred to as the "Data") or Derived Data (that is, a set of data that is a derivation made by a User from the Data, resulting from the applications of formulas, analytics or any other method) may be resold by the User only for the purpose of providing third-party analysis within an established research platform under the following conditions: (However, Users may not extract or integrate any portion of the Data or Derived Data for any other purpose.)

a) Users may utilize the Data only as described herein. b) User may not export more than an insubstantial portion of the Data or Derived Data, c) Any Data exported by the User may only be distributed if the following conditions are met:

   i) Data must be incorporated in added-value reports or presentations, either of which are part of the regular services offered by the User and not as stand-alone products.
   ii) Data may not be used as part of a general mailing or included in external websites or other mass communication vehicles or formats, including, but not limited to, advertisements.
   iii) Except as provided herein, Data may not be resold by User.

"Insubstantial Portions" shall mean an amount of the Data that (1) has no independent commercial value, (2) could not be used by User, its clients, Authorized Users and/or its agents as a substitute for the Data or any part of it, (3) is not separately marketed by the User, an affiliate of the User or any third-party source (either alone or with other data), and (4) is not retrieved by User, its clients, Authorized Users and/or its Agents via regularly scheduled, systematic batch jobs.

LIMITED WARRANTY; DISCLAIMER OF LIABILITY: While Plunkett Research, Ltd. ("PRL") has made an effort to obtain the Data from sources deemed reliable, PRL makes no warranties, expressed or implied, regarding the Data contained herein. This book and its Data are provided to the End-User "AS IS" without warranty of any kind. No oral or written information or advice given by PRL, its employees, distributors or representatives will create a warranty or in any way increase the scope of this Limited Warranty, and the Customer or End-User may not rely on any such information or advice. Customer Remedies: PRL's entire liability and your exclusive remedy shall be, at PRL's sole discretion, either (a) return of the price paid, if any, or (b) repair or replacement of a book that does not meet PRL's Limited Warranty and that is returned to PRL with sufficient evidence of or receipt for your original purchase.

NO OTHER WARRANTIES: TO THE MAXIMUM EXTENT PERMITTED BY APPLICABLE LAW, PRL AND ITS DISTRIBUTORS DISCLAIM ALL OTHER WARRANTIES AND CONDITIONS, EITHER EXPRESSED OR IMPLIED, INCLUDING, BUT NOT LIMITED TO, IMPLIED WARRANTIES OR CONDITIONS OF MERCHANTABILITY, FITNESS FOR A PARTICULAR PURPOSE, TITLE AND NON-INFRINGEMENT WITH REGARD TO THE BOOK AND ITS DATA, AND THE PROVISION OF OR FAILURE TO PROVIDE SUPPORT SERVICES. LIMITATION OF LIABILITY: TO THE MAXIMUM EXTENT PERMITTED BY APPLICABLE LAW, IN NO EVENT SHALL PRL BE LIABLE FOR ANY SPECIAL, INCIDENTAL OR CONSEQUENTIAL DAMAGES WHATSOEVER (INCLUDING, WITHOUT LIMITATION, DAMAGES FOR LOSS OF BUSINESS PROFITS, BUSINESS INTERRUPTION, ABILITY TO OBTAIN OR RETAIN EMPLOYMENT OR REMUNERATION, ABILITY TO PROFITABLY MAKE AN INVESTMENT, OR ANY OTHER PECUNIARY LOSS) ARISING OUT OF THE USE OF, OR RELIANCE UPON, THE BOOK OR DATA, OR THE INABILITY TO USE THIS DATA OR THE FAILURE OF PRL TO PROVIDE SUPPORT SERVICES, EVEN IF PRL HAS BEEN ADVISED OF THE POSSIBILITY OF SUCH DAMAGES. IN ANY CASE, PRL'S ENTIRE LIABILITY SHALL BE LIMITED TO THE AMOUNT ACTUALLY PAID BY YOU FOR THE BOOK.

PLUNKETT'S INTERNET OF THINGS (IoT) & DATA ANALYTICS INDUSTRY ALMANAC 2022

CONTENTS

Continued on next page

Continued from previous page

INTRODUCTION

PLUNKETT'S INTERNET OF THINGS (IOT) & DATA ANALYTICS INDUSTRY ALMANAC is designed to be used as a general source for researchers of all types.

The data and areas of interest covered are intentionally broad, ranging from the trends relating to machine communications, robotics, networks and predictive analysis, to emerging technology, to an in-depth look at the major for-profit firms (which we call "THE INTERNET OF THINGS 400") within the many industry sectors that make up the IoT and data analytics arena.

This reference book is designed to be a general source for researchers. It is especially intended to assist with market research, strategic planning, employment searches, contact or prospect list creation and financial research, and as a data resource for executives and students of all types.

PLUNKETT'S INTERNET OF THINGS (IOT) & DATA ANALYTICS INDUSTRY ALMANAC takes a rounded approach for the general reader. This book presents a complete overview of the entire IoT and data analytics industry (see "How To Use This Book"). For example, you will find trends in the artificial intelligence (AI), machine to machine (M2M) communications, remote sensor and wireless networks and big data and data mining markets, along with easy-to-use charts and tables on all facets of IoT and data analytics in general, from the sales and profits of the providers to projected growth in the industry.

THE INTERNET OF THINGS 400 is our unique grouping of the biggest, most successful corporations in all segments of the IoT and data analytics industry, including AI, robotics and automation, cellular telephone networks, satellite communications and cloud computing. Tens of thousands of pieces of information, gathered from a wide variety of sources, have been researched and are presented in a unique form that can be easily understood. This section includes thorough indexes to THE INTERNET OF THINGS 400, by geography, industry, sales, brand names, subsidiary names and many other topics. (See Chapter 4.)

Especially helpful is the way in which PLUNKETT'S INTERNET OF THINGS (IOT) & DATA ANALYTICS INDUSTRY ALMANAC enables readers who have no business background to readily compare the financial records and growth plans of IoT and data analytics companies and major industry groups. You'll see the mid-term financial record of each firm, along with the impact of earnings, sales and strategic plans on each company's potential to fuel growth, to serve new markets and to provide investment and employment opportunities.

No other source provides this book's easy-to-understand comparisons of growth, expenditures, technologies, corporations and many other items of great importance to people of all types who may be studying this, one of the fastest growing industries in the world today.

By scanning the data groups and the unique indexes, you can find the best information to fit your personal research needs. The major companies in the IoT and data analytics field are profiled and then ranked using several different groups of specific criteria. Which firms are the biggest employers? Which companies earn the most profits? These things and much more are easy to find.

In addition to individual company profiles, an overview of IoT and data analytics markets and trends is provided. This book's job is to help you sort through easy-to-understand summaries of today's trends in a quick and effective manner.

Whatever your purpose for researching the IoT and data analytics field, you'll find this book to be a valuable guide. Nonetheless, as is true with all resources, this volume has limitations that the reader should be aware of:

- Financial data and other corporate information can change quickly. A book of this type can be no more current than the data that was available as of the time of editing. Consequently, the financial picture, management and ownership of the firm(s) you are studying may have changed since the date of this book. For example, this almanac includes the most up-to-date sales figures and profits available to the editors as of early 2022. That means that we have typically used corporate financial data as of the end of 2021.

- Corporate mergers, acquisitions and downsizing are occurring at a very rapid rate. Such events may have created significant change, subsequent to the publishing of this book, within a company you are studying.

- Some of the companies in THE INTERNET OF THINGS 400 are so large in scope and in variety of business endeavors conducted within a parent organization, that we have been unable to completely list all subsidiaries, affiliations, divisions and activities within a firm's corporate structure.

- This volume is intended to be a general guide to a quickly evolving industry. That means that researchers should look to this book for an overview and, when conducting in-depth research, should contact the specific corporations or industry associations in question for the very latest changes and data. Where possible, we have listed contact names, toll-free telephone numbers and internet site addresses for the companies, government agencies and industry associations involved so that the reader may get further details without unnecessary delay.

- Tables of industry data and statistics used in this book include the latest numbers available at the time of printing, generally through the end of 2021. In a few cases, the only complete data available was for earlier years.

- We have used exhaustive efforts to locate and fairly present accurate and complete data. However, when using this book or any other source for business and industry information, the reader should use caution and diligence by conducting further research where it seems appropriate. We wish you success in your endeavors, and we trust that your experience with this book will be both satisfactory and productive.

Jack W. Plunkett
Houston, Texas
April 2022

HOW TO USE THIS BOOK

The two primary sections of this book are devoted first to the automotive industry as a whole and then to the "Individual Data Listings" for THE INTERNET OF THINGS 400. If time permits, you should begin your research in the front chapters of this book. Also, you will find lengthy indexes in Chapter 4 and in the back of the book.

THE INTERNET OF THINGS (IoT) & DATA ANALYTICS INDUSTRY

Chapter 1: Major Trends Affecting the Internet of Things (IoT) & Data Analytics Industry. This chapter presents an encapsulated view of the major trends that are creating rapid changes in the IoT and data analytics industry today.

Chapter 2: Internet of Things (IoT) and Data Analytics Statistics. This chapter presents in-depth statistics on artificial intelligence (AI), robotics and animation, remote sensors and wireless networks and cloud computing revenues, the growth of data analytics services and more.

Chapter 3: Important Internet of Things (IoT) and Data Analytics Industry Contacts – Addresses, Telephone Numbers and Internet Sites. This chapter covers contacts for important government agencies, IoT and data analytics organizations and trade groups. Included are numerous important internet sites.

THE INTERNET OF THINGS 400

Chapter 4: THE INTERNET OF THINGS 400: Who They Are and How They Were Chosen. The companies compared in this book were carefully selected from the IoT and data analytics industry, largely in the United States. Many of the firms are based outside the U.S. For a complete description, see THE INTERNET OF THINGS 400 indexes in this chapter.

Individual Data Listings:

Look at one of the companies in THE INTERNET OF THINGS 400's Individual Data Listings. You'll find the following information fields:

Company Name:

The company profiles are in alphabetical order by company name. If you don't find the company you are seeking, it may be a subsidiary or division of one of the firms covered in this book. Try looking it up in the Index by Subsidiaries, Brand Names and Selected Affiliations in the back of the book.

Industry Code:

Industry Group Code: An NAIC code used to group companies within like segments.

Types of Business:

A listing of the primary types of business specialties conducted by the firm.

Brands/Divisions/Affiliations:

Major brand names, operating divisions or subsidiaries of the firm, as well as major corporate affiliations—such as another firm that owns a significant portion of the company's stock. A complete Index by Subsidiaries, Brand Names and Selected Affiliations is in the back of the book.

Contacts:

The names and titles up to 27 top officers of the company are listed, including human resources contacts.

Growth Plans/ Special Features:

Listed here are observations regarding the firm's strategy, hiring plans, plans for growth and product development, along with general information regarding a company's business and prospects.

Financial Data:

Revenue (2021 or the latest fiscal year available to the editors, plus up to five previous years): This figure represents consolidated worldwide sales from all operations. These numbers may be estimates.

R&D Expense (2021 or the latest fiscal year available to the editors, plus up to five previous years): This figure represents expenses associated with the research and development of a company's goods or services. These numbers may be estimates.

Operating Income (2021 or the latest fiscal year available to the editors, plus up to five previous years): This figure represents the amount of profit realized from annual operations after deducting operating expenses including costs of goods sold, wages and depreciation. These numbers may be estimates.

Operating Margin % (2021 or the latest fiscal year available to the editors, plus up to five previous years): This figure is a ratio derived by dividing operating income by net revenues. It is a measurement of a firm's pricing strategy and operating efficiency. These numbers may be estimates.

SGA Expense (2021 or the latest fiscal year available to the editors, plus up to five previous years): This figure represents the sum of selling, general and administrative expenses of a company, including costs such as warranty, advertising, interest, personnel, utilities, office space rent, etc. These numbers may be estimates.

Net Income (2021 or the latest fiscal year available to the editors, plus up to five previous years): This figure represents consolidated, after-tax net profit from all operations. These numbers may be estimates.

Operating Cash Flow (2021 or the latest fiscal year available to the editors, plus up to five previous years): This figure is a measure of the amount of cash generated by a firm's normal business operations. It is calculated as net income before depreciation and after income taxes, adjusted for working capital. It is a prime indicator of a company's ability to generate enough cash to pay its bills. These numbers may be estimates.

Capital Expenditure (2021 or the latest fiscal year available to the editors, plus up to five previous years): This figure represents funds used for investment in or improvement of physical assets such as offices, equipment or factories and the purchase or creation of new facilities and/or equipment. These numbers may be estimates.

EBITDA (2021 or the latest fiscal year available to the editors, plus up to five previous years): This figure is an acronym for earnings before interest, taxes, depreciation and amortization. It represents a company's financial performance calculated as revenue minus expenses (excluding taxes, depreciation and interest), and is a prime indicator of profitability. These numbers may be estimates.

Return on Assets % (2021 or the latest fiscal year available to the editors, plus up to five previous years): This figure is an indicator of the profitability of a company relative to its total assets. It is calculated by dividing annual net earnings by total assets. These numbers may be estimates.

Return on Equity % (2021 or the latest fiscal year available to the editors, plus up to five previous years): This figure is a measurement of net income as a percentage of shareholders' equity. It is also called the rate of return on the ownership interest. It is a vital indicator of the quality of a company's operations. These numbers may be estimates.

Debt to Equity (2021 or the latest fiscal year available to the editors, plus up to five previous years): A ratio of the company's long-term debt to its shareholders' equity. This is an indicator of the overall financial leverage of the firm. These numbers may be estimates.

Address:

The firm's full headquarters address, the headquarters telephone, plus toll-free and fax numbers where available. Also provided is the internet address.

Stock Ticker, Exchange: When available, the unique stock market symbol used to identify this firm's common stock for trading and tracking purposes is indicated. Where appropriate, this field may contain "private" or "subsidiary" rather than a ticker symbol. If the firm is a publicly-held company headquartered outside of the U.S., its international ticker and exchange are given.

Total Number of Employees: The approximate total number of employees, worldwide, as of the end of 2021 (or the latest data available to the editors).

Parent Company: If the firm is a subsidiary, its parent company is listed.

Salaries/Bonuses:

(The following descriptions generally apply to U.S. employers only.)

Highest Executive Salary: The highest executive salary paid, typically a 2021 amount (or the latest year available to the editors) and typically paid to the Chief Executive Officer.

Highest Executive Bonus: The apparent bonus, if any, paid to the above person.

Second Highest Executive Salary: The next-highest executive salary paid, typically a 2021 amount (or the latest year available to the editors) and typically paid to the President or Chief Operating Officer.

Second Highest Executive Bonus: The apparent bonus, if any, paid to the above person.

Other Thoughts:

Estimated Female Officers or Directors: It is difficult to obtain this information on an exact basis, and employers generally do not disclose the data in a public way. However, we have indicated what our best efforts reveal to be the apparent number of women who either are in the posts of corporate officers or sit on the board of directors. There is a wide variance from company to company.

Hot Spot for Advancement for Women/Minorities: A "Y" in appropriate fields indicates "Yes." These are firms that appear either to have posted a substantial number of women and/or minorities to high posts or that appear to have a good record of going out of their way to recruit, train, promote and retain women or minorities. (See the Index of Hot Spots For Women and Minorities in the back of the book.) This information may change frequently and can be difficult to obtain and verify. Consequently, the reader should use caution and conduct further investigation where appropriate.

Glossary: A short list of IoT and data analytics industry terms.

Chapter 1

MAJOR TRENDS AFFECTING THE INTERNET OF THINGS (IoT) & DATA ANALYTICS INDUSTRY

Major Trends Affecting the Internet of Things (IoT) & Data Analytics Industry:

1) Introduction to the Internet of Things (IoT) and Data Analytics Industry
2) Smart Cities Utilize Sensors and Artificial Intelligence (AI)/Create Privacy and Security Issues
3) The Internet of Things (IoT) and M2M to Boom, Enhanced by Artificial Intelligence (AI)
4) Wireless Information Systems Surge Ahead in Vehicles: Telematics, Intelligent Transportation (ITS) and Real Time Traffic Information
5) Self-Driving, Autonomous Cars Receive Massive Investments in Research and Development Worldwide
6) Introduction to the Artificial Intelligence (AI) & Machine Learning Industry
7) A Brief History of Artificial Intelligence (AI) and the State of the Industry Today
8) The Pros & Cons of Artificial Intelligence (AI) & Machine Learning
9) Robotics, Artificial Intelligence (AI) and Automation Revolutionize Supply Chain and Logistics Systems
10) Voice and Face Recognition Change the Wireless World, Enhanced Through Artificial Intelligence (AI)
11) Artificial Intelligence (AI), Deep Learning and Machine Learning Advance into Commercial Applications, Including Health Care and Robotics
12) Industrial Robots and Factory Automation Advance Through Artificial Intelligence (AI)
13) RFID Drives Inventory Management Evolution
14) The Future of Transportation and Supply Chains: Massive Investments in Infrastructure, Mobility Services and Hyperloop
15) Digital Assistants Include Amazon's Echo and Google's Home/Alexa and Similar Software Power Third-Party Developers
16) Wi-Fi Enables Wireless Traffic Growth, Including the Internet of Things (IoT)
17) Global Internet Market Tops 5.2 Billion Users/Ultrafast Broadband Expands, both Fixed and Wireless
18) Cloud Computing and Software as a Service (SaaS) Point the Way to the Future
19) Virtual Reality/Augmented Reality and 3-D Games Create Opportunities for the Tech Industry/Immersion Games to Grow
20) Wearable Sensors Track Exercise Data/Apparel and Shoe Manufacturers Adopt Technologies
21) Growth in Big Data Supported by Expansion of Cloud Computing and Predictive Analytics
22) Precision Agriculture Technologies (AgTech), Farm Robotics, GPS and Irrigation Market Grows Worldwide/Hi Tech Greenhouses
23) 5G Wireless Networks to Rollout Worldwide, Enabling the Internet of Things (IoT)/Massive Investments Required
24) Cybersecurity Challenges for the Internet of Things (IoT)
25) The Internet of Things (IoT) in Factories, Robotics and Equipment

1) Introduction to the Internet of Things (IoT) & Data Analytics Industry

To put the massive scale and potential of Internet of Things (IoT) technology in perspective, consider the following: In a world of roughly 5 billion people with access to the internet (about two-thirds of the world's population), about six times as many (29.3 billion) objects will be connected to the internet by 2023, according to projections by network device firm Cisco. Over the very long term, trillions of objects, points of geography, buildings, devices, appliances, vehicles, etc. may eventually be communicating with each other and with major computer systems via networks, fixed or wireless, over the IoT. Spending on IoT-specific hardware, software and services worldwide was estimated at $250 billion for 2021 by Plunkett Research.

Selected Technologies that Have Deep Synergies with the IoT & Data Analytics

Artificial Intelligence (AI)
Autonomous Vehicles and Intelligent Transportation
Robotics and Automation
Cellular Telephone Networks and Smartphones
Sensors of Most Types
Smart Meters and Energy Systems
Wi-Fi and Wireless Networks
RFID
Predictive Analytics
Satellite Communications
Big Data and Data Mining
Cloud Computing
Machine to Machine (M2M) Communications
Source: Plunkett Research, Ltd.

How the IoT Works: Simply put, IoT is a method of enabling objects to communicate with each other. Most aspects of this process can also be described as machine-to-machine (M2M) communications. A network of some sort is always involved, thus the use of the descriptor "internet of things."

The IoT "Network of Networks"

Eventually, IoT will become a massive, all-encompassing "network of networks." That is, IoT networks that will be based within individual home Wi-Fi networks, individual business locations, plus the networks within organizations and systems in education, health care, transportation, the environment, the supply chain, the industrial base, government, etc. will interconnect and communicate with each other in myriad ways.

The global technology sector has long recognized what is called the "network effect." This phrase evolved to define the fact that the value of a network increases exponentially as the number of users (people, devices, sensors) on the network grows. For example, an early, developmental network that enabled only a few people to email each other was of limited value. On the other hand, once the global email network grew to encompass billions of users, it was of extraordinary value. That's the track that IoT is on today—a limited number of devices in the network that will, over time, grow to hundreds of billions of devices, thereby creating extraordinary value and efficiency.

Imagine a modern cargo ship, a behemoth that may transport 18,000 cargo containers plus crew members over long distances. The vast number of complex on-board machines and systems are both mission-critical and subject to potential failures. Consequently, the use of digital, M2M communications via an on-board network is a logical way to keep the ship operating smoothly while ensuring safety and efficiency. Sensors can gather multiple points of data on the massive engines that power the ship—temperature, oil condition, fuel use and vibration. Such sensors might detect vibrations that indicate a potential bearing failure that could lead to an engine shut down. Preventative maintenance could be planned.

Other sensors might determine that the air conditioning system is having difficulty maintaining the correct temperature in the crew's quarters. Yet another sensing system might detect a leak in a fuel bunker. Continuous gathering and analyzing of such data can not only boost safety but also lead to savings of massive amounts of time, fuel and expense. Crew members on board can take appropriate preventive actions in many cases. Other situations may require dockside repairs. At the same time, imagine this ship communicating its location, speed and direction 24/7 to other ships nearby for safer passage. This occurs today via AIS (Automatic Identification Systems).

Now, imagine the same types of sensors applied to a manufacturing plant, a refinery, an airport, a commercial airliner, a hotel or a shopping mall. IoT will be utilized in all types of facilities and systems.

Finally, imagine the remote gathering of such data from an entire fleet of cruise ships, aircraft, refineries or manufacturing facilities. Highly advanced computers at company headquarters can analyze massive amounts of data coming in from thousands of remote facilities at once, apply AI to the data and make predictions ("predictive analytics") about changes needed or future equipment problems. Analysis of IoT data can show what challenges loom, what supplies are needed, which items of equipment need repair or replacement, or which theoretical new ideas will prove to be effective once they are applied to real-life situations.

The larger the pool of data, the more observable the patterns and the better the accuracy and outcomes of the process. IoT data is limited only by the number of sensors that are embedded in a system or structure, and the price and capabilities of such sensors are improving constantly.

IoT isn't only about industrial or transportation systems. It can also be applied to highly personal situations. For example, watch-like devices, worn on the wrist, can gather a wearer's information such as heart rate, exercise and sleep. The information can be transmitted to systems in the cloud where the wearer's health can be monitored 24/7. M2M systems in sophisticated parking lots are already alerting drivers to the locations of empty parking places. "Smart meters" that monitor electricity usage at homes are sending usage data to electric utilities' headquarters utilizing IoT. In fact, this was the first widespread home application of IoT.

At a 2019 National Hockey League game, chip-maker Intel attached sensors to pucks as well as to players' uniforms. This enabled viewers with smartphones to watch enhanced real-time stats, such as how fast a puck is traveling or how long it took a player to move from one end of the rink to the other. Eventually, advanced sensors may become standard at major league games, enabling fans to enjoy a radically altered viewing experience.

One of the more promising advancements is the synergy between M2M communications and a technology known as "machine learning" (one of the keys to AI). In 2014, Google spent nearly $600 million to acquire UK-based DeepMind, an intensive machine learning research group. The main point is that software can be trained by being constantly fed data, queried as to its meaning, and then receiving feedback a machine's decisions. It is essentially training a machine to respond correctly to data of a given nature or to data within a given set of circumstances. This makes M2M the vital link in many types of machine learning efforts, because M2M is the first step in gathering many types of data.

Industry Sectors with Significant Near-Term Benefits from AI, IoT and M2M

Health Care

- Remote gathering and monitoring of patients' vital signs

Agriculture

- Remote gathering of field conditions, eventually even down to the square meter basis, for monitoring of moisture/irrigation, sunlight and nutrients

Transportation

- Remote gathering of and feeding data to transportation planners, control systems, AI platforms and predictive analytics systems
- Utilizing RFID and similar systems plus M2M to track containers and shipments
- Creating M2M Intelligent Transportation Systems (ITS)
- Providing traffic flow management
- Enabling self-driving cars and trucks—instantaneous analysis, over IoT, of real-time data is vital to self-driving vehicles
- Optimizing operations for aircraft, truck fleets, railroads and ships—monitoring engine conditions and fuel usage, and predicting needed maintenance or possible failures
- Remote monitoring of vibration, stress and other conditions in bridges and other infrastructure

Energy Efficiency and Production/Environmental Controls

- Remote gathering of and feeding environmental and energy production/usage data to control systems, AI platforms and predictive analytics systems
- Monitoring a wide variety of local conditions in order to create technologically-advanced "smart cities" and green buildings
- Improving energy efficiency in air conditioning, lighting and other systems

- Improving operations and outcomes at all types of energy production operations, from selecting better sites for drilling oil wells to gaining optimum output from windmills and refineries
- Enhancing air and water quality monitoring and control; creating water usage efficiencies

Manufacturing

- Remote gathering of and feeding plant, equipment and operations data to control systems, AI platforms and predictive analytics systems
- Monitoring of manufacturing equipment conditions such as temperature, vibration, energy efficiency, materials input and product output
- Reducing plant downtime and operating costs
- Increasing efficient use of materials and personnel
- Optimizing actions of robotic equipment

Supply Chain

- Utilizing RFID and similar systems for remote gathering of and feeding data to control systems, AI platforms and predictive analytics systems
- Monitoring changes in inventory
- Optimizing the timing of orders and shipping
- Reducing inventory wastage and delays

Source: Plunkett Research Ltd.

SPOTLIGHT: Internet Protocol Version 6 (IPv6)

Internet Protocol Version 6 (IPv6) is the latest generation of IP standard. Individual IP addresses are key to the operation of the internet, as they are required for each device, smartphone, tablet, computer, sensor, etc. that is connected to the internet. IPv6 is intended to first work with, and eventually replace, IPv4. Version 6 will enable a vastly larger number of devices to each utilize one internet address (an IP address) at one time. Specifically, it will allow for 340 trillion, trillion, trillion addresses. It is vital to the implementation of the immense number of sensors that will eventually be connected to IoT.

The rapid growth of cloud computing at reasonable cost has been among the biggest accelerators to the development of IoT. The rapidly growing need of AI systems for data provides another big boost. Today, massive investments in research, development and applications of IoT, AI and machine learning are being made by government and industry on a global scale. For example, in 2018 Samsung announced it would invest more than $22 billion over the following three years in development of advanced technologies, including AI. It planned to create a staff of at least 1,000 researchers and engineers dedicated to AI by 2020.

Elsewhere, the semiconductor industry is especially focused on creating advanced chips capable of delivering on the full potential of IoT and AI. An ever-accelerating amount of data to be gathered by IoT and then filtered and analyzed via machine learning and AI will require ever more powerful chips that can operate at blinding speed. Intel, AMD and other leading chip makers are in a race to create the industry's best semiconductors for AI computing

2) Smart Cities Utilize Sensors and Artificial Intelligence (AI)/Create Privacy and Security Issues

A growing number of cities around the world are investing in sensors, software and networks that monitor everything from noise, to road traffic, to air quality and pedestrian movement. These "smart cities" analyze reams of data and adjust a wide variety of services to maximize efficiency and minimize waste in a number of sectors including energy (such as street lighting), infrastructure, transportation, mobility and architecture/construction. Data generated by these sensors and systems will rely on both the Internet of things (IoT) and machine learning to greatly enhance efficiencies in the way that people live, work, shop and commute.

For example, networks of embedded sensors are reducing energy consumption by street lights and traffic signals. The city of Copenhagen led the way with a cutting-edge wireless network of streetlamps and sensors. Bike lanes are marked with embedded green lights that sense oncoming cyclists and illuminate long enough for riders to proceed safely through (called the "Green Wave"). LED streetlights brighten as vehicles approach and then dim when traffic passes. Smartphone apps alert drivers to light changes to ease congestion. Other cities and communities are following suit. Los Angeles is switching to outdoor LED lighting with traffic sensors that detect congestion and synchronize signals.

In Barcelona, sensors alert garbage collectors only when trash containers are full. Parking-space sensors transmit data to drivers via smartphone apps as to where available spaces are, reducing the need to spend time and fuel looking for spots. Barcelona's bus service has been updated to run on a more efficient route structure, increasing ridership 30% in four years. Monitors in street lights can track noise and crowd movement, even alerting police to crowds when necessary. The city of Boston has instituted similar sensors, while Hamburg's port computerized its loading systems to streamline offloading and reduce traffic jams. Singapore is also deploying sensors for virtual mapping, vehicle tracking, crowd measurement and the level of cleanliness in public places.

The McKinsey Global Institute conducted a recent study in which it found that smart city applications could reduce fatalities by 8%-10%; accelerate emergency response times by 20%-35%; cut average commutes by 15%-20%; lower the disease burden by 8%-15%; and cut greenhouse gas emissions by 10%-15%. McKinsey Global estimates that by 2025, cities that adopt such smart technologies will save up to $1.7 trillion per year on all city services. Sensor manufacturers, software companies and data analysis firms, including IBM, Cisco and Microsoft, are rushing to get in on the smart city bonanza.

Top technology firms like Google and its parent firm called Alphabet are well aware of the business potential from these trends. Alphabet has a subsidiary called Sidewalk Labs that is working closely with U.S. cities to develop cutting edge, technology-based services that can ease car and truck traffic congestion, improve pedestrian flow and make cities safer and more enjoyable. In this regard, Sidewalk Labs has developed a software platform called Flow, aimed at diagnosing traffic patterns and avoiding congestion.

The U.S. Department of Transportation launched, in December 2015, an initiative called Smart City Challenge, with a grant of $40 million to the city that submitted the best proposal for implementation of smart city technologies within a given locale. Sidewalk Labs worked with the finalists to refine their proposals. It was a joint learning exercise that helped Sidewalk Labs better understand the goals of the cities, and helped the cities to better understand the potential of traffic analysis sensors and software. Columbus, Ohio was awarded the $40 million with a plan to deploy three self-driving electric shuttles to link a bus rapid transit center and a retail district, as well as using data analytics to improve health access in a neighborhood with an abnormally high infant mortality rate. Also, Columbus plans to create what it calls a "Smart Columbus Operating System." It will be focused on transportation at first, but may be widely expanded in the future. The city won an additional $10 million from the late Paul Allen's Vulcan, Inc. and $90 million from a number of private partners.

A proposed $50 million project in Toronto, Canada hoped to transform 12 flood-prone acres called Quayside into a testing area for urban problem solving. (Initially, the plan also included the adjacent 150-acre River District.) Sidewalk Labs was working with government agency Waterfront Toronto to test technologies including robotics, thermal power generation and self-driving vehicles. For example, robots could be used to deliver packages and haul away trash using underground tunnels. Private cars would not be allowed in the area, with robo-taxis and self-driving vehicles providing transportation. Some buildings are to be made of wood prefabricated in a Sidewalk-funded factory and meet exacting environmental standards. Automatic awnings would extend during wet weather and walking paths would quickly melt snow. Beneath the ground, Quayside would build a digital layer of sensors to monitor use of everything from streets to sidewalks to park benches, in addition to noise levels and water and power consumption.

Smart city detractors are concerned about privacy issues. In the case of Quayside, some people criticize the plan as a way for Sidewalk Labs' parent company Google to expand its surveillance reach from internet searches into the physical world. The project was scaled back in late 2019 after a vote by Canadian government agency Waterfront Toronto unanimously limited the project to its original 12 acres. The agency announced plans to further evaluate the project.

Privacy and Cybersecurity Issues with Smart City Networks, Devices and Data

Maintaining individual citizens' privacy is a major issue for smart city initiatives in the EU, U.S. and Canada. The use of cameras to monitor foot traffic and vehicle traffic patterns implies the ability to capture data on the exact location of people (facial recognition) and their vehicles (license plates) at a given time and place. That includes where a trip (or walk) may have started, what stops were made and where the trip ended. The possibilities for abuse are endless. For example, if criminals hack into such systems, they could monitor the locations and habits of people to target for sex abuse (including children), kidnapping, blackmail or mugging.

There are many issues to resolve in this area, and one of the most vital is making smart city networks safe from intruders.

Asia and Europe generally dominate the smart city trend, although interest is high in the U.S. and Canada. For example, Singapore's Smart Nation Vision is a widely copied model for smart city development. Dubai also set a high standard for smart city evolution with heavy emphasis on IoT.

SPOTLIGHT: Top Cities Adopting Smart City Strategies are Typically Agreed to Include:
Many analysts are attempting to evaluate special city-wide efforts to adopt smart city projects. Top cities listed often include:

- Singapore, Singapore
- Dubai, UAE
- Seoul, S. Korea
- Helsinki, Finland
- Oslo, Norway
- Copenhagen, Denmark
- Boston, Mass., U.S.
- Amsterdam, Netherlands
- New York City, NY., U.S.
- London, UK
- Barcelona, Spain
- Hong Kong, Hong Kong

3) The Internet of Things (IoT) and M2M to Boom, Enhanced by Artificial Intelligence (AI)/Open New Avenues for Hacking

The phrase "Internet of Things" or "IoT" will become increasingly commonplace. It refers to wireless communications known as M2M or machine-to-machine. M2M can be as simple as a refrigerator that lets a smartphone app know when you are running low on milk (via Wi-Fi) to a vast, exceedingly complex network of wireless devices connecting all of the devices in a massive factory. Analysts at network device giant Cisco expect M2M connections to grow dramatically and rapidly, to 14.7 billion by 2023, while they expect the consumer segment to have almost 75% of total devices and connections.

A Wireless Sensor Network (WSN) consists of a grouping of remote sensors that transmit data wirelessly to a receiver that is collecting information into a database. Special controls may alert the network's manager to changes in the environment, traffic or hazardous conditions within the vicinity of the sensors. Long-term collection of data from remote sensors can be used to establish patterns and make predictions, as well as to manage surveillance in real time. Another term that is coming into wide use is M2M2P or machine-to-machine-to-people. The "to-people" part refers to the fact that consumers, workers and professionals will increasingly be actively involved in the gathering of data, its analysis and its usage. For example, M2M2P systems that automatically collect data from patients' bedsides; analyze, chart and store that data; and make the data available to doctors or nurses so that they may take any necessary actions are becoming increasingly powerful. Such systems, part of the growing trend of electronic health records (EHR), can also include bedside comments spoken into tablet computers by physicians that are transcribed automatically by voice recognition software and then stored into EHR.

Connected Devices are a Notorious Channel for Hackers' Entry into Networks and Data

The Internet of Things (IoT) is a vital component of machine-to-machine (M2M) communications, and will become even more important with the rollout of fast, urban 5G wireless networks. IoT sensors, monitors and cameras can gather the types of data that can make cities more efficient (in a wide range of areas, from traffic flow to lighting efficiency); make agricultural technology advance (such as better efficiency in irrigation and fertilization) and enhance operations in manufacturing and distribution facilities of all types. However, connected devices such as these are notorious nodes through which hackers have had stunning and costly success at taking over networks and stealing data. There is a massive need, and an accompanying business opportunity, to make M2M networks as cybersafe as possible.

The long-term trend of miniaturization is playing a vital role in M2M. Intel and other firms are working on convergence of MEMS (microelectromechanical systems—tiny devices or switches that can measure changes such as acceleration or vibration), RFID (wireless radio frequency identification devices) and sometimes tiny computer processors (microprocessors embedded with software). In a small but powerful package, such remote sensors can monitor and transmit the stress level or metal fatigue in a highway bridge or an aircraft wing, or monitor manufacturing processes and product quality in a factory. In our age of growing focus on environmental quality, they can be designed to analyze surrounding air for chemicals, pollutants or particles, using lab on a chip technology that already largely exists. Some observers have referred to these wireless sensors as "smart dust," expecting vast quantities of them to be scattered about the Earth as the sensors become smaller and less expensive over the near future. Energy efficiency is going to benefit greatly, particularly in newly-built offices and factories. An important use of advanced sensors will be to monitor and control energy efficiency on a room-by-room, or even square meter-by-square meter, basis in large buildings.

In an almost infinite variety of possible, efficiency-enhancing applications, artificial intelligence (AI) software can use data gathered from smart dust to forecast needed changes, and robotics or microswitches can then act upon that data, making adjustments in processes automatically. For example, such a system of sensors and controls could make adjustments to the amount of an ingredient being added to the assembly line in a paint factory or food processing plant; increase fresh air flow to a factory room; or adjust air conditioning output in one room while leaving a nearby hallway as is. The ability to monitor conditions such as these 24/7, and provide instant analysis and reporting to engineers, means that potential problems can be deterred, manufacturing defects can be avoided and energy efficiency can be enhanced dramatically. Virtually all industry sectors and processes will benefit.

Look for data sensors in homes to proliferate over the near- to mid-term. In the insurance business, live data emanating from sensors in homes could lead to more intelligent policies. Monitoring data via smartphone could be a significant opportunity for companies in the senior care, childcare and pet care sectors.

Internet Research Tip: The Internet of Things Connections Counter and Infographic:

Network equipment maker Cisco has posted a "Connections Counter" online, which provides a running count of people and things connected to the internet, newsroom.cisco.com/ioe . This page also provides many useful links to Internet of Things resources.

In addition, Cisco posts a highly informative Internet of Things page at www.cisco.com/web/solutions/trends/iot/overview.html which includes a one-minute IoT video.

Meanwhile, French technology firm SigFox offers a simple, inexpensive wireless network, designed specifically for M2M needs. The network transmits data at a rate of 100 bits per second, which is slower by a factor of 1,000 than most smartphone networks, but does so cheaply while it fills simple transmission needs such as those from many wireless sensors (such as Whistle, a clip-on collar sensor that tracks dog activity levels). Base stations use a wireless chip that costs only $1 to $2, and customers pay modest service charges per year per device. As of early-2020, SigFox had deployed its technology in about 63 countries.

Intel and other firms have developed methods that enable such remote sensors to bypass the need for internal batteries. Instead, they can run on "power harvesting circuits" that are able to reap power from nearby television signals, FM radio signals, Wi-Fi networks or RFID readers.

Memory chips used in sensors are much smaller than those in smartphones and laptops, opening a major opportunity for manufacturers such as Adesto Technologies. The firm makes chips that store between 32 kilobits and one megabit of data, making them a good fit for small monitors such as fitness data tracking wristbands. Future applications might include location-based beacons in retail stores that alert nearby customers to selected items by cellphone. Smoke detectors with small memory chips could sense battery life, while blood transfusion bags could track their locations, ages and content viabilities.

Internet Research Tip: Internet of Things (IoT) Networks:

For more information on wireless network systems and remote sensors, see:

Analog Devices, Inc. (which acquired Linear Technology Corp.), www.analog.com/en/applications/technology/smartmesh-pavilion-home.html%20#

Moog, Inc., www.moog.com

C3ai, c3iot.com/industries

4) Wireless Information Systems Surge Ahead in Vehicles: Telematics, Intelligent Transportation (ITS) and Real Time Traffic Information

Telematics: Many near-term advances in car and truck technology will lie in on-board software, wireless communications and convenience features known broadly as "telematics." Using cellular telephone technology, fee-based telematics networks, which allow drivers to check e-mail and online services for weather, stock quotes or driving directions merely by voicing a command, are already in place. Many other features are also provided. GM's OnStar is a leading telematics system. Such systems offer varying degrees of networked services linking cars to external systems such as global positioning systems (GPS). The external systems monitor the position of each vehicle and perform tasks such as unlocking doors or switching off lights remotely upon request. They also dispatch service vehicles or medical aid when necessary. More recent innovations include ultrasonic rear sensors that warn drivers when they are about to back into something, and voice-activated phone dialing and navigation plotting.

OnStar services (www.onstar.com) are available in GM cars worldwide. The OnStar RemoteLink App affords users the ability to view vehicle diagnostics, such as tire pressure, oil life and gasoline levels, start the vehicle remotely and get navigation assistance.

Significant improvements to OnStar's accident-reporting system have been developed. The system is able to notify 911 of further details regarding automobile accidents, including the force and direction of impact and whether the car has rolled over. Through an Advanced Automatic Crash Notification (AACN) system, such data travels in real time to an internet database that alerts hospitals, police and similar emergency responders.

OnStar's 4G LTE service is standard equipment on all new GM vehicles. Most other major car manufacturers are following suit with similar products. As the technology grows, it will be able to provide more and more options, both safety- and entertainment-related.

Apple's CarPlay software displays an iPhone's screen on a vehicle's dashboard, offering access to apps such as Apple's mapping tool.

Porsche's Porsche Communication Management (PCM) system uses Wi-Fi, Bluetooth and cable to connect smartphones with its vehicles. Dashboard touchscreens are sensitive to handwriting, and links written letters or numbers to contacts or addresses automatically.

Car rental giant Avis uses a device located on the underside of a vehicle's hood that senses the car's location, fuel level, tire pressure and break pad status. This data is vital for Avis to maintain its fleet efficiently. It also affords the company the ability to make its cars more accessible to customers by creating self-service, counter-free hubs away from airports.

Predictive Diagnostics: Telematics systems that include sensors connected to engines and transmissions are now capable of providing real time diagnostics to fleet headquarters. This can be particularly valuable to owners of truck fleets, where diesel engines represent immense investments, and predictive software can alert owners to potential failures and the need for preventive maintenance. PACCAR, a major maker of trucks, worked with the former Sprint Nextel to create an onboard package that includes telematics, navigation, GPS location reporting and predictive analytics.

ITS (Intelligent Transportation Systems): The FCC set aside the 5.9-gigahertz spectrum for wireless networks providing in-car services known as Intelligent Transportation Systems (ITS). ITS includes a broad number of information technologies that can provide an electronic communications link to cars and trucks, enabling drivers to be alerted to road hazards, delays, construction and accidents. At the same time, ITS can transmit driving directions and a wealth of additional driving-related information. (Services such as this have been available to drivers in Japan for a few years.) The U.S. Department of Transportation has a serious effort underway to cooperate with a variety of industries to develop ITS. (See its ITS-specific web site at www.its.dot.gov.)

"V2V" or vehicle-to-vehicle communications systems and "V2I" (vehicle-to-infrastructure) systems are under intense development and research. The 2017 Cadillac CTS sedan was the first vehicle on the road with the technology which can transmit data such as hard braking in the vehicle ahead. They may soon be required in all new vehicles as a basis for collision avoidance.

Advanced Onboard Traffic Information: Satellite Radio provider Sirius XM, though best known for satellite-based music, has jumped into advanced onboard traffic information provided by satellite. Previously, GPS navigation systems calculated routes to a destination, with no knowledge of true traffic conditions along the planned route. Sirius XM NavTraffic provides detailed traffic information overlaid on the navigation road map, allowing the navigation system to show the traffic conditions between the driver and his or her destination. The display can show traffic delays, such as accidents or construction, and the average speed of vehicles along the way.

Waze, Inc. offers a social driving app through which drivers share traffic data, maps and other travel information, such as where to find the cheapest gas, or a friend's location on route to common destinations. Google acquired Waze in 2013.

The ever-increasing amounts of data, known as "big data," require more and more sophisticated technology for tracking and analysis. Take, for example, Inrix, Inc. (inrix.com), which gathers data from a community of millions of vehicles, including locations, speeds, weather conditions and nearby events such as highly attended concerts or sporting events. Inrix crunches the data and produces detailed maps used by drivers, city and state authorities and emergency services providers. Drivers can use Inrix to avoid congested areas, traffic authorities are able to post information on highway signs relating to problems and emergency services can respond more quickly when needed.

5) Self-Driving, Autonomous Cars Receive Massive Investments in Research and Development Worldwide

The U.S. National Highway Traffic Safety Administration (NHTSA)announced a 15-point safety assessment guideline to be used by manufacturers planning to produce self-driving vehicles. The list covers data sharing, data privacy, safety systems, crashworthiness and consumer education, among other things. A car's systems must be able to easily switch from machine driving to human driving when needed. All features must be submitted to the NHTSA for certification.

The Levels of Self-Driving Technologies

Level 0: The driver is always in total control, with no assistance. However most new cars today come with automated safety features that may adjust traction and braking under certain circumstances.

Level 1: Very simple driver assistance, such as cruise control and parking assist. The driver always controls the direction of the car on the road.

Level 2: The car can steer itself under certain situations, such as a slow-moving traffic jam. Requires constant monitoring by the driver.

Level 3: The car can largely steer, brake and adjust speed by itself. However, the car realizes its own limitations and may ask the driver to retake control at any moment. Technologies employed may include such items as adaptive cruise control and automatic lane centering.

Level 4: This is the lowest level of truly autonomous driving. The car is able to perform all driving tasks under most driving conditions.

Level 5: This is full automation, as no driver is required at all. The vehicle may be operated unoccupied.

Today, self-driving technology is largely a reality, although it will require continuous refinement to make it capable of meeting the demands of day-to-day transportation in a safe manner. Armed with sensors, cameras and cutting-edge software, these vehicles can navigate themselves completely. Machine learning and artificial intelligence are key to the development and operation of reasonably safe, practical autonomous vehicles. The more that such vehicles are tested on the road, the greater the ability of their systems to learn the endless variations of road conditions, traffic flow, pedestrian activities and highway hazards. Ford Motor Co. acquired Argo AI, an artificial intelligence research and development firm. GM has invested in Cruise Automation, a similar firm. The company was running a fully driverless test fleet in San Francisco, California starting in December 2020.

Driverless technology also relies on maps that are constantly updated as roads and conditions change. A company called Here (originally owned by Nokia but acquired by BMW, Daimler and Audi) is mapping roads in the U.S. and Europe using data acquired from truckers equipped with scanners. Google's self-driving unit is also working on precise mapping using technology that uses lasers transmitted from specially outfitted cars that create images of roads and their surroundings. Another company, Mobileye, makes camera systems that enable vehicles to detect obstacles and apply the brakes to avoid collisions. Volkswagen and BMW are equipping models with Mobileye, and will gather and analyze the images to create maps in a crowdsourcing model.

Google has been testing its driverless cars, which have logged millions of road miles. (A driver/observer is in each car when it is on the road.) The onboard equipment includes an $80,000 3-D video camera that watches for things like pedestrians and traffic lights, radar and car position sensors. Equipment costs will plummet when these units go into volume production.

Google's self-driving effort has been placed into a special subsidiary named Waymo. It has been conducting tests of self-driving cars for several years. Passengers have the use of buttons to start the vehicle, pull the vehicle over, lock or unlock doors and contact a call center. Waymo has been partnering with Lyft to offer rides in the Phoenix metro area in 10 driverless Waymo One vehicles (with human safety observers onboard). In July 2019, the firm received permission from California legislators to transport passengers as part of the state's Autonomous Vehicle Passenger Service pilot. In October 2020, Waymo began offering rides in fully driverless vehicles in the Phoenix area. Thousands of driverless rides have been provided since then without incident.

Uber instituted a test program for driverless vehicles in Pittsburgh, Pennsylvania in September 2016, and later launched tests in the Phoenix, Arizona area. Tragically, in March 2018, an Uber self-driving car (while under minimal supervision by an observer riding in the car) struck and killed a woman who was pushing a bicycle in a street in Arizona. Uber has realigned its effort by agreeing to work with Toyota in the self-driving field. Toyota announced that it would invest $500 million in Uber and that technology from both firms will be integrated into Toyota vehicles to be built for use on Uber's ride-sharing platform.

Taking the driver out of the vehicle would save approximately two-thirds of the cost. It's no surprise that Uber, Lyft and Didi Chuxing (in addition to Google and Chinese search engine firm Baidu) are all investing in driverless technology.

Proponents of driverless cars argue that they are infinitely safer than traditional vehicles. Such automated cars may be able to react to potential crashes and safety hazards much more quickly and effectively than human drivers. In addition, their constant communication with nearby vehicles would enable more cars to be safely moving at a steady speed on a given stretch of road at one time, cutting traffic jams and enhancing transportation efficiency. McKinsey & Co. estimated that a widespread adoption of self-driving cars and trucks could eliminate 90% of all auto accidents in the U.S. and prevent up to $190 billion in damages and health care costs yearly. Waymo, GM's Cruise and Apple are working on expanding autonomous vehicle service in carefully selected areas including California, Florida and Nevada.

A $6.5 million, 23-acre testing site opened at the University of Michigan where AVs are tested in simulated congested urban conditions. Robotic pedestrians and cyclists dart into traffic while vehicles navigate any number of potentially hazardous conditions including traffic circles, bridges, tunnels, gravel roads and obstructed views.

Texas A&M University's Transportation Institute oversees the Center for Transportation Safety, an organization that conducts research and outreach programs funded at approximately $5 million per year. The school has recently launched its new RELLIS campus on 2,000 acres for research, testing, training and development related to advanced transportation.

Driverless trucks (18-wheelers) are also on the horizon. Although truckers and the firms they drive for tend to be slow to adopt new technologies, some are using automation to enable "platooning," or a caravan of two to three trucks equipped with video cameras, advanced cruise control systems and radar-based braking systems. The lead truck on a convoy controls acceleration and braking for all trucks in the line which are precisely spaced at distances as close as 30 feet. A real-time video camera beams a feed to the following truck drivers so that they can see the road ahead. Traveling single file affords aerodynamic drag reduction resulting in fuel savings of up to 10%.

The U.S. Postal Service (USPS) tested self-driving trucks on five 1,000-mile routes between Phoenix and Dallas in May 2019. The trucks were provided by TuSimple, an autonomous trucking firm.

Driverless vehicles raise significant safety concerns. The software necessary to run the vehicles is vulnerable to hacking.

6) Introduction to the Artificial Intelligence (AI) & Machine Learning Industry

Artificial intelligence (AI) spending worldwide was estimated at $85.3 billion for 2020 by analysts at IDC and is expected to grow to $204.0 billion by 2023. This is an estimate on a broad basis that includes spending on software and services. Plunket Research estimates the U.S. market for AI on this basis at $80 billion for 2021. Researchers at Gartner estimated that the global business value derived yearly from AI had already reached $2.9 trillion by 2021, while analysts at McKinsey Global Institute estimated that AI's contribution to the global economy could soar to $13.0 trillion by 2030.

In many ways, artificial intelligence (AI) is a logical extension of recent technology trends. A combination of ever-more-powerful computer chips, cloud computing, continued miniaturization of devices such as sensors, and the growth of the big data/data analytics sector are major enablers of AI on what is now a cost-effective basis.

Artificial intelligence (AI) and machine learning will create vast changes in nearly all segments of business and industry over the mid-term. The effect of AI on consumers and households is already in broad evidence, although the people benefitting from such technologies may not be aware of the process or the significance of what's going on around them. For example, utilizing machine learning, Amazon.com pioneered the development of advanced software that learns from a shopper's actions online and then makes product recommendations tailored to the individual. In its early years, Netflix famously offered a $1 million prize to anyone who could engineer an algorithm that would learn from a subscriber's movie rental habits in a manner that would increase the accuracy and usefulness of its online recommendation engine by 10%. The more that Amazon or Netflix can display perfectly curated products for individual shoppers, the happier the consumer and the greater the amount of sales completed. (Yes, Netflix paid off on this Progress Prize offer, selecting the work of a team of engineers that called themselves "BellKor's Programmatic Chaos.")

Search engines like Google and Bing utilize similar technology to serve up billions of dollars' worth of online ads weekly to carefully-targeted readers of news, entertainment and data online. These recommendation engines run in the background 24/7; they learn more and more as time goes by and interactions with consumers increase; they benefit from frequent, incremental improvements made by software engineers; and they make the owners of these technologies highly efficient, effective and profitable in their business operations.

Today, Amazon's incredibly popular cloud computing subsidiary, Amazon Web Services (AWS), offers the "SageMaker" tool to enable companies of all sizes to quickly build machine learning tools. AWS also offers easy-to-deploy AI-based tools for speech recognition, image recognition personalization engines, face recognition, forecasting and much more. Many other firms also offer rapid-deployment AI platforms so that institutions and corporations of all types to easily put AI to work.

Consider the implications of machine learning for critical industrial processes. For example, airlines around the world spend hundreds of millions of dollars monthly on fuel. Imagine the benefit, both financially and in terms of reduced carbon emissions, if the air transport sector can reduce fuel usage a mere five percent through the utilization of machine learning—determinizing the most efficient air routes in light of current weather, setting the optimum engine speeds for fuel efficiency and assigning the most efficient flight paths in and out of airports by computer-aided air traffic controllers. Airlines will thereby reduce both total time in the air and total fuel burnt. This is but one possibility from tens of thousands of potential applications—virtually all factory, supply chain, and transportation sectors can benefit through such uses of AI.

Technologies that Have Deep Synergies with Artificial Intelligence

Big Data and Data Mining
Cloud Computing
Digital Assistants (Siri, Alexa, etc.)
Imaging and Facial Recognition
Predictive Analytics
Robotics and Automation
Semiconductors
Sensors and Wireless Networks
The Internet of Things (IoT)
Voice Recognition
Source: Plunkett Research, Ltd.

<u>*How AI works:*</u> Simply put, AI and machine learning work by finding patterns in data. The larger the pool of data, the more observable the patterns and the better the accuracy and outcomes of the machine learning process. Amazon, for example, not only uses AI broadly in its online services, it is successfully applying it in physical retail stores. Amazon operates several AI-assisted, brick and mortar convenience store called Amazon Go in major U.S. cities. Customers may pick up drinks, snacks and prepared meals. Shoppers scan an app on their smartphones when they enter the store, so that they can be properly identified as individual shoppers. Cameras throughout the store track shoppers and note which products they have selected while totaling the cost. The store runs without cashiers, utilizing electronic checkout and payment, while sensors based on AI determine which products were removed from the shelves by which customer, facilitating both checkout and restocking. There is the potential for a very large rollout of these Amazon Go stores worldwide, with a UK launch possible in the near future. Technologies refined in the Amazon Go stores may show up in stores at Amazon's Whole Foods subsidiary, and in its specialty stores that sell books and electronics. Based on the experience of Amazon and a few other pioneers, AI will have a very significant effect on the way we shop in stores.

One of the more promising advancements is called "deep learning." In 2014, Google spent nearly $600 million to acquire UK-based DeepMind, an intensive learning research group. Deep learning is sometimes referred to in conjunction with phrases such as "machine learning" and "neural networking."

The main point is that software can be trained by being constantly fed data, queried as to its meaning, and receiving feedback to its responses. It is essentially training a machine to respond correctly to data of a given nature or to data within a given set of circumstances.

Industry Sectors with Significant Benefits from Artificial Intelligence and Machine Learning

(The higher the amount, recency and frequency of data available, the more useful the outcomes from applying AI to such data. Health care is a perfect example, with vast amounts of patient and outcome data captured daily on a global basis.)

Health Care
- Disease diagnosis and analysis of scans, samples, symptoms and imaging
- Recommendations for optimum treatment
- Drug development

Agriculture
- Enhancement of the "Precision Agriculture" trend, for more effective irrigation, planting and harvesting
- Prediction of weather and rain

Transportation
- Providing traffic flow management
- Enabling self-driving cars and trucks
- Optimizing operations for aircraft, truck fleets, railroads and ships

Energy Efficiency and Production/Environmental Controls
- Developing technologically-advanced "smart cities" and green buildings
- Improving energy efficiency in air conditioning, lighting and other systems
- Improving operations and outcomes at all types of energy production operations, from selecting better sites for drilling oil wells to gaining optimum output from windmills
- Enhancing air and water quality monitoring and control

Manufacturing
- Reducing plant downtime
- Increasing efficient use of materials and personnel
- Optimizing actions of robotic equipment

Financial Services
- Better analyzing risk for insurance underwriting
- Analyzing optimum investments for specific goals
- Approving loans and controlling credit risk

Supply Chain
- Optimizing timing of orders and shipping
- Reducing inventory wastage and delays

Cybersecurity
- Providing the ability to rapidly analyze and react to potential cybersecurity threats
- Enabling online log-in systems and networks, to better determine whether the party attempting to log-in should be authorized

Source: Plunkett Research Ltd.

7) A Brief History of Artificial Intelligence (AI) and the State of the Industry Today

The concept of artificial intelligence (often referred to as "AI") continues to evolve, as scientists and software engineers gain a greater understanding of reasonably possible goals for this technology. In 1956, John McCarthy may have been the first to use the phrase, describing artificial intelligence as "the science and engineering of making intelligent machines." This was a pretty dramatic statement, considering the barely advanced state of computers and robotics at the time.

In 1950, computer pioneer Alan Turing proposed, in a paper titled *Computing Machinery and Intelligence*, a test that could determine whether or not a machine could "think." Essentially, he suggested that, in a situation where a person asked the same questions of both a machine and a human being, if he couldn't tell the difference between text answers coming from the machine and the human in blind results, then it might be reasonable to call the machine "intelligence." The Turing Test clearly avoids any discussion of what "consciousness" is.

Gary Marcus, a scientist at New York University, proposed another test, the Ikea Construction Challenge, to see whether or not a machine could assemble a piece of Ikea furniture when provided with a pile of parts and related instructions.

Near the end of 2015, a group of well-known Silicon Valley investors, including Elon Musk and Peter Thiel, announced a long-term commitment to raise funds of as much a $1 billion for a new organization to be known as OpenAI, www.openai.com. OpenAI is a nonprofit group, dedicated to moving AI ahead to the point that it "will benefit humanity."

Another well-funded AI organization is the Allen Institute for Artificial Intelligence (AI2). Located in Seattle, the group was co-founded by Paul Allen, one of the co-founders of Microsoft, and scientist Oren Etzioni. AI2 has developed its own complex test for artificial intelligence called a GeoSolver.

The rapid growth of cloud computing at reasonable cost has been among the biggest accelerators to the development of AI. The extension of the internet of things (IoT) will likewise boost AI. However, one of the most interesting boosters has been the advent of an open-source software coding language known as Python. Hundreds of thousands of pre-written parcels of code are available to Python developers via a simple online portal known as the "CheeseShop." Among them are a large number of code packs that enable users to rapidly create neural networks and other AI tools with limited effort.

Massive investments in research, development and applications of AI and machine learning are being made by government and industry on a global scale. Global spending on AI on a broad basis, including software, hardware and services, has been estimated for 2021 at $341.8 billion by analysts at IDC. This amount could triple by 2022. For example, in 2018 Samsung announced it would invest more than $22 billion over the following three years in development of advanced technologies, including AI. It planned to create a staff of at least 1,000 researchers and engineers dedicated to artificial intelligence by 2020.

Elsewhere, the semiconductor industry is especially focused on creating advanced chips capable of delivering on the full potential of AI. An ever-accelerating amount of data to be filtered and analyzed via machine learning and AI will require ever more powerful chips that can operate at blinding speed. Leading chip makers are in a race to create the industry's best semiconductors for AI computing. (Consider, for example, the processing power required to learn from the billions of internet searches conducted by business and consumers daily, or to analyze the billions of photos and comments posted to social media and other web sites each month.) Nvidia is considered to be the leading maker of high-powered chips for AI, with its competitors trying hard to keep pace. Other companies, such as startup Run:AI are developing software that will help AI chips run more efficiently.

Today, a serious battle is in place between the United States and China for long-term dominance of the AI sector. While the U.S. has long made the highest total investments in AI research, China, in July 2017, announced that it wants to grow the output of its AI-based industries to 10 trillion yuan (about $1.5 trillion in U.S. currency) by 2030. Firms based in China with very significant and growing reliance on AI include Alibaba, Baidu, Tencent, Huawei and iFlyTek, along with specialty firms Megvii and SenseTime that have superb capabilities in applying AI to facial recognition. In 2020, AI proved its use in rapid development of Coronavirus vaccines and in tracking the disease.

8) The Pros & Cons of Artificial Intelligence (AI) & Machine Learning

While the business and investment world are generally extremely excited about artificial intelligence, many observers are deeply concerned about AI's potential to dilute personal privacy, while others see AI potentially destroying jobs or diminishing the value of workers. The advantages of AI are relatively easy to determine and analyze. However, determining the disadvantages is not an easy task.

Clearly, AI is a revolutionary, very disruptive technology. Its effects on the economy, as well as the workplace, will be profound. The potential for employment disruption by AI is creating controversy similar to the controversy surrounding the potential effect of robotics on jobs. (The robotics sector is becoming more and more closely linked to AI—each is a vital part of the global trend of "automation," whether that automation is in the factory, online or in driverless vehicles.) A recent, in-depth study by analysts at McKinsey & Co. estimated that roughly 15% of the global workforce, or about 400 million workers, could be displaced by automation from 2016 to 2030. This isn't to say that total global employment will drop, but the type and nature of available jobs will evolve. While some tasks may be completely automated due to a combination of AI and robotics, other tasks will simply be made more accurate and efficient, and many other types of tasks will remain reasonably completed only by human workers. McKinsey further estimated that only about 5% of today's jobs could be completely replaced through today's known AI-enhanced technologies.

As AI becomes more advanced, its use is moving toward much more critical situations and processes. Over the mid-term, machines will not only be able to make human tasks more efficient and accurate, to a growing extent they will assist and cooperate in the completion of work that humans cannot reasonably accomplish on their own. (The word "Cobots," short for collabòrative robots, has already evolved to describe such synergy between humans and machines in the field of robotics.) This enhancement of labor productivity can be of critical value in a world where nearly all major nations, from Europe to Asia and North America, are facing aging populations, modest birth rates and the looming prospect of labor shortages.

Among the greatest benefits to mankind will be AI's ability to help solve many of society's most pressing and critical problems—AI will help to increase data security, reduce online fraud, reduce physical crimes, lower the cost of some types of consumer products and services, improve health care outcomes and improve environmental quality. (Unfortunately, large-scale, technology-oriented criminals and state-sponsored hackers may also utilize AI. A cybersecurity AI-arms race may quickly evolve in such practices as ransomware and malware.)

At the same time, there are many observers who are concerned about the potential misuse of artificial intelligence. The greatest single concern may be the way that AI incentivizes companies to capture more and more personal data about people and their individual actions and interests. Since AI becomes more effective and more powerful as the size of a data pool grows, AI-driven firms, such as social media and advertising platforms, are driven to capture and utilize ever-greater amounts of personal data. This invasion of privacy has advanced dramatically in recent years, and there is always the potential for significant abuse. This growing pool of personal data will also become even more appealing to hackers and criminals.

Facial recognition software and cameras that can identify and track the actions of individuals are already in wide use, particularly in China. Facial recognition can boost security at airports and help stop crime on the streets. On the other hand, some people think it is the ultimate invasion of privacy. As AI expands and grows in everyday use, such controversies will expand. Advancing technologies will boost both capabilities and ethical concerns. Cloud computing, ultra-fast 5G wireless networks and the Internet of Things will work hand-in-hand with AI and machine learning. This will be a great advantage to some firms. At the same time, ethical and privacy concerns may drive a new level of regulatory control by governments worldwide.

During 2018, executives at Microsoft advocated for establishment of appropriate government regulations covering how facial recognition can be utilized. Microsoft's President and Chief Legal Officer argued that delays of such regulations could exacerbate societal problems. Specifically, he pointed out the need to regulate gender and racial bias in facial recognition platforms, as well as the need for protection of privacy. At the same time, he addressed potential benefits of such technology, including the fact that Microsoft's "Face" product is utilized by Uber to verify the identities of its drivers each time they log into the Uber app.

9) Robotics, Artificial Intelligence (AI) and Automation Revolutionize Supply Chain and Logistics Systems

To a growing extent, the transportation industry now includes the use of robotics and artificial intelligence in terms of self-driving cars and trucks, and eventually may include a significant level of robotic delivery vehicles. Robotics are already providing a high level of automation in ports and warehousing, while artificial intelligence is being applied widely to the supply chain.

Innovative firms are manufacturing robots that make cargo transport, fulfillment and delivery services cheaper and more efficient than ever before. Take the Port of Los Angeles, for example, where terminal operator TraPac (www.trapac.com) provides autonomous carriers that double the speed of loading and unloading containers from cargo ships. The carriers are four-stories tall and can move at speeds up to 18 miles per hour using advanced algorithms to plot routes that avoid collisions and save time.

In warehouses and distribution centers, Symbotic LLC (www.symbotic.com) uses autonomous robots that move untethered among storage racks to stack and retrieve packing cases, unlike earlier warehouse automation systems that use robots on tracks with fixed routes. Symbotic's robots afford customers denser storage since they can position products on any shelf in a warehouse and document locations for easy retrieval. The company claims that its robots can cut distribution labor costs by 80%, and enable warehouses that can be 25% to 40% smaller than normal.

Vital tasks in distribution centers include 1) the efficient shelving or storing of inventory; 2) locating and picking items from inventory on an as-needed basis; 3) moving and sorting items once they have been picked; 4) packing items in appropriate boxes; and 4) grouping packed items in appropriate spots or pallets so that they will end up on the correct truck with the right carrier. Robotics, automation and artificial intelligence are rapidly taking over many of these tasks, often in collaboration with human workers. The net effect is a dramatic boosting of output while reducing operating costs. Worker safety is also improved, since robots assist with much of the heavy lifting.

The latest robots used in logistics and distribution centers are somewhat like small self-driving cars. They drive themselves from warehouse shelves to packing or shipping stations. They can tow very heavy pallets or containers of goods and materials. Managers can use data collected by the robots to improve on-site efficiency. Mobile robots from Fetch Robotics, Inc. can map existing inventory in a warehouse by reading RFID tags, and provide input to managers about items that need to be reordered.

Autonomous, mobile robots manufactured by firms such Singapore-based GreyOrange are being deployed by leading logistics centers such as those operated by XPO Logistics, Inc. These advanced, small robots learn the locations of specific inventory items throughout a warehouse. Using artificial intelligence, they can rapidly move inventory items to the correct shipping station, following the most efficient route to move from place to place within the facility. Many other robot manufacturers are competing in this space and advancements in technology and capabilities are continuous.

The ability of robots to identify objects that are in front of them has advanced hand-in-hand with the ability of computers to conduct facial recognition. This means that commercial robots can be trained, through machine learning, to identify and grasp the correct object for a given task, such as assembly or packing. This technology is being tested on robots designed to be used for cooking in fast food restaurants. A robot called SORT, manufactured by Kindred, Inc., utilizes advanced machine vision to determine how to best grasp an item of inventory and put it in a bin.

In retail stores, one of the most critical tasks is to determine and maintain correct levels of inventory of the most popular items. Giant retailer Kohl's is combining the ability of RFID tags, to track in-house items, with software analytics enhanced by machine learning, to predict and maintain optimum inventories.

While many people worry that robots will take jobs away from humans, the opposite is occurring in e-commerce sales where business is booming. While robots may be able to pack boxes, humans are necessary to process orders and fulfill additional warehouse functions. The U.S. Department of Labor reported that warehouses added hundreds of thousands of jobs between 2012 and 2019, bringing total employment in the sector to 1.2 million.

As for personal deliveries, Starship Technologies (www.starship.xyz) has small wheeled units in testing around the world. Unlike drones, Starship Technologies' robots stay firmly on the ground, maneuvering along sidewalks at speeds of up to four miles per hour with a range of two miles, making them applicable for the last mile delivery stage of consumer or business shipping. When the units reach a delivery address, the addressee is alerted and uses a smartphone app to unlock the knee-high robot and remove the package(s) inside. The robots can carry up to 40 pounds. The company's founders also started Skype.

In 2019, several U.S. grocery store chains owned by Koninklijke Ahold Delhaize NV of The Netherlands implemented technology from Relex Solutions to speed inventory replenishment and cut out-of-stocks as well as spoilage of fresh foods. By 2022, the system is expected to be in operation in all of the Dutch firm's U.S. stores, including the Food Lion, Hannaford, Stop & Shop, Giant Food and Giant/Martin's chains.

SPOTLIGHT: Micro-Fulfillment Centers

The Coronavirus brought sweeping changes to the retail sector—basically a rapid restructuring of the entire sector. Retail foot traffic slumped while ecommerce soared for everything from groceries to household items to apparel. These changes have significant implications for supply chain and distribution. Since consumers frequently demand same-day (and often two-hour) availability of goods that they have ordered online, a superior level of rapid distribution may, in many cases, only be provided by creating "micro-fulfillment centers." These centers are small, local warehousing, packing and distribution areas that may be only a few hundred square meters in size. They may be located in a special area within a retail store, or they may be free-standing facilities, often near the store. Thus, the centers are typically within dense population areas. (This is a sharp contrast to traditional fulfilment centers that typically are of massive size and often located a significant drive-time away from densely populated markets.) Micro-Fulfillment works best when coupled with systems and equipment designed especially for this purpose, and specialized robotics and related software are a great tool for this strategy.

10) Voice, Face & Image Recognition Change the Wireless World, Enhanced Through Artificial Intelligence (AI)

With the advent of voice recognition via Siri, Apple's virtual personal iPhone assistant, the wireless market changed irrevocably. Siri not only translates spoken words into text in the form of e-mails, text messages and reminders, it responds to voice commands for such tasks as making phone calls, and it searches the internet for answers to spoken questions. Siri created a major boost to both business and consumer interest in voice recognition.

Significant advancements in voice recognition on the latest smartphone software from Microsoft, Apple and other leading firms continue to be introduced. Using technology originally developed by Nuance Communications as an app, Siri and similar technologies turn voice recognition capability into a mobile everyday tool. It understands natural language including colloquialisms and some nuances of context. For example, ask Siri "Will the weather be nice?" and the response might be "No, probably not so nice today through this Wednesday," along with the display of the local weather forecast for the next six days. Ask it to find the calorie count in a Big Mac and Siri searches online for nutritional information from McDonald's and displays it.

Siri continues to evolve with subsequent updates to Apple's mobile operating system. Siri's voice can now be either male or female, there are new animations, and the system has faster response times. In addition, Siri checks more sources for answers to queries, and performs more tasks such as returning calls, voicemail playback and controlling iTunes Radio. This technology has been incorporated in Apple's HomePod digital assistant, intended to compete with similar products pioneered by Google and Amazon. Most importantly, these technologies rely on artificial intelligence and machine learning in order to continuously improve accuracy and capabilities.

Smartphones are only the beginning of the voice recognition revolution. This capability is rapidly being added to all types of electronics, appliances and much more. Voice recognition is already available in advanced entertainment systems in many automobiles. The fuel for this trend will be state-of-the-art technologies that are available to third-party developers, including Microsoft's Cortana, Google's Home and Amazon's Lex (Alexa, which powers the extremely popular Amazon Echo digital assistant device.)

Facial Recognition and Voice Print Potential for Safer Account Login and Customer Authentication

A very important benefit of the evolving capabilities of face and voice recognition is their use in cybersecurity. Facial ID is slowly being rolled out as an additional method of login identification, for everything from smartphones to the apps that reside on them. Meanwhile, call centers, such as those at banks and investment companies, are enthusiastic about capturing voice prints from their customers, and then utilizing artificial intelligence to match up their voices on future telephone calls. Although some hackers, with great effort, may be able to fake facial or voice attributes, these methods are, at the very least, a reasonable additional layer of login security for multi-factor authentication.

The newest smartphones have cutting-edge cameras capable of scanning 3-D objects. Samsung and Apple both offer models (the Galaxy and the iPhone respectively) with cameras that can scan faces to unlock phone screens, rather than relying on fingerprint recognition or a manually typed passcode. In the near future, smartphone cameras will be able to scan text and translate it into different languages. Apple acquired PrimeSense, a company that developed depth-sensing camera systems used in Microsoft's Kinect motion-sensitive devices, to help build its face recognition technology.

OpenAI (openai.com) created GPT-3, or Generative Pre-trained Transformer 3. It uses language-processing algorithms mined from roughly 570 gigabytes of data gathered by internet crawling, enabling it to answer questions, write essays and summaries, translate languages, create memos or program computer code.

Elsewhere, the Allen Institute for Artificial Intelligence (AI2, allenai.org) developed a model that can create images from a text caption. In the same vein, the University of North Carolina, Chapel Hill's scientists came up with a method that combines images with existing language models, resulting in amped up reading comprehension. These are breakthroughs that will greatly enhance machines' ability to perform complex tasks.

11) Artificial Intelligence (AI), Deep Learning and Machine Learning Advance into Commercial Applications, Including Health Care and Robotics

While the practical definition and ultimate capabilities of AI are debated, industry has put AI to work and continues to invest very heavily in advanced development. Today, AI has synergies with many highly advanced technologies such as virtual reality, factory automation, robotics, self-driving cars, speech recognition and predictive analytics.

One of the more promising advancements is called "deep learning." Google spent nearly $600 million to acquire UK-based DeepMind, an intensive learning research group. Deep learning is sometimes referred to in conjunction with phrases such as "machine learning" and "neural networking." The main point is that software can be trained by being constantly fed data, queried as to its meaning, and receiving feedback to its responses. It is essentially training a machine to respond correctly to data of a given nature or to data within a given set of circumstances.

The most compelling opportunities for the development and use of artificial intelligence software may be in engineering/research, investment analysis and, especially, health care. Simply put, health care is one of the world's largest and fastest-growing industries, and virtually all of the government and private health initiatives that pay for health care are desperately seeking ways to improve patient care outcomes, cut billing fraud, create operating efficiencies and generally slow the growth of costs overall.

Google and U.S. hospital chain HCA Healthcare, Inc. signed a deal in May 2021 to develop algorithms that will analyze data from digital health care records for 32 million patients. The goal is to improve operating efficiency and promote better medical efficacy. The technology may boost patient monitoring and assist medical personnel in making treatment decisions. Google also signed a similar deal with the Mayo Clinic

IBM created a business unit called Watson Health, based on its advanced "Watson" supercomputing-artificial intelligence hardware/software technology, combined with massive health care database firms that it acquired. In early 2016, IBM announced the acquisition of Truven Health Analytics, Inc. for $2.6 billion, for the Watson Health unit. In early 2022, IBM agreed to sell some of its Watson Health unit data and analytics to private equity firm Francisco Partners for more than $1 billion to increase IBM's focus on its hybrid cloud and AI strategy. Nonetheless, technology firms have found that AI faces multiple challenges in analyzing complicated medical conditions in a manner that can improve treatments and outcomes.

By some estimates, the amount of digital health care data doubles every 60 days. One of the first commercial applications of AI to medical equipment to be approved by the FDA was the Acumen Hypotension Prediction Index. This system utilizes machine learning based to alert doctors in real time to the probability that a patient's blood pressure might plummet. It is applicable to patients in life-threatening situations, such as those that doctors are attempting to stabilize after surgery or a trauma. Likewise, AI has tremendous promise for enhancing the ability of ambulance and emergency room personnel to instantly diagnose patient conditions and suggest the best possible treatment—even before the patient arrives at the hospital.

Elsewhere, demand is growing for advanced data tools in factories in order to monitor operations and equipment performance. This will increase efficiency and speed as well as reduce waste. According to some analysts, global manufacturers are expected to increase spending on data management and analytics to $20 billion by 2026, up from approximately $5 billion in 2020.

However, a significant portion of the investment in systems that gather and analyze data needs to focus on cybersecurity. Data gathering via sensors, customer/patient records, webcams and monitors is an invitation for hackers to attempt to use such devices and records as ways to hack into networks for ransomware or data theft. Connected devices at homes and government/commercial facilities (including everything from webcams to digital door locks to smart thermostats) are extremely susceptible to easy hacking, unless they are properly installed with strong passwords and protected by firewalls or similar authentication systems.

12) Industrial Robots and Factory Automation Advance Through Artificial Intelligence (AI)

The ISO 8373 defines industrial robots as being automatically controlled, reprogrammable, featuring a multipurpose manipulator capable of movement in three or more directions, including linear or rotational movement. It may be either fixed or mobile.

The type of joints used industrial robots indicate the classification and potential uses of a robot. The primary types of joints include:

Revolute joints—may include a hinge, a pin or an axle. They have one degree of freedom (DoF). That is, they can move in one direction or one manner.

Prismatic joints—also have one DoF. They move along a fixed axis. That is, they are pistons or similar sliding objects.

Spherical joints—with three DoFs. They can rotate or pivot around a round bearing. Ball joints used in automobiles are spherical joints.

Industrial robots are further classified by their mechanical organization:

- Articulated robots—feature an arm that can closely resemble the movement of a human arm. The arm may have several joints that are revolute joints.
- Cylindrical robots—feature an arm and design that do well in circular workspaces. They may include a combination of revolute and prismatic joints.
- Cartesian robots—feature an arm that has prismatic joints only and tend to be linear in action. This type of robot typically has great strength and lifting capacity. A gantry robot is a related type of cartesian robot.
- Parallel robots (also known as "parallel manipulators")—consist of three or more rotary or prismatic rotation points (axes). They can be used to manipulate large loads. A flight simulator (used to train pilots on the ground in a virtual environment) may be manipulated by a parallel robot.
- SCARA robots (Selective Compliance Arm for Robotic Assembly, or Selective Compliance Articulated Robot Arm)—a robot used to install components and move parts. It can mimic the motions of a human arm.

An additional, informal classification of robots is collaborative robots, or "cobots." This refers to robots that work closely alongside human workers, with the intent of making repetitive tasks easier and faster to complete.

The International Federation of Robotics (IFR) estimated the total, worldwide base of operational industrial robots at the end of 2020 would be about 3 million, growing to 4 million by 2022.

The automotive and electronics industries have been prime drivers of robot sector growth in recent years. The largest markets for sales of robots are China, Korea, Japan, the U.S. and Germany. U.S. investment in factory automation and robotics is expected to be very substantial in coming years. China is investing very heavily in both robots within its factories and the development of its own robotic technologies.

China used its massive population base (1.4 billion), low wages and heavy investment of funds by both government agencies and corporations (domestic and foreign), to become a massive manufacturing engine over several decades. Today, however, China is at a dramatic point of change, with rapidly rising wages, an aging population, a shrinking workforce and very effective competition from lower-cost nations such as Vietnam. Consequently, China is seen as one of the highest growth markets in the world for factory automation. Chinese government policies focus on automating many key manufacturing and technology sectors, including automobiles, electronics, home appliances, logistics and food production. Chinese robotics makers such as Anhui Effort Intelligent Equipment and Siasun Robot & Automation are expected to compete heavily against Western companies like Adept Technology for dominance in the global robotics market. Artificial intelligence and automation are a particular focus of China's long-term plans. Robotics companies plan significant investments in China-based factories and marketing efforts to capture their share of this market.

China's government launched an initiative to make billions of yuan available for manufacturers to upgrade their facilities and technology with robots. The region of Guangdong pledged to invest $150 billion in industrial robotic equipment and the creation of two centers for advanced automation.

Robotics will not only help China with its workforce challenges while restraining total wage costs, it will also assist China in its vital effort to move its manufacturing upmarket into aerospace, medical technology and other sectors requiring very high levels of manufacturing precision and quality.

Pros and Cons-Are Robots Stealing Jobs?

Taiwanese venture capitalist and artificial intelligence (AI) expert Kai-Fu Lee forecasted in early 2019 that 40% of global jobs will be replaced by robots capable of automating tasks, particularly those relating to self-driving cars and trucks over the next 15 years. It remains to be seen whether such a high level of jobs might be affected. On the positive side, if prices decrease due to robotics in sectors such as auto manufacturing, consumers may have more to spend which will create jobs in other sectors. Deloitte Consulting expects 2 million new positions in the manufacturing sector by 2025 through the development of new technologies.

In order to fill those jobs, workers will require extensive training in advanced factory automation systems and computerized machine tools. Meanwhile, faster, cheaper robots are becoming available, making them affordable (as little as $25,000) for small to medium-sized factories. What remains to be seen is if the expected wave of new robotic technologies, such as drones and driverless cars, will spill over with further negative effects on employment and wages.

In the automotive sector, General Motors (GM) is working with Fanuc, a Japanese robotics manufacturer, Cisco Systems and Rockwell Automation to monitor robots and plant working conditions (such as temperature and humidity). Gathered data, stored in a cloud network, is analyzed and workers can service robots before they break or alter conditions to limit costly downtime when robots fail.

The future of the robotics and factory automation industry is extremely bright. China is a perfect example of the types of trends that will drive the industry forward: rising wages, a rapidly growing manufacturing sector, soaring global trade in manufactured goods and demographic challenges. Combined with today's very low penetration of robotics in most of the world's nations, dramatic increases in industrial robotics sales will occur for decades to come. Industries that will rely more and more on robotics and automation include food processing, pharmaceuticals, oil and gas, logistics and warehousing, automobile manufacturing, chemicals and textiles.

New cutting-edge robots allow humans to work alongside them. Thought to be too dangerous until recently, new models such as Baxter, made by Rethink Robotics, "learns" new tasks when a human moves the robot's arms through an operation. Baxter is in use on U.S. conveyor lines helping package items. Auto maker BMW uses heavy assembly robots made by Universal Robots to help humans complete final vehicle door assembly.

The transportation and logistics sector will be heavily influenced by robotics. For example, giant robots are in use at the Port of Los Angeles and the Port of Long Beach in the U.S. to unload container ships and move cargo containers on the docks. The Port of Long Beach has an automated terminal with a capacity of handling 3.3 million 20-foot container units yearly. Industry analysts estimate that robots can improve dock productivity by as much as 30%.

New U.S. tax rules are spurring the modernization of American factories, through incentives to invest in plants and machinery. Between 2018 and 2023, the new tax code allows companies to take an immediate write-off of the cost of new equipment, which will boost the installation of robots.

13) RFID Drives Inventory Management Evolution

The biggest technology breakthrough in inventory management is RFID (radio frequency identification)—the placement of microchips in product containers, cartons and packaging, combined with the use of special sensors in warehouses, hand-held scanners or store shelves that alert a central inventory management system as to shipment arrivals, product purchases and the need to restock inventory, communicating via wireless means. From loading docks to cash registers to parking lots, RFID readers have the potential to wirelessly track the movement of each and every item of inventory. Bar codes will be replaced by Electronic Product Codes (EPC), which are stored in RFID microchips. In retail stores, the chips could even eliminate the need to scan each item at checkout. Checkout stations will be equipped with receivers that automatically calculate purchases of an entire cart of merchandise at a time, rather than each individual item. These systems can lead to reductions in shoplifting and the elimination of costly manual inventory counts.

Leading suppliers of RFID equipment include:

Alien Technology, www.alientechnology.com
Avery Dennison, www.averydennison.com
Dust Networks, www.linear.com/products/wireless_sensor_networks_-_dust_networks (a subsidiary of Linear Technology)
Intermec Technologies, www.intermec.com (a subsidiary of Honeywell International, Inc.)
Millennial Net, www.millennialnet.com
ODIN, www.odinrfid.com
Radiant RFID, www.radiantrfid.com
Savi, www.savi.com
SSE Technologies, www.ssetechnologies.com
Texas Instruments, www.ti.com
Thinfilm, www.thinfilm.no/

Another potential advantage of RFID is that manufacturers and distributors are able to reduce overall inventory, thanks to greater supply chain efficiency. Walmart is heavily invested in this new technology. The greatest advantage of RFID implementation in stores such as Walmart may be a reduction of out-of-stock situations. The ability to keep popular items properly in stock means higher revenues.

At MIT, experts are endeavoring to enhance RFID systems by continuing work on a project originally called the Auto-ID Center. Now called EPCglobal, the initiative is backed by more than 50 companies including Walmart, Procter & Gamble and Coca-Cola. (See www.gs1.org/epcglobal.) The project developed a common language for all RFID chips, thereby substantially reducing costs. It is estimated that costs must fall to between one and five cents per chip for this new wave of technology to be universally adopted. (As of 2016, costs in actual commercial RFID use were between 5 cents and 15 cents per tag for typical volume purchases, according to the RFID Journal.) EPCglobal has been at the forefront of design standards for all components of RFID systems, including electronic product codes for the tags and software to look after them.

Thinfilm is a Norway-based firm that uses printing to manufacture simple integrated electronics at a fraction of the cost of conventional electronics, in highly scalable processes compatible with high-volume, low-cost markets. Thinfilm has integrated sensing, data storage and display in a label format. Addition of a printed near-field communication (NFC) interface will allow Thinfilm's sensor labels to link sensor data to apps on mobile devices and/or cloud-based analytics.

Yet another breakthrough in technology is the result of efforts made by Telmex Lab for Communications and Development, also at MIT. The lab has created a tiny dot called a Bokode that, while only 3 millimeters wide, can hold more than 10 megabytes of data. The data can be read by the camera installed in most smartphones.

The next step in RFID may be a nanoparticle-based covert barcode system that can be embedded in a wide variety of objects from polymers to drugs to inks to explosives. The nanoparticles are embedded during manufacturing and can be tracked by thermal analysis to follow the life of the object. Practical applications may include document authentication, manufacturer and/or vendor identification and location verification. Researchers at the Worcester Polytechnic Institute are studying the concept.

When fully implemented, advanced RFID and electronic sensor/monitor systems will be more than mere inventory management systems. They will be able to track virtually every item made, from the factory to the freight container to the shipping line to the warehouse to the store, even from the checkout lane to the home. They could even be used to sort recyclable items for reuse by the manufacturers, following the entire lifecycle of every product.

14) The Future of Transportation and Supply Chains: Massive Investments in Infrastructure, Mobility Services and Hyperloop

Rapidly advancing technologies will relieve some of the pressure and potential congestion caused by ever-growing automobile, truck, ship and airplane traffic. These technologies can be grouped in three broad areas: 1) self-driving cars and trucks, 2) improved traffic control in the skies and on the roads, and 3) improvements in freight handling and tracking technologies. Many of these advances will be based upon utilizing remote data sensors and the Internet of Things (IoT) to gather data 24/7, analyze that input and make rapid changes or recommendations in order to reduce congestion, improve conditions or project supply chain needs.

Self-driving (autonomous) automobiles and trucks will be of particular benefit on today's highly congested roads and highways. It is relatively easy for self-driving vehicles to understand and respond to road conditions on long stretches of divided highway, with prominent striping, little or no cross-traffic and fewer impediments like stop signs and sharp turns than found on city streets. These vehicles will be able to travel while closely spaced on highways, reducing the need for new highway construction. They will also travel together at consistent speeds, meaning less stop and go driving. Fully self-driving vehicles will become so advanced that they can provide passenger transportation on crowded city streets, with safety records that will far exceed those of human drivers. The term Mobility Services is widely used to describe car-sharing strategies like ZipCar, ride-hailing systems like Uber and other alternative personal transportation systems, including bicycle sharing.

Autonomous vehicles capable of driving themselves will have very profound effects on automobile manufacturing, usage, sales and ownership patterns. At least in dense urban environments, the result is very likely to be a large proportion of individuals who opt to use shared vehicles rather than user-owned cars. Automobile makers are keenly aware that individual car ownership may decline over the long term. These firms are positioning themselves to build and distribute cars best suited for the sharing economy and mobility services market.

While self-driving technology may enable cars to be spaced very close together on roadways, incredibly tight, bumper-to-bumper traffic already exists on busy streets in many of the world's largest cities. Variable pricing ("congestion pricing") for toll roads, toll bridges and tunnels may be one answer, by charging vehicles, self-driving or not, much higher tolls during times of highest congestion. This strategy gives drivers economic incentive to delay trips until hours with lighter traffic. Cities including London, Singapore and Stockholm have been testing variable toll systems in this regard. London instituted congestion pricing in 2003 and initially reduced traffic congestion by as much as 30%. New York City will be the first U.S. city to impose congestion tolls upon drivers starting in 2021. As of early 2022, the Triborough Bridge and Tunnel Authority was still considering fee amounts and how to enforce them. Fees are expected to be $11 to $14 for cars, and around $25 for trucks, during prime business hours, and less at night and on weekends. A congestion zone will be drawn in the city from 60th Street south to the Battery. The city already charges fees of $2.50 for yellow taxis and $2.75 for ride hailing services such as Uber for trips that start, end or pass through Manhattan south of 96th Street (as well as $0.75 for shared car pools including UberPool and Via).

In addition to the traffic control advantages of self-driving car technology, other advanced technologies will improve traffic efficiency at airports and on congested city streets. Closely spaced traffic sensors in cities will alert ITS (intelligent transportation system) systems within cars and trucks in order to warn of congestion and suggest better routes. Advanced systems will also be able to control traffic lights for better demand-based timing.

At airports, highly advanced technologies will enable air traffic control to safely space aircraft closer together, reduce delays and route airlines so they can travel more directly to destinations with less circling and less fuel burned. Basic routing technologies such as these have already been applied to many railroad systems, greatly improving operating efficiencies.

Meanwhile, advancements in technology will improve the efficiencies of freight handling and tracking. RFID tags are already in widespread use, enabling freight systems to electronically receive vital details about freight containers, such as contents, shipper, date shipped and intended routing. Gathering big data from RFIDs and then analyzing that data with predictive software will enable more efficient warehousing and freight routing. An additional boost is now widely seen from warehouse robotics, efficiently moving the right pallet or parcel to the right place with greater speed and safety. Amazon.com, in its massive warehouses, is a world leader in this area. Automation is rapidly being adopted in ocean shipping ports as well.

While ride dispatch services like Uber and Lyft have dramatically changed the way that consumers get local transport on-demand, such technologies will soon revolutionize freight trucking as well, including the Uber Freight system. As the world speeds towards roughly 10 billion in global population by 2050, and the rapidly expanding global middle class buys more, consumes more, ships more and travels more, the opportunities for technology companies to fulfill these needs will spur innovation and investment on a very major scale worldwide.

Technologies for high-speed long-distance trains as well as light rail will continue to advance. Ultra-fast Maglev trains may eventually be funded in select markets.

While various engineering associations and global think tanks have long pointed out this dire need for engineering and construction, one massive problem is constantly in the way of progress: funding. To begin with, governments are poor planners and savers. While voters are faced with crowded, out-of-date airports, potholes in roads and leaks in water mains, governments rarely have amassed reserves for replacement and expansion of infrastructure. This means that funding most often comes through borrowing via the issuance of bonds.

Another avenue for construction, ownership and funding of infrastructure is through private companies, such as Australia's massive Macquarie Infrastructure Company, which owns and operates such facilities as airport hangars and solar power generation plants. Elsewhere, private company Heathrow Airport Holdings owns and operates London's Heathrow Airport, as well as the airports at Glasgow, Aberdeen and Southampton.

Such projects are often funded through public-private partnerships. Since governments have generally failed to reserve sufficient funds for future infrastructure replacement and maintenance, and there is some practical limit to how much of future needs can be filled by private companies, such partnerships may be increasingly vital to the transportation and utilities sectors. Examples of such public-private partnerships include a deal between the Milwaukee Metropolitan Sewage District and United Water to improve the city's sewage system and multiple new toll roads in Texas, California and Virginia. However, government assistance is not necessarily a guarantee of financial success for private investors, and some joint projects have fallen into bankruptcy due to lower usage and toll revenue than originally forecasted.

SPOTLIGHT: Hyperloop

A futuristic alternative to high speed trains could be on the distant horizon thanks to a concept from Tesla Motors and SpaceX founder Elon Musk. His idea is to build a giant, above-ground tube atop pylons in which a 28-passenger pod would move at speeds up to 760 mph. The solar powered pod would travel through the tube, in which fans would remove sufficient air to eliminate most of the drag that naturally slows moving objects. Musk envisions a route between Los Angeles and San Francisco, which could take as little as 30 minutes to travel. The tube would be built along existing roads making construction and maintenance easier, and safety features would include pod wheels in case of system failure.

Initially, Musk invited other companies to bid for building funding. Two companies competing in this field are Virgin Hyperloop (virginhyperloop.com), associated with Sir Richard Branson, and Hyperloop Transportation Technologies (www.hyperlooptt.com), branded as HyperloopTT.

In late 2020, two Virgin Hyperloop employees completed an important test run on a track in Las Vegas. The experimental pod reached 100 mph on the 500-meter track. The company plans to build a $500 million test facility in West Virginia.

Musk indicated that he was interested in building a project himself, specifically a 29-minute route between New York City and Washington, D.C. Boring Co., a tunnel-carving firm owned by Musk, will likely help develop the plans. The company initially proposed projects including a tunnel connecting Baltimore, Maryland and Washington, D.C. (35 miles) and downtown Chicago with O'Hare International Airport (17 miles). By early 2022, the Boring Co. appeared to have shifted its sights to a twin-tunnel Loop system for the massive Las Vegas Convention Center, along with an R&D tunnel in Hawthorne, California.

15) Digital Assistants Include Amazon's Echo and Google's Home/Alexa and Similar Software Power Third-Party Developers

Apple, Google, Amazon and Microsoft are competing to offer the best voice-activated systems that can do anything from reporting the time and weather, to playing music on request, to performing web searches, to telling jokes, to making purchases from internet sites. These platforms utilize the latest in artificial intelligence in order to become more useful over time. Apple's Siri is available on iPhones, iPads, Apple Watches and through an app in some vehicles. Google Now is an app available on a variety of mobile devices as is Microsoft's Cortana app. Amazon's Alexa web app is installed on a gadget called Amazon Echo that sits on a countertop, desk or shelf. Alexa software can be installed on other devices as well. Google offers a similar device called Google Home. All of these apps and platforms are voice-activated, and use connections to other apps and systems to find information such as directions, time, date, weather and trivia, or make purchases, which are reported audibly (users can choose their device's voice gender and language). The next step for these handy assistants is the ability to connect with apps relating to climate control, lighting and/or security enabling users to simply say, for example,

"Set home temperature to 72 degrees," or "Activate alarm system," and have the action performed, even from remote locations.

Importantly, most systems are open to third-party developers. For example, Amazon has opened "Lex" to developers, which is the artificial intelligence engine behind the Alexa and Echo platforms. Lex is tied into Amazon's AWS cloud computing system. Software and product developers can incorporate Lex, enabling voice-activated or click-activated responsiveness (often in the form of specific task-oriented icons or apps known as "bots"). This gives these developers instant access to extremely powerful cloud computing, artificial intelligence and voice-activation in one easy-to-launch package. Amazon charges a modest fee per thousand uses or data accesses. This ease-of-use has spurred a tidal wave of new product development worldwide, with the potential to revolutionize the manner in which consumers interface with their digital devices and the internet.

Top Voice-Activated Technology Platforms and their Unique Advantages:

Alexa: Owned by Amazon. Connects to Amazon AWS Cloud services, making it easy to embed Alexa software in third-party products.

Siri: Owned by Apple. Siri, already familiar to hundreds of millions of iPhone users worldwide, has evolved into a very sophisticated digital assistant.

Cortana: Owned by Microsoft. Microsoft had deep partnerships and experience with third-party corporate software and technology firms, making this an easy platform for others to embed.

Google Assistant: Owned by Google. Assistant capitalizes on Google's constantly evolving expertise in search and artificial intelligence.

Source: Plunkett Research, Ltd.

16) Wi-Fi Enables Wireless Traffic Growth, Including the Internet of Things (IoT)

While cellular phone companies are investing billions of dollars in technologies to give their subscribers enhanced services such and 4G mobile internet, Wi-Fi is more vital than ever for wireless access. As the number of cellular device subscriptions for smartphones, tablets, laptops and aircards has soared, so has the demand placed upon cellular networks. Wi-Fi acts as a vital relief valve. Wireless device owners increasingly want to access immense files, such as Netflix movies on demand. If the world's rapidly increasing wireless data traffic relied solely on cellular networks, the system would be under severe stress. However, since wireless device owners frequently have access to Wi-Fi as an alternative for a large portion of the day, they can switch to Wi-Fi from cellular as needed, reducing their total cellular subscription costs and dramatically reducing the load placed on cellular networks. The role played by Wi-Fi will remain vitally important, even as ultrafast 5G cellular networks are rolled out. At the same time, Wi-Fi will become even more important to the world's technology users as connected devices proliferate in the rapidly growing Internet of Things (IoT).

Experts at Cisco, with their Cisco Visual Networking Index, estimated that by 2022, the global number of internet-connected mobile devices will reach 3.6 per capita (nearly 28.5 billion devices). Smartphones will represent about 44% of these devices and connections. More than 50% of mobile traffic is offloaded to Wi-Fi rather than remaining on cellular networks.

Wi-Fi routers have very high theoretical data transfer speeds, but actual speeds rely on local internet connections. On the fixed end, each Wi-Fi network is tied into an internet router. This means that the actual download speed enjoyed by the Wi-Fi user is limited to the speed of the internet service connected to the router. If a user has a local internet connection with a 50 meg download speed via a cable modem, then the local Wi-Fi system will also be limited to 50 meg.

Wi-Fi is now advancing through enhanced technologies. Recent enhancements include MU-MIMO (multi-user, multiple-input, multiple-output), which allows a Wi-Fi device to handle data requests from multiple sources at once. Another recent technology known as OFDMA (orthogonal frequency-division multiple access) can split a Wi-Fi channel into many data pipes simultaneously. Kumu Networks, Inc., a startup based in Santa Clara, California (kumunetworks.com), has developed "full duplex" technology that enables Wi-Fi to transmit and receive simultaneously, effectively doubling the speed and capability of the network.

In early 2019, Amazon acquired Eero, a Wi-Fi startup that makes small wireless routers for home use, promising no Wi-Fi dead zones within the home. The acquisition enables Amazon to compete with Google's OnHub Wi-Fi routers.

Amazon and Apple are using devices such as iPhones, smartwatches, "smart" speakers and personal digital assistants such as Alexa to provide connectivity and power wireless networks. The companies use their wireless networks, such as Amazon's Sidewalk, as well as Apple's AirTag and Find My Network, to allow the devices to transmit tiny bits of data from any available wireless connection, thereby supplementing Wi-Fi networks and reducing wireless communication problems. Data is encrypted for security.

17) Global Internet Market Tops 5.2 Billion Users/Ultrafast Broadband Expands, both Fixed and Wireless

The majority of American cellphones are now smartphones. Big improvements in the devices, such as the latest iPhones and Android-based units, along with enhanced high-speed access via 4G networks, are fueling this growth. In addition, most major e-commerce, news and entertainment sites have carefully designed their web pages to perform reasonably well on the "third screen," that is, cellphones (with TV being the first screen and desktop or laptop computers being the second screen). Globally, the number of internet users was 5.2 billion as of March 2021, (including wireless) according to Internetworldstats.com.

Internet access speeds continue to increase dramatically. Google launched its "Google Fiber" ultra-high-speed internet service in Kansas City, Kansas in 2012, and soon expanded into Austin, Texas; Provo, Utah; and Atlanta, Georgia. This system allows homes and businesses to have 1 gigabit per second access, roughly 100 to 200 times the speed of typical DSL or mobile broadband. More than 1,000 U.S. towns and cities applied for the service when it was first announced, but Google is gauging the results of this initial effort before making any decisions about rolling it out.

AT&T initially launched a similar 1 gigabit service in competition with Google in the Austin area called AT&T FIBER. The firm offers this fast service in dozens of cities across the U.S.

What will widespread use of fast internet access mean to consumers? The opportunities for new or enhanced products and services are endless, and the amount of entertainment, news, commerce and personal services designed to take advantage of broadband will continue to grow rapidly. For example, education support and classes via broadband is rapidly growing into a major industry.

Broadband in the home is essential for everyday activities ranging from children's homework to shopping to managing financial accounts. Online entertainment and information options, already vast, will grow daily. Some online services are becoming indispensable, and always-on is the new accepted standard. The quality of streaming video and audio is becoming clear and reliable, making music and movie downloads extremely fast, and allowing internet telephone users to see their parties on the other end as if they were in the same room. Compression and caching techniques are evolving, and distribution and storage costs are expected to plummet. A very significant portion of today's radio, television and movie entertainment is migrating to the web.

18) Cloud Computing and Software as a Service (SaaS) Point the Way to the Future

There is a now-unstoppable trend toward downplaying the role of packaged software that is installed on the desktop, relying instead on internet-based applications hosted in the cloud. This accelerated dramatically with the onset of the Coronavirus and working-from-home. The trend is called Software as a Service (SaaS). In fact, Sun Microsystem's famous positioning line of long standing, "The network is the computer," pretty well sums up this movement, a thought that "uses the internet as the computing platform of the future." Microsoft, Google, IBM, Salesforce, Oracle and other leading firms are quickly enhancing their own suites of internet-based applications.

Cloud computing is the use of remote servers, often owned and operated by third-party service providers, to store and access data and software, as opposed to servers owned by the user. Firms that offer cloud services run clusters of computers networked together, often based on open standards. Such cloud networks can consist of thousands of computers. Cloud services enable a client company to immediately increase computing capability without any investment in physical infrastructure. (The word "cloud" is also broadly used to describe any data or application that runs via the internet.) The concept of cloud computing is key to the growing use of SaaS.

The Coronavirus pandemic accelerated movement of data from in-house servers to the cloud significantly. Gartner forecasted that global spending on public cloud services of all types, on a broad basis, would reach $397.5 billion in 2022.

Spending on cloud infrastructure is spiraling as well. Gartner reported global infrastructure investment of $59.2 billion in 2021, up 32% from 2020. For 2022, Gartner forecasted spending of $106.8 billion.

Amazon.com was one of the earliest companies to offer cloud services, and it remains a leader in this field. Since it must operate immense server capacity anyway, Amazon decided in early 2006 to offer cloud computing services, on its servers, to outside parties. Amazon Web Services (AWS) have been extremely popular. Using AWS requires no long-term contract or up-front investment. Charges are reasonable and usage-based (a few cents per gigabyte per month, in the U.S.). Remote servers, remote storage and the Amazon SimpleDB database are among the most popular AWS tools. Amazon, Microsoft and Google are investing vast sums to build new data centers for cloud services.

Software that is sold and operates only via the cloud is a growing trend. Adobe Systems, Inc., for example, a maker of extremely popular design software, is selling its biggest software products as online services only available by subscription to Adobe Creative Cloud.

SPOTLIGHT: Hybrid Cloud

The hybrid cloud is a data strategy where some applications and data are moved to cloud-based systems, while highly sensitive data or certain functions are kept on client-owned, local systems. Microsoft began offering hybrid cloud services in 2017 by allowing customers to run a portion of its Azure cloud on in-house servers (built to Microsoft specifications) which work smoothly with Azure data centers. In late 2019, the firm added Azure Stack, a rugged platform designed to support military data needs. Another option is Azure Arc, which affords customers the ability to store more data on their own servers. In 2020, Amazon joined the hybrid cloud movement by offering AWS (Amazon Web Services) server racks called Outposts for local use combined with software that connects it to the AWS cloud. Outposts customers include Disney animators (who demand almost instantaneous connections between in-house data and cloud data), Verizon Communications (needing faster 5G browsing speeds) and Fox Corp. (for video production needs).

2021 saw Microsoft launching Windows 365 (in July) and Windows 11 (in October). Both are cloud-based and part of Microsoft's efforts to regain global operating system market share (which was 85% in 2011 but only 30% in 2021). Windows 365 can be utilized by Apple users without the need to go through Apple's proprietary App Store.

The result of these efforts has become a wide variety of software that is accessed only via the internet instead of the desktop. Some software can be accessed for free, but many rich software applications are rented to the user by subscription or by fees based on the amount of time used. The growing use of smartphones is accelerating this trend. Also, the sharing of data, whether for business collaboration (such as Microsoft's Office 365 and Salesforce's customer management solution) or simply for fun (such as Facebook), has simplified dramatically thanks to the cloud. Business models and profit streams are being altered as a result.

A major goal of publishing software in the cloud is for the user to be able to eliminate much of the money and staff effort that an organization typically invests in building, managing and updating software in the traditional manner on a computer network. At the same time, the cloud enables software providers to build steady streams of renewable subscription revenues. Salesforce, a customer relationship management (CRM) software leader, has achieved great success by selling only internet-based (SaaS) access to its tools. NetSuite is another major provider of internet-based applications. Its offering for businesses includes CRM, enterprise resource planning (ERP), accounting, ecommerce and much more, all on a subscription basis. Among the advantages of SaaS are no software to purchase and no software to install or maintain.

19) Virtual Reality/Augmented Reality and 3-D Technologies Create Opportunities for the Tech Industry/Immersion Games to Grow

One of the most closely watched developments in the technology sector, especially in electronic games, is virtual reality, or "VR." Analysts at TrendForce reported global shipments of VR devices were expected to reach 5.12 million units in 2020, and further expand to 43.2 million units in 2025. In addition to gaming, potential major uses for VR include training/education as well as entertainment in general. Growth will be boosted by the ability to connect VR and augmented reality (AR) devices to IoT.

California-based Oculus VR headsets make virtual reality seem startlingly lifelike. Its Oculus Rift S headset makes stereoscopic 3-D gaming players using PCs feel immersed in the game, using some components that are commonly found in smartphones and tablets. This is sometimes referred to as "immersion" gaming. The Oculus Go headset requires no PC, no wires and no controller, while the

Oculus Quest headset works with an app and a game controller.

Facebook acquired Oculus VR for $2 billion in March 2014, and it created the Rift headsets to bring a realistic feeling to virtual meetings and entertainment, in addition to the obvious advantages for games. Rift is compatible with Microsoft Windows and the Xbox. Samsung has partnered with Oculus to launch the Gear VR, powered by an Android-based Galaxy device.

Sony's virtual reality headset, the PlayStation VR, was released in October 2016. Another virtual reality headset is HTC Corporation's Vive. Its price tag includes two wireless controllers and two base stations for 360-degree room-scale motion-tracking.

Google has had a major focus on the potential of VR since 2014. It was the lead investor in a $542 million funding round for Magic Leap, Inc., the developer of an eyeglass-based device that can project computer generated images over real settings (a twist on VR called augmented reality). The Magic Leap One device was released in early 2019.

Microsoft's 3D offering, HoloLens, made its debut in 2015. Another device that promises augmented reality, HoloLens imposes holograms over real views. The headset is designed to allow users to play electronic games, build 3D models and conduct immersive videoconferencing. Microsoft offers a HoloLens Commercial Suite for organizations and a Development Edition for individual developers. In late 2019, Microsoft released Hololens 2, a next generation version designed for the enterprise sector with a wider field of view and hand and eye-tracking. Microsoft's Windows 10 operating system supports VR headsets from a variety of manufacturers including Acer, Dell, HP, Lenovo Group and Samsung. Samsung's HMD Odyssey headset, for example, features OLED displays and includes headphones and a built-in microphone.

Augmented Reality (AR) is a technology that superimposes computer-generated, digital images on a real-time view, creating a composite view. For example, health technicians may use smart glasses, with AR installed, to see the location of a patient's veins before drawing blood, or technicians may wear smart glasses to see schematics and instructions relating to nearby equipment that needs fixing. The Daqri Smart Helmet enables factory workers to do just that in addition to providing protection. Analysts expect rapid growth among major corporations in adopting this technology. Forrester Research forecasted that 14.4 million U.S. workers will use AR related smart glasses such as Google Glass and HoloLens in 2025, up from 400,000 in 2016. Goldman Sachs Group, Inc. projected that AR and VR combined would generate $80 billion in hardware sales by 2025. Walmart was already using VR headsets in all of its roughly 4,600 U.S. stores to train workers to stock shelves and use online pickup machines as of 2018.

The Coronavirus pandemic vastly accelerated the adoption of AR since social distancing requires people to stay far apart. Business travel virtually shut down for several months and will likely continue to be curtailed even as businesses reopen. AR technology allows team members to interact from a distance. For example, due to a global curtailment of travel, an Intel engineer in Germany was unable to fly to a chip plant in Arizona that needed his expertise. Intel relayed a video to the engineer of real-time work at the plant via AR goggles, and he was able to walk the plant workers through a vital repair. Volkswagen AG's Porsche subsidiary reported that use of AR glasses in U.S. service departments more than tripled during the pandemic when technicians got virtual help from counterparts in different cities and different countries. Other sector that are embracing the technology include health care and defense.

Apple, Inc. is investing heavily in both VR and AR technology. Its headset, codenamed T288, is expected to offer an 8K display for each eye, and could be ready for release as early as 2022. The company is also focusing on AR features for iPhones and iPads which, as of mid-2018, were already equipped with cameras that enable composite images.

VR uses are stretching far beyond gaming. Surgeons can practice complicated techniques before cutting into patients. Corporate training is another area where VR is coming into play. Wal-Mart, Inc., for example, now utilizes VR training in all 200 of its training centers, which serve 140,000 new hires per year.

SPOTLIGHT: NextVR

NextVR, Inc. developed and patented a technology platform capable of delivering live events in virtual reality. The NextVR platform captures, compresses, transmits and displays immersive virtual reality content over the internet, primarily delivering live sports and music to fans globally. The NextVR experience requires either a Google Daydream View, Samsung Gear VR, Oculus Go, PlayStation VR Windows Mixed Reality or Mirage Solo headset and compatible phone. Users then download the free NextVR App, put the VR headset on and become engaged and immersed in the content. Inside the app is a range of regularly-scheduled content via partners. NextVR partners includes the NBA, FOX Sports, Live Nation, International Champions Cup and more. NextVR was acquired by Apple in May 2020 in a deal that was worth an estimated $100 million.

20) Wearable Sensors Track Exercise Data/Apparel and Shoe Manufacturers Adopt Technologies

The big news in sports equipment is wearable sensors that can measure anything from heart rates to speed achieved to physical exertion. Sensors are being embedded in all kinds of apparel, shoes and accessories. This sector will evolve very quickly by adopting the latest breakthroughs in the Internet of Things (IoT) and machine learning, in order to capitalize on data generated by device wearers.

A private company called Catapult Sports makes a matchbook-sized GPS device called Vector that professional and amateur athletes wear to measure performance. The firm also offers the ClearSky local positioning system (LPS) and the Catapult One athlete monitoring system. The devices are paired with analytical software capable of tracking multiple athletes both indoors and out. Catapult acquired sports monitoring device company GPSports.

Sporting goods manufacturers such as Nike are using sensors to entice customers. Nike and other shoemakers, including Adidas, have long offered sensors that can be worn on running shoes to collect data on steps, mileage or calories burned. Nike provides a technology called Nike+ that is incorporated in certain running shoes and can communicate with Apple or Android smart phones. Users can see total running time, distance, pace and calories burned. It can provide feedback during the run to let the runner know whether or not personal goals are being met. If you don't want to buy the special shoes, you can buy standalone sensors that can be attached to your favorite shoes from other makers. The Nike FuelBand (a wristband that can track a user's walking, dancing, basketball playing and many other activities via a built-in accelerometer) was a pioneer in this field. However, after a few short years Nike dropped the band itself while maintaining the underlying technology. Nike now makes its Fuel software available to outside firms for incorporation in a wide variety of activity trackers. Nike's Fuel Band was widely admired but did not rack up impressive sales. One of the trends causing the firm to change gears was the development of the Apple Watch. Nike Fuel is now available as an Apple Watch app.

GPS company TomTom offers a watch with a large screen and built-in GPS. Nikeplus.com enables users to upload complete running and workout information, compete with friends, store personal exercise history and find popular running routes. A large number of TomTom editions are available specifically for golfers, hikers and participants in other types of activities.

The system can also be used by people using exercise equipment indoors. Compatible cardio machines such as treadmills, elliptical machines and stationary bikes made by firms such as LifeFitness, Precor and Cybex have ports to which iPods can be connected to record pace, time and distance. In addition, iTunes is featuring upbeat music for workouts, favorite playlists from famous athletes and even real-time voice feedback during exercise. The sensor and transmitter retail at a modest price. The result has been a massive online running community, with millions of members. Members can post comments about their runs, share tips and engage in friendly competition to see who makes the best time for a given distance or track.

Eyewear is also utilizing sensors for a variety of uses. Luxottica's Oakley offers athletes the Radar Pace sunglasses and attached earphones with a voice-activated system that tracks heart rate, power output, speed, cadence, distance and times, while it partners with Intel for data analysis. The OrCam MyEye integrates glasses with earphones and cameras that read text to assist the visually impaired. Vuzix's smart glasses are Android-based wearable computers for industrial and medical applications, with the ability to take still photos, record and playback video, track timed events and link to other devices such as smartphones.

Apparel and fabrics are also being redesigned to incorporate sensors or at least provide connectivity to personal electronics. Textronics, Inc. makes fabric with circuitry, sensors and a functional component woven in that render the material capable of sending signals to heart rate monitors, which are popular among serious athletes. Textronics makes a sports bra under the NuMetrex brand which senses the wearer's heart rate and communicates that data to a wrist monitor. The bras free female athletes from wearing separate heart rate monitor straps and sensors.

Adidas has been innovating with sensors as well. Its latest effort is a line of smart products under the miCoach brand, including fit smart, a wristband which measures heart rate, calories, pace and speed, distance and stride rate; smart run, which is an all-in-one running watch; smart ball, a soccer training ball embedded with a sensor that measures speed, spin and strike force; x_cell, a wearable sensor that measures vertical movement in addition to heart rate and running speed; speed cell, an on-shoe sensor; and the Adidas heart rate monitor with strap. Most Adidas miCoach sensors link to selected smartphones. OMsignal, a Montreal-based company, makes machine-washable t-shirts that measure the wearer's heart rate, breathing and body temperature.

Fitness apparel maker Under Armour invested $710 million buying fitness app companies MapMyFitness, MyFitnessPal and Endomondo. MapMyFitness is U.S. firm that offers an app aimed at runners and cyclists. MyFitnessPal is a calorie counting app with a massive community of users. Endomondo is European app for logging exercise data for a variety of sports. Analysts expect Under Armour to develop clothing that tracks and analyzes fitness data.

Another twist on wearable electronics is the use of conductive fibers, which are typically substrate fibers such as cotton, polyester or nylon coated or embedded with electrically conductive elements. The result is lighter and more flexible than using metal wires as conductors, making it easily wearable and washable. Conductive fibers can be used in a wide variety of applications, including in military uniforms (which can power equipment), RFID tags in clothing and sensors in active wear that can measure heart rate and distance covered.

Internet Research Tip:

For more about conductive fibers, see the web site for the Conductive Fibers Manufacturing Council, www.cfibermfg.com.

The Massachusetts Institute of Technology (MIT) announced the founding of the Advanced Functional Fabrics of America Institute (AFFOA), a public-private consortium of manufacturers, universities, agencies and companies to accelerate innovation in high-tech, U.S.-based manufacturing involving fibers and textiles. AFFOA includes dozens of universities, industry members, manufacturers and startup incubators across 29 U.S. states and Puerto Rico.

Electronic components, which are becoming smaller and smaller, are now easily incorporated into articles of clothing. Industrial applications for wearable electronics will also evolve. For example, police officers, soldiers and emergency medical technicians may benefit from the ability to see up-to-date data on a wearable dashboard such as Google Glass, while built-in cameras and microphones may exchange vital real-time information with experts and analysts in remote locations. This could move remote collaboration in highly-critical situations to a new level.

SPOTLIGHT: CuteCircuit

London-based CuteCircuit is a fashion house that produces women's and men's clothing made of fabric embedded with micro-electronics that create changing, lighted patterns, shapes and texts. CuteCircuit projects include the Sound Shirt, with micro-actuators embedded in the fabric that receive music transmissions that the wearer can feel; and the Hug Shirt, which captures the strength, duration and location of touches such as hugs and actuators that recreate the sensations. CuteCircuit produces custom clothing through its Haute Couture line, and offers ready-to-wear through its website, cutecircuit.com.

21) Growth in Big Data Supported by Expansion of Cloud Computing and Predictive Analytics

"Big data" refers to the massive sets of digital information that are generated and captured at an accelerating rate by a wide variety of enterprises. For example, the digitization of health care records for hundreds of millions of patients is creating massive data sets. Likewise, the recording of activities of billions of monthly users of Facebook creates big data that is key to Facebook's ability to generate advertising revenues. Today, advertising of all types is being adjusted on a continuous basis due to the analysis of big data, often in real-time. Top technology companies such as IBM are seeing tremendous growth in this segment.

A growing trend is the generation of big data sets by remote wireless sensors in heavy industry, transportation and agriculture. The analysis of big data is creating enormous opportunities for greater efficiency in such areas as manufacturing, energy, finance, and marketing, as well as the development of intelligent transportation systems and better outcomes in health care. At the same time, challenges in the big data trend include the capture, storage, visualization and analysis of immense amounts of information in a rapid and cost-effective manner. Security and privacy are additional concerns.

Big data is, unfortunately, a big lure to hackers and criminals. Massive data sets have tremendous value to criminals and are often the target of major network breaches. For example, such data may be useful for military espionage, theft of intellectual property such as engineering designs and theft of vital consumer data such as credit bureau files.

The hand-in-hand partner of big data is analytical software, sometimes referred to as "predictive analytics." Gaining advantage from increasing amounts of data is accomplished via extremely powerful software algorithms that can parse reams of data at extremely high speed. That software then must present results, predictions and viewpoints that solve the needs of the organization in question. Statisticians and other professionals who can manage these tasks are in very high demand. Big data is also closely linked to the rapidly developing field of artificial intelligence (AI), and the related study of machine learning.

At the same time, however, big data is, unfortunately, a lure to hackers and criminals.

SAS, a global corporation known for its analytical software, recently wrote about the power of this trend at work in a major retail chain that is able to analyze data gathered from past customer transactions to determine the optimum prices to set in each of its stores. By using the latest data capture and analysis tools, the company reduced the amount of time for this weekly project from 30 hours of work to only two hours. Another example from SAS discusses a major bank that was able to reduce its regularly scheduled analysis of loan portfolios, looking for potential loan default, from 96 hours of work to only 4 hours. Such savings in time can represent very large boosts to productivity and profits.

The online advertising industry has been a prime beneficiary of the big data trend. As search engines, e-commerce sites and social media have been able to capture immense amounts of information about people who are online (often extending to consumers' locations, tastes and demographics), they have developed highly targeted advertising opportunities for firms that want to reach specific types of consumers. Media networks including Comcast Corp.'s NBCUniversal are offering advertisers data analytics tools to target ads more effectively. Called Audience Targeting Platform, it links data in set-top boxes to buying patterns of the people who use them.

The global financial industry is also a key player in big data. Now that all types of banking, investment, insurance and trading activities have been digitized and globalized, the amount of data that financial institutions must deal with offers both headaches and opportunities. On the challenges side, financial companies are faced with an ever-increasing need to fend off hackers, scam artists and major fraud schemes from their digital repositories, while providing highly regulated levels of consumer privacy. At the same time, having access to reams of information about their customers enables these institutions to better tailor targeted advertising and marketing, and to make better credit and lending decisions. On the investment side, big data enables traders, hedge fund managers and mutual funds, as well as financial analysts and money managers, to conduct real-time analysis of big data sets to maximize return on investment while minimizing risk. Insurance underwriters likewise benefit greatly from the risk analysis and risk management afforded by the proper analysis of big data.

The health care industry is beginning to rely heavily on big data. One of the major initiatives within the industry is the digitization of patient records. Similarly, the compilation of massive databases containing the outcomes of all types of treatments, drug therapies and surgeries will increase reliance on big data analysis. The goals include making patient records portable and readily accessible by any caregiver, along with using state-of-the-art analysis tools to determine the most effective treatments for specific types of patients and illnesses. In addition, big data will be used to pinpoint the most effective health care organizations based on cost of care, mortality, readmission to the hospital and other factors. Such studies will help identify best practices and potentially increase cost-effectiveness. At the same time, the industry will be able to create incentives for organizations shown to provide the best care.

An excellent example of a big data project is NEON, the National Ecological Observatory Network. The $434 million project is being overseen by the U.S. National Science Foundation. NEON became fully operational in 2019. It has 15,000 sensors across the U.S. will collect more than 500 types of daily data from 81 field sites (47 terrestrial and 34 aquatic) such as temperature, air pressure, wind speed and direction, ozone levels and soil and water nutrients. The data not only helps boost the effectiveness of government programs, it also is available to the public free of charge, as an aid to weather forecasting and agriculture. The system generates 200 terabytes of data each year, or four times that collected and transmitted by the Hubble telescope.

Technologies that have Synergies with Big Data:

- Artificial Intelligence (AI)
- Autonomous vehicles
- Cloud computing
- Cybersecurity
- Data visualization software
- Drug and vaccine development
- E-Commerce product recommendations
- ERP (Enterprise Resource Planning) software
- Financial Technology (FinTech)
- Health care technologies
- IoT (Internet of Things)
- M2M (Machine-to-Machine) communications
- Online advertising
- Predictive analytics software
- Remote wireless sensors
- Search engines
- Semiconductor manufacturing
- Social media
- Software-as-a-Service (SaaS)

Source: Plunkett Research, Ltd.

The rapidly escalating trend of big data across a broad range of industries is a perfect fit with the expansion of cloud computing. Now, massive databases can be hosted by remote databases (in the cloud) and then accessed via the internet for analysis and action.

Network technology leader Cisco Systems publishes the Cisco Global Cloud Index. In its latest release, it forecast that data center internet-based traffic will grow more than threefold, or a 27% compound annual growth rate, from 2017-2022. Traffic will reach 20.6 zettabytes (a zettabyte is about 909 million terabytes) in 2021. By 2021, 95% of all traffic will come from cloud systems.

Self-Driving Cars and the IoT Require Edge Computing as an Adjunct to Cloud Computing

While computing via the cloud is clearly a dominant trend today, a concept called edge computing is also growing in popularity as a supplement to cloud-based data processing. Edge computing is a local technology strategy whereby digital processing is done near the point where the data is first acquired. For example, a self-driving car generates vast amounts of data constantly.

Sending that data to the cloud to be processed would create small delays in analyzing road conditions and safety threats. Such delays, even if tiny, could imperil the car and its occupants.

In contrast, computing at the "edge" of the in-car laser detection system (LIDAR) and other devices would be nearly instantaneous, and portions of the data could still be transmitted via wireless networks to the cloud for further analysis. (Recent analysis shows that autonomous vehicles could generate as much as 25 gigabytes of data hourly.)

Many other technology trends will drive the use of edge computing forward. M2M (machine-to-machine) communications is rapidly emerging in the form of IoT (the Internet of Things). Here, remote sensors gather vast amounts of data from machinery, aircraft, trucks, ships, infrastructure and other vital components of day-to-day life. The intent is to capture data that can be rapidly analyzed in order to optimize both safety and operating efficiencies. Here, too, sending the data to the cloud may not be fast or efficient enough for the intended purpose. For example, conducting edge computing of data continuously gathered from industrial machinery, and later sending the resulting analysis on to a cloud computing center, may save factories from breakdowns and significantly reduce maintenance costs.

22) Precision Agriculture Technologies (AgTech), Farm Robotics, GPS and Irrigation Market Grows Worldwide/Hi Tech Greenhouses

Around the world, researchers, agricultural equipment firms, GPS makers and other technology firms are investing heavily in the development of advanced technology for the agricultural sector. These new technologies range from robotic systems to plant, nurture and harvest crops, fruit and vegetables, to wireless sensors that control irrigation via state of the art automated drip systems. The technology comes at a time when it is extremely difficult for many farmers in the U.S. to find fruit and vegetable pickers and other manual laborers.

Farm Robotics: The Massachusetts Institute of Technology (MIT) operates an experimental greenhouse where cherry tomatoes are grown entirely under the care of small robots. Sensors attached to each plant gauge water, food and/or fertilizer needs, while robots water and feed the plants as necessary. Vision sensors measure when a plant is ripe, and the fruit is then picked by a mechanical arm. Other examples of robotic agriculture systems include a rice planter developed by the National Agricultural Research Centre in Japan and a grapevine pruning prototype made by San Diego, California-based Vision Robotics.

The University of Sydney, Australia recently developed the Robot for Intelligent Perception and Precision Application (RIPPA). It's a four-wheeled, solar-powered unit that finds weeds in vegetable fields and targets them precisely with herbicide. Meanwhile, Rowbot Systems of Minneapolis is working on a device that can navigate rows of maize and apply fertilizer without damaging the plants. For fruit cultivation, the E-Series, manufactured by AGROBOT (www.agrobot.com), uses cameras to determine when strawberries are ripe and then harvests the berries for packaging by humans. AGROBOT also offers the Bug Vacuum, an autonomous robot for lygus pest control in orchards.

The cost for new robotic systems is substantial, yet the savings on the cost of human labor, over time, could be significant. Meanwhile, farm equipment manufacturer Kinze Manufacturing, Inc. and Jaybridge Robotics partnered to develop tractors that run without a human driver. Another company, Robotic Harvesting LLC, has developed technology for harvesting strawberries that relies on cameras and robotic arms. An inventor in Oxnard, California created the Agrobot, a $100,000 fruit picking machine with 14 arms, and plans to build a larger 60-armed unit. Yet another firm, Small Robot Company (www.smallrobotcompany.com), offers "agribots" designed to perform tasks such as weeding, seeding and fertilizing as well as scanning for soil and plant conditions.

Faculty at Britain's Harper Adams University cobbled together robotic equipment starting in 2016 with the goal of farming a roughly 2.5-acre plot (one hectare) without human assistance. In its first year, the group harvested 4.5 metric tons of spring barley and 6.5 metric tons of winter wheat in 2018. Their next goal is hands-free farming of 35 non-contiguous hectares.

Robotic systems are still in an early stage, since the wide varieties of crops grown around the world require highly specialized equipment (picking oranges, for example, is a very different activity than harvesting rice). Also, systems perfected in greenhouses may prove faulty when working in varied weather conditions and on rough terrain. However, high-end farming equipment such as commercial tractors are already equipped with real-time GPS software which would enable a certain degree of automation.

SPOTLIGHT: Agricultural Drones

Low-cost aerial camera drones (flying platforms in the form of small, fixed-wing airplanes or helicopters called quadcopters) can be seen flying over growing numbers of farms to monitor crops and field conditions. They can cost as little as $1,000, and are equipped with an autopilot, GPS and cameras. Images analyzed by software on the ground can reveal irrigation problems, soil variation, pests and fungal infestations. Infrared images highlight potential problems such as chlorophyll levels that can't be seen with the naked eye.

Low altitudes afford farmers much better resolution than satellite imagery (which is far more expensive at about $1,000 per hour). Drones can fly at any time, so farmers can compare images shot on a monthly, weekly, daily or even hourly basis to study changes in crop growth. Key drone manufacturers include 3D Robotics, Yamaha and PrecisionHawk.

Agricultural Big Data: Technology is also impacting crop forecasting. A Chicago-based firm, Lanworth (a unit of Thomson Reuters), has developed a system using satellite images, analytical software and eyewitness reports to compete with agriculture output estimates issued by the U.S. Department of Agriculture (USDA). Lanworth's data, culled at no charge from NASA's landsat satellite system (which was built in 1972 to record images of Soviet crop production), uses historical reports to compare current images to the quantity and ripeness of past crops.

High-Tech Commercial Greenhouses Grow Crops Indoors: Another technology of note is vertical farming, in which indoor fields and orchards are built, floor upon floor, in urban areas. Led by boosters such as Columbia University professor Dickson Despommier, the idea is eco-friendly in many ways. If food is grown in urban areas, little transportation is necessary to get produce to consumers.

AeroFarms (aerofarms.com) is a greenhouse venture based on aeroponics, which is the practice of soil-free vertical farming. Seeds are scattered over permeable microfleece cloth, placed under LED lights and sprayed with a super-rich nutrient solution. A membrane forms on the microfleece in which the seeds germinate. Roots form and pierce down through the microfleece where they are further treated with nutrient solution. AeroFarms operates its aeroponic farm and global headquarters in a 70,000 square-foot former steel mill in Newark, New Jersey, where it produces more than 2 million pounds of leafy greens annually.

Freight Farms (www.freightfarms.com) is a Boston-based startup that repurposes shipping containers into arable square footage. The firm fills the containers, which could be located in any vacant lot or alleyway, with LED lights, sensors and hydroponic systems. The firm claims that an average Freight Farms box, called a Leafy Green Machine (LGM) can produce 48,568 mini-heads of lettuce per year, or about the same yield as two acres of farmland.

The Coronavirus pandemic spurred interest in vertical farming due to concerns about food security. These farms can be located in urban areas, simplifying logistics and speeding delivery times. Empty commercial buildings may possibly be converted to agricultural use post-pandemic. Vertical farms may also see greater variety in the crops they produce, including root and vine vegetables and bush fruits.

GPS and Precision Agriculture: Precision agriculture, also called precision farming, is in use to a growing extent across the globe. The intent is to increase yield, decrease costs (including manpower and water usage) and avoid problems in the field. Today, it primarily involves the use of GPS to guide tractors for precise tilling and planting. Eventually, it will evolve to include the use of remote wireless sensors, GPS, satellite imagery, predictive databases and other advanced technologies to monitor and react to soil, weather and crop conditions, such as the local level of soil moisture and soil nutrients. Robotics and nanotechnology will eventually be part of this trend.

GPS maker Trimble operates a large agricultural division. It offers a wide variety of location-based technologies and data analytics for farmers. The goal is to maximize efficiency while reducing waste of farm chemicals and water. One tool improves irrigation, drainage and land leveling. Another provides high efficiency tractor guidance via GPS. Trimble also offers drones for aerial mapping and crop management and overall farm management software. It recently acquired the HarvestMark technology that enables food supply chain transparency and tracking of food products by origin, from the exact farm location to the supermarket shelf.

Irrigation Technologies: Agriculture is by far the world's biggest user of water, and water scarcity is without doubt one of the greatest problems the world will face in coming years. Out of sheer necessity, vast amounts of money are being invested in research, development and implementation of advanced crop irrigation technologies. Leading nations in this field include Israel and China, both facing significant water scarcity issues. American companies and investors also have a keen interest in this field. In California's Central Valley, for example, water from the Sacramento River is diverted into canals fitted with control structures and gates. Any excess is allowed to percolate down into the groundwater basin or diverted to a small structure with pumps, filters and pressure gauges in a drip irrigation system. Microsprinklers can also be attached to drip systems to disperse water in longer arcs covering more territory. This is part of the concept of micro-irrigation, pioneered by Israeli-American scientist Daniel Hillel, which exposes crops to frequent, small amounts of water rather than less frequent, heavy watering.

23) 5G Wireless Networks to Rollout Worldwide, Enabling the Internet of Things (IoT)/Massive Investments Required

Fast wireless systems make it possible for subscribers to receive high-quality music, video and other features, and to connect interactively with the internet at high speeds. Fast wireless, combined with high-resolution color screens and cameras on smartphones, means that subscribers are using their handsets to play games, access Facebook, get detailed news or financial data, watch mobile TV and shop online. Smartphone owners are filming videos with their phones and then posting them to social media. They are also viewing internet sites featuring store and restaurant listings, as well as advertising, based on the location of the user. Film and video sites Netflix, Hulu and YouTube are immense drivers of traffic.

The next big thing in wireless internet service is 5G technology. The concept enables blinding download speeds from one gigabyte per second (Gbps), to perhaps as high as 10 Gbps. Part of the appeal is 5G's low latency (response time) of as little as one millisecond, compared to 4G's 50 milliseconds.

Ultrafast 5G wireless service will be the critical backbone that will enable IoT on a vast scale. Far beyond simply improving smartphone services, 5G will connect sensors and devices to networks, gathering data and enabling machine-to-machine communications at near instantaneous speeds. For example, it will be of vital, real-time use in robotics and self-driving cars and trucks.

In theory, 5G wireless can be more than 50 times faster than 4G. A test in New York City found that 5G enabled the download of a 2.1 GB movie file in two minutes, 57 seconds, compared to about one hour for a 4G download of the same film. However, actual 5G downloads achieved vary from city-to-city and carrier-to-carrier, and the movie download cited above may take a much longer tie to complete in some places. Actual users of 5G in 2020 often found lower than expected speed increases, as 5G networks and equipment are still in early stages of roll-out.

In the U.S., Sprint and T-Mobile completed a merger in April 2020. The combined businesses, operating under the T-Mobile name, planned to invest approximately $40 billion in infrastructure by 2022, developing what they expect to be one of the first nationwide 5G networks. Sprint and T-Mobile hope that the combined companies, with 90 million total customers, can operate more efficiently while aggressively establishing advanced 5G wireless services.

South Korea's largest mobile carriers (SK Telecom Co. and KT Corp.), manufacturers including Samsung Electronics Co. and LG Electronics, Inc. and the South Korean government have been true 5G pioneers. In April 2019, both SK Telecom and KT Corp. launched their first 5G commercial services.

The EU and South Korea agreed to cooperate to develop systems, establish standards and acquire radio frequencies necessary to implement 5G networks. The partnership will be led by Europe's 5G PPP (backed by Telefonica SA and Nokia Oyj) and South Korea's 5G Forum.

The United Nations' International Telecommunication Union (ITU) agreed on a set of requirements for 5G technology in 2018. Download speeds should be at least 20 gigabits per second, response times should be less than 1 millisecond, and at least 1 million devices should be able to connect within a high-traffic area equal to one square kilometer. In practical terms, a full-length, high-resolution movie should transmit in two seconds. Carriers, equipment manufacturers and tech companies must agree to work together to establish seamless connections around the world, along with methods of managing these connections.

U.S. cellphone service providers have invested billions of dollars in enhancing their networks over recent years. Subscribers wanting 5G were initially limited to a small number of devices capable of using the service. However, by 2021 5G had been rolled out, at least to some extent, in most major metro markets and was in use on a variety of devices.

However, all major wireless device makers are investing heavily in the design of 5G-capable handsets. As services roll out to more and more cities worldwide, consumers' demand for new handsets will accelerate and will generate tremendous new revenues for handset makers. Apple launched its first 5G iPhone (the iPhone 12) in late 2020, and later introduced the iPhone 13 and the iPhone SE, both of which support 5G. The earliest models of true 5G handsets were expensive, and, due to high energy consumption, lacked the long battery endurance enjoyed by typical smartphones. (5G smartphones are designed to work with lower speed 4G networks when necessary. For example, if the handsets reach high temperatures, they will switch to 4G to conserve power.) However, 5G will improve rapidly, and consumers will eventually adopt them in massive quantities, as long as monthly subscription fees are reasonable and handset prices fall to reasonable levels. All-in-all, this is terrific news for handset manufacturers, as it has become more and more daunting to create improvements to today's smartphones that are compelling enough to get consumers to upgrade.

Despite these positives, 5G infrastructure faces a long and expensive rollout. In a recent report, Deloitte Consulting estimated that U.S. conversion to 5G would require carriers to invest a combined $130 billion to $150 billion. Other analysts believe that deployment of 5G (outside of urban areas with the highest population densities) will take more than 10 years due to the expense and the necessity of cooperation among carriers and local municipalities. According to CTIA, in 2020, the U.S. had 154,000 cellular service towers. However, an additional 769,000 transmission must be created by 2026 to achieve full 5G coverage, due to the fact that 5G has shorter range and requires more antennas. Analysts at Evercore estimated in 2021 that it could be two years before two-thirds of Americans can have 5G service that is notably better than 4G.

While 4G mobile phone service can travel fairly long distances and transmissions come and go from tall towers, the fastest-service (known as high-band) 5G antennae must be spaced fairly close together. Carriers will be competing to offer the fastest possible speeds within dense cities. Consequently, carriers will be placing small 5G antennae on street lights, the sides of buildings and other unique spots. Seeing this boom of new antenna locations as a potential source of tax revenue, some U.S. cities have been attempting to charge high permit fees to the carriers for each new antenna deployed. Unfortunately, the super-fast high-band systems may not be able to penetrate walls, creating the need for even more antennae. Slower low- and mid-band systems are likely to be used in areas that are not as densely populated.

5G may also increase cybersecurity threats since it will eventually connect to vast numbers of devices, pieces of equipment and remote sensors as the Internet of Things grows. Its potential use in autonomous vehicles, factories, transportation systems, utilities and smart-city infrastructure raises security concerns.

Chinese mobile equipment manufacturer Huawei Technologies Co., which was previously a dominant player in the global 5G market, faced cybersecurity doubts among certain foreign governments in recent years, resulting in U.S. and Australian government bans of Huawei 5G equipment. The bans, in addition to other Huawei restrictions in the U.K. and a number of EU countries, have opened doors for other cellular equipment makers to gain market share and play larger roles in establishing global standards. In the U.S., a number of smaller companies such as Airspan Networks (www.airspan.com), Mavenir (www.mavenir.com), JMA Wireless (jmawireless.com), Parallel Wireless (www.parallelwireless.com) and Rakuten Symphony (symphony.rakuten.com), which acquired Altiostar in 2019, are pushing ahead using open-standard 5G software.

Satellite provider Dish is spending an estimated $10 billion to launch a 5G wireless service. The service will be focused on creating wide-area networks for major enterprises, capable of powering the Internet of Things (IoT). Dish will be working with Dell Technologies' RAN (Radio Access Network) architecture and a strategy known as "edge" computing which enables faster IoT data processing. Dish is hoping that its service will cost much less to operate than those of traditional competitors.

Meanwhile, some carriers have been advertising a "lite" version of 5G, optimistically referred to as 5GE—the E stands for "evolution." Such service is technically based on an enhanced 4G system. Another technology is 5G NR ("new radio"), which upgrades existing 4G networks with regard to home internet access. For example, Verizon offers the 5G NR Enhanced Gateway modem made by D-Link.

High speed mobile access is a global phenomenon. China ranks number one in the world in the total number of high-speed internet subscribers. India's high-speed wireless count is soaring, thanks to massive investments in infrastructure, along with intense competition that keeps prices low. China's Huawei Technologies is investing heavily in 5G technology development and plans to compete head-on with the world's other technology giants in hopes to own very significant market share in 5G equipment.

Faster speed may also be achieved through new routers which support Wi-Fi 6 (also known as 802.11ax). They enable more devices in crowded areas to exchange data, such as texts and tweets, more quickly. Peak download speeds max out at 9.6 gigabits per second. In addition, Bluetooth 5 is a new standard with improved wireless range and reliability. Growing numbers of devices are compatible with Bluetooth 5.

SPOTLIGHT: pCell

Artemis Networks, www.artemis.com, may solve wireless network traffic jams with a technology called the pCell mobile wireless data transmission system. Compared to conventional cell towers, which share spectrum capacity and suffer slow performance when many users are on the network simultaneously, pCell uses interference caused by closely placed antennas to create a unique and clear wireless signal for each user on the network. The firm claims that all pCell service is full speed, no matter how many users are involved.

24) Cybersecurity Challenges for the Internet of Things (IoT)

IoT is a revolutionary, disruptive technological concept. It is also potentially invasive of our homes, offices, automobiles and even our outdoor surroundings. Since the whole point of IoT is to gather data at the "endpoint," that is at the point where the data is created, and then analyze that data in remote computer systems, often with ultra-powerful artificial intelligence, it is designed to surround us. IoT will gather and transmit data about mundane things like what temperature we set on our thermostats and what items we put in refrigerators. On a more personal basis, it will know where we are heading in our vehicles, what we look like as we pass by a digital camera and perhaps what we weigh when we get on a bathroom scale. The possibilities are endless. Unfortunately, the possibilities for abuse are likewise endless, including the potential for hackers to enter our homes and offices via IoT devices. Used well, IoT will make the world more convenient, efficient, environmentally sound and "safer". But, that potential for "safer" has a big "IF" in front of it.

Radical new ways of blocking hackers, spyware, malware, abuse of personal data and uninvited invasion of privacy are called for if consumers and businesses are going to feel enthusiastic enough about IoT to invest in and utilize new devices, such as IoT-enabled appliances and health monitors in the home, intelligent transportation technologies in cars and advanced inventory or machinery management in factories and offices. This means an urgent need for improved network and device security at all levels, from firewalls and Wi-Fi routers to advanced software on devices and nodes.

One pioneer in developing secure technologies for the world of IoT is Boston-based Cybereason, Inc., www.cybereason.com, which is focused on securing connected endpoint devices. Companies that can solve security needs may eventually have a global market of 1 trillion connected devices or more. Likewise, Veridify Security, www.veridify.com, formerly SecureRF, is developing innovative security solutions for IoT devices.

IoT relies heavily on Wi-Fi, which is notoriously open to hacking, as well as on advanced 5G wireless services. Unfortunately, security and malware on smartphones and wireless monitors are already a great concern. Thousands of stories already abound in the news media of clever ways that hackers have utilized thermostats and other devices connected to business networks in order to enter servers and extract critical data files. One example is hackers that utilized a connection made to a non-secure thermostat on a large aquarium in a U.S. casino.

Traditionally, connected devices in the home or office, such as alarm systems, smart thermostats and webcams, have not been well protected from hacking. Consumers of IoT at all levels, from individual households to government agencies, businesses and industrial giants, will soon face a significant challenge: What device and wireless service brands can they trust? At what level are they willing to trade privacy for the potential efficiencies of IoT-enabled devices?

25) The Internet of Things (IoT) in Factories, Robotics and Equipment

IoT will enable many industries to meet goals that are vital in today's evolving global economy. This includes rapid changes in factories, and new revenue sources for manufacturers of equipment.

On the factory floor, automation is the driving trend today. Factory managers want to get the highest level of error-free output with the lowest number of employees. This means that robots completely take over some tasks, but work closely with human workers as "cobots" in others. It also means highly efficient supply chains and parts inventories, as well as rapid movement through distribution to end customers. All-in-all, this adds up to optimum lean production, which puts a well-thought-out factory in an excellent competitive position.

IoT will be a very significant enabler of efficient factories, and at least initially, it will be the manufacturing sector that is making the largest investments in the technology, followed by the transportation sector. For example, ultrafast 5G wireless will mean that data can be sent to, and gathered from, sensors and robotic devices in a near instantaneous fashion. Conditions within factory machinery and production lines can be monitored and improved on a 24/7 basis. IoT sensors can gather vital data such as machinery temperature, vibration, output and input, and can monitor conditions within products, such as processed foods or paints, while they are in production.

Internet Research Tip: The Industrial Internet Consortium

This industry group, focused on IoT, offers a wealth of news, trends and research on its website, www.iiconsortium.org.

Microsoft is working with manufacturers to install technology that enables them to measure such factors as moisture content in food products while they are on the processing line. Microsoft sees the Industrial IoT as a massive future user of cloud services, and is reaching out to manufacturers, including Siemens, to establish relationships that will boost Microsoft's Azure cloud platform for all types of connected machinery and equipment. Microsoft offers what it calls "Azure IoT Solution Accelerators" online: a set of templates that enable users to readily create customized IoT platforms within their own businesses or factories. These templates enable firms to start connecting and monitoring devices with less cost and effort.

Likewise, chip industry leader Intel offers system design resources to enable all types of businesses to accelerate their use of IoT. Of course, Intel is investing heavily in the design and manufacture of chips that support IoT activities.

Caterpillar is one of many massive global equipment and machinery manufacturers making huge bets on the potential of IoT. The firm's latest bulldozers, front-end loaders and other heavy equipment are connected to its cloud services. This includes items like engine sensors and even oil-level sensors in oil caps that can alert operators when they need to add more lubricant. The intent is not only to add value for end-customers, but also to boost sales of replacement parts and services.

A major challenge facing robotics is the ability to correctly select needed items and to manipulate an item's position (such as turning it so that it can fit properly into a shipping box). A San Francisco-based nonprofit called OpenAI (openai.com) is working on developing robots that can train themselves to complete various tasks. It has a robot "hand" called Dactyl, that uses an array of lights, cameras and neural-network software to try out different actions in a simulated environment before attempting it for real. The process is called reinforcement learning, and it allows the robot to randomly experiment. Dactyl successfully taught itself to flip a toy building block in its mechanical fingers.

A new category of wearable robotics helps fulfillment center personnel reduce injuries. Called exosuits, the devices are strapped onto workers and include sensors and algorithms to measure movement and loads lifted, in addition to skeleton-like attachments that support the wearer's back and hips. Verve Motion (vervemotion.com), based in Cambridge, Massachusetts, offers a battery-powered exosuit called SafeLift that promises to take 30% of strain off of people when they perform physically strenuous tasks.

26) The Internet of Things (IoT) and the Smart Home

Homeowners have been early adopters of connected devices, utilizing IoT to improve property security and energy efficiency. Google saw this trend coming as early as 2014 when it purchased connected thermostat maker Nest for $3.2 billion. Nest's devices collect data at the thermostat level and utilize artificial intelligence and IoT to learn how to best set the temperature in the home in a manner that coincides with the residents' typical daily patterns. That is, Nest can learn to change settings when all family members have left for the day, say by 8:30 AM, and to alter settings in time for the kids to be home by 3:00 P.M. Meanwhile it communicates via Wi-Fi and IoT with software on central servers.

Nest includes motion detectors as well as sensors for temperature, humidity and light. The long-term game for the firm is to gather data about consumer power usage that will be of high value to electric utilities. Consumers at home can opt into special rebate programs if they allow Nest to reduce their power usage during times of peak utility loads.

Amazon purchased connected doorbell/webcam company Ring for $1 billion. It also invested in the ecobee smart thermostat firm. Amazon uses its Alexa and Echo digital assistants platform to offer a wide variety of connected devices and services to the home, via Wi-Fi and IoT.

Homeowners expect to benefit from the smart home trend through improved home security, alarms and webcams; greater convenience through connected devices that help to manage access to news and entertainment; easier ecommerce orders of a wide variety of products; and greater household energy efficiency.

27) Hot Fields Within Computers, Hardware & Software Include Artificial Intelligence (AI), Cybersecurity and the Internet of Things (IoT)

- Data and network security (Cybersecurity)—This remains a top concern among technology consumers and manufacturers alike. Whether it's security when conducting online banking or security in using e-mail and online collaboration, technology users are fed up with being hacked, spammed, cheated and abused by fraud. Security is also a major concern for social media networks, smartphones and cloud computing.
- Artificial Intelligence (AI) and Machine Learning—One of the greatest areas of investment and research in the entire technology field is AI and related machine learning, deep learning and neural networks. Simply put, AI will boost the effectiveness and reach of many other technologies, from robotics to gaming to personal digital assistants.
- The Internet of Things (IoT)—Remote wireless sensors, 5G, Wi-Fi connections, Bluetooth connections and other advanced technologies are

enabling a boom in machine-to-machine (M2M) communications that will soon reach stunning proportions.

- Electronic games—Mobile access and interactive online game playing continue to fuel global sales in this sector.
- Virtual Reality—The ability to use advanced software and displays in order to create an immersion environment of extremely high-quality promises to drive changes in gaming, advertising, entertainment and training.
- Augmented Reality (AR)—a technology that superimposes computer-generated, digital images on a real time view, creating a composite view.
- Autonomous Vehicles—cars, trucks and utility vehicles with self-driving capabilities.
- Voice recognition—Advanced software to enable a user to use verbal commands in everything from smartphones to automobile dashboard commands.
- Personal Digital Assistants—Amazon's Alexa, Apple's Siri and Google Home are ushering in a new era of voice-activated user interfaces to search and entertainment.
- Face recognition and other biometrics are growing as a means of digital log-in.
- Mobile computing—ultra-fast 5G service is slowly being rolled out.
- Denser, faster, more energy-efficient chips continue to be announced, particularly important to artificial intelligence systems.
- Fiber-to-the-premises (FTTP)—Fiber-optic cable installed all the way through to the living room is becoming standard for very high-speed internet. Businesses take advantage of similar systems.
- Cloud computing—Clusters of inexpensive servers power remote data centers for software applications, search, data storage and data sharing. This is a cost-effective alternative to storing software and data on a local device or server. A twist on this technology is called "hybrid cloud," where an enterprise uses a combination of local servers for highly sensitive data, along with cloud-based files and software.
- Software as a Service (SaaS)—Software for business or consumer use that is accessed via the internet rather than installed on a local computer. Generally, this remote software can be considered to be accessed via the cloud.
- Quantum computing is slowing moving closer to becoming practical for specialized digital research.
- Data science, which is collecting, analyzing and interpreting large amounts of data to identify ways to help a business improve operations or marketing, and gain a competitive edge.
- AI in Health Care—increasingly used in all facets of health care from analysis of patient outcomes, to drug development, to vaccine development.

Sites with the latest information on worldwide markets in InfoTech:

Gartner, www.gartner.com
Forrester Research, www.forrester.com
International Data Corporation, www.idc.com
451 Research, 451research.com

Sites with the latest statistics on internet usage:

ClickZ, www.clickz.com and click Stats & Tools.
eMarketer, www.emarketer.com
International Telecommunication Union, www.itu.int
Pew Internet & American Life, www.pewresearch.org/internet

Chapter 2

INTERNET OF THINGS (IoT) & DATA ANALYTICS INDUSTRY STATISTICS

Contents:

Internet of Things (IoT) & Data Analytics Industry Statistics and Market Size Overview

Global Market	Amount	Unit	Date	Source
Worldwide Spending on IoT	250	Bil. US$	2022	PRE
Networked Devices and Connections	29.3	Bil.	2023	Cisco
Internet Users, Worldwide	6.5	Bil.	2022	PRE
Global Artificial Intelligence Market	327.5	Bil. US$	2021	IDC

U.S.	Amount	Unit	Date	Source
IoT Spending	62.0	Bil. US$	2022	PRE
U.S. Artificial Intelligence Spending	100.0	Bil. US$	2022	PRE
U.S. IT Spending (forecast)	920.5	Bil. US$	2022	PRE
Software Publishing Industry Revenue	399.6	Bil. US$	2022	PRE
Data Processing, Hosting, and Related Services Industry Revenue	212.6	Bil. US$	2022	PRE
High Speed Internet Subscribers, U.S., Fixed, Home & Business	121.2	Mil.	2022	PRE
High Speed Internet Subscribers, U.S., Wireless, incl. Smartphone	328.6	Mil.	2022	PRE

IDC = International Data Corporation

PRE = Plunkett Research Estimate

PRE = Plunkett Research Estimate

Software Publishing Industry, U.S.: Estimated Revenue, Inventories & Expenses: 2016-2021

(In Millions of US$; Latest Year Available)

NAICS Code: 5112	2021*	2020	2019	2018	2017	2016
Total Operating Revenue	**357,037**	**360,605**	**331,512**	**303,590**	**276,234**	**249,847**
System software publishing		86,552	71,789	86,869	75,137	67,097
Operating systems software		36,493	27,826	28,207	25,627	23,126
Network software		27,340	23,070	23,896	18,144	16,554
Database management software		19,548	18,388	17,665	17,240	16,172
Development tools & programming languages software		3,171	2,505	2,694	2,637	2,670
Other systems software		S	S	14,407	11,489	8,575
Application software publishing		140,172	159,663	137,169	122,545	111,903
General business productivity & home use applications		91,842	86,542	67,104	60,415	52,631
Cross-industry application software		S	32,798	35,187	31,807	31,244
Vertical market application software		22,166	16,807	17,832	16,581	14,290
Utilities software		5,274	4,564	4,182	3,047	3,029
Other application software		20,890	18,952	12,864	10,695	10,709
Custom application design & development services		8,792	S	6,245	4,613	4,253
IT technical consulting services		S	11,561	11,172	10,996	8,505
Re-sale of computer hardware & software		S	15,439	11,294	10,128	10,219
IT related training services		4,078	4,047	4,071	4,133	4,135
All other operating revenue		44,022	48,308	46,770	48,682	43,735
Breakdown of Revenue by Software Sales Type						
System software		98,513	85,197	86,869	75,137	67,097
Personal computer software		27,511	18,977	18,658	19,256	18,133
Enterprise or network software		46,974	43,563	46,010	35,492	30,529
Mainframe computer software		14,774	15,467	14,786	13,830	11,449
Other system software		9,254	7,190	7,415	6,559	6,986
Application software		172,291	159,663	137,169	122,545	111,903
Personal computer software		43,465	45,141	37,416	31,556	28,958
Enterprise or network software		89,495	81,023	67,636	59,902	54,204
Mainframe computer software		S	S	S	5,488	5,986
Other application software		S	31,727	S	25,599	22,755
Inventories at End of Year						
Total		**8,570**	**5,834**	**4,738**	**4,100**	**4,130**
Finished goods		S	4,965	3,554	2,563	2,679
Work-in-process		1,067	S	939	1,122	999
Materials, fuel, supplies, etc.		9,846	671	245	S	452
Expenses						
Total	**194,897**	**237,107**	**145,179**	**142,807**	**133,462**	**121,120**

Notes: Estimates are based on data from the 2020 Service Annual Survey and administrative data. Dollar volume estimates are published in millions of dollars; consequently, results may not be additive.

* Plunkett Research Estimate.

S = Estimate does not meet publication standards because of high sampling variability (coefficient of variation is greater than 30%) or poor response quality (total quantity response rate is less than 50%). Unpublished estimates derived from this table by subtraction are subject to these same limitations and should not be attributed to the U.S. Census Bureau.

Source: U.S. Census Bureau

Plunkett Research,® Ltd.

www.plunkettresesarch.com

Software Publishing Industry, U.S.: Estimated Selected Expenses: 2016-2021

(In Millions of US$; Latest Year Available)

NAICS Code: 5112	2021*	2020	2019	2018	2017	2016
Total	**258,190**	**237,107**	**232,392**	**212,400**	**185,112**	**168,092**
Gross annual payroll		105,543	104,591	98,520	85,189	75,158
Employer's cost for fringe benefits		25,862	S	S	23,030	20,259
Temporary staff and leased employee expense		5,179	5,731	6,108	4,839	4,298
Expensed equipment, materials, parts, and supplies		831	S	S	3,101	2,636
Expensed purchases of software		4,057	S	S	2,525	2,245
Purchased software reproduction		S	1,108	983	830	858
Depreciation and amortization charges		18,104	17,080	15,517	12,237	11,708
All other operating expenses		40,963	72,306	61,577	53,361	50,930

Notes: Estimates are based on data from the 2020 Service Annual Survey and administrative data. Dollar volume estimates are published in millions of dollars; consequently, results may not be additive.

* Plunkett Research Estimate.

S = Estimate does not meet publication standards because of high sampling variability (coefficient of variation is greater than 30%) or poor response quality (total quantity response rate is less than 50%). Unpublished estimates derived from this table by subtraction are subject to these same limitations and should not be attributed to the U.S. Census Bureau.

Source: U.S. Census Bureau
Plunkett Research,® Ltd.
www.plunkettresesarch.com

Data Processing, Hosting, and Related Services Industry, U.S.: Estimated Revenue & Expenses: 2016-2021

(In Millions of US$; Latest Year Available)

NAICS Code: 518	2021*	2020	2019	2018	2017	2016
Total Operating Revenue	**230,399**	**205,869**	**193,228**	**175,261**	**157,477**	**139,288**
Data processing, information technology (IT) infrastructure provisioning, and hosting services		146,405	134,969	126,158	111,206	97,877
Information technology (IT) design and development services		S	S	S	S	6,630
Information technology (IT) technical support services		6,289	6,207	S	4,302	4,216
Information technology (IT) technical consulting services		S	S	S	S	3,967
Information and document transformation services		S	S	S	2,779	S
Software publishing		5,589	6,350	4,089	S	S
Reselling of computer hardware and software		S	S	S	3,318	2,611
All other operating revenue		31,046	28,301	S	S	S
Total Expenses	**204,042**	**155,026**	**145,179**	**142,807**	**133,462**	**121,120**

Notes: Estimates are based on data from the 2020 Service Annual Survey and administrative data. Dollar volume estimates are published in millions of dollars; consequently, results may not be additive.

* Plunkett Research Estimate.

S = Estimate does not meet publication standards because of high sampling variability (coefficient of variation is greater than 30%) or poor response quality (total quantity response rate is less than 50%). Unpublished estimates derived from this table by subtraction are subject to these same limitations and should not be attributed to the U.S. Census Bureau.

Source: U.S. Census Bureau

Plunkett Research,® Ltd.

www.plunkettresesarch.com

Data Processing, Hosting, and Related Services Industry, U.S.: Estimated Selected Expenses: 2015-2020

(In Millions of US$; Latest Year Available)

NAICS Code: 518	2020	2019	2018	2017	2016	2015
Total	**155,026**	**148,256**	**142,548**	**133,147**	**120,800**	**126,827**
Gross annual payroll	72,199	63,211	59,197	54,666	49,885	47,092
Employer's cost for fringe benefits	10,970	S	S	10,742	9,761	S
Temporary staff and leased employee expense	S	S	S	S	2,449	S
Expensed equipment, materials, parts, and supplies	2,135	S	S	S	3,110	S
Expensed purchases of software	5,559	S	S	3,585	3,078	S
Depreciation and amortization charges	15,117	14,414	16,735	14,089	11,443	S
All other operating expenses	S	S	S	44,558	41,394	S

Notes: Estimates are based on data from the 2020 Service Annual Survey and administrative data. Dollar volume estimates are published in millions of dollars; consequently, results may not be additive.

* Plunkett Research Estimate.

S = Estimate does not meet publication standards because of high sampling variability (coefficient of variation is greater than 30%) or poor response quality (total quantity response rate is less than 50%). Unpublished estimates derived from this table by subtraction are subject to these same limitations and should not be attributed to the U.S. Census Bureau.

Source: U.S. Census Bureau

Plunkett Research,® Ltd.

www.plunkettresesarch.com

Number of Business & Residential High Speed Internet Lines, U.S.: 2016-2021

(In Thousands)

Types of Technology	Dec-16	Dec-17	Dec-18	Dec-19	Dec-20*	Dec-21*
ADSL	23,891	21,653	19,691	18,462	16,942	15,547
SDSL	8	9	4	3	2	2
Other Wireline[1]	32	68	74	98	142	206
Cable Modem	59,145	61,567	63,788	65,415	65,415	67,650
FTTP[2]	10,956	12,702	14,621	16,097	18,300	20,804
Satellite	1,676	1,688	1,787	1,826	1,878	1,933
Fixed Wireless	1,099	1,146	1,318	1,400	1,518	1,646
Total Fixed	**96,907**	**98,832**	**101,283**	**101,283**	**104,198**	**107,787**
Mobile Wireless (Smartphone)	253,000	266,208	267,191	272,096	278,777	285,621
Total Lines	**349,607**	**365,040**	**368,473**	**368,473**	**382,975**	**393,408**

Notes: High-speed lines are connections to end-user locations that deliver services at speeds exceeding 200 kbps in at least one direction. Advanced services lines, which are a subset of high-speed lines, are connections that deliver services at speeds exceeding 200 kbps in both directions. Line counts presented in this report are not adjusted for the number of persons at a single end-user location who have access to, or who use, the Internet-access services that are delivered over the high-speed connection to that location.

[1] Power Line and Other are summarized with Other Wireline to maintain firm confidentiality.

[2] Fiber to the premises.

* Plunkett Research Estimate.

Source: U.S. Federal Communications Bureau (FCC)

Plunkett Research, Ltd.

www.plunkettresearch.com

Internet Access Technologies Compared

(In Millions of Bits per Second - Mbps)

Type of Access	Maximum Data Rate (In Mbps)	Characteristics
Dialup		
Dialup	.0288, .0336, .056	Analog modems that require dialup connection. Slowest method of Internet access.
ISDN	.064, .128	Integrated Services Digital Network. Digital access that requires dialup connection.
Wired Broadband		
ADSL	1.5 - 24 Downstream .5 - 3.5 Upstream	Asymmetrical Digital Subscriber Line. Highest speeds are on ADSL2+ (ULL).
SDSL	2.3	Symmetric Digital Subscriber Line. Downstream and upstream data transfer rates are similar. Ideal for businesses because of synchronous speed and high-speed router capabilities.
VDSL	24 - 100 Downstream 2.3 - 16 Upstream	Very High bit-Rate DSL.
Cable Modem	4 - 2,000 Downstream .384 - 50 Upstream	2 Gigabyte (2 GB) speeds are possible with DOCSIS 3.1 technology.
FTTH	15 to 1,000 Downstream 5 to 1,000 Upstream	Fiber to the Home (Home, Node, Premises, etc). Google Fiber is a leading provider. Google is developing 10 Gigabyte (10 GB) technologies.
T1/DS1	1.544	Ideal for businesses with high bandwidth requirements.
T3/DS3	44.736	Equivalent to 30 T1 circuits.
E1 (Europe)	2.048	European version of T1.
E3 (Europe)	34.368	European version of T3.
OC3	155.52	High-speed access. Uses optical fiber technology.
OC12	622.08	Offers higher speed access than OC3. Uses optical fiber technology.
OC48	2,488.32	Offers one of the fastest data rates. Uses optical fiber technology. Extremely expensive to setup and maintain.
OC768	39,813.12	Network line used by AT&T, Cisco and others.
Wireless Broadband		
802.15.3 (UWB)	100 - 2,000	UWB stands for ultrawideband. It is useful for high-speed, short distance data transfer.
802.11b-g (Wi-Fi)	11 - 54	Typical home and office wireless networks.
802.11n (MIMO), 802.11ac	100 - 2,000	Faster data transmission rates and broader area coverage than other 802.11 technologies.
802.15 (Bluetooth) versions 1.0 - 2.0	1 - 3	Useful for high-speed, short distance data transfer.
802.15 Bluetooth version 3.0	24	Bluetooth 3.0 offers high speed data transfer at short range of up to 10 meters.
802.16e (WiMAX)	15 - 70	Has the potential to be useful for distances of up to 30 miles.
802.16m (WiMAX2)	110-365 Download 70-376 Upload	Also known as WiMAX Advanced, this technology is classified by the ITU as true 4G.
Satellite	5 to 20	Limited upstream speeds. Low-Earth Orbit satellites may offer faster speeds.
CDMA2000 EV-DO	2.4	Popular cellular technology. EV-DO Rev. A is 3.1 Mbps, Rev. B is 14.7 Mbps
HSPA	14.4	Popular 3G cellular
LTE Advanced (4G -5G)	100-1,000 Download up to 500 Upload	An upgraded version of LTE. Sometimes called an IMT-Advanced technology.
5G	1,000 to 10,000	5G NR (2017-18) improves existing 4G networks as a modest speed upgrade. 5G 15 was the first standalone 5G specification (2017-19).
HSPA+	42 - 168	Advanced cellular, Release 8 is 42 Mbps, Release 9 is 84 Mbps and Release 10 is 168 Mbps.
LTE (3G-4G)	36 to 326	"Long Term Evolution" technology for cellular networks.
LTE Advanced (4G, Release 10)	100-1,000 Download up to 500 Upload	An upgraded version of LTE that is classified by the ITU as 4G. Sometimes called an IMT-Advanced technology.
5G	200 - 10,000	Download speeds of as much 10 Gigabytes are theoretically possible.

Note: 1 Mbps = 1,000 Kbps; 1,000 Mbps = 1 Gigabyte (1 GB)

Research Funding for Engineering, U.S. National Science Foundation: Fiscal Years 2020-2022

(In Millions of US$)

Engineering: Subactivity Area	FY 2020 Actual	FY 2021 (TBD)	FY 2022 Request	Change over 2020 Actual	
				Amount	Percent
Chemical, Bioengineering, Environmental & Transport Systems (CBET)	197.92	199.96	241.05	41.09	20.5%
Civil, Mechanical & Manufacturing Innovation (CMMI)	238.58	241.13	290.50	49.37	20.5%
Electrical, Communications & Cyber Systems (ECCS)	122.86	124.05	149.52	25.47	20.5%
Engineering Education & Centers (EEC)	124.06	125.02	149.30	24.28	19.4%
Emerging Frontiers and Multidisciplinary Activities (EFMA)	70.88	71.69	86.42	14.73	20.5%
Total, Engineering Activity	**754.31**	**761.85**	**916.79**	**154.94**	**20.3%**

Note: Totals may not add due to rounding.

Source: U.S. National Science Foundation
Plunkett Research, Ltd.
www.plunkettresearch.com

Chapter 3

IMPORTANT INTERNET OF THINGS (IoT) & DATA ANALYTICS INDUSTRY CONTACTS

Addresses, Telephone Numbers and Internet Sites

Contents:

1) Aerospace & Defense Industry Associations

Aerospace Industries Association
1000 Wilson Blvd., Ste. 1700
Arlington, VA 22209-3928 US
Phone: 703-358-1000
E-mail Address: *aia@aia-aerospace.org*
Web Address: www.aia-aerospace.org
The Aerospace Industries Association represents the nation's leading manufacturers and suppliers of civil, military, and business aircraft, helicopters, unmanned aerial vehicles, space systems, aircraft engines, missiles, materiel, and related components, equipment, services, and information technology.

Council of Defense & Space Industry Associations (CODSIA)
1000 Wilson Blvd., Ste. 1800
Arlington, VA 22209 USA
Phone: 703-243-2020
Fax: 703-243-8539
E-mail Address: info@codsia.org
Web Address: www.codsia.org
The Council of Defense and Space Industry Associations (CODSIA) provides a central channel of communications for improving industry-wide consideration of the many policies, regulations, implementation problems, procedures and questions involved in federal procurement actions.

Defense MicroElectronics Activity (DMEA)
4234 54th St.
McClellan, CA 95652-2100 USA
Phone: 916-231-1555
Fax: 916-231-2855
Web Address: www.dmea.osd.mil
Defense MicroElectronics Activity (DMEA) was established by the Department of Defense to provide a broad spectrum of microelectronics services.

Federal Association of German Aerospace Industry (BDLI)
Bundesverband der Deutschen Luft- und Raumfahrtindustrie eV (BDLI)
ATRIUM Friedrichstrasse 60
Berlin, D-10117 Germany
Phone: 49-30-2061-40-0
Fax: 49-30-2061-40-90
E-mail Address: kontakt@bdli.de
Web Address: www.bdli.de
The German Aerospace Industries Association (BDLI) represents the German aviation and aerospace industry at the national and international levels.

National Defense Industrial Association (NDIA)
2101 Wilson Blvd., Ste. 700
Arlington, VA 22201 USA
Phone: 703-522-1820
Fax: 703-522-1885
E-mail Address: trice@ndia.org
Web Address: www.ndia.org
The National Defense Industrial Association (NDIA), an association with more than 47,000 individuals as well as 1,375 corporate members, is dedicated to discussing defense industry concerns and promoting national security.

2) Aerospace Resources

Defense Science Technology Lab (DSTL)
Porton Down
Salisbury, Wiltshire SP4 0JQ UK
Phone: 44-1980-613000
Fax: 44-1980-613004
E-mail Address: centralenquiries@dstl.gov.uk
Web Address: www.dstl.gov.uk
Defense Science Technology Lab (DSTL) supplies scientific research and advice to the Ministry of Defense (MOD) and other government departments.

NASA Learning Technologies Project (LTP)
NASA Headquarters, Ste. 2R40
Washington, DC 20546 USA
Phone: 301-286-1112

E-mail Address: daniel.laughlin@gsfc.nasa.gov
Web Address:
www.nasa.gov/offices/education/programs/national/ltp/home/index.html
The NASA Learning Technologies Project (LTP) is the space association's educational technology research and development division.

3) Artificial Intelligence Associations

Allen Institute for Artificial Intelligence (AI2)
2157 N. Northlake Way, Ste. 110
Seattle, WA 98103 USA
Phone: 206-548-5600
E-mail Address: ai2-info@allenai.org
Web Address: allenai.org
AI2 was founded in 2014 with the singular focus of conducting high-impact research and engineering in the field of artificial intelligence, all for the common good. AI2 was the creation of late Paul Allen, Microsoft co-founder. Situated on the shores of Lake Union, AI2 employs over 40 of the world's best scientific talent in the field of AI, attracting individuals of varied interests and backgrounds from across the globe.

Neural Information Processing System Foundation, Inc. (NIPS)
1269 Law Str.
San Diego, CA 92109 USA
Toll Free: 858-208-3810
E-mail Address: meperry@salk.edu
Web Address: https://nips.cc
NIPS is a leading organization gathering leaders from academia and the corporate world together for a highly regarded annual conference on artificial intelligence (AI), machine learning and related topics.

OpenAI
E-mail Address: info@openai.com
Web Address: www.openai.com
Near the end of 2015, a group of well-known Silicon Valley investors, including Elon Musk and Peter Thiel, announced a long-term commitment to raise funds of as much a $1 billion for a new organization to be known as OpenAI, www.openai.com. OpenAI is a nonprofit research organization consisting of 60 people focused on long-term, fundamental AI projects.

4) Automotive Industry Associations

Alliance of Automobile Manufacturers
803 7th St. NW, Ste. 300
Washington, DC 20001 USA
Phone: 202-326-5500
Fax: 202-326-5598
E-mail Address: info@autoalliance.org
Web Address: www.autoalliance.org
The Alliance of Automobile Manufacturers is a trade association composed of 9 car manufacturing companies including BMW Group, DaimlerChrysler, Ford Motor Company, General Motors, Mazda, Mitsubishi Motors, Porsche, Toyota and Volkswagen. Alliance members account for more than 90% of vehicles sold in the U.S.

Association of Global Automakers (Global Automakers)
1050 K St. NW, Ste. 650
Washington, DC 20001 USA
Phone: 202-650-5555
E-mail Address: info@globalautomakers.org
Web Address: www.globalautomakers.org
The Association of Global Automakers (Global Automakers), formerly the Association of International Automobile Manufacturers, Inc., is a trade association representing 14 international motor vehicle manufacturers. Members concentrate on improving the safety and efficiency of vehicles, as well as investing in American communities.

Canadian Transportation Equipment Association (CTEA)
16 Barrie Blvd., Unit 3B
St. Thomas, ON N5P 4B9 Canada
Phone: 519-631-0414
Fax: 519-631-1333
E-mail Address: ccowell@atminc.on.ca
Web Address: www.ctea.ca
The Canadian Transportation Equipment Association (CTEA) standardizes the commercial vehicle equipment manufacturing industry in Canada.

Canadian Vehicle Manufacturers' Association (CVMA)
170 Attwell Dr., Ste. 400
Toronto, ON M9W 5Z5 Canada
Phone: 416-364-9333
Fax: 416-367-3221
Toll Free: 800-758-7122
E-mail Address: info@cvma.ca
Web Address: www.cvma.ca

The Canadian Vehicle Manufacturers' Association (CVMA) is the industry organization representing manufacturers of light and heavy duty motor vehicles in Canada. Association members collaborate to solve industry objectives in the way of consumer protection, the environment and vehicle safety.

United States Council for Automotive Research Inc. (USCAR)
1000 Town Center Dr., Ste. 300
Southfield, MI 48075 USA
Phone: 248-223-9000
E-mail Address: sbairley@uscar.org
Web Address: www.uscar.org
The United States Council for Automotive Research (USCAR) was founded in 1992. Its goal is to further strengthen the technology base of the U.S. auto industry through cooperative research and development. Its main focus is to create, support and direct U.S. cooperative research and development to advance automotive technologies. USCAR is composed of a number of specialized groups that focus on specific research areas. USCAR is governed by the three-member USCAR Council, whose membership includes the R&D vice presidents from each of the U.S. automakers.

5) Automotive Industry Resources

Automotive Center
1800 Crooks Rd.
Troy, MI 48084 USA
Phone: 248-244-8920
Web Address: www.plastics-car.com
The Automotive Center, sponsored by the American Chemistry Council's Plastics Division, strives to provide the automobile designer, stylist or engineer with up-to-the-minute research and information on plastics applications in cars.

6) Automotive Safety

American Traffic Safety Services Institute (The) (ATSSA)
15 Riverside Pkwy., Ste. 100
Fredericksburg, VA 22406-1077 USA
Phone: 540-368-1701
Fax: 540-368-1717
Toll Free: 800-272-8772
E-mail Address: communications@atssa.com
Web Address: www.atssa.com
The American Traffic Safety Services Institute (ATSSA) is an international trade association whose members provide pavement markings, signage, work zone traffic control devices and other safety features on our nation's roadways.

7) Blockchain Associations

Enterprise Ethereum Alliance
401 Edgewater Pl., Ste. 600
Wakefield, MA 01880 USA
Web Address: https://entethalliance.org/
The Enterprise Ethereum Alliance connects Fortune 500 enterprises, startups, academics and technology vendors with Ethereum virtual currency network subject matter experts. Members learn from and build upon the blockchain network to define enterprise-grade software capable of handling complex, highly demanding applications at the speed of business.

Hyperledger
E-mail Address: info@hyperledger.org
Web Address: www.hyperledger.org
Hyperledger is an open source collaborative effort created to advance cross-industry blockchain technologies. It is a global collaboration, hosted by The Linux Foundation, including leaders in finance, banking, Internet of Things, supply chains, manufacturing and technology.

8) Canadian Government Agencies-General

Canadian Intellectual Property Office (CIPO)
Place du Portage, 50 Victoria St., Rm. C-229
Gatineau, QC K1A 0C9 Canada
Phone: 819-934-0544
Fax: 819-953-2476
Toll Free: 866-997-1936
Web Address: www.cipo.ic.gc.ca
The Canadian Intellectual Property Office (CIPO) is the agency responsible for the administration and processing of intellectual property in Canada, including patents, trademarks, copyrights, industrial designs and integrated circuit topographies.

9) Canadian Government Agencies-Scientific

Institute for Microstructural Sciences (IMS)
1200 Montreal Rd., Bldg. M-58
Ottawa, ON K1A 0R6 Canada

Phone: 613-993-9101
Fax: 613-952-9907
Toll Free: 877-672-2672
E-mail Address: info@nrc-cnrc.gc.ca
Web Address: www.nrc-cnrc.gc.ca
The Institute for Microstructural Sciences (IMS) is a branch of Canada's National Research Council (NRC) that focuses its research on the information and telecommunications technology sector.

10) Careers-Computers/Technology

ComputerJobs.com, Inc.
675 Alpha Dr., Ste. E
Highland Heights, OH 44143 USA
Toll Free: 800-850-0045
Web Address: www.computerjobs.com
ComputerJobs.com, Inc. is an employment web site that offers users a links to computer-related job opportunities organized by skill and market.

Dice.com
6465 S. Greenwood Plaza Blvd., Ste. 400
Centennial, CO 80111 USA
Phone: 515-280-1144
Fax: 515-280-1452
Toll Free: 888-321-3423
E-mail Address: techsupport@dice.com
Web Address: www.dice.com
Dice.com provides free employment services for IT jobs. The site includes advanced job searches by geographic location and category, availability announcements and resume postings, as well as employer profiles, a recruiter's page and career links. It is maintained by Dice Holdings, Inc., a publicly traded company.

Institute for Electrical and Electronics Engineers (IEEE) Job Site
445 Hoes Ln.
Piscataway, NJ 08855-1331 USA
Phone: 732-981-0060
Toll Free: 800-678-4333
E-mail Address: candidatejobsite@ieee.org
Web Address: careers.ieee.org
The Institute for Electrical and Electronics Engineers (IEEE) Job Site provides a host of employment services for technical professionals, employers and recruiters. The site offers job listings by geographic area, a resume bank and links to employment services.

Pencom Systems, Inc.
152 Remsen St.
Brooklyn, NY 11201 USA
Phone: 718-923-1111
Fax: 718-923-6065
E-mail Address: tom@pencom.com
Web Address: www.pencom.com
Pencom Systems, Inc., an open system recruiting company, hosts a career web site geared toward high-technology and scientific professionals, featuring an interactive salary survey, career advisor, job listings and technology resources. Its focus is the financial services industry within the New York City area.

11) Careers-First Time Jobs/New Grads

CollegeGrad.com, Inc.
950 Tower Ln., Fl. 6
Foster City, CA 94404 USA
E-mail Address: info@quinstreet.com
Web Address: www.collegegrad.com
CollegeGrad.com, Inc. offers in-depth resources for college students and recent grads seeking entry-level jobs.

National Association of Colleges and Employers (NACE)
62 Highland Ave.
Bethlehem, PA 18017-9085 USA
Phone: 610-868-1421
E-mail Address: customerservice@naceweb.org
Web Address: www.naceweb.org
The National Association of Colleges and Employers (NACE) is a premier U.S. organization representing college placement offices and corporate recruiters who focus on hiring new grads.

12) Careers-General Job Listings

CareerBuilder, Inc.
200 N La Salle Dr., Ste. 1100
Chicago, IL 60601 USA
Phone: 773-527-3600
Fax: 773-353-2452
Toll Free: 800-891-8880
Web Address: www.careerbuilder.com
CareerBuilder, Inc. focuses on the needs of companies and also provides a database of job openings. The site has over 1 million jobs posted by 300,000 employers, and receives an average 23 million unique visitors monthly. The company also operates online career centers for 140 newspapers

and 9,000 online partners. Resumes are sent directly to the company, and applicants can set up a special e-mail account for job-seeking purposes. CareerBuilder is primarily a joint venture between three newspaper giants: The McClatchy Company, Gannett Co., Inc. and Tribune Company.

CareerOneStop
Toll Free: 877-872-5627
E-mail Address: info@careeronestop.org
Web Address: www.careeronestop.org
CareerOneStop is operated by the employment commissions of various state agencies. It contains job listings in both the private and government sectors, as well as a wide variety of useful career resources and workforce information. CareerOneStop is sponsored by the U.S. Department of Labor.

LaborMarketInfo (LMI)
Employment Development Dept.
P.O. Box 826880, MIC 57
Sacramento, CA 94280-0001 USA
Phone: 916-262-2162
Fax: 916-262-2352
Web Address: www.labormarketinfo.edd.ca.gov
LaborMarketInfo (LMI) provides job seekers and employers a wide range of resources, namely the ability to find, access and use labor market information and services. It provides statistics for employment demographics on both a local and regional level, as well as career searching tools for California residents. The web site is sponsored by California's Employment Development Office.

Recruiters Online Network
E-mail Address: rossi.tony@comcast.net
Web Address: www.recruitersonline.com
The Recruiters Online Network provides job postings from thousands of recruiters, Careers Online Magazine, a resume database, as well as other career resources.

USAJOBS
USAJOBS Program Office
1900 E St. NW, Ste. 6500
Washington, DC 20415-0001 USA
Phone: 818-934-6600
Web Address: www.usajobs.gov
USAJOBS, a program of the U.S. Office of Personnel Management, is the official job site for the U.S. Federal Government. It provides a comprehensive list of U.S. government jobs, allowing users to search for employment by location; agency; type of work; or by senior executive positions. It also has special employment sections for individuals with disabilities, veterans and recent college graduates; an information center, offering resume and interview tips and other information; and allows users to create a profile and post a resume.

13) Careers-Job Reference Tools

Vault.com, Inc.
132 W. 31st St., Fl. 16
New York, NY 10001 USA
Fax: 212-366-6117
Toll Free: 800-535-2074
E-mail Address: customerservice@vault.com
Web Address: www.vault.com
Vault.com, Inc. is a comprehensive career web site for employers and employees, with job postings and valuable information on a wide variety of industries. Its features and content are largely geared toward MBA degree holders.

14) Chinese Government Agencies-Informational Technology

Ministry of Industry and Information Technology (MIIT)
13 W. Chang'an Ave.
Beijing, 100804 China
Phone: 86-10-68205985
Web Address: www.miit.gov.cn
The Ministry of Industry and Information Technology of the People's Republic of China was established in 2008 as a department under the State Council responsible for the administration of China's industrial branches and information industry. The main responsibilities of the ministry are to determine China's industrial planning, policies and standards; to monitor the daily operation of industrial branches; to promote the development of major technological equipment and innovation concerning the communication sector; to guide the construction of information system; and to safeguard China's information security.

15) Chinese Government Agencies-Science & Technology

China Ministry of Science and Technology (MOST)
15B Fuxing Rd.
Beijing, 100862 China

Web Address: www.most.gov.cn
The China Ministry of Science and Technology (MOST) is the PRC's official body for science and technology related activities. It drafts laws, policies and regulations regarding science and technology; oversees budgeting and accounting for funds; and supervises research institutes operating in China, among other duties.

16) Computer & Electronics Industry Associations

Armed Force Communications and Electronics Association
4114 Legato Rd., Ste. 1000
Fairfax, VA 22033-3899 USA
Phone: 703-631-6100
Fax: 703-631-6169
Toll Free: 800-336-4583
E-mail Address: service@afcea.org
Web Address: www.afcea.org
AFCEA provides a forum for military, government and industry communities to collaborate so that technology and strategy align with the needs of those who serve.

Asian-Oceanian Computing Industry Organization (ASOCIO)
No. 2, Jalan PJU 8/8A,
c/o PIKOM, Block E1, Empire Damansara E-01-G,
Petaling Jaya, Selangor 47820 Malaysia
Phone: 603-7622-0079
Fax: 603-7622-4879
E-mail Address: secretariat@asocio.org
Web Address: www.asocio.org
The Asian-Oceanian Computing Industry Organization's (ASOCIO) objective is to promote the development of the computing industry in the region.

Association for Computing Machinery (ACM)
1601 Broadway, Fl. 10
New York, NY 10019-7434 USA
Phone: 212-626-0500
Fax: 212-944-1318
Toll Free: 800-342-6626
E-mail Address: acmhelp@acm.org
Web Address: www.acm.org
The Association for Computing Machinery (ACM) is dedicated to advancing the arts, sciences and applications of computing and information technology. ACM's online Digital Library offers visitors access to journal publications and other educational materials.

Association for Information Systems (AIS)
35 Broad St., Ste. 917
Atlanta, GA 30303 USA
Phone: 404-413-7445
Fax: 404-413-7443
E-mail Address: membership@aisnet.org
Web Address: www.aisnet.org
The Association for Information Systems (AIS) is an organization for information system researchers and educators working in colleges and universities worldwide. Its web site offers substantial resources regarding computer systems research and new developments.

Association of Information Technology Professionals (AITP)
3500 Lacey Rd., Ste. 100
Downers Grove, IL 60515 USA
Phone: 630-678-8300
Fax: 630-678-8384
Toll Free: 866-835-8020
E-mail Address: aitp_hq@aitp.org
Web Address: www.aitp.org
The Association of Information Technology Professionals (AITP) is a trade organization that provides training and education through partnerships within the information technology industry.

Association of the Computer and Multimedia Industry of Malaysia (PIKOM)
E1, Empire Damansara, E-01-G
No.2, Jalan PJU 8/8A, Damansara Perdana
Petaling Jaya, Selangor Darul Ehsan 47820 Malaysia
Phone: 603-7622-0079
Fax: 603-7622-4879
E-mail Address: info@pikom.org.my
Web Address: www.pikom.org.my
The Association of the Computer and Multimedia Industry of Malaysia, or, in Malay, Persatuan Industri Komputer dan Multimedia Malaysia (PIKOM), is the national association representing more than 1,000 companies active in the information and communications technology (ICT) industry in Malaysia.

Business Technology Association (BTA)
12411 Wornall Rd., Ste. 200
Kansas City, MO 64145 USA
Phone: 816-941-3100
Fax: 816-941-4843
Toll Free: 800-505-2821
E-mail Address: info@bta.org
Web Address: www.bta.org

The Business Technology Association (BTA) is an organization for resellers and dealers of business technology products. Its site offers buying groups, message boards, legal advice, news on industry trends and live chats.

Canadian Advanced Technology Alliances (CATAAlliance)
207 Bank St., Ste. 416
Ottawa, ON K2P 2N2 Canada
Phone: 613-236-6550
E-mail Address: info@cata.ca
Web Address: www.cata.ca
The Canadian Advanced Technology Alliances (CATAAlliance) is one of Canada's leading trade organizations for the research, development and technology sectors.

China Electronic Components Association (CECA)
23 Shijingshan Rd.
ZhongChu Building
Beijing, 100049 China
Phone: 86-10-6887-1587
E-mail Address: icceca@ic-ceca.org.cn
Web Address: www.ic-ceca.org.cn
The China Electronic Components Association (CECA) acts as the representative of the Chinese electronics components industry. Its web site provides consultation services and research reports on components for a wide variety of markets.

Computer & Communications Industry Association (CCIA)
25 Massachusetts Ave., Ste. 300C
Washington, DC 20001 USA
Phone: 202-783-0070
Fax: 202-783-0534
Web Address: www.ccianet.org
The Computer & Communications Industry Association (CCIA) is a non-profit membership organization for companies and senior executives representing the computer, Internet, information technology (IT) and telecommunications industries.

Computer Technology Industry Association (CompTIA)
3500 Lacey Rd., Ste. 100
Downers Grove, IL 60515 USA
Phone: 630-678-8300
Fax: 630-678-8384
Toll Free: 866-835-8020
Web Address: www.comptia.org
The Computer Technology Industry Association (CompTIA) is the leading association representing the international technology community. Its goal is to provide a unified voice, global advocacy and leadership, and to advance industry growth through standards, professional competence, education and business solutions.

Electronic Industries Association of India (ELCINA)
422 Okhla Industrial Estate
ELCINA House
New Delhi, Delhi 110020 India
Phone: 91-11-2692-4597
Fax: 91-11-2692-3440
E-mail Address: info@elcina.com
Web Address: www.elcina.com
The Electronic Industries Association of India (ELCINA) is an organization for the promotion of electronic hardware manufacturing through active representation and advice to the Indian government.

Electronics and Computer Software Export Promotion Council (ESC)
ESC House, 155 Okhla Industrial Estate
New Delhi, Delhi 110020 India
Phone: 91-11-47480000
Fax: 91-11-2685-3412
E-mail Address: info@escindia.com
Web Address: www.escindia.in
The Electronics and Computer Software Export Promotion Council (ESC) represents the info-communication technology industry through electronics and IT trade facilitation.

Electronics Technicians Association international (ETA International)
5 Depot St.
Greencastle, IN 46135 USA
Phone: 765-653-8262
Fax: 765-653-4287
Toll Free: 800-288-3824
E-mail Address: eta@eta-i.org
Web Address: www.eta-i.org
The Electronics Technicians Association International (ETA International) is a nonprofit professional association for electronics technicians worldwide. The organization provides recognized professional credentials for electronics technicians.

European Electronic Component Manufacturers Association (EECA)
11/13 rue de la Duchesse

Brussels, 1150 Belgium
Phone: 32-2-290-36-60
Fax: 32-2-290-36-65
E-mail Address: secretariat.gen@eeca.be
Web Address: www.eeca.eu
The European Electronic Component Manufacturers Association (EECA) is comprised of two more specific industry associations: the European Semiconductor Industry Association (ESIA) and the European Passive Components Industry Association (EPCIA). The mission of the EECA is to promote and support the electronic components industry of Europe in the global marketplace.

German Association for Information Technology, Telecom and New Media (BITKOM)
Bundersverband Informationswirtschaft Telekommunikation und neue Medien
Albrechtstr. 10A
Berlin-Mitte, 10117 Germany
Phone: 49-30-27576-0
Fax: 49-30-27576-400
E-mail Address: bitkom@bitkom.org
Web Address: www.bitkom.org
German Association for Information Technology, Telecom and New Media (BITKOM) represents information technology and telecommunications specialists and companies.

German Electrical and Electronic Manufacturers' Association (ZVEI)
Zentralverband Elektrotechnik- und Elektronikindustrie e.V.
Lyoner St. 9
Frankfurt am Main, 60528 Germany
Phone: 49-69-6302-0
Fax: 49-69-6302-317
E-mail Address: zvei@zvei.org
Web Address: www.zvei.org
The German Electrical and Electronic Manufacturers' Association (ZVEI) represents its members' interests at the national and international level.

Global Semiconductor Alliance (GSA)
12400 Coit Rd., Ste. 650
Dallas, TX 75251 USA
Phone: 972-866-7579
Fax: 972-239-2292
Toll Free: 888-322-5195
E-mail Address: contact@gsaglobal.org
Web Address: www.gsaglobal.org
The Global Semiconductor Alliance (GSA) serves the entire supply chain of the global semiconductor industry, including intellectual property (IP), electronic design automation (EDA)/design, wafer manufacturing, test and packaging activities.

Hong Kong Electronic Industries Association (HKEIA)
Harbor Crystal Ctr., 100 Granville Rd.
Rm. 1201, Fl. 12
Kowloon, Hong Kong Hong Kong
Phone: 852-2778-8328
Fax: 852-2788-2200
E-mail Address: hkeia@hkeia.org
Web Address: www.hkeia.org
The Hong Kong Electronic Industries Association Limited (HKEIA) is a non-profit trade organization dedicated to the promotion and development of the electronics industry.

Indian Electrical & Electronics Manufacturers Association (IEEMA)
501 Kakad Chambers
132 Dr. Annie Besant Rd., Worli
Mumbai, 400018 India
Phone: 91-22-2493-0532
Fax: 91-22-2493-2705
E-mail Address: mumbai@ieema.org
Web Address: www.ieema.org
The Indian Electrical & Electronics Manufacturers Association (IEEMA) represents all sectors of the electrical and allied products businesses of the Indian electrical industry.

Information Technology Association of Canada (ITAC)
5090 Explorer Dr., Ste. 801
Mississauga, ON L4W 4T9 Canada
Phone: 905-602-8345
Fax: 905-602-8346
E-mail Address: dwhite@itac.ca
Web Address: www.itac.ca
The Information Technology Association of Canada (ITAC) represents the IT, software, computer and telecommunications industries in Canada.

Information Technology Industry Council (ITI)
700 K St. NW, Ste. 600
Washington, DC 20001 USA
Phone: 202-737-8888
Fax: 202-638-4922
E-mail Address: info@itic.org
Web Address: www.itic.org
The Information Technology Industry Council (ITI) is a premier group of the nation's leading high-tech

companies and widely recognized as one of the tech industry's most effective lobbying organization in Washington, in various foreign capitals and the World Trade Organization (WTO).

Information Technology Management Association (ITMA)
Robinson Rd.
P.O. Box 3297
Singapore, 905297 Singapore
Phone: 65-8171-4456
Fax: 65-6410-8008
E-mail Address: secretariat@itma.org.sg
Web Address: www.itma.org.sg
Information Technology Management Association (ITMA) represents professionals working in the field of IT management in Singapore.

Institute for Interconnecting and Packaging Electronic Circuits (IPC)
3000 Lakeside Dr., Ste. 105 N
Bannockburn, IL 60015 USA
Phone: 847-615-7100
Fax: 847-615-7105
E-mail Address: answers@ipc.org
Web Address: www.ipc.org
The Institute for Interconnecting and Packaging Electronic Circuits (IPC) is a trade association for companies in the global printed circuit board and electronics manufacturing services industries.

International Microelectronics Assembly and Packaging Society (IMAPS)
P.O. Box 110127
Research Triangle Park, NC 27709-5127 USA
Phone: 919-293-5000
Fax: 919-287-2339
E-mail Address: info@imaps.org
Web Address: www.imaps.org
The International Microelectronics Assembly and Packaging Society (IMAPS) is dedicated to the advancement and growth of the use of microelectronics and electronic packaging through professional education, workshops and conferences.

International Technology Roadmap for Semiconductors (ITRS)
Web Address: www.itrs2.net
The International Technology Roadmap for Semiconductors (ITRS) aims to ensure the continued development of the semiconductor industry through the assessment of industry technologies. ITRS strives to foster teamwork and collaboration within the industry, and holds annual public conferences on the current state and future of the semiconductor industry. It is sponsored by the five leading chip manufacturing regions in the world: Europe, Japan, Korea, Taiwan and the U.S.

Japan Business Federation (Nippon Keidanren)
Keidanren Kaikan
1-3-2 Otemachi
Tokyo, Chiyoda-ku 100-8188 Japan
Phone: 81-3-6741-0171
Fax: 81-3-6741-0301
E-mail Address: webmaster@keidanren.or.jp
Web Address: www.keidanren.or.jp/
Japan Business Federation (Nippon Keidanren) is an amalgamation of Japan Federation of Economic Organizations (Keidanren) and Japan Federation of Employers' Associations (Nikkeiren). The group focuses on the technological development of Japanese industry and the promotion of trade.

Japan Electronics and Information Technology Industries Association (JEITA)
Ote Cen. Bldg.
1-1-3, Otemachi
Tokyo, Chiyoda-ku 100-0004 Japan
Phone: 81-3-5218-1050
Fax: 81-3-5218-1070
Web Address: www.jeita.or.jp/english
Japan Electronics and Information Technology Industries Association (JEITA) promotes the manufacturing and international trade and consumption of electronics and electronic components in Japan.

Korea Association of Information and Telecommunications (KAIT)
NO. 1678-2, 2nd Fl. Dong-Ah Villat 2 Town
Seocho-dong, Seocho-gu
Seoul, 137-070 Korea
Phone: 82-2-580-0582
E-mail Address: webmaster@kait.or.kr
Web Address: www.kait.or.kr/eng
The Korea Association of Information and Telecommunications (KAIT) was created to develop and promote the InfoTech, computer, consumer electronics, wireless, software and telecommunications sectors in Korea.

Korea Electronics Association (KEA)
World Cup buk-ro 54-gil, Mapo-gu, Fl. 11
Seoul, 03924 Korea
Phone: 82-2-6388-6000

Fax: 82-02-6388-6009
Web Address: www.gokea.org
The Korea Electronics Association (KEA) was established by Korea's Ministry of Commerce to promote the growth and development of the nation's electronics industry.

Korea Semiconductor Industry Association (KSIA)
182, Pangyoyeok-ro, Bundang-gu, Seongnam-si
Fl. 9-12, KSIA Bldg.
Gyeonggi-do, Korea
Phone: 82-2-576-3472
Fax: 82-2-570-5269
E-mail Address: admin@ksia.or.kr
Web Address: www.ksia.or.kr
The Korean Semiconductor Industry Association (KSIA) represents the interests of Korean semiconductor manufacturers.

Manufacturers' Association for Information Technology (MAIT)
4/2, Siri Institutional Area, August Kranti Marg
Fl. 4, PHD House, Ramakrishna Dalmia Wing
New Delhi, Delhi 110-016 India
Phone: 91-11-2685-5487
Fax: 91-11-2685-1321
E-mail Address: contact@mait.com
Web Address: www.mait.com
The Manufacturers' Association for Information Technology (MAIT) is an organization that focuses on the promotion of the hardware, training, design/R&D and the associated services sectors of the Indian IT industry.

National Electrical Manufacturers Association (NEMA)
1300 N. 17th St., Ste. 900
Arlington, VA 22209 USA
Phone: 703-841-3200
E-mail Address: press@nema.org
Web Address: www.nema.org
The National Electrical Manufacturers Association (NEMA) develops standards for the electrical manufacturing industry and promotes safety in the production and use of electrical products.

Network Professional Association (NPA)
3517 Camino Del Rio S., Ste. 215
San Diego, CA 92108-4089 USA
Fax: 888-672-6720
Toll Free: 888-672-6720
Web Address: www.npanet.org
The Network Professionals Association (NPA) is a self-regulating, nonprofit association of network computing professionals that sets standards of technical expertise and professionalism.

North America Chinese Clean-tech & Semiconductor Association (NACSA)
809-B Cuesta Dr., Ste. 208
Mountain View, CA 94040 USA
Web Address: www.nacsa.com
The North America Chinese Clean-tech & Semiconductor Association (NACSA), founded in Silicon Valley in 1996, is dedicated to the advancement of Chinese professionals in high-tech and related industries, including chip design, chip manufacture, system manufacture, equipment manufacture and software.

Retail Solutions Providers Association (RSPA)
9920 Couloak Dr., Ste. 120
Charlotte, NC 28216 USA
Phone: 704-357-3124
Fax: 704-357-3127
Toll Free: 800-782-2693
E-mail Address: Info@GoRSPA.org
Web Address: www.gorspa.org
The Retail Solutions Providers Association (RSPA) is a trade association composed of businesses involved in the purchase, resale, enhancement, installation and maintenance of point-of-sale systems to and for end users.

Semiconductor & Electronics Industries in the Philippines, Inc. (SEIPI)
117-A Technology Ave., Fl. 2, Building 2
Binan, 4024 Philippines
Phone: 63906-559-4584
Fax: 02-869-0000
E-mail Address: helpdesk@seipi.org.ph
Web Address: www.seipi.org.ph
The SEIPI Foundation is an organization of foreign and local semiconductor and electronics companies in the Philippines.

Semiconductor Equipment and Materials International (SEMI)
673 S. Milpitas Blvd.
Milpitas, CA 95035 USA
Phone: 408-943-6900
Fax: 408-428-9600
E-mail Address: semihq@semi.org
Web Address: www.semi.org

Semiconductor Equipment and Materials International (SEMI) is a trade association serving the global semiconductor equipment, materials and flat-panel display industries.

Semiconductor Equipment Association of Japan (SEAJ)
3 Rokubancho Chiyoda-ku
6F Rokubancho SK Bldg.
Tokyo, 102-0085 Japan
Phone: 81-3-3261-8260
Fax: 81-3-3261-8263
Web Address: www.seaj.or.jp
The Semiconductor Equipment Association of Japan (SEAJ) represents the semiconductor manufacturing equipment industry in Japan. The association is an organization of semiconductor manufacturing and flat panel display (FPD) manufacturing equipment manufacturers.

Semiconductor Industry Association (SIA)
1101 K St. NW, Ste. 450
Washington, DC 20005 USA
Phone: 202-446-1700
Fax: 202-216-9745
Toll Free: 866-756-0715
Web Address: www.semiconductors.org
The Semiconductor Industry Association (SIA) is a trade association representing the semiconductor industry in the U.S. Through its coalition of more than 60 companies, SIA members represent roughly 80% of semiconductor production in the U.S. The coalition aims to advance the competitiveness of the chip industry and shape public policy on issues particular to the industry.

Shenzhen Electronics Industries Association (SZEIA)
Guangdong Shenzhen SEG 4 W., Fl. 11
Shenzhen, 518031 China
Phone: 86-755-3300-5162
Fax: 86-755-3300-5155
E-mail Address: szseia@szeia.com
Web Address: www.szeia.com
The Shenzhen Electronics Industries Association (SZEIA) is one of China's primary organizations for the electronics industry. Its web site contains information regarding policies and regulations affecting the electronics industry, as well as news and career opportunities.

Singapore Computer Society
53/53A Neil Rd.
Singapore, 088891 Singapore
Phone: 65-6226-2567
Fax: 65-6226-2569
E-mail Address: scs.secretariat@scs.org.sg
Web Address: www.scs.org.sg
The Singapore Computer Society is a membership society for infocomm professionals in Singapore.

Storage Network Industry Association (SNIA)
5201 Great America Pkwy., Ste. 320
Santa Clara, CA 95054 USA
Phone: 719-694-1380
Fax: 719-694-1385
E-mail Address: emerald@snia.org
Web Address: www.snia.org
The Storage Network Industry Association (SNIA) is a trade associated dedicated to viability of storage networks within the IT industry. SNIA sponsors technical work groups, produces the Storage Networking Conference series and maintains a Technology Center in Colorado Springs, Colorado.

Surface Mount Technology Association (SMTA)
6600 City West Pkwy., Ste. 300
Eden Prairie, MN 55424 USA
Phone: 952-920-7682
Fax: 952-926-1819
E-mail Address: smta@smta.org
Web Address: www.smta.org
The Surface Mount Technology Association (SMTA) is an international network of professionals whose careers encompass electronic assembly technologies, microsystems, emerging technologies and associated business operations.

Taiwan Electrical and Electronic Manufacturers' Association (TEEMA)
Min Chuan E. Rd., Fl. 6, No. 109, Sec. 6
Taipei, 11490 Taiwan
Phone: 886-2-8792-6666
Fax: 886-2-8792-6088
E-mail Address: teema@teema.org.tw
Web Address: www.teema.org.tw
The Taiwan Electrical and Electronic Manufacturers' Association (TEEMA) works as an intermediary between its members and the government to help the industry to succeed.

Taiwan Semiconductor Industry Association (TSIA)
195 Sec. 4, Zhongxing Rd.
Rm. 1246, Hall. 51
Zhudong, Hsinchu 31040 Taiwan

Phone: 886-3-591-5574
Fax: 886-3-582-0056
Web Address: www.tsia.org.tw
The TSIA is Taiwan's national trade organization, containing more than 130 member companies that represent all aspects of the semiconductor industry.

World Information Technology and Services Alliance (WITSA)
8300 Boone Blvd., Ste. 450
Vienna, VA 22182 USA
Phone: 571-265-5964
Fax: 703-893-1269
E-mail Address: admin@witsa.org
Web Address: www.witsa.org
The World Information Technology and Services Alliance (WITSA) is a consortium of over 70 information technology (IT) industry associations from economies around the world. WITSA members represent over 90% of the world IT market. Founded in 1978 and originally known as the World Computing Services Industry Association, WITSA is an advocate in international public policy issues affecting the creation of a robust global information infrastructure.

17) Computer & Electronics Industry Resources

Centre for Development of Advanced Computing (C-DAC)
Pune University Campus
Ganesh Khind
Pune, 411 007 India
Phone: 91-20-2570-4100
Fax: 91-20-2569-4004
Web Address: www.cdac.in
The Centre for Development of Advanced Computing (C-DAC) is a research and development institution created for the design, development and deployment information technology solutions for economic and human advancement. C-DAC is a branch of India's Department of Information Technology (DIT), Ministry of Communications & Information Technology (MCIT).

Cisco Cloud Index
170 W. Tasman Dr.
San Jose, CA 95134 USA
Toll Free: 800-553-6387
Web Address: www.cisco.com/go/cloudindex
The Cisco Cloud Index covers three areas focused on data center and cloud traffic trends and next-generation service or application adoption. They include: Data center and cloud traffic forecast; Workload transition, which provides projections for workloads moving from traditional IT to cloud-based architectures; and Cloud readiness, which provides regional statistics on broadband adoption as a precursor for cloud services.

EETimes
Web Address: www.eetimes.com
The EETimes is an online magazine devoted to electronic engineers in the semiconductor, systems and software design fields.

Information Technology and Innovation Foundation (ITIF)
700 K St. NW, Ste. 600
Washington, DC 20001 USA
Phone: 202-449-1351
E-mail Address: mail@itif.org
Web Address: www.itif.org
Information Technology and Innovation Foundation (ITIF) is a non-partisan research and educational institute (a think tank) with a mission to formulate and promote public policies to advance technological innovation and productivity internationally, in Washington, and in the States. Recognizing the vital role of technology in ensuring American prosperity, ITIF focuses on innovation, productivity, and digital economy issues.

Ministry of Electronics and Information Technology (India)
Electronics Niketan
6 CGO Complex, Lodhi Rd.
New Delhi, 110003 India
Phone: 91-11-2430-1851
E-mail Address: webmaster@deity.gov.in
Web Address: www.meity.gov.in
Ministry of Communications & Information Technology (MIT) of the Government of India, is charged with promoting the information technology and communications industries.

18) Computer-Aided Engineering Resources

Center for Design Research (CDR) at Stanford University
Center for Design Research
Bldg. 560, 424 Panama Mall
Stanford, CA 94305-2232 USA
Phone: 650-723-9233

Fax: 650-725-8475
E-mail Address: tunison@stanford.edu
Web Address: www-cdr.stanford.edu
The web site of the Center for Design Research (CDR) at Stanford University provides information on the center's staff, laboratories and projects on design process and design tool development for engineering.

19) Consulting Industry Associations

TechServe Alliance
1420 King St., Ste. 610
Alexandria, VA 22314 USA
Phone: 703-838-2050
E-mail Address: staff@techservealliance.org
Web Address: www.techservealliance.org
The TechServe Alliance, is an association that aims to advance excellence and ethics within the IT & engineering staffing and solutions industry. Its membership offers collaborative networking and knowledge sharing, updated operational and market trends and commitment to fair business practices and ethical code of conducts.

20) Corporate Information Resources

Business Journals (The)
120 W. Morehead St., Ste. 400
Charlotte, NC 28202 USA
Toll Free: 866-853-3661
E-mail Address: gmurchison@bizjournals.com
Web Address: www.bizjournals.com
Bizjournals.com is the online media division of American City Business Journals, the publisher of dozens of leading city business journals nationwide. It provides access to research into the latest news regarding companies both small and large. The organization maintains 42 websites and 64 print publications and sponsors over 700 annual industry events.

Business Wire
101 California St., Fl. 20
San Francisco, CA 94111 USA
Phone: 415-986-4422
Fax: 415-788-5335
Toll Free: 800-227-0845
E-mail Address: info@businesswire.com
Web Address: www.businesswire.com
Business Wire offers news releases, industry- and company-specific news, top headlines, conference calls, IPOs on the Internet, media services and access to tradeshownews.com and BW Connect On-line through its informative and continuously updated web site.

Edgar Online, Inc.
35 W. Wacker Dr.
Chicago, IL 60601 USA
Phone: 301-287-0300
Fax: 301-287-0390
Toll Free: 800-823-5304
Web Address: www.edgar-online.com
Edgar Online, Inc. is a gateway and search tool for viewing corporate documents, such as annual reports on Form 10-K, filed with the U.S. Securities and Exchange Commission.

PR Newswire Association LLC
200 Vesey St., Fl. 19
New York, NY 10281 USA
Fax: 800-793-9313
Toll Free: 800-776-8090
E-mail Address: mediainquiries@cision.com
Web Address: www.prnewswire.com
PR Newswire Association LLC provides comprehensive communications services for public relations and investor relations professionals, ranging from information distribution and market intelligence to the creation of online multimedia content and investor relations web sites. Users can also view recent corporate press releases from companies across the globe. The Association is owned by United Business Media plc.

Silicon Investor
E-mail Address: si.admin@siliconinvestor.com
Web Address: www.siliconinvestor.com
Silicon Investor is focused on providing information about technology companies. Its web site serves as a financial discussion forum and offers quotes, profiles and charts.

21) Drone Associations

Unmanned Systems Technology (UST)
Office 1 Ste. C, Mulberry Ct.
Christchurch, BH23 1PS UK
Phone: 44-01202-485884
E-mail Address: hello@ust.team
Web Address:
www.unmannedsystemstechnology.com
Unmanned Systems Technology (UST) is a dedicated directory of component, service and platform

suppliers within the unmanned systems industry. All categories of unmanned systems are included: Air vehicles (UAV/UAS/RPAS), Ground Vehicles and Robotic Systems (UGVs), Surface and Subsea vehicles (USV, UUV) and Space vehicles.

22) Ecommerce and Data Interchange Technology Associations

Center for Research in Electronic Commerce
McCombs School of Business
CBA 6.426, 2100 Speedway, Stop B6500
Austin, TX 78712-1170 USA
Phone: 512-471-7962
Fax: 512-471-3034
E-mail Address: abw@uts.cc.utexas.edu
Web Address: cism.mccombs.utexas.edu/
The Center for Research in Electronic Commerce at the University of Texas is a leading research institution in generating critical knowledge and understanding in the fields of information systems and management, electronic commerce and the digital economy.

RosettaNet
7877 Washington Village Dr., Ste. 300
Dayton, OH 45459 USA
Phone: 937-435-3870
E-mail Address: info@gs1us.org
Web Address: www.resources.gs1us.org/rosettanet
RosettaNet, a subsidiary of GS1 US, is a nonprofit organization whose mission is to develop e-business process standards that serve as a frame of reference for global trading networks. The organization's standards provide a common language for companies within the global supply chain.

23) Economic Data & Research

Centre for European Economic Research (The, ZEW)
L 7, 1
Mannheim, 68161 Germany
Phone: 49-621-1235-01
Fax: 49-621-1235-224
E-mail Address: empfang@zew.de
Web Address: www.zew.de/en
Zentrum fur Europaische Wirtschaftsforschung, The Centre for European Economic Research (ZEW), distinguishes itself in the analysis of internationally comparative data in a European context and in the creation of databases that serve as a basis for scientific research. The institute maintains a special library relevant to economic research and provides external parties with selected data for the purpose of scientific research. ZEW also offers public events and seminars concentrating on banking, business and other economic-political topics.

Economic and Social Research Council (ESRC)
Polaris House
North Star Ave.
Swindon, SN2 1UJ UK
Phone: 44-01793 413000
E-mail Address: esrcenquiries@esrc.ac.uk
Web Address: www.esrc.ac.uk
The Economic and Social Research Council (ESRC) funds research and training in social and economic issues. It is an independent organization, established by Royal Charter. Current research areas include the global economy; social diversity; environment and energy; human behavior; and health and well-being.

Eurostat
5 Rue Alphonse Weicker
Joseph Bech Bldg.
Luxembourg, L-2721 Luxembourg
Phone: 352-4301-1
E-mail Address: eurostat-pressoffice@ec.europa.eu
Web Address: ec.europa.eu/eurostat
Eurostat is the European Union's service that publishes a wide variety of comprehensive statistics on European industries, populations, trade, agriculture, technology, environment and other matters.

Federal Statistical Office of Germany
Gustav-Stresemann-Ring 11
Wiesbaden, D-65189 Germany
Phone: 49-611-75-2405
Fax: 49-611-72-4000
Web Address: www.destatis.de
Federal Statistical Office of Germany publishes a wide variety of nation and regional economic data of interest to anyone who is studying Germany, one of the world's leading economies. Data available includes population, consumer prices, labor markets, health care, industries and output.

India Brand Equity Foundation (IBEF)
Fl. 20, Jawahar Vyapar Bhawan
Tolstoy Marg
New Delhi, 110001 India
Phone: 91-11-43845500
Fax: 91-11-23701235

E-mail Address: info.brandindia@ibef.org
Web Address: www.ibef.org
India Brand Equity Foundation (IBEF) is a public-private partnership between the Ministry of Commerce and Industry, the Government of India and the Confederation of Indian Industry. The foundation's primary objective is to build positive economic perceptions of India globally. It aims to effectively present the India business perspective and leverage business partnerships in a globalizing marketplace.

National Bureau of Statistics (China)
57, Yuetan Nanjie, Sanlihe
Xicheng District
Beijing, 100826 China
Fax: 86-10-6878-2000
E-mail Address: info@gj.stats.cn
Web Address: www.stats.gov.cn/english
The National Bureau of Statistics (China) provides statistics and economic data regarding China's economy and society.

Organization for Economic Co-operation and Development (OECD)
2 rue Andre Pascal, Cedex 16
Paris, 75775 France
Phone: 33-1-45-24-82-00
Fax: 33-1-45-24-85-00
E-mail Address: webmaster@oecd.org
Web Address: www.oecd.org
The Organization for Economic Co-operation and Development (OECD) publishes detailed economic, government, population, social and trade statistics on a country-by-country basis for over 30 nations representing the world's largest economies. Sectors covered range from industry, labor, technology and patents, to health care, environment and globalization.

Statistics Bureau, Director-General for Policy Planning (Japan)
19-1 Wakamatsu-cho
Shinjuku-ku
Tokyo, 162-8668 Japan
Phone: 81-3-5273-2020
E-mail Address: toukeisoudan@soumu.go.jp
Web Address: www.stat.go.jp/english
The Statistics Bureau, Director-General for Policy Planning (Japan) and Statistical Research and Training Institute, a part of the Japanese Ministry of Internal Affairs and Communications, plays the central role of producing and disseminating basic official statistics and coordinating statistical work under the Statistics Act and other legislation.

Statistics Canada
150 Tunney's Pasture Driveway
Ottawa, ON K1A 0T6 Canada
Phone: 514-283-8300
Fax: 514-283-9350
Toll Free: 800-263-1136
E-mail Address: STATCAN.infostats-infostats.STATCAN@canada.ca
Web Address: www.statcan.gc.ca
Statistics Canada provides a complete portal to Canadian economic data and statistics. Its conducts Canada's official census every five years, as well as hundreds of surveys covering numerous aspects of Canadian life.

24) Electronic Health Records/Continuity of Care Records

American Health Information Management Association (AHIMA)
233 N. Michigan Ave., Fl. 21
Chicago, IL 60601-5809 USA
Phone: 312-233-1100
Fax: 312-233-1090
Toll Free: 800-335-5535
E-mail Address: info@ahima.org
Web Address: www.ahima.org
The American Health Information Management Association (AHIMA) is a professional association that consists health information management professionals who work throughout the health care industry.

25) Engineering Industry Resources

Cornell Engineering Library (The)
Engineering Library Cornell University
Carpenter Hall, Fl. 1
Ithaca, NY 14853 USA
Phone: 607-254-6261
E-mail Address: engrref@cornell.edu
Web Address: engineering.library.cornell.edu
Cornell University's Engineering Library web site has a number of resources concerning engineering research, as well as links to other engineering industry information sources.

26) Engineering, Research & Scientific Associations

Agency For Science, Technology And Research (A*STAR)
1 Fusionopolis Way
20-10 Connexis N. Twr.
Singapore, 138632 Singapore
Phone: 65-6826-6111
Fax: 65-6777-1711
E-mail Address: contact@a-star.edu.sg
Web Address: www.a-star.edu.sg
The Agency For Science, Technology And Research (A*STAR) of Singapore comprises the Biomedical Research Council (BMRC), the Science and Engineering Research Council (SERC), A*STAR Joint Council (A*JC), the A*STAR Graduate Academy (A*GA) and the Corporate Group. Both Councils fund the A*STAR public research institutes which conducts research in specific niche areas in science, engineering and biomedical science.

Alfred P. Sloan Foundation
630 Fifth Ave., Ste. 2550
New York, NY 10111 USA
Phone: 212-649-1649
Fax: 212-757-5117
E-mail Address: myerson@sloan.org
Web Address: www.sloan.org
The Alfred P. Sloan Foundation funds science and technology, economic performance, education, national issues and civics programs through research fellowships and grants.

American National Standards Institute (ANSI)
1899 L St. NW, Fl. 11
Washington, DC 20036 USA
Phone: 202-293-8020
Fax: 202-293-9287
E-mail Address: info@ansi.org
Web Address: www.ansi.org
The American National Standards Institute (ANSI) is a private, nonprofit organization that administers and coordinates the U.S. voluntary standardization and conformity assessment system. Its mission is to enhance both the global competitiveness of U.S. business and the quality of life by promoting and facilitating voluntary consensus standards and conformity assessment systems and safeguarding their integrity.

American Society for Engineering Education (ASEE)
1818 North St. NW, Ste. 600
Washington, DC 20036-2479 USA
Phone: 202-331-3500
Fax: 202-265-8504
E-mail Address: board@asee.org
Web Address: www.asee.org
The American Society for Engineering Education (ASEE) is nonprofit organization dedicated to promoting and improving engineering and technology education.

Association for Electrical, Electronic & Information Technologies (VDE)
Stresemannallee 15
Frankfurt, 60596 Germany
Phone: 49-69-6308-0
Fax: 49-69-6308-9865
E-mail Address: service@vde.com
Web Address: www.vde.com
The Association for Electrical, Electronic & Information Technologies (VDE) is a German organization with roughly 36,000 members, representing one of the largest technical associations in Europe.

Association for Facilities Engineering (AFE)
8200 Greensboro Dr., Ste. 400
McLean, VA 22102 USA
Phone: 571-395-8777
Fax: 571-766-2142
Web Address: www.afe.org
The Association for Facilities Engineering (AFE) provides education, certification, technical information and other relevant resources for plant and facility engineering, operations and maintenance professionals worldwide.

Association of German Engineers (The, VDI)
VDI e.V.
VDI-Platz 1
Dusseldorf, 40468 Germany
Phone: 49-(0)-211-6214-0
Fax: 49 (0) 211-6214-575
Web Address: www.vdi.de
The Association of German Engineers (VDI) promotes innovation and technology in Germany and represents one of the largest technical-scientific associations in Europe.

Association of German Machinery and Equipment Engineering (VDMA)
Friedrichstrasse 95
Berlin, 10117 Germany
Phone: 49-30-30-69-46-0
Fax: 49-30-30-69-46-20
E-mail Address: berlin@vdma.org
Web Address: www.vdma.org
The Association of German Machinery and Equipment Engineering (VDMA) represents the machinery and plant manufacturing industry and the associated information technology and system engineering sector. The website includes product database, and member company lists as well as publications and links.

Center for Innovative Technology (CIT)
2214 Rock Hill Rd., Ste. 600
Herndon, VA 20170-4228 USA
Phone: 703-689-3000
Fax: 703-689-3041
E-mail Address: info@cit.org
Web Address: www.cit.org
The Center for Innovative Technology is a nonprofit organization designed to enhance the research and development capabilities by creating partnerships between innovative technology start-up companies and advanced technology consumers.

Chemical Industry and Engineering Society of China (CIESC)
Fl. 7, Block B, No. 33
Beijing Anding Rd., Chaoyang District
Beijing, 100029 China
Phone: 86-10-6444-1885
E-mail Address: yyangyh@ciesc.cn
Web Address: www.ciesc.cn
The Chemical Industry and Engineering Society of China (CIESC) aims to advance chemical engineering professionals and the chemical industry through academic and educational development. CIESC is affiliated with the China Association for Science and Technology.

China Association for Science and Technology (CAST)
3 Fuxing Rd.
Beijing, 100863 China
Phone: 8610-6857-1898
Fax: 8610-6857-1897
E-mail Address: cast-liasion@cast.org.cn
Web Address: english.cast.org.cn
The China Association for Science and Technology (CAST) is the largest national non-governmental organization of scientific and technological workers in China. The association has nearly 207 member organizations in the fields of engineering, science and technology.

Chinese Academy of Sciences (CAS)
52 Sanlihe Rd.
Beijing, 100864 China
Phone: 86-10-6859-7521
Fax: 86-10-6851-1095
E-mail Address: cas_en@cas.cn
Web Address: english.cas.ac.cn
The Chinese Academy of Sciences (CAS) is an academic institution and research center active within the fields of natural and technological sciences. It brings together the operations of 124 science institutions, including five universities and supporting entities and over 104 research institutes throughout China.

Community Research and Development Information Service (CORDIS)
Office for Official Publications of the European Union Communities
2 rue Mercier
Luxembourg, L-2985 Luxembourg
Phone: 352-2929-42210
E-mail Address: cordis@publications.europa.eu
Web Address: cordis.europa.eu
The Community Research and Development Information Service (CORDIS) provides information about research and development sponsored and supported by the European Union. It is managed by the Office for Official Publications of the European Union Communities (Publications Office).

Federation of Technology Industries (FHI)
Leusderend 12
Leusden, 3832 RC The Netherlands
Phone: 31-33-465-7507
Fax: 31-33-461-6638
E-mail Address: info@fhi.nl
Web Address: federatie.fhi.nl
The Federation of Technology Industries (FHI) is the Dutch trade organization representing the industrial electronics, automation, laboratory technology and medical technology sectors in the Netherlands.

IEEE Broadcast Technological Society (IEEE BTS)
445 Hoes Ln.

Piscataway, NJ 08854 USA
Phone: 732-562-6061
Fax: 732-235-1627
E-mail Address: a.temple@ieee.org
Web Address: bts.ieee.org
The IEEE Broadcast Technological Society (IEEE BTS) is the arm of the Institute of Electrical & Electronics Engineers (IEEE) devoted to devices, equipment, techniques and systems related to broadcast technology.

IEEE Communications Society (ComSoc)
3 Park Ave., Fl. 17
New York, NY 10016 USA
Phone: 212-705-8900
Fax: 212-705-8999
Web Address: www.comsoc.org
The IEEE Communications Society (ComSoc) is composed of industry professionals with a common interest in advancing communications technologies.

Indian Institute of Technology - Roorkee
Roorkee, Uttarakhand 247 667 India
Phone: 91-1332-285311
E-mail Address: registar@iitr.ernet.in
Web Address: www.iitr.ac.in
Indian Institute of Technology - Roorkee is among the foremost institutes in higher technological education and engineering in India for basic and applied research.

Industrial Research Institute (IRI)
P.O. Box 13968
Arlington, VA 22219 USA
Phone: 703-647-2580
Fax: 703-647-2581
E-mail Address: information@iriweb.org
Web Address: www.iriweb.org
The Innovation Research Interchange (IRI) is a nonprofit organization of over 200 leading industrial companies, representing industries such as aerospace, automotive, chemical, computers and electronics, which carry out industrial research efforts in the U.S. manufacturing sector. IRI helps members improve research and development capabilities.

Institute of Electrical and Electronics Engineers (IEEE)
3 Park Ave., Fl. 17
New York, NY 10016-5997 USA
Phone: 212-419-7900
Fax: 212-752-4929
Toll Free: 800-678-4333
E-mail Address: society-info@ieee.org
Web Address: www.ieee.org
The Institute of Electrical and Electronics Engineers (IEEE) is a nonprofit, technical professional association of more than 430,000 individual members in approximately 160 countries. The IEEE sets global technical standards and acts as an authority in technical areas ranging from computer engineering, biomedical technology and telecommunications to electric power, aerospace and consumer electronics.

Institution of Engineering and Technology (The) (IET)
Michael Faraday House, Six Hills Way
Stevenage, Herts SG1 2AY UK
Phone: 44-1438-313-311
Fax: 44-1438-765-526
E-mail Address: postmaster@theiet.org
Web Address: www.theiet.org
The Institution of Engineering and Technology (IET) is an innovative international organization for electronics, electrical, manufacturing and IT professionals.

International Electrotechnical Commission (IEC)
3, rue de Varembe
P.O. Box 131
Geneva 20, CH-1211 Switzerland
Phone: 41-22-919-02-11
Fax: 41-22-919-03-00
E-mail Address: info@iec.ch
Web Address: www.iec.ch
The International Electrotechnical Commission (IEC), based in Switzerland, promotes international cooperation on all questions of standardization and related matters in electrical and electronic engineering.

International Standards Organization (ISO)
Chemin de Blandonnet 8
1214 Vernier
Geneva, CP 401 Switzerland
Phone: 41-22-749-01-11
Fax: 41-22-733-34-30
E-mail Address: central@iso.org
Web Address: www.iso.org
The International Standards Organization (ISO) is a global consortium of national standards institutes from 162 countries. The established International Standards are designed to make products and services more efficient, safe and clean.

Japan Science and Technology Agency (JST)
Kawaguchi Ctr. Bldg.
4-1-8 Honcho, Kawaguchi-shi
Saitama, 332-0012 Japan
Phone: 81-48-226-5601
Fax: 81-48-226-5651
Web Address: www.jst.go.jp/EN
The Japan Science and Technology Agency (JST) acts as a core organization for implementation of the nation's science and technology policies by conducting research and development, with particular emphasis on new technological needs.

National Academy of Engineering (NAE)
500 5th St. NW
Washington, DC 20001 USA
Phone: 202-334-3200
E-mail Address: dmote@nae.edu
Web Address: www.nae.edu
The National Academy of Engineering (NAE) is a nonprofit institution that conducts independent studies to examine important topics in engineering and technology. It is the portal for all engineering activities at the National Academies, which include the National Academy of Sciences, the Institute of Medicine and the National Research Council.

National Academy of Science (NAS)
500 5th St. NW
Washington, DC 20001 USA
Phone: 202-334-2000
E-mail Address: worldwidefeedback@nas.edu
Web Address: www.nasonline.org
The National Academy of Science (NAS) is a private, nonprofit, self-perpetuating society of scholars engaged in scientific and engineering research. Three organizations comprise the NAS: The National Academy of Engineering, the National Academy of Sciences and the National Academy of Medicine.

Netherlands Organization for Applied Scientific Research (TNO)
Anna van Buerenplein 1
The Hague, NL-2595 DA The Netherlands
Phone: 31-88-866-0000
E-mail Address: wegwijzer@tno.nl
Web Address: www.tno.nl
The Netherlands Organization for Applied Scientific Research (TNO) is a contract research organization that provides a link between fundamental research and practical application.

Optical Society of America (OSA)
2010 Massachusetts Ave. NW
Washington, DC 20036-1023 USA
Phone: 202-223-8130
Fax: 202-223-1096
E-mail Address: info@osa.org
Web Address: www.osa.org
The Optical Society of America (OSA) is an interdisciplinary society offering synergy between all components of the optics industry, from basic research to commercial applications such as fiber-optic networks. It has a membership group of over 16,000 individuals from over 100 countries. Members include scientists, engineers, educators, technicians and business leaders.

Professional Engineers Board Singapore (PEB)
52 Jurong Gateway Rd.
Singapore, 608550 Singapore
Phone: 65-6334-2310
Fax: 65-6334-2347
E-mail Address: registrar@peb.gov.sg
Web Address: www.peb.gov.sg
The Professional Engineers Board Singapore (PEB) is a statutory board in the Ministry of National Development. PEB was established since 1971 under the Professional Engineers Act in order to keep and maintain a register of professional engineers, a register of practitioners and a register of licensed corporations.

Research in Germany, German Academic Exchange Service (DAAD)
Kennedyallee 50
Bonn, 53175 Germany
Phone: 49-228-882-743
Web Address: www.research-in-germany.de
The Research in Germany portal, German Academic Exchange Service (DAAD), is an information platform and contact point for those looking to find out more about Germany's research landscape and its latest research achievements. The portal is an initiative of the Federal Ministry of Education and Research.

Royal Society (The)
6-9 Carlton House Ter.
London, SW1Y 5AG UK
Phone: 44-20-7451-2500
E-mail Address: science.policy@royalsociety.org
Web Address: royalsociety.org
The Royal Society, originally founded in 1660, is the UK's leading scientific organization and the oldest

scientific community in continuous existence. It operates as a national academy of science, supporting scientists, engineers, technologists and researchers. Its web site contains a wealth of data about the research and development initiatives of its fellows and foreign members.

Society of Automotive Engineers (SAE)
755 W. Big Beaver, Ste. 1600
Troy, MA 48084 USA
Phone: 248-273-2455
Fax: 248-273-2494
Toll Free: 877-606-7323
E-mail Address: automotive_hq@sae.org
Web Address: www.sae.org
The Society of Automotive Engineers (SAE) is a resource for technical information and expertise used in designing, building, maintaining and operating self-propelled vehicles for use on land, sea, air or space.

Society of Broadcast Engineers, Inc. (SBE)
9102 N. Meridian St., Ste. 150
Indianapolis, IN 46260 USA
Phone: 317-846-9000
E-mail Address: jporay@sbe.org
Web Address: www.sbe.org
The Society of Broadcast Engineers (SBE) exists to increase knowledge of broadcast engineering and promote its interests, as well as to continue the education of professionals in the industry.

SPIE
1000 20th St.
Bellingham, WA 98225-6705 USA
Phone: 360-676-3290
Fax: 360-647-1445
Toll Free: 888-504-8171
E-mail Address: customerservice@spie.org
Web Address: www.spie.org
SPIE is a nonprofit technical society aimed at the advancement and dissemination of knowledge in optics, photonics and imaging.

World Federation of Engineering Organizations
Maison de l'UNESCO
1, rue Miollis
Paris, 75015 France
Phone: 33-1-45-68-48-47
Fax: 33-1-45-68-48-65
E-mail Address: secretariat@wfeo.net
Web Address: www.wfeo.org
World Federation of Engineering Organizations (WFEO) is an international non-governmental organization that represents major engineering professional societies in over 90 nations. It has several standing committees including engineering and the environment, technology, communications, capacity building, education, energy and women in engineering.

27) Entertainment & Amusement Associations-General

Entertainment Technology Center (ETC)
313 S. Figueroa St.
Los Angeles, CA 90089 USA
Phone: 213-821-6163
E-mail Address: info@etcenter.org
Web Address: www.etcenter.org
The Entertainment Technology Center at the University of Southern California (ETC@USC) exists to discover, research, develop and accelerate entertainment, consumer electronics, technology and services industries. This research center brings together senior executives, thought leaders and innovators to explore issues related to creation, distribution and consumption of creative content. It provides research and publications, as well as conducts events, collaborative projects, shared exploratory labs and demonstrations.

28) Environmental Organizations

Center for Environmental Systems Research (CESR)
University of Kassel
Wilhelmshoher Allee 47, Raum 1130
Kassel, 34109 Germany
Phone: 0561-804-6110
Fax: 0561-804-6112
E-mail Address: info@cesr.de
Web Address: www.usf.uni-kassel.de/cesr/
The Center for Environmental Systems Research (CESR) is part of the University of Kassel. It operates four research groups: Global and Regional Dynamics, covering water and land use changes; Socio-Environmental Systems; Integrated Water Management; and Sustainable Energy and Material Flow Management. The CESR publishes many important papers and boosts education and research.

29) Environmental Resources

Environment Canada
10 Wellington, Fl. 23
Gatineau, QC K1A 0H3 Canada
Phone: 819-997-2800
Fax: 819-994-1412
Toll Free: 800 668-6767
E-mail Address: enviroinfo@ec.gc.ca
Web Address: www.ec.gc.ca
Environment Canada is the Canadian government's natural environment preservation department.

30) Financial Technology Associations, FinTech

Association for Financial Technology
3525 Piedmont Rd. NE, Ste. 300
Atlanta, GA 30305 USA
Phone: 404-789-3154
Fax: 404-240-0998
E-mail Address: aft@aftweb.com
Web Address: www.aftweb.com
Association for Financial Technology (AFT) is a premier resource for networking and professional development for those companies and executives serving U.S. financial institutions (FI's), including banks, credit unions, lenders and payment companies. Founded in 1972, the organization members represent virtually every area of technology, data or services needed to help FI's succeed.

31) FinTech Resources

FinTech Breakthrough
E-mail Address: info@fintechbreakthrough.com
Web Address: https://fintechbreakthrough.com/
FinTech Breakthrough runs an annual technology awards program that recognizes outstanding technology platforms and executives in areas such as payments, mortgages, banking and investments. Its website is an excellent source for learning about outstanding companies in this field.

32) Games Industry Associations

Association for UK Interactive Entertainment (UKIE)
24-28 Hatton Wall
London, EC1N 8JH UK
Phone: 44-20-7534-0580
E-mail Address: info@ukie.org.uk
Web Address: www.ukie.org.uk
The Association for UK Interactive Entertainment (UKIE) is the UK's leading trade body for games and wider interactive entertainment industry. Membership includes almost all major companies involved with the publishing and development of videogames in the UK.

Entertainment Software Association (ESA)
601 Massachusetts Ave. NW, Ste. 300
Washington, DC 20001 USA
Phone: 202-223-2400
E-mail Address: esa@theesa.com
Web Address: www.theesa.com
The Entertainment Software Association (ESA) is a U.S. trade association for companies that publish video and computer games for consoles, personal computers and the Internet. The ESA owns the E3 Media & Business Summit, a major invitation-only annual trade show for the video game industry.

Hong Kong Digital Entertainment Industry Support Centre
78 Tat Chee Ave.
HKPC Building
Kowloon, Hong Kong Hong Kong
Phone: 852-2788-5678
Fax: 852-2788-5900
E-mail Address: hkpcenq@hkpc.org
Web Address: www.hkpc.org/en/industry-support-services/support-centres/hong-kong-software-industry-information-centre
The Hong Kong Digital Entertainment Industry Support Centre comprises three major sectors in Hong Kong, namely entertainment software, computer animation and digital effects in the production of videos and films. The center supports the development of professionals in the field of animation, design and programming, as well as promotes traditional industries through business development, marketing and branding.

Independent Game Developers Association Limited (The, TIGA)
One London Wall, Fl. 6
London, EC2Y 5EB UK
Phone: 44-845-468-2330
E-mail Address: info@tiga.org
Web Address: www.tiga.org
The Independent Game Developers Association (TIGA) is the trade association representing the UK's games industry. Its members include independent games developers, in-house publisher owned

developers, outsourcing companies, technology businesses and universities.

33) Health Care Business & Professional Associations

Advanced Medical Technology Association (AdvaMed)
701 Pennsylvania Ave. NW, Ste. 800
Washington, DC 20004-2654 USA
Phone: 202-783-8700
Fax: 202-783-8750
E-mail Address: info@advamed.org
Web Address: www.advamed.org
The Advanced Medical Technology Association (AdvaMed) strives to be the advocate for a legal, regulatory and economic climate that advances global health care by assuring worldwide access to the benefits of medical technology.

34) Industry Research/Market Research

Forrester Research
60 Acorn Park Dr.
Cambridge, MA 02140 USA
Phone: 617-613-5730
Toll Free: 866-367-7378
E-mail Address: press@forrester.com
Web Address: www.forrester.com
Forrester Research is a publicly traded company that identifies and analyzes emerging trends in technology and their impact on business. Among the firm's specialties are the financial services, retail, health care, entertainment, automotive and information technology industries.

Gartner, Inc.
56 Top Gallant Rd.
Stamford, CT 06902 USA
Phone: 203-964-0096
E-mail Address: info@gartner.com
Web Address: www.gartner.com
Gartner, Inc. is a publicly traded IT company that provides competitive intelligence and strategic consulting and advisory services to numerous clients worldwide.

MarketResearch.com
6116 Executive Blvd., Ste. 550
Rockville, MD 20852 USA
Phone: 240-747-3093
Fax: 240-747-3004
Toll Free: 800-298-5699
E-mail Address: customerservice@marketresearch.com
Web Address: www.marketresearch.com
MarketResearch.com is a leading broker for professional market research and industry analysis. Users are able to search the company's database of research publications including data on global industries, companies, products and trends.

Plunkett Research, Ltd.
P.O. Drawer 541737
Houston, TX 77254-1737 USA
Phone: 713-932-0000
Fax: 713-932-7080
E-mail Address: customersupport@plunkettresearch.com
Web Address: www.plunkettresearch.com
Plunkett Research, Ltd. is a leading provider of market research, industry trends analysis and business statistics. Since 1985, it has served clients worldwide, including corporations, universities, libraries, consultants and government agencies. At the firm's web site, visitors can view product information and pricing and access a large amount of basic market information on industries such as financial services, InfoTech, ecommerce, health care and biotech.

35) Internet & Online Business Resources

InternetNews.com
3343 Perimeter Hill Dr., Ste. 100
Nashville, TN 37211 USA
Phone: 877-822-9526
E-mail Address: info@technologyadvice.com
Web Address: www.internetnews.com
InternetNews.com offers real-time business news specifically designed for Internet technology managers. News categories include hardware, software, mobility, content, networking and search.

36) Internet Industry Associations

Asia & Pacific Internet Association (APIA)
P.O. Box 1908
Milton, 4064 Australia
E-mail Address: apiasec@apia.org
Web Address: www.apia.org
Asia & Pacific Internet Association (APIA) is a nonprofit trade association whose aim is to promote the business interests of the Internet-related service

industry in the Asia Pacific region. The site contains a list of organizations, standards, regional Internet registries and related Asia Pacific organizations.

China Internet Network Information Center
4, S. 4th St., Zhongguancun
Fl. 1, Bldg. 1, Software Park
Beijing, 100190 China
Phone: 86-10-58813000
Fax: 86-10-58812666
E-mail Address: service@cnnic.cn
Web Address: www.cnnic.cn
The China Internet Network Information Center compiles Internet information and databases regarding the Internet community and facilitates the development and application of Internet resources and relevant technologies in China.

Cooperative Association for Internet Data Analysis (CAIDA)
9500 Gilman Dr.
Mail Stop 0505
La Jolla, CA 92093-0505 USA
Phone: 858-534-5000
E-mail Address: info@caida.org
Web Address: www.caida.org
The Cooperative Association for Internet Data Analysis (CAIDA), representing organizations from the government, commercial and research sectors, works to promote an atmosphere of greater cohesion in the engineering and maintenance of the Internet. CAIDA is located at the San Diego Supercomputer Center (SDSC) on the campus of the University of California, San Diego (UCSD).

Cyber Threat Alliance (CTA)
3033 Wilson Blvd., Ste. 700
Arlington, VA 22201 USA
E-mail Address: PR@cyberthreatalliance.org
Web Address: https://www.cyberthreatalliance.org/
The Cyber Threat Alliance (CTA) goal is to improve the cybersecurity of the global digital ecosystem by enabling near real-time, high-quality cyber threat information sharing among companies and organizations in the cybersecurity field.

Federation of Internet Service Providers of the Americas (FISPA)
c/o Jim Hollis
8200 Raintree Ln., Ste. 100
Charlotte, NC 28277 USA
Phone: 704-844-2540
Fax: 704-844-2728
Toll Free: 813-574-2556
E-mail Address: executive.director@fipsa.org
Web Address: www.fispa.org
The Federation of Internet Service Providers of the Americas (FISPA) encourages discussion, education and collective buying power for organizations involved in providing Internet access, web hosting, web design and other Internet products and services.

International Academy of Digital Arts and Sciences (IADAS)
22 W. 21st St., Fl. 7
New York, NY 10010 USA
Phone: 212-675-4890
E-mail Address: dmdavies@iadas.net
Web Address: www.iadas.net
The International Academy of Digital Arts and Sciences (IADAS) is dedicated to the progress of new media worldwide. It runs The Webby Awards, honoring web sites for technological and creative achievements, as well as The Lovie Awards, honoring individuals involved in managing, designing, marketing online web sites, advertising, mobile apps and social content for European market.

Internet Association
Phone: 202-869-8680
E-mail Address: info@internetassociation.org
Web Address: https://internetassociation.org
The Internet Association is a trade association that exclusively represents leading global internet companies on matters of public policy. It offers posts, reports and resources relating to election advertising, patents, net neutrality, trade, privacy, data security, sharing economy and global internet governance.

Internet Law & Policy Forum (ILPF)
2440 Western Ave., Ste. 709
Seattle, WA 98121 USA
Phone: 206-727-0700
Fax: 206-374-2263
E-mail Address: admin@ilpf.org
Web Address: www.ilpf.org
The Internet Law & Policy Forum (ILPF) is dedicated to the global development of the Internet through legal and public policy initiatives. It is an international nonprofit organization whose member companies develop and deploy the Internet in every aspect of business today.

Internet Society (ISOC)
11710 Plaza America Dr., Ste. 400
Reston, VA 20190 USA

Phone: 703-439-2120
Fax: 703-326-9881
E-mail Address: isoc@isoc.org
Web Address: www.isoc.org
The Internet Society (ISOC) is a nonprofit organization that provides leadership in public policy issues that influence the future of the Internet. The organization is the home of groups that maintain infrastructure standards for the Internet, such as the Internet Engineering Task Force (IETF) and the Internet Architecture Board (IAB).

Internet Systems Consortium, Inc. (ISC)
P.O. Box 360
Newmarket, NH 03857 USA
Phone: 650-423-1300
Fax: 650-423-1355
E-mail Address: info@isc.org
Web Address: www.isc.org
The Internet Systems Consortium, Inc. (ISC) is a nonprofit organization with extensive expertise in the development, management, maintenance and implementation of Internet technologies.

Organization for the Advancement of Structured Information Standards (OASIS)
35 Corporate Dr., Ste. 150
Burlington, MA 01803-4238 USA
Phone: 781-425-5073
Fax: 781-425-5072
E-mail Address: info@oasis-open.org
Web Address: www.oasis-open.org
The Organization for the Advancement of Structured Information Standards (OASIS) is a consortium which drives the development and adoption of e-business standards. It produces Web services standards, along with standards for security, e-business, and standardization efforts in the public sector and for application-specific markets. Founded in 1993, OASIS has more than 5,000 participants representing over 600 organizations and individual members in 100 countries.

US Internet Service Provider Association (US ISPA)
700 12th St. NW, Ste. 700E
Washington, DC 20005 USA
Phone: 202-904-2351
E-mail Address: kdean@usispa.org
Web Address: www.usispa.org
US Internet Service Provider Association (US ISPA) is a leading provider of technical, business, policy and regulatory support to ISPs (Internet service providers).

W3C (World Wide Web Consortium)
32 Vassar St., Bldg. 32-G515
Cambridge, MA 02139 USA
Phone: 617-253-2613
Fax: 617-258-5999
E-mail Address: susan@w3.org
Web Address: www.w3.org
The World Wide Web Consortium (W3C) develops technologies and standards to enhance the performance and utility of the World Wide Web. The W3C is hosted by three different organizations: the European Research Consortium for Informatics and Mathematics (ERICM) handles inquiries about the W3C in the EMEA region; Keio University handles W3C's Japanese and Korean correspondence; and the Computer Science & Artificial Intelligence Lab (CSAIL) at MIT handles all other countries, include Australia and the U.S.

37) Internet Industry Resources

American Registry for Internet Numbers (ARIN)
P.O. Box 232290
Centreville, VA 20120 USA
Phone: 703-227-9840
Fax: 703-263-0417
E-mail Address: info@arin.net
Web Address: www.arin.net
The American Registry for Internet Numbers (ARIN) is a nonprofit organization that administers and registers Internet protocol (IP) numbers. The organization also develops policies and offers educational outreach services.

Berkman Center for Internet & Society
23 Everett St., Fl. 2
Cambridge, MA 02138 USA
Phone: 617-495-7547
Fax: 617-495-7641
E-mail Address: cyber@law.harvard.edu
Web Address: cyber.law.harvard.edu
The Berkman Center for Internet & Society, housed at Harvard University's law school, focuses on the exploration of the development and inner-workings of laws pertaining to the Internet. The center offers Internet courses, conferences, advising and advocacy.

CommerceNet
5050 El Camino Real, Ste. 215
Los Altos, CA 94022 USA

Phone: 650-289-4040
Fax: 650-289-4041
E-mail Address: info@commerce.net
Web Address: www.commerce.net
CommerceNet, an entrepreneurial research institute, is also an industry consortium for companies using, promoting and building electronic commerce solutions on the Internet.

Congressional Internet Caucus Advisory Committee (CICA)
1440 G St. NW
Washington, DC 20005 USA
Phone: 202-638-4370
E-mail Address: tlordan@netcaucus.org
Web Address: www.netcaucus.org
The Congressional Internet Caucus Advisory Committee (ICAC) works to educate the public, as well as a bipartisan group from the U.S. House and Senate about Internet-related policy issues.

InformationWeek
5 Howick Pl.
London, SW1P 1WG UK
Phone: 415-947-6000
Web Address: www.informationweek.com
InformationWeek is an online community comprising of a diverse range of IT professionals who offer insights and share their experiences with technologies, products and technology trends. It mainly consists of nine technology and vertical communities: strategic CIO, software, cloud, big data, mobile, government, security, healthcare and infrastructure.

Internet Assigned Numbers Authority (IANA)
12025 Waterfront Dr., Ste. 300
Los Angeles, CA 90094 USA
Phone: 424-254-5300
Fax: 424-254-5033
E-mail Address: iana@iana.org
Web Address: www.iana.org
The Internet Assigned Numbers Authority (IANA) serves as the central coordinator for the assignment of parameter values for Internet protocols. IANA is operated by the Internet Corporation for Assigned Names and Numbers (ICANN).

Internet Education Foundation
1440 G St. NW
Washington, DC 20005 USA
Phone: 202-638-4370
Fax: 202-637-0968
E-mail Address: tlordan@neted.org
Web Address: www.neted.org
The Internet Education Foundation is a nonprofit organization dedicated to educating the public and policymakers about the potential of the global Internet to promote democracy, communications and commerce.

InterNIC
Web Address: www.internic.net
InterNIC provides public information regarding Internet domain name registration services.

National Informatics Centre (NIC)
Lodhi Rd.
A-Block, CGO Complex
New Delhi, Delhi 110 003 India
Phone: 91-11-24305000
E-mail Address: wim@nic.in
Web Address: www.nic.in
The National Informatics Centre (NIC), under the Department of Information Technology of the Government of India, provides support to India's governmental agencies through the applications of information technology and technological activities.

38) Internet of Things Resources

IoT For All
Web Address: www.iotforall.com
IoT For All provides a wealth of entertaining and easy-to-understand articles, news and graphics regarding leading Internet of Things applications and devices.

IoT World Today
5 Howick Place
% Informa PLC
London, SW1P 1WG UK
Phone: 44 20 7017 5000
E-mail Address: customersupport@informa.com
Web Address: www.iotworldtoday.com
IoT World Today publishes a constantly updated stream of internet of things related stories, news and resources on its website. It is published by Informa PLC.

39) Internet Usage Statistics

Pew Internet & American Life Project
1615 L St. NW, Ste. 800
Washington, DC 20036 USA

Phone: 202-419-4300
Fax: 202-857-8562
E-mail Address: info@pewinternet.org
Web Address: www.pewinternet.org
The Pew Internet & American Life Project, an initiative of the Pew Research Center, produces reports that explore the impact of the Internet on families, communities, work and home, daily life, education, health care and civic and political life.

40) Manufacturing Associations-Machinery & Technology

National Center for Manufacturing Sciences (NCMS)
3025 Boardwalk Dr.
Ann Arbor, MI 48108-3230 USA
Fax: 734-995-1150
Toll Free: 800-222-6267
E-mail Address: contact@ncms.org
Web Address: www.ncms.org
The National Center for Manufacturing Sciences (NCMS) is a non-profit membership organization dedicated to advancing the global competitiveness of North American manufacturing industry.

41) MBA Resources

MBA Depot
Web Address: www.mbadepot.com
MBA Depot is an online community and information portal for MBAs, potential MBA program applicants and business professionals.

42) Nanotechnology Associations

International Association of Nanotechnology (IANT)
NASA Ames Research Center
P.O. Box 151
Moffett Field, CA 94035 USA
Phone: 408-280-6222
Fax: 877-636-6266
E-mail Address: info@ianano.org
Web Address: www.ianano.org
The International Association of Nanotechnology is a non-profit organization that promotes research collaboration in nanoscience worldwide for the benefit of society. The IANT sponsors panel discussions, regional meetings and an international congress to discuss the development of nanotechnology.

43) Nanotechnology Resources

National Institute of Advanced Industrial Science and Technology-Nanomaterials Research Institute
1-1-1 Higashi
AIST Tusukubs Central 5
Tsukuba, Ibaraki 305-8565 Japan
E-mail Address: nmri-info-ml@aist.go.jp
Web Address:
https://unit.aist.go.jp/nmri/index_en.html
The National Institute of Advanced Industrial Science and Technology-Nanomaterials Research Institute is Japan's foremost nanomaterials research institute.

National Nanotechnology Initiative (NNI)
4201 Wilson Blvd.
Stafford II, Rm. 405
Arlington, VA 22230 USA
Phone: 703-292-8626
Fax: 703-292-9312
E-mail Address: info@nnco.nano.gov
Web Address: www.nano.gov
The National Nanotechnology Initiative (NNI) is a federal R&D program established to coordinate the multiagency efforts in nanoscale science, engineering and technology. 20 department and independent agencies participate in the NNI. Other federal organizations contribute with studies, applications of the results from those agencies performing R&D and other collaborations. The NNI is part of the National Nanotechnology Coordination Office within the Nanoscale Science Engineering and Technology (NSET) subcommittee of the National Science and Technology Council (NSTC).

44) Participatory Sensing Resources

Center for Embedded Networked Sensing (CENS) at UCLA
UCLA 3563 Boelter Hall
Los Angeles, CA 90095-1596 USA
Phone: 310-206-2476
Fax: 310-206-3053
E-mail Address: xuanmai@cens.ucla.edu
Web Address: research.cens.ucla.edu
The Center for Embedded Networked Sensing (CENS) at UCLA is a research department focused on developing wireless sensing systems applicable to scientific and societal issues. The center maintains a multidisciplinary approach, with faculty and students from such diverse fields as Computer Science,

Electrical Engineering, Civil and Environmental Engineering, Biology, Statistics, Education, Urban Planning and Theater, Film, and Television.

45) Patent Organizations

European Patent Office
Bob-van-Benthem-Platz 1
Munich, 80469 Germany
Phone: 49 89 2399-0
Toll Free: 08-800-80-20-20-20
E-mail Address: press@epo.org
Web Address: www.epo.org
The European Patent Office (EPO) provides a uniform application procedure for individual inventors and companies seeking patent protection in up to 38 European countries. It is the executive arm of the European Patent Organization and is supervised by the Administrative Council.

World Intellectual Property Organization (WIPO)
34 chemin des Colombettes
Geneva, CH-1211 Switzerland
Phone: 41-22-338-9111
Fax: 41-22-733-5428
Web Address: www.wipo.int
The World Intellectual Property Organization (WIPO) has a United Nations mandate to assist organizations and companies in filing patents and other intellectual property data on a global basis. At its web site, users can download free copies of its WIPO magazine and search its international patent applications.

46) Patent Resources

Patent Board (The)
Web Address: www.patentboard.com
The Patent Board is an online platform, which offers tools and metrics for patent analysis and intellectual property investing. Its services include technology landscape analysis, portfolio assessment and merger and acquisition due diligence. The Patent Board platform is owned by Global Ventures, LLC.

47) Privacy & Consumer Matters

Electronic Frontier Foundation (EFF)
815 Eddy St.
San Francisco, CA 94109 USA
Phone: 415-436-9333
Fax: 415-436-9993
E-mail Address: info@eff.org
Web Address: www.eff.org
The Electronic Frontier Foundation (EFF) is a nonprofit, non-partisan organization that strives to protect user privacy and free speech online, fight illegal surveillance, support freedom-enhancing technologies and advocate for users and innovators. It advances its mission through impact litigation, policy analysis, grassroots activism and technology development.

Electronic Privacy Information Center (EPIC)
1519 New Hampshire Ave. NW
Washington, DC 20036 USA
Phone: 202-483-1140
Fax: 202-483-1248
E-mail Address: info@epic.org
Web Address: www.epic.org
The Electronic Privacy Information Center (EPIC) is public interest research center, established to focus public attention on emerging civil liberties issues and to protect privacy, the First Amendment and constitutional values.

Federal Trade Commission-Privacy and Security
600 Pennsylvania Ave. NW
Washington, DC 20580 USA
Phone: 202-326-2222
Web Address: business.ftc.gov/privacy-and-security
Federal Trade Commission-Privacy and Security is responsible for many aspects of business-to-consumer and business-to-business trade and regulation.

Internet Crime Complaint Center (IC3)
Web Address: www.ic3.gov
The Internet Crime Complaint Center (IC3) is a joint venture between the FBI and the National White Collar Crime Center. It provides a central collection point for Internet crime complaints, which are then sent on to the appropriate government agency. At the IC3 website, consumers may file a complaint online. IC3 accepts Internet crime complaints either from the person who believes they were defrauded, or from third parties.

Privacy International
62 Britton St.
London, EC1M 5UY UK
Phone: 44-20-3422-4321
E-mail Address: info@privacy.org
Web Address: www.privacyinternational.org

Privacy International is a government and business watchdog, alerting individuals to wiretapping and national security activities, medical privacy infringement, police information systems and the use of ID cards, video surveillance and data matching.

TRUSTe
111 Sutter St., Ste. 600
San Francisco, CA 94104 USA
Phone: 415-520-3490
Fax: 415-520-3420
Toll Free: 888-878-7830
E-mail Address: trustarc-info@trustarc.com
Web Address: trustarc.com/consumer-info/privacy-certification-standards/
TRUSTe formed an alliance with all major portal sites to launch the Privacy Partnership campaign, a consumer education program designed to raise the awareness of Internet privacy issues. The organization works to meet the needs of business web sites while protecting user privacy.

48) Research & Development, Laboratories

Advanced Technology Laboratory (ARL)
10000 Burnet Rd.
University of Texas at Austin
Austin, TX 78758 USA
Phone: 512-835-3200
Fax: 512-835-3259
Web Address: www.arlut.utexas.edu
Advanced Technology Laboratory (ARL) at the University of Texas at Austin provides research programs dedicated to improving the military capability of the United States in applications of acoustics, electromagnetic and information technology.

Commonwealth Scientific and Industrial Research Organization (CSRIO)
CSIRO Enquiries
Private Bag 10
Clayton South, Victoria 3169 Australia
Phone: 61-3-9545-2176
Toll Free: 1300-363-400
Web Address: www.csiro.au
The Commonwealth Scientific and Industrial Research Organization (CSRIO) is Australia's national science agency and a leading international research agency. CSRIO performs research in Australia over a broad range of areas including agriculture, minerals and energy, manufacturing, communications, construction, health and the environment.

Council of Scientific & Industrial Research (CSIR)
2 Rafi Marg
Anusandhan Bhawan
New Delhi, 110001 India
Phone: 91-11-2373-7889
Fax: 91-11-2371-0618
E-mail Address: itweb@csir.res.in
Web Address: www.csir.res.in
The Council of Scientific & Industrial Research (CSIR) is a government-funded organization that promotes research and development initiatives in India. It operates in the fields of energy, biotechnology, space, science and technology.

Electronics and Telecommunications Research Institute (ETRI)
218 Gajeongno
Yuseong-gu
Daejeon, 34129 Korea
Phone: 82-42-860-6114
E-mail Address: k21human@etri.re.kr
Web Address: www.etri.re.kr
Established in 1976, the Electronics and Telecommunications Research Institute (ETRI) is a nonprofit government-funded research organization that promotes technological excellence. The research institute has successfully developed information technologies such as TDX-Exchange, High Density Semiconductor Microchips, Mini-Super Computer (TiCOM), and Digital Mobile Telecommunication System (CDMA). ETRI's focus is on information technologies, robotics, telecommunications, digital broadcasting and future technology strategies.

Fraunhofer-Gesellschaft (FhG) (The)
Fraunhofer-Gesellschaft zur Forderung der angewandten Forschung e.V.
Postfach 20 07 33
Munich, 80007 Germany
Phone: 49-89-1205-0
Fax: 49-89-1205-7531
Web Address: www.fraunhofer.de
The Fraunhofer-Gesellschaft (FhG) institute focuses on research in health, security, energy, communication, the environment and mobility. FhG includes over 80 research units in Germany. Over 70% of its projects are derived from industry contracts.

Helmholtz Association
Anna-Louisa-Karsch-Strasse 2
Berlin, 10178 Germany
Phone: 49-30-206329-0
E-mail Address: info@helmholtz.de
Web Address: www.helmholtz.de/en
The Helmholtz Association is a community of 18 scientific-technical and biological-medical research centers. Helmholtz Centers perform top-class research in strategic programs in several core fields: energy, earth and environment, health, key technologies, structure of matter, aeronautics, space and transport.

Idaho National Laboratory (INL)
1955 N. Fremont Ave.
Idaho Falls, ID 83415 USA
Toll Free: 866-495-7440
Web Address: www.inl.gov
Idaho National Laboratory (INL) is a multidisciplinary, multiprogram laboratory that specializes in developing nuclear energy with research concerning the environment, energy, science and national defense.

Industrial Technology Research Institute (ITRI)
195, Sec. 4, Chung Hsing Rd
Chutung, 31040 Taiwan
Phone: 886-3-582-0100
Fax: 886-3-582-0045
Web Address: www.itri.org.tw
The Industrial Technology Research Institute (ITRI) is a nonprofit R&D organization founded in 1973 by the Ministry of Economic Affairs (MOEA) of Taiwan. It engages in applied research and technical service for Taiwan's industrial development. ITRI focuses on six areas of development: Information and Communications; Electronics and Optoelectronics; Material, Chemical and Nanotechnology; Medical devices and biomedical; Mechanical Systems; and Green Energy and Environment.

Institute for Telecommunication Sciences (ITS)
325 Broadway
Boulder, CO 80305-3337 USA
Phone: 303-497-3571
E-mail Address: info@its.bldrdoc.gov
Web Address: www.its.bldrdoc.gov
The Institute for Telecommunication Sciences (ITS) is the research and engineering branch of the National Telecommunications and Information Administration (NTIA), a division of the U.S. Department of Commerce (DOC). Its research activities are focused on advanced telecommunications and information infrastructure development.

Leibniz Association of German Research Institutes (WGL)
Chaussee Strasse 111
Berlin, D-10115 Germany
Phone: 49-030/20-60-49-0
Fax: 49-030/20-60-49-55
E-mail Address: info@leibniz-gemeinschaft.de
Web Address: www.leibniz-gemeinschaft.de
The Leibniz Association of German Research Institutes (WGL) is a research organization that comprises over 89 institutes. WGL works on international interdisciplinary research and acts as a bridge between traditional research and customer oriented applications. The association focuses on scientific excellence and social relevance.

Max Planck Society (MPG)
Hofgartenstr. 8
Munich, 80539 Germany
Phone: 49-89-2108-0
Fax: 49-89-2108-1111
E-mail Address: post@gv.mpg.de
Web Address: www.mpg.de
The Max Planck Society (MPG) currently maintains 83 institutes, research units and working groups that are devoted to basic research in the natural sciences, life sciences, social sciences, and the humanities. Max Planck Institutes work largely in an interdisciplinary setting and in close cooperation with universities and research institutes in Germany and abroad.

MITRE Corporation
202 Burlington Rd.
Bedford, MA 01730-1420 USA
Phone: 781-271-2000
E-mail Address: media@mitre.org
Web Address: www.mitre.org
MITRE Corporation is a nonprofit engineering institution offering expertise in communications, information, space, environmental and aviation systems. It operates three federally funded research and development centers for the U.S. government.

National Renewable Energy Laboratory (NREL)
15013 Denver W. Pkwy.
Golden, CO 80401 USA
Phone: 303-275-3000
Web Address: www.nrel.gov

The National Renewable Energy Laboratory (NREL) reduces nuclear danger, transfers applied environmental technology to government and non-government entities and forms economic and industrial alliances.

National Research Council Canada (NRC)
1200 Montreal Rd., Bldg. M-58
Ottawa, ON K1A 0R6 Canada
Phone: 613-993-9101
Fax: 613-952-9907
Toll Free: 877-672-2672
E-mail Address: info@nrc-cnrc.gc.ca
Web Address: www.nrc-cnrc.gc.ca
National Research Council Canada (NRC) is comprised of 12 government organization, research institutes and programs that carry out multidisciplinary research. It maintains partnerships with industries and sectors key to Canada's economic development.

Oak Ridge National Laboratory (ORNL)
1 Bethel Valley Rd.
P.O. Box 2008
Oak Ridge, TN 37831 USA
Phone: 865-576-7658
Web Address: www.ornl.gov
The Oak Ridge National Laboratory (ORNL) is a multi-program science and technology laboratory managed for the U.S. Department of Energy by U.T.-Battelle, LLC. It conducts basic and applied research and development to create scientific knowledge and technological solutions.

Pacific Northwest National Laboratory (PNNL)
902 Battelle Blvd.
Richland, WA 99352 USA
Phone: 509-375-2121
Toll Free: 888-375-7665
E-mail Address: inquiry@pnl.gov
Web Address: www.pnnl.gov
The Pacific Northwest National Laboratory (PNNL) is a Department of Energy facility that conducts research in 10 areas of focus: Chemical and Molecular Sciences; Biological Systems Science; Climate Change Science; Subsurface Science; Chemical Engineering; Applied Materials Science and Engineering; Applied Nuclear Science and Technology; Advanced Computer Science, Visualization and Data; Systems Engineering and Integration; and Large-Scale User Facilities and Advanced Instrumentation.

Program on Vehicle and Mobility Innovation (PVMI)
1050 Steinberg Hall-Dietrich Hall
3620 Locust Walk
Philadelphia, PA 19104-6371 USA
Phone: 215-746-4831
E-mail Address: mackinstitute@wharton.upenn.edu
Web Address: pvmi.wharton.upenn.edu
The Program on Vehicle and Mobility Innovation (PVMI), formerly the International Motor Vehicle Program (IMVP), is a research project, funded by leading global car makers as well as government agencies, focused on enhancing automotive design and manufacturing methods. In 2013, the IMVP changed its name to the PVMI and was integrated into the Mack Institute for Innovation Management at the Wharton School, University Pennsylvania.

Sandia National Laboratories
1515 Eubank SE
Albuquerque, NM 87125 USA
Phone: 505-844-8066
Web Address: www.sandia.gov
Sandia National Laboratories is a national security laboratory operated for the U.S. Department of Energy by the Sandia Corporation. It designs all nuclear components for the nation's nuclear weapons and performs a wide variety of energy research and development projects.

Sloan Automotive Laboratory
60 Vassar St., Bldg. 31-153
Cambridge, MA 02139-4307 USA
Phone: 617-253-4529
Fax: 617-253-9453
Web Address: web.mit.edu/sloan-auto-lab
The Sloan Automotive Laboratory at MIT was founded in 1929 by Professor C.F. Taylor, with a grant from Alfred P. Sloan, Jr., CEO of General Motors, as a major laboratory for automotive research in the US and the world. The goals of the Laboratory are to provide the fundamental knowledge base for automotive engineering and to educate students to become technological leaders in the automotive industry.

SRI International
1100 Wilson Blvd., Ste. 2800
Arlington, VA 22209 USA
Phone: 650-859-2000
Web Address: www.sri.com
SRI International is a nonprofit research organization that offers contract research services to government

agencies, as well as commercial enterprises and other private sector institutions. It is organized around broad divisions including biosciences, global partnerships, education, products and solutions division, advanced technology and systems and information and computing sciences division.

49) RFID Industry Associations

Association for Automatic Identification and Mobility (AIM)
20399 Rte. 19, Ste. 203
Cranberry Township, PA 16066 USA
Phone: 724-742-4470
E-mail Address: info@aimglobal.org
Web Address: www.aimglobal.org
The Association for Automatic Identification and Mobility (AIM) is a global trade organization dedicated to accelerating the growth and use of RFID and other automated identification and data capture/collection (AIDC) technologies and services. Its more than 900 members are manufacturers or service providers of RFID, bar code, card, biometrics and electronic article surveillance technologies.

EPCglobal Inc.
300 Princeton S. Corporate Ctr.
Ewing Township, NJ 08628 USA
Phone: 937-435-3870
E-mail Address: info@gs1us.org
Web Address: www.gs1.org/epcglobal
EPCglobal Inc. is a global standards organization for the Electronic Product Code (EPC), which supports the use of RFID. It was initially developed by the Auto-ID Center, an academic research project at the Massachusetts Institute of Technology (MIT). Today, offices and affiliates of EPCglobal are based in nearly every nation of the world. The nonprofit organization is a joint venture between GS1, formerly known as EAN International, and GS1 US, formerly known as the Uniform Code Council.

50) RFID Resources

RFID.org
20399 Rte. 19, Ste. 203
Cranberry Township, PA 16066 USA
Phone: 724-742-4470
Fax: 724-742-4476
E-mail Address: info@aimglobal.org
Web Address: www.aimglobal.org/?RFID
RFID.org is a link to news, events, case studies and commentary relating to radio frequency identification (RFID) technologies and applications. The site is sponsored by the global branch of the Association for Automatic Identification and Mobility (AIM GLOBAL).

51) Robotic Process Automation (RPA) Associations

Institute for Robotic Process Automation & Artificial Intelligence
E-mail Address: helpdesk@irpanetwork.com
Web Address: www.irpaai.com
Founded in 2013, the Institute for Robotic Process Automation and Artificial Intelligence (IRPA AI) is an independent professional association and knowledge forum for the buyers, sellers, influencers and analysts of robotic process automation, cognitive computing and artificial intelligence.

52) Robotics & Automation Industry Associations

Continental Automated Buildings Association (CABA)
1173 Cyrville Rd., Ste. 210
Ottawa, ON K1J 7S6 Canada
Phone: 613-686-1814
Fax: 613-744-7833
Toll Free: 888-798-2222
E-mail Address: caba@caba.org
Web Address: www.caba.org
The Continental Automated Buildings Association (CABA) is an international not-for-profit industry association dedicated to the advancement of intelligent home and intelligent building technologies. The organization is supported by an international membership of nearly 335 companies involved in the design, manufacture, installation and retailing of products relating to home automation and building automation. Public organizations, including utilities and government are also members.

Industrial Wireless at Work (WINA)
1500 Sunday Dr., Ste. 102
Raleigh, NC 27607 USA
Phone: 919-314-6560
Fax: 919-314-6561
E-mail Address: info@wina.org
Web Address: www.wina.org

WINA's mission is to provide unbiased information and education about industrial wireless technologies and applications to accelerate the widespread deployment of wireless in the industrial market.

International Federation of Robotics (IFR)
Lyoner St. 18
Frankfurt am Main, 60528 Germany
Phone: 49-69-6603-1502
Fax: 49-69-6603-2502
E-mail Address: secretariat@ifr.org
Web Address: www.ifr.org
The International Federation of Robotics (IFR) promotes the robotics industry worldwide, including the fields of industrial robots for manufacturing and other purposes, service robots and robotics research. Among other things, it is focused on research, development, use and international co-operation in the entire field of robotics, and it seeks to act as a focal point for organizations and governmental representatives in activities related to robotics.

Singapore Industrial Automation Association (SIAA)
9, Town Hall Rd., Ste. 02-23
Singapore, 609431 Singapore
Phone: 65-6749-1822
Fax: 65-6841-3986
E-mail Address: secretariat@siaa.org
Web Address: www.siaa.org
The Singapore Industrial Automation Association (SIAA) is a non-profit organization which promotes the application of industrial automation with reference to business, technology & information services.

53) Satellite-Related Professional Organizations

Society of Satellite Professionals International (SSPI)
250 Park Ave., Fl. 7
The New York Information Technology Ctr.
New York, NY 10177 USA
Phone: 212-809-5199
Fax: 212-825-0075
E-mail Address: rbell@sspi.org
Web Address: www.sspi.org
The Society of Satellite Professionals International (SSPI) is a nonprofit member-benefit society that serves satellite professionals worldwide.

54) Science & Technology Resources

Technology Review
1 Main St., Fl. 13
Cambridge, MA 02142 USA
Phone: 617-475-8000
Fax: 617-475-8000
Web Address: www.technologyreview.com
Technology Review, an MIT enterprise, publishes tech industry news, covers innovation and writes in-depth articles about research, development and cutting-edge technologies.

55) Science Parks

International Association of Science Parks (IASP)
Calle Maria Curie 35, Campanillas
Malaga, 29590 Spain
Phone: 34-95-202-83-03
Fax: 34-95-202-04-64
E-mail Address: iasp@iasp.ws
Web Address: www.iasp.ws
The International Association of Science Parks (IASP) is a worldwide network of science and technology parks. It enjoys Special Consultative status with the Economic and Social Council of the United Nations. Its 394 members represent science parks in 75 nations. It is also a founding member of the World Alliance for Innovation (WAINOVA). Its world headquarters are located in Spain, with an additional office in the Tsinghua University Science Park, Beijing, China.

56) Sensors Industry Associations

International Frequency Sensor Association (IFSA)
548 Beaver Creek Cres.
Waterloo, ON N2V 2J6 Canada
Phone: 289-439-2493
E-mail Address: info@sensorsportal.com
Web Address: www.sensorportal.com
International Frequency Sensor Association (IFSA) is a non-profit, international society for supporting research and development in physical and chemical, electrical and non-electrical sensors and biosensors. It was founded in 1999. The main aim of IFSA is to provide a platform for academicians, researchers and engineers to present and discuss their latest research results, experiences and future trends in the area of design and application of different smart sensors with

digital, frequency (period), duty-cycle, PWM, time interval, phase-shift or pulse number output.

57) Software Industry Associations

Apache Software Foundation
401 Edgewater Pl., Ste. 600
Wakefield, MA 01880 USA
Fax: 919-573-9199
E-mail Address: apache@apache.org
Web Address: www.apache.org
Apache Software Foundation is one of the largest open software successes. Apache is used by about two-thirds of all web sites worldwide. Its software manages the interaction between a web site and the viewer's browser.

Business Software Alliance (BSA)
20 F St. NW, Ste. 800
Washington, DC 20001 USA
Phone: 202-872-5500
Fax: 202-872-5501
E-mail Address: info@bsa.org
Web Address: www.bsa.org
The Business Software Alliance (BSA) is a leading global software industry association. BSA educates consumers regarding software management, copyright protection, cyber security, trade, ecommerce and other Internet-related issues.

Colorado Technology Association
1245 Champa St., Ste. 200
Denver, CO 80204 USA
Phone: 303-592-4070
E-mail Address: info@coloradotechnology.org
Web Address: www.coloradotechnology.org/
The Colorado Technology Association, formerly the Colorado Software & Internet Association, promotes the technology industry in Colorado through networking and organization.

Enterprise Data Management Council (EDM)
Phone: 646-722-4381
E-mail Address: info@edmcouncil.org
Web Address: www.edmcouncil.org
The EDM Council is a non-profit trade association created by leading financial industry participants. Its primary purpose is to address the issues and challenges associated with managing data content as a business and operational priority.

European Software Institute (ESI)
Parque Tecnologico de Bizkaia
Edificio 202
Zamudio, Bizkaia E-48170 Spain
Phone: 34-946-430-850
Fax: 34-901-706-009
Web Address: www.esi.es
The European Software Institute (ESI) is a nonprofit foundation launched as an initiative of the European Commission, with the support of leading European companies working in the information technology field.

Information Systems Security Association (ISSA)
1964 Gallows Rd., Ste. 210
Vienna, VA 22182 USA
Phone: 703-982-8205
Fax: 703-495-2973
Toll Free: 866-349-5818
E-mail Address: mdelacruz@issa.org
Web Address: www.issa.org
The Information Systems Security Association (ISSA) is an international nonprofit organization of information security professionals. It offers educational forums, publishes resources and networking opportunities to its members.

Irish Software Association (ISA)
Confederation House
84-86 Lower Baggot St.
Dublin, 2 Ireland
Phone: 353-1-605-1500
E-mail Address: info@technology-ireland.ie
Web Address: www.software.ie
The Irish Software Association (ISA) promotes the interests of IT services and software companies in Ireland. It helps software companies grow and become competitive internationally.

Korea Software Industry Association (KOSA)
IT Venture Tower W., 12F
135 Jung-daero, Songpa-gu
Seoul, 05717 South Korea
Phone: 82-2-2188-6900
Fax: 82-2-2188-6901
E-mail Address: choicy@sw.or.kr
Web Address: www.sw.or.kr
The Korea Software Industry Association (KOSA) is Korea's nonprofit trade organization representing more than 1,200 member companies in the software industry.

Linux Foundation (The)
1 Letterman Dr.
Building D, Ste. D4700

San Francisco, CA 94129 USA
Phone: 415-723-9709
E-mail Address: info@linuxfoundation.org
Web Address: www.linuxfoundation.org
The Linux Foundation, founded in 2007 by the merger of Open Source Development Labs (OSDL) and the Free Standards Group, is a nonprofit organization that standardizes, protects and promotes the work of Linux creator Linus Torvalds. It provides necessary services and resources to make and keep open source software competitive with closed platforms. The foundation is supported by a global consortium of global open source IT industry leaders, with facilities in the U.S. and Japan.

National Association of Software and Service Companies of India (NASSCOM)
Plot No. 7-10 NASSCOM Campus, Sector 126
Noida, 201303 India
Phone: 91-120-4990111
Fax: 91-120-4990119
E-mail Address: north@nasscom.in
Web Address: www.nasscom.im
The National Association of Software and Service Companies (NASSCOM) is the trade body and chamber of commerce for the IT and business process outsourcing (BPO) industry in India. The association's 1,400 members consist of corporations located around the world involved in software development, software services, software products, IT-enabled/BPO services and e-commerce.

New Mexico Technology Council (NMTC)
200 Broadway Blvd. NE
Albuquerque, NM 87102 USA
Phone: 505-847-6840
E-mail Address: info@nmtechcouncil.org
Web Address: www.nmtechcouncil.org
The New Mexico Technology Council (NMTC) represents the interests of the software industry in New Mexico. Its members include businesses, tech professionals and organizations who work to promote technology industry in New Mexico.

Object Management Group (OMG)
9C Medway Rd., PMB 274
Milford, MA 01757 USA
Phone: 781-444-0404
Fax: 781-444-0320
E-mail Address: info@omg.org
Web Address: www.omg.org
The Object Management Group (OMG) is a not-for-profit organization devoted to the interoperability of enterprise software. It acts as a technology standard consortium, wherein standards are driven by end-users, vendors, academic institutions and government agencies.

Singapore Infocomm Technology Federation (SiTF)
79 Ayer Rajah Crescent
Ste. 02-03/04/05
Singapore, 139955 Singapore
Phone: 65-6325-9700
Fax: 65-6325-4993
E-mail Address: info@sitf.org.sg
Web Address: sitf.org.sg
Singapore Infocomm Technology Federation (SiTF) is an infocom industry association that has four chapters: Cloud Computing Chapter, Digital Media Wireless Chapter, Security and Governance Chapter and Singapore Enterprise Chapter.

Software & Information Industry Association (SIIA)
1090 Vermont Ave. NW, Fl. 6
Washington, DC 20005-4095 USA
Phone: 202-289-7442
Fax: 202-289-7097
Web Address: www.siia.net
The Software & Information Industry Association (SIIA) is a principal trade association for the software and digital content industry.

Software Association of Oregon (SAO)
123 NE Third Ave., Ste. 210
Portland, OR 97232 USA
Phone: 503-228-5401
Web Address: www.techoregon.org
The Technology Association of Oregon, formerly Software Association of Oregon (SAO) promotes the growth of technology industry by offering opportunities, such as networking, professional and business development programs, advocacy, industry promotions and talent development.

Software Contractors' Guild
9725 Richland Hills Ln.
Bakersfield, CA 93306 USA
E-mail Address: scguild.service@gmail.com
Web Address: www.scguild.com
The Software Contractors' Guild is a collection of U.S. and international databases regarding available software contractors and organizations seeking to place contract work. Membership requires a small annual fee.

Washington Technology Industry Association
1721 8th Ave. N
Seattle, WA 98109 USA
Phone: 206-448-3033
E-mail Address: info@washingtontechnology.org
Web Address: www.washingtontechnology.org
The Washington Technology Industry Association promotes and helps coordinate the software industry in the state of Washington.

58) Software Industry Resources

Software Engineering Institute (SEI)-Carnegie Mellon
4500 5th Ave.
Pittsburgh, PA 15213-2612 USA
Phone: 412-268-5800
Fax: 412-268-5758
Toll Free: 888-201-4479
E-mail Address: info@sei.cmu.edu
Web Address: www.sei.cmu.edu
The Software Engineering Institute (SEI) is a federally funded research and development center at Carnegie Mellon University, sponsored by the U.S. Department of Defense through the Office of the Under Secretary of Defense for Acquisition, Technology, and Logistics [OUSD (AT&L)]. The SEI's core purpose is to help users make measured improvements in their software engineering capabilities.

59) Stocks & Financial Markets Data

SiliconValley.com
4 N. Second St., Ste. 700
San Jose, CA 95113 USA
Phone: 408-920-5000
Fax: 408-228-8060
E-mail Address: svfeedback@mercurynews.com
Web Address: www.siliconvalley.com
SiliconValley.com, run by San Jose Mercury News and owned by MediaNews Group, offers a summary of current financial news and information regarding the field of technology.

60) Supercomputing

Top 500 Supercomputer Sites
Prometeus GmbH
Fliederstr. 2
Waibstadt-Daisbach, D-74915 Germany
Phone: 49-7261-913-160
E-mail Address: info@top500.org
Web Address: www.top500.org
The Top 500 project was started in 1993 to provide a reliable basis for tracking and detecting trends in high-performance computing. Twice a year, a list of the sites operating the 500 most powerful computer systems is assembled and released. The Linpack benchmark is used as a performance measure for ranking the computer systems. The list contains a variety of information including system specifications and major application areas. The Top 500 web site is promoted by Prometeus GmbH.

61) Sustainable Transportation

Transportation Sustainability Research Center (TSRC)
University of California Richmond Field Station
1301 S. 46th St., Building 190
Richmond, CA 94804 USA
E-mail Address: sshaheen@berkeley.edu
Web Address: tsrc.berkeley.edu/
The Transportation Sustainability Research Center (TSRC) was formed in 2006 to combine the research forces of six campus groups at UC Berkeley: the University of California Transportation Center, the University of California Energy Institute, the Institute of Transportation Studies, the Energy and Resources Group, the Center for Global Metropolitan Studies, and the Berkeley Institute of the Environment. Research efforts are primarily concentrated in six main areas: advanced vehicles and fuels; energy and infrastructure; goods movement; innovative mobility; Mobility for special populations; and transportation and energy systems analysis.

62) Technology Law Associations

International Technology Law Association (ITechLaw)
7918 Jones Branch Dr., Ste. 300
McLean, VA 22102 USA
Phone: 703-506-2895
Fax: 703-506-3266
E-mail Address: memberservices@itechlaw.org
Web Address: www.itechlaw.org
The International Technology Law Association (ITechLaw) offers information concerning Internet and converging technology law. It represents lawyers in the field of technology law.

63) Technology Transfer Associations

Association of University Technology Managers (AUTM)
111 W. Jackson Blvd., Ste. 1412
Chicago, IL 60604 USA
Phone: 847-686-2244
Fax: 847-686-2253
E-mail Address: info@autm.net
Web Address: www.autm.net
The Association of University Technology Managers (AUTM) is a nonprofit professional association whose members belong to over 300 research institutions, universities, teaching hospitals, government agencies and corporations. The association's mission is to advance the field of technology transfer and enhance members' ability to bring academic and nonprofit research to people around the world.

Federal Laboratory Consortium for Technology Transfer
111 W. Jackson Blvd., Ste. 1412
Chicago, IL 60604 USA
Phone: 847-686-2298
E-mail Address: info@federallabs.org
Web Address: www.federallabs.org
In keeping with the aims of the Federal Technology Transfer Act of 1986 and other related legislation, the Federal Laboratory Consortium (FLC) works to facilitate the sharing of research results and technology developments between federal laboratories and the mainstream U.S. economy. FLC affiliates include federal laboratories, large and small businesses, academic and research institutions, state and local governments and various federal agencies. The group has regional support offices and local contacts throughout the U.S.

Licensing Executives Society (USA and Canada), Inc.
11130 Sunrise Valley Dr., Ste. 350
Reston, VA 20191 USA
Phone: 703-234-4058
Fax: 703-435-4390
E-mail Address: info@les.org
Web Address: www.lesusacanada.org
Licensing Executives Society (USA and Canada), Inc., established in 1965, is a professional association composed of about 3,000 members who work in fields related to the development, use, transfer, manufacture and marketing of intellectual property. Members include executives, lawyers, licensing consultants, engineers, academic researchers, scientists and government officials. The society is part of the larger Licensing Executives Society International, Inc. (same headquarters address), with a worldwide membership of some 12,000 members from approximately 80 countries.

State Science and Technology Institute (SSTI)
5015 Pine Creek Dr.
Westerville, OH 43081 USA
Phone: 614-901-1690
E-mail Address: contactus@ssti.org
Web Address: www.ssti.org
The State Science and Technology Institute (SSTI) is a national nonprofit group that serves as a resource for technology-based economic development. In addition to the information on its web site, the Institute publishes a free weekly digest of news and issues related to technology-based economic development efforts, as well as a members-only publication listing application information, eligibility criteria and submission deadlines for a variety of funding opportunities, federal and otherwise.

64) Telecommunications Industry Associations

Alliance for Telecommunications Industry Solutions (ATIS)
1200 G St. NW, Ste. 500
Washington, DC 20005 USA
Phone: 202-628-6380
E-mail Address: moran@atis.org
Web Address: www.atis.org
The Alliance for Telecommunications Industry Solutions (ATIS) is a U.S.-based body committed to rapidly developing and promoting technical and operations standards for the communications and related information technologies industry worldwide.

Asia-Pacific Telecommunity (APT)
Chaengwattana Rd., 12/49 Soi 5
Bangkok, 10210 Thailand
Phone: 66-2-573-0044
Fax: 66-2-573-7479
E-mail Address: aptmail@apt.int
Web Address: www.aptsec.org
The Asia-Pacific Telecommunity (APT) is an organization of governments, telecom service providers, manufacturers of communication equipment, research & development organizations and other stakeholders active in the field of communication and information technology. APT

serves as the focal organization for communication and information technology in the Asia-Pacific region.

China Communications Standards Association (CCSA)
52 Garden Rd., Haidian District
Beijing, 100083 China
Phone: 86-10-6230-2730
Fax: 86-10-6230-1849
Web Address: www.ccsa.org.cn/english
The China Communications Standards Association (CCSA) is a nonprofit organization that works to standardize the field of communications technology across China. Its membership includes operators, telecom equipment manufacturers and universities and academies from across China.

DigitalEurope
Rue de la Science 14
Brussels, 1040 Belgium
Phone: 32-2-609-5310
Fax: 32-2-609-5339
E-mail Address: info@digitaleurope.org
Web Address: www.digitaleurope.org
DigitalEurope is dedicated to improving the business environment for the European information and communications technology and consumer electronics sector. Its members include 57 leading corporations and 37 national trade associations from across Europe.

European Telecommunications Standards Institute (ETSI)
ETSI Secretariat
650, route des Lucioles
Sophia-Antipolis Cedex, 06921 France
Phone: 33-4-92-94-42-00
Fax: 33-4-93-65-47-16
E-mail Address: info@etsi.org
Web Address: www.etsi.org
The European Telecommunications Standards Institute (ETSI) is a non-profit organization whose mission is to produce the telecommunications standards to be implemented throughout Europe.

INCOMPAS
1100 G St. NW, Ste. 800
Washington, DC 20005 USA
Phone: 202-296-6650
E-mail Address: gnorris@comptel.org
Web Address: www.incompas.org
CompTel is a trade organization representing voice, data and video communications service providers and their supplier partners. Members are supported through education, networking, policy advocacy and trade shows.

International Federation for Information Processing (IFIP)
Hofstrasse 3
Laxenburg, A-2361 Austria
Phone: 43-2236-73616
Fax: 43-2236-73616-9
E-mail Address: ifip@ifip.org
Web Address: www.ifip.org
The International Federation for Information Processing (IFIP) is a multinational, apolitical organization in information & communications technologies and sciences recognized by the United Nations and other world bodies. It represents information technology societies from 56 countries or regions, with over 500,000 members in total.

International Telecommunications Union (ITU)
Place des Nations
Geneva 20, 1211 Switzerland
Phone: 41-22-730-5111
Fax: 41-22-733-7256
E-mail Address: itumail@itu.int
Web Address: www.itu.int
The International Telecommunications Union (ITU) is an international organization for the standardization of the radio and telecommunications industry. It is an agency of the United Nations (UN).

Pacific Telecommunications Council (PTC)
914 Coolidge St.
Honolulu, HI 96826-3085 USA
Phone: 808-941-3789
Fax: 833-944-0749
E-mail Address: info@ptc.org
Web Address: www.ptc.org
The Pacific Telecommunications Council (PTC), through its member network, promotes the development and use of telecommunications and information and communications technologies to enhance the lives of people living in the Pacific hemisphere.

Telecommunications Industry Association (TIA)
1310 N. Courthouse Rd., Ste. 890
Arlington, VA 22201 USA
Phone: 703-907-7700
Fax: 703-907-7727

E-mail Address: smontgomery@tiaonline.org
Web Address: www.tiaonline.org
The Telecommunications Industry Association (TIA) is a leading trade association in the information, communications and entertainment technology industry. TIA focuses on market development, trade promotion, trade shows, domestic and international advocacy, standards development and enabling e-business.

Voice On the Net (VON) Coalition, Inc.
1200 Seventh St. NW
Pillsbury Winthrop Shaw Pittman LLP
Washington, DC 20036-3006 USA
Phone: 202-663-8215
E-mail Address: glenn.richards@pillsburylaw.com
Web Address: www.von.org
Voice On the Net (VON) Coalition, Inc. is an organization is an advocate for the IP telephony industry. The VON Coalition supports that the IP industry should remain free of governmental regulations. It also serves to educate consumers and the media on Internet communications technologies.

65) Telecommunications Resources

Center for Democracy and Technology (CDT)
1401 K St. NW, Ste. 200
Washington, DC 20005 USA
Phone: 202-637-9800
Fax: 202-637-0968
Web Address: www.cdt.org
The Center for Democracy and Technology (CDT) works to promote democratic values and constitutional liberties in the digital age.

Department of Telecommunication (Gov. of India)
20 Ashoka Rd.
Sanchar Bhawan
New Delhi, 110001 India
Phone: 91-11-2373-9191
Fax: 91-11-2372-3330
E-mail Address: secy-dot@nic.in
Web Address: www.dot.gov.in
The Government of India's Department of Telecommunication web site provides information, directories, guidelines, news and information related to the telecom, Internet, Wi-Fi and wireless communication industries. It is a branch of India's Ministry of Communications & Information Technology.

Infocomm Development Authority of Singapore (IMDA)
10 Pasir Panjang Rd.
#10-01 Mapletree Business City
Singapore, 117438 Singapore
Phone: 65-6211-0888
Fax: 65-6211-2222
E-mail Address: info@imda.gov.sg
Web Address: www.imda.gov.sg
The goal of the Infocomm Media Development Authority of Singapore (IMDA) is to actively seek opportunities to grow infocomm industry in both the domestic and international markets.

International Communications Project (The)
Unit 2, Marine Action
Birdhill Industrial Estate
Birdhill, Co Tipperary Ireland
Phone: 353-86-108-3932
Fax: 353-61-749-801
E-mail Address: robert.alcock@intercomms.net
Web Address: www.intercomms.net
The International Communications Project (InterComms) is an authoritative policy, strategy and reference publication for the international telecommunications industry.

Ministry of Communications and Information (Gov. of Singapore)
140 Hill St. #01-01A
Old Hill St. Police Station
Singapore, 179369 Singapore
Fax: 65-6837-9480
Toll Free: 800-837-9655
E-mail Address: MCI_Connects@mci.gov.sg
Web Address: www.mci.gov.sg
The Ministry of Communications and Information, is the department of the Singapore government responsible for the development of the nation as a global hub for information, communication and arts related endeavors through the promotion of creativity in the arts, design, media and infocomm technology sectors.

Total Telecom
Wren House
43 Hatton Garden
London, EC1N 8 EL UK
Phone: 44-20-7092-100
Fax: 44-20-7242-1508
E-mail Address: info@totaltele.com
Web Address: www.totaltele.com

Total Telecom offers information, news and articles on the telecommunications industry in the U.K. and worldwide through its web site and the Total Telecom Magazine. Total Telecom is owned by Terrapinn Ltd.

66) Temporary Staffing Firms

Allegis Group
7301 Parkway Dr.
Hanover, MD 21076 USA
Toll Free: 800-927-8090
Web Address: www.allegisgroup.com
The Allegis Group provides technical, professional and industrial recruiting and staffing services. Allegis specializes in information technology staffing services. The firm operates in the United Kingdom, Germany and The Netherlands as Aerotek and TEKsystems, and in India as Allegis Group India. Aerotek provides staffing solutions for aviation, engineering, automotive and scientific personnel markets.

CDI Corporation
1735 Market St., Ste. 200
Philadelphia, PA 190103 USA
Phone: 215-636-1240
E-mail Address: engineeringsolutions@cdicorp.com
Web Address: www.cdicorp.com
CDI Corporation specializes in engineering and information technology staffing services. Company segments include CDI IT Solutions, specializing in information technology; CDI Engineering Solutions, specializing in engineering outsourcing services; AndersElite Limited, operating in the United Kingdom and Australia; and MRINetwork, specializing in executive recruitment.

Glotel Inc.
8700 W. Bryn Mawr Ave., Ste. 400N
Chicago, IL 60631 USA
Phone: 312-612-7480
E-mail Address: info@glotelinc.com
Web Address: www.glotel.com
Glotel is a global technology staffing and managed projects solutions company specializing in the placement of contract and permanent personnel within all areas of technology. Glotel has a network of offices throughout Europe, the U.S. and Asia-Pacific.

Harvey Nash
110 Bishopgate
London, EC2N 4AY UK
Phone: 44-20-7333-0033
Fax: 44-20-7333-0032
E-mail Address: info@harveynash.com
Web Address: www.harveynash.com
Harvey Nash provides professional recruitment, interim executive leadership services and outsourcing services. The firm specializes in information technology staffing on a permanent and contract basis in US, UK and Europe. It also offers outsourcing services including offshore software development services, information technology systems management, workforce risk management and managed services for network administration.

Robert Walters plc
11 Slingsby Pl.
St. Martin's Courtyard
London, WC2E 9AB UK
Phone: 44-20-7379-3333
Fax: 44-20-7509-8714
E-mail Address: london@robertwalters.com
Web Address: www.robertwalters.com
Robert Walters PLC is a professional recruitment specialist, outsourcing and human resource consultant. The firm provides services for the temporary, contract and permanent placement of individuals in the sectors of finance, operations, legal, information technology, marketing and administration support. It has offices in 24 countries including the US.

67) Trade Associations-General

BUSINESSEUROPE
168 Ave. de Cortenbergh 168
Brussels, 1000 Belgium
Phone: 32-2-237-65-11
Fax: 32-2-231-14-45
E-mail Address: main@businesseurope.eu
Web Address: www.businesseurope.eu
BUSINESSEUROPE is a major European trade federation that operates in a manner similar to a chamber of commerce. Its members are the central national business federations of the 34 countries throughout Europe from which they come. Companies cannot become direct members of BUSINESSEUROPE, though there is a support group which offers the opportunity for firms to encourage BUSINESSEUROPE objectives in various ways.

Federation of Hong Kong Industries
8 Cheung Yue St.

Fl. 31, Billion Plz., Cheung Sha Wan
Kowloon, Hong Kong Hong Kong
Phone: 852-2732-3188
Fax: 852-2721-3494
E-mail Address: fhki@fhki.org.hk
Web Address: www.industryhk.org
The Federation of Hong Kong Industries promotes the trade, investment advancement and development of opportunities for the industrial and business communities of Hong Kong. The web site hosts a trade enquiry on products and services and publishes research reports and trade publications.

Pacific Economic Cooperation Council (PECC)
29 Heng Mui Keng Terr.
Singapore, 119 620 Singapore
Phone: 65-6737-9823
Fax: 65-6737-9824
E-mail Address: info@pecc.org
Web Address: www.pecc.org
The Pacific Economic Cooperation Council (PECC) aims to serve as a regional forum for cooperation and policy coordination to promote economic development in the Asia-Pacific region. It is a unique tripartite partnership of senior individuals from business, industry, government and other intellectual fields.

68) Trade Resources

Enterprise Singapore
1 Fusionopolis Walk
#01-02 S. Tower, Solaris
Singapore, 138628 Singapore
Phone: 65-6898-1800
Fax: 65-6278-6667
E-mail Address: enquiry@enterprisesg.gov.sg
Web Address: www.spring.gov.sg
International Enterprise Singapore and SPRING came together on 1 April 2018 as a single agency to form Enterprise Singapore. Enterprise Singapore is an enterprise development agency for growing, innovative companies. It works with partners to help small and medium enterprises with financing; capabilities and management development; technology and innovation; and access to markets.

69) Transportation Industry Associations

Intelligent Transportation Society of America (ITS America)
1100 New Jersey Ave. SE, Ste. 850
Washington, DC 20003 USA
Phone: 202-484-4847
Toll Free: 800-374-8472
E-mail Address: info@itsa.org
Web Address: www.itsa.org
The Intelligent Transportation Society of America (ITS America) is a nonprofit organization made up of members interested in the development of intelligent transportation systems technologies.

70) Transportation Industry Resources

Institute of Transportation Studies
University of California
109 McLaughlin Hall, MC1720
Berkeley, CA 94720 USA
Phone: 510-642-3585
E-mail Address: its@its.berkeley.edu
Web Address: its.berkeley.edu/
The UC Berkeley Institute of Transportation Studies is one of the world's leading centers for transportation research, education, and scholarship. Areas of research focus include: transportation planning, logistics, infrastructure management, safety, transportation economics and public transportation.

71) U.S. Government Agencies

Bureau of Economic Analysis (BEA)
4600 Silver Hill Rd.
Washington, DC 20233 USA
Phone: 301-278-9004
E-mail Address: customerservice@bea.gov
Web Address: www.bea.gov
The Bureau of Economic Analysis (BEA), is an agency of the U.S. Department of Commerce, is the nation's economic accountant, preparing estimates that illuminate key national, international and regional aspects of the U.S. economy.

Bureau of Labor Statistics (BLS)
2 Massachusetts Ave. NE
Washington, DC 20212-0001 USA
Phone: 202-691-5200
Fax: 202-691-7890
Toll Free: 800-877-8339
E-mail Address: blsdata_staff@bls.gov
Web Address: stats.bls.gov
The Bureau of Labor Statistics (BLS) is the principal fact-finding agency for the Federal Government in the field of labor economics and statistics. It is an independent national statistical agency that collects,

processes, analyzes and disseminates statistical data to the American public, U.S. Congress, other federal agencies, state and local governments, business and labor. The BLS also serves as a statistical resource to the Department of Labor.

Cybersecurity & Infrastructure Security Agency (CISA)
245 Murray Ln.
Washington, D.C. 20528-0380 USA
Phone: 888-282-0870
E-mail Address: central@cisa.gov
Web Address: www.cisa.gov
The Cybersecurity & Infrastructure Security Agency (CISA) is the U.S. government agency focused on defending against cyber attacks and the development of new cybersecurity tools. The CISA also responds to attacks against the U.S. Government.

FCC-VoIP Division
445 12th St. SW
Washington, DC 20554 USA
Fax: 866-418-0232
Toll Free: 888-225-5322
E-mail Address: FOIA@fcc.gov
Web Address: www.fcc.gov/voip
The FCC-VoIP Division is dedicated to the promotion and regulation of the VoIP (Voice over Internet Protocol) industry. It operates as part of the Federal Communications Commission (FCC). VoIP allows users to call from their computer (or adapters) over the Internet to regular telephone numbers.

Federal Communications Commission (FCC)
445 12th St. SW
Washington, DC 20554 USA
Fax: 866-418-0232
Toll Free: 888-225-5322
E-mail Address: PRA@fcc.gov
Web Address: www.fcc.gov
The Federal Communications Commission (FCC) is an independent U.S. government agency established by the Communications Act of 1934 responsible for regulating interstate and international communications by radio, television, wire, satellite and cable.

Federal Communications Commission (FCC)-Wireless Telecommunications Bureau
445 12th St. SW
Washington, DC 20554 USA
Phone: 202-418-0600
Fax: 202-418-0787
Toll Free: 888-225-5322
E-mail Address: PRA@fcc.gov
Web Address: www.fcc.gov/wireless-telecommunications#block-menu-block-4
The Federal Communications Commission (FCC)-Wireless Telecommunications Bureau handles nearly all FCC domestic wireless telecommunications programs and policies, including cellular and smarftphones, pagers and two-way radios. The bureau also regulates the use of radio spectrum for businesses, aircraft/ship operators and individuals.

National Science Foundation (NSF)
2415 Eisenhower Ave.
Alexandria, VA 22314 USA
Phone: 703-292-5111
Toll Free: 800-877-8339
E-mail Address: info@nsf.gov
Web Address: www.nsf.gov
The National Science Foundation (NSF) is an independent U.S. government agency responsible for promoting science and engineering. The foundation provides colleges and universities with grants and funding for research into numerous scientific fields.

National Telecommunications and Information Administration (NTIA)
1401 Constitution Ave. NW
Herbert C. Hoover Bldg.
Washington, DC 20230 USA
Phone: 202-482-2000
Web Address: www.ntia.doc.gov
The National Telecommunications and Information Administration (NTIA), an agency of the U.S. Department of Commerce, is the Executive Branch's principal voice on domestic and international telecommunications and information technology issues.

U.S. Census Bureau
4600 Silver Hill Rd.
Washington, DC 20233-8800 USA
Phone: 301-763-4636
Toll Free: 800-923-8282
E-mail Address: pio@census.gov
Web Address: www.census.gov
The U.S. Census Bureau is the official collector of data about the people and economy of the U.S. Founded in 1790, it provides official social, demographic and economic information. In addition to the Population & Housing Census, which it conducts every 10 years, the U.S. Census Bureau conducts numerous other surveys annually.

U.S. Department of Commerce (DOC)
1401 Constitution Ave. NW
Washington, DC 20230 USA
Phone: 202-482-2000
E-mail Address: publicaffairs@doc.gov
Web Address: www.commerce.gov
The U.S. Department of Commerce (DOC) regulates trade and provides valuable economic analysis of the economy.

U.S. Department of Labor (DOL)
200 Constitution Ave. NW
Washington, DC 20210 USA
Phone: 202-693-4676
Toll Free: 866-487-2365
E-mail Address: m-DOLPublicAffairs@dol.gov
Web Address: www.dol.gov
The U.S. Department of Labor (DOL) is the government agency responsible for labor regulations. The Department of Labor's goal is to foster, promote, and develop the welfare of the wage earners, job seekers, and retirees of the United States; improve working conditions; advance opportunities for profitable employment; and assure work-related benefits and rights.

U.S. Department of Transportation (US DOT)-Intelligent Transportation Systems (ITS)
1200 New Jersey Ave. SE, HOIT
Washington, DC 20590 USA
Toll Free: 866-367-7487
E-mail Address: ITSHelp@dot.gov
Web Address: www.its.dot.gov
The U.S. Department of Transportation's (US DOT) Intelligent Transportation System (ITS) program was established to support the development of intelligent transportation systems through the integration of intelligent vehicles and an intelligent infrastructure. The Federal ITS program supports the overall advancement of ITS through investments in major initiatives, exploratory studies and a crosscutting core program.

U.S. Patent and Trademark Office (PTO)
600 Dulany St.
Madison Bldg.
Alexandria, VA 22314 USA
Phone: 571-272-1000
Toll Free: 800-786-9199
E-mail Address: usptoinfo@uspto.gov
Web Address: www.uspto.gov
The U.S. Patent and Trademark Office (PTO) administers patent and trademark laws for the U.S. and enables registration of patents and trademarks.

U.S. Securities and Exchange Commission (SEC)
100 F St. NE
Washington, DC 20549 USA
Phone: 202-942-8088
Fax: 202-772-9295
Toll Free: 800-732-0330
E-mail Address: help@sec.gov
Web Address: www.sec.gov
The U.S. Securities and Exchange Commission (SEC) is a nonpartisan, quasi-judicial regulatory agency responsible for administering federal securities laws. These laws are designed to protect investors in securities markets and ensure that they have access to disclosure of all material information concerning publicly traded securities. Visitors to the web site can access the EDGAR database of corporate financial and business information.

U.S. Trade Representative (USTR)
600 17th St. NW
Washington, DC 20508 USA
Phone: 202-395-3230
Fax: 202-395-6121
E-mail Address: media@ustr.eop.gov
Web Address: www.ustr.gov
The U.S. Trade Representative (USTR) is the nation's chief trade negotiator and the principal trade policy advisor to the President.

72) Wireless & Cellular Industry Associations

3GPP (The 3rd Generation Partnership Project)
3GPP Mobile Competence Centre, c/o ETSI
650, route des Lucioles
Sophia-Antipolis, Cedex 06921 France
E-mail Address: info@3gpp.org
Web Address: www.3gpp.org
The 3GPP is engaged in study, discussion and information approval through its members, which includes seven telecommunications standard development organizations (ARIB, ETSI, ATIS, CCSA, TTA, TSDSI and TTC) and mainly covers topics, such as cellular telecommunications network technologies, including radio access, the core transport network and service capabilities.

4GAmericas
1750 112th Ave. NE, Ste. B220

Bellevue, WA 98004 USA
Phone: 425-372-8922
Fax: 425-372-8923
Web Address: www.4gamericas.org
4G Americas is an industry trade organization composed of leading telecommunications service providers and manufacturers. The organization's mission is to promote, facilitate and advocate for the deployment and adoption of the 3GPP family of technologies throughout the Americas. The organization aims to develop the expansive wireless ecosystem of networks, devices, and applications enabled by GSM and its evolution to LTE. The organization publishes a significant amount of research and holds important conferences.

5G Automotive Association (5GAA)
E-mail Address: oflore@qti.qualcomm.com
Web Address: www.5gaa.org
The 5G Automotive Association (5GAA) is comprised ot AUDI AG, BMW Group, Daimler AG, Ericsson, Huawei, Intel, Nokia and Qualcomm. The association develops, tests and promotes communications solutions, support standardization and accelerate commercial availability and global market penetration. The goal is to address connected mobility and road safety needs with applications such as connected automated driving, ubiquitous access to services and integration into smart cities and intelligent transportation.

Bluetooth Special Interest Group (SIG)
5209 Lake Washington Blvd. NE, Ste. 350
Kirkland, WA 98033 USA
Phone: 425-691-3535
Fax: 425-691-3524
Web Address: www.bluetooth.com
The Bluetooth Special Interest Group (SIG) is a trade association comprised of leaders in the telecommunications, computing, automotive, industrial automation and network industries that is driving the development of Bluetooth wireless technology, a low cost short-range wireless specification for connecting mobile devices and bringing them to market.

Broadband Wireless Association (BWA)
Phone: 44-7765-250610
E-mail Address: Stephen@thebwa.eu
Web Address: www.thebwa.eu
The Broadband Wireless Association (BWA) provides representation, news and information for the European broadband wireless industry.

Canada Wireless Telecommunications Association (CWTA)
80 Elgin St., Ste. 300
Ottawa, ON K1P 6R2 Canada
Phone: 613-233-4888
Fax: 613-233-2032
E-mail Address: info@cwta.ca
Web Address: www.cwta.ca
The Canada Wireless Telecommunications Association (CWTA) seeks to be the pre-eminent source of input to government policy and public opinion on behalf of the wireless communications industry in Canada, in order to establish and maintain a positive economic environment for the wireless industry.

CDMA Development Group (CDG)
P.O. Box 22249
San Diego, CA 92129-2249 USA
Phone: 714-987-2362
Fax: 714-545-4601
Toll Free: 888-800-2362
E-mail Address: info@mobilitydg.org
Web Address: www.cdg.org
The CDMA Development Group (CDG) is composed of the world's leading code division multiple access (CDMA) service providers and manufacturers that have joined together to lead the adoption and evolution of CDMA wireless systems around the world.

Cellular Telecommunications & Internet Association (CTIA)
1400 16th St. NW, Ste. 600
Washington, DC 20036 USA
Phone: 202-785-0081
Web Address: www.ctia.org
The Cellular Telecommunications & Internet Association (CTIA) is an international nonprofit membership organization that represents a variety of wireless communications sectors including cellular service providers, manufacturers, wireless data and Internet companies. CTIA's industry committees study spectrum allocation, homeland security, taxation, safety and emerging technology.

Global System for Mobile Communication Association (GSMA)
The Wallbrook Bldg.
Fl. 2, 25 Wallbrook
London, EC4N 8AF UK
Phone: 44-207-356-0600
Fax: 44-20-7356-0601

E-mail Address: info@gsma.com
Web Address: www.gsmworld.com
The Global System for Mobile Communications Association (GSMA) is a global trade association representing nearly 800 GSM mobile phone operators from 219 countries.

Hong Kong Wireless Technology Industry Association
16 Cheung Yue St.
Unit B & D, Fl. 11, Gee Hing
Hong Kong, Hong Kong
Phone: 582-2989-9164
E-mail Address: contact@hkwtia.org
Web Address: www.hkwtia.org
The Hong Kong Wireless Technology Industry Association (WTIA), established in 2001, is a nonprofit trade association intended to provide a platform for wireless-related businesses to work together for the development and growth of the wireless industry.

Industrial Internet Consortium
9C Medway Rd., PMB 274
Milford, MA 01757 USA
Phone: 781-444-0404
E-mail Address: info@iiconsortium.org
Web Address: www.iiconsortium.org
The Industrial Internet Consortium was founded in 2014 to further development, adoption and wide-spread use of interconnected machines, intelligent analytics and people at work. Through an independently-run consortium of technology innovators, industrial companies, academia and government, the goal of the IIC is to accelerate the development and availability of intelligent industrial automation for the public good.

Li-Fi Consortium
E-mail Address: info@lificonsortium.org
Web Address: www.lificonsortium.org
The Li-Fi Consortium is a membership group founded to set standards and promote utilization of next-generation optical wireless networks, which are sometimes referred to as Li-Fi. Li-Fi is somewhat like Wi-Fi, except that it utilizes light as a means to transmit data.

NFC Forum (Near Field Communications Forum)
401 Edgewater Pl., Ste. 600
Wakefield, MA 01880 USA
Phone: 781-876-8955
Fax: 781-610-9864
E-mail Address: info@nfc-forum.org
Web Address: www.nfc-forum.org
The NFC Forum is an industry organization that promotes standards for Near Field Communication (NFC) technology. NFC is used by smart cards, smart phones and similar devices to exchange information and make payments wirelessly, with a touch.

Open Mobile Alliance (OMA)
2907 Shelter Island, Ste. 105-273
San Diego, CA 92106 USA
Phone: 858-623-0742
Fax: 858-623-0743
E-mail Address: snewberry@omaorg.org
Web Address: www.openmobilealliance.org
The Open Mobile Alliance (OMA) facilitates global user adoption of mobile data services by specifying market driven mobile service enablers that ensure service interoperability across devices, geographies, service providers, operators and networks, while allowing businesses to compete through innovation and differentiation.

Personal Communications Industry Association (PCIA)
500 Montgomery St., Ste. 500
Alexandria, VA 22314 USA
Phone: 703-739-0300
Fax: 703-836-1608
Toll Free: 800-759-0300
E-mail Address: jennifer.blasi@pcia.com
Web Address: www.pcia.com
The Personal Communications Industry Association (PCIA) is an association of companies that own and operate tower, rooftop and other kinds of wireless broadcasting and telecommunications equipment.

Small Cell Forum
P.O. Box 23
Dursley, Gloucestershire GL11 5WA UK
E-mail Address: info@smallcellforum.org
Web Address: www.smallcellforum.org
The Small Cell Forum, formerly the Femto Forum is a not-for-profit membership organization founded in 2007 to promote femtocell deployment worldwide. Comprised of mobile operators, telecoms hardware and software vendors, content providers and innovative start-ups, the group's mission is to advance the development and adoption of femtocell products and services within the residential and small to medium business markets.

Wi-Fi Alliance
10900-B Stonelake Blvd., Ste. 126
Austin, TX 78759 USA
Phone: 512-498-9434
Fax: 512-498-9435
Web Address: www.wi-fi.org
The Wi-Fi Alliance is a non-profit group that promotes wireless interoperability via Wi-Fi (802.11 standards). It also provides consumers with current information about Wi-Fi systems. The alliance currently includes over 350 member organizations.

WiMAX Forum
9009 SE Adams St., Ste. 2259
Clackamas, OR 97015 USA
Phone: 858-605-0978
Fax: 858-461-6041
Web Address: www.wimaxforum.org
The WiMAX Forum supports the implementation and standardization of long-range wireless Internet connections. It is a non-profit organization dedicated to the promotion and certification of interoperability and compatibility of broadband wireless products.

WiMedia Alliance, Inc.
2400 Camino Ramon, Ste. 375
San Ramon, CA 94583 USA
Phone: 925-275-6604
Fax: 925-886-3809
E-mail Address: help@wimedia.org
Web Address: www.wimedia.org
WiMedia Alliance, Inc. is an open, nonprofit wireless industry association that promotes the adoption and standardization of ultrawideband (UWB) worldwide for use in the personal computer, consumer electronics and mobile market segments.

Wireless Communications Alliance (WCA)
1510 Page Mill Rd.
Palo Alto, CA 94304-1125 USA
E-mail Address: promote@wca.org
Web Address: www.wca.org
The Wireless Communications Alliance (WCA) is a non-profit business association for companies and organizations working with wireless technologies. It promotes networking, education and the exchange of information amongst its members.

Wireless Communications Association International (WCAI)
1333 H St. NW, Ste. 700 W
Washington, DC 20005-4754 USA
Phone: 202-452-7823
Web Address: www.wcainternational.com/
The Wireless Communications Association International (WCAI) is a nonprofit trade association representing the wireless broadband industry.

ZigBee Alliance
508 Second St., Ste. 206
Davis, CA 95616 USA
Phone: 530-564-4565
Fax: 530-564-4721
E-mail Address: zigbee_media@mail.zigbee.org
Web Address: www.zigbee.org
The ZigBee Alliance is an association of companies working together to enable reliable, cost-effective, low-power, wirelessly networked monitoring and control products based on an open global standard.

73) Wireless & Cellular Industry Resources

Hong Kong Wireless Development Centre (HKWDC)
31 Wylie Rd.
Room 1814, Fl. 18, Tung Wah College
Homantin, Kowloon Hong Kong
Phone: 852-3190-6630
E-mail Address: po@twc.edu.hk
Web Address: www.hkwdc.org
The Hong Kong Wireless Development Centre (HKWDC) aims to facilitate mobile and wireless application development in Hong Kong.

IoT Now
70 Churchill Sq., Ste. 138
Kings Hill, Kent ME19 4YU UK
Phone: 44-1420-588638
E-mail Address: j.cowan@wkm-global.com
Web Address: www.iot-now.com
IoT Now is an online resource for people who are interested in machine-to-machine communications and information regarding business -to-business users and consumers' connected devices.

Wi-Fi Planet
Web Address: www.wi-fiplanet.com
Wi-Fi Planet is a web site devoted to wireless networking protocols. The site features daily news, reviews, tutorials, forums and event and product listings related to the Wi-Fi performance.

Wireless Design Online
5340 Fryling Rd., Ste. 300
Erie, PA 16510 USA

Phone: 814-897-7700
Fax: 814-897-9555
E-mail Address: info@wirelessdesignonline.com
Web Address: www.wirelessdesignonline.com
Wireless Design Online is an Internet resource for technical information covering the wireless industry.

74) Wireless Networks Resources

University of Washington Networks & Mobile Systems
University of Washington
Seattle, WA 98195 USA
Web Address: http://netlab.cs.washington.edu/
This website at the school of Computer Science at the University of Washington offers a wealth of information regarding state-of-the-art projects in remote wireless sensors, self-powered wireless networks, smart cities, smart cars and much more.

Chapter 4

THE INTERNET OF THINGS 400: WHO THEY ARE AND HOW THEY WERE CHOSEN

Includes Indexes by Company Name, Industry & Location

The companies chosen to be listed in PLUNKETT'S INTERNET OF THINGS (IOT) & DATA ANALYTICS INDUSTRY ALMANAC comprise a unique list. THE INTERNET OF THINGS 400 were chosen specifically for their dominance in the many facets of the machine communications, robotics, networks and predictive analytics industry in which they operate. Complete information about each firm can be found in the "Individual Profiles," beginning at the end of this chapter. These profiles are in alphabetical order by company name.

THE INTERNET OF THINGS 400 companies are from all parts of the United States, Canada, Europe, Asia/Pacific and beyond. THE INTERNET OF THINGS 400 includes companies that are deeply involved in the technologies, services and trends that keep the entire industry forging ahead.

Simply stated, THE INTERNET OF THINGS 400 contains the largest, most successful, fastest growing firms in machine communications, robotics, networks, predictive analysis and related industries in the world. To be included in our list, the firms had to meet the following criteria:

1) Generally, these are corporations based in the U.S., however, the headquarters of many firms are located in other nations.
2) Prominence, or a significant presence, in the machine communications, robotics, network and predictive analysis industry, and also in related services, equipment and supporting fields. (See the following Industry Codes section for a complete list of types of businesses that are covered).
3) The companies in THE INTERNET OF THINGS 400 do not have to be exclusively in the machine communications, robotics, network and predictive analysis field.
4) Financial data and vital statistics must have been available to the editors of this book, either directly from the company being written about or from outside sources deemed reliable and accurate by the editors. A small number of companies that we would like to have included are not listed because of a lack of sufficient, objective data.

INDEXES TO THE INTERNET OF THINGS 400, AS FOUND IN THIS CHAPTER AND IN THE BACK OF THE BOOK:

INDEX OF COMPANIES WITHIN INDUSTRY GROUPS

The industry codes shown below are based on the 2012 NAIC code system (NAIC is used by many analysts as a replacement for older SIC codes because NAIC is more specific to today's industry sectors, see www.census.gov/NAICS). Companies are given a primary NAIC code, reflecting the main line of business of each firm.

Industry Group/Company	Industry Code	2020 Sales	2020 Profits
Advertising Agencies and Marketing Services			
Wieden+Kennedy	541810		
Advertising/Marketing - Online			
Marketo	541810E	355,000,000	
Aircraft Engine and Engine Parts Manufacturing			
GE Aviation	336412	22,042,000,000	1,229,000,000
Honeywell International Inc	336412	32,636,999,680	4,778,999,808
Raytheon Technologies Corporation	336412	56,587,001,856	-3,519,000,064
Rolls-Royce plc	336412	15,743,711,232	-4,220,869,632
Aircraft Manufacturing (Aerospace), including Passenger Airliners and Military Aircraft,			
Airbus SE	336411	56,367,804,416	-1,279,546,368
Boeing Company (The)	336411	58,157,998,080	-11,873,000,448
Bombardier Inc	336411		
General Dynamics Corporation	336411	37,924,999,168	3,167,000,064
Lockheed Martin Corporation	336411	65,398,001,664	6,832,999,936
Northrop Grumman Corporation	336411	36,799,000,576	3,188,999,936
Textron Inc	336411	11,651,000,320	309,000,000
Aircraft, Missile and Space Vehicle (including Rockets), Drones, Satellites Manufacturing			
BAE Systems plc	336410	25,667,418,112	1,729,624,704
Kongsberg Gruppen ASA	336410	2,842,272,256	320,826,560
Automobile (Car) and Truck Electrical and Electronic Equipment Manufacturing			
Sumitomo Electric Industries Ltd	336320	27,301,560,320	638,993,344
Automobile (Car) and Truck Parts, Components and Systems Manufacturing, Including Gasoline Engines, Interiors and Electronics,			
Aptiv PLC	336300	13,066,000,384	1,804,000,000
Robert Bosch GmbH	336300	87,812,100,000	2,158,862,000
Automobile (Car) and Truck Transmission and Power Train Parts Manufacturing			
ZF Friedrichshafen AG (ZF)	336350	40,054,300,000	1,285,970,000
Automobile (Car) Manufacturing (incl. Autonomous or Self-Driving)			
Audi AG	336111	55,700,000,000	4,500,000,000
Bayerische Motoren Werke AG (BMW Group)	336111	111,793,733,632	4,263,272,704
FAW Group Corporation (First Automotive Works)	336111	106,848,000,000	
Ford Motor Company	336111	127,144,001,536	-1,279,000,064
General Motors Company (GM)	336111	122,484,998,144	6,426,999,808
Honda Motor Co Ltd	336111	131,199,328,256	4,004,656,896
Hyundai Motor Company	336111	87,338,631,168	1,196,261,120
Isuzu Motors Limited	336111	18,276,474,880	713,788,608
Jaguar Land Rover Limited	336111	22,170,100,000	-6,176,680,000

Industry Group/Company	Industry Code	2020 Sales	2020 Profits
Kia Corporation	336111	49,690,189,824	1,249,294,592
Mazda Motor Corporation	336111	30,142,042,112	106,595,544
Mercedes-Benz Group AG	336111	174,267,908,096	4,096,129,792
Mitsubishi Motors Corporation	336111	19,949,000,704	-226,521,024
NIO Inc	336111	2,545,472,512	-829,672,768
Nissan Motor Co Ltd	336111	86,805,962,752	-5,897,999,360
Nissan North America Inc	336111	47,671,100,000	-147,792,000
Renault SA	336111	49,098,219,520	-9,043,784,704
SAIC Motor Corporation Limited	336111	113,698,000,000	4,471,750,000
Stellantis North America (FCA US LLC)	336111	74,090,200,000	
Stellantis NV	336111	97,886,994,432	32,750,968
Subaru Corporation	336111	29,384,808,448	1,340,787,584
Suzuki Motor Corporation	336111	30,652,989,440	1,179,413,632
Tata Motors Limited	336111	34,564,714,496	-1,518,092,672
Tesla Inc	336111	31,536,001,024	690,000,000
Toyota Industries Corporation	336111	19,079,776,256	1,281,861,760
Toyota Motor Corporation	336111	262,995,935,232	18,243,495,936
Toyota Motor Sales USA Inc (TMS)	336111	95,587,830,000	
Volkswagen AG (VW)	336111	251,712,651,264	10,013,891,584
WM Motor Technology Co Ltd	336111		
Zoox Inc	336111		
Automobile (Car) Reservations (e.g. Uber), Car Sharing, Sharing Economy, Ticket Offices, Time Share and Vacation Club Rentals and Specialty Reservation Services			
DiDi Global Inc	561599	22,191,347,712	-1,646,234,112
Lyft Inc	561599	2,364,680,960	-1,752,856,960
Uber Technologies Inc	561599	11,139,000,320	-6,768,000,000
Computer and Data Systems Design, Consulting and Integration Services			
Accenture plc	541512	44,327,038,976	5,107,838,976
Atos SE	541512	12,627,191,808	621,139,072
CACI International Inc	541512	5,720,041,984	321,480,000
Capgemini SE	541512	17,897,838,592	1,080,781,952
Cognizant Technology Solutions Corporation	541512	16,652,000,256	1,392,000,000
Getronics NV	541512	569,400,000	
Happiest Minds Technologies Private Limited	541512	94,930,500	9,531,200
Infosys Limited	541512	12,780,000,256	2,331,000,064
Long View Systems	541512	275,500,000	
NTT DATA Corporation	541512	19,918,524,416	660,328,256
Publicis Sapient	541512	1,877,871,996	
Science Applications International Corporation (SAIC)	541512	6,378,999,808	226,000,000
Symbio Group (The)	541512		
Tata Consultancy Services Limited (TCS)	541512	21,470,898,933	4,312,628,111
Tech Mahindra Limited	541512	5,058,680,000	518,015,000
Unisys Corporation	541512	2,026,300,032	750,700,032
Wipro Limited	541512	8,130,474,496	1,295,291,776

Industry Group/Company	Industry Code	2020 Sales	2020 Profits
Computer Manufacturing, Including PCs, Laptops, Mainframes and Tablets			
Dell Technologies Inc	334111	92,154,003,456	4,616,000,000
Fujitsu Limited	334111	33,898,604,544	1,406,294,912
Hewlett Packard Enterprise Company	334111	26,982,000,640	-322,000,000
Hitachi Limited	334111	77,038,264,320	769,709,248
HP Inc	334111	56,639,000,576	2,844,000,000
NEC Corporation	334111	28,703,776,308	927,047,973
Omron Automation Americas	334111	59,659,031	
Computer Networking & Related Equipment Manufacturing (may incl. Internet of Things, IoT)			
Cisco Systems Inc	334210A	49,301,000,192	11,214,000,128
Digi International Inc	334210A	279,271,008	8,411,000
D-Link Corporation	334210A	536,339,000	44,097,900
Extreme Networks Inc	334210A	948,019,008	-126,845,000
Fortinet Inc	334210A	2,594,400,000	488,500,000
Juniper Networks Inc	334210A	4,445,100,032	257,800,000
NETGEAR Inc	334210A	1,255,202,048	58,293,000
Zoom Telephonics Inc (dba Minim)	334210A	47,988,548	-3,858,415
Computer Programming and Custom Software Development and Consulting			
FPT Software Company Limited	541511	726,777,000	
Nexient	541511		
Program-Ace	541511		
Sigma Software	541511		
SoftServe Inc	541511	261,843,750	
Computer Software (Business and Consumer), Packaged Software, Artificial Intelligence (AI), Software as a Service (Saas) Industry			
Aurora Innovation Inc	511210		
Waymo LLC	511210		
Computer Software: Business Management & Enterprise Resource Planning (ERP)			
ASG Technologies Group Inc	511210H	425,000,000	
C3.ai Inc	511210H	156,666,000	-69,378,000
Micro Focus International Plc	511210H	3,000,999,936	-2,969,499,904
Microsoft Corporation	511210H	143,015,002,112	44,280,999,936
Oracle Corporation	511210H	39,068,000,256	10,135,000,064
Oracle NetSuite	511210H	1,008,291,375	
PAR Technology Corporation	511210H	213,786,000	-36,562,000
Pegasystems Inc	511210H	1,017,516,992	-61,373,000
SAP SE	511210H	30,873,999,360	5,810,473,472
SAS Institute Inc	511210H	3,000,000,000	
Symphony Technology Group	511210H	2,998,125,000	
UKG Inc (Ultimate Kronos Group)	511210H	3,000,000,000	770,000,000
Computer Software: Data Base & File Management			
Actifio Inc	511210J	176,800,000	
Cloudera Inc	511210J	794,190,976	-336,582,016
DataStax Inc	511210J	126,000,000	
Embarcadero Technologies Inc	511210J	174,636,000	

Industry Group/Company	Industry Code	2020 Sales	2020 Profits
MongoDB Inc	511210J	421,720,000	-175,522,000
Orbital Insight	511210J		
Palantir Technologies Inc	511210J	1,092,673,024	-1,166,391,040
Qualtrics International Inc	511210J	763,521,984	-272,502,016
Computer Software: E-Commerce, Web Analytics & Applications Management			
EAG Global Tech Services Ltd (Eastern Peak)	511210M		
Magneto IT Solutions LLC	511210M		
Placemeter Inc	511210M		
VironIT	511210M		
Computer Software: Healthcare & Biotechnology			
Aeon Global Health Corp	511210D		
Allscripts Healthcare Solutions Inc	511210D	1,502,700,032	700,406,976
Cegedim SA	511210D	610,315,000	13,265,000
Cerner Corporation	511210D	5,505,787,904	780,088,000
eClinicalWorks	511210D	646,000,000	
Epic Systems Corporation	511210D	3,300,000,000	
Medical Information Technology Inc (MEDITECH)	511210D	502,851,197	74,542,923
Computer Software: Multimedia, Advertising, Graphics & Publishing			
Adobe Inc	511210F	12,867,999,744	5,260,000,256
Computer Software: Network Management, System Testing, & Storage			
Affirmed Networks Inc	511210B		
Citrix Systems Inc	511210B	3,236,699,904	504,446,016
F5 Networks Inc	511210B	2,350,821,888	307,440,992
HQSoftware	511210B		
LaQuest Inc	511210B		
NetScout Systems Inc	511210B	891,820,032	-2,754,000
Nutanix Inc	511210B	1,307,682,048	-872,883,008
OSDB Ltd	511210B		
Particle Industries Inc	511210B	10,197,000	
Radware Ltd	511210B	250,027,008	9,636,000
Rocket Software Inc	511210B	500,000,000	
R-STYLE LAB Company (R-Style Lab)	511210B		
ScienceSoft USA Corporation	511210B		
SolarWinds Corporation	511210B	1,019,241,024	158,475,008
Telenor Connexion AB	511210B		
TP-Link Technologies Co Ltd	511210B	2,400,000,000	
Tyler Technologies Inc	511210B	1,116,663,040	194,820,000
UIB Holdings Pte Ltd	511210B		
UNICOM Engineering Inc	511210B	333,230,625	
VMware Inc	511210B	10,810,999,808	6,412,000,256
VMware Tanzu Labs	511210B	605,209,968	
Computer Software: Operating Systems, Languages & Development Tools, Artificial Intelligence (AI)			
ACCESS Co Ltd	511210I	87,375,294	-23,303,100
FogHorn Systems	511210I		
GlobeRanger Corporation	511210I		

Industry Group/Company	Industry Code	2020 Sales	2020 Profits
Preferred Networks Inc	511210I		
Progress Software Corporation	511210I	442,150,016	79,722,000
Computer Software: Sales & Customer Relationship Management			
LiveRamp Holdings Inc	511210K	380,572,000	-124,511,000
salesforce.com inc	511210K	17,098,000,384	126,000,000
Trilogy Inc	511210K		
Computer Software: Security & Anti-Virus			
AhnLab Inc	511210E	163,716,795	16,996,413
Beijing Qihu Keji Co Ltd (Qihoo 360)	511210E	1,779,434,863	434,780,776
Carbon Black Inc	511210E	264,252,240	
Check Point Software Technologies Ltd	511210E	2,064,899,968	846,600,000
Cloudflare Inc	511210E	431,059,008	-119,370,000
CrowdStrike Holdings Inc	511210E	481,412,992	-141,779,008
Cybereason Inc	511210E		
CYREN Ltd	511210E	36,388,000	-17,263,000
Darktrace PLC	511210E	199,100,000	-28,672,000
Entrust Corporation	511210E	840,000,000	
Forcepoint LLC	511210E	700,000,000	
Illumio	511210E		
Lookout Inc	511210E		
Mandiant Inc	511210E	940,584,000	-207,303,008
McAfee Corp	511210E	2,905,999,872	-289,000,000
NortonLifeLock Inc	511210E	2,489,999,872	3,887,000,064
Okta Inc	511210E	586,067,008	-208,912,992
OneSpan Inc	511210E	215,691,008	-5,455,000
Palo Alto Networks Inc	511210E	3,408,399,872	-267,000,000
ProofPoint Inc	511210E	1,050,009,984	-163,808,992
SecureWorks Corporation	511210E	552,764,992	-31,666,000
SentinelOne Inc	511210E		
Tanium Inc	511210E	500,000,000	
Trend Micro Inc	511210E	1,529,480,320	236,406,448
VeriSign Inc	511210E	1,265,052,032	814,888,000
WatchGuard Technologies Inc	511210E		
Zscaler Inc	511210E	431,268,992	-115,116,000
Computer Software: Supply Chain & Logistics, (may incl. Artificial Intelligence, AI)			
American Software Inc	511210A	115,466,000	6,742,000
Aspen Technology Inc	511210A	598,716,992	229,671,008
Blue Yonder Group Inc	511210A	1,240,312,500	
Manhattan Associates Inc	511210A	586,371,968	87,240,000
Samsara Inc	511210A	119,865,000	-225,224,000
Computer Software: Telecom, Communications & VOIP, Internet of Things (IoT)			
Aruba Networks Inc	511210C	3,000,000,000	
BlackBerry Limited	511210C	1,040,000,000	-152,000,000
Location Labs Inc	511210C	52,093,125	
Slack Technologies Inc	511210C	630,422,016	-571,057,984
XIUS	511210C	507,385,000	-3,782,000

Industry Group/Company	Industry Code	2020 Sales	2020 Profits
Computers, Peripherals, Software and Accessories Distribution			
TESSCO Technologies Incorporated	423430	540,298,304	-21,568,900
Connectors for Electronics Manufacturing			
TE Connectivity Ltd	334417	12,172,000,256	-241,000,000
Consumer Electronics Manufacturing, Including Audio and Video Equipment, Stereos, TVs and Radios			
Invoxia	334310		
Koninklijke Philips NV (Royal Philips)	334310	22,061,729,792	1,340,531,072
Panasonic Corporation	334310	65,820,188,672	1,983,295,744
Pioneer Corporation	334310	3,193,021,383	
Ring Protect Inc	334310		
Samsung Electronics Co Ltd	334310	198,873,792,512	21,911,455,744
Sharp Corporation	334310	19,957,540,864	184,158,704
SkyBell Technologies Inc	334310		
Sony Group Corporation	334310	79,900,000,000	
Contract Electronics Manufacturing Services (CEM) and Printed Circuits Assembly			
Accton Technology Corporation	334418	1,936,970,000	179,555,000
Flex Ltd	334418	24,209,870,848	87,579,000
Foxconn Technology Co Ltd	334418	3,726,840,000	166,662,000
Hon Hai Precision Industry Company Ltd	334418	193,112,539,136	3,668,863,232
HTC Corporation	334418	206,480,000	-214,194,000
Inventec Corporation	334418	14,490,420,369	268,444,087
Jabil Inc	334418	27,266,437,120	53,912,000
Quanta Computer Inc	334418	39,316,463,616	912,852,160
Samsung Electro-Mechanics Co Ltd	334418	7,541,537,908	5,731,006,550
Sanmina Corporation	334418	6,960,370,176	139,712,992
Electric Motor and Power & Motor Generator Manufacturing			
YASKAWA Electric Corporation	335312	3,611,094,272	136,831,728
Electric Signal, Electricity, and Semiconductor Test and Measuring Equipment Manufacturing			
Agilent Technologies Inc	334515	5,338,999,808	719,000,000
Itron Inc	334515	2,173,349,888	-57,955,000
Electrical Appliance Manufacturing, Small			
Dyson Singapore Pte Ltd	335210	498,419,012	7,739,004
Electricity Control Panels, Circuit Breakers and Power Switches Equipment (Switchgear) Manufacturing			
ABB Ltd	335313	26,133,999,616	5,145,999,872
Broadcom Inc	335313	23,887,998,976	2,960,000,000
Factory Automation, Robots (Robotics) Industrial Process, Thermostat, Flow Meter and Environmental Quality Monitoring and Control Manufacturing (incl. Artificial Intelligence, AI)			
Advanced Energy Industries Inc	334513	1,415,826,048	134,675,008
Ametek Inc	334513	4,540,028,928	872,438,976
Cemtrex Inc	334513	43,518,384	-9,933,775
CTS Corporation	334513	424,065,984	34,686,000
Electro-Sensors Inc	334513	7,621,000	-124,000

Industry Group/Company	Industry Code	2020 Sales	2020 Profits
Emerson Electric Co	334513	16,785,000,448	1,964,999,936
Faro Technologies Inc	334513	303,768,000	629,000
Ideal Power Inc	334513	428,129	-7,793,897
II-VI Incorporated	334513	2,380,070,912	-67,029,000
Keyence Corporation	334513	4,849,064,960	1,740,922,880
Mesa Laboratories Inc	334513	117,687,000	1,349,000
MKS Instruments Inc	334513	2,329,999,872	350,100,000
Onto Innovation Inc	334513	556,496,000	31,025,000
Perceptron Inc	334513	62,262,000	-3,971,000
Powell Industries Inc	334513	518,499,008	16,660,000
Roper Technologies Inc	334513	5,527,099,904	949,699,968
Schmitt Industries Inc	334513	4,189,924	3,880,575
Siemens AG	334513	64,529,571,840	4,551,255,552
Siemens Limited	334513	1,389,970,000	104,112,000
Vishay Precision Group Inc	334513	269,812,000	10,787,000
Woodward Inc	334513	2,495,664,896	240,395,008
Yokogawa Electric Corporation	334513	3,553,758,976	129,046,424
Zygo Corporation	334513		
Heavy Duty Truck (including Buses) Manufacturing			
Daimler Trucks North America LLC	336120	16,741,000,000	
Navistar International Corporation	336120	7,503,000,064	-347,000,000
PACCAR Inc	336120	18,728,499,200	1,298,400,000
Volvo AB	336120	37,350,543,360	2,131,914,112
Internet Search Engines, Online Publishing, Sharing, Gig and Consumer Services, Online Radio, TV and Entertainment Sites and Social Media			
Alphabet Inc (Google)	519130	182,527,000,576	40,269,000,704
Machine Tool and Laser Manufacturing (for Bending, Buffing, Boring, Pressing, Grinding or Forming)			
Fanuc Corporation	333517	4,466,029,056	644,713,664
Nachi-Fujikoshi Corporation	333517	1,930,330,000	23,599,300
Management of Businesses & Enterprises			
LG Corporation	551114	6,206,060,000	1,524,570,000
Market Research, Business Intelligence and Opinion Polling			
Forrester Research Inc	541910	448,984,000	9,990,000
Gartner Inc	541910	4,099,403,008	266,744,992
Medical Equipment and Supplies Manufacturing			
3M Company	339100	32,184,000,512	5,384,000,000
Office Administrative Services			
Conduent Incorporated	561110	4,163,000,064	-118,000,000
Online Sales, B2C Ecommerce, Sharing Economy Platforms			
Amazon.com Inc	454111	386,063,990,784	21,330,999,296
Outdoor, Underwater, Decorative, Stage and Stadium Lighting Equipment Manufacturing			
Click & Grow LLC	335129		
Outsourced Computer Facilities Management and Operations Services			
International Business Machines Corporation (IBM)	541513	73,620,996,096	5,590,000,128

Industry Group/Company	Industry Code	2020 Sales	2020 Profits
Power, Distribution and Specialty Transformer Manufacturing			
Mitsubishi Electric Corporation	335311	39,212,228,608	1,949,263,616
Schneider Electric SA	335311	28,413,159,424	2,400,984,832
Radar, Navigation, Sonar, Space Vehicle Guidance, Flight Systems and Marine Instrument Manufacturing			
Electro Optic Systems Holdings Limited	334511	139,747,648	-18,926,476
Garmin Ltd	334511	4,186,573,056	992,323,968
TomTom International BV	334511	596,502,400	-290,963,008
Trimble Inc	334511	3,147,699,968	389,900,000
Rolling Mill and Other Metalworking Machinery Manufacturing			
Bosch Rexroth AG	333519	6,386,870,000	
KUKA AG	333519	2,906,365,952	-116,435,344
Satellite Telecommunications			
Gilat Satellite Networks Ltd	517410	165,884,992	34,911,000
Globalstar Inc	517410	128,487,000	-109,639,000
Inmarsat Global Limited	517410	1,137,300,000	218,400,000
Intelsat SA	517410	1,913,080,064	-911,664,000
Iridium Communications Inc	517410	583,438,976	-56,054,000
OneWeb Ltd	517410	26,520,760	
SES SA	517410	2,073,475,072	-97,123,560
Scientific Research and Development (R&D) in Physics, Engineering, Telecommunications and Computers			
Amazon Lab126 Inc	541712		
Fujitsu Laboratories Ltd	541712		
Hewlett Packard Laboratories (HP Labs)	541712		
Hitachi High Technologies America Inc	541712		
IBM Research	541712		
NEC Laboratories America Inc	541712		
Nokia Bell Labs	541712		
Siemens USA	541712	17,791,100,000	
Toshiba Corporate R&D Center	541712		
Security Guard, Security Patrol, Armored Car, Security System, Locksmith and Other Security Services			
Johnson Controls International plc	561600	22,317,000,704	631,000,000
Security Systems Services (except Locksmiths)			
Vivint Smart Home Inc	561621	1,260,729,984	-484,240,000
Security, Detection, Burglar Alarms, Sensors & Intercom System Manufacturing			
ECSI International Inc	334290		
George Risk Industries Inc	334290	14,809,000	2,104,000
Iteris Inc	334290	114,117,000	-5,610,000
Universal Security Instruments Inc	334290	14,803,024	-5,813,891
Semiconductor and Solar Cell Manufacturing, Including Chips, Memory, LEDs, Transistors and Integrated Circuits, Artificial Intelligence (AI), & Internet of Things (IoT)			
Advanced Micro Devices Inc (AMD)	334413	9,763,000,320	2,489,999,872
Analog Devices Inc	334413	5,603,056,128	1,220,760,960

Industry Group/Company	Industry Code	2020 Sales	2020 Profits
Arm Holdings plc	334413	1,825,600,000	
Arteris IP	334413	31,812,000	-3,260,000
ASE Technology Holding Co Ltd	334413	17,191,147,520	972,067,008
Cambricon Technologies Corporation Limited	334413	70,309,900	-66,568,900
CEVA Inc	334413	100,326,000	-2,379,000
Cirrus Logic Inc	334413	1,281,123,968	159,498,000
Cypress Semiconductor Corporation	334413	2,469,951,680	
Diodes Incorporated	334413	1,229,214,976	98,088,000
DSP Group Inc	334413	114,480,000	-6,790,000
GLOBALFOUNDRIES Inc	334413	4,850,505,216	-1,347,570,944
Hoya Corporation	334413	5,118,185,472	1,005,289,728
Infineon Technologies AG	334413	9,675,087,872	415,598,496
Intel Corporation	334413	77,866,999,808	20,899,000,320
Lattice Semiconductor Corporation	334413	408,120,000	47,392,000
Macronix International Co Ltd	334413	1,415,520,680	186,204,541
Marvell Technology Group Ltd	334413	2,699,161,088	1,584,391,040
Maxim Integrated Products Inc	334413	2,191,395,072	654,694,016
MediaTek Inc	334413	11,610,704,896	1,474,713,088
Microchip Technology Incorporated	334413	5,274,200,064	570,600,000
Micron Technology Inc	334413	21,435,000,832	2,687,000,064
Novatek Microelectronics Corp	334413	2,843,618,069	420,280,105
NVIDIA Corporation	334413	10,917,999,616	2,796,000,000
NXP Semiconductors NV	334413	8,611,999,744	52,000,000
OmniVision Technologies Inc	334413	1,890,000,000	
ON Semiconductor Corporation	334413	5,255,000,064	234,200,000
Qualcomm Incorporated	334413	23,530,999,808	5,198,000,128
Renesas Electronics America Inc	334413	629,955,000	
Renesas Electronics Corporation	334413	6,288,644,608	400,917,344
Semiconductor Manufacturing International Corporation	334413	3,906,975,000	669,098,000
Silicon Laboratories Inc	334413	886,676,992	12,531,000
Silicon Motion Technology Corporation	334413	539,521,024	79,746,000
SK Hynix Inc	334413	26,790,414,336	3,993,400,576
Skyworks Solutions Inc	334413	3,355,699,968	814,800,000
STMicroelectronics NV	334413	10,218,999,808	1,106,000,000
Taiwan Semiconductor Manufacturing Co Ltd (TSMC)	334413	48,268,500,992	18,408,108,032
Texas Instruments Incorporated	334413	14,460,999,680	5,594,999,808
Toshiba Corporation	334413	29,786,923,008	-1,007,284,416
UNISOC Communications Inc	334413	1,595,261,850	
United Microelectronics Corporation	334413	6,372,935,168	823,941,248
VIA Technologies Inc	334413	231,269,059	172,306,521
Wolfspeed Inc	334413	903,900,032	-191,700,000
Xilinx Inc	334413	3,162,665,984	792,721,024
Xperi Holding Corporation	334413	892,019,968	146,762,000
Telecommunications, Telephone and Network Equipment Manufacturing, including PBX, Routers, Switches, Internet of Things (IoT), and Handsets Manufacturing			
Ciena Corporation	334210	3,532,156,928	361,291,008
Datang Telecom Technology Co Ltd	334210	184,950,836	-266,214,215

Industry Group/Company	Industry Code	2020 Sales	2020 Profits
Fujitsu Network Communications Inc	334210		
Huawei Technologies Co Ltd	334210		
Tellabs Inc	334210	1,610,256,375	
ZTE Corporation	334210	15,883,930,624	666,940,928
Telephone, Internet Access, Broadband, Data Networks, Server Facilities and Telecommunications Services Industry			
Akamai Technologies Inc	517110	3,198,149,120	557,054,016
Amazon Web Services Inc (AWS)	517110	45,370,000,000	13,531,000,000
AT&T Inc	517110	171,759,992,832	-5,176,000,000
BCE Inc (Bell Canada Enterprises)	517110	17,964,359,680	2,067,828,480
BT Group plc	517110		
China Telecom Corporation Limited	517110	60,295,513,005	3,194,324,250
China Unicom (Hong Kong) Limited	517110		
KT Corporation	517110	20,525,596,672	588,616,320
Nippon Telegraph and Telephone Corporation (NTT)	517110	104,560,590,848	7,515,605,504
Orange	517110	47,737,360,384	5,445,695,488
Reliance Communications Ltd	517110	230,471,000	-5,675,650,000
Singapore Technologies Telemedia Pte Ltd	517110	2,970,803,015	68,702,179
Singtel Optus Pty Limited	517110	4,768,040,000	1,570,080,000
SoftBank Group Corp	517110	54,348,640,256	-8,449,403,392
Speedcast International Limited	517110	685,300,000	
Swisscom AG	517110	12,027,696,128	1,657,871,616
TDS Telecommunications LLC	517110	976,000,000	100,000,000
Telecom Italia SpA	517110	17,849,278,464	8,158,379,008
Telefonica SA	517110	48,647,614,464	1,786,621,824
Telstra Corporation Limited	517110	16,268,843,008	1,299,821,056
Verizon Communications Inc	517110	128,292,003,840	17,801,000,960
Wireless Communications and Radio and TV Broadcasting Equipment Manufacturing, including Cellphones (Handsets) and Internet of Things (IoT)			
Alien Technology Corporation	334220	60,196,500	
Anaren Inc	334220	242,676,000	
Apple Inc	334220	274,515,001,344	57,410,998,272
Aviat Networks Inc	334220	238,642,000	257,000
Beijing Tianyu Communication Equipment Co Ltd (K-Touch)	334220	367,500,000	
Comtech Telecommunications Corp	334220	616,715,008	7,020,000
CyberTAN Technology Inc	334220	171,926,580	838,445
InterDigital Inc	334220	358,991,008	44,801,000
L3Harris Technologies Inc	334220	18,193,999,872	1,119,000,064
LG Electronics Inc	334220	53,128,343,552	1,653,032,576
LG Electronics USA Inc	334220	12,429,400,000	152,231,000
LM Ericsson Telephone Company (Ericsson)	334220	25,646,315,520	1,929,405,440
Maxar Technologies Inc	334220	1,723,000,064	303,000,000
Motorola Mobility LLC	334220	5,218,000,000	
Motorola Solutions Inc	334220	7,414,000,128	949,000,000
Nokia Corporation	334220	24,678,420,480	-2,841,428,992
OPPO Electronics Corporation	334220		
Phazar Antenna Corp	334220	13,837,500	

Industry Group/Company	Industry Code	2020 Sales	2020 Profits
Potevio Corporation	334220	12,618,112,500	
PowerFleet Inc	334220	113,593,000	-9,007,000
Proxim Wireless Corporation	334220		
Sony Electronics Inc	334220	5,995,464,166	
TCI International Inc	334220	1,449,350,000	
Telesat Corporation	334220		
Telular Corporation	334220	160,875,000	
Uniden Holdings Corporation	334220	185,786,000	-4,284,380
ViaSat Inc	334220	2,309,238,016	-212,000
vivo Mobile Communication Co Ltd	334220		
Wireless Telecom Group Inc	334220	41,748,000	-8,088,000
Xiaomi Corporation	334220	37,667,800,000	3,112,000,000
Wireless Telecommunications Carriers (except Satellite)			
Agero Inc	517210	664,350,000	
Altice Europe NV	517210	16,862,064,312	
America Movil SAB de CV	517210	46,902,632,448	2,161,018,368
AT&T Mobility LLC	517210	72,564,000,000	22,372,000,000
Bharti Airtel Limited	517210	11,458,722,139	-4,075,670,815
China Mobile Limited	517210	117,674,000,000	16,567,600,000
Deutsche Telekom AG	517210		
Jio (Reliance Jio Infocomm Limited)	517210	8,504,180,000	734,478,000
KDDI Corporation	517210	46,019,653,632	5,621,656,576
LG Uplus Corp	517210	11,268,308,992	391,994,912
NTT DOCOMO Inc	517210	43,134,016,602	5,485,300,000
OnStar LLC	517210	1,874,250,000	
SK Telecom Co Ltd	517210	15,641,241,600	1,263,375,744
Telenor ASA	517210	13,628,857,344	1,924,404,352
T-Mobile US Inc	517210	68,396,998,656	3,064,000,000
Vodafone Group plc	517210	50,791,104,512	-1,038,996,224
Wireless Telecommunications Resellers			
Telit Communications PLC	517911	343,620,992	6,220,000

ALPHABETICAL INDEX

Ford Motor Company
Forrester Research Inc
Fortinet Inc
Foxconn Technology Co Ltd
FPT Software Company Limited
Fujitsu Laboratories Ltd
Fujitsu Limited
Fujitsu Network Communications Inc
Garmin Ltd
Gartner Inc
GE Aviation
General Dynamics Corporation
General Motors Company (GM)
George Risk Industries Inc
Getronics NV
Gilat Satellite Networks Ltd
GLOBALFOUNDRIES Inc
Globalstar Inc
GlobeRanger Corporation
Happiest Minds Technologies Private Limited
Hewlett Packard Enterprise Company
Hewlett Packard Laboratories (HP Labs)
Hitachi High Technologies America Inc
Hitachi Limited
Hon Hai Precision Industry Company Ltd
Honda Motor Co Ltd
Honeywell International Inc
Hoya Corporation
HP Inc
HQSoftware
HTC Corporation
Huawei Technologies Co Ltd
Hyundai Motor Company
IBM Research
Ideal Power Inc
II-VI Incorporated
Illumio
Infineon Technologies AG
Infosys Limited
Inmarsat Global Limited
Intel Corporation
Intelsat SA
InterDigital Inc
International Business Machines Corporation (IBM)
Inventec Corporation
Invoxia
Iridium Communications Inc
Isuzu Motors Limited
Iteris Inc
Itron Inc
Jabil Inc
Jaguar Land Rover Limited
Jio (Reliance Jio Infocomm Limited)
Johnson Controls International plc
Juniper Networks Inc
KDDI Corporation
Keyence Corporation
Kia Corporation
Kongsberg Gruppen ASA
Koninklijke Philips NV (Royal Philips)
KT Corporation
KUKA AG
L3Harris Technologies Inc
LaQuest Inc
Lattice Semiconductor Corporation
LG Corporation
LG Electronics Inc
LG Electronics USA Inc
LG Uplus Corp
LiveRamp Holdings Inc
LM Ericsson Telephone Company (Ericsson)
Location Labs Inc
Lockheed Martin Corporation
Long View Systems
Lookout Inc
Lyft Inc
Macronix International Co Ltd
Magneto IT Solutions LLC
Mandiant Inc
Manhattan Associates Inc
Marketo
Marvell Technology Group Ltd
Maxar Technologies Inc
Maxim Integrated Products Inc
Mazda Motor Corporation
McAfee Corp
MediaTek Inc
Medical Information Technology Inc (MEDITECH)
Mercedes-Benz Group AG
Mesa Laboratories Inc
Micro Focus International Plc
Microchip Technology Incorporated
Micron Technology Inc
Microsoft Corporation
Mitsubishi Electric Corporation
Mitsubishi Motors Corporation
MKS Instruments Inc
MongoDB Inc
Motorola Mobility LLC
Motorola Solutions Inc
Nachi-Fujikoshi Corporation
Navistar International Corporation
NEC Corporation
NEC Laboratories America Inc
NETGEAR Inc
NetScout Systems Inc
Nexient
NIO Inc
Nippon Telegraph and Telephone Corporation (NTT)
Nissan Motor Co Ltd
Nissan North America Inc
Nokia Bell Labs
Nokia Corporation
Northrop Grumman Corporation
NortonLifeLock Inc
Novatek Microelectronics Corp

NTT DATA Corporation
NTT DOCOMO Inc
Nutanix Inc
NVIDIA Corporation
NXP Semiconductors NV
Okta Inc
OmniVision Technologies Inc
Omron Automation Americas
ON Semiconductor Corporation
OneSpan Inc
OneWeb Ltd
OnStar LLC
Onto Innovation Inc
OPPO Electronics Corporation
Oracle Corporation
Oracle NetSuite
Orange
Orbital Insight
OSDB Ltd
PACCAR Inc
Palantir Technologies Inc
Palo Alto Networks Inc
Panasonic Corporation
PAR Technology Corporation
Particle Industries Inc
Pegasystems Inc
Perceptron Inc
Phazar Antenna Corp
Pioneer Corporation
Placemeter Inc
Potevio Corporation
Powell Industries Inc
PowerFleet Inc
Preferred Networks Inc
Program-Ace
Progress Software Corporation
ProofPoint Inc
Proxim Wireless Corporation
Publicis Sapient
Qualcomm Incorporated
Qualtrics International Inc
Quanta Computer Inc
Radware Ltd
Raytheon Technologies Corporation
Reliance Communications Ltd
Renault SA
Renesas Electronics America Inc
Renesas Electronics Corporation
Ring Protect Inc
Robert Bosch GmbH
Rocket Software Inc
Rolls-Royce plc
Roper Technologies Inc
R-STYLE LAB Company (R-Style Lab)
SAIC Motor Corporation Limited
salesforce.com inc
Samsara Inc
Samsung Electro-Mechanics Co Ltd
Samsung Electronics Co Ltd
Sanmina Corporation
SAP SE
SAS Institute Inc
Schmitt Industries Inc
Schneider Electric SA
Science Applications International Corporation (SAIC)
ScienceSoft USA Corporation
SecureWorks Corporation
Semiconductor Manufacturing International Corporation
SentinelOne Inc
SES SA
Sharp Corporation
Siemens AG
Siemens Limited
Siemens USA
Sigma Software
Silicon Laboratories Inc
Silicon Motion Technology Corporation
Singapore Technologies Telemedia Pte Ltd
Singtel Optus Pty Limited
SK Hynix Inc
SK Telecom Co Ltd
SkyBell Technologies Inc
Skyworks Solutions Inc
Slack Technologies Inc
SoftBank Group Corp
SoftServe Inc
SolarWinds Corporation
Sony Electronics Inc
Sony Group Corporation
Speedcast International Limited
Stellantis North America (FCA US LLC)
Stellantis NV
STMicroelectronics NV
Subaru Corporation
Sumitomo Electric Industries Ltd
Suzuki Motor Corporation
Swisscom AG
Symbio Group (The)
Symphony Technology Group
Taiwan Semiconductor Manufacturing Co Ltd (TSMC)
Tanium Inc
Tata Consultancy Services Limited (TCS)
Tata Motors Limited
TCI International Inc
TDS Telecommunications LLC
TE Connectivity Ltd
Tech Mahindra Limited
Telecom Italia SpA
Telefonica SA
Telenor ASA
Telenor Connexion AB
Telesat Corporation
Telit Communications PLC
Tellabs Inc
Telstra Corporation Limited
Telular Corporation

Tesla Inc
TESSCO Technologies Incorporated
Texas Instruments Incorporated
Textron Inc
T-Mobile US Inc
TomTom International BV
Toshiba Corporate R&D Center
Toshiba Corporation
Toyota Industries Corporation
Toyota Motor Corporation
Toyota Motor Sales USA Inc (TMS)
TP-Link Technologies Co Ltd
Trend Micro Inc
Trilogy Inc
Trimble Inc
Tyler Technologies Inc
Uber Technologies Inc
UIB Holdings Pte Ltd
UKG Inc (Ultimate Kronos Group)
UNICOM Engineering Inc
Uniden Holdings Corporation
UNISOC Communications Inc
Unisys Corporation
United Microelectronics Corporation
Universal Security Instruments Inc
VeriSign Inc
Verizon Communications Inc
VIA Technologies Inc
ViaSat Inc
VironIT
Vishay Precision Group Inc
Vivint Smart Home Inc
vivo Mobile Communication Co Ltd
VMware Inc
VMware Tanzu Labs
Vodafone Group plc
Volkswagen AG (VW)
Volvo AB
WatchGuard Technologies Inc
Waymo LLC
Wieden+Kennedy
Wipro Limited
Wireless Telecom Group Inc
WM Motor Technology Co Ltd
Wolfspeed Inc
Woodward Inc
Xiaomi Corporation
Xilinx Inc
XIUS
Xperi Holding Corporation
YASKAWA Electric Corporation
Yokogawa Electric Corporation
ZF Friedrichshafen AG (ZF)
Zoom Telephonics Inc (dba Minim)
Zoox Inc
Zscaler Inc
ZTE Corporation
Zygo Corporation

INDEX OF HEADQUARTERS LOCATION BY U.S. STATE

To help you locate the firms geographically, the city and state of the headquarters of each company are in the following index.

AT&T Mobility LLC; Atlanta
Manhattan Associates Inc; Atlanta
SecureWorks Corporation; Atlanta

IDAHO
Micron Technology Inc; Boise

ILLINOIS
Allscripts Healthcare Solutions Inc; Chicago
Boeing Company (The); Chicago
CTS Corporation; Lisle
Hitachi High Technologies America Inc; Schaumburg
Motorola Mobility LLC; Chicago
Motorola Solutions Inc; Chicago
Navistar International Corporation; Lisle
Omron Automation Americas; Hoffman Estates
OneSpan Inc; Chicago
Telular Corporation; Chicago

MARYLAND
CEVA Inc; Rockville
Ciena Corporation; Hanover
Lockheed Martin Corporation; Bethesda
TESSCO Technologies Incorporated; Hunt Valley
Universal Security Instruments Inc; Owings Mills

MASSACHUSETTS
Actifio Inc; Waltham
Affirmed Networks Inc; Acton
Agero Inc; Medford
Akamai Technologies Inc; Cambridge
Analog Devices Inc; Wilmington
Aspen Technology Inc; Bedford
Carbon Black Inc; Waltham
Cybereason Inc; Boston
eClinicalWorks; Westborough
Forrester Research Inc; Cambridge
Medical Information Technology Inc (MEDITECH); Westwood
MKS Instruments Inc; Andover
NetScout Systems Inc; Westford
Onto Innovation Inc; Wilmington
Pegasystems Inc; Cambridge
Progress Software Corporation; Bedford
Publicis Sapient; Boston
Raytheon Technologies Corporation; Waltham
Rocket Software Inc; Waltham
UNICOM Engineering Inc; Canton
XIUS; North Chelmsford

MICHIGAN
Ford Motor Company; Dearborn
General Motors Company (GM); Detroit
OnStar LLC; Warren
Perceptron Inc; Plymouth
Stellantis North America (FCA US LLC); Auburn Hills

MINNESOTA
3M Company; St. Paul
Digi International Inc; Minnetonka
Electro-Sensors Inc; Minnetonka
Entrust Corporation; Shakopee

MISSOURI
Cerner Corporation; North Kansas City
Emerson Electric Co; St. Louis

NEBRASKA
George Risk Industries Inc; Kimball

NEW HAMPSHIRE
Zoom Telephonics Inc (dba Minim); Manchester

NEW JERSEY
Cognizant Technology Solutions Corporation; Teaneck
Conduent Incorporated; Florham Park
ECSI International Inc; Clifton
LG Electronics USA Inc; Englewood Cliffs
NEC Laboratories America Inc; Princeton
Nokia Bell Labs; Murray Hill
PowerFleet Inc; Woodcliff Lake
Siemens USA; Princeton
Wireless Telecom Group Inc; Parsippany

NEW YORK
Anaren Inc; East Syracuse
Cemtrex Inc; Brooklyn
Comtech Telecommunications Corp; Melville
GLOBALFOUNDRIES Inc; Malta
HQSoftware; New York
IBM Research; Yorktown Heights
International Business Machines Corporation (IBM); Armonk
Magneto IT Solutions LLC; New York
MongoDB Inc; New York
PAR Technology Corporation; New Hartford
Placemeter Inc; New York
Verizon Communications Inc; New York

NORTH CAROLINA
Extreme Networks Inc; Morrisville
Honeywell International Inc; Charlotte
SAS Institute Inc; Cary
Wolfspeed Inc; Durham

OHIO
GE Aviation; Cincinnati

OREGON
Daimler Trucks North America LLC; Portland
Lattice Semiconductor Corporation; Hillsboro
Schmitt Industries Inc; Portland
Wieden+Kennedy; Portland

PENNSYLVANIA
Ametek Inc; Berwyn
Aurora Innovation Inc; Pittsburgh
II-VI Incorporated; Saxonburg
Unisys Corporation; Blue Bell
Vishay Precision Group Inc; Malvern

RHODE ISLAND
Textron Inc; Providence

TENNESSEE
Nissan North America Inc; Franklin

TEXAS
AT&T Inc; Dallas
Aviat Networks Inc; Austin
Cirrus Logic Inc; Austin
Dell Technologies Inc; Round Rock
Diodes Incorporated; Plano
Embarcadero Technologies Inc; Austin
Forcepoint LLC; Austin
Fujitsu Network Communications Inc; Richardson
GlobeRanger Corporation; Richardson
Hewlett Packard Enterprise Company; Houston
Ideal Power Inc; Austin
Oracle Corporation; Austin
Oracle NetSuite; Austin
Phazar Antenna Corp; Mineral Wells
Powell Industries Inc; Houston
ScienceSoft USA Corporation; McKinney
Silicon Laboratories Inc; Austin
SoftServe Inc; Austin
SolarWinds Corporation; Austin
Speedcast International Limited; Houston
Tellabs Inc; Carrollton
Texas Instruments Incorporated; Dallas
Toyota Motor Sales USA Inc (TMS); Plano
Trilogy Inc; Austin
Tyler Technologies Inc; Plano

UTAH
Qualtrics International Inc; Provo
Vivint Smart Home Inc; Provo

VIRGINIA
CACI International Inc; Reston
General Dynamics Corporation; Renton
Iridium Communications Inc; McLean
Northrop Grumman Corporation; Falls Church
Science Applications International Corporation (SAIC); Reston
VeriSign Inc; Reston

WASHINGTON
Amazon Web Services Inc (AWS); Seattle
Amazon.com Inc; Seattle
F5 Networks Inc; Seattle
Itron Inc; Liberty Lake
Microsoft Corporation; Redmond
PACCAR Inc; Bellevue
Tanium Inc; Kirkland
T-Mobile US Inc; Bellevue
WatchGuard Technologies Inc; Seattle

WISCONSIN
Epic Systems Corporation; Verona
TDS Telecommunications LLC; Madison

INDEX OF NON-U.S. HEADQUARTERS LOCATION BY COUNTRY

Hoya Corporation; Tokyo
Isuzu Motors Limited; Tokyo
KDDI Corporation; Tokyo
Keyence Corporation; Osaka
Mazda Motor Corporation; Hiroshima
Mitsubishi Electric Corporation; Tokyo
Mitsubishi Motors Corporation; Tokyo
Nachi-Fujikoshi Corporation; Minato-ku, Tokyo
NEC Corporation; Tokyo
Nippon Telegraph and Telephone Corporation (NTT); Tokyo
Nissan Motor Co Ltd; Kanagawa
NTT DATA Corporation; Tokyo
NTT DOCOMO Inc; Tokyo
Panasonic Corporation; Osaka
Pioneer Corporation; Tokyo
Preferred Networks Inc; Tokyo
Renesas Electronics Corporation; Tokyo
Sharp Corporation; Sakai City, Osaka
SoftBank Group Corp; Tokyo
Sony Group Corporation; Tokyo
Subaru Corporation; Tokyo
Sumitomo Electric Industries Ltd; Osaka
Suzuki Motor Corporation; Hamamatsu
Toshiba Corporate R&D Center; Kawasaki-shi
Toshiba Corporation; Tokyo
Toyota Industries Corporation; Aichi
Toyota Motor Corporation; Toyota
Trend Micro Inc; Tokyo
Uniden Holdings Corporation; Tokyo
YASKAWA Electric Corporation; Kitakyushu
Yokogawa Electric Corporation; Tokyo

KOREA
AhnLab Inc; Seoul
Hyundai Motor Company; Seoul
Kia Corporation; Seoul
KT Corporation; Gyeonggi-do
LG Corporation; Seoul
LG Electronics Inc; Seoul
LG Uplus Corp; Seoul
Samsung Electro-Mechanics Co Ltd; Suwon
Samsung Electronics Co Ltd; Suwon-si
SK Hynix Inc; Icheon-si
SK Telecom Co Ltd; Seoul

LUXEMBOURG
Intelsat SA; Luxembourg
SES SA; Luxembourg

MEXICO
America Movil SAB de CV; Mexico City

NORWAY
Kongsberg Gruppen ASA; Kongsberg
Telenor ASA; Fornebu

PHILIPPINES
LaQuest Inc; Taguig

SINGAPORE
Dyson Singapore Pte Ltd; Singapore
Flex Ltd; Singapore
Singapore Technologies Telemedia Pte Ltd; Singapore
UIB Holdings Pte Ltd; Singapore

SPAIN
Telefonica SA; Madrid

SWEDEN
LM Ericsson Telephone Company (Ericsson); Stockholm
Telenor Connexion AB; Solna
Volvo AB; Gothenburg

SWITZERLAND
ABB Ltd; Zurich
Garmin Ltd; Schaffhausen
STMicroelectronics NV; Geneva
Swisscom AG; Bern
TE Connectivity Ltd; Schaffhausen

TAIWAN
Accton Technology Corporation; Hsinchu
ASE Technology Holding Co Ltd; Kaohsiung
CyberTAN Technology Inc; Hsinchu
D-Link Corporation; Taipei
Foxconn Technology Co Ltd; Taipei
Hon Hai Precision Industry Company Ltd; Tu-Chen City, Taipei
HTC Corporation; Taoyuan
Inventec Corporation; Taipei
Macronix International Co Ltd; Hsinchu City
MediaTek Inc; Hsinchu City
Novatek Microelectronics Corp; Hsinchu
Quanta Computer Inc; Taoyuan City
Taiwan Semiconductor Manufacturing Co Ltd (TSMC); Hsinchu
United Microelectronics Corporation; Hsinchu City
VIA Technologies Inc; Xindian District, New Taipei City

THE NETHERLANDS
Airbus SE; Leiden
Altice Europe NV; Amsterdam
Getronics NV; Amsterdam
Koninklijke Philips NV (Royal Philips); Amsterdam
NXP Semiconductors NV; Eindhoven
Stellantis NV; Lijnden
TomTom International BV; Amsterdam

UKRAINE
OSDB Ltd; Kharkiv
Program-Ace; Kharkiv
Sigma Software; Kyiv

UNITED KINGDOM

Arm Holdings plc; Cambridge
BAE Systems plc; London
BT Group plc; London
Darktrace PLC; Cambridge
Inmarsat Global Limited; London
Jaguar Land Rover Limited; Coventry
Micro Focus International Plc; Newbury
OneWeb Ltd; London
Rolls-Royce plc; London
Telit Communications PLC; London
Vodafone Group plc; Newbury

VIETNAM

FPT Software Company Limited; Hanoi

Individual Profiles On Each Of THE INTERNET OF THINGS 400

3M Company

www.3m.com

NAIC Code: 339100

TYPES OF BUSINESS:

Health Care Products
Specialty Materials & Textiles
Industrial Products
Safety, Security & Protection Products
Display & Graphics Products
Consumer & Office Products
Electronics & Communications Products
Fuel Cell Technology

BRANDS/DIVISIONS/AFFILIATES:

Scotch
Post-it
Nexcare
Filtrete
Command
Futuro
Littmann
Ace

GROWTH PLANS/SPECIAL FEATURES:

3M is a multinational conglomerate that has operated since 1902 when it was known as Minnesota Mining and Manufacturing. The company is well-known for its research and development laboratory, and the firm leverages its science and technology across multiple product categories. As of 2020, 3M is organized into four business segments: safety and industrial, transportation and electronics, healthcare, and consumer. Nearly 50% of the company's revenue comes from outside the Americas, with the safety and industrial segment constituting a plurality of the firm's net sales. Many of the company's 60,000-plus products touch and concern a variety of consumers and end markets.

3M offers its employees medical and dental insurance, tuition reimbursement, flexible spending accounts, disability coverage, a 401(k), adoption assistance and more.

CONTACTS: *Note: Officers with more than one job title may be intentionally listed here more than once.*

Michael Roman, CEO
Denise Rutherford, Sr. VP, Divisional
Monish Patolawala, CFO
Theresa Reinseth, Chief Accounting Officer
Ivan Fong, Chief Legal Officer
John Banovetz, Chief Technology Officer
Michael Vale, Executive VP, Divisional
Ashish Khandpur, Executive VP, Divisional
Mojdeh Poul, Executive VP, Divisional
Jeffrey Lavers, Executive VP, Divisional
Eric Hammes, President, Divisional
Kristen Ludgate, Senior VP, Divisional
Veena Lakkundi, Senior VP, Divisional

FINANCIAL DATA: *Note: Data for latest year may not have been available at press time.*

In U.S. $	2021	2020	2019	2018	2017	2016
Revenue		32,184,000,000	32,136,000,000	32,765,000,000	31,657,000,000	30,109,000,000
R&D Expense		1,878,000,000	1,911,000,000	1,821,000,000	1,850,000,000	1,735,000,000
Operating Income		6,822,000,000	6,128,000,000	6,733,000,000	7,234,000,000	7,223,000,000
Operating Margin %						
SGA Expense		6,879,000,000	6,961,000,000	7,529,000,000	6,572,000,000	6,111,000,000
Net Income		5,384,000,000	4,570,000,000	5,349,000,000	4,858,000,000	5,050,000,000
Operating Cash Flow		8,113,000,000	7,070,000,000	6,439,000,000	6,240,000,000	6,662,000,000
Capital Expenditure		1,501,000,000	1,699,000,000	1,577,000,000	1,373,000,000	1,420,000,000
EBITDA		9,151,000,000	7,753,000,000	8,838,000,000	9,414,000,000	8,726,000,000
Return on Assets %						
Return on Equity %						
Debt to Equity						

CONTACT INFORMATION:

Phone: 651 733-1110 Fax: 651 733-9973
Toll-Free: 800-364-3577
Address: 3M Center, St. Paul, MN 55144-1000 United States

STOCK TICKER/OTHER:

Stock Ticker: MMM
Employees: 95,000
Parent Company:
Exchange: NYS
Fiscal Year Ends: 12/31

SALARIES/BONUSES:

Top Exec. Salary: $1,299,948 Bonus: $
Second Exec. Salary: $442,500 Bonus: $700,000

OTHER THOUGHTS:

Estimated Female Officers or Directors: 7
Hot Spot for Advancement for Women/Minorities: Y

ABB Ltd

NAIC Code: 335313

www.abb.com

TYPES OF BUSINESS:

Diversified Engineering Services
Power Transmission & Distribution Systems
Control & Automation Technology Products
Industrial Robotics
Energy Trading Software
Artificial Intelligence

BRANDS/DIVISIONS/AFFILIATES:

GROWTH PLANS/SPECIAL FEATURES:

ABB is a global supplier of electrical equipment and automation products. Founded in the late 19th century, the company was created out of the merger of two old industrial companies--ASEA and BBC--and is now called Asea Brown Boveri Group, or ABB. The company is the number-one or number-two supplier in all of its core markets and the number-two robotic arm supplier globally. In automation, it offers a full suite of products for both discrete and process automation as well as industrial robotics.

CONTACTS: *Note: Officers with more than one job title may be intentionally listed here more than once.*

Bjorn Rosengren, CEO
Timo Ihamuotila, CFO
Sylvia Hill, Chief Human Resources Officer
Diane de Saint Victor, General Counsel
Brice Koch, Head-Power Systems Div.
Bernhard Jucker, Head-Power Prod. Div.
Veli-Matti Reinikkala, Head-Process Automation Div.
Tarak Mehta, Head-Low Voltage Prod. Div.
Peter Voser, Chmn.
Frank Duggan, Head-Global Markets

FINANCIAL DATA: *Note: Data for latest year may not have been available at press time.*

In U.S. $	2021	2020	2019	2018	2017	2016
Revenue		26,134,000,000	27,978,000,000	27,662,000,000	34,312,000,000	33,828,000,000
R&D Expense		1,127,000,000	1,198,000,000	1,147,000,000	1,365,000,000	1,300,000,000
Operating Income		2,007,000,000	2,261,000,000	2,102,000,000	3,294,000,000	3,098,000,000
Operating Margin %						
SGA Expense		4,895,000,000	5,447,000,000	5,295,000,000	5,607,000,000	5,349,000,000
Net Income		5,146,000,000	1,439,000,000	2,173,000,000	2,213,000,000	1,899,000,000
Operating Cash Flow		1,693,000,000	2,325,000,000	2,924,000,000	3,799,000,000	3,843,000,000
Capital Expenditure		694,000,000	762,000,000	772,000,000	949,000,000	831,000,000
EBITDA		1,996,000,000	3,038,000,000	3,297,000,000	4,609,000,000	4,195,000,000
Return on Assets %						
Return on Equity %						
Debt to Equity						

CONTACT INFORMATION:

Phone: 41-43-317-7111 Fax: 41-43-317-4420
Toll-Free:
Address: Affolternstrasse 44, Zurich, CH-8050 Switzerland

STOCK TICKER/OTHER:

Stock Ticker: ABB Exchange: NYS
Employees: 105,600 Fiscal Year Ends: 12/31
Parent Company:

SALARIES/BONUSES:

Top Exec. Salary: $1,629,851 Bonus: $1,059,396
Second Exec. Salary: $977,936 Bonus: $756,916

OTHER THOUGHTS:

Estimated Female Officers or Directors: 2
Hot Spot for Advancement for Women/Minorities: Y

Accenture plc

www.accenture.com

NAIC Code: 541512

TYPES OF BUSINESS:

IT Consulting
Technology
Artificial Intelligence
Data
Analytics
Supply Chain Management
Cloud
Automation

BRANDS/DIVISIONS/AFFILIATES:

Zestgroup

GROWTH PLANS/SPECIAL FEATURES:

Accenture is a leading global IT-services firm that provides consulting, strategy, and technology and operational services. These services run the gamut from aiding enterprises with digital transformation to procurement services to software system integration. The company provides its IT offerings to a variety of sectors, including communications, media and technology, financial services, health and public services, consumer products, and resources. Accenture employs just under 500,000 people throughout 200 cities in 51 countries.

CONTACTS: *Note: Officers with more than one job title may be intentionally listed here more than once.*

Julie Sweet, CEO
Jo Deblaere, COO
KC McClure, CFO
Jill Kramer, CMO
Ellyn J. Shook, Chief Human Resources Officer
Paul R. Daugherty, CTO
Martin I. Cole, Group CEO-Tech.
Sander vant Noordende, Group CEO-Prod.
Richard Lumb, Group CEO-Financial Services
Stephen J Rohleder, Group CEO-Health & Public Service
Michael J Salvino, Group CEO-Business Process Outsourcing
Julie Spellman Sweet, General Counsel
David C. Thomlinson, Chief Oper. & Geographic Strategy Officer
Shawn Collinson, Chief Strategy Officer
Michael R. Sutcliff, Group CEO-Accenture Digital
Robert E. Sell, Group CEO-Comm., Media & Tech.
Mark A. Knickrehm, Group CEO-Accenture Strategy
Gianfranco Casati, Group CEO-Growth Markets
Adrian Lajtha, Chief Leadership Officer
Jean-Marc Ollagnier, Group CEO-Resources
Julie Sweet, Chmn.

FINANCIAL DATA: *Note: Data for latest year may not have been available at press time.*

In U.S. $	2021	2020	2019	2018	2017	2016
Revenue	50,533,390,000	44,327,040,000	43,215,010,000	41,603,430,000	36,765,480,000	34,797,660,000
R&D Expense						
Operating Income	7,621,529,000	6,513,644,000	6,305,074,000	5,841,041,000	4,632,609,000	4,810,445,000
Operating Margin %						
SGA Expense	8,742,599,000	7,462,514,000	7,009,614,000	6,601,872,000	6,397,883,000	5,466,982,000
Net Income	5,906,809,000	5,107,839,000	4,779,112,000	4,059,907,000	3,445,149,000	4,111,892,000
Operating Cash Flow	8,975,148,000	8,215,152,000	6,626,953,000	6,026,691,000	4,973,039,000	4,575,115,000
Capital Expenditure	580,132,000	599,132,000	599,009,000	619,187,000	515,919,000	496,566,000
EBITDA	9,711,850,000	8,580,526,000	7,167,520,000	6,754,408,000	5,433,366,000	6,348,882,000
Return on Assets %						
Return on Equity %						
Debt to Equity						

CONTACT INFORMATION:

Phone: 353-1-646-2000 Fax:
Toll-Free:
Address: 1 Grand Canal Sq., Dublin, 2 Ireland

STOCK TICKER/OTHER:

Stock Ticker: ACN
Employees: 506,000
Parent Company:
Exchange: NYS
Fiscal Year Ends: 08/31

SALARIES/BONUSES:

Top Exec. Salary: $1,250,000 Bonus: $
Second Exec. Salary: $1,136,125 Bonus: $

OTHER THOUGHTS:

Estimated Female Officers or Directors: 6
Hot Spot for Advancement for Women/Minorities: Y

ACCESS Co Ltd

www.access-company.com

NAIC Code: 511210I

TYPES OF BUSINESS:

Web Browser Technologies
Internet of Things
Network Technology
Multi-Screen Products
Network Operating System
Digital Publishing
eBook store
eTextbooks

BRANDS/DIVISIONS/AFFILIATES:

IP Infusion Inc
ZebOS
OcNOS
VirNOS
PUBLUS
PUBLUS Reader
PUBLIS Lite

CONTACTS: *Note: Officers with more than one job title may be intentionally listed here more than once.*

Kiyo Oishi, CEO
Ryuji Natsuumi, VP-Software Solution
Kiyoyasu Oishi, Sr. VP-Bus. Dev.
Kiyoyasu Oishi, VP-Global Bus.

GROWTH PLANS/SPECIAL FEATURES:

ACCESS Co., Ltd. develops and provides advanced software technologies to mobile, PC and other markets worldwide. The company's products and services make internet connectivity happen. ACCESS' three primary solutions encompass Internet of Things (IoT), networks and digital publishing. IoT products include an IoT gateway, an HMI engine for LCD touch panels, a range of browsers and related browser products and solutions, and multi-screen products and solutions. The networks division operates through wholly-owned IP Infusion, Inc., which provides network technology that can handle mission-critical requirements for world-leading carriers, telecommunications equipment manufacturers, and enterprise data centers. IP Infusion's network products include: ZebOS, an embedded network operating system (OS) that supports a range of protocols; OcNOS, an open compute project (OCP)-compliant integrated network OS supporting multi-protocol label switching, supporting the networking needs of public clouds, private clouds and hybrid cloud networks; and VirNOS, a virtual software platform that helps to reduce capital expenditures and operating expenditures for mobile operators and corporate data centers, while simultaneously reducing the time to new service delivery and supporting agility requirements of networks. Last, the digital publishing division offers PUBLUS (publishing businesses), an electronic bookstore solution to major publishers and electronic book service providers in Japan and abroad. Digital publishing offers EPUB3-compliant package sales of books, micro-content distribution of single stories, free online magazines and ad-supported electronic book business models. PUBLUS Reader reproduces complex vertical or reflow text and offers a fast process of fixed format electronic books. PUBLIS Lite is an electronic textbook distribution system that meets instructional material needs, such as displaying PDFs or files comprised of thousands of pages and searching for books in the cloud's bookshelf. Headquartered in Tokyo, Japan, ACCESS operates throughout Asia, Europe and the U.S. via subsidiaries and affiliates.

FINANCIAL DATA: *Note: Data for latest year may not have been available at press time.*

In U.S. $	2021	2020	2019	2018	2017	2016
Revenue	68,197,854	87,375,294	74,446,200	71,877,200	57,857,300	61,763,611
R&D Expense						
Operating Income						
Operating Margin %						
SGA Expense						
Net Income	-23,019,952	-23,303,100	4,571,855	2,244,770	2,753,030	-11,918,903
Operating Cash Flow						
Capital Expenditure						
EBITDA						
Return on Assets %						
Return on Equity %						
Debt to Equity						

CONTACT INFORMATION:

Phone: 81-3-68639088 Fax: 81-3-68539089
Toll-Free:
Address: Daito Bldg., Kandaneribei-cho 3, Chiyoda-ku, Tokyo, 101-0022 Japan

STOCK TICKER/OTHER:

Stock Ticker: 4813
Employees: 774
Parent Company:
Exchange: Tokyo
Fiscal Year Ends: 01/31

SALARIES/BONUSES:

Top Exec. Salary: $ Bonus: $
Second Exec. Salary: $ Bonus: $

OTHER THOUGHTS:

Estimated Female Officers or Directors:
Hot Spot for Advancement for Women/Minorities:

Accton Technology Corporation

www.accton.com

NAIC Code: 334418

TYPES OF BUSINESS:

Contract Electronics Manufacturing
Technical & Communications Outsourcing
IP Network Switches
Semiconductors & Chipsets
Wireless Hardware
Online Portal
VoIP Hardware

BRANDS/DIVISIONS/AFFILIATES:

CONTACTS:

Note: Officers with more than one job title may be intentionally listed here more than once.

Edgar Masri, CEO
Fanny Chen, CFO
George Tchaparian, Sr. VP-R&D
Edward Lin, Contact-News & Media Rel.
Fai-Long Kuo, Exec. VP
Kuo-Tai Choiu, Sr. VP
Meen-Ron Lin, Chmn.
Sheng-Shun Liou, VP-Logistics

GROWTH PLANS/SPECIAL FEATURES:

Accton Technology Corporation is a Taiwan-based company that researches, develops, manufactures and markets computer network system products. The company also manufactures network computers and network peripheral equipment. Accton's solutions are divided into five categories: cloud data center, carrier access, campus network, Internet of Things (IoT) integration and SD-WAN. The firm's cloud data center solution comprises high-speed, high-density, standardized OCP-compliant (open compute project) platforms, which provide an open hardware network fabric for cloud data centers. Accton has developed a full range of Top-of-Rack and spine switches that support interface speeds from 1G up to 400G. Carrier access solutions are provided to carrier, service provider and multiple system operator (MS) customers, with products ranging from passive optical networks for residential broadband access to NEBS-compliant (network equipment building system) aggregation switches and routers, as well as 3G/4G mobile and enterprise IP backhaul devices. Campus network solutions consist of flexible wired connectivity and high-density wireless access for campus and enterprise networks. IoT integration solutions cover three main areas: integrating networking protocols and developing service applications; creating a database for big data applications services; and partnership and collaboration with alliances in the IoT ecosystem. By connecting IoT demands from different communities and through virtualized, digitalized solutions, Accton aims to enhance the quality of life with all alliances. Last, SD-WAN solutions include open software-defined network platforms that provide the foundation for next-generation networks, and involve the transformation of WAN networks into SD-WANs. Accton's R&D division is continually engaged in design and development, with more than 1,000 patents related to network product design and manufacturing.

FINANCIAL DATA:

Note: Data for latest year may not have been available at press time.

In U.S. $	2021	2020	2019	2018	2017	2016
Revenue		1,936,970,000	1,842,250,000	1,433,710,000	1,180,920,704	951,584,448
R&D Expense						
Operating Income						
Operating Margin %						
SGA Expense						
Net Income		179,555,000	164,602,000	96,409,500	82,924,760	61,170,752
Operating Cash Flow						
Capital Expenditure						
EBITDA						
Return on Assets %						
Return on Equity %						
Debt to Equity						

CONTACT INFORMATION:

Phone: 886 35770270 Fax: 886 35780764
Toll-Free:
Address: No.1 Creation 3rd Rd., Hsinchu Science Park, Hsinchu, 30077 Taiwan

STOCK TICKER/OTHER:

Stock Ticker: 2345
Exchange: TWSE
Employees: 5,200
Fiscal Year Ends: 12/31
Parent Company:

SALARIES/BONUSES:

Top Exec. Salary: $ Bonus: $
Second Exec. Salary: $ Bonus: $

OTHER THOUGHTS:

Estimated Female Officers or Directors:
Hot Spot for Advancement for Women/Minorities:

Actifio Inc

NAIC Code: 511210J

www.actifio.com

TYPES OF BUSINESS:

Computer Software, Data Base & File Management
Copy Data Management
Cloud Backup
Enterprise Cloud
Disaster Recovery Solution
Hybrid Workload Solution

BRANDS/DIVISIONS/AFFILIATES:

Alphabet Inc
Google LLC
Google Cloud
Actifio GO

GROWTH PLANS/SPECIAL FEATURES:

Actifio, Inc. has designed a Google Cloud offering called Actifio GO, which enables enterprise-class backup and disaster recovery for Google Cloud and hybrid workloads. Actifio serves approximately 3,600 customers in 38 countries through its single platform. Actifio GO's copy data management solutions are extended to new challenges enterprises face as they modernize their applications, on-premises, in hybrid or multi-cloud. Actifio is owned by Google LLC, itself is a subsidiary of Alphabet, Inc.

CONTACTS: *Note: Officers with more than one job title may be intentionally listed here more than once.*

Ash Ashutosh, CEO

FINANCIAL DATA: *Note: Data for latest year may not have been available at press time.*

In U.S. $	2021	2020	2019	2018	2017	2016
Revenue	180,000,000	176,800,000	170,000,000	100,000,000	95,000,000	78,000,000
R&D Expense						
Operating Income						
Operating Margin %						
SGA Expense						
Net Income						
Operating Cash Flow						
Capital Expenditure						
EBITDA						
Return on Assets %						
Return on Equity %						
Debt to Equity						

CONTACT INFORMATION:

Phone: 781-790-7500 Fax:
Toll-Free:
Address: 333 Wyman St., Waltham, MA 02451 United States

STOCK TICKER/OTHER:

Stock Ticker: Subsidiary
Employees: 400
Parent Company: Alphabet Inc
Exchange:
Fiscal Year Ends: 12/31

SALARIES/BONUSES:

Top Exec. Salary: $ Bonus: $
Second Exec. Salary: $ Bonus: $

OTHER THOUGHTS:

Estimated Female Officers or Directors:
Hot Spot for Advancement for Women/Minorities:

Adobe Inc

www.adobe.com

NAIC Code: 511210F

TYPES OF BUSINESS:

Computer Software, Multimedia, Graphics & Publishing
Document Management Software
Photo Editing & Management Software
Graphic Design Software
Digital Media Solutions
Marketing Solutions
Workflow Solutions
Cloud Solutions

BRANDS/DIVISIONS/AFFILIATES:

Adobe Experience Cloud
Adobe LiveCycle
Adobe Connect
Frame.io

GROWTH PLANS/SPECIAL FEATURES:

Adobe provides content creation, document management, and digital marketing and advertising software and services to creative professionals and marketers for creating, managing, delivering, measuring, optimizing and engaging with compelling content multiple operating systems, devices and media. The company operates with three segments: digital media content creation, digital experience for marketing solutions, and publishing for legacy products (less than 5% of revenue).

Adobe offers its employees comprehensive benefits.

CONTACTS: *Note: Officers with more than one job title may be intentionally listed here more than once.*

Shantanu Narayen, CEO
John Murphy, CFO
Mark Garfield, Chief Accounting Officer
Ann Lewnes, Chief Marketing Officer
Abhay Parasnis, Chief Technology Officer
John Warnock, Co-Founder
Scott Belsky, Executive VP, Divisional
Gloria Chen, Executive VP, Divisional
Dana Rao, Executive VP
Anil Chakravarthy, Executive VP

FINANCIAL DATA: *Note: Data for latest year may not have been available at press time.*

In U.S. $	2021	2020	2019	2018	2017	2016
Revenue		12,868,000,000	11,171,300,000	9,030,008,000	7,301,505,000	5,854,430,000
R&D Expense		2,188,000,000	1,930,228,000	1,537,812,000	1,224,059,000	975,987,000
Operating Income		4,237,000,000	3,268,121,000	2,840,369,000	2,168,095,000	1,492,094,000
Operating Margin %						
SGA Expense		4,559,000,000	4,124,984,000	3,365,727,000	2,822,298,000	2,487,907,000
Net Income		5,260,000,000	2,951,458,000	2,590,774,000	1,693,954,000	1,168,782,000
Operating Cash Flow		5,727,000,000	4,421,813,000	4,029,304,000	2,912,853,000	2,199,728,000
Capital Expenditure		419,000,000	394,479,000	266,579,000	178,122,000	203,805,000
EBITDA		5,049,000,000	4,098,624,000	3,229,610,000	2,538,040,000	1,837,115,000
Return on Assets %						
Return on Equity %						
Debt to Equity						

CONTACT INFORMATION:

Phone: 408 536-6000 Fax: 408 536-6799
Toll-Free: 800-833-6687
Address: 345 Park Ave., San Jose, CA 95110-2704 United States

STOCK TICKER/OTHER:

Stock Ticker: ADBE
Employees: 22,516
Parent Company:
Exchange: NAS
Fiscal Year Ends: 11/30

SALARIES/BONUSES:

Top Exec. Salary: $641,346 Bonus: $3,000,000
Second Exec. Salary: $1,000,000 Bonus: $

OTHER THOUGHTS:

Estimated Female Officers or Directors: 5
Hot Spot for Advancement for Women/Minorities: Y

Advanced Energy Industries Inc

www.advanced-energy.com

NAIC Code: 334513

TYPES OF BUSINESS:

Instruments and Related Products Manufacturing for Measuring, Displaying, and Controlling Industrial Process Variables
Industrial Power Conversion
Plasma Power Generator

BRANDS/DIVISIONS/AFFILIATES:

Versatile Power

GROWTH PLANS/SPECIAL FEATURES:

Advanced Energy Industries Inc provides precision power-conversion measurement and control solutions that transform power into various forms for use in manufacturing and industrial equipment and applications. The firm serves original equipment manufacturers and end customers in the semiconductor, flat panel display, solar panel, and other industrial capital equipment markets. Products include thin-film power-conversion systems, which control and modify raw electrical power into a customizable, predictable power source, and power control modules, which control and measure temperature during manufacturing cycles. A majority of the firm's revenue is generated in the United States, with the rest primarily from Asia and Europe.

CONTACTS: *Note: Officers with more than one job title may be intentionally listed here more than once.*

Yuval Wasserman, CEO
Stephen Kelley, CEO
Paul Oldham, CFO
Grant Beard, Chairman of the Board
Thomas McGimpsey, Chief Administrative Officer

FINANCIAL DATA: *Note: Data for latest year may not have been available at press time.*

In U.S. $	2021	2020	2019	2018	2017	2016
Revenue		1,415,826,000	788,948,000	718,892,000	671,012,000	483,704,000
R&D Expense		143,961,000	101,503,000	76,008,000	57,999,000	44,445,000
Operating Income		189,189,000	59,426,000	175,792,000	200,770,000	126,857,000
Operating Margin %						
SGA Expense		188,590,000	142,555,000	108,033,000	93,262,000	77,678,000
Net Income		134,675,000	64,941,000	147,025,000	137,861,000	127,454,000
Operating Cash Flow		201,236,000	48,392,000	151,271,000	182,701,000	119,287,000
Capital Expenditure		36,483,000	25,188,000	20,330,000	9,042,000	6,821,000
EBITDA		236,959,000	85,573,000	189,384,000	210,194,000	134,670,000
Return on Assets %						
Return on Equity %						
Debt to Equity						

CONTACT INFORMATION:

Phone: 970 221-4670 Fax:
Toll-Free:
Address: 1595 Wynkoop St., Ste. 800, Denver, CO 80202 United States

STOCK TICKER/OTHER:

Stock Ticker: AEIS
Employees: 10,000
Parent Company:
Exchange: NAS
Fiscal Year Ends: 12/31

SALARIES/BONUSES:

Top Exec. Salary: $800,000 Bonus: $
Second Exec. Salary: $535,217 Bonus: $

OTHER THOUGHTS:

Estimated Female Officers or Directors:
Hot Spot for Advancement for Women/Minorities:

Advanced Micro Devices Inc (AMD)

www.amd.com

NAIC Code: 334413

TYPES OF BUSINESS:

Microprocessors
Semiconductors
Chipsets
Wafer Manufacturing
Multimedia Graphics

BRANDS/DIVISIONS/AFFILIATES:

AMD
ATI
Athlon
EPYC
Radeon
Ryzen
Threadripper

CONTACTS: *Note: Officers with more than one job title may be intentionally listed here more than once.*

Lisa Su, CEO
Devinder Kumar, CFO
Darla Smith, Chief Accounting Officer
Mark Papermaster, Chief Technology Officer
John Caldwell, Director
Richard Bergman, Executive VP, Divisional
Darren Grasby, Executive VP
Forrest Norrod, General Manager, Divisional
Harry Wolin, Senior VP

GROWTH PLANS/SPECIAL FEATURES:

Advanced Micro Devices designs microprocessors for the computer and consumer electronics industries. The majority of the firm's sales are in the personal computer and data center markets via CPUs and GPUs. Additionally, the firm supplies the chips found in prominent game consoles such as the Sony PlayStation and Microsoft Xbox. AMD acquired graphics processor and chipset maker ATI in 2006 in an effort to improve its positioning in the PC food chain. In 2009, the firm spun out its manufacturing operations to form the foundry GlobalFoundries. In 2020, the firm agreed to acquire FPGA-leader Xilinx to diversify its business and augment its opportunities in key end markets such as the data center.

FINANCIAL DATA: *Note: Data for latest year may not have been available at press time.*

In U.S. $	2021	2020	2019	2018	2017	2016
Revenue		9,763,000,000	6,731,000,000	6,475,000,000	5,329,000,000	4,272,000,000
R&D Expense		1,983,000,000	1,547,000,000	1,434,000,000	1,160,000,000	1,008,000,000
Operating Income		1,369,000,000	631,000,000	451,000,000	204,000,000	-382,000,000
Operating Margin %						
SGA Expense		995,000,000	750,000,000	562,000,000	511,000,000	460,000,000
Net Income		2,490,000,000	341,000,000	337,000,000	43,000,000	-497,000,000
Operating Cash Flow		1,071,000,000	493,000,000	34,000,000	68,000,000	90,000,000
Capital Expenditure		294,000,000	217,000,000	163,000,000	113,000,000	77,000,000
EBITDA		1,676,000,000	724,000,000	621,000,000	339,000,000	-159,000,000
Return on Assets %						
Return on Equity %						
Debt to Equity						

CONTACT INFORMATION:

Phone: 408 749-4000 Fax:
Toll-Free:
Address: 2485 Augustine Dr., Santa Clara, CA 95054 United States

STOCK TICKER/OTHER:

Stock Ticker: AMD
Employees: 12,600
Parent Company:
Exchange: NAS
Fiscal Year Ends: 12/31

SALARIES/BONUSES:

Top Exec. Salary: $1,095,574 Bonus: $
Second Exec. Salary: $649,037 Bonus: $

OTHER THOUGHTS:

Estimated Female Officers or Directors: 3
Hot Spot for Advancement for Women/Minorities: Y

Aeon Global Health Corp

aeonglobalhealth.com

NAIC Code: 511210D

TYPES OF BUSINESS:

Computer Software, Healthcare & Biotechnology
Clinical Services
Medical Tests
Software
Records Management Software
Revenue Cycle Software

BRANDS/DIVISIONS/AFFILIATES:

CONTACTS:

Note: Officers with more than one job title may be intentionally listed here more than once.

Hanif Roshan, CEO
Peter Hellwig, CFO

GROWTH PLANS/SPECIAL FEATURES:

Aeon Global Health Corp. and its subsidiaries provide clinical services to healthcare professionals. These services include, but are not limited to: medical tests used for monitoring both therapeutic drugs as well as drugs of abuse; the ability of an individual to metabolize or potentially have an adverse reaction to a number of drugs and other compounds; and the potential risk of an individual to develop certain cancers based on their genetic makeup. Aeon also provides web-based revenue cycle management applications and telehealth products and services, which enable health care clinical testing organizations to increase revenues, improve productivity, reduce costs, coordinate patient care, enhance related administrative and clinical workflows, and comply with regulatory requirements. The web-based services interface seamlessly with billing, information and records management systems. Primary client groups serviced by Aeon include physicians, clinics, medical centers, hospitals, accountable care organizations, rehab centers, intensive outpatient care centers and employer health programs. The company's services are paid through a mix of reimbursement from Medicare, Medicaid and private health insurance carriers, along with direct-paying clientele.

FINANCIAL DATA:

Note: Data for latest year may not have been available at press time.

In U.S. $	2021	2020	2019	2018	2017	2016
Revenue			12,932,305	16,301,144	20,198,772	34,576,916
R&D Expense						
Operating Income						
Operating Margin %						
SGA Expense						
Net Income			-7,975,387	-8,000,377	-32,073,514	5,265,028
Operating Cash Flow						
Capital Expenditure						
EBITDA						
Return on Assets %						
Return on Equity %						
Debt to Equity						

CONTACT INFORMATION:

Phone: 678 276-8412 Fax:
Toll-Free: 888-661-0225
Address: 2225 Centennial Dr., Gainesville, GA 30504 United States

STOCK TICKER/OTHER:

Stock Ticker: AGHC Exchange: PINX
Employees: 52 Fiscal Year Ends: 06/30
Parent Company:

SALARIES/BONUSES:

Top Exec. Salary: $ Bonus: $
Second Exec. Salary: $ Bonus: $

OTHER THOUGHTS:

Estimated Female Officers or Directors:
Hot Spot for Advancement for Women/Minorities:

Affirmed Networks Inc

www.affirmednetworks.com

NAIC Code: 511210B

TYPES OF BUSINESS:

Computer Software: Network Management (IT), System Testing & Storage
Virtualized Cloud
Technology
Wireless
Internet of Things
Wi-Fi
5G
Automation

BRANDS/DIVISIONS/AFFILIATES:

Microsoft Corporation

CONTACTS:

Note: Officers with more than one job title may be intentionally listed here more than once.

Anand Krishnamurthy, CEO

GROWTH PLANS/SPECIAL FEATURES:

Affirmed Networks, Inc. develops new technologies for the wireless industry. The company's virtualized, cloud-native mobile core solution offers mobile network operators the agility and flexibility necessary to keep up with traffic demand, to create, provide and launch new services in a matter of days. Affirmed Networks' end-to-end Internet of Things (IoT) mobile solution is built on an open architecture and delivers virtualized connectivity (LTE-M, NB-IoT (Narrowband), SCEF), an IoT service platform and IoT integration services. The firm's virtualized dot-per-inch (DPI) and GiLAN solution allows mobile operators to quickly and easily build new services from a broad library of security, optimization, routing and other network functions. Affirmed Networks' Wi-Fi gateway solution offers evolved packet data gateway (ePDG) and trusted Wi-Fi access gateway (TWAG) functionality to enable virtualized Wi-Fi access, more revenue opportunities and enhanced subscriber experience via a seamless, integrated and fully-virtualized solution. The combination of Wi-Fi with cellular services on a single platform allows operators unified radio access network (RAN) access for mobile services and allows fixed and mobile operators to expand their network coverage, add new services and improve overall consumer experience. The company's 5G mobile core solution is built on a webscale, cloud-native architecture that enables rapid creation and delivery of new services, unlimited scale and superior customer experience. The Affirmed service automation platform (ASAP) is a network-wide service automation and orchestration platform that simplifies service creation, service provisioning and the turn-up of new virtual network function instances in the network. The firm's virtual probe embeds probe/packet brokering functions into its virtualized evolved packet core (vEPC) rather than a separate network appliance, reducing costs by as much as 50%. Last, Affirmed Networks' virtual slice function enables fine-grained 5G network slicing across legacy, virtualized and multi-vendor environments. Affirmed Networks is a subsidiary of Microsoft Corporation.

FINANCIAL DATA:

Note: Data for latest year may not have been available at press time.

In U.S. $	2021	2020	2019	2018	2017	2016
Revenue						
R&D Expense						
Operating Income						
Operating Margin %						
SGA Expense						
Net Income						
Operating Cash Flow						
Capital Expenditure						
EBITDA						
Return on Assets %						
Return on Equity %						
Debt to Equity						

CONTACT INFORMATION:

Phone: 978-268-0800 Fax:
Toll-Free:
Address: 35 Nagog Park, Acton, MA 01720 United States

STOCK TICKER/OTHER:

Stock Ticker: Subsidiary
Employees: 200
Parent Company: Microsoft Corporation
Exchange:
Fiscal Year Ends:

SALARIES/BONUSES:

Top Exec. Salary: $ Bonus: $
Second Exec. Salary: $ Bonus: $

OTHER THOUGHTS:

Estimated Female Officers or Directors:
Hot Spot for Advancement for Women/Minorities:

Agero Inc

NAIC Code: 517210

www.agero.com

TYPES OF BUSINESS:

Automotive Telematics
Roadside Assistance
Location-based Telematics
Accident Management
Towing Software
Dispatch Management
Artificial Intelligence
Communication Services and Solutions

BRANDS/DIVISIONS/AFFILIATES:

Cross Country Group (LLC The)

CONTACTS: *Note: Officers with more than one job title may be intentionally listed here more than once.*

Dave Ferrick, CEO
George Horvat, COO
Bill Gerraughty, CFO
Beth Davidson, CMO
Emma Barnes Brown, Chief People Officer
Bernie Gracy, Chief Digital Officer
Peter Necheles, Sr. VP-Corp. Dev.
Michael A. Saxton, Sr. Advisor
Tom Metzger, Sr. VP
Jeffrey Blecher, Chief Strategy Officer

GROWTH PLANS/SPECIAL FEATURES:

Agero, Inc. provides telematics (location-based voice and data communication services) and roadside assistance for motorists. With operations throughout North America, the firm serves millions of drivers each year, and its technology is incorporated into new passenger vehicles that are sold in the U.S. Agero divides its products and services into five categories: roadside assistance, accident management, consumer affairs, towing software and dispatch management. Roadside assistance delivers scalable, transparent and digitally-enabled assistance, including different options for communicating, seamless data transfer, inbound contact center, artificial intelligent (AI)-enabled algorithms for event and situational data to identify the best provider match for every service event as well as to communicate with consumers during a vehicle breakdown, and application programming interface (API) integrations that can assist consumers with electric vehicles about locating nearby charging stations. The accident management category delivers technology and services during the accident event, including on-scene management, vehicle release services and crash assistance. The consumer affairs category delivers communications solutions and services to automotive industry clients, helping them maximize customer satisfaction by resolving questions and concerns at the earliest state of intervention. These solutions include: telematics, uniting connected vehicles with a contact center; recall management, for maintaining consumer satisfaction; sales support, for both inbound or outbound vehicles; and customer care service center, offering integrated solutions that can be fulfilled seamlessly. The consumer affairs category offers solutions and services for resolving questions and concerns. The towing software category consists of software for managing a towing business, including: a dashboard for managing and storing dispatch sites; and digital dispatching, enabling dispatch to and from the screen or mobile app. Last, the dispatch management category offers a software-as-a-service (SaaS) platform for delivering vertically-integrated, digital, and transparent roadside solutions worldwide. Agero is privately-owned by The Cross Country Group LLC.

FINANCIAL DATA: *Note: Data for latest year may not have been available at press time.*

In U.S. $	2021	2020	2019	2018	2017	2016
Revenue	700,000,000	664,350,000	772,500,000	735,000,000	700,000,000	675,000,000
R&D Expense						
Operating Income						
Operating Margin %						
SGA Expense						
Net Income						
Operating Cash Flow						
Capital Expenditure						
EBITDA						
Return on Assets %						
Return on Equity %						
Debt to Equity						

CONTACT INFORMATION:

Phone: 781-393-9300 Fax: 781-393-6706
Toll-Free:
Address: 400 River's Edge Dr., Medford, MA 02155 United States

STOCK TICKER/OTHER:

Stock Ticker: Private
Exchange:
Employees: 3,500
Fiscal Year Ends: 12/31
Parent Company: Cross Country Group (LLC The)

SALARIES/BONUSES:

Top Exec. Salary: $ Bonus: $
Second Exec. Salary: $ Bonus: $

OTHER THOUGHTS:

Estimated Female Officers or Directors: 1
Hot Spot for Advancement for Women/Minorities: Y

Agilent Technologies Inc

www.agilent.com

NAIC Code: 334515

TYPES OF BUSINESS:

Test Equipment
Communications Test Equipment
Integrated Circuits Test Equipment
Bioanalysis Equipment
Laboratory Automation and Robotics
Bioinstrumentation
Software Products
Informatics Products

BRANDS/DIVISIONS/AFFILIATES:

Agilent CrossLab
Agilent Technologies Research Laboratories
Resolution Bioscience

GROWTH PLANS/SPECIAL FEATURES:

Originally spun out of Hewlett-Packard in 1999, Agilent has evolved into a leading life sciences and diagnostics firm. Today, Agilent's measurement technologies serve a broad base of customers with its three operating segments: life science and applied tools (45% of fiscal 2020 sales), cross lab (36% of sales consisting of consumables and services related to its life science and applied tools), and diagnostics and genomics (20%). Just over half of its sales are generated from the biopharmaceutical, chemical, and energy end markets, but it also supports clinical lab, environmental, forensics, food, academic, and government-related organizations. The company is geographically diverse, with operations in the U.S. (33%) and China (20%) representing the largest country concentrations.

Agilent offers its employees health and financial benefits as well as on-site amenities and services.

CONTACTS: *Note: Officers with more than one job title may be intentionally listed here more than once.*

Michael McMullen, CEO
Robert McMahon, CFO
Koh Hwee, Chairman of the Board
Rodney Gonsalves, Chief Accounting Officer
Michael Tang, General Counsel
Jacob Thaysen, President, Divisional
Henrik Ancher-Jensen, President, Divisional
Samraat Raha, President, Divisional
Padraig McDonnell, President, Divisional
Dominique Grau, Senior VP, Divisional

FINANCIAL DATA: *Note: Data for latest year may not have been available at press time.*

In U.S. $	2021	2020	2019	2018	2017	2016
Revenue		5,339,000,000	5,163,000,000	4,914,000,000	4,472,000,000	4,202,000,000
R&D Expense		495,000,000	404,000,000	385,000,000	339,000,000	329,000,000
Operating Income		846,000,000	941,000,000	928,000,000	841,000,000	615,000,000
Operating Margin %						
SGA Expense		1,496,000,000	1,460,000,000	1,374,000,000	1,229,000,000	1,253,000,000
Net Income		719,000,000	1,071,000,000	316,000,000	684,000,000	462,000,000
Operating Cash Flow		921,000,000	1,021,000,000	1,087,000,000	889,000,000	793,000,000
Capital Expenditure		119,000,000	156,000,000	177,000,000	176,000,000	139,000,000
EBITDA		1,228,000,000	1,231,000,000	1,231,000,000	1,094,000,000	862,000,000
Return on Assets %						
Return on Equity %						
Debt to Equity						

CONTACT INFORMATION:

Phone: 408 345-8886 Fax:
Toll-Free: 800-227-9770
Address: 5301 Stevens Creek Blvd., Santa Clara, CA 95051 United States

STOCK TICKER/OTHER:

Stock Ticker: A
Employees: 17,000
Parent Company:
Exchange: NYS
Fiscal Year Ends: 10/31

SALARIES/BONUSES:

Top Exec. Salary: $1,172,853 Bonus: $
Second Exec. Salary: $316,538 Bonus: $500,000

OTHER THOUGHTS:

Estimated Female Officers or Directors: 6
Hot Spot for Advancement for Women/Minorities: Y

AhnLab Inc

NAIC Code: 511210E

global.ahnlab.com

TYPES OF BUSINESS:

Computer Software: Network Security, Managed Access, Digital ID, Cybersecurity & Anti-Virus
Computer Network Security Consulting
Personalized Software Development
Mobile Device Software Protection
Malware Detection
Remediation Solution

BRANDS/DIVISIONS/AFFILIATES:

V3
AhnLab EPP
AhnLab EDR
AhnLab EPS
AhnLab TS Engine
AhnLab TrusGuard
AhnLab TrusGuard DPX
AhnLab MDS

CONTACTS: *Note: Officers with more than one job title may be intentionally listed here more than once.*

Chi Jung Gwon, CEO

GROWTH PLANS/SPECIAL FEATURES:

AhnLab, Inc. is a Korean company that specializes in developing information security software products. The firm offers a comprehensive portfolio of security software, from endpoint security to network, web and transaction security software, as well as consulting and security services. In the endpoint security market, AhnLab offers the V3 family of products for enterprises and home users, which includes anti-virus solutions preserving the safety of all information environments that viruses can infiltrate. This family is comprised of V3 Internet Security software for protecting desktops, V3 Mobile to protect against threats to mobile devices and the V3 Net series for file servers. Other endpoint security products include: AhnLab EPP (endpoint protection platform), AhnLab EDR (endpoint detection and response), AhnLab EPS (endpoint protection security), AhnLab Xcanner (malware detection and remediation) and AhnLab TS Engine (addressing security threats such as viruses, malicious codes, Trojan horses, spyware programs and phishing). Network security products include AhnLab TrusGuard and AhnLab TrusGuard DPX, which offer protection against evolving distributed-denial-of-service (DDoS) attacks, various cyber attacks and integrated network security. For advanced threats, the AhnLab MDS product is the company's ultimate threat defense against targeted threats and Zero-day attacks. This solution delivers fast, comprehensive endpoint and network protection against known and unknown malware. Other services by the company include managed security services, IT security consulting services and forensic services. AhnLab is headquartered in South Korea, with global locations in Japan and China. During 2021, AhnLab acquired NAONWORKS, an operation technology security solution provider.

FINANCIAL DATA: *Note: Data for latest year may not have been available at press time.*

In U.S. $	2021	2020	2019	2018	2017	2016
Revenue		163,716,795	144,219,530	143,063,000	140,742,273	118,449,810
R&D Expense						
Operating Income						
Operating Margin %						
SGA Expense						
Net Income		16,996,413	16,494,569	20,451,300	15,243,800	12,101,940
Operating Cash Flow						
Capital Expenditure						
EBITDA						
Return on Assets %						
Return on Equity %						
Debt to Equity						

CONTACT INFORMATION:

Phone: 82-31-722-8000 Fax: 82-31-722-8901
Toll-Free:
Address: 220, Pangyoyeok-ro, Bundang-gu, Seongnam-si, Gyeon, Seoul, 463-400 South Korea

STOCK TICKER/OTHER:

Stock Ticker: 53800
Employees: 900
Parent Company:
Exchange: Seoul
Fiscal Year Ends: 12/31

SALARIES/BONUSES:

Top Exec. Salary: $ Bonus: $
Second Exec. Salary: $ Bonus: $

OTHER THOUGHTS:

Estimated Female Officers or Directors:
Hot Spot for Advancement for Women/Minorities:

Airbus SE

www.airbus.com

NAIC Code: 336411

TYPES OF BUSINESS:

Aircraft Manufacturing
Helicopter Manufacturing
Transport Aircraft
Military Aircraft
Defense Communications Systems
Satellites
Space Systems
Maintenance Services

BRANDS/DIVISIONS/AFFILIATES:

Hforce
Hcare
SmartForce
ArianeGroup

GROWTH PLANS/SPECIAL FEATURES:

Airbus is a major aerospace and defense firm. The company designs, develops, and manufactures commercial and military aircraft, as well as space launch vehicles and satellites. The company operates its business through three divisions: commercial, defense and space, and helicopters. Commercial offers a full range of aircraft ranging from the narrow-body (130-200 seats) A320 series to the much larger A350-1000 wide body. The defense and space segment supplies governments with military hardware, including transport aircraft, aerial tankers, and fighter aircraft (Eurofighter). The helicopter division manufactures turbine helicopters for the civil and parapublic markets.

CONTACTS: *Note: Officers with more than one job title may be intentionally listed here more than once.*

Guillaume Faury, CEO
Alberto Gutierrez, COO
Dominik Asam, CFO
Christian Scherer, Chief Commercial Officer
Thierry Baril, Chief Human Resources Officer
Sabine Kauke, CTO
Marwan Lahoud, Chief Strategy Officer
Fabrice Bregier, CEO-Airbus
Bernhard Gerwert, CEO-Airbus Defense & Space
Guillaume Faury, CEO-Airbus Helicopters
Francois Auque, Exec. VP-Space Systems
Rene Obermann, Chmn.

FINANCIAL DATA: *Note: Data for latest year may not have been available at press time.*

In U.S. $	2021	2020	2019	2018	2017	2016
Revenue		56,367,800,000	79,593,880,000	71,947,100,000	75,402,900,000	75,192,840,000
R&D Expense		3,227,664,000	3,792,336,000	3,633,099,000	3,170,068,000	3,354,151,000
Operating Income		749,884,200	1,154,189,000	3,540,493,000	2,666,381,000	-484,488,500
Operating Margin %						
SGA Expense		2,416,796,000	6,917,231,000	2,749,952,000	2,754,469,000	3,075,203,000
Net Income		-1,279,546,000	-1,538,166,000	3,449,016,000	3,244,604,000	1,123,697,000
Operating Cash Flow		-6,121,043,000	4,238,427,000	2,617,819,000	5,018,804,000	4,934,103,000
Capital Expenditure		1,986,516,000	2,642,664,000	2,580,550,000	2,888,861,000	3,455,792,000
EBITDA		2,413,407,000	4,942,008,000	8,096,265,000	8,340,204,000	4,638,215,000
Return on Assets %						
Return on Equity %						
Debt to Equity						

CONTACT INFORMATION:

Phone: 31 715245600 Fax: 31 715232807
Toll-Free:
Address: Mendelweg 30, Leiden, ZH 2333 CS Netherlands

STOCK TICKER/OTHER:

Stock Ticker: EADSF
Employees: 126,495
Parent Company:
Exchange: PINX
Fiscal Year Ends: 12/31

SALARIES/BONUSES:

Top Exec. Salary: $ Bonus: $
Second Exec. Salary: $ Bonus: $

OTHER THOUGHTS:

Estimated Female Officers or Directors: 1
Hot Spot for Advancement for Women/Minorities:

Akamai Technologies Inc

NAIC Code: 517110

www.akamai.com

TYPES OF BUSINESS:

Online Information Service-Streaming Content
Content Delivery Protection
Business Content Applications
Internet Protection
Security Solutions
Edge Computing
Cloud Optimization

BRANDS/DIVISIONS/AFFILIATES:

Guardicore Ltd

CONTACTS:

Note: Officers with more than one job title may be intentionally listed here more than once.

F. Leighton, CEO
Edward McGowan, CFO
Daniel Hesse, Chairman of the Board
Laura Howell, Chief Accounting Officer
Mani Sundaram, Chief Information Officer
Kim Salem-Jackson, Chief Marketing Officer
Robert Blumofe, Chief Technology Officer
Adam Karon, COO
Paul Joseph, Executive VP, Divisional
Aaron Ahola, Executive VP
Anthony Williams, Executive VP
Rick Mcconnell, General Manager, Divisional

GROWTH PLANS/SPECIAL FEATURES:

Akamai operates a content delivery network, or CDN, which entails locating servers at the edges of networks so its customers, which store content on Akamai servers, can reach their own customers faster, more securely, and with better quality. Akamai has over 325,000 servers distributed over 4,000 points of presence in more than 1,000 cities worldwide. Its customers generally include media companies, which stream video content or make video games available for download, and other enterprises that run interactive or high-traffic websites, such as e-commerce firms and financial institutions. Akamai also has a significant security business, which is integrated with its core web and media businesses to protect its customers from cyber threats.

Akamai offers its employees health and dental care, time off, fitness/wellness options and more.

FINANCIAL DATA:

Note: Data for latest year may not have been available at press time.

In U.S. $	2021	2020	2019	2018	2017	2016
Revenue		3,198,149,000	2,893,617,000	2,714,474,000	2,502,996,000	2,340,049,000
R&D Expense		269,315,000	261,365,000	246,165,000	222,434,000	167,628,000
Operating Income		701,674,000	577,991,000	416,052,000	394,476,000	470,923,000
Operating Margin %						
SGA Expense		966,696,000	947,545,000	982,775,000	900,087,000	798,840,000
Net Income		557,054,000	478,035,000	298,373,000	218,321,000	316,132,000
Operating Cash Flow		1,215,000,000	1,058,304,000	1,008,327,000	800,983,000	866,298,000
Capital Expenditure		731,872,000	562,077,000	405,741,000	414,778,000	316,289,000
EBITDA		1,163,591,000	1,022,519,000	820,811,000	707,274,000	812,386,000
Return on Assets %						
Return on Equity %						
Debt to Equity						

CONTACT INFORMATION:

Phone: 617 444-3000 Fax:
Toll-Free: 877-425-2624
Address: 145 Broadway, Cambridge, MA 02142 United States

STOCK TICKER/OTHER:

Stock Ticker: AKAM
Employees: 8,368
Parent Company:
Exchange: NAS
Fiscal Year Ends: 12/31

SALARIES/BONUSES:

Top Exec. Salary: $580,000 Bonus: $
Second Exec. Salary: $505,000 Bonus: $

OTHER THOUGHTS:

Estimated Female Officers or Directors: 4
Hot Spot for Advancement for Women/Minorities: Y

Alien Technology Corporation

www.alientechnology.com

NAIC Code: 334220

TYPES OF BUSINESS:

RFID Equipment
RFID Products
Integrated Circuits
Tags
Readers
Antenna
RFID Solutions Center

BRANDS/DIVISIONS/AFFILIATES:

Fluidic Self Assembly
Higgs
Squiggle
Alien Custom Product (ACP)
RFID Solutions Center

CONTACTS: *Note: Officers with more than one job title may be intentionally listed here more than once.*

Terrel Pruett, VP-Mktg.
David A. Aaron, Chief Legal Officer
David A. Aaron, VP-Bus. Dev.
Zhongrui Xia, Chmn.

GROWTH PLANS/SPECIAL FEATURES:

Alien Technology Corporation is a leading provider of UHF (ultra-high frequency) Gen-2 radio frequency identification (RFID) products. Alien's patented Fluidic Self Assembly (FSATM) manufacturing process allows the firm to manufacture high-volume, low-cost RFID tags. The company's products solve the identification of things via Internet of Things (IoT) technology. These products are categorized into four groups: integrated circuits (ICs), tags, readers and antennas. Alien's UHF EPCglobal Class-1 Generation-2 RFID ICs include large memory, mass-market and extended reach/robustness ICs marketed under the Higgs brand name. Its Squiggle family of tags span a broad range of applications. This division also specializes in retail/apparel, item-level tagging, transportation, life sciences, special form-factors and tags for mounting on challenging surfaces or in challenging environments. Readers are built for challenging environments and comprise advanced filtering and intelligence capabilities for less network traffic, fewer equipment add-ons and lower setup and maintenance costs. Reader products are available for the enterprise, for commercial use and for handheld purposes. The handheld RFID reader can be utilized with Alien's all-day battery life for use with current smart devices. This division's range of circular polarized antenna products are designed to meet challenging applications, and designed to be paired efficiently with Alien's readers. The antennas also work with any RFID reader. In addition, Alien Technology offers custom products created expressly for feature-packet, complex installations. They include the Alien Custom Product (ACP) series of hardware solutions, which enable swift and efficient installations for advanced applications and next-generation requirements. Alien has offices worldwide, including the U.S., and regional offices for Latin America, Europe/Middle East/Africa/India, China and Asia Pacific. Its RFID Solutions Center, which offers training and specialized services, is located in Dayton, Ohio, USA.

Alien Technology offers its employees health plans, life and disability insurance, 401(k) and a variety of assistance programs and plans.

FINANCIAL DATA: *Note: Data for latest year may not have been available at press time.*

In U.S. $	2021	2020	2019	2018	2017	2016
Revenue	62,604,360	60,196,500	57,330,000	54,600,000	52,000,000	50,100,000
R&D Expense						
Operating Income						
Operating Margin %						
SGA Expense						
Net Income						
Operating Cash Flow						
Capital Expenditure						
EBITDA						
Return on Assets %						
Return on Equity %						
Debt to Equity						

CONTACT INFORMATION:

Phone: 408-782-3900 Fax: 408-782-3908
Toll-Free:
Address: 845 Embedded Way, San Jose, CA 95138-1030 United States

STOCK TICKER/OTHER:

Stock Ticker: Private
Employees: 240
Parent Company:
Exchange:
Fiscal Year Ends: 09/30

SALARIES/BONUSES:

Top Exec. Salary: $ Bonus: $
Second Exec. Salary: $ Bonus: $

OTHER THOUGHTS:

Estimated Female Officers or Directors: 1
Hot Spot for Advancement for Women/Minorities:

Allscripts Healthcare Solutions Inc

www.allscripts.com

NAIC Code: 511210D

TYPES OF BUSINESS:

Computer Software, Healthcare & Biotechnology
Interactive Education Services
Clinical Software
Electronic Records Systems
Care Management Software

BRANDS/DIVISIONS/AFFILIATES:

Sunrise
Paragon
Allscripts TouchWorks EHR
Allscripts Professional EHR
Veradigm
FollowMyHealth
Allscripts CareInMotion
2bPrecise

GROWTH PLANS/SPECIAL FEATURES:

Allscripts Healthcare Solutions provides information technology and offerings to acute and ambulatory providers as well as hospital services. The company supports electric medical records, private cloud hosting, and other clinical services that support patient engagement and better outcomes. Additionally, the company offers administrative tools and services to improve operations, such as practice management, revenue cycle management, and clinical care coordination. Allscripts was founded in 1986 and is headquartered in Chicago.

Allscripts offers its employees medical, dental and vision insurance; flex spending accounts; 401(k); adoption assistance; and education assistance.

CONTACTS: *Note: Officers with more than one job title may be intentionally listed here more than once.*

Paul Black, CEO
Richard Poulton, CFO
Michael Klayko, Director
Lisa Khorey, Executive VP
Tejal Vakharia, Other Corporate Officer

FINANCIAL DATA: *Note: Data for latest year may not have been available at press time.*

In U.S. $	2021	2020	2019	2018	2017	2016
Revenue		1,502,700,000	1,771,677,000	1,749,962,000	1,806,342,000	1,549,899,000
R&D Expense		206,061,000	254,509,000	268,409,000	220,219,000	187,906,000
Operating Income		-55,911,000	12,081,000	-21,420,000	41,917,000	64,421,000
Operating Margin %						
SGA Expense		389,941,000	419,774,000	450,967,000	486,271,000	392,865,000
Net Income		700,407,000	-182,178,000	363,740,000	-196,459,000	-25,652,000
Operating Cash Flow		-106,715,000	46,254,000	67,891,000	279,415,000	269,004,000
Capital Expenditure		105,018,000	130,436,000	144,617,000	185,271,000	137,982,000
EBITDA		97,782,000	66,296,000	256,398,000	96,398,000	220,523,000
Return on Assets %						
Return on Equity %						
Debt to Equity						

CONTACT INFORMATION:

Phone: 866 358-6869 Fax:
Toll-Free: 800-654-0889
Address: 222 Merchandise Mart Plz., Ste. 2024, Chicago, IL 60654 United States

STOCK TICKER/OTHER:

Stock Ticker: MDRX
Employees: 8,400
Parent Company:
Exchange: NAS
Fiscal Year Ends: 12/31

SALARIES/BONUSES:

Top Exec. Salary: $630,000 Bonus: $560,070
Second Exec. Salary: $1,030,000 Bonus: $

OTHER THOUGHTS:

Estimated Female Officers or Directors: 2
Hot Spot for Advancement for Women/Minorities: Y

Alphabet Inc (Google)

abc.xyz/investor

NAIC Code: 519130

TYPES OF BUSINESS:

Search Engine-Internet
Paid Search Listing Advertising Services
Online Software and Productivity Tools
Online Video and Photo Services
Travel Booking
Web Analytical Tools
Venture Capital
Online Ad Exchanges

BRANDS/DIVISIONS/AFFILIATES:

Google LLC
Android
YouTube
GooglePlay
Gmail
Google Ad Manager
AdSense
AdMob

GROWTH PLANS/SPECIAL FEATURES:

Alphabet is a holding company, with Google, the Internet media giant, as a wholly owned subsidiary. Google generates 99% of Alphabet revenue, of which more than 85% is from online ads. Google's other revenue is from sales of apps and content on Google Play and YouTube, as well as cloud service fees and other licensing revenue. Sales of hardware such as Chromebooks, the Pixel smartphone, and smart homes products, which include Nest and Google Home, also contribute to other revenue. Alphabet's moonshot investments are in its other bets segment, where it bets on technology to enhance health (Verily), faster Internet access to homes (Google Fiber), self-driving cars (Waymo), and more. Alphabet's operating margin has been 25%-30%, with Google at 30% and other bets operating at a loss.

CONTACTS: *Note: Officers with more than one job title may be intentionally listed here more than once.*

Sundar Pichai, CEO
Ruth Porat, CFO
John Hennessy, Chairman of the Board
Amie OToole, Chief Accounting Officer
Sergey Brin, Co-Founder
Larry Page, Co-Founder
Kent Walker, Other Executive Officer
Philipp Schindler, Other Executive Officer
Prabhakar Raghavan, Senior VP, Subsidiary

FINANCIAL DATA: *Note: Data for latest year may not have been available at press time.*

In U.S. $	2021	2020	2019	2018	2017	2016
Revenue		182,527,000,000	161,857,000,000	136,819,000,000	110,855,000,000	90,272,000,000
R&D Expense		27,573,000,000	26,018,000,000	21,419,000,000	16,625,000,000	13,948,000,000
Operating Income		41,224,000,000	35,928,000,000	31,392,000,000	28,882,000,000	23,716,000,000
Operating Margin %						
SGA Expense		28,998,000,000	28,015,000,000	24,459,000,000	19,765,000,000	17,470,000,000
Net Income		40,269,000,000	34,343,000,000	30,736,000,000	12,662,000,000	19,478,000,000
Operating Cash Flow		65,124,000,000	54,520,000,000	47,971,000,000	37,091,000,000	36,036,000,000
Capital Expenditure		22,281,000,000	23,548,000,000	25,139,000,000	13,184,000,000	10,212,000,000
EBITDA		61,914,000,000	51,506,000,000	44,062,000,000	34,217,000,000	30,418,000,000
Return on Assets %						
Return on Equity %						
Debt to Equity						

CONTACT INFORMATION:

Phone: 650 253-0000 Fax: 650 253-0001
Toll-Free:
Address: 1600 Amphitheatre Pkwy., Mountain View, CA 94043 United States

STOCK TICKER/OTHER:

Stock Ticker: GOOGL
Employees: 135,301
Parent Company:
Exchange: NAS
Fiscal Year Ends: 12/31

SALARIES/BONUSES:

Top Exec. Salary: $2,015,385 Bonus: $
Second Exec. Salary: $655,000 Bonus: $

OTHER THOUGHTS:

Estimated Female Officers or Directors: 3
Hot Spot for Advancement for Women/Minorities: Y

Altice Europe NV

NAIC Code: 517210

www.altice.net

TYPES OF BUSINESS:

Wireless Telecommunications Carriers
Telecommunications
Media
Data Technology
Live Broadcasting
Advertising Solutions
Digital Solutions
Fiber-to-the-Home

BRANDS/DIVISIONS/AFFILIATES:

Altice

GROWTH PLANS/SPECIAL FEATURES:

Altice Europe NV is a multinational fiber, broadband, telecommunications, contents and media company. Its global presence covers France, Israel, the Dominican Republic and Portugal. The firm's activities are divided into three segments: telecom, media and content, and data and advertising. The telecom segment distributes, invests and services high speed broadband. The media and content segment provides original content, high-quality TV shows and international, national and local news channels. The firm delivers live broadcast premium sports events as well as well-known media and entertainment. The data and advertising segment innovates with technology in its labs across the world; links leading brands to audiences through its premium advertising solutions; and provides enterprise digital solutions to businesses. All of the company's products are marketed under the Altice brand name.

CONTACTS: *Note: Officers with more than one job title may be intentionally listed here more than once.*

Armando Pereira, COO
Malo Corbin, CFO
Patrick Drahi, Pres. of the Board

FINANCIAL DATA: *Note: Data for latest year may not have been available at press time.*

In U.S. $	2021	2020	2019	2018	2017	2016
Revenue	17,536,546,884	16,862,064,312	17,383,571,456	16,747,968,512	25,401,894,912	24,498,884,608
R&D Expense						
Operating Income						
Operating Margin %						
SGA Expense						
Net Income			288,312,416	-391,113,312	-590,193,728	-1,838,505,216
Operating Cash Flow						
Capital Expenditure						
EBITDA						
Return on Assets %						
Return on Equity %						
Debt to Equity						

CONTACT INFORMATION:

Phone: 41-79946 4931 Fax:
Toll-Free:
Address: Prins Bernhardplein 200, Amsterdam, 1097JB Netherlands

STOCK TICKER/OTHER:

Stock Ticker: Private
Employees: 35,328
Parent Company:
Exchange:
Fiscal Year Ends:

SALARIES/BONUSES:

Top Exec. Salary: $ Bonus: $
Second Exec. Salary: $ Bonus: $

OTHER THOUGHTS:

Estimated Female Officers or Directors:
Hot Spot for Advancement for Women/Minorities:

Amazon Lab126 Inc

www.lab126.com

NAIC Code: 541712

TYPES OF BUSINESS:

Research and Development in the Physical, Engineering and Life Sciences (except Biotechnology)
Innovative Consumer Electronic Products
Product Engineering
Product Development
Product Design
Research
Consumer Electronic Devices
Cloud-based Solutions and Services

BRANDS/DIVISIONS/AFFILIATES:

Amazon.com Inc
Kindle
Kindle Touch
Kindle Voyage
Kindle Oasis
Amazon Dash
Amazon Fire TV
Amazon Echo

CONTACTS: *Note: Officers with more than one job title may be intentionally listed here more than once.*

Mike Grothus, Sr. Mgr. - Oper.

GROWTH PLANS/SPECIAL FEATURES:

Amazon Lab126, Inc., a subsidiary of Amazon.com, Inc., operates as a lab focusing on research, innovation and development of consumer electronic products. The Lab126 name originated from the arrow in the Amazon logo, which draws a line from A to Z; the 1 stands for A and the 26 stands for Z. Since the launch of Amazon's first eReader, the Kindle, in 2007, the firm has expanded its product range and added Kindle Keyboard, Kindle Touch, Kindle Paperwhite eReaders, Kindle Fire tablets, Kindle Voyage and Kindle Oasis to its portfolio. In addition, the company also offers Amazon Fire TV, a streaming media player which can be connected to a HDTV and supports services such as Hulu, Netflix, Pandora, YouTube and Spotify; and Amazon Echo, which is an audio streaming device offering immersive, omni-directional audio and powered by Alexa app (a cloud-based service). Through the app, the device interacts with a user's voice, which it can recognize across the room and can play music, answer questions, read audiobooks, news, report traffic and weather and controls lights and other switches. The device is compatible with WeMo, Wink, Samsung and other smart home devices. The Amazon Dash is a handheld, push-button consumer goods ordering device. The customer can either scan the barcode of the product or voice request it into their Amazon shopping cart. Additionally, the one-click button allows shoppers to reorder their favorite, frequently used products. Lab126 is headquartered in Sunnyvale, California.

FINANCIAL DATA: *Note: Data for latest year may not have been available at press time.*

In U.S. $	2021	2020	2019	2018	2017	2016
Revenue						
R&D Expense						
Operating Income						
Operating Margin %						
SGA Expense						
Net Income						
Operating Cash Flow						
Capital Expenditure						
EBITDA						
Return on Assets %						
Return on Equity %						
Debt to Equity						

CONTACT INFORMATION:

Phone: 650-456-1100 Fax:
Toll-Free:
Address: 1100 Enterprise Way, Sunnyvale, CA 94043 United States

STOCK TICKER/OTHER:

Stock Ticker: Subsidiary
Employees: 4,000
Parent Company: Amazon.com Inc
Exchange:
Fiscal Year Ends: 12/31

SALARIES/BONUSES:

Top Exec. Salary: $ Bonus: $
Second Exec. Salary: $ Bonus: $

OTHER THOUGHTS:

Estimated Female Officers or Directors:
Hot Spot for Advancement for Women/Minorities:

Amazon Web Services Inc (AWS)

www.aws.amazon.com

NAIC Code: 517110

TYPES OF BUSINESS:

Cloud Computing Services
Cloud Software
Cloud Computing Services
Database Storage
Cloud Applications
Internet Solutions
Virtual Servers
Machine Learning

BRANDS/DIVISIONS/AFFILIATES:

Amazon.com Inc
Amazon EC2
Amazon Simple Storage Service
Amazon Aurora
Amazon DynamoDB
Amazon RDS
Amazon VPC
Amazon Lightsail

CONTACTS: *Note: Officers with more than one job title may be intentionally listed here more than once.*

Adam Selipsky, CEO

GROWTH PLANS/SPECIAL FEATURES:

Amazon Web Services, Inc. (AWS) is a business unit within Amazon.com, Inc. that offers a suite of cloud-computing services. Cloud computing is the on-demand delivery of compute power, database storage, applications and other IT resources through a cloud services platform via the internet. AWS' platform offers more than 200 fully featured services, which operate from strategically located data centers worldwide, including North America, South America, Europe, and Asia Pacific. AWS' services help clients build applications with increased flexibility, scalability and reliability. Solutions by industry include advertising/marketing, automotive, consumer packaged goods, education, energy, financial services, game technology, government, health care, life sciences, manufacturing, media/entertainment, nonprofit, power/utilities, retail, telecommunications, and travel/hospitality. Featured services by AWS include Amazon EC2 virtual servers in the cloud, Amazon Simple Storage Service for storage in the cloud, Amazon Aurora for a high-performance managed relational database, Amazon DynamoDB for a managed NoSQL database, Amazon RDS for a managed relational database service for MySQL and other servers, AWS Lambda for a run code, Amazon VPC for isolated cloud resources, Amazon LightSail for launching and managing virtual private servers, and Amazon SageMaker for building and deploying machine learning and Internet of Things (IoT) models at scale. AWS offers price options without long-term contracts, as well as free short-term offers.

FINANCIAL DATA: *Note: Data for latest year may not have been available at press time.*

In U.S. $	2021	2020	2019	2018	2017	2016
Revenue	62,200,000,000	45,370,000,000	35,026,000,000	25,655,000,000	17,459,000,000	12,219,000,000
R&D Expense						
Operating Income						
Operating Margin %						
SGA Expense						
Net Income	18,500,000,000	13,531,000,000	9,201,000,000	7,296,000,000	4,331,000,000	3,108,000,000
Operating Cash Flow						
Capital Expenditure						
EBITDA						
Return on Assets %						
Return on Equity %						
Debt to Equity						

CONTACT INFORMATION:

Phone: 206-266-1000 Fax:
Toll-Free:
Address: 410 Terry Ave. N., Seattle, WA 98109 United States

STOCK TICKER/OTHER:

Stock Ticker: Subsidiary
Employees:
Parent Company: Amazon.com Inc
Exchange:
Fiscal Year Ends: 12/31

SALARIES/BONUSES:

Top Exec. Salary: $ Bonus: $
Second Exec. Salary: $ Bonus: $

OTHER THOUGHTS:

Estimated Female Officers or Directors:
Hot Spot for Advancement for Women/Minorities:

Amazon.com Inc

www.amazon.com

NAIC Code: 454111

TYPES OF BUSINESS:

Online Retailing and Related Services
Robotics
Cloud Computing Services
Logistics Services
Retail Supermarkets & Grocery Delivery
Online Household Goods Retail
Online Auto & Industrial Retail
E-Commerce Support & Hosting

BRANDS/DIVISIONS/AFFILIATES:

Amazon Web Services (AWS)
Amazon Marketplace
Amazon Prime
Echo
Whole Foods Market
Amazon Go
Amazon Go Grocery
Kindle Direct Publishing

GROWTH PLANS/SPECIAL FEATURES:

Amazon is a leading online retailer and one of the highest-grossing e-commerce aggregators, with $386 billion in net sales and approximately $482 billion in estimated physical/digital online gross merchandise volume, or GMV, in 2020. Retail related revenue represented approximately 83% of total, followed by Amazon Web Services' cloud computing, storage, database, and other offerings (12%), and advertising services and cobranded credit cards (6%). International segments constituted 27% of Amazon's non-AWS sales in 2020, led by Germany, the United Kingdom, and Japan.

CONTACTS: *Note: Officers with more than one job title may be intentionally listed here more than once.*

David Clark, CEO, Divisional
Andrew Jassy, CEO
Brian Olsavsky, CFO
Jeffrey Bezos, Chairman of the Board
Shelley Reynolds, Chief Accounting Officer
David Zapolsky, General Counsel
Jeffrey Blackburn, On Leave

FINANCIAL DATA: *Note: Data for latest year may not have been available at press time.*

In U.S. $	2021	2020	2019	2018	2017	2016
Revenue		386,064,000,000	280,522,000,000	232,887,000,000	177,866,000,000	135,987,000,000
R&D Expense						
Operating Income		22,899,000,000	14,541,000,000	12,421,000,000	4,106,000,000	4,186,000,000
Operating Margin %						
SGA Expense		71,416,000,000	60,012,000,000	46,987,000,000	36,363,000,000	25,750,000,000
Net Income		21,331,000,000	11,588,000,000	10,073,000,000	3,033,000,000	2,371,000,000
Operating Cash Flow		66,064,000,000	38,514,000,000	30,723,000,000	18,434,000,000	16,443,000,000
Capital Expenditure		40,140,000,000	16,861,000,000	13,427,000,000	11,955,000,000	6,737,000,000
EBITDA		51,076,000,000	37,365,000,000	28,019,000,000	16,132,000,000	12,492,000,000
Return on Assets %						
Return on Equity %						
Debt to Equity						

CONTACT INFORMATION:

Phone: 206 266-1000 Fax:
Toll-Free:
Address: 410 Terry Ave. N., Seattle, WA 98109 United States

STOCK TICKER/OTHER:

Stock Ticker: AMZN
Employees: 1,298,000
Parent Company:
Exchange: NAS
Fiscal Year Ends: 12/31

SALARIES/BONUSES:

Top Exec. Salary: $175,000 Bonus: $
Second Exec. Salary: $160,000 Bonus: $

OTHER THOUGHTS:

Estimated Female Officers or Directors: 3
Hot Spot for Advancement for Women/Minorities: Y

America Movil SAB de CV

NAIC Code: 517210

www.americamovil.com

TYPES OF BUSINESS:

Wireless Telecommunications Carriers (except Satellite)
Wireless Internet
Local & Long Distance
Satellite & Cable TV

BRANDS/DIVISIONS/AFFILIATES:

Telcel
Telmex
Claro
TracFone
A1
Straight Talk
KPN

GROWTH PLANS/SPECIAL FEATURES:

America Movil is the largest telecom carrier in Latin America, serving about 270 million wireless customers across the region. It also provides fixed-line phone, Internet access, and television services in most of the countries it serves. Mexico is the firm's largest market, providing about 30% of revenue. Movil dominates the Mexican wireless market with about 63% customer share and also serves about half of fixed-line Internet access customers in the country. Brazil, its second most important market, provides about 20% of revenue. Movil has agreed to sell its low-margin wireless resale business in the U.S., which operates under the Tracfone and Straight Talk brands, to Verizon. The firm holds a 51% stake in Telekom Austria and a 20% stake in Dutch carrier KPN.

CONTACTS: *Note: Officers with more than one job title may be intentionally listed here more than once.*

Daniel Hajj Aboumrad, CEO
Carlos Garcia Moreno Elizondo, CFO
Patric Slim Domit, Vice Chmn.
Alejandro Cantu Jimenez, General Counsel
Salvador Cortes Gomez, COO-Mexico
Fernando Ocampo Carapia, CFO-Mexico
Juan Antonio Aguilar, CEO-Central America
Enrique Luna Roshard, CFO-Central America
Juan Carlos Archila Cabal, CEO-Colombia
Fernando Gonzalez Apango, CFO-Colombia
Carlos Slim Domit, Chmn.

FINANCIAL DATA: *Note: Data for latest year may not have been available at press time.*

In U.S. $	2021	2020	2019	2018	2017	2016
Revenue		46,902,630,000	46,462,670,000	47,886,050,000	47,121,580,000	44,989,690,000
R&D Expense						
Operating Income		7,626,790,000	7,141,828,000	6,436,902,000	4,618,986,000	5,055,640,000
Operating Margin %						
SGA Expense		9,784,503,000	9,962,449,000	10,478,970,000	11,098,960,000	10,520,880,000
Net Income		2,161,018,000	3,124,004,000	2,424,551,000	1,352,622,000	398,944,100
Operating Cash Flow		12,952,820,000	10,805,800,000	11,453,940,000	10,044,480,000	10,875,890,000
Capital Expenditure		5,975,563,000	7,003,764,000	7,002,587,000	6,306,210,000	7,150,285,000
EBITDA		12,992,680,000	15,120,930,000	13,697,930,000	11,758,060,000	9,798,009,000
Return on Assets %						
Return on Equity %						
Debt to Equity						

CONTACT INFORMATION:

Phone: 52-55-2581-4449 Fax: 52-55-2581-4422
Toll-Free:
Address: Lago Zurich 245, Colonia Granada, Ampliacion, Mexico City, DF 11529 Mexico

STOCK TICKER/OTHER:

Stock Ticker: AMOV
Exchange: NYS
Employees: 186,851
Fiscal Year Ends: 12/31
Parent Company:

SALARIES/BONUSES:

Top Exec. Salary: $ Bonus: $
Second Exec. Salary: $ Bonus: $

OTHER THOUGHTS:

Estimated Female Officers or Directors: 2
Hot Spot for Advancement for Women/Minorities:

American Software Inc

www.amsoftware.com

NAIC Code: 511210A

TYPES OF BUSINESS:

Computer Software, Supply Chain & Logistics
Enterprise Resource Planning Software
Supply Chain Management
Enterprise Software Solutions
IT Consulting
Product Lifecycle Management
IT Staffing Services

BRANDS/DIVISIONS/AFFILIATES:

Logility Inc
Demand Management Inc
Proven Method Inc (The)
American Software ERP

GROWTH PLANS/SPECIAL FEATURES:

American Software Inc develops enterprise management and supply chain-related software and services. Its software and services bring business value to companies by supporting their operations over cloud-based Internet-architected solutions. The company's operating segment inlcude Supply Chain Management (SCM); Information Technology Consulting (IT Consulting) and Other. It generates maximum revenue from the Supply Chain Management segment. SCM segment provides collaborative supply chain solutions to streamline and optimize the production, distribution, and management of products between trading partners. Its solutions consist of global sourcing, workflow management, customer service applications, and ERP solutions.

CONTACTS: *Note: Officers with more than one job title may be intentionally listed here more than once.*

H. Dow, CEO
Vincent Klinges, CFO
James Edenfield, Chairman of the Board
Bryan Sell, Chief Accounting Officer
James Mcguone, Secretary

FINANCIAL DATA: *Note: Data for latest year may not have been available at press time.*

In U.S. $	2021	2020	2019	2018	2017	2016
Revenue	111,408,000	115,466,000	108,706,000	112,703,000	106,286,000	113,889,000
R&D Expense	16,964,000	15,348,000	13,078,000	11,877,000	11,889,000	11,248,000
Operating Income	4,361,000	6,048,000	5,276,000	13,531,000	7,766,000	13,527,000
Operating Margin %						
SGA Expense	39,443,000	41,477,000	37,998,000	36,715,000	34,506,000	34,613,000
Net Income	8,089,000	6,742,000	6,803,000	12,053,000	14,621,000	10,242,000
Operating Cash Flow	17,756,000	25,982,000	23,930,000	6,754,000	19,780,000	18,291,000
Capital Expenditure	1,298,000	3,590,000	7,213,000	6,232,000	4,455,000	3,901,000
EBITDA	9,971,000	14,151,000	12,995,000	19,561,000	14,406,000	19,145,000
Return on Assets %						
Return on Equity %						
Debt to Equity						

CONTACT INFORMATION:

Phone: 404 261-4381 Fax: 404 264-5514
Toll-Free: 800-726-2946
Address: 470 E. Paces Ferry Rd., NE, Atlanta, GA 30305 United States

STOCK TICKER/OTHER:

Stock Ticker: AMSWA
Employees: 424
Parent Company:
Exchange: NAS
Fiscal Year Ends: 04/30

SALARIES/BONUSES:

Top Exec. Salary: $660,000 Bonus: $655,900
Second Exec. Salary: $598,448 Bonus: $205,195

OTHER THOUGHTS:

Estimated Female Officers or Directors:
Hot Spot for Advancement for Women/Minorities:

Ametek Inc

NAIC Code: 334513

www.ametek.com

TYPES OF BUSINESS:

Monitoring, Testing, Calibration and Display Electronic Device Manufacturing
ElectromechanicalÂ Device Manufacturing

BRANDS/DIVISIONS/AFFILIATES:

Magnetrol International
Crank Software
EGS Automation

GROWTH PLANS/SPECIAL FEATURES:

Ametek is a diversified industrial conglomerate with about $4.5 billion in sales. The firm operates through two segments: electronic instruments, or EIG, and electromechanical, or EMG. EIG designs and manufactures differentiated and advanced instruments for the process, aerospace, power, and industrial end markets. EMG is a focused, niche supplier of highly engineered automation solutions, thermal management systems, specialty metals, and electrical interconnects, among other products. About half of the firm's sales are made in the United States. The firm's asset-light strategy in place for nearly two decades emphasizes growth through acquisitions, new product development through research and development, driving operational efficiencies, and global and market expansion.

CONTACTS: *Note: Officers with more than one job title may be intentionally listed here more than once.*

David Zapico, CEO
William Burke, CFO
Thomas Montgomery, Chief Accounting Officer
Ronald Oscher, Chief Administrative Officer
Emanuela Speranza, General Manager, Geographical
David Hermance, General Manager
John Hardin, President, Divisional
Tony Ciampitti, President, Divisional
Timothy Jones, President, Divisional
Thomas Marecic, President, Divisional

FINANCIAL DATA: *Note: Data for latest year may not have been available at press time.*

In U.S. $	2021	2020	2019	2018	2017	2016
Revenue		4,540,029,000	5,158,557,000	4,845,872,000	4,300,170,000	3,840,087,000
R&D Expense						
Operating Income		1,027,884,000	1,177,380,000	1,075,540,000	915,094,000	801,897,000
Operating Margin %						
SGA Expense		515,630,000	610,280,000	584,022,000	533,645,000	462,970,000
Net Income		872,439,000	861,297,000	777,933,000	681,470,000	512,158,000
Operating Cash Flow		1,280,980,000	1,114,422,000	925,518,000	833,259,000	756,835,000
Capital Expenditure		74,199,000	102,346,000	82,076,000	75,074,000	63,280,000
EBITDA		1,423,646,000	1,392,271,000	1,269,415,000	1,077,985,000	967,123,000
Return on Assets %						
Return on Equity %						
Debt to Equity						

CONTACT INFORMATION:

Phone: 610 647-2121 Fax:
Toll-Free:
Address: 1100 Cassatt Rd., Berwyn, PA 19312-1177 United States

STOCK TICKER/OTHER:

Stock Ticker: AME
Employees: 18,100
Parent Company:
Exchange: NYS
Fiscal Year Ends: 12/31

SALARIES/BONUSES:

Top Exec. Salary: $1,122,000 Bonus: $660,000
Second Exec. Salary: $582,750 Bonus: $100,800

OTHER THOUGHTS:

Estimated Female Officers or Directors:
Hot Spot for Advancement for Women/Minorities:

Analog Devices Inc

www.analog.com

NAIC Code: 334413

TYPES OF BUSINESS:

Integrated Circuits-Analog & Digital
MEMS Products
DSP Products
Accelerometers & Gyroscopes

BRANDS/DIVISIONS/AFFILIATES:

GROWTH PLANS/SPECIAL FEATURES:

Analog Devices is a leading analog, mixed signal, and digital signal processing chipmaker. The firm has a significant market share lead in converter chips, which are used to translate analog signals to digital and vice versa. The company serves tens of thousands of customers, and more than half of its chip sales are made to industrial and automotive end markets. Analog Devices' chips are also incorporated into wireless infrastructure equipment.

ADI offers its employees medical, dental and vision coverage; life insurance; and various employee assistance programs.

CONTACTS: *Note: Officers with more than one job title may be intentionally listed here more than once.*

Vincent Roche, CEO
Prashanth Mahendra-Rajah, CFO
Ray Stata, Chairman of the Board
Michael Sondel, Chief Accounting Officer
Gregory Henderson, Senior VP, Divisional
Joseph Hassett, Senior VP, Divisional
Martin Cotter, Senior VP, Divisional

FINANCIAL DATA: *Note: Data for latest year may not have been available at press time.*

In U.S. $	2021	2020	2019	2018	2017	2016
Revenue		5,603,056,000	5,991,065,000	6,200,942,000	5,107,503,000	3,421,409,000
R&D Expense		1,050,519,000	1,130,348,000	1,165,410,000	968,602,000	653,816,000
Operating Income		1,550,581,000	1,806,267,000	1,943,053,000	1,104,597,000	1,041,796,000
Operating Margin %						
SGA Expense		659,923,000	648,094,000	695,937,000	691,046,000	461,438,000
Net Income		1,220,761,000	1,363,011,000	1,495,432,000	727,259,000	861,664,000
Operating Cash Flow		2,008,487,000	2,253,100,000	2,442,361,000	1,112,592,000	1,280,895,000
Capital Expenditure		165,692,000	275,372,000	254,876,000	204,098,000	127,397,000
EBITDA		2,315,845,000	2,526,054,000	2,691,169,000	1,663,384,000	1,255,468,000
Return on Assets %						
Return on Equity %						
Debt to Equity						

CONTACT INFORMATION:

Phone: 781 935-5565 Fax:
Toll-Free: 800-262-5643
Address: One Analog Way, Wilmington, MA 01887 United States

STOCK TICKER/OTHER:

Stock Ticker: ADI
Employees: 15,900
Parent Company:
Exchange: NAS
Fiscal Year Ends: 10/31

SALARIES/BONUSES:

Top Exec. Salary: $1,050,000 Bonus: $
Second Exec. Salary: $575,000 Bonus: $

OTHER THOUGHTS:

Estimated Female Officers or Directors: 3
Hot Spot for Advancement for Women/Minorities: Y

Anaren Inc

www.anaren.com

NAIC Code: 334220

TYPES OF BUSINESS:

Wireless Telecommunications Components
Radio Frequency
Microwave Microelectronics
Components
Beamforming Networks
Unicircuit
Printed Circuit Board Fabrication
Ceramic Solutions

BRANDS/DIVISIONS/AFFILIATES:

TTM Technologies Inc

CONTACTS: *Note: Officers with more than one job title may be intentionally listed here more than once.*

Thomas T. Edman, CEO
David M. Ferrara, General Counsel
Timothy P. Ross, Pres., Space & Defense
George A. Blanton, Treas.
Gert Thygesen, Sr. VP-Tech.
Mark Burdick, Pres., Wireless Group

GROWTH PLANS/SPECIAL FEATURES:

Anaren, Inc., a subsidiary of TTM Technologies, Inc., is a global designer and manufacturer of high-frequency radio frequency (RF) and microwave microelectronics, components and assemblies. The firm's engineering expertise and products are utilized by major manufacturers around the world, which are primarily engaged in the space, defense and telecommunications sectors. Anaren's capabilities span beamforming networks, integrated RF solutions, complex build-to-print (unicircuit), high-reliability printed circuit board (PCB) fabrication, thick film substrates, low temperature co-fired ceramic (LTCC) solutions and multi-chip modules. The company's standard RF components include couplers, power dividers, baluns, and radio transceivers, as well as build-to-print complex subassemblies including beamformers, RF modules, hybrid microelectronics, ceramic substrates and more. Products that can be customized include beamforming networks, integrated RF solutions, ceramic circuits and packaging, microelectronics and high-reliability PCB. Anaren's diverse portfolio delivers innovations in design and solutions for military, satellite and telecommunications applications.

Anaren offers its employees health and wealth benefits, as well as a variety of employee assistance programs.

FINANCIAL DATA: *Note: Data for latest year may not have been available at press time.*

In U.S. $	2021	2020	2019	2018	2017	2016
Revenue	250,000,000	242,676,000	226,800,000	189,000,000	180,000,000	175,000,000
R&D Expense						
Operating Income						
Operating Margin %						
SGA Expense						
Net Income						
Operating Cash Flow						
Capital Expenditure						
EBITDA						
Return on Assets %						
Return on Equity %						
Debt to Equity						

CONTACT INFORMATION:

Phone: 315 432-8909 Fax: 315 432-9121
Toll-Free: 800-544-2414
Address: 6635 Kirkville Rd., East Syracuse, NY 13057 United States

STOCK TICKER/OTHER:

Stock Ticker: Subsidiary
Employees: 1,100
Parent Company: TTM Technologies Inc
Exchange:
Fiscal Year Ends: 12/31

SALARIES/BONUSES:

Top Exec. Salary: $ Bonus: $
Second Exec. Salary: $ Bonus: $

OTHER THOUGHTS:

Estimated Female Officers or Directors: 2
Hot Spot for Advancement for Women/Minorities:

Apple Inc

www.apple.com

NAIC Code: 334220

TYPES OF BUSINESS:

Electronics Design and Manufacturing
Software
Computers and Tablets
Retail Stores
Smartphones
Online Music Store
Apps Store
Home Entertainment Software & Systems

BRANDS/DIVISIONS/AFFILIATES:

iPhone
iPad
Apple Watch
Apple TV
iOS
watchOS
HomePod
AirPods

GROWTH PLANS/SPECIAL FEATURES:

Apple designs a wide variety of consumer electronic devices, including smartphones (iPhone), tablets (iPad), PCs (Mac), smartwatches (Apple Watch), AirPods, and TV boxes (Apple TV), among others. The iPhone makes up the majority of Apple's total revenue. In addition, Apple offers its customers a variety of services such as Apple Music, iCloud, Apple Care, Apple TV+, Apple Arcade, Apple Card, and Apple Pay, among others. Apple's products run internally developed software and semiconductors, and the firm is well known for its integration of hardware, software and services. Apple's products are distributed online as well as through company-owned stores and third-party retailers. The company generates roughly 40% of its revenue from the Americas, with the remainder earned internationally.

Apple offers employees comprehensive health benefits, retirement plans and various employee assistance programs.

CONTACTS: *Note: Officers with more than one job title may be intentionally listed here more than once.*

Timothy Cook, CEO
Luca Maestri, CFO
Arthur Levinson, Chairman of the Board
Chris Kondo, Chief Accounting Officer
Jeffery Williams, COO
Katherine Adams, General Counsel
Deirdre OBrien, Senior VP, Divisional

FINANCIAL DATA: *Note: Data for latest year may not have been available at press time.*

In U.S. $	2021	2020	2019	2018	2017	2016
Revenue	365,817,000,000	274,515,000,000	260,174,000,000	265,595,000,000	229,234,000,000	215,639,000,000
R&D Expense	21,914,000,000	18,752,000,000	16,217,000,000	14,236,000,000	11,581,000,000	10,045,000,000
Operating Income	108,949,000,000	66,288,000,000	63,930,000,000	70,898,000,000	61,344,000,000	60,024,000,000
Operating Margin %						
SGA Expense	21,973,000,000	19,916,000,000	18,245,000,000	16,705,000,000	15,261,000,000	14,194,000,000
Net Income	94,680,000,000	57,411,000,000	55,256,000,000	59,531,000,000	48,351,000,000	45,687,000,000
Operating Cash Flow	104,038,000,000	80,674,000,000	69,391,000,000	77,434,000,000	63,598,000,000	65,824,000,000
Capital Expenditure	11,085,000,000	7,309,000,000	10,495,000,000	13,313,000,000	12,795,000,000	13,548,000,000
EBITDA	123,136,000,000	81,020,000,000	81,860,000,000	87,046,000,000	76,569,000,000	73,333,000,000
Return on Assets %						
Return on Equity %						
Debt to Equity						

CONTACT INFORMATION:

Phone: 408 996-1010 Fax: 408 974-2483
Toll-Free: 800-692-7753
Address: One Apple Park Way, Cupertino, CA 95014 United States

STOCK TICKER/OTHER:

Stock Ticker: AAPL Exchange: NAS
Employees: 147,000 Fiscal Year Ends: 09/30
Parent Company:

SALARIES/BONUSES:

Top Exec. Salary: $3,000,000 Bonus: $
Second Exec. Salary: $1,000,000 Bonus: $

OTHER THOUGHTS:

Estimated Female Officers or Directors:
Hot Spot for Advancement for Women/Minorities:

Aptiv PLC

NAIC Code: 336300

www.aptiv.com

TYPES OF BUSINESS:

Motor Vehicle Parts Manufacturing
Vehicle Components
Safety Technology Solutions
Signal and Power Solutions
Advanced Safety
User Experience
Autonomous Vehicles
Autonomous Technologies

BRANDS/DIVISIONS/AFFILIATES:

Motional

GROWTH PLANS/SPECIAL FEATURES:

Aptiv's signal and power solutions segment supplies components and systems that make up a vehicle's electrical system backbone, including wiring assemblies and harnesses, connectors, electrical centers, and hybrid electrical systems. The advanced safety and user experience segment provides body controls, infotainment and connectivity systems, passive and active safety electronics, advanced driver-assist technologies, and displays, as well as the development of software for these systems. Aptiv's largest customer is General Motors at roughly 13% of revenue, including sales to GM's Shanghai joint venture. North America and Europe represented approximately 38% and 33% of total 2019 revenue, respectively.

CONTACTS:

Note: Officers with more than one job title may be intentionally listed here more than once.

Kevin P. Clark, CEO
Joseph R. Massaro, Sr. VP
Wendy F. Miller, Sr. VP
Glen De Vos, Sr. VP

FINANCIAL DATA:

Note: Data for latest year may not have been available at press time.

In U.S. $	2021	2020	2019	2018	2017	2016
Revenue		13,066,000,000	14,357,000,000	14,435,000,000	12,884,000,000	16,661,000,000
R&D Expense						
Operating Income		820,000,000	1,424,000,000	1,582,000,000	1,545,000,000	2,275,000,000
Operating Margin %						
SGA Expense		976,000,000	1,076,000,000	993,000,000	952,000,000	1,145,000,000
Net Income		1,804,000,000	990,000,000	1,067,000,000	1,355,000,000	1,257,000,000
Operating Cash Flow		1,413,000,000	1,624,000,000	1,628,000,000	1,468,000,000	1,941,000,000
Capital Expenditure		586,000,000	781,000,000	846,000,000	698,000,000	828,000,000
EBITDA		2,882,000,000	2,007,000,000	2,151,000,000	1,941,000,000	2,285,000,000
Return on Assets %						
Return on Equity %						
Debt to Equity						

CONTACT INFORMATION:

Phone: 353-1-259-7013 Fax:
Toll-Free:
Address: 5 Hanover Quay, Grand Canal Dock, Dublin, D02 VY79 Ireland

STOCK TICKER/OTHER:

Stock Ticker: APTV
Employees: 151,000
Parent Company:
Exchange: NYS
Fiscal Year Ends: 12/31

SALARIES/BONUSES:

Top Exec. Salary: $1,141,924 Bonus: $
Second Exec. Salary: $857,917 Bonus: $

OTHER THOUGHTS:

Estimated Female Officers or Directors:
Hot Spot for Advancement for Women/Minorities:

Arm Holdings plc

www.arm.com

NAIC Code: 334413

TYPES OF BUSINESS:

Semiconductors Manufacturing

BRANDS/DIVISIONS/AFFILIATES:

SoftBank Group Corp

CONTACTS:

Note: Officers with more than one job title may be intentionally listed here more than once.

Simon Segars, CEO
Inder M. Singh, CFO
Kirsty Gill, Chief People Officer
Dipesh Patel, CTO
Phil David, General Counsel
Thomas P. Lantzsch, Exec. VP-Strategy
Ian Thornton, VP-Investor Rel.
Mike Inglis, Chief Commercial Officer
Dipesh Patel, Exec. VP
John Cornish, Exec. VP
Antonio J. Viana, Exec. VP-Global & Commercial Dev.

GROWTH PLANS/SPECIAL FEATURES:

Arm Holdings plc is a designer of processors, physical IP and related technology and software. The firm also sells development tools intended to enhance the cost-effectiveness, performance and energy-efficiency of high-volume embedded applications. Arm licenses and sells development tools directly to systems companies and provides support services to its systems firms, licensees and other systems designers. In addition, the company licenses and sells its products and technology to international electronics firms; these firms then manufacture and market application-specific integrated circuits, microprocessors and standard processors that utilize ARM's technology to systems companies. Arm's products are grouped into six categories, namely, Internet of Things (IoT) solutions, processors, AI technologies , graphics/multimedia, development tools and custom system on chips (SoCs). Its Pelion IoT platform is a flexible, secure and efficient foundation spanning connectivity, device and data management. The company's IoT SoC solutions are tools designed to accelerate time to security for SoC designers, device makers and developers. Its Mbed open-source embedded operating system is used in IoT connected products. Processor IPs are used for a wide range of devices, from sensors and servers; and graphics processors offer a complete multimedia solution for SoC. Wireless IP products include low-power, low-voltage solutions for WPAN and LPWAN. Security IP is designed to protect against a variety of threats and vulnerabilities. Industries served by the firm include automotive, logistics, smart cities, smart buildings, smart homes, health care, storage, industrial, wearables, utilities, energy, mobile and infrastructure. Arm Holdings operates as a subsidiary of SoftBank Group Corp. In December of 2021, the Federal Trade Commission (FTC) sued to block Nvidia Corp.'s September 2020 acquisition of Arm Holdings plc from SoftBank Group Corp. over antitrust concerns.

FINANCIAL DATA:

Note: Data for latest year may not have been available at press time.

In U.S. $	2021	2020	2019	2018	2017	2016
Revenue	2,000,000,000	1,825,600,000	1,630,000,000	1,625,000,000	1,500,000,000	1,400,000,000
R&D Expense						
Operating Income						
Operating Margin %						
SGA Expense						
Net Income						
Operating Cash Flow						
Capital Expenditure						
EBITDA						
Return on Assets %						
Return on Equity %						
Debt to Equity						

CONTACT INFORMATION:

Phone: 44 1223400400 Fax: 44 1223400410
Toll-Free:
Address: 110 Fulbourn Rd., Cambridge, CB1 9NJ United Kingdom

STOCK TICKER/OTHER:

Stock Ticker: Subsidiary
Employees: 6,300
Parent Company: SoftBank Group Corp
Exchange:
Fiscal Year Ends: 12/31

SALARIES/BONUSES:

Top Exec. Salary: $ Bonus: $
Second Exec. Salary: $ Bonus: $

OTHER THOUGHTS:

Estimated Female Officers or Directors: 3
Hot Spot for Advancement for Women/Minorities: Y

Arteris IP

www.arteris.com

NAIC Code: 334413

TYPES OF BUSINESS:

Network-On-A-Chip Technology
Network-on-Chip Technology
Intellectual Property Solutions
Semiconductor IP
IP Deployment Technology
Cache Systems
Artificial Intelligence
Machine Learning

GROWTH PLANS/SPECIAL FEATURES:

Arteris Inc is a provider of network-on-chip interconnect semiconductor intellectual property (IP) and IP deployment technology to accelerate system-on-chip semiconductor development and integration for a wide range of applications from AI to automobiles, mobile phones, IoT, cameras, SSD controllers, and servers for customers such as Bosch, Baidu, Mobileye, Samsung, Toshiba and NXP.

BRANDS/DIVISIONS/AFFILIATES:

Ncore Cache Coherent IP
FlexNoC Interconnect IP
CodaCache
FlexNoC Resilience Package
FlexNoC AI Package
PIANO Timing Closure Package
IP-XACT
Arteris Harmony Trace

CONTACTS: *Note: Officers with more than one job title may be intentionally listed here more than once.*

K. Janac, CEO
Nicholas Hawkins, CFO
Evin Kebebew, Controller
Laurent Moll, COO
Isabelle Geday, Director
Paul Alpern, General Counsel

FINANCIAL DATA: *Note: Data for latest year may not have been available at press time.*

In U.S. $	2021	2020	2019	2018	2017	2016
Revenue		31,812,000	31,501,000			
R&D Expense		17,020,000	10,051,000			
Operating Income		-3,777,000	7,273,000			
Operating Margin %						
SGA Expense		17,078,000	12,315,000			
Net Income		-3,260,000	4,618,000			
Operating Cash Flow		2,163,000	12,199,000			
Capital Expenditure		654,000	242,000			
EBITDA		-1,249,000	8,029,000			
Return on Assets %						
Return on Equity %						
Debt to Equity						

CONTACT INFORMATION:

Phone: 408-470-7300 Fax: 408-470-7301
Toll-Free:
Address: 595 Millich Dr., Ste. 200, Campbell, CA 95008 United States

STOCK TICKER/OTHER:

Stock Ticker: AIP
Exchange: NAS
Employees: 200
Fiscal Year Ends: 12/31
Parent Company: Arteris Holdings Inc

SALARIES/BONUSES:

Top Exec. Salary: $302,636 Bonus: $
Second Exec. Salary: $197,902 Bonus: $

OTHER THOUGHTS:

Estimated Female Officers or Directors:
Hot Spot for Advancement for Women/Minorities:

Aruba Networks Inc

www.arubanetworks.com

NAIC Code: 511210C

TYPES OF BUSINESS:

Computer Software: Telecom, Communications & VOIP
Wireless Security Systems
Mobility Software
Internet of Things Solutions
Artificial Intelligence
Network Management
Cloud Management
Edge Infrastructure

BRANDS/DIVISIONS/AFFILIATES:

Hewlett-Packard Enterprise Company
ClearPass
Silver Peak Systems

CONTACTS: *Note: Officers with more than one job title may be intentionally listed here more than once.*

Richard Gough, Head-Bus. Oper.
Andrew Schultz, Sr. VP-Finance
Alain Carpentier, Head.-Global Sales
Kristin Major, Head-Human Resources
David Hughes, Chief Product & Technology Officer
John Dilullo, Executive VP, Divisional
Ava Hahn, General Counsel
Ash Chowdappa, Head-Software Engineering

GROWTH PLANS/SPECIAL FEATURES:

Aruba Networks, Inc., part of Hewlett Packard Enterprise Company, manufactures and markets unified mobility, Edge and Internet of Things (IoT) software solutions. The firm's solutions empower organizations to serve mobile users who rely on internal and Edge-/cloud-based apps for their work and personal lives. Aruba's vertical solutions are industry specific in regards to networking and security, and include financial services, hospitality, federal government, primary and higher education, healthcare, retail, service providers and large public venues. Its technology solutions are technology specific in regards to helping businesses stay ahead of the curve, and include the Aruba architecture, 5G and Wi-Fi 6, artificial intelligent (AI)-powered solutions, cloud managed networking, Edge infrastructure, dynamic segmentation, indoor wireless coverage, IoT, unified communications and wireless technologies. These vertical and technology solutions span the digital workplace, software-defined branch, data center and small/medium businesses. Network products include access points, switches, gateways, controllers, network management, software-defined wide area network (SD-WAN), analytics and assurance. Security products provide analytics-driven visibility, detection, control and response across the entire network architecture. Aruba's dynamic segmentation feature allows IT organizations to define and enforce secure traffic segmentation policies for IoT, users and their traffic. Its ClearPass offering provides AI-powered visibility and policy enforcement to manage and control access for mobile and IoT on any vendor's wired and wireless networks. Aruba is based in the U.S., with global offices in North America, Latin America, Europe, Middle East, Africa and Asia Pacific.

FINANCIAL DATA: *Note: Data for latest year may not have been available at press time.*

In U.S. $	2021	2020	2019	2018	2017	2016
Revenue	3,120,000,000	3,000,000,000	2,625,000,000	2,500,000,000	2,600,000,000	2,000,000,000
R&D Expense						
Operating Income						
Operating Margin %						
SGA Expense						
Net Income						
Operating Cash Flow						
Capital Expenditure						
EBITDA						
Return on Assets %						
Return on Equity %						
Debt to Equity						

CONTACT INFORMATION:

Phone: 408 941-4300 Fax: 408 752-0626
Toll-Free: 800-943-4526
Address: 6280 America Center Dr., San Jose, CA 95002 United States

STOCK TICKER/OTHER:

Stock Ticker: Subsidiary Exchange:
Employees: 7,000 Fiscal Year Ends: 10/31
Parent Company: Hewlett Packard Enterprise Company

SALARIES/BONUSES:

Top Exec. Salary: $ Bonus: $
Second Exec. Salary: $ Bonus: $

OTHER THOUGHTS:

Estimated Female Officers or Directors:
Hot Spot for Advancement for Women/Minorities:

ASE Technology Holding Co Ltd

NAIC Code: 334413

www.aseglobal.com

TYPES OF BUSINESS:

Semiconductor Manufacturing
Semiconductor Packaging Services
Design & Testing Services

BRANDS/DIVISIONS/AFFILIATES:

Advanced Semiconductor Engineering Inc
Siliconware Precision Industries Co Ltd
Universal Scientific Industrial Co Ltd

GROWTH PLANS/SPECIAL FEATURES:

ASE Technology Holding Co Ltd is a semiconductor assembly and testing firm. The company operates in segments: Packaging, Testing, and Electronic Manufacturing Services. Of these, packaging services contribute the most revenue. It involves packaging bare semiconductors into completed semiconductors with improved electrical and thermal characteristics. The Testing Segment includes front-end engineering testing, wafer probing, and final testing services. In the EMS segment, the company designs manufacture and sells electronic components and telecommunication equipment motherboards. The company is based in Taiwan but garners over half its sales from firms in the United States.

CONTACTS: *Note: Officers with more than one job title may be intentionally listed here more than once.*

Jason C.S. Chang, CEO
Tien Wu, COO
Richard H.P. Chang, Pres.
Joseph Tung, CFO
Richard H.P. Chang, Pres.
Joseph Su, Mgr.-Investor Rel.
Raymond Lo, Pres., Kaohsiung Plant Area
Jason C.S. Chang, Chmn.
Rutherford Chang, Pres., ASE China

FINANCIAL DATA: *Note: Data for latest year may not have been available at press time.*

In U.S. $	2021	2020	2019	2018	2017	2016
Revenue		17,191,150,000	14,891,810,000	13,374,820,000	10,468,010,000	9,907,304,000
R&D Expense		695,693,000	663,000,100	539,285,400	423,368,500	410,556,900
Operating Income		1,314,237,000	885,568,800	973,442,600	936,025,600	980,967,900
Operating Margin %						
SGA Expense		858,001,500	806,940,800	704,706,400	568,271,900	544,034,700
Net Income		972,067,000	614,893,600	945,040,700	822,441,000	769,909,700
Operating Cash Flow		2,705,317,000	2,605,936,000	1,840,821,000	1,709,489,000	1,878,059,000
Capital Expenditure		2,277,062,000	2,108,777,000	1,512,464,000	902,385,400	981,346,800
EBITDA		3,265,919,000	2,812,948,000	2,819,348,000	2,243,316,000	2,160,978,000
Return on Assets %						
Return on Equity %						
Debt to Equity						

CONTACT INFORMATION:

Phone: 886 287805489 Fax: 886 227576121
Toll-Free:
Address: 26 Chin Third Rd., Nantze Export Processing Zone, Kaohsiung, 811 Taiwan

STOCK TICKER/OTHER:

Stock Ticker: ASX Exchange: NYS
Employees: 101,981 Fiscal Year Ends: 12/31
Parent Company:

SALARIES/BONUSES:

Top Exec. Salary: $ Bonus: $
Second Exec. Salary: $ Bonus: $

OTHER THOUGHTS:

Estimated Female Officers or Directors:
Hot Spot for Advancement for Women/Minorities: Y

ASG Technologies Group Inc

www.asg.com

NAIC Code: 511210H

TYPES OF BUSINESS:

Computer Software, Enterprise Productivity
Enterprise Software
Information Management Solutions
IT Systems Management
Content Services
Data Intelligence
Digital Automation

BRANDS/DIVISIONS/AFFILIATES:

Rocket Software Inc

GROWTH PLANS/SPECIAL FEATURES:

ASG Technologies Group, Inc. is a global enterprise software vendor, providing solutions for information management and IT systems management. The company's information management solutions capture, manage, govern and enable companies to understand and support all types of information. Its IT systems management solutions ensure that the systems and infrastructure supporting that information lifecycle are always available and performing as needed. Other products by ASG include content services, data intelligence and digital automation. ASG's products and solutions primarily serve the financial services, government and insurance sectors. During 2021, ASG Technologies was acquired by private technology company Rocket Software, Inc.

CONTACTS:

Note: Officers with more than one job title may be intentionally listed here more than once.

Charles Sansbury, CEO
Dilip Upmanyu, CFO
Chuck Neal, Exec. VP-Sales & Mktg.
Licia Williams, Exec. VP-Human Resources
Swamy Viswanathan, Exec. VP-Chief Product Officer
John Connor, CTO
Derek Eckelman, General Counsel
Richard Vance, Exec. VP-Oper.
Alex Derby, Sr. VP-Sales Oper.

FINANCIAL DATA:

Note: Data for latest year may not have been available at press time.

In U.S. $	2021	2020	2019	2018	2017	2016
Revenue	430,000,000	425,000,000	420,000,000	400,000,000	350,000,000	300,000,000
R&D Expense						
Operating Income						
Operating Margin %						
SGA Expense						
Net Income						
Operating Cash Flow						
Capital Expenditure						
EBITDA						
Return on Assets %						
Return on Equity %						
Debt to Equity						

CONTACT INFORMATION:

Phone: 239-435-2200 Fax: 239-263-3692
Toll-Free: 800-325-2555
Address: 708 Goodlette Rd. N., Naples, FL 34102 United States

STOCK TICKER/OTHER:

Stock Ticker: Private
Exchange:
Employees: 1,000
Fiscal Year Ends: 12/31
Parent Company: Rocket Software Inc

SALARIES/BONUSES:

Top Exec. Salary: $ Bonus: $
Second Exec. Salary: $ Bonus: $

OTHER THOUGHTS:

Estimated Female Officers or Directors:
Hot Spot for Advancement for Women/Minorities:

Aspen Technology Inc

NAIC Code: 511210A

www.aspentech.com

TYPES OF BUSINESS:

Computer Software-Manufacturing Automation
Decision Support Software
Support Services
Petroleum & Chemical Process Software

BRANDS/DIVISIONS/AFFILIATES:

aspenONE

GROWTH PLANS/SPECIAL FEATURES:

Aspen Technology is a leading global supplier of software solutions that optimize asset design, operations, and maintenance in complex industrial environments. The company's AspenOne software platform helps improve process-oriented plant efficiency, and thereby lower capital intensity, increase working capital efficiency, and improve margins. Aspen was founded in 1981 and serves more than 2,300 customers in 32 countries.

CONTACTS: *Note: Officers with more than one job title may be intentionally listed here more than once.*

Antonio Pietri, CEO
Chantelle Breithaupt, CFO
Jill Smith, Chairman of the Board
Christopher Stagno, Chief Accounting Officer
John Hague, Executive VP, Divisional
Frederic Hammond, General Counsel

FINANCIAL DATA: *Note: Data for latest year may not have been available at press time.*

In U.S. $	2021	2020	2019	2018	2017	2016
Revenue	709,376,000	598,717,000	598,345,000	499,514,000	482,942,000	472,344,000
R&D Expense	94,229,000	92,230,000	83,122,000	82,076,000	79,530,000	67,152,000
Operating Income	358,401,000	257,359,000	282,802,000	209,641,000	212,016,000	211,381,000
Operating Margin %						
SGA Expense	196,595,000	187,521,000	174,605,000	157,153,000	143,930,000	145,200,000
Net Income	319,803,000	229,671,000	262,734,000	148,688,000	162,196,000	139,951,000
Operating Cash Flow	276,134,000	243,258,000	238,313,000	206,936,000	182,386,000	153,744,000
Capital Expenditure	2,366,000	1,419,000	1,567,000	660,000	3,125,000	3,752,000
EBITDA	402,249,000	300,769,000	320,066,000	215,578,000	220,538,000	217,912,000
Return on Assets %						
Return on Equity %						
Debt to Equity						

CONTACT INFORMATION:

Phone: 781-221-6400 Fax: 781-221-6410
Toll-Free: 855-882-7736
Address: 20 Crosby Dr., Bedford, MA 01730 United States

STOCK TICKER/OTHER:

Stock Ticker: AZPN Exchange: NAS
Employees: 1,710 Fiscal Year Ends: 06/30
Parent Company:

SALARIES/BONUSES:

Top Exec. Salary: $800,000 Bonus: $
Second Exec. Salary: $600,000 Bonus: $

OTHER THOUGHTS:

Estimated Female Officers or Directors: 3
Hot Spot for Advancement for Women/Minorities: Y

AT&T Inc

www.att.com

NAIC Code: 517110

TYPES OF BUSINESS:

Local Telephone Service
Telecommunications
Media Services
Technology
Video Services
Broadband
Television and Film Production
Entertainment Services

BRANDS/DIVISIONS/AFFILIATES:

WanerMedia
HBO Max
Home Box Office
Warner Bros
Xandr
Otter Media Holdings
Vrio

GROWTH PLANS/SPECIAL FEATURES:

Wireless is AT&T's largest business,contributing about 40% of revenue. The firm is the third- largest U.S. wireless carrier, connecting 66 million postpaid and 17 million prepaid phone customers. WarnerMedia contributes a bit less than 20% of revenue with media assets that include HBO, the Turner cable networks, and the Warner Brothers studios. AT&T plans to spin Warner off and merge it with Discovery to create a new stand-alone media firm. The firm recently sold a 30% stake in its traditional television business, which serves 15 million customers and generates about 17% of sales. This business will be removed from AT&T's financials going forward. Fixed-line telecom services provided to businesses and consumers account for about 20% of revenue, serving about 15 million broadband customers.

CONTACTS: *Note: Officers with more than one job title may be intentionally listed here more than once.*

Jason Kilar, CEO, Subsidiary
Jeffery McElfresh, CEO, Subsidiary
Lori Lee, CEO, Subsidiary
John Stankey, CEO
Pascal Desroches, CFO
William Kennard, Chairman of the Board
David Huntley, Chief Compliance Officer
David McAtee, General Counsel
Angela Santone, Senior Executive VP, Divisional
Edward Gillespie, Senior Executive VP, Subsidiary

FINANCIAL DATA: *Note: Data for latest year may not have been available at press time.*

In U.S. $	2021	2020	2019	2018	2017	2016
Revenue		171,760,000,000	181,193,000,000	170,756,000,000	160,546,000,000	163,786,000,000
R&D Expense						
Operating Income		25,285,000,000	29,413,000,000	26,142,000,000	23,863,000,000	24,708,000,000
Operating Margin %						
SGA Expense		38,039,000,000	39,422,000,000	36,765,000,000	34,917,000,000	36,347,000,000
Net Income		-5,176,000,000	13,903,000,000	19,370,000,000	29,450,000,000	12,976,000,000
Operating Cash Flow		43,130,000,000	48,668,000,000	43,602,000,000	39,151,000,000	39,344,000,000
Capital Expenditure		15,675,000,000	19,435,000,000	20,758,000,000	20,647,000,000	21,516,000,000
EBITDA		42,188,000,000	64,694,000,000	65,032,000,000	45,826,000,000	50,569,000,000
Return on Assets %						
Return on Equity %						
Debt to Equity						

CONTACT INFORMATION:

Phone: 210 821-4105 Fax:
Toll-Free:
Address: 208 S. Akard St., Dallas, TX 75202 United States

STOCK TICKER/OTHER:

Stock Ticker: T
Employees: 230,000
Parent Company:
Exchange: NYS
Fiscal Year Ends: 12/31

SALARIES/BONUSES:

Top Exec. Salary: $2,050,000 Bonus: $
Second Exec. Salary: $1,666,667 Bonus: $

OTHER THOUGHTS:

Estimated Female Officers or Directors: 4
Hot Spot for Advancement for Women/Minorities: Y

Sales, profits and employees may be estimates. Financial information, benefits and other data can change quickly and may vary from those stated here.

AT&T Mobility LLC

NAIC Code: 517210

www.att.com/wireless

TYPES OF BUSINESS:

Mobile Phone and Wireless Services
Wireless Data Services
Cell Phone Services

BRANDS/DIVISIONS/AFFILIATES:

AT&T Inc
AT&T Wireless

GROWTH PLANS/SPECIAL FEATURES:

AT&T Mobility, LLC, also referred to as AT&T Wireless, is a leading wireless telecommunications service provider predominantly serving the U.S. The wholly-owned subsidiary of AT&T, Inc. provides wireless voice and data services to consumer and wholesale subscribers. AT&T Mobility offers a comprehensive range of nationwide wireless voice and data communications services in a variety of pricing plans, including postpaid and prepaid service plans. The firm provides 5G services in select locations throughout the U.S., which offers seamless connection and ultra-fast speeds at home, business or on-the-go. AT&T also offers 5G phones and devices for 5G connection and compatibility.

CONTACTS: *Note: Officers with more than one job title may be intentionally listed here more than once.*

John T. Stankey, CEO-Corporate
Ralph de la Vega, Pres.

FINANCIAL DATA: *Note: Data for latest year may not have been available at press time.*

In U.S. $	2021	2020	2019	2018	2017	2016
Revenue	73,000,000,000	72,564,000,000	71,056,000,000	70,521,000,000	70,259,000,000	72,587,000,000
R&D Expense						
Operating Income						
Operating Margin %						
SGA Expense						
Net Income		22,372,000,000	22,321,000,000	21,568,000,000	20,204,000,000	20,743,000,000
Operating Cash Flow						
Capital Expenditure						
EBITDA						
Return on Assets %						
Return on Equity %						
Debt to Equity						

CONTACT INFORMATION:

Phone: 404-236-7895 Fax:
Toll-Free:
Address: 1025 Lenox Park Blvd., Atlanta, GA 30319 United States

STOCK TICKER/OTHER:

Stock Ticker: Subsidiary
Employees: 40,000
Parent Company: AT&T Inc
Exchange:
Fiscal Year Ends: 12/31

SALARIES/BONUSES:

Top Exec. Salary: $ Bonus: $
Second Exec. Salary: $ Bonus: $

OTHER THOUGHTS:

Estimated Female Officers or Directors:
Hot Spot for Advancement for Women/Minorities:

Atos SE

www.atos.net

NAIC Code: 541512

TYPES OF BUSINESS:

IT Consulting
Business Process Outsourcing
Payment Solutions
e-Commerce Consulting
Supply Chain Management
Customer Relationship Management
Product Lifecycle Management
Web Design

BRANDS/DIVISIONS/AFFILIATES:

Atos
Atos Syntel
Unify
Worldgrid

GROWTH PLANS/SPECIAL FEATURES:

Atos SE is a France-based IT services provider. The company generates over EUR 11 billion in annual revenue (the majority of which is generated in Europe), employs approximately 100,000 staff, and operates in 72 countries. Atos provides managed services, consulting and systems integration, Big Data and security, and Worldline (transactional services) across the manufacturing, retail and transportation, public health, telecom, media and utilities, and financial services markets.

CONTACTS: *Note: Officers with more than one job title may be intentionally listed here more than once.*

Pierre Barnabe, Co-CEO
Adrian Gregory, Co-CEO
Robert Goegele, Head-Mfg., Retail & Svcs
Philippe Mareine, Gen. Sec.
Charles Dehelly, Sr. Exec. VP-Global Oper.
Marc Meyer, Head-Talent & Comm.
Michel-Alain Proch, Head-Finance
Francis Meston, Head-System Integration
Eric Grall, Head-Managed Svcs.
Ingo Juraske, Head-Public Sector, Health Care & Transport
Jeremy Hore, Head-Siemens Account
Gilles Grapinet, Sr. Exec. VP-Global Functions

FINANCIAL DATA: *Note: Data for latest year may not have been available at press time.*

In U.S. $	2021	2020	2019	2018	2017	2016
Revenue		12,627,190,000	13,086,830,000	13,843,500,000	14,332,610,000	13,233,090,000
R&D Expense						
Operating Income		994,951,900	973,494,300	1,216,303,000	1,213,028,000	1,153,173,000
Operating Margin %						
SGA Expense		548,861,100	553,378,400	369,295,400	354,388,100	325,025,100
Net Income		621,139,100	3,838,639,000	711,486,600	678,396,800	653,664,200
Operating Cash Flow		1,376,670,000	1,535,907,000	1,260,348,000	1,397,224,000	1,120,083,000
Capital Expenditure		361,390,000	365,907,400	537,567,600	594,373,600	475,566,700
EBITDA		1,687,240,000	1,547,201,000	1,513,321,000	1,574,757,000	1,442,285,000
Return on Assets %						
Return on Equity %						
Debt to Equity						

CONTACT INFORMATION:

Phone: 33 173260000 Fax:
Toll-Free:
Address: River Ouest 80, Quai Voltaire, Bezons, 95877 France

STOCK TICKER/OTHER:

Stock Ticker: AEXAY Exchange: PINX
Employees: 105,000 Fiscal Year Ends: 12/31
Parent Company:

SALARIES/BONUSES:

Top Exec. Salary: $ Bonus: $
Second Exec. Salary: $ Bonus: $

OTHER THOUGHTS:

Estimated Female Officers or Directors: 5
Hot Spot for Advancement for Women/Minorities: Y

Audi AG

NAIC Code: 336111

www.audi.com

TYPES OF BUSINESS:

Automobile Manufacturing
Luxury & Sports Cars
Automobile Customization & Accessories
Engine Manufacturing
Automotive Electronics

BRANDS/DIVISIONS/AFFILIATES:

Volkswagen AG
Audi Sport GmbH
Automobili Lamborghini SpA
Ducati Motor Holding SpA
Q3
A1
e-tron
R8

CONTACTS: *Note: Officers with more than one job title may be intentionally listed here more than once.*

Frank Dreves, Dir.-Prod.
Bernd Martens, Dir.-Procurement
Markus Duesmann, Chmn.
Ulf Berkenhagen, Dir.-Purchasing

GROWTH PLANS/SPECIAL FEATURES:

Audi AG, a wholly-owned subsidiary of Volkswagen AG, is a Germany-based designer and manufacturer of high-end luxury cars. The firm participates in companies like sports car manufacturer Lamborghini, motorcycle manufacturer Ducati, and vehicle upgrade and technology firm Audi Sport GmbH. Audi AG's current (2022) serial models include the Q3, Q4 e-tron, Q5, Q7, Q8, e-tron, A3, A4, A5, A6, A7, A8, TT and R8. These models come in a range of body styles, including sport utility vehicles (SUVs), wagons, sedans, sportbacks, couples, convertibles, sport, electric and hybrid. Audi's vehicles comprise alternative drive systems, digital services such as connected navigation, infotainment, emergency calling/servicing, vehicle control and more. Audi is present in more than 100 markets worldwide and procures at 20 locations in 12 countries via Audi AG, Audi Sport GmbH, Automobili Lamborghini SpA and Ducati Motor Holding SpA.

FINANCIAL DATA: *Note: Data for latest year may not have been available at press time.*

In U.S. $	2021	2020	2019	2018	2017	2016
Revenue	60,000,000,000	55,700,000,000	65,414,262,784	69,610,889,216	64,994,811,904	70,015,705,088
R&D Expense						
Operating Income						
Operating Margin %						
SGA Expense						
Net Income		4,500,000,000	4,523,238,912	3,973,401,344	3,842,744,832	2,342,984,704
Operating Cash Flow						
Capital Expenditure						
EBITDA						
Return on Assets %						
Return on Equity %						
Debt to Equity						

CONTACT INFORMATION:

Phone: 49-800-2834444 Fax:
Toll-Free:
Address: Grosskunden-Platz, Ingolstadt, D-85045 Germany

STOCK TICKER/OTHER:

Stock Ticker: Subsidiary
Employees: 90,640
Parent Company: Volkswagen AG
Exchange:
Fiscal Year Ends: 12/31

SALARIES/BONUSES:

Top Exec. Salary: $ Bonus: $
Second Exec. Salary: $ Bonus: $

OTHER THOUGHTS:

Estimated Female Officers or Directors:
Hot Spot for Advancement for Women/Minorities:

Aurora Innovation Inc

aurora.tech

NAIC Code: 511210

TYPES OF BUSINESS:

Technology for Self-Driving Vehicles
Artificial Intelligence
Autonomous Vehicle
Self-Driving Technology

BRANDS/DIVISIONS/AFFILIATES:

Aurora Driver
Aurora Horizon
Aurora Connect

GROWTH PLANS/SPECIAL FEATURES:

Aurora Innovation Inc is engaged in the self-driving technology business. Aurora is involved in the development of the Aurora Drive, a suite of self-driving hardware, software, and data services in the world to transform the global transportation market. The Aurora Driver is designed as a platform to adapt and interoperate amongst a multitude of vehicle types and applications.

CONTACTS:

Note: Officers with more than one job title may be intentionally listed here more than once.

Chris Urmson, CEO
James Bagnell, Co-Founder
Sterling Anderson, Co-Founder
William Mouat, General Counsel
Richard Tame, Vice President, Divisional

FINANCIAL DATA:

Note: Data for latest year may not have been available at press time.

In U.S. $	2021	2020	2019	2018	2017	2016
Revenue						
R&D Expense						
Operating Income						
Operating Margin %						
SGA Expense						
Net Income						
Operating Cash Flow						
Capital Expenditure						
EBITDA						
Return on Assets %						
Return on Equity %						
Debt to Equity						

CONTACT INFORMATION:

Phone: Fax:
Toll-Free: 888-583-9506
Address: 50 33rd St., Pittsburgh, PA 15201 United States

STOCK TICKER/OTHER:

Stock Ticker: AUR
Employees: 1,600
Parent Company:
Exchange: NAS
Fiscal Year Ends: 12/31

SALARIES/BONUSES:

Top Exec. Salary: $ Bonus: $
Second Exec. Salary: $ Bonus: $

OTHER THOUGHTS:

Estimated Female Officers or Directors:
Hot Spot for Advancement for Women/Minorities:

Aviat Networks Inc

www.aviatnetworks.com

NAIC Code: 334220

TYPES OF BUSINESS:

Wireless Transmission Systems
Network Management Services
Network Operations Centers

BRANDS/DIVISIONS/AFFILIATES:

GROWTH PLANS/SPECIAL FEATURES:

Aviat Networks Inc is a networking solutions provider. It designs, manufactures and sells wireless networking products, solutions, and services to mobile and fixed operators, private network operators, government agencies, transportation and utility companies, public safety agencies and broadcast network operators around the world. The company's product categories include point-to-point microwave and millimeter wave radios that are licensed (subject to local frequency regulatory requirements), lightly-licensed and license-exempt (operating in license-exempt frequencies), and element and network management software. Primarily the firm's concentrations for most of the Sales and Service resources are in the United States, Western and Southern Africa, the Philippines, and the European Union.

CONTACTS: *Note: Officers with more than one job title may be intentionally listed here more than once.*

Peter Smith, CEO
David Gray, CFO
John Mutch, Director
Bryan Tucker, Senior VP, Geographical

FINANCIAL DATA: *Note: Data for latest year may not have been available at press time.*

In U.S. $	2021	2020	2019	2018	2017	2016
Revenue	274,911,000	238,642,000	243,858,000	242,506,000	241,874,000	268,690,000
R&D Expense	21,810,000	19,284,000	21,111,000	19,750,000	18,684,000	20,806,000
Operating Income	24,481,000	7,427,000	2,104,000	2,596,000	-396,000	-24,991,000
Operating Margin %						
SGA Expense	56,324,000	57,985,000	56,055,000	58,157,000	57,184,000	65,902,000
Net Income	110,139,000	257,000	9,738,000	1,845,000	-823,000	-29,907,000
Operating Cash Flow	17,298,000	17,493,000	2,944,000	8,209,000	9,405,000	-126,000
Capital Expenditure	2,847,000	4,608,000	5,246,000	6,563,000	4,021,000	1,574,000
EBITDA	27,823,000	8,150,000	6,120,000	6,494,000	5,285,000	-21,791,000
Return on Assets %						
Return on Equity %						
Debt to Equity						

CONTACT INFORMATION:

Phone: 408 941-7100 Fax: 512-582-4605
Toll-Free:
Address: 200 Parker Dr., Ste. C100A, Austin, TX 78728 United States

STOCK TICKER/OTHER:

Stock Ticker: AVNW Exchange: NAS
Employees: 708 Fiscal Year Ends: 07/01
Parent Company:

SALARIES/BONUSES:

Top Exec. Salary: $444,231 Bonus: $
Second Exec. Salary: $315,000 Bonus: $

OTHER THOUGHTS:

Estimated Female Officers or Directors: 1
Hot Spot for Advancement for Women/Minorities:

BAE Systems plc

www.baesystems.com/en-uk/home

NAIC Code: 336410

TYPES OF BUSINESS:

Defense and Aerospace Systems
Military Vehicles
Military Aircraft
Naval Vessels & Submarines
Satellite Manufacturing
Electronic Systems
Advanced Materials & Technologies
Security & Surveillance Technology

BRANDS/DIVISIONS/AFFILIATES:

BAE Systems Applied Intelligence
BAE Systems Australia
BAE Systems US
BAE Systems Saudi Arabia

GROWTH PLANS/SPECIAL FEATURES:

BAE Systems is a British global defense company. BAE has a dominant position in the U.K., is a top-six supplier to the U.S. Department of Defense, and has a strong presence in key defense markets (eg. Saudi Arabia and Australia). Exposure to programmes is well diversified. BAE derives 45% of sales from services and support and 35% from major programmes such as the F-35 Lightning II and Eurofighter Typhoon fighter jets. The balance of sales is derived from electronic systems and cyber intelligence.

CONTACTS: *Note: Officers with more than one job title may be intentionally listed here more than once.*

Charles Woodburn, CEO
Brad Greve, Dir.-Group Finance
Mark Phillips, Dir.-Communications
Karin Hoeing, Dir.-Human Resources
Ben Hudson, CTO
Phillip Bramwell, General Counsel
Alan Garwood, Dir.-Bus. Dev.
Claire Divver, Dir.-Comm.
Nigel Whitehead, Managing Dir.-Programs & Support
Tom Arseneault, COO-BAE Systems, Inc.
Kevin Taylor, Dir.-Strategy
Jerry Demuro, CEO
Roger Carr, Chmn.
Guy Griffiths, Managing Dir.-Intl

FINANCIAL DATA: *Note: Data for latest year may not have been available at press time.*

In U.S. $	2021	2020	2019	2018	2017	2016
Revenue		25,667,420,000	24,373,190,000	22,397,240,000	24,395,830,000	23,687,470,000
R&D Expense						
Operating Income		2,339,454,000	2,306,166,000	1,974,622,000	1,768,238,000	2,121,087,000
Operating Margin %						
SGA Expense						
Net Income		1,729,625,000	1,965,301,000	1,331,505,000	1,137,105,000	1,215,664,000
Operating Cash Flow		1,552,535,000	2,126,413,000	1,597,806,000	2,525,864,000	1,636,419,000
Capital Expenditure		635,127,700	625,807,200	661,757,800	633,796,200	652,437,300
EBITDA		3,433,951,000	3,508,515,000	2,585,782,000	2,967,924,000	2,493,908,000
Return on Assets %						
Return on Equity %						
Debt to Equity						

CONTACT INFORMATION:

Phone: 44 1252373232 Fax: 44 1252383991
Toll-Free:
Address: Stirling Square, 6 Carlton Gardens, London, SW1Y 5AD United Kingdom

STOCK TICKER/OTHER:

Stock Ticker: BAESY
Exchange: PINX
Employees: 89,600
Fiscal Year Ends: 12/31
Parent Company:

SALARIES/BONUSES:

Top Exec. Salary: $1,308,869 Bonus: $2,316,818
Second Exec. Salary: $769,610 Bonus: $995,966

OTHER THOUGHTS:

Estimated Female Officers or Directors: 4
Hot Spot for Advancement for Women/Minorities: Y

Bayerische Motoren Werke AG (BMW Group) www.bmwgroup.com

NAIC Code: 336111

TYPES OF BUSINESS:

Automobile Manufacturing
Financial Services
Motorcycles
Software
Consulting Services
Fleet Management
IT Solutions
Engines

BRANDS/DIVISIONS/AFFILIATES:

MINI
Rolls-Royce Motor Cars
BMW Motoren
Bavaria Wirtschaftsagentur GmbH
BMW Technik
X1
i4
C 650 GT

GROWTH PLANS/SPECIAL FEATURES:

In addition to being one of the world's leading premium light-vehicle manufacturers, BMW Group produces BMW motorcycles and provides financial services. Premium light-vehicle brands include BMW, Mini, and ultraluxury brand Rolls-Royce. Operations include 31 production facilities in 15 countries, with a sales network reaching over 140 countries. In 2020, worldwide sales volume exceeded 2.3 million automobiles and more than 179,000 motorcycles.

CONTACTS: *Note: Officers with more than one job title may be intentionally listed here more than once.*

Frank-Peter Arndt, Head-Prod.
Herbert Diess, Dir.-Dev.
Friedrich Eichner, Dir.-Finance
Harald Kruger, Dir.-MINI, Motorcycles, Rolls-Royce & After Sales
Peter Schwarzenbauer, Head-MINI, Rolly-Royce & Aftersales
Oliver Zipse, Chmn.
Klaus Draeger, Chief Purchasing & Supplier Network Officer

FINANCIAL DATA: *Note: Data for latest year may not have been available at press time.*

In U.S. $	2021	2020	2019	2018	2017	2016
Revenue		111,793,700,000	117,688,900,000	110,088,400,000	111,441,400,000	106,342,400,000
R&D Expense						
Operating Income		5,375,676,000	8,546,873,000	10,173,130,000	11,050,630,000	10,507,410,000
Operating Margin %						
SGA Expense		9,932,578,000	10,578,560,000	10,794,270,000	10,796,530,000	10,342,530,000
Net Income		4,263,273,000	5,550,724,000	8,037,540,000	9,734,944,000	7,750,686,000
Operating Cash Flow		14,964,930,000	4,135,657,000	5,704,315,000	6,673,292,000	3,583,408,000
Capital Expenditure		6,945,464,000	7,794,730,000	8,782,906,000	8,031,893,000	6,576,169,000
EBITDA		13,347,710,000	15,397,470,000	17,294,770,000	17,944,140,000	17,111,820,000
Return on Assets %						
Return on Equity %						
Debt to Equity						

CONTACT INFORMATION:

Phone: 49 89 3822 5858   Fax: 49 89 3821 4661
Toll-Free:
Address: Petuelring 130, BMW-HAUS, Munich, BY 80788 Germany

STOCK TICKER/OTHER:

Stock Ticker: BMWYY   Exchange: PINX
Employees: 118,909   Fiscal Year Ends: 12/31
Parent Company:

SALARIES/BONUSES:

Top Exec. Salary: $ Bonus: $
Second Exec. Salary: $ Bonus: $

OTHER THOUGHTS:

Estimated Female Officers or Directors: 5
Hot Spot for Advancement for Women/Minorities: Y

BCE Inc (Bell Canada Enterprises)

www.bce.ca

NAIC Code: 517110

TYPES OF BUSINESS:

Telecommunication Service Provider
Telecommunications
Media
Wireless
Internet
Television Services
Retail

BRANDS/DIVISIONS/AFFILIATES:

GROWTH PLANS/SPECIAL FEATURES:

BCE is both a wireless and Internet service provider, offering wireless, broadband, television, and landline phone services in Canada. It is one of the big three national wireless carriers, with its roughly 10 million customers constituting about 30% of the market. It is also the ILEC (incumbent local exchange carrier--the legacy telephone provider) throughout much of the eastern half of Canada, including in the most populous Canadian provinces--Ontario and Quebec. Additionally, BCE has a media segment, which holds television, radio, and digital media assets. BCE licenses the Canadian rights to movie channels including HBO, Showtime, and Starz. In 2020, the wireline segment accounted for 55% of total EBITDA, while wireless composed 38%, and media provided the remainder.

CONTACTS: *Note: Officers with more than one job title may be intentionally listed here more than once.*

Mirko Bibic, CEO
Claire Gillies, Pres., Subsidiary
Glen LeBlanc, CFO
Gordon Nixon, Chairman of the Board
Robert Malcolmson, Chief Legal Officer
Bernard le Duc, Executive VP, Divisional
Michael Cole, Executive VP, Subsidiary
Stephen Howe, Executive VP, Subsidiary
Devorah Lithwick, Other Executive Officer
Rizwan Jamal, President, Subsidiary
Blaik Kirby, President, Subsidiary
Thomas Little, President, Subsidiary
John Watson, President, Subsidiary
Wade Oosterman, President, Subsidiary

FINANCIAL DATA: *Note: Data for latest year may not have been available at press time.*

In U.S. $	2021	2020	2019	2018	2017	2016
Revenue		17,964,360,000	18,813,000,000	18,423,610,000	17,835,610,000	17,050,560,000
R&D Expense						
Operating Income		4,084,628,000	4,589,417,000	4,271,471,000	4,182,760,000	4,145,078,000
Operating Margin %						
SGA Expense			-108,337,300	62,804,210		
Net Income		2,067,828,000	2,505,103,000	2,299,419,000	2,287,643,000	2,379,494,000
Operating Cash Flow		6,087,298,000	6,247,449,000	5,796,828,000	5,776,417,000	5,215,104,000
Capital Expenditure		3,366,306,000	3,130,790,000	3,161,407,000	3,166,902,000	2,961,218,000
EBITDA		6,928,089,000	7,834,040,000	7,105,511,000	6,975,977,000	6,809,546,000
Return on Assets %						
Return on Equity %						
Debt to Equity						

CONTACT INFORMATION:

Phone: 514-870-8777 Fax: 514 766-5735
Toll-Free: 800-339-6353
Address: 1, carrefour Alexander-Graham Bell, Bldg. A, 7/Fl, Verdun, QC H3E 3B3 Canada

STOCK TICKER/OTHER:

Stock Ticker: BCE
Employees: 49,781
Parent Company:
Exchange: NYS
Fiscal Year Ends: 12/31

SALARIES/BONUSES:

Top Exec. Salary: $1,300,000 Bonus: $
Second Exec. Salary: $900,000 Bonus: $

OTHER THOUGHTS:

Estimated Female Officers or Directors: 4
Hot Spot for Advancement for Women/Minorities: Y

Beijing Qihu Keji Co Ltd (Qihoo 360)

www.360.cn

NAIC Code: 511210E

TYPES OF BUSINESS:

Computer Software: Network Security, Managed Access, Digital ID, Cybersecurity & Anti-Virus
Security Services
Internet and Mobile Security
Virus Protection
Connected Device Protection
Data Shredding
Threat Detection
Cryptocurrency Protection

BRANDS/DIVISIONS/AFFILIATES:

Qihoo 360
360

CONTACTS:

Note: Officers with more than one job title may be intentionally listed here more than once.

Hongzhang Zhou, CEO

GROWTH PLANS/SPECIAL FEATURES:

Beijing Qihu Keji Co., Ltd. does business as Qihoo 360 and is a provider of security services to consumers and businesses. The firm's core internet and mobile security product is 360, which offers personal computers (PCs) protection from viruses, Trojans and other emerging threats. 360 begins with a full check of the overall condition of the device's health and safety; then scans for viruses via antivirus engines; manages and optimizes the computer's system services in order to shorten boot time; cleans up disk space by removing junk files and plugins; and then protects the four modes of performance, balance, security and custom, each of which offer a level of protection from malware, phishing attacks and backdoors. 360 is available for Mac and Android devices. 360 integrates antivirus engines; provides layered protection against phishing, Trojan and data theft; and enables the execution of risky programs in the Sandbox by keeping threats separate from the system and via automatic updates and theme support. 360 is free and can be downloaded from the company's website or mobile app. Its Premium Membership offers data shredding, privacy cleaner, disk analyzer, driver updater, firewall, scheduled cleanup protection, ad-free and more for a minimal annual fee. 360 for governments and businesses is a Qihoo cyber security product that protects against all types of threats in one easy-to-manage scalable solution. It features 360's multi-layered protection against malware and viruses; instant deployment protection; and mobile and web controls that extend management flexibility without resource overheads. 360 also offers a cryptocurrency protection solution, a blockchain wallet protector, an anti-ransomware tool and high-speed compression software. 360 offers home security products, routing products, smart wear products, car products and more.

FINANCIAL DATA:

Note: Data for latest year may not have been available at press time.

In U.S. $	2021	2020	2019	2018	2017	2016
Revenue		1,779,434,863	1,837,600,000	1,908,830,000	1,879,120,000	1,841,851,520
R&D Expense						
Operating Income						
Operating Margin %						
SGA Expense						
Net Income		434,780,776	851,393,000	510,062,000	525,403,000	
Operating Cash Flow						
Capital Expenditure						
EBITDA						
Return on Assets %						
Return on Equity %						
Debt to Equity						

CONTACT INFORMATION:

Phone: 86 1058781000 Fax:
Toll-Free:
Address: Bldg 2, 6 Haoyuan, Jiuxianqiao Rd., Chaoyang Dist, Beijing, 100015 China

STOCK TICKER/OTHER:

Stock Ticker: 601360
Employees: 6,639
Parent Company:
Exchange: Shanghai
Fiscal Year Ends: 12/31

SALARIES/BONUSES:

Top Exec. Salary: $ Bonus: $
Second Exec. Salary: $ Bonus: $

OTHER THOUGHTS:

Estimated Female Officers or Directors:
Hot Spot for Advancement for Women/Minorities:

Beijing Tianyu Communication Equipment Co Ltd (K-Touch)

www.k-touch.cn

NAIC Code: 334220

TYPES OF BUSINESS:

Mobile Phone Research, Development & Manufacturing

BRANDS/DIVISIONS/AFFILIATES:

K-Touch
M1

CONTACTS: *Note: Officers with more than one job title may be intentionally listed here more than once.*

Rong Xiuli, CEO

GROWTH PLANS/SPECIAL FEATURES:

Beijing Tianyu Communication Equipment Co., Ltd. (K-Touch) is a developer, manufacturer and marketer of cell phones and other technological products, and is one of the largest mobile phone manufacturers in China. Founded in 2002, the firm operates through offices across the country, as well as through more than 700 after-sales authorized service centers. It also runs state-of-the-art research and development laboratories which provide up-to-date, in-demand products to the market; and maintains hundreds of technical support service stations across China. K-Touch's current (mid-2019) product line includes flagship phone models K-Touch i9 and i10 mini smartphones, as well as the K-Touch 8848, K-Touch X11, K-Touch 8818 and M1s, featuring various Chinese telecom 3G and 4G networks. Products have been sold in 50 countries and regions, including Asia, Africa and Europe, and can be purchased in retail stores as well as through eCommerce channels. The firm's headquarters are located in the industrial base of the 161,458-square-foot Zhongguan County Technology Garden in Tongzhou, Beijing.

FINANCIAL DATA: *Note: Data for latest year may not have been available at press time.*

In U.S. $	2021	2020	2019	2018	2017	2016
Revenue	380,000,000	367,500,000	350,000,000	336,000,000	320,000,000	300,000,000
R&D Expense						
Operating Income						
Operating Margin %						
SGA Expense						
Net Income						
Operating Cash Flow						
Capital Expenditure						
EBITDA						
Return on Assets %						
Return on Equity %						
Debt to Equity						

CONTACT INFORMATION:

Phone: 8610-589-28888 Fax: 8610-589-29999
Toll-Free: 400-700-9966
Address: No. 55 Jiachuang Ave., 2nd Rd., Beijing, 100111 China

STOCK TICKER/OTHER:

Stock Ticker: Private
Employees: 1,000
Parent Company:
Exchange:
Fiscal Year Ends:

SALARIES/BONUSES:

Top Exec. Salary: $ Bonus: $
Second Exec. Salary: $ Bonus: $

OTHER THOUGHTS:

Estimated Female Officers or Directors: 1
Hot Spot for Advancement for Women/Minorities:

Bharti Airtel Limited

NAIC Code: 517210

www.airtel.in

TYPES OF BUSINESS:

Cell Phone Service
Telecommunications
Mobile Services
Digital TV
Telephone Services
Broadband Services
ICT Services

BRANDS/DIVISIONS/AFFILIATES:

Bharti Enterprises Limited
Singapore Telecommunications Limited

CONTACTS:

Note: Officers with more than one job title may be intentionally listed here more than once.

Gopal Vittal, CEO
Soumen Ray, CFO
Jyoti Pawar, Dir.-Legal & Regulatory
Raghunath Mandava, Dir.-Customer Experience
Manoj Kohli, CEO-International
Jagbir Singh, Dir.-Network Svcs. Group
Sunil Bharti Mittal, Chmn.

GROWTH PLANS/SPECIAL FEATURES:

Bharti Airtel Limited is an Indian telecommunications service provider. With customers and operations spanning India, as well as countries across south Asia and Africa, Airtel is one of India's largest telecommunications firms. The company is divided into four business units: mobile services, home services, Airtel business and digital TV services. The mobile services unit offers prepaid and postpaid voice, data (2G, 3G, 4G LTE and 4G+) and other services, including news updates, mobile internet and email. The home services business unit offers fixed-line telephone and broadband services across pan-India. Product offerings include voice connectivity over fixed-line and high-speed broadband on copper and fiber with speeds up to 100 megabits per second. The Airtel business unit provides information and communication technology (ICT) services in India, and offers a portfolio of services to enterprises, governments, carriers and small/medium businesses. Services include voice, data and video, as well as network integration, data centers, managed services, enterprise mobility applications, digital media, international toll-free services and short-message-system (SMS) hubbing. The digital TV services business unit offers standard and high-definition (HD) digital TV services with 3D capabilities and Dolby surround sound. This division offers hundreds of channels, including HD channels, international channels and interactive services. The firm is 64%-owned by Bharti Enterprises Limited and 36%-owned by Singapore Telecommunications Limited (SingTel).

Bharti Airtel offers its employees sabbaticals, onsite day care and fitness center, concierge service and maternity leave.

FINANCIAL DATA:

Note: Data for latest year may not have been available at press time.

In U.S. $	2021	2020	2019	2018	2017	2016
Revenue	13,800,838,370	11,458,722,139	11,652,878,750	12,741,896,310	14,709,500,000	14,791,625,789
R&D Expense						
Operating Income						
Operating Margin %						
SGA Expense						
Net Income	-1,685,126,652	-4,075,670,815	242,554,500	335,658,538	585,452,000	840,076,842
Operating Cash Flow						
Capital Expenditure						
EBITDA						
Return on Assets %						
Return on Equity %						
Debt to Equity						

CONTACT INFORMATION:

Phone: 91-11-4666-6100 Fax: 91-11-4166-6137
Toll-Free:
Address: 1 Nelson Mandela Rd., Vasant Kunj, Phase II, New Delhi, 110 070 India

STOCK TICKER/OTHER:

Stock Ticker: 532454
Employees: 14,000
Parent Company: Bharti Enterprises
Exchange: Bombay
Fiscal Year Ends: 03/31

SALARIES/BONUSES:

Top Exec. Salary: $ Bonus: $
Second Exec. Salary: $ Bonus: $

OTHER THOUGHTS:

Estimated Female Officers or Directors: 4
Hot Spot for Advancement for Women/Minorities: Y

BlackBerry Limited

www.blackberry.com

NAIC Code: 511210C

TYPES OF BUSINESS:

Computer Software: Telecom, Communications & VOIP
Security Software & Services
Internet of Things
Machine Learning
Endpoint Security
Artificial Intelligence
Intelligent Vehicle Solutions

BRANDS/DIVISIONS/AFFILIATES:

BlackBerry Spark
BlackBerry Protect
BlackBerry Persona
BlackBerry QNX
BlackBerry IVY
BlackBerry AtHoc
BlackBerry Alert
Cylance Inc

CONTACTS: *Note: Officers with more than one job title may be intentionally listed here more than once.*

John Chen, CEO
Steve Rai, CFO
Randall Cook, Chief Legal Officer
Mark Wilson, Chief Marketing Officer
Thomas Eacobacci, COO
Sai Yuen Ho, Executive VP, Divisional
Mattias Eriksson, General Manager, Divisional
Nita White-Ivy, Other Executive Officer
Marjorie Dickman, Other Executive Officer
John Giamatteo, President, Divisional

GROWTH PLANS/SPECIAL FEATURES:

BlackBerry, once known for being the world's largest smartphone manufacturer, is now exclusively a software provider with a stated goal of end-to-end secure communication for enterprises. The firm provides endpoint management and protection to enterprises, specializing in regulated industries like government, as well as embedded software to the automotive, medical, and industrial markets.

BlackBerry's employee benefits vary by location, but can include comprehensive health benefits, reimbursement programs, stock purchase and savings plans, as well as a variety of employee assistance programs.

FINANCIAL DATA: *Note: Data for latest year may not have been available at press time.*

In U.S. $	2021	2020	2019	2018	2017	2016
Revenue	893,000,000	1,040,000,000	904,000,000	932,000,000	1,309,000,000	2,160,000,000
R&D Expense	215,000,000	259,000,000	219,000,000	239,000,000	306,000,000	469,000,000
Operating Income	-98,000,000	-183,000,000	-63,000,000	-189,000,000	-428,000,000	-517,000,000
Operating Margin %						
SGA Expense	344,000,000	493,000,000	406,000,000	467,000,000	553,000,000	712,000,000
Net Income	-1,104,000,000	-152,000,000	93,000,000	405,000,000	-1,206,000,000	-208,000,000
Operating Cash Flow	82,000,000	26,000,000	100,000,000	704,000,000	-224,000,000	257,000,000
Capital Expenditure	44,000,000	44,000,000	49,000,000	45,000,000	69,000,000	102,000,000
EBITDA	100,000,000	29,000,000	86,000,000	-12,000,000	-189,000,000	99,000,000
Return on Assets %						
Return on Equity %						
Debt to Equity						

CONTACT INFORMATION:

Phone: 519 888-7465 Fax: 519 888-7884
Toll-Free:
Address: 2200 University Ave. E., Waterloo, ON N2K 0A7 Canada

STOCK TICKER/OTHER:

Stock Ticker: BB
Employees: 3,497
Parent Company:
Exchange: NYS
Fiscal Year Ends: 02/28

SALARIES/BONUSES:

Top Exec. Salary: $1,000,000 Bonus: $2,000,000
Second Exec. Salary: $555,581 Bonus: $19,719

OTHER THOUGHTS:

Estimated Female Officers or Directors:
Hot Spot for Advancement for Women/Minorities: Y

Blue Yonder Group Inc

NAIC Code: 511210A

blueyonder.com

TYPES OF BUSINESS:

Computer Software: Supply Chain & Logistics
Digital Supply Chain
Commerce
Logistics
Business Planning
Artificial Intelligence
Machine Learning
Internet of Things

BRANDS/DIVISIONS/AFFILIATES:

Panasonic Corporation
Luminate

CONTACTS: *Note: Officers with more than one job title may be intentionally listed here more than once.*

Girish Rishi, CEO
Sue Savage, CFO
Kevin Iaquinto, CMO
David King, Exec. VP-Prod. Dev.
David Kennedy, Chief Legal Officer
David Gai, Exec. VP-Svcs.
Yasu Higuchi, Chmn.

GROWTH PLANS/SPECIAL FEATURES:

Blue Yonder Group, Inc. offers a digital supply chain platform that delivers dynamic commerce experiences from beginning to end. The Luminate platform helps clients predict potential disruptions, find growth opportunities and optimize inventory replenishment. It provides synchronized business planning, execution, delivery and labor solutions by leveraging artificial intelligence (AI) and machine learning (ML) capabilities, as well as workflow-driven user experiences across the entire workplace. Other technologies include cloud transformation, data management, microservices, Internet of Things (IoT), infrastructure orchestration and more. Solutions by Luminate include planning for the delivery of goods to market, inventory optimization, financial management, warehouse integration, transportation/logistics and labor/operations planning and fulfillment information. Blue Yonder serves more than 3,000 customers worldwide, and comprises over 400 granted patents and patents pending. Services by Blue Yonder include cloud transformation, discovery services, education, enablement and expansion. Blue Yonder has offices in more than 40 locations worldwide, including major cities in the U.S., Asia Pacific, Canada, Latin America, Europe, Australia and the Middle East. During 2021, Blue Yonder was fully-acquired by Panasonic Corporation, accelerating both company's vision for an autonomous supply chain. Panasonic will unify its sensing technologies and edge devices with Blue Yonder's AI/ML solutions to create smarter and more connected strategies across ecommerce, retail stores, warehouses, transportation and workplaces.

FINANCIAL DATA: *Note: Data for latest year may not have been available at press time.*

In U.S. $	2021	2020	2019	2018	2017	2016
Revenue	1,300,000,000	1,240,312,500	1,181,250,000	1,125,000,000	935,000,000	850,000,000
R&D Expense						
Operating Income						
Operating Margin %						
SGA Expense						
Net Income						
Operating Cash Flow						
Capital Expenditure						
EBITDA						
Return on Assets %						
Return on Equity %						
Debt to Equity						

CONTACT INFORMATION:

Phone: 480 308-3000 Fax: 480 308-3001
Toll-Free: 800-438-5301
Address: 15059 N. Scottsdale Rd., Ste. 400, Scottsdale, AZ 85254-2666 United States

STOCK TICKER/OTHER:

Stock Ticker: Subsidiary
Employees: 5,500
Parent Company: Panasonic Corporation
Exchange:
Fiscal Year Ends: 12/31

SALARIES/BONUSES:

Top Exec. Salary: $ Bonus: $
Second Exec. Salary: $ Bonus: $

OTHER THOUGHTS:

Estimated Female Officers or Directors: 2
Hot Spot for Advancement for Women/Minorities:

Boeing Company (The)

www.boeing.com

NAIC Code: 336411

TYPES OF BUSINESS:

Aircraft Manufacturing
Aerospace Technology & Manufacturing
Military Aircraft
Satellite Manufacturing
Communications Products & Services
Air Traffic Management Technology
Financing Services
Research & Development

BRANDS/DIVISIONS/AFFILIATES:

Boeing Capital Corporation
737
747
767
777
787

GROWTH PLANS/SPECIAL FEATURES:

Boeing is a major aerospace and defense firm. With headquarters in Chicago, the firm operates in four segments, commercial airplanes, defense, space & security, global services, and Boeing capital. Boeing's commercial airplanes segment generally produces about 60% of sales and two-thirds of operating profit, and it competes with Airbus in the production of aircraft ranging from 130 seats upwards. Boeing's defense, space & security segment competes with Lockheed, Northrop, and several other firms to create military aircraft and weaponry. The defense segment produces about 25% of sales and 13% of operating profit, respectively. Boeing's global services segment provides aftermarket servicing to commercial and military aircraft and produces about 15% of sales and 21% of operating profit.

Boeing offers its employees health and retirement plans, tuition assistance and other programs.

CONTACTS: *Note: Officers with more than one job title may be intentionally listed here more than once.*

Leanne Caret, CEO, Divisional
Gregory Hyslop, Exec. VP, Divisional
Theodore Colbert, CEO, Divisional
Stanley Deal, CEO, Divisional
David Calhoun, CEO
Gregory Smith, CFO
David Dohnalek, Chairman of the Board, Subsidiary
Lawrence Kellner, Chairman of the Board
Carol Hibbard, Chief Accounting Officer
Susan Doniz, Chief Information Officer
Brett Gerry, Chief Legal Officer
Bertrand-Marc Allen, Chief Strategy Officer
Timothy Keating, Executive VP, Divisional
Michael DAmbrose, Executive VP, Divisional
Michael Arthur, President, Divisional
Edward Dandridge, Senior VP, Divisional
Jenette Ramos, Senior VP, Divisional

FINANCIAL DATA: *Note: Data for latest year may not have been available at press time.*

In U.S. $	2021	2020	2019	2018	2017	2016
Revenue		58,158,000,000	76,559,000,000	101,127,000,000	93,392,000,000	94,571,000,000
R&D Expense		2,476,000,000	3,219,000,000	3,269,000,000	3,179,000,000	4,627,000,000
Operating Income		-12,978,000,000	-2,662,000,000	11,801,000,000	10,053,000,000	5,538,000,000
Operating Margin %						
SGA Expense		4,817,000,000	3,909,000,000	4,567,000,000	4,094,000,000	3,616,000,000
Net Income		-11,873,000,000	-636,000,000	10,460,000,000	8,197,000,000	4,895,000,000
Operating Cash Flow		-18,410,000,000	-2,446,000,000	15,322,000,000	13,344,000,000	10,499,000,000
Capital Expenditure		1,303,000,000	1,961,000,000	1,791,000,000	1,870,000,000	2,613,000,000
EBITDA		-10,074,000,000	734,000,000	14,193,000,000	12,476,000,000	7,784,000,000
Return on Assets %						
Return on Equity %						
Debt to Equity						

CONTACT INFORMATION:

Phone: 312 544-2000 Fax:
Toll-Free:
Address: 100 N. Riverside Plz., Chicago, IL 60606-1596 United States

STOCK TICKER/OTHER:

Stock Ticker: BA
Exchange: NYS
Employees: 142,000
Fiscal Year Ends: 12/31
Parent Company:

SALARIES/BONUSES:

Top Exec. Salary: $1,150,000 Bonus: $
Second Exec. Salary: $366,154 Bonus: $750,000

OTHER THOUGHTS:

Estimated Female Officers or Directors: 7
Hot Spot for Advancement for Women/Minorities: Y

Bombardier Inc

www.bombardier.com

NAIC Code: 336411

TYPES OF BUSINESS:

Aircraft Manufacturing
Aircraft
Aircraft Manufacturing
Pre-Owned Aircraft
Business Jets

BRANDS/DIVISIONS/AFFILIATES:

Global
Challenger
Learjet
Bombarider Specialized Aircraft

GROWTH PLANS/SPECIAL FEATURES:

Bombardier Inc is engaged in the manufacture of business aircraft. It designs, manufactures, markets, and provides aftermarket support for Learjet, Challenger, and Global business jets, spanning from the light to large categories; designs manufactures, and provides aftermarket support for a broad portfolio of commercial aircraft in the 50- to 100-seat categories, including the CRJ550, CRJ700, CRJ900, CRJ1000 regional jets, and the Q400 turboprop. The company mainly operates in Europe, North America, Asia-Pacific, and others. The majority of the revenue is generated from North America.

CONTACTS: *Note: Officers with more than one job title may be intentionally listed here more than once.*

Alain Bellemare, CEO
David Coleal, Pres., Divisional
John Di Bert, CFO
Pierre Beaudoin, Chairman of the Board
FranCois Caza, Chief Technology Officer
J. R. Bombardier, Director
Jean-Louis Fontaine, Director
Sameh Abdelmalek, Other Executive Officer
Dimitrios Vounassis, Other Executive Officer
Danny Perna, President, Divisional
Paul Sislian, President, Divisional
Frederick Cromer, President, Divisional
Nico Buchholz, Senior VP, Divisional
Louis Veronneau, Senior VP, Divisional

FINANCIAL DATA: *Note: Data for latest year may not have been available at press time.*

In U.S. $	2021	2020	2019	2018	2017	2016
Revenue		6,487,000,000	15,757,000,000	16,236,000,000	16,218,000,000	16,339,000,000
R&D Expense		320,000,000	292,000,000	217,000,000	240,000,000	287,000,000
Operating Income		-269,000,000	222,000,000	905,000,000	508,000,000	-195,000,000
Operating Margin %						
SGA Expense		420,000,000	1,013,000,000	1,156,000,000	1,194,000,000	1,133,000,000
Net Income		-868,000,000	-1,797,000,000	232,000,000	-516,000,000	-1,022,000,000
Operating Cash Flow		-2,821,000,000	-680,000,000	597,000,000	531,000,000	137,000,000
Capital Expenditure		364,000,000	552,000,000	1,164,000,000	1,389,000,000	1,255,000,000
EBITDA		1,120,000,000	-249,000,000	1,020,000,000	203,000,000	-51,000,000
Return on Assets %						
Return on Equity %						
Debt to Equity						

CONTACT INFORMATION:

Phone: 514 861-9481 Fax: 514 861-2746
Toll-Free:
Address: 800 Rene-Levesque Blvd. W., Montreal, QC H3B 1Y8 Canada

STOCK TICKER/OTHER:

Stock Ticker: BDRXF Exchange: PINX
Employees: 13,800 Fiscal Year Ends: 12/31
Parent Company:

SALARIES/BONUSES:

Top Exec. Salary: $ Bonus: $
Second Exec. Salary: $ Bonus: $

OTHER THOUGHTS:

Estimated Female Officers or Directors: 3
Hot Spot for Advancement for Women/Minorities: Y

Bosch Rexroth AG

www.boschrexroth.com

NAIC Code: 333519

TYPES OF BUSINESS:

Assembly Machines Manufacturing
Engineering Equipment
Manufacturing
Technologies

BRANDS/DIVISIONS/AFFILIATES:

Robert Bosch GmbH

CONTACTS: *Note: Officers with more than one job title may be intentionally listed here more than once.*

Bertram Hoffmann, Head-Production & Quality Mgmt.
Paul Cooke, Sr. VP-Eng.
Stefan Spindler, Head-Mobile Application
Rolf Najork, Chmn.
Rolf-Dieter Amann, Head-Purchasing & Logistics

GROWTH PLANS/SPECIAL FEATURES:

Bosch Rexroth AG is a company specializing in the manufacture of large-scale engineering equipment. Products are manufactured worldwide and sold through sales associates in more than 80 countries. Bosch Rexroth divides its sales between the regions of Asia Pacific & Africa, the Americas and Europe, with over 50% of sales coming out of the European market. The company operates through three segments based on the industries it serves: mobile applications, machinery application & engineering and factory automation. The mobile applications segment sells equipment for several uses, including construction machinery, excavators, materials handling and agricultural and forestry equipment. Products in this segment aim to provide the most power with the lowest emissions. The machinery applications & engineering segment sells machines for a wide range of purposes and for a long list of industries. Some of the products sold in this segment include machines for civil engineering, marine, mining, oil and gas drilling, stage technology, energy technology and machine tools and presses. The factory automation segment manufactures machines used in a variety of factories, including assembly and handling, automotive, semiconductor, electronics, printing, converting, packaging, processing, machine tools (cutting) and solar. This division implements Internet of Things (IoT) technology and connectivity in regards to hydraulic products. Bosch Rexroth's technologies span applications such as assembly, electric drives and controls, industrial hydraulics, linear motion, mobile hydraulics, electronics, IoT, gear, molding and casting, tightening, resistance welding, automated production assistance and mobile robotic components. Bosch Rexroth is a wholly-owned subsidiary of Robert Bosch GmbH.

FINANCIAL DATA: *Note: Data for latest year may not have been available at press time.*

In U.S. $	2021	2020	2019	2018	2017	2016
Revenue	6,500,000,000	6,386,870,000	6,953,130,000	6,917,662,500	6,588,250,000	7,785,898,393
R&D Expense						
Operating Income						
Operating Margin %						
SGA Expense						
Net Income						
Operating Cash Flow						
Capital Expenditure						
EBITDA						
Return on Assets %						
Return on Equity %						
Debt to Equity						

CONTACT INFORMATION:

Phone: 49-9352-18-0 Fax: 49-9352-18-3972
Toll-Free:
Address: Maria-Theresien Strabe 23, Lohr, 97816 Germany

STOCK TICKER/OTHER:

Stock Ticker: Private
Exchange:
Employees: 29,600
Fiscal Year Ends: 12/31
Parent Company: Robert Bosch GmbH

SALARIES/BONUSES:

Top Exec. Salary: $ Bonus: $
Second Exec. Salary: $ Bonus: $

OTHER THOUGHTS:

Estimated Female Officers or Directors:
Hot Spot for Advancement for Women/Minorities:

Broadcom Inc

www.broadcom.com

NAIC Code: 335313

TYPES OF BUSINESS:

Electrical Switches, Sensors, MEMS, Optomechanicals
Semiconductors
Connectivity Technology
Wireless Applications
Optical Products
Mainframe Software
Enterprise Software
Security Software

BRANDS/DIVISIONS/AFFILIATES:

AppNeta Inc

GROWTH PLANS/SPECIAL FEATURES:

Broadcom--the combined entity of Broadcom and Avago--boasts a highly diverse product portfolio across an array of end markets. Avago focused primarily on radio frequency filters and amplifiers used in high-end smartphones, such as the Apple iPhone and Samsung Galaxy devices, in addition to an assortment of solutions for wired infrastructure, enterprise storage, and industrial end markets. Legacy Broadcom targeted networking semiconductors, such as switch and physical layer chips, broadband products (such as television set-top box processors), and connectivity chips that handle standards such as Wi-Fi and Bluetooth. The company has acquired Brocade, CA Technologies, and Symantec's enterprise security business to bolster its offerings in infrastructure software.

CONTACTS: *Note: Officers with more than one job title may be intentionally listed here more than once.*

Hock Tan, CEO
Kirsten Spears, CFO
Henry Samueli, Chairman of the Board
Mark Brazeal, Chief Legal Officer
Charles Kawwas, COO
Thomas Krause, President, Divisional

FINANCIAL DATA: *Note: Data for latest year may not have been available at press time.*

In U.S. $	2021	2020	2019	2018	2017	2016
Revenue		23,888,000,000	22,597,000,000	20,848,000,000	17,636,000,000	13,240,000,000
R&D Expense		4,968,000,000	4,696,000,000	3,768,000,000	3,292,000,000	2,674,000,000
Operating Income		4,212,000,000	4,180,000,000	5,368,000,000	2,666,000,000	587,000,000
Operating Margin %						
SGA Expense		1,935,000,000	1,709,000,000	1,056,000,000	787,000,000	806,000,000
Net Income		2,960,000,000	2,724,000,000	12,259,000,000	1,692,000,000	-1,739,000,000
Operating Cash Flow		12,061,000,000	9,697,000,000	8,880,000,000	6,551,000,000	3,411,000,000
Capital Expenditure		463,000,000	432,000,000	635,000,000	1,069,000,000	723,000,000
EBITDA		11,125,000,000	9,478,000,000	9,254,000,000	7,016,000,000	2,520,000,000
Return on Assets %						
Return on Equity %						
Debt to Equity						

CONTACT INFORMATION:

Phone: 408-433-8000 Fax:
Toll-Free:
Address: 1320 Ridder Park Dr., San Jose, CA 95131-2313 United States

STOCK TICKER/OTHER:

Stock Ticker: AVGO
Employees: 21,000
Parent Company:
Exchange: NAS
Fiscal Year Ends: 10/31

SALARIES/BONUSES:

Top Exec. Salary: $1,171,154 Bonus: $
Second Exec. Salary: $485,577 Bonus: $455,062

OTHER THOUGHTS:

Estimated Female Officers or Directors: 5
Hot Spot for Advancement for Women/Minorities: Y

BT Group plc

www.btplc.com

NAIC Code: 517110

TYPES OF BUSINESS:

Telecommunications Services
Communications Networks
Telecommunications Equipment Distribution
International Broadband Networks
Consulting Services
Internet Service Provider
Local & Long-Distance Phone Service
Networking Services

BRANDS/DIVISIONS/AFFILIATES:

British Telecommunications plc
BT
EE
Plusnet
Openreach

GROWTH PLANS/SPECIAL FEATURES:

BT Group is the incumbent fixed-line phone company in the U.K., providing phone, Internet access, and television services to residential and business customers. The firm acquired wireless carrier EE in 2016. It also runs a global services business that is still one of the largest international providers of managed networks and information technology services. The firm is organized into four segments: consumer services (46% of reported revenue), enterprise services (26%), global services (18%), and Openreach (11%, net of sales to other BT units). Openreach holds much of BT's network infrastructure and sells access to BT's retail units and other carriers.

Most BT employees in the UK can receive broadband, BT TV, BT Sport and BT Mobile products either for free or at discounted rates. The firm also offers a retirement savings scheme and optional health benefits.

CONTACTS: *Note: Officers with more than one job title may be intentionally listed here more than once.*

Philip Jansen, CEO
Simon Lowth, CFO
Dan Fitz, General Counsel
Jan du Plessis, Chmn.
Stephen Yeo, CEO-South East Asia

FINANCIAL DATA: *Note: Data for latest year may not have been available at press time.*

In U.S. $	2021	2020	2019	2018	2017	2016
Revenue	28,402,330,000	30,498,120,000	31,194,490,000	31,587,280,000	32,038,660,000	25,354,510,000
R&D Expense						
Operating Income	4,232,854,000	4,922,573,000	5,079,691,000	5,283,410,000	5,479,142,000	5,436,534,000
Operating Margin %						
SGA Expense	2,359,426,000	2,732,248,000	3,170,313,000	3,070,450,000	3,532,482,000	2,910,669,000
Net Income	1,959,975,000	2,308,829,000	2,874,719,000	2,705,618,000	2,540,511,000	3,445,934,000
Operating Cash Flow	7,939,762,000	8,349,866,000	5,666,884,000	6,560,324,000	8,220,710,000	6,895,863,000
Capital Expenditure	6,528,368,000	5,465,827,000	4,897,274,000	4,476,518,000	4,187,582,000	3,283,490,000
EBITDA	9,164,747,000	10,048,870,000	9,267,273,000	9,148,769,000	8,982,330,000	8,524,293,000
Return on Assets %						
Return on Equity %						
Debt to Equity						

CONTACT INFORMATION:

Phone: 44 2073565000 Fax: 44 2073565520
Toll-Free:
Address: 81 Newgate St., London, EC1A 7AJ United Kingdom

STOCK TICKER/OTHER:

Stock Ticker: BTGOF
Employees: 99,700
Parent Company:
Exchange: PINX
Fiscal Year Ends: 03/31

SALARIES/BONUSES:

Top Exec. Salary: $1,464,655 Bonus: $1,757,586
Second Exec. Salary: $978,656 Bonus: $1,175,719

OTHER THOUGHTS:

Estimated Female Officers or Directors: 1
Hot Spot for Advancement for Women/Minorities: Y

C3.ai Inc

c3.ai

NAIC Code: 511210H

TYPES OF BUSINESS:

Computer Software, Business Management & ERP
Enterprise Artificial Intelligence Software
Digital Transformation Solutions

BRANDS/DIVISIONS/AFFILIATES:

C3 AI

GROWTH PLANS/SPECIAL FEATURES:

C3.ai Inc is an enterprise artificial intelligence company. The company provides software-as-a-service applications that enable customers to rapidly develop, deploy, and operate large-scale Enterprise AI applications across any infrastructure. It provides solutions under three divisions namely, The C3 AI Suite, is a comprehensive application development and runtime environment that is designed to allow customers to rapidly design, develop, and deploy Enterprise AI applications of any type; C3 AI Applications, include a large and growing family of industry-specific and application-specific turnkey AI solutions that can be immediately installed and deployed; and C3.ai Ex Machina, analytics for applying data science to every-day business decisions.

C3.ai offers comprehensive health benefits, life insurance, 401K, education assistance, career training and more.

CONTACTS: *Note: Officers with more than one job title may be intentionally listed here more than once.*

Thomas Siebel, CEO
David Barter, CFO
Bruce Cleveland, Chief Marketing Officer
Edward Abbo, Chief Technology Officer
Patricia House, Co-Founder
Brady Mickelsen, General Counsel
Houman Behzadi, Other Executive Officer

FINANCIAL DATA: *Note: Data for latest year may not have been available at press time.*

In U.S. $	2021	2020	2019	2018	2017	2016
Revenue	183,217,000	156,666,000	91,605,000			
R&D Expense	68,856,000	64,548,000	37,318,000			
Operating Income	-60,258,000	-71,497,000	-36,042,000			
Operating Margin %						
SGA Expense	130,100,000	124,828,000	59,943,000			
Net Income	-55,696,000	-69,378,000	-33,346,000			
Operating Cash Flow	-37,553,000	-61,281,000	-34,876,000			
Capital Expenditure	1,628,000	2,879,000	6,811,000			
EBITDA	-55,961,000	-70,195,000	-35,492,000			
Return on Assets %						
Return on Equity %						
Debt to Equity						

CONTACT INFORMATION:

Phone: 650-503-2200 Fax:
Toll-Free:
Address: 1300 Seaport Blvd., Ste. 500, Redwood City, CA 94063 United States

STOCK TICKER/OTHER:

Stock Ticker: AI
Employees: 714
Parent Company:
Exchange: NYS
Fiscal Year Ends: 04/30

SALARIES/BONUSES:

Top Exec. Salary: $550,000 Bonus: $
Second Exec. Salary: $223,398 Bonus: $100,000

OTHER THOUGHTS:

Estimated Female Officers or Directors:
Hot Spot for Advancement for Women/Minorities:

CACI International Inc

www.caci.com

NAIC Code: 541512

TYPES OF BUSINESS:

Consulting-InfoTech Related
Enterprise Technology
Mission Technology
Security
Information Technology
Cloud
Command and Control
Electronic Warfare

BRANDS/DIVISIONS/AFFILIATES:

SA Photonics Inc

GROWTH PLANS/SPECIAL FEATURES:

CACI International is an information solutions and services provider, offering a variety of information solutions and services to its customers. The company's primary customers are agencies and departments of the U.S. government, which account for the vast majority of the firm's revenue. It provides information solutions and services supporting national security missions and government modernization/transformation for intelligence, defense, and federal civilian customers. The firm conducts its operations through a variety of subsidiaries in the United States and Europe.

CONTACTS: *Note: Officers with more than one job title may be intentionally listed here more than once.*

Gregory Bradford, CEO, Subsidiary
John Mengucci, CEO
Thomas Mutryn, CFO
Michael Daniels, Chairman of the Board
Christopher Voci, Chief Accounting Officer
J. Koegel, Executive VP
Todd Probert, President, Divisional
Meisha Lutsey, President, Divisional
DeEtte Gray, President, Divisional

FINANCIAL DATA: *Note: Data for latest year may not have been available at press time.*

In U.S. $	2021	2020	2019	2018	2017	2016
Revenue	6,044,135,000	5,720,042,000	4,986,341,000	4,467,860,000	4,354,617,000	3,744,053,000
R&D Expense						
Operating Income	539,451,000	457,696,000	377,867,000	340,700,000	297,261,000	264,750,000
Operating Margin %						
SGA Expense						
Net Income	457,443,000	321,480,000	265,604,000	301,171,000	163,671,000	142,799,000
Operating Cash Flow	592,215,000	518,705,000	555,297,000	325,127,000	281,250,000	242,577,000
Capital Expenditure	73,129,000	72,303,000	47,902,000	41,594,000	43,268,000	20,835,000
EBITDA	664,814,000	568,384,000	463,744,000	412,896,000	369,021,000	329,502,000
Return on Assets %						
Return on Equity %						
Debt to Equity						

CONTACT INFORMATION:

Phone: 703 841-7800 Fax: 703 841-7882
Toll-Free:
Address: 12021 Sunset Hills Rd., Reston, VA 20190 United States

STOCK TICKER/OTHER:

Stock Ticker: CACI
Employees: 22,900
Parent Company:
Exchange: NYS
Fiscal Year Ends: 06/30

SALARIES/BONUSES:

Top Exec. Salary: $995,833 Bonus: $
Second Exec. Salary: $642,417 Bonus: $

OTHER THOUGHTS:

Estimated Female Officers or Directors: 5
Hot Spot for Advancement for Women/Minorities: Y

Cambricon Technologies Corporation Limited www.cambricon.com

NAIC Code: 334413

TYPES OF BUSINESS:

Semiconductor and Related Device Manufacturing
Artificial Intelligence
Processor Chips
Machine Learning Processor Chip
Cloud AI Chips
Circuit Board Products
Smart Accelerator Cards
Computing Power Support Products

BRANDS/DIVISIONS/AFFILIATES:

Cambrian 1A
Cambricon-1M
Cambricon-1H
Silu 100
Siyuan
Xuansi

CONTACTS: *Note: Officers with more than one job title may be intentionally listed here more than once.*

Tianshi Chen, CEO

GROWTH PLANS/SPECIAL FEATURES:

Cambricon Technologies Corporation Limited develops global artificial intelligence (AI) chips. The firm is dedicated to building core processor chips for intelligent cloud servers, smart terminals and intelligent robots. Cambricon launched its first processor the year the company was founded, 2016, the Cambrian 1A, which is a terminal AI special processor that has been applied to tens of millions of smart phones and other terminal devices. Other intelligent terminal processors include Cambricon-1M and 1H. The company's Silu 100 (MLU100) machine learning processor chip has a performance-to-power ratio that surpasses CPU (central processing unit) and GPU (graphics processing unit) when running mainstream intelligent algorithms. MLU stands for mean length utterance, which measures linguistic utterances spoken within a given timeframe. Cambricon's Siyuan brand offers next-generation cloud AI chips and board products, which process the theoretical peak performance of non-sparse deep learning models to improve the previous generation chip. Siyuan 270, 290 and 370 series of smart accelerator cards provide customers with energy-efficient solutions in various fields such as intelligent video analysis, speech synthesis, recommendation engine, AI cloud and more. Xuansi 1000 is a smart accelerator used as a basic building unit of automatic identification and data capture (AIDC), and integrates with Siyuan 290 smart chips in a 2U classis. Cambricon's edge AI series products include the Siyuan 220, which offers three-dimensional coverage in the cloud, edge and end, which further enriches and improves its end-cloud integrated product system. The Siyuan 220 series also provides customers with highly-optimized AI computing power support. Based in Beijing, China, the firm has offices in Shanghai, Shenzhen, Hefei and Xi'an.

FINANCIAL DATA: *Note: Data for latest year may not have been available at press time.*

In U.S. $	2021	2020	2019	2018	2017	2016
Revenue		70,309,900	63,528,900			
R&D Expense						
Operating Income						
Operating Margin %						
SGA Expense						
Net Income		-66,568,900	-168,736,000			
Operating Cash Flow						
Capital Expenditure						
EBITDA						
Return on Assets %						
Return on Equity %						
Debt to Equity						

CONTACT INFORMATION:

Phone: 86-10-83030003 Fax:
Toll-Free:
Address: Fl. 11-17, Block D, Zhizhen Bldg., No.7 Zhichun Rd., Beijing, 100000 China

STOCK TICKER/OTHER:

Stock Ticker: 688256
Employees: 1,268
Parent Company:
Exchange: Shanghai
Fiscal Year Ends: 12/31

SALARIES/BONUSES:

Top Exec. Salary: $ Bonus: $
Second Exec. Salary: $ Bonus: $

OTHER THOUGHTS:

Estimated Female Officers or Directors:
Hot Spot for Advancement for Women/Minorities:

Capgemini SE

www.capgemini.com

NAIC Code: 541512

TYPES OF BUSINESS:

IT Consulting
Business Consulting
Digital Transformation
Technology
Engineering Services
Cloud
Managed Services

BRANDS/DIVISIONS/AFFILIATES:

Capgemini Invent
Empired Limited

GROWTH PLANS/SPECIAL FEATURES:

Capgemini is a French IT services company with a global presence. The firm has over 450 offices globally, with more than half of its employees based in India. Capgemini provides services related to IT consulting, infrastructure management, and business process outsourcing.

CONTACTS: *Note: Officers with more than one job title may be intentionally listed here more than once.*

Aiman Ezzat, CEO
Olivier Sevillia, COO
Carole Ferrand, CFO
Anne Lebel, Chief Human Resources Officer
Jean-Baptiste Massignon, Gen. Sec.
Pierre-Yves Cros, Chief Dev. Officer
Philippe Grangeon, Head-Comm.
John Brahim, Deputy CEO
Francois Hucher, Dir.-Delivery
Christopher Stancombe, Head-Bus. Process Outsourcing
Paul Nannetti, Global Sales & Portfolio
Aruna Jayanthi, Head-India

FINANCIAL DATA: *Note: Data for latest year may not have been available at press time.*

In U.S. $	2021	2020	2019	2018	2017	2016
Revenue		17,897,840,000	15,951,980,000	14,903,950,000	14,446,570,000	14,160,840,000
R&D Expense						
Operating Income		1,985,386,000	1,767,423,000	1,593,504,000	1,526,873,000	1,490,734,000
Operating Margin %						
SGA Expense		2,548,929,000	2,382,915,000	2,228,195,000	2,135,589,000	2,163,823,000
Net Income		1,080,782,000	966,718,300	824,420,900	926,061,900	1,040,126,000
Operating Cash Flow		1,875,840,000	2,026,043,000	1,576,564,000	1,502,027,000	1,489,604,000
Capital Expenditure		232,644,800	250,714,300	266,525,100	272,171,800	222,480,700
EBITDA		2,464,228,000	2,273,369,000	1,762,905,000	1,695,145,000	1,656,747,000
Return on Assets %						
Return on Equity %						
Debt to Equity						

CONTACT INFORMATION:

Phone: 33 147545000 Fax: 33 142273210
Toll-Free:
Address: 11 rue de Tilsitt, Paris, 75017 France

STOCK TICKER/OTHER:

Stock Ticker: CGEMY
Employees: 219,314
Parent Company:
Exchange: PINX
Fiscal Year Ends: 12/31

SALARIES/BONUSES:

Top Exec. Salary: $ Bonus: $
Second Exec. Salary: $ Bonus: $

OTHER THOUGHTS:

Estimated Female Officers or Directors: 4
Hot Spot for Advancement for Women/Minorities: Y

Carbon Black Inc

NAIC Code: 511210E

www.carbonblack.com

TYPES OF BUSINESS:

Computer Software, Network Security, Managed Access, Digital ID, Cybersecurity & Anti-Virus

BRANDS/DIVISIONS/AFFILIATES:

VMWare Inc
Cb Defense
Cb Defense for Vmware
Cb Response
Cb Protection
VMWare Carbon Black Cloud

CONTACTS: *Note: Officers with more than one job title may be intentionally listed here more than once.*

Patrick Morley, CEO
Ryan Polk, Senior VP

GROWTH PLANS/SPECIAL FEATURES:

Carbon Black, Inc. is a security solutions company. Its next-generation endpoint security enables organizations to disrupt advanced attacks. Carbon Black's products include: VMWare Carbon Black Cloud, Cb Defense, Db Defense for VMware, Cb Response and Cb Protection. VMWare Carbon Black Cloud is a consolidated endpoint security platform that delivers innovative security services through the cloud. It applies big data analytics across all endpoints to make predictions about, and provide protection from, current, future and unknown attacks. CB Defense is a next-generation antivirus plus endpoint detection and response (EDR) in one cloud-delivered platform. Its stops commodity malware, advanced malware, non-malware attacks and ransomware. Cb Defense for VMware is an integrated solution with VMware AppDefense that provides threat detection and in-depth application behavior insight to stop attacks in-progress and accelerate response. Cb Response is a high-scalable, real-time EDR with visibility for top security operations centers and incident response teams. Cb Protection locks down servers and critical systems with 100% efficacy; its stopped 100% of attacks in NSS Labs' Advanced Endpoint Protection test. In addition, Cb Protection enables: continuous compliance for key frameworks including PCI-DSS, HIPAA, SOX, FISMA and NERC; the monitoring of critical activity and the enforcement of configurations for assessing risk and maintaining system integrity; and the security of end-of-life systems with change-control and whitelisting policies. Industries that utilize Carbon Black products include finance, local and federal governments, healthcare, manufacturing, oil/gas/utilities, retail and hospitality. Carbon Black is headquartered in Waltham, Massachusetts, with additional U.S. offices located in Boston, Colorado California and Texas as well as internationally in the U.K., Singapore, Japan and Australia.

FINANCIAL DATA: *Note: Data for latest year may not have been available at press time.*

In U.S. $	2021	2020	2019	2018	2017	2016
Revenue	272,000,000	264,252,240	251,668,800	209,724,000	162,014,000	112,857,000
R&D Expense						
Operating Income						
Operating Margin %						
SGA Expense						
Net Income			-77,954,150	-82,057,000	-55,827,000	-44,709,000
Operating Cash Flow						
Capital Expenditure						
EBITDA						
Return on Assets %						
Return on Equity %						
Debt to Equity						

CONTACT INFORMATION:

Phone: 617-393-7400 Fax: 617-393-7499
Toll-Free:
Address: 1100 Winter St., Waltham, MA 02451 United States

STOCK TICKER/OTHER:

Stock Ticker: Subsidiary
Exchange:
Employees: 932
Fiscal Year Ends: 12/31
Parent Company: VMWare Inc

SALARIES/BONUSES:

Top Exec. Salary: $ Bonus: $
Second Exec. Salary: $ Bonus: $

OTHER THOUGHTS:

Estimated Female Officers or Directors:
Hot Spot for Advancement for Women/Minorities:

Cegedim SA

NAIC Code: 511210D

www.cegedim.com/Pages/default.aspx

TYPES OF BUSINESS:

Computer Software, Healthcare & Biotechnology
Databases
Pharmaceuticals Marketing & Tracking Software
Compliance Services
Market Research
Sales Force Optimization Services
Consulting
Outsourcing

BRANDS/DIVISIONS/AFFILIATES:

CONTACTS:

Note: Officers with more than one job title may be intentionally listed here more than once.

Jean-Claude Labrune, CEO
Pierre Marucchi, Managing Dir.
Laurent Labrune, Managing Dir.
Bruno Sarfati, CEO-Cegedim Strategic Data
Arnaud Guyon, Dir.-e-bus.
Daniel Flis, Dir.-Comm.
Laurent Labrune, CEO-Cegedim Relationship Mgmt.
Jean-Louis Lompre, Dir.-Customer Info.
Alain Missoffe, Dir.-Health Care Software
Jean-Claude Labrune, Chmn.

GROWTH PLANS/SPECIAL FEATURES:

Cegedim SA is a global technology and services company. The firm supplies services, technological tools, specialized software, data flow management services and databases. Its offerings primarily serve the healthcare industry across insurance, digitization, human resource, payroll, outsourcing and hosting business divisions. Cegedim Healthcare Software offers a complete range of IT solutions such as medical software, pharmacist software and a drug database. Innovative solutions are provided for optimizing sales outlets, digital promotion, information, training, remote management or implementing services based on real-time data and sales statistics. Cegedim's insurance solutions support social protection professionals in the management and marketing of offers, covering the entire health and welfare value chain. Cegedim's eBusiness software supports companies in dematerializing their management documents and automating their processes, from order to payment through the invoice, with more than 120,000 globally-connected companies in the database. Cegedim SRH intervenes in the human resource outsourcing market by proposing innovative solutions and services, from payroll management to HR management, based on smart capabilities and features. Last, Cegedim Outsourcing is a cloud-based outsourcing and hosting application that covers business and IT processes, enabling an agile operational workflow. Cegedim is based in France, and operates in 10 countries.

FINANCIAL DATA:

Note: Data for latest year may not have been available at press time.

In U.S. $	2021	2020	2019	2018	2017	2016
Revenue		610,315,000	564,074,000	534,951,000	547,903,000	452,293,000
R&D Expense						
Operating Income						
Operating Margin %						
SGA Expense						
Net Income		13,265,000	4,031,500	6,633,990	8,504,830	-31,080,000
Operating Cash Flow						
Capital Expenditure						
EBITDA						
Return on Assets %						
Return on Equity %						
Debt to Equity						

CONTACT INFORMATION:

Phone: 33-1-49-09-22-00 Fax: 33-1-46-03-45-95
Toll-Free:
Address: 137 rue d'Aguesseau, Boulogne-Billancourt, 92100 France

STOCK TICKER/OTHER:

Stock Ticker: CGDM
Employees: 5,300
Parent Company:
Exchange: Paris
Fiscal Year Ends: 12/31

SALARIES/BONUSES:

Top Exec. Salary: $ Bonus: $
Second Exec. Salary: $ Bonus: $

OTHER THOUGHTS:

Estimated Female Officers or Directors: 2
Hot Spot for Advancement for Women/Minorities:

Cemtrex Inc

www.cemtrex.com

NAIC Code: 334513

TYPES OF BUSINESS:

Instruments and Related Products Manufacturing for Measuring, Displaying, and Controlling Industrial Process Variables
Internet of Things
Advanced Technologies
Industrial Services
Smart Devices
Security and Surveillance

BRANDS/DIVISIONS/AFFILIATES:

Vicon Industries
Virtual Driver Interactive

GROWTH PLANS/SPECIAL FEATURES:

Cemtrex Inc is a multi-industry technology company that is engaged in the development of markets such as Internet of Things, Augmented and Virtual Reality, and Artificial Intelligence and Computer Vision in a wide range of sectors, including consumer products, industrial manufacturing, digital applications, and intelligent security and surveillance systems. The company's operating segment includes Advanced Technologies and Industrial Services. It generates maximum revenue from the Advanced Technologies segment.

CONTACTS: *Note: Officers with more than one job title may be intentionally listed here more than once.*

Saagar Govil, CEO
Christopher Moore, CFO

FINANCIAL DATA: *Note: Data for latest year may not have been available at press time.*

In U.S. $	2021	2020	2019	2018	2017	2016
Revenue		43,518,380	39,265,040	89,936,520	120,628,200	93,704,560
R&D Expense		1,827,286	1,481,879	5,558,682		
Operating Income		-4,033,505	-7,447,350	-10,900,670	5,115,678	5,063,898
Operating Margin %						
SGA Expense		21,570,670	21,528,140	36,727,240	34,797,870	24,149,770
Net Income		-9,933,775	-22,364,940	-9,240,409	4,389,915	4,994,045
Operating Cash Flow		-4,093,057	3,935,474	-2,802,336	1,107,727	7,895,211
Capital Expenditure		1,566,014	1,659,480	12,207,320	5,677,666	663,834
EBITDA		1,502,473	-4,838,845	-5,196,104	8,571,125	9,053,839
Return on Assets %						
Return on Equity %						
Debt to Equity						

CONTACT INFORMATION:

Phone: 631 756-9116 Fax: 631 420-4985
Toll-Free:
Address: 276 Greenpoint Ave., Ste. 208, Brooklyn, NY 11222 United States

STOCK TICKER/OTHER:

Stock Ticker: CETX
Employees: 344
Parent Company:
Exchange: NAS
Fiscal Year Ends: 09/30

SALARIES/BONUSES:

Top Exec. Salary: $376,923 Bonus: $612,303
Second Exec. Salary: $276,923 Bonus: $243,140

OTHER THOUGHTS:

Estimated Female Officers or Directors:
Hot Spot for Advancement for Women/Minorities:

Cerner Corporation

www.cerner.com

NAIC Code: 511210D

TYPES OF BUSINESS:

Computer Software, Healthcare & Biotechnology
Medical Information Systems
Application Hosting
Integrated Delivery Networks
Access Management
Consulting Services
Safety & Risk Management

BRANDS/DIVISIONS/AFFILIATES:

Cerner Millennium
HealtheIntent
Cerner Health Services Inc
CernerWorks
Kantar Health

GROWTH PLANS/SPECIAL FEATURES:

Cerner is a leading supplier of healthcare information technology solutions and tech-enabled services. The company is a long-standing market leader in the electronic health record industry, and along with rival Epic Systems corners a majority of the market for acute care EHR within health systems. The company is guided by the mission of the founding partners to provide seamless medical records across all healthcare providers to improve outcomes. Beyond medical records, the company offers a wide range of technology that supports the clinical, financial, and operational needs of healthcare facilities.

CONTACTS: *Note: Officers with more than one job title may be intentionally listed here more than once.*

Mark Erceg, CFO
Brent Shafer, Chairman of the Board
Michael Battaglioli, Chief Accounting Officer
Daniel Devers, Chief Legal Officer
Jerome Labat, Chief Technology Officer
Travis Dalton, Executive VP
Tracy Platt, Executive VP
Donald Trigg, President

FINANCIAL DATA: *Note: Data for latest year may not have been available at press time.*

In U.S. $	2021	2020	2019	2018	2017	2016
Revenue		5,505,788,000	5,692,598,000	5,366,325,000	5,142,272,000	4,796,473,000
R&D Expense		749,007,000	737,136,000	683,663,000	605,046,000	551,418,000
Operating Income		694,044,000	600,669,000	774,785,000	960,471,000	911,013,000
Operating Margin %						
SGA Expense		3,074,201,000	3,195,935,000	2,883,165,000	2,632,088,000	2,464,380,000
Net Income		780,088,000	529,454,000	630,059,000	866,978,000	636,484,000
Operating Cash Flow		1,436,705,000	1,313,099,000	1,454,009,000	1,307,675,000	1,155,612,000
Capital Expenditure		617,501,000	780,976,000	757,440,000	665,877,000	771,595,000
EBITDA		1,717,976,000	1,356,947,000	1,451,429,000	1,555,864,000	1,427,149,000
Return on Assets %						
Return on Equity %						
Debt to Equity						

CONTACT INFORMATION:

Phone: 816 221-1024 Fax:
Toll-Free:
Address: 2800 Rock Creek Pkwy., North Kansas City, MO 64117 United States

STOCK TICKER/OTHER:

Stock Ticker: CERN
Employees: 27,400
Parent Company:
Exchange: NAS
Fiscal Year Ends: 12/31

SALARIES/BONUSES:

Top Exec. Salary: $849,176 Bonus: $
Second Exec. Salary: $697,115 Bonus: $

OTHER THOUGHTS:

Estimated Female Officers or Directors: 13
Hot Spot for Advancement for Women/Minorities: Y

CEVA Inc

www.ceva-dsp.com

NAIC Code: 334413

TYPES OF BUSINESS:

Semiconductor and Related Device Manufacturing
Digital Signal Processing
System on Chip
Technology
Artificial Intelligence
Machine Learning

BRANDS/DIVISIONS/AFFILIATES:

Intrinsix Corp

GROWTH PLANS/SPECIAL FEATURES:

CEVA Inc is a licensor of signal-processing intellectual property. Through partnerships with semiconductor companies and original equipment manufacturers globally, the company helps produce devices for a range of end markets. OEMs and semiconductor companies choose to sell products with CEVA equipment to wireless, consumer, automotive, and Internet of Things companies. Revenue is derived primarily from licensing fees and related revenue, and royalties generated from the shipments of products utilizing its intellectual properties. CEVA also engages in the training and sale of development systems.

CONTACTS: *Note: Officers with more than one job title may be intentionally listed here more than once.*

Gideon Wertheizer, CEO
Yaniv Arieli, CFO
Peter Mcmanamon, Chairman of the Board
Michael Boukaya, COO
Issachar Ohana, Executive VP, Divisional

FINANCIAL DATA: *Note: Data for latest year may not have been available at press time.*

In U.S. $	2021	2020	2019	2018	2017	2016
Revenue		100,326,000	87,152,000	77,877,000	87,507,000	72,653,000
R&D Expense		62,010,000	52,843,000	47,755,000	40,385,000	30,838,000
Operating Income		-763,000	-1,924,000	-1,245,000	15,873,000	14,386,000
Operating Margin %						
SGA Expense		26,023,000	24,204,000	22,515,000	23,060,000	20,107,000
Net Income		-2,379,000	28,000	574,000	17,028,000	13,100,000
Operating Cash Flow		15,163,000	9,674,000	8,612,000	24,469,000	14,459,000
Capital Expenditure		2,935,000	10,825,000	5,279,000	4,135,000	2,387,000
EBITDA		5,058,000	3,345,000	2,912,000	19,123,000	17,021,000
Return on Assets %						
Return on Equity %						
Debt to Equity						

CONTACT INFORMATION:

Phone: 240-308-8328 Fax:
Toll-Free:
Address: 15245 Shady Grove Rd., Ste. 400, Rockville, MD 20850 United States

STOCK TICKER/OTHER:

Stock Ticker: CEVA
Employees: 404
Parent Company:
Exchange: NAS
Fiscal Year Ends: 12/31

SALARIES/BONUSES:

Top Exec. Salary: $475,729 Bonus: $
Second Exec. Salary: $293,456 Bonus: $

OTHER THOUGHTS:

Estimated Female Officers or Directors:
Hot Spot for Advancement for Women/Minorities:

Check Point Software Technologies Ltd

www.checkpoint.com

NAIC Code: 511210E

TYPES OF BUSINESS:

Computer Software: Network Security, Managed Access, Digital ID, Cybersecurity & Anti-Virus
Security Software Development
Network Security
Cloud Security
User Access Security
Software Management Solutions

BRANDS/DIVISIONS/AFFILIATES:

Quantum
CloudGuard
Harmony
Infinity-Vision
Avanan

GROWTH PLANS/SPECIAL FEATURES:

Check Point Software Technologies is a pure-play cybersecurity vendor. The company offers solutions for network, endpoint, cloud, and mobile security in addition to security management. Check Point, a software specialist, sells to enterprises, businesses, and consumers. At the end of 2020, 45% of its revenue was from the Americas, 43% from Europe, and 12% from Asia-Pacific, Middle East, and Africa. The firm, based in Tel Aviv, Israel, was founded in 1993 and has about 5,000 employees.

CONTACTS: *Note: Officers with more than one job title may be intentionally listed here more than once.*

Gil Shwed, CEO
Tal Payne, CFO
Peter Alexander, CMO
Yiftah Yoffe, Chief Human Resources Officer
Dorit Dor, Chief Product Officer
Jerry Ungerman, Chmn.

FINANCIAL DATA: *Note: Data for latest year may not have been available at press time.*

In U.S. $	2021	2020	2019	2018	2017	2016
Revenue		2,064,900,000	1,994,800,000	1,916,475,000	1,854,658,000	1,741,301,000
R&D Expense		252,800,000	239,200,000	211,523,000	192,386,000	178,372,000
Operating Income		904,200,000	881,800,000	913,774,000	923,917,000	852,270,000
Operating Margin %						
SGA Expense		681,400,000	658,400,000	589,799,000	525,392,000	508,656,000
Net Income		846,600,000	825,700,000	821,305,000	802,923,000	724,847,000
Operating Cash Flow		1,161,000,000	1,104,300,000	1,143,081,000	1,109,608,000	946,237,000
Capital Expenditure		19,300,000	25,900,000	17,149,000	28,784,000	24,050,000
EBITDA		931,300,000	905,800,000	934,562,000	940,553,000	867,006,000
Return on Assets %						
Return on Equity %						
Debt to Equity						

CONTACT INFORMATION:

Phone: 972 37534555   Fax: 972 35759256
Toll-Free: 800-429-4391
Address: 5 Shlomo Kaplan St., Tel Aviv, 6789159 Israel

STOCK TICKER/OTHER:

Stock Ticker: CHKP   Exchange: NAS
Employees: 5,198   Fiscal Year Ends: 12/31
Parent Company:

SALARIES/BONUSES:

Top Exec. Salary: $400,200   Bonus: $276,700
Second Exec. Salary: $352,200   Bonus: $254,600

OTHER THOUGHTS:

Estimated Female Officers or Directors: 3
Hot Spot for Advancement for Women/Minorities: Y

China Mobile Limited

NAIC Code: 517210

www.chinamobileltd.com

TYPES OF BUSINESS:

Mobile Phone Service
Wireless Music Service
News & Information Service
Instant Messaging Service
Data Services

BRANDS/DIVISIONS/AFFILIATES:

China Mobile Communications Group Co Ltd

CONTACTS:

Note: Officers with more than one job title may be intentionally listed here more than once.

Xin Dong, CEO
Ronghua Li, CFO
Huang Wnelin, VP
Sha Yuejia, VP
Liu Aili, VP
Jie Yang, Chmn.

GROWTH PLANS/SPECIAL FEATURES:

China Mobile Limited (CML) is a leading provider of mobile telecommunications services in Mainland China. CML is one of the largest wireless communications providers in the world in terms of total subscribers, with more than 940 million mobile customers and 210 million wireline broadband customers. The firm is a publicly-traded subsidiary of China Mobile Communications Group Co., Ltd., owning a majority 72.72%. CML provides wireless products and services in all 31 Chinese provinces, regions and municipalities, including Hong Kong, through several wholly-owned subsidiaries. The company offers voice services comprising local calls, domestic long-distance calls, international long-distance calls, intra-provincial roaming, inter-provincial roaming and international roaming, as well as providing voice value-added services such as caller identity display, caller restrictions, call waiting, call forwarding, call holding, voice mail, conference calls and more. The company also offers: SMS (short message services) and other data services; and MMS (multimedia message services), which allows users to combine and deliver several types of messages, including graphics, sounds, text, and motion pictures over wireless networks. In addition, CML provides high-speed internet through wireless local area networks (WLAN) throughout Mainland China. The company's 4G and 5G business is based on the FDD (frequency division duplex) mode long-term evolution (LTE) technology.

FINANCIAL DATA:

Note: Data for latest year may not have been available at press time.

In U.S. $	2021	2020	2019	2018	2017	2016
Revenue		117,674,000,000	110,869,217,280	109,516,939,264	104,327,135,232	104,893,775,872
R&D Expense						
Operating Income						
Operating Margin %						
SGA Expense						
Net Income		16,567,600,000	15,850,562,560	17,506,353,152	16,100,168,704	16,100,953,088
Operating Cash Flow						
Capital Expenditure						
EBITDA						
Return on Assets %						
Return on Equity %						
Debt to Equity						

CONTACT INFORMATION:

Phone: 85 231218888 Fax: 85 225119092
Toll-Free:
Address: 99 Queen's Rd. Central, The Center, Fl. 60, Hong Kong, Hong Kong 999077 Hong Kong

STOCK TICKER/OTHER:

Stock Ticker: 941 Exchange: Hong Kong
Employees: 454,332 Fiscal Year Ends: 12/31
Parent Company: China Mobile Communications Group Co Ltd

SALARIES/BONUSES:

Top Exec. Salary: $ Bonus: $
Second Exec. Salary: $ Bonus: $

OTHER THOUGHTS:

Estimated Female Officers or Directors: 1
Hot Spot for Advancement for Women/Minorities: Y

China Telecom Corporation Limited

www.chinatelecom-h.com

NAIC Code: 517110

TYPES OF BUSINESS:

Fixed-Line & Wireless Telecommunications Services
Internet & Ecommerce Services
Outsourcing Services
Telecommunications
Broadband
Wireless Networks
Internet of Things
Optical Broadband

BRANDS/DIVISIONS/AFFILIATES:

CONTACTS:

Note: Officers with more than one job title may be intentionally listed here more than once.

Ruiwen Ke, CEO
Zhengmao Li, Pres.
Yung Shun Loy, Jacky, Sec.
Gao Jinxing, Financial Controller
Li Ping, Exec. VP
Zhang Jiping, Exec. VP
Yang Xiaowei, Exec. VP
Sun Kangmin, Exec. VP

GROWTH PLANS/SPECIAL FEATURES:

China Telecom Corporation Limited is one of the largest telecommunications and broadband service providers in China. With approximately 160 million wireline access lines in service, over 350 million mobile subscribers, 153 million wireline broadband subscribers and 108 million access lines in service. China Telecom operates in 31 provinces, municipalities and autonomous regions. The company focuses on government, financial and large enterprise customers. China Telecom's wireline telephone services consist of local telephone; domestic long distance; and international, Hong Kong, Macau and Taiwan long distance and interconnection. Mobile voice services include local calls, domestic long-distance calls, international long-distance calls, intra-provincial roaming, inter-provincial roaming and international roaming. The firm is focused on further developing high speed services. It is a leader in 4G and 5G wireless within China. The company also provides industry-specific applications for government and enterprise subscribers. Internet access services consist of wireline internet access services, including dial-up and broadband services, and wireless internet access services. Services are offered through integrated and customized plans. China Telecom continually expanded its fiber network coverage and deployed its Gigabit optical broadband network. Value added services are offered for the wireline and mobile services, and include caller ID, color ringtone, mobile MMS (multimedia messaging service) and industry-specific applications for government and enterprises. Additionally, the company provides integrated information application services and managed data and leased line services.

FINANCIAL DATA:

Note: Data for latest year may not have been available at press time.

In U.S. $	2021	2020	2019	2018	2017	2016
Revenue		60,295,513,005	55,847,145,472	56,053,747,712	51,596,083,200	52,161,781,760
R&D Expense						
Operating Income						
Operating Margin %						
SGA Expense						
Net Income		3,194,324,250	3,049,539,840	3,152,543,744	2,622,851,584	2,665,798,400
Operating Cash Flow						
Capital Expenditure						
EBITDA						
Return on Assets %						
Return on Equity %						
Debt to Equity						

CONTACT INFORMATION:

Phone: 86 10 5850 1800 Fax: 86 10 6601 0728
Toll-Free:
Address: 31 Jinrong St., Xicheng Dist., Beijing, 100033 China

STOCK TICKER/OTHER:

Stock Ticker: 728
Employees: 281,192
Parent Company:
Exchange: Hong Kong
Fiscal Year Ends: 12/31

SALARIES/BONUSES:

Top Exec. Salary: $ Bonus: $
Second Exec. Salary: $ Bonus: $

OTHER THOUGHTS:

Estimated Female Officers or Directors: 3
Hot Spot for Advancement for Women/Minorities: Y

China Unicom (Hong Kong) Limited

www.chinaunicom.com.hk/en/global/home.php

NAIC Code: 517110

TYPES OF BUSINESS:

Wireless Phone Service
Fixed Line Services
Mobile Services
Digital Transformation
Omnichannel
Internet of Things
Cloud Computing
Industrial IT

BRANDS/DIVISIONS/AFFILIATES:

China United Network Communications Group Co Ltd

CONTACTS: *Note: Officers with more than one job title may be intentionally listed here more than once.*

Liehong Liu, CEO
Zhongyue Chen, Pres.
Yuzhuo Li, CFO
Chu Ka Yee, Sec.
Tong Jilu, Sr. VP
Liehong Liu, Chmn.

GROWTH PLANS/SPECIAL FEATURES:

China Unicom (Hong Kong) Limited is an integrated telecommunications operator in China. The company focuses on promoting comprehensive digital transformation led by 5G services, upgrading existing customers and expanding scale in new user markets. The firm's 5G strategy helps to drive mobile service growth, including bundled services across internet, cloud and more. China Unicom coordinates network with business, service interaction and information regarding its fixed-line service, ranging from 3G to 5G capabilities. The firm therefore sells broadband and marketing services as well as network deployment. China Unicom offers a cloud management product, which is cloud-network integrated, secure, reliable, private, customizable and multi-cloud collaborative. Big data services span data application, data technology, artificial intelligence and blockchain, with a focus on key industries such as government, finance, cultural, tourism and transportation. Its Internet of Things (IoT) system for business is driven by 4G and 5G capabilities; and its industrial IT services span areas such as smart city, digital government, big data, IT, innovation and more to further promote digital transformation. China Unicom's marketing services promote 5G and smart living solutions via brand strategies across all marketing channels. The firm actively implements comprehensive digital transformation, online-to-offline integration and end-to-end customer experience services. China Unicom operates as a subsidiary of China United Network Communications Group Company Limited, which holds a majority, 52.1% share.

FINANCIAL DATA: *Note: Data for latest year may not have been available at press time.*

In U.S. $	2021	2020	2019	2018	2017	2016
Revenue			43,180,634,112	43,234,443,264	38,719,217,664	40,599,527,424
R&D Expense						
Operating Income						
Operating Margin %						
SGA Expense						
Net Income			1,684,032,128	1,515,629,056	257,537,328	92,541,872
Operating Cash Flow						
Capital Expenditure						
EBITDA						
Return on Assets %						
Return on Equity %						
Debt to Equity						

CONTACT INFORMATION:

Phone: 852 21262018 Fax:
Toll-Free:
Address: 99 Queens Rd. Central, The Center, Fl. 75, Hong Kong, Hong Kong 999077 Hong Kong

STOCK TICKER/OTHER:

Stock Ticker: 762 Exchange: Hong Kong
Employees: 254,702 Fiscal Year Ends: 12/31
Parent Company: China United Network Communications Group Co Ltd

SALARIES/BONUSES:

Top Exec. Salary: $ Bonus: $
Second Exec. Salary: $ Bonus: $

OTHER THOUGHTS:

Estimated Female Officers or Directors:
Hot Spot for Advancement for Women/Minorities:

Ciena Corporation

www.ciena.com

NAIC Code: 334210

TYPES OF BUSINESS:

Communications Networking Equipment
Software & Support Services
Consulting Services
Switching Platforms
Packet Interworking Products
Access Products
Network & Service Management Tools

BRANDS/DIVISIONS/AFFILIATES:

Blue Planet Automation
Adaptive Network

GROWTH PLANS/SPECIAL FEATURES:

Ciena Corp is a network strategy and technology company. It provides network hardware, software, and services that support the transport, switching, aggregation, service delivery, and management of video, data, and voice traffic on communications networks. It serves various industries such as communication services providers, web-scale providers, cable operators, government, and large enterprises worldwide. The business activities function through Networking Platforms; Platform Software and Services; Blue Planet Automation Software, and Global Services segments. Geographically, its presence is seen in the markets of the United States, Canada, the Caribbean, Latin America, Europe, the Middle East, Africa, the Asia Pacific, Japan, and India.

CONTACTS: *Note: Officers with more than one job title may be intentionally listed here more than once.*

Gary Smith, CEO
James Moylan, CFO
Patrick Nettles, Chairman of the Board
Andrew Petrik, Chief Accounting Officer
Mary Yang, Chief Strategy Officer
Stephen Alexander, Chief Technology Officer
David Rothenstein, General Counsel
Scott McFeely, Senior VP, Divisional
Jason Phipps, Senior VP, Divisional
Rick Hamilton, Senior VP, Divisional

FINANCIAL DATA: *Note: Data for latest year may not have been available at press time.*

In U.S. $	2021	2020	2019	2018	2017	2016
Revenue		3,532,157,000	3,572,131,000	3,094,286,000	2,801,687,000	2,600,573,000
R&D Expense		529,888,000	548,139,000	491,564,000	475,329,000	451,794,000
Operating Income		513,647,000	374,674,000	253,196,000	238,655,000	165,715,000
Operating Margin %						
SGA Expense		585,973,000	597,445,000	554,193,000	498,773,000	482,559,000
Net Income		361,291,000	253,434,000	-344,690,000	1,261,953,000	72,584,000
Operating Cash Flow		493,654,000	413,140,000	229,261,000	234,882,000	289,520,000
Capital Expenditure		82,667,000	62,579,000	67,616,000	94,600,000	107,185,000
EBITDA		619,809,000	473,354,000	314,050,000	334,880,000	285,066,000
Return on Assets %						
Return on Equity %						
Debt to Equity						

CONTACT INFORMATION:

Phone: 410 694-5700 Fax: 410 694-5750
Toll-Free: 800-921-1144
Address: 7035 Ridge Rd., Hanover, MD 21076 United States

STOCK TICKER/OTHER:

Stock Ticker: CIEN
Employees: 7,032
Parent Company:
Exchange: NYS
Fiscal Year Ends: 10/31

SALARIES/BONUSES:

Top Exec. Salary: $988,462 Bonus: $
Second Exec. Salary: $571,888 Bonus: $

OTHER THOUGHTS:

Estimated Female Officers or Directors: 2
Hot Spot for Advancement for Women/Minorities:

Sales, profits and employees may be estimates. Financial information, benefits and other data can change quickly and may vary from those stated here.

Cirrus Logic Inc

www.cirrus.com

NAIC Code: 334413

TYPES OF BUSINESS:

Integrated Circuits-Analog & Digital
Integrated Circuit Development
Integrated Circuit Manufacturing
Semiconductor Chips
Software

BRANDS/DIVISIONS/AFFILIATES:

SoundClear
Lion Semiconductor inc

GROWTH PLANS/SPECIAL FEATURES:

Cirrus Logic Inc is a provider of integrated circuits for audio and voice signal processing applications. The firm's products are organized into two streams: portable audio products, and non-portable audio and other products. These products include analog and mixed-signal components targeting mobile devices, smart homes, and applications in the automotive, energy, and industrial markets. Roughly half of the firm's revenue is generated in China, with the rest coming from the United States, Europe, South Korea, Japan, Taiwan, and countries across the world.

Cirrus offers its employees health insurance, 401(k) and employee assistance plans and programs.

CONTACTS: *Note: Officers with more than one job title may be intentionally listed here more than once.*

John Forsyth, CEO
Thurman Case, CFO
David Tupman, Chairman of the Board
Jo-Dee Benson, Other Executive Officer
Scott Anderson, Senior VP, Divisional
Gregory Thomas, Senior VP
Andrew Brannan, Vice President, Divisional
Allan Hughes, Vice President, Divisional
Carl Alberty, Vice President, Divisional
Jeffrey Baumgartner, Vice President, Divisional

FINANCIAL DATA: *Note: Data for latest year may not have been available at press time.*

In U.S. $	2021	2020	2019	2018	2017	2016
Revenue	1,369,230,000	1,281,124,000	1,185,524,000	1,532,186,000	1,538,940,000	1,169,251,000
R&D Expense	342,759,000	347,647,000	375,139,000	366,444,000	303,658,000	269,217,000
Operating Income	237,534,000	195,405,000	95,856,000	262,461,000	326,892,000	168,541,000
Operating Margin %						
SGA Expense	127,008,000	131,115,000	126,502,000	131,811,000	127,265,000	117,082,000
Net Income	217,344,000	159,498,000	89,991,000	161,995,000	261,209,000	123,630,000
Operating Cash Flow	348,945,000	295,815,000	206,694,000	318,711,000	369,751,000	155,282,000
Capital Expenditure	20,475,000	21,576,000	35,758,000	84,503,000	51,296,000	46,088,000
EBITDA	293,386,000	250,560,000	174,627,000	347,651,000	382,080,000	237,357,000
Return on Assets %						
Return on Equity %						
Debt to Equity						

CONTACT INFORMATION:

Phone: 512 851-4000 Fax: 512 912-3977
Toll-Free: 800-888-5016
Address: 800 W. 6th St., Austin, TX 78701 United States

STOCK TICKER/OTHER:

Stock Ticker: CRUS
Employees: 1,481
Parent Company:
Exchange: NAS
Fiscal Year Ends: 03/31

SALARIES/BONUSES:

Top Exec. Salary: $692,308 Bonus: $
Second Exec. Salary: $443,077 Bonus: $

OTHER THOUGHTS:

Estimated Female Officers or Directors: 4
Hot Spot for Advancement for Women/Minorities: Y

Cisco Systems Inc

www.cisco.com

NAIC Code: 334210A

TYPES OF BUSINESS:

Computer Networking Equipment
Routers & Switches
Real-Time Conferencing Technology
Server Virtualization Software
Data Storage Products
Security Products
Teleconference Systems and Technology
Unified Communications Systems

BRANDS/DIVISIONS/AFFILIATES:

AppDynamics Inc
Acacia Communications Inc

GROWTH PLANS/SPECIAL FEATURES:

Cisco Systems, Inc. is the world's largest hardware and software supplier within the networking solutions sector. The infrastructure platforms group includes hardware and software products for switching, routing, data center, and wireless applications. Its applications portfolio contains collaboration, analytics, and Internet of Things products. The security segment contains Cisco's firewall and software-defined security products. Services are Cisco's technical support and advanced services offerings. The company's wide array of hardware is complemented with solutions for software-defined networking, analytics, and intent-based networking. In collaboration with Cisco's initiative on growing software and services, its revenue model is focused on increasing subscriptions and recurring sales.

CONTACTS: *Note: Officers with more than one job title may be intentionally listed here more than once.*

Charles Robbins, CEO
R. Herren, CFO
Prat Bhatt, Chief Accounting Officer
Deborah Stahlkopf, Chief Legal Officer
Maria Martinez, COO
Geraldine Elliott, Executive VP

FINANCIAL DATA: *Note: Data for latest year may not have been available at press time.*

In U.S. $	2021	2020	2019	2018	2017	2016
Revenue	49,818,000,000	49,301,000,000	51,904,000,000	49,330,000,000	48,005,000,000	49,247,000,000
R&D Expense	6,549,000,000	6,347,000,000	6,577,000,000	6,332,000,000	6,059,000,000	6,296,000,000
Operating Income	13,719,000,000	14,101,000,000	14,541,000,000	12,667,000,000	12,729,000,000	12,928,000,000
Operating Margin %						
SGA Expense	11,411,000,000	11,094,000,000	11,398,000,000	11,386,000,000	11,177,000,000	11,433,000,000
Net Income	10,591,000,000	11,214,000,000	11,621,000,000	110,000,000	9,609,000,000	10,739,000,000
Operating Cash Flow	15,454,000,000	15,426,000,000	15,831,000,000	13,666,000,000	13,876,000,000	13,570,000,000
Capital Expenditure	692,000,000	770,000,000	909,000,000	834,000,000	964,000,000	1,146,000,000
EBITDA	15,558,000,000	16,363,000,000	17,327,000,000	16,174,000,000	15,434,000,000	15,746,000,000
Return on Assets %						
Return on Equity %						
Debt to Equity						

CONTACT INFORMATION:

Phone: 408 526-4000 Fax: 408 526-4100
Toll-Free: 800-553-6387
Address: 170 W. Tasman Dr., San Jose, CA 95134-1706 United States

STOCK TICKER/OTHER:

Stock Ticker: CSCO
Employees: 79,500
Parent Company:
Exchange: NAS
Fiscal Year Ends: 07/31

SALARIES/BONUSES:

Top Exec. Salary: $495,385 Bonus: $8,000,000
Second Exec. Salary: $1,416,731 Bonus: $

OTHER THOUGHTS:

Estimated Female Officers or Directors: 10
Hot Spot for Advancement for Women/Minorities: Y

Citrix Systems Inc

NAIC Code: 511210B

www.citrix.com

TYPES OF BUSINESS:

Computer Software: Network Management (IT), System Testing & Storage
IT Development
Cloud
Workspace Organization
Application Programming
Collaboration
Security
Delivery Management

BRANDS/DIVISIONS/AFFILIATES:

Wrangler Topco LLC
Wrike Inc

GROWTH PLANS/SPECIAL FEATURES:

Citrix Systems provides virtualization software, including Virtual Apps and Desktops for desktop virtualization and Citrix Virtual Apps for application virtualization. The company also provides Citrix Endpoint Management for mobile device management and Citrix ADC for application delivery and Citrix SDWAN for routing, security, and WAN monitoring.

Citrix offers its employees health benefits, wellness programs, job development, 401(k), a bonus program and flexible workstyles.

CONTACTS: *Note: Officers with more than one job title may be intentionally listed here more than once.*

Paul Hough, CEO
Arlen Shenkman, CFO
Robert Calderoni, Chairman of the Board
Jessica Soisson, Chief Accounting Officer
Antonio Gomes, Chief Legal Officer
Timothy Minahan, Chief Marketing Officer
Woong Kim, Chief Technology Officer
Mark Schmitz, COO
Sridhar Mullapudi, Executive VP, Divisional
Hector Lima, Executive VP, Divisional
Donna Kimmel, Executive VP
Mark Ferrer, Executive VP

FINANCIAL DATA: *Note: Data for latest year may not have been available at press time.*

In U.S. $	2021	2020	2019	2018	2017	2016
Revenue		3,236,700,000	3,010,564,000	2,973,903,000	2,824,686,000	3,418,265,000
R&D Expense		538,080,000	518,877,000	439,984,000	415,801,000	489,265,000
Operating Income		620,789,000	558,365,000	694,685,000	645,910,000	776,904,000
Operating Margin %						
SGA Expense		1,576,486,000	1,453,385,000	1,389,577,000	1,308,677,000	1,563,382,000
Net Income		504,446,000	681,813,000	575,667,000	-20,719,000	536,112,000
Operating Cash Flow		935,809,000	783,070,000	1,035,345,000	908,276,000	1,115,830,000
Capital Expenditure		50,019,000	66,954,000	72,564,000	88,280,000	160,512,000
EBITDA		769,977,000	744,946,000	851,513,000	771,970,000	910,751,000
Return on Assets %						
Return on Equity %						
Debt to Equity						

CONTACT INFORMATION:

Phone: 954 267-3000 Fax: 954 267-9319
Toll-Free: 800-424-8749
Address: 851 W. Cypress Creek Rd., Fort Lauderdale, FL 33309 United States

STOCK TICKER/OTHER:

Stock Ticker: CTXS
Employees: 9,000
Parent Company:
Exchange: NAS
Fiscal Year Ends: 12/31

SALARIES/BONUSES:

Top Exec. Salary: $575,000 Bonus: $500,000
Second Exec. Salary: $1,000,000 Bonus: $

OTHER THOUGHTS:

Estimated Female Officers or Directors: 2
Hot Spot for Advancement for Women/Minorities:

Click & Grow LLC

www.clickandgrow.com

NAIC Code: 335129

TYPES OF BUSINESS:

Lighting Equipment Manufacturing
Smart Garden
Indoor Fresh Food Garden
Indoor Fresh Flower Garden
Technology

BRANDS/DIVISIONS/AFFILIATES:

CONTACTS:

Note: Officers with more than one job title may be intentionally listed here more than once.

Mattias Lepp, CEO

GROWTH PLANS/SPECIAL FEATURES:

Click & Grow, LLC creates transformative technologies that enable the growth of fresh food locally and sustainably. The firm offers smart gardens that provide people, especially those living in urban communities, with a starting point of growing their own fresh food indoors. Through its innovative smart soil, automated system and other products, Click & Grow plants grow quickly and easily, without any genetically-modified organisms (GMOs), pesticides, insecticides or other harmful substances. The company's smart soil was inspired by NASA technology, and creates an environment that allows plants to survive by: releasing nutrients in sync with the plant's life cycle, keeping soil pH balanced and employing tiny oxygen pockets so the plants can breathe. The smart garden's adjustable light-emitting diode (LED) lamp furnishes the plants with an enhanced light spectra that spurs growth. A variety of plants can be grown in Click & Grow's smart gardens, including mini tomatoes, peppers, leafy greens, peas and herbs, as well as petunias and other flowers and plants. A smart garden with three plant pods costs about $140, a garden that grows nine plants simultaneously is priced from $230, and a garden that grows 27 plant pods costs about $600. Plant pods can be delivered to one's doorstep, and frequent subscribers can save money via free shipping and discounts on pods. Subscriptions can be cancelled at any time. Accessories are offered as well, including herb shears, herb saver container, extension arms, garden float, plastic water cup, domes, transmitting wicks and more. Click & Grow store-within-stores (resellers) are located throughout the U.S. and Canada.

FINANCIAL DATA:

Note: Data for latest year may not have been available at press time.

In U.S. $	2021	2020	2019	2018	2017	2016
Revenue						
R&D Expense						
Operating Income						
Operating Margin %						
SGA Expense						
Net Income						
Operating Cash Flow						
Capital Expenditure						
EBITDA						
Return on Assets %						
Return on Equity %						
Debt to Equity						

CONTACT INFORMATION:

Phone: 917-675--4973 Fax:
Toll-Free:
Address: 2443 Fillmore St., Ste. 380-8505, San Francisco, CA 94115 United States

STOCK TICKER/OTHER:

Stock Ticker: Private
Employees: 40
Parent Company:
Exchange:
Fiscal Year Ends:

SALARIES/BONUSES:

Top Exec. Salary: $ Bonus: $
Second Exec. Salary: $ Bonus: $

OTHER THOUGHTS:

Estimated Female Officers or Directors:
Hot Spot for Advancement for Women/Minorities:

Cloudera Inc

NAIC Code: 511210J

www.cloudera.com

TYPES OF BUSINESS:

Computer Software, Data Base & File Management
Enterprise Data Cloud Solutions
Edge
Artificial Intelligence
Machine Learning
Data Analytics
Opensource Software
Data Management

BRANDS/DIVISIONS/AFFILIATES:

Clayton Dubilier & Rice LLC
KKR & Co
Cloudera Enterprise Data Hub
Cloudera Data Warehouse
Cloudera Engineering
Cloudera DataFlow
Cloudera Fast Forward Research
Cloudera Science Workbench

CONTACTS: *Note: Officers with more than one job title may be intentionally listed here more than once.*

Robert Bearden, CEO
Scott Aronson, COO
Kevin Cook, CFO
Sudhir Menon, Chief Product Officer
Bob Mahan, Chief Human Resources Officer
Ram Venkatesh, CTO
Arun Murthy, Other Executive Officer
Mick Hollison, Pres.

GROWTH PLANS/SPECIAL FEATURES:

Cloudera, Inc. is an enterprise data cloud company. From the edge to artificial intelligence (AI), the firm's integrated suite of data analytics and management products enable clients to transform data into actionable insights. Cloudera's portable, multi-cloud platform features security, governance and management functions, including machine learning. These offerings are based predominantly on opensource software, utilizing data stored natively in public cloud object stores as well as in various opensource data stores. As a result, organizations are able to capitalize on vast amounts of data from a variety of sources to serve customers better, design connected products and services, and protect their enterprises. Cloudera's software is offered on a subscription basis, and primarily serves corporate enterprises and public sector organizations globally. Current product offerings include: Cloudera Enterprise Data Hub, which combines the data warehouse, operational database and data science and engineering products with shared data experience (SDX) technology; Cloudera Data Warehouse, which delivers an enterprise-grade, hybrid cloud solution for self-service analytics; Cloudera Engineering, which enables users to streamline, simplify and scale big data processing regardless of where data is stored; Cloudera DataFlow, a scalable, real-time streaming data platform that collects, curates and analyzes data; Cloudera Fast Forward Research, which researches emerging machine learning trends and their working prototypes; Hortonworks Data Platform, a scalable data management platform that helps organizations securely store, process and analyze any data sheet; and Cloudera Science Workbench, a multi-user, multi-language development environment for data science and machine learning applications. In late-2021, Cloudera was acquired by Clayton, Dubilier & Rice LLC and KKR & Co. in an approximately $4.7 billion all-cash transaction, and subsequently ceased from being publicly traded.

Cloudera offers its employees health and financial benefits.

FINANCIAL DATA: *Note: Data for latest year may not have been available at press time.*

In U.S. $	2021	2020	2019	2018	2017	2016
Revenue	869,258,000	794,190,976	479,940,992	367,443,008	261,026,000	166,048,000
R&D Expense						
Operating Income						
Operating Margin %						
SGA Expense						
Net Income	-162,734,000	-336,582,016	-192,648,992	-385,792,992	-187,316,992	-203,143,008
Operating Cash Flow						
Capital Expenditure						
EBITDA						
Return on Assets %						
Return on Equity %						
Debt to Equity						

CONTACT INFORMATION:

Phone: 650-362-0488 Fax:
Toll-Free: 888-789-1488
Address: 5470 Great America Pkwy., Santa Clara, CA 95054 United States

STOCK TICKER/OTHER:

Stock Ticker: Private
Employees: 2,728
Parent Company: KKR & Co Inc
Exchange:
Fiscal Year Ends: 01/31

SALARIES/BONUSES:

Top Exec. Salary: $ Bonus: $
Second Exec. Salary: $ Bonus: $

OTHER THOUGHTS:

Estimated Female Officers or Directors:
Hot Spot for Advancement for Women/Minorities:

Cloudflare Inc

www.cloudflare.com

NAIC Code: 511210E

TYPES OF BUSINESS:

Computer Software, Network Security, Managed Access, Digital ID, Cybersecurity & Anti-Virus
Web Content Delivery
Cloud Platform
Business Network Services
Software

BRANDS/DIVISIONS/AFFILIATES:

GROWTH PLANS/SPECIAL FEATURES:

Cloudflare Inc is a United States-based company engaged in the software business. It has built a cloud platform that delivers a range of network services to businesses. The product offerings of the company include Argo Smart Routing, Load Balancing, Web Optimizations, Mobile Software Development Kit, Cloudflare Access, and Cloudflare Spectrum among others.

Cloudflare offers health benefits and other employee assistance programs.

CONTACTS: *Note: Officers with more than one job title may be intentionally listed here more than once.*

Matthew Prince, CEO
Thomas Seifert, CFO
Paul Underwood, Chief Accounting Officer
Michelle Zatlyn, Co-Founder
Douglas Kramer, General Counsel

FINANCIAL DATA: *Note: Data for latest year may not have been available at press time.*

In U.S. $	2021	2020	2019	2018	2017	2016
Revenue		431,059,000	287,022,000	192,674,000	134,915,000	84,791,000
R&D Expense		127,144,000	90,669,000	54,463,000	33,650,000	23,663,000
Operating Income		-106,768,000	-107,946,000	-84,899,000	-9,730,000	-17,029,000
Operating Margin %						
SGA Expense		309,628,000	240,876,000	179,573,000	82,207,000	54,195,000
Net Income		-119,370,000	-105,828,000	-87,164,000	-10,748,000	-17,334,000
Operating Cash Flow		-17,129,000	-38,917,000	-43,281,000	3,167,000	-13,318,000
Capital Expenditure		74,962,000	57,279,000	34,839,000	22,975,000	18,558,000
EBITDA		-50,622,000	-74,122,000	-66,190,000	3,321,000	-8,256,000
Return on Assets %						
Return on Equity %						
Debt to Equity						

CONTACT INFORMATION:

Phone: 888-993-5273 Fax:
Toll-Free:
Address: 101 Townsend St., San Francisco, CA 94107 United States

STOCK TICKER/OTHER:

Stock Ticker: NET
Employees: 1,788
Parent Company:
Exchange: NYS
Fiscal Year Ends: 12/31

SALARIES/BONUSES:

Top Exec. Salary: $650,000 Bonus: $
Second Exec. Salary: $550,000 Bonus: $

OTHER THOUGHTS:

Estimated Female Officers or Directors: 1
Hot Spot for Advancement for Women/Minorities:

Cognizant Technology Solutions Corporation www.cognizant.com

NAIC Code: 541512

TYPES OF BUSINESS:

Computer Systems Design Services
Outsourced Services
Software Engineering
Artificial Intelligence
Machine Learning
Data Analytics

BRANDS/DIVISIONS/AFFILIATES:

Linium
Magenic
Servian
ESG Mobility
TSQ
Hunter
Devbridge

CONTACTS: *Note: Officers with more than one job title may be intentionally listed here more than once.*

Brian Humphries, CEO
Jan Siegmund, CFO
Michael Patsalos-Fox, Chairman of the Board
Matthew Friedrich, Executive VP
Andrew Stafford, Executive VP
Pradeep Shilige, Executive VP
Becky Schmitt, Executive VP
Balu Ayyar, Executive VP
Malcolm Frank, Executive VP
Gregory Hyttenrauch, Executive VP
Ursula Morgenstern, Executive VP
Robert Telesmanic, Senior VP

GROWTH PLANS/SPECIAL FEATURES:

Cognizant is a global IT services provider, offering consulting and outsourcing services to some of the world's largest enterprises spanning the financial services, media and communications, healthcare, natural resources, and consumer products industries. Cognizant employs nearly 300,000 people globally, roughly 70% of whom are in India, although the company's headquarters are in Teaneck, New Jersey.

Cognizant offers health plans and employee assistance programs.

FINANCIAL DATA: *Note: Data for latest year may not have been available at press time.*

In U.S. $	2021	2020	2019	2018	2017	2016
Revenue		16,652,000,000	16,783,000,000	16,125,000,000	14,810,000,000	13,487,000,000
R&D Expense						
Operating Income		2,329,000,000	2,670,000,000	2,801,000,000	2,481,000,000	2,289,000,000
Operating Margin %						
SGA Expense		3,100,000,000	2,972,000,000	3,026,000,000	2,769,000,000	2,731,000,000
Net Income		1,392,000,000	1,842,000,000	2,101,000,000	1,504,000,000	1,553,000,000
Operating Cash Flow		3,299,000,000	2,499,000,000	2,592,000,000	2,407,000,000	1,621,000,000
Capital Expenditure		398,000,000	392,000,000	377,000,000	284,000,000	300,000,000
EBITDA		2,679,000,000	3,095,000,000	3,322,000,000	3,121,000,000	2,755,000,000
Return on Assets %						
Return on Equity %						
Debt to Equity						

CONTACT INFORMATION:

Phone: 201 801-0233 Fax: 201 801-0243
Toll-Free: 888-937-3277
Address: 300 Frank W. Burr Blvd., Teaneck, NJ 07666 United States

STOCK TICKER/OTHER:

Stock Ticker: CTSH
Employees: 289,500
Parent Company:
Exchange: NAS
Fiscal Year Ends: 12/31

SALARIES/BONUSES:

Top Exec. Salary: $595,845 Bonus: $600,000
Second Exec. Salary: $1,026,681 Bonus: $

OTHER THOUGHTS:

Estimated Female Officers or Directors: 1
Hot Spot for Advancement for Women/Minorities:

Comtech Telecommunications Corp

www.comtechtel.com

NAIC Code: 334220

TYPES OF BUSINESS:

Communications Equipment-Microwave & RF
Satellite Equipment & Technologies
Communication Solutions
Next-Generation 911 Solutions

GROWTH PLANS/SPECIAL FEATURES:

Comtech Telecommunications Corp is a provider of advanced communications solutions. The company is engaged in designing, developing, producing and marketing products, systems, and services for communications solutions. It is engaged in two business segments, Commercial Solutions, and Government Solutions Segment.

BRANDS/DIVISIONS/AFFILIATES:

UHP Networks Inc

CONTACTS:

Note: Officers with more than one job title may be intentionally listed here more than once.

Fred Kornberg, CEO
Michael Bondi, CFO
Michael Porcelain, COO
Yelena Simonyuk, Other Corporate Officer
Nancy Stallone, Secretary

FINANCIAL DATA:

Note: Data for latest year may not have been available at press time.

In U.S. $	2021	2020	2019	2018	2017	2016
Revenue	581,695,000	616,715,000	671,797,000	570,589,000	550,368,000	411,004,000
R&D Expense	49,148,000	52,180,000	56,407,000	53,869,000	54,260,000	42,190,000
Operating Income	31,994,000	35,928,000	44,074,000	35,075,000	25,022,000	20,700,000
Operating Margin %						
SGA Expense	111,796,000	117,130,000	128,639,000	113,922,000	116,080,000	94,932,000
Net Income	-73,480,000	7,020,000	25,041,000	29,769,000	15,827,000	-7,738,000
Operating Cash Flow	-40,638,000	52,764,000	68,031,000	50,344,000	66,655,000	14,970,000
Capital Expenditure	16,037,000	7,225,000	8,785,000	8,642,000	8,150,000	5,667,000
EBITDA	-37,760,000	47,520,000	68,437,000	69,805,000	74,287,000	22,803,000
Return on Assets %						
Return on Equity %						
Debt to Equity						

CONTACT INFORMATION:

Phone: 631 962-7000 Fax: 631 777-8877
Toll-Free:
Address: 68 S. Service Rd., Ste. 230, Melville, NY 11747 United States

STOCK TICKER/OTHER:

Stock Ticker: CMTL
Employees: 2,038
Parent Company:
Exchange: NAS
Fiscal Year Ends: 07/31

SALARIES/BONUSES:

Top Exec. Salary: $840,000 Bonus: $
Second Exec. Salary: $525,000 Bonus: $

OTHER THOUGHTS:

Estimated Female Officers or Directors:
Hot Spot for Advancement for Women/Minorities:

Conduent Incorporated

NAIC Code: 561110

www.conduent.com

TYPES OF BUSINESS:

Business Process Outsourcing
Business Process Outsourcing
Mission-Critical Digital Platforms
Internet of Things
Cloud
Mobile
Automation
Blockchain

BRANDS/DIVISIONS/AFFILIATES:

GROWTH PLANS/SPECIAL FEATURES:

Conduent Inc acts as a provider of business process services with expertise in transaction-intensive processing, analytics, and automation. The company provides industry-focused service offerings in growth markets such as Healthcare and Transportation as well as provides multi-industry services such as transaction processing, customer care, and payment services. It operates through three segments namely Commercial Industries, Government Service, Transportation. The services provided by the company includes industry-centric business process services, government-centric business process services, business process services, and others. The company operates its business in the US, Europe, and other areas. Most of the company's revenue is generated in the US.

Conduent offers its employees healthcare benefits and discount and development programs.

CONTACTS: *Note: Officers with more than one job title may be intentionally listed here more than once.*

Clifford Skelton, CEO
Stephen Wood, CFO
Scott Letier, Chairman of the Board
Mark Prout, Chief Information Officer
Mark Brewer, Executive VP, Divisional
Michael Krawitz, Executive VP
Louis Keyes, Executive VP

FINANCIAL DATA: *Note: Data for latest year may not have been available at press time.*

In U.S. $	2021	2020	2019	2018	2017	2016
Revenue		4,163,000,000	4,467,000,000	5,393,000,000	6,022,000,000	6,408,000,000
R&D Expense		1,000,000	8,000,000	11,000,000	13,000,000	31,000,000
Operating Income		26,000,000	27,000,000	180,000,000	174,000,000	-87,000,000
Operating Margin %						
SGA Expense		468,000,000	479,000,000	560,000,000	615,000,000	686,000,000
Net Income		-118,000,000	-1,934,000,000	-416,000,000	181,000,000	-983,000,000
Operating Cash Flow		161,000,000	132,000,000	283,000,000	302,000,000	108,000,000
Capital Expenditure		139,000,000	215,000,000	224,000,000	132,000,000	188,000,000
EBITDA		380,000,000	-1,569,000,000	177,000,000	618,000,000	-574,000,000
Return on Assets %						
Return on Equity %						
Debt to Equity						

CONTACT INFORMATION:

Phone: 844-663-2638 Fax:
Toll-Free:
Address: 100 Campus Dr., Ste. 200, Florham Park, NJ 07932 United States

STOCK TICKER/OTHER:

Stock Ticker: CNDT
Employees: 67,000
Parent Company:
Exchange: NAS
Fiscal Year Ends: 12/31

SALARIES/BONUSES:

Top Exec. Salary: $697,693 Bonus: $
Second Exec. Salary: $487,770 Bonus: $

OTHER THOUGHTS:

Estimated Female Officers or Directors:
Hot Spot for Advancement for Women/Minorities:

CrowdStrike Holdings Inc

www.crowdstrike.com

NAIC Code: 511210E

TYPES OF BUSINESS:

Computer Software, Network Security, Managed Access, Digital ID, Cybersecurity & Anti-Virus
Cloud Solutions
Cloud Modules
Security Solutions
Remediation Solutions
Threat Detection Solutions
Network Security Monitoring

BRANDS/DIVISIONS/AFFILIATES:

Falcon
CrowdStrike Threat Graph
Falcon Prevent
Falcon X
Falcon Insight
Falcon Device Control
Falcon Overwatch
Secure Circle LLC

GROWTH PLANS/SPECIAL FEATURES:

CrowdStrike Holdings, Inc. is a cybersecurity vendor that specializes in endpoint protection, threat intelligence and hunting, attack remediation, and offers various solutions to supplement security and network operations teams. Its cloud-based architecture collects data across all its endpoint agents, analyzes the information within its cloud platform, and updates all of its customers' security posture. CrowdStrike sells packaged tiers of cybersecurity protection and offers individual security modules via its online marketplace. The company was founded in 2011, went public in 2019, and is based in California.

CONTACTS: *Note: Officers with more than one job title may be intentionally listed here more than once.*

George Kurtz, CEO
Burt Podbere, CFO
Gerhard Watzinger, Chairman of the Board
Shawn Henry, Other Executive Officer
Michael Carpenter, President, Divisional

FINANCIAL DATA: *Note: Data for latest year may not have been available at press time.*

In U.S. $	2021	2020	2019	2018	2017	2016
Revenue	874,438,000	481,413,000	249,824,000	118,752,000	52,745,000	
R&D Expense	214,670,000	130,188,000	84,551,000	58,887,000	39,145,000	
Operating Income	-92,529,000	-146,065,000	-136,864,000	-131,440,000	-90,556,000	
Operating Margin %						
SGA Expense	522,752,000	355,663,000	214,899,000	136,819,000	70,150,000	
Net Income	-92,629,000	-141,779,000	-140,077,000	-135,490,000	-91,340,000	
Operating Cash Flow	356,566,000	99,943,000	-22,968,000	-58,766,000	-51,998,000	
Capital Expenditure	63,843,000	87,487,000	42,645,000	29,755,000	12,647,000	
EBITDA	-46,167,000	-115,827,000	-122,884,000	-125,174,000	-87,617,000	
Return on Assets %						
Return on Equity %						
Debt to Equity						

CONTACT INFORMATION:

Phone: 408-462-9439 Fax:
Toll-Free: 888-512-8906
Address: 150 Mathilda Place, Ste. 300, Sunnyvale, CA 94086 United States

STOCK TICKER/OTHER:

Stock Ticker: CRWD
Employees: 3,394
Parent Company:
Exchange: NAS
Fiscal Year Ends: 01/31

SALARIES/BONUSES:

Top Exec. Salary: $550,000 Bonus: $
Second Exec. Salary: $550,000 Bonus: $

OTHER THOUGHTS:

Estimated Female Officers or Directors:
Hot Spot for Advancement for Women/Minorities:

CTS Corporation

www.ctscorp.com

NAIC Code: 334513

TYPES OF BUSINESS:

Electronic Sensors for Automobiles
Components & Sensors
Manufacturing & Assembly Services
Electronics Manufacturing Services
Supply Chain Services
Component Design Services (ODM)

GROWTH PLANS/SPECIAL FEATURES:

CTS Corp operates in the electronics industry. The company is a global manufacturer of sensors, electronic components, and actuators. It designs, manufacture, and sell a broad line of sensors, electronic components, and actuators primarily to original equipment manufacturers (OEM) for the aerospace and defense, industrial, information technology, medical, telecommunications, and transportation markets. Geographically, it derives a majority of revenue from the United States and also has a presence in China; Singapore; Czech Republic; Taiwan, and other countries.

BRANDS/DIVISIONS/AFFILIATES:

CONTACTS:

Note: Officers with more than one job title may be intentionally listed here more than once.

Kieran OSullivan, CEO
Ashish Agrawal, CFO
Thomas White, Chief Accounting Officer
Scott D'Angelo, General Counsel

FINANCIAL DATA:

Note: Data for latest year may not have been available at press time.

In U.S. $	2021	2020	2019	2018	2017	2016
Revenue		424,066,000	468,999,000	470,483,000	422,993,000	396,679,000
R&D Expense		24,317,000	25,967,000	25,304,000	25,146,000	24,040,000
Operating Income		46,959,000	61,200,000	66,100,000	43,342,000	54,764,000
Operating Margin %						
SGA Expense		67,787,000	70,408,000	73,569,000	71,943,000	61,624,000
Net Income		34,686,000	36,146,000	46,532,000	14,448,000	34,380,000
Operating Cash Flow		76,783,000	64,405,000	58,152,000	58,048,000	47,202,000
Capital Expenditure		14,858,000	21,733,000	28,488,000	18,094,000	20,500,000
EBITDA		75,421,000	77,533,000	82,702,000	64,270,000	79,939,000
Return on Assets %						
Return on Equity %						
Debt to Equity						

CONTACT INFORMATION:

Phone: 630-577-8800 Fax:
Toll-Free:
Address: 4925 Indiana Ave., Lisle, IL 60532 United States

STOCK TICKER/OTHER:

Stock Ticker: CTS
Employees: 3,786
Parent Company:
Exchange: NYS
Fiscal Year Ends: 12/31

SALARIES/BONUSES:

Top Exec. Salary: $721,850 Bonus: $
Second Exec. Salary: $355,135 Bonus: $75,000

OTHER THOUGHTS:

Estimated Female Officers or Directors:
Hot Spot for Advancement for Women/Minorities:

Cybereason Inc

www.cybereason.com

NAIC Code: 511210E

TYPES OF BUSINESS:

Computer Software: Network Security, Managed Access, Digital ID, Cybersecurity & Anti-Virus
Cyber Security
Cyber Technology
Technology Development
Software Development
Endpoint Detection Platform

BRANDS/DIVISIONS/AFFILIATES:

empow

CONTACTS: *Note: Officers with more than one job title may be intentionally listed here more than once.*

Lior Div, CEO
Emmy Linder, COO
Russell Stein, CFO
Meg O'Leary, CMO
Marisa Ianelli, VP-People
Israel Barak, CIO
Yonatan Striem-Amit, CTO

GROWTH PLANS/SPECIAL FEATURES:

Cybereason, Inc. develops technology and software that protects customers against cyberattacks. The firm has developed an endpoint detection platform that exposes the attacker's vulnerable points. The platform is built to utilize that insight to locate the primary component of the attack, connect it with other pieces of information to reveal an entire campaign and create a way to shut it down. Many Cybereason employees have served in the military and therefore specialize in hacking operations, with expertise in defending against the most advanced attacks. Cybereason's products are grouped into three categories: endpoint prevention, which encompasses next-generation antivirus threat detection and endpoint controls for threat management purposes; endpoint detection and response, which mitigates security threat before they cause harm and includes advanced tools for investigation and remediation purposes; and endpoint security analytics, which enables clients to easily hunt threats at scale and to investigate historical data. Services by Cybereason are also grouped into three categories, including: managed detection and response, breach response and cyber/compromise assessment. With headquarters in the U.S. and London, U.K., the firm has global offices in Israel, Tokyo, France, Germany and South Africa. During 2021, Cybereason acquired empow, a security analytics company based in Tel Aviv, Israel.

FINANCIAL DATA: *Note: Data for latest year may not have been available at press time.*

In U.S. $	2021	2020	2019	2018	2017	2016
Revenue						
R&D Expense						
Operating Income						
Operating Margin %						
SGA Expense						
Net Income						
Operating Cash Flow						
Capital Expenditure						
EBITDA						
Return on Assets %						
Return on Equity %						
Debt to Equity						

CONTACT INFORMATION:

Phone: 855-695-8200 Fax:
Toll-Free:
Address: 200 Clarendon St., Fl. 18, Boston, MA 02116 United States

STOCK TICKER/OTHER:

Stock Ticker: Private
Employees: 952
Parent Company:
Exchange:
Fiscal Year Ends:

SALARIES/BONUSES:

Top Exec. Salary: $ Bonus: $
Second Exec. Salary: $ Bonus: $

OTHER THOUGHTS:

Estimated Female Officers or Directors:
Hot Spot for Advancement for Women/Minorities:

CyberTAN Technology Inc

NAIC Code: 334220

www.cybertan.com.tw

TYPES OF BUSINESS:

Wireless Networking Equipment
Broadband Equipment
Wireless Network Equipment
Product Manufacture
Internet of Things Solutions
Artificial Intelligence
Wi-Fi Solutions
Cameras and Sensors

BRANDS/DIVISIONS/AFFILIATES:

GEO
LEO

CONTACTS: *Note: Officers with more than one job title may be intentionally listed here more than once.*

Roger Wu, Pres.
Hank Hsieh, VP
K.C. Kuo, VP
Teddy Chen, Chmn.

GROWTH PLANS/SPECIAL FEATURES:

CyberTAN Technology, Inc. manufactures broadband and wireless networking equipment. The company's products are primarily used for home and/or business connectivity, networking and communication purposes. CyberTAN offers six main products lines: 5G broadband, satellite broadband, home connectivity and entertainment, fixed broadband, NFV/SDN and enterprise, and Internet of Things (IoT) solutions. 5G products include: fixed wireless access (FWA) devices, enabling network operators to deliver fast broadband to homes and businesses where fiber is unavailable or too expensive to maintain; SD-WAN (software-defined wide area network) devices, providing encryption solutions for communicating over the internet; and 5G radio access network devices, for mobile communication connectivity. Satellite broadband products offer satellite internet everywhere, including rural areas. This division's products include geostationary satellite GEO, low-earth router LEO and an SD-WAN satellite. Home connectivity and entertainment products deliver Wi-Fi solutions such as whole-home mesh Wi-Fi systems, managed Wi-Fi devices, Wi-Fe traffic boosters and over-the-top/set-top-box (OTT/STB) devices. CyberTAN's fixed broadband products provide fiber access technology to deliver gigabit internet services to residences and businesses. NFV (network functions virtualization) and SDN enterprise products provide networking solutions for telecommunications edge and enterprise applications. This division's virtual customer premises equipment (vCPE) products are offered for small, medium and large enterprises, and other products include access point (AP) network solutions, access switch solutions and voice-over-internet protocol (VoIP) devices. Last, IoT solutions include IoT gateways, IoT sensors, IP cameras, mobile trackers and video/audio artificial intelligence (AI) devices. Headquartered in Taiwan, CyberTAN has a domestic office in New Taipei City and an international office in California, USA.

FINANCIAL DATA: *Note: Data for latest year may not have been available at press time.*

In U.S. $	2021	2020	2019	2018	2017	2016
Revenue		171,926,580	266,777,100	280,818,000	310,899,000	338,959,159
R&D Expense						
Operating Income						
Operating Margin %						
SGA Expense						
Net Income		838,445	5,845,091	5,620,280	4,766,060	11,078,829
Operating Cash Flow						
Capital Expenditure						
EBITDA						
Return on Assets %						
Return on Equity %						
Debt to Equity						

CONTACT INFORMATION:

Phone: 886-3-577-7777 Fax: 886-3-577-7788
Toll-Free:
Address: 99 Park Ave. III, Science Park, Hsinchu, 308 Taiwan

STOCK TICKER/OTHER:

Stock Ticker: 3062
Employees: 2,440
Parent Company:
Exchange: TWSE
Fiscal Year Ends: 12/31

SALARIES/BONUSES:

Top Exec. Salary: $ Bonus: $
Second Exec. Salary: $ Bonus: $

OTHER THOUGHTS:

Estimated Female Officers or Directors:
Hot Spot for Advancement for Women/Minorities:

Cypress Semiconductor Corporation

www.cypress.com

NAIC Code: 334413

TYPES OF BUSINESS:

Integrated Circuits
Embedded Systems
Systems-on-Chip
Microcontrollers
Wireless
Memory
Power Management
Touch Sensing

BRANDS/DIVISIONS/AFFILIATES:

Infineon Technologies AG

CONTACTS:

Note: Officers with more than one job title may be intentionally listed here more than once.

Thad Trent, CFO
Sam Geha, Executive VP, Divisional
Sudhir Gopalswamy, Executive VP, Divisional
Wolfgang Eder, Chmn.-Corporate

GROWTH PLANS/SPECIAL FEATURES:

Cypress Semiconductor Corporation manufactures advanced embedded system solutions for automotive, industrial and consumer products. The company's systems on-chip, general-purpose microcontrollers, analog integrated circuits (ICs), wireless and USB-C-based connectivity solutions and memories help engineers design differentiated products. Cypress operates through two business segments: microcontroller and connectivity, and memory products. The microcontroller and connectivity segment focuses on high-performance microcontroller (MCU), analog and wireless and wired connectivity solutions. This division also includes the company's power management business unit, the touch sensing business unit and its timing solutions business. The memory products segment focuses on high-performance parallel and serial NOR flash memories, NAND flash memories, static random access memory (SRAM), F-RAM ferroelectric memory devices and other specialty memories. Cypress operates as a subsidiary of semiconductor manufacturer, Infineon Technologies AG.

FINANCIAL DATA:

Note: Data for latest year may not have been available at press time.

In U.S. $	2021	2020	2019	2018	2017	2016
Revenue	2,650,000,000	2,469,951,680	2,205,314,000	2,483,840,000	2,327,770,880	1,923,107,968
R&D Expense						
Operating Income						
Operating Margin %						
SGA Expense						
Net Income			40,413,000	354,592,000	-80,915,000	-686,251,008
Operating Cash Flow						
Capital Expenditure						
EBITDA						
Return on Assets %						
Return on Equity %						
Debt to Equity						

CONTACT INFORMATION:

Phone: 408 943-2600 Fax: 408 943-4730
Toll-Free: 800-541-4736
Address: 198 Champion Ct., San Jose, CA 95134 United States

STOCK TICKER/OTHER:

Stock Ticker: Subsidiary
Employees: 6,546
Parent Company: Infineon Technologies AG
Exchange:
Fiscal Year Ends: 12/31

SALARIES/BONUSES:

Top Exec. Salary: $ Bonus: $
Second Exec. Salary: $ Bonus: $

OTHER THOUGHTS:

Estimated Female Officers or Directors:
Hot Spot for Advancement for Women/Minorities:

CYREN Ltd

NAIC Code: 511210E

www.cyren.com

TYPES OF BUSINESS:

Computer Software: Network Security, Managed Access, Digital ID, Cybersecurity & Anti-Virus
Anti-Virus Software
URL Filtering Software
Web Protection
Cybersecurity

BRANDS/DIVISIONS/AFFILIATES:

GROWTH PLANS/SPECIAL FEATURES:

CYREN Ltd provides information security solutions for protecting the web, email, and mobile transactions. It is a security as a service provider of cloud-based security technology solutions that mitigate cyber threats, advanced malware attacks, information leaks, legal liability, and productivity loss through the application of cyber intelligence. The firm's customers include OEM and service provider distribution partners and service providers. Its products and services are categorized in security as a service, cyber intelligence suite, and embedded threat intelligence services. The company derives its revenues from the sale of real-time cloud-based services.

CONTACTS: *Note: Officers with more than one job title may be intentionally listed here more than once.*

Brett Jackson, CEO
Kenneth Tarpey, CFO
Mike Fleck, VP-Mktg.
Eva Markowitz, VP-Human Resources
Eva Markowitz, Vice President, Divisional
Boris Bogod, Vice President, Divisional
Michael Tamir, Vice President, Divisional
Einat Glik, Vice President, Divisional
Sigurdur Stefnisson, Vice President, Divisional
Dan Maier, Vice President, Divisional
Mickey DiPietro, Vice President, Divisional
Atif Ahmed, Vice President, Geographical
Eric Spindel, Vice President

FINANCIAL DATA: *Note: Data for latest year may not have been available at press time.*

In U.S. $	2021	2020	2019	2018	2017	2016
Revenue		36,388,000	38,391,000	35,900,000	30,799,000	30,983,000
R&D Expense		16,083,000	15,801,000	16,116,000	9,825,000	8,656,000
Operating Income		-15,742,000	-17,669,000	-19,301,000	-13,762,000	-5,174,000
Operating Margin %						
SGA Expense		21,261,000	24,702,000	24,545,000	22,837,000	17,459,000
Net Income		-17,263,000	-18,018,000	-19,414,000	-15,648,000	-6,213,000
Operating Cash Flow		-8,410,000	-6,882,000	-11,457,000	-7,214,000	2,418,000
Capital Expenditure		3,248,000	5,166,000	5,304,000	5,338,000	4,113,000
EBITDA		-10,953,000	-10,533,000	-13,291,000	-8,557,000	-2,113,000
Return on Assets %						
Return on Equity %						
Debt to Equity						

CONTACT INFORMATION:

Phone: 011-972-9-863688 Fax:
Toll-Free:
Address: 10 Ha-Menofim St., Fl. 5, Herzliya, 4672561 Israel

STOCK TICKER/OTHER:

Stock Ticker: CYRN
Employees: 222
Parent Company:
Exchange: NAS
Fiscal Year Ends: 12/31

SALARIES/BONUSES:

Top Exec. Salary: $263,172 Bonus: $
Second Exec. Salary: $260,125 Bonus: $

OTHER THOUGHTS:

Estimated Female Officers or Directors: 3
Hot Spot for Advancement for Women/Minorities: Y

Daimler Trucks North America LLC www.daimler-trucksnorthamerica.com

NAIC Code: 336120

TYPES OF BUSINESS:

Truck Manufacturing
Custom-Built Chassis
Van & Bus Manufacturing
Automobile Parts Manufacturing
Specialty Vehicle Manufacturing
Military Vehicle Manufacturing
Used Truck Dealerships
Truck Stops

BRANDS/DIVISIONS/AFFILIATES:

Daimler AG
Freightliner Trucks
Western Star Truck Sales Inc
Detroit Diesel Corporation
Thomas Built Buses
SelecTrucks
Alliance Truck Parts
Daimler Truck Financial

CONTACTS: *Note: Officers with more than one job title may be intentionally listed here more than once.*

John O'Leary, CEO
Jeff Allen, SR. VP-Oper. & Specialty Vehicles
Stefan Kurschner, CFO
David Carson, Sr. VP-Sales & Mktg.
Eileen Frack, Sr. VP-People
Rainer Mueller-Finkeldei, Sr. VP-Eng. & Technology
Friedrich Baumann, Sr. VP-Aftermarket
Albert Kirchmann, Head-Daimler Truck Asia, Finance & Control

GROWTH PLANS/SPECIAL FEATURES:

Daimler Trucks North America, LLC (Daimler NA), a wholly owned subsidiary of Daimler AG, is one of the largest manufacturers of medium- and heavy-duty trucks and specialized commercial vehicles in North America. The company is comprised of nine businesses. Freightliner Trucks manufactures Class 5-8 models of Freightliner-branded trucks with pickup and delivery, towing, municipal, construction and long-haul on-highway applications. Western Star Truck Sales, Inc. manufactures the Western Star brand of trucks, which are targeted at small and medium fleets, as well as owner-operators, with a focus on vocational and extreme-duty segments. Detroit Diesel Corporation manufactures a full portfolio of heavy-duty and mid-range diesel engines, as well as transmissions, axles, safety systems and telematics products for the on-highway and vocational commercial truck markets. Thomas Built Buses designs and builds school buses, including light- and medium-duty lines. Freightliner Custom Chassis Corporation manufactures premium chassis for recreational vehicles, walk-in vans, delivery vehicles, commercial vehicles, shuttle buses and school buses. SelecTrucks is Daimler Trucks' remarketing retail distributor, engaged in selling Freightliner-branded used trucks through retail locations in the U.S. and Canada. Alliance Truck Parts offers new and remanufactured parts to the commercial transportation industry. It has more than 30 product lines for all makes and all models of trucks and buses. Daimler Truck Financial offers financing for commercial vehicles such as Freightliner, Western Star, SelecTrucks, Thomas Built Buses, Mitsubishi Fuso and Sprinter. The firm customizes its financing solutions with a broad range of loan, lease and payment options. Daimler Truck Financial is a business unit of Mercedes-Benz Financial Services USA, LLC. Last, Elite Support are certified delivers that sell, maintain and repair Freightliner and Western Star trucks. In late-2021, Daimler AG approved a spinoff of its truck division since luxury cars and trucks are pursuing different technological approaches: battery versus hydrogen powered vehicles.

FINANCIAL DATA: *Note: Data for latest year may not have been available at press time.*

In U.S. $	2021	2020	2019	2018	2017	2016
Revenue	18,000,000,000	16,741,000,000	21,257,200,000	19,012,100,000	17,688,900,000	14,165,100,000
R&D Expense						
Operating Income						
Operating Margin %						
SGA Expense						
Net Income			2,758,220,000	1,345,100,000	1,068,490,000	1,943,440,000
Operating Cash Flow						
Capital Expenditure						
EBITDA						
Return on Assets %						
Return on Equity %						
Debt to Equity						

CONTACT INFORMATION:

Phone: 503-745-8000 Fax: 503-745-8921
Toll-Free:
Address: 4555 N. Channel Ave., Portland, OR 97217 United States

STOCK TICKER/OTHER:

Stock Ticker: Subsidiary
Employees: 23,709
Parent Company: Daimler Truck Holding AG
Exchange:
Fiscal Year Ends: 12/31

SALARIES/BONUSES:

Top Exec. Salary: $ Bonus: $
Second Exec. Salary: $ Bonus: $

OTHER THOUGHTS:

Estimated Female Officers or Directors:
Hot Spot for Advancement for Women/Minorities:

Sales, profits and employees may be estimates. Financial information, benefits and other data can change quickly and may vary from those stated here.

Darktrace PLC

NAIC Code: 511210E

www.darktrace.com

TYPES OF BUSINESS:

Computer Software: Network Security, Managed Access, Digital ID, Cybersecurity & Anti-Virus
Autonomous Response Technology
Artificial Intelligence
Cyber Security Solutions
Threat Detection Solutions

BRANDS/DIVISIONS/AFFILIATES:

Enterprise Immune System
Darktrace Antigena
Antigena Cloud
Antigena Network
Antigena Email
Darktrace Industrial

CONTACTS: *Note: Officers with more than one job title may be intentionally listed here more than once.*

Poppy Gustafsson, CEO
Nick Trim, COO
Cathy Graham, CFO
Emily Orton, CMO
Jack Stockdale, CTO
Dave Palmer, Chief Product Officer

GROWTH PLANS/SPECIAL FEATURES:

Darktrace PLC is a world-leading artificial intelligence (AI) company for cyber security. The firm was founded in 2013 by mathematicians from the University of Cambridge and government cyber intelligence experts in the U.S. and U.K. Darktrace was formed to empower organizations to defend their systems against the most advanced of cyber threats. Its Enterprise Immune System technology applies AI to detect a range of threats at their earliest stages, including insider attacks, latent vulnerabilities, slow-developing threats and even state-sponsored espionage. Darktrace's autonomous response technology, Darktrace Antigena, allows the Enterprise Immune System to react to in-progress cyberattacks in a highly precise way, giving security teams the time needed to catch up and react. Antigena Cloud provides 24/7 autonomous protection of data in the cloud, stopping insider threats, account takeovers and critical misconfigurations. Antigena Network delivers autonomous response AI across the enterprise and Internet of Things (IoT), generating measured and proportionate responses when a significantly threatening incident arises. Antigena Email allows Darktrace's cyber AI to neutralize malicious emails in Office 365, including advanced spear phishing, impersonation attempts, data loss and high-risk user behaviors. The company's Darktrace Industrial business unit focuses on fighting threats in the industrial and SCADA (supervisory control and data acquisition) networks, and builds on the customer base that utilize Darktrace AI to protect critical national infrastructure and operational technology. Darktrace easily integrates with existing infrastructure, including SIEM dashboards, SOC environments or any other downstream ticketing and alerting tool. This allows security teams to adopt Darktrace without changing existing business processes and working practices. Darktrace serves more than 5,500 customers in over 110 countries.

FINANCIAL DATA: *Note: Data for latest year may not have been available at press time.*

In U.S. $	2021	2020	2019	2018	2017	2016
Revenue	281,300,000	199,100,000	135,781,000	40,000,000	30,000,000	15,000,000
R&D Expense						
Operating Income						
Operating Margin %						
SGA Expense						
Net Income	-149,588,000	-28,672,000				
Operating Cash Flow						
Capital Expenditure						
EBITDA						
Return on Assets %						
Return on Equity %						
Debt to Equity						

CONTACT INFORMATION:

Phone: 440 1223 394100 Fax:
Toll-Free:
Address: Maurice Wilkes Bldg., Cowley Rd., Cambridge, CB4 0DS United Kingdom

STOCK TICKER/OTHER:

Stock Ticker: DARK
Employees: 1,600
Parent Company:
Exchange: London
Fiscal Year Ends: 06/30

SALARIES/BONUSES:

Top Exec. Salary: $ Bonus: $
Second Exec. Salary: $ Bonus: $

OTHER THOUGHTS:

Estimated Female Officers or Directors:
Hot Spot for Advancement for Women/Minorities:

Datang Telecom Technology Co Ltd

www.datang.com

NAIC Code: 334210

TYPES OF BUSINESS:

Telecommunications Equipment
Mobile Communications Products
Optical Communications Products
Digital Microwave Products
Software
Integrated Circuits
Internet of Things
Microelectronics

BRANDS/DIVISIONS/AFFILIATES:

CONTACTS:

Note: Officers with more than one job title may be intentionally listed here more than once.

Xincheng Lei, Managing Dir.
Gui Xue, CFO
Xiubin Qi, Corp. Sec.
Desheng Zhou, Vice Chmn.
Kun Jiang, Deputy Gen. Mgr.
Hongyan Wang, Deputy Gen. Mgr.
Pengfei Wang, Deputy Gen. Mgr.
Bin Cao, Chmn.

GROWTH PLANS/SPECIAL FEATURES:

Datang Telecom Technology Co., Ltd., owned by the Chinese government, is principally engaged in integrated circuit (IC) design, terminal design, software, applications, mobile internet services, communication devices and Internet of Things. Datang's IC design solutions include security chips and mobile terminal security chips. The firm implements hardware system-level terminal security solutions that comply with GP International Standards and UnionPay specifications. They can be used for enterprise applications, industrial applications, financial payments, digital rights, personal privacy and more. Terminal design products and services include smartphones, data terminals and industry terminals. Software solutions include wireless access, operation support systems, information security and platform products. Related applications include smart city, smart business, smart traffic, tourism, energy conservation, government information and more. Mobile internet products and services include custom-designed terminals, custom services and mobile applications. Datang's communication devices offer wired access, wireless access and optical communication. Its Internet of Things (IoT) and smart device products and solutions include smart cards, smart cities, car networking, sensor networks, information security, converged communication systems and video surveillance. In addition, Datang offers a core cloud integrated security+ solution based on loading a domestic cryptographic algorithm security chip, expanding the IoT category to include solutions such as smart door locks.

FINANCIAL DATA:

Note: Data for latest year may not have been available at press time.

In U.S. $	2021	2020	2019	2018	2017	2016
Revenue		184,950,836	204,780,000	340,788,000	667,468,000	1,052,584,806
R&D Expense						
Operating Income						
Operating Margin %						
SGA Expense						
Net Income		-266,214,215	-128,650,000	81,998,400	-406,745,000	-258,531,837
Operating Cash Flow						
Capital Expenditure						
EBITDA						
Return on Assets %						
Return on Equity %						
Debt to Equity						

CONTACT INFORMATION:

Phone: 86-10-5891-9000 Fax: 86-10 58919131
Toll-Free:
Address: Yongjia N. Rd., No. 6, Haidian Dist., Beijing, 100094 China

STOCK TICKER/OTHER:

Stock Ticker: 600198
Exchange: Shanghai
Employees: 918
Fiscal Year Ends: 12/31
Parent Company:

SALARIES/BONUSES:

Top Exec. Salary: $ Bonus: $
Second Exec. Salary: $ Bonus: $

OTHER THOUGHTS:

Estimated Female Officers or Directors:
Hot Spot for Advancement for Women/Minorities:

DataStax Inc

www.datastax.com

NAIC Code: 511210J

TYPES OF BUSINESS:

Computer Software, Data Base & File Management
Software Development
Enterprise Opensource Software
Database Management Systems
Database Security Solutions
Cloud Deployment
Streaming Services

BRANDS/DIVISIONS/AFFILIATES:

Astra DB

CONTACTS:

Note: Officers with more than one job title may be intentionally listed here more than once.

Chet Kapoor, CEO
Mala Tejwani, Dir.-Bus, Dev. & Oper.
Don Dixon, Dir.-Finance
Thomas Been, Dir. Mktg.
Chris Vogel, Dir.-People
Jonathan Ellis, Dir.-Technology
Chet Kapoor, Chmn.

GROWTH PLANS/SPECIAL FEATURES:

DataStax, Inc. is a software company that develops and provides commercial support for an enterprise edition of the Apache Cassandra database. Apache Cassandra is an opensource distributed database management system designed to handle large amounts of data across many commodity servers, providing high availability with no single point of failure. Its NoSQL (not-only-SQL/structured query language) database technology is built for the performance and availability demands of modern web, mobile and Internet of Things (IoT) applications. This gives enterprises a secure database that remains operationally simple when scaled in a single datacenter or across multiple datacenters and clouds. DataStax offers on-premises, hybrid and multi-cloud deployments, as well as a suite of distributed data management products and cloud services. DataStax's marquee offering is Astra DB, an open, multi-cloud serverless database built on a Kubernetes-based architecture. DataStax also offers Astra Streaming, a multi-cloud messaging and event streaming platform built on Apache Pulsar. DataStax has nearly 500 customers including The Home Depot, T-Mobile and Intuit. The firm is based in California, USA, with a EMEA (Europe/Middle East/Africa) regional headquarter in London, U.K., as well as offices in France, Japan, Australia and Singapore. DataStax partners include IBM, Microsoft, Google, VMware, Deloitte, Publicis Sapient, Accenture, DataNaya Inc., Expero, Pivotal, Imanis Data, Feedzai, Mesosphere and Atos.

DataStax offers its employees various company fitness and social options.

FINANCIAL DATA:

Note: Data for latest year may not have been available at press time.

In U.S. $	2021	2020	2019	2018	2017	2016
Revenue	130,000,000	126,000,000	105,000,000	100,000,000	95,000,000	
R&D Expense						
Operating Income						
Operating Margin %						
SGA Expense						
Net Income						
Operating Cash Flow						
Capital Expenditure						
EBITDA						
Return on Assets %						
Return on Equity %						
Debt to Equity						

CONTACT INFORMATION:

Phone: 650-389-6000 Fax:
Toll-Free:
Address: 3975 Freedom Circle, Fl. 4, Santa Clara, CA 95054 United States

STOCK TICKER/OTHER:

Stock Ticker: Private
Employees: 600
Parent Company:
Exchange:
Fiscal Year Ends: 12/31

SALARIES/BONUSES:

Top Exec. Salary: $ Bonus: $
Second Exec. Salary: $ Bonus: $

OTHER THOUGHTS:

Estimated Female Officers or Directors:
Hot Spot for Advancement for Women/Minorities:

Sales, profits and employees may be estimates. Financial information, benefits and other data can change quickly and may vary from those stated here.

Dell Technologies Inc

www.delltechnologies.com/en-us/index.htm

NAIC Code: 334111

TYPES OF BUSINESS:

Computer Manufacturing
Information Technology
IT Device Development
IT Device Production
Hardware
Software
Storage Solutions
Networking Products

BRANDS/DIVISIONS/AFFILIATES:

Client Solutions Group
Infrastructure Solutions Group
Dell EMC
Virtustream

GROWTH PLANS/SPECIAL FEATURES:

Dell Technologies, born from Dell's 2016 acquisition of EMC, is a leading provider of servers, storage, and networking products through its ISG segment, and PCs, monitors, and peripherals via its CSG division. Its brands include Dell, Dell EMC, Secureworks, and Virtustream. The company focuses on supplementing its traditional mainstream servers and PCs with hardware and software products for hybrid-cloud environments. The Texas-based company employs around 158,000 people and sells globally.

CONTACTS: *Note: Officers with more than one job title may be intentionally listed here more than once.*

Michael Dell, CEO
Thomas Sweet, CFO
Brunilda Rios, Chief Accounting Officer
Allison Dew, Chief Marketing Officer
Jeffrey Clarke, COO
Richard Rothberg, General Counsel
Jennifer Saavedra, Other Executive Officer
Howard Elias, Other Executive Officer
William Scannell, President, Divisional

FINANCIAL DATA: *Note: Data for latest year may not have been available at press time.*

In U.S. $	2021	2020	2019	2018	2017	2016
Revenue	94,224,000,000	92,154,000,000	90,621,000,000	78,660,000,000	61,642,000,000	50,911,000,000
R&D Expense	5,275,000,000	4,992,000,000	4,604,000,000	4,384,000,000	2,636,000,000	1,051,000,000
Operating Income	5,144,000,000	2,622,000,000	-191,000,000	-3,333,000,000	-3,252,000,000	-514,000,000
Operating Margin %						
SGA Expense	18,998,000,000	21,319,000,000	20,640,000,000	19,003,000,000	13,575,000,000	7,850,000,000
Net Income	3,250,000,000	4,616,000,000	-2,310,000,000	-3,728,000,000	-1,672,000,000	-1,104,000,000
Operating Cash Flow	11,407,000,000	9,291,000,000	6,991,000,000	6,810,000,000	2,222,000,000	2,162,000,000
Capital Expenditure	2,082,000,000	2,576,000,000	1,497,000,000	1,581,000,000	906,000,000	482,000,000
EBITDA	11,449,000,000	8,814,000,000	7,873,000,000	5,352,000,000	1,333,000,000	2,266,000,000
Return on Assets %						
Return on Equity %						
Debt to Equity						

CONTACT INFORMATION:

Phone: 512 338-4400 Fax: 512 283-6161
Toll-Free: 800-289-3355
Address: One Dell Way, Round Rock, TX 78682 United States

STOCK TICKER/OTHER:

Stock Ticker: DELL
Employees: 158,000
Parent Company:
Exchange: NYS
Fiscal Year Ends: 01/31

SALARIES/BONUSES:

Top Exec. Salary: $881,160 Bonus: $
Second Exec. Salary: $750,000 Bonus: $

OTHER THOUGHTS:

Estimated Female Officers or Directors: 1
Hot Spot for Advancement for Women/Minorities: Y

Deutsche Telekom AG

www.telekom.com

NAIC Code: 517210

TYPES OF BUSINESS:

Local & Long-Distance Telephone Service
Telecommunications
Mobile Communications
Network Products and Services
Broadband Products and Services
Internet Products and Services
IPTV Products and Services
ICT Solution

BRANDS/DIVISIONS/AFFILIATES:

Deutsche Telekom (UK) Ltd
T-Systems South Africa (Pty) Limited
T-Systems PR China Ltd
T-Systems North America Inc
T-Systems Argentina SA
T-Systems do Brasil Ltda
T-Mobile

GROWTH PLANS/SPECIAL FEATURES:

Deutsche Telekom AG (DT) is one of the world's largest telecommunications companies, with roughly 242 million mobile customers, 27 million fixed-network lines and 22 million broadband lines. DT offers its products and services in more than 50 countries worldwide while operating domestically out of Germany. The firm generally operates under the T-Mobile brand. DT provides fixed-network/broadband, mobile communications, internet and IPTV (internet protocol TV) products and services for consumers, and information and communication technology (ICT) solutions for business and corporate customers. The company's core business is the operation and sale of networks and connections.

CONTACTS: *Note: Officers with more than one job title may be intentionally listed here more than once.*

Timotheus Hottges, CEO
Thomas Kremer, Dir.-Legal Affairs, Compliance & Data Privacy
Claudia Nemat, Dir.-Europe & Technology
Reinhard Clemens, Dir.-T-Systems
Niek Jan van Damme, Dir.-Germany

FINANCIAL DATA: *Note: Data for latest year may not have been available at press time.*

In U.S. $	2021	2020	2019	2018	2017	2016
Revenue			86,675,243,008	81,449,975,808	81,013,276,672	80,808,132,608
R&D Expense						
Operating Income						
Operating Margin %						
SGA Expense						
Net Income			4,179,998,208	2,341,317,888	3,741,136,128	2,957,271,552
Operating Cash Flow						
Capital Expenditure						
EBITDA						
Return on Assets %						
Return on Equity %						
Debt to Equity						

CONTACT INFORMATION:

Phone: 49 2281814949 Fax: 49 2281819400
Toll-Free:
Address: Friedrich-Ebert-Allee 140, Bonn, GM 53113 Germany

STOCK TICKER/OTHER:

Stock Ticker: DTEGF
Employees: 226,000
Parent Company:
Exchange: OTC
Fiscal Year Ends: 12/31

SALARIES/BONUSES:

Top Exec. Salary: $ Bonus: $
Second Exec. Salary: $ Bonus: $

OTHER THOUGHTS:

Estimated Female Officers or Directors: 6
Hot Spot for Advancement for Women/Minorities: Y

DiDi Global Inc

www.didiglobal.com

NAIC Code: 561599

TYPES OF BUSINESS:

Car Ride Dispatch Service, Mobile App-Based
Mobility Technology
Mobile Apps
Ride Hailing
Taxi Hailing
Shared Mobility
Automotive Solutions
Artificial Intelligence

BRANDS/DIVISIONS/AFFILIATES:

DiDi
DiDi Finance
DiDi Consumer Loans
DiDi Driver Insurance

GROWTH PLANS/SPECIAL FEATURES:

DiDi Global Inc is a mobility technology platform. It is building four key components of its platform that work together to improve the consumer experience: shared mobility, auto solutions, electric mobility, and autonomous driving. It is a go-to brand in China for shared mobility, providing consumers with a range of safe, affordable, and convenient mobility services, including ride-hailing, taxi-hailing, chauffeur, hitch, and other forms of shared mobility.

CONTACTS: *Note: Officers with more than one job title may be intentionally listed here more than once.*

Will Wei Cheng, CEO
Jean Qing Liu, Pres.

FINANCIAL DATA: *Note: Data for latest year may not have been available at press time.*

In U.S. $	2021	2020	2019	2018	2017	2016
Revenue		22,191,350,000	24,234,560,000	21,181,780,000		
R&D Expense		989,009,200	837,235,000	685,369,000		
Operating Income		-2,158,751,000	-1,254,639,000	-1,948,102,000		
Operating Margin %						
SGA Expense		3,661,059,000	2,784,927,000	2,428,472,000		
Net Income		-1,646,234,000	-1,523,166,000	-2,345,042,000		
Operating Cash Flow		178,115,200	226,186,000	-1,444,880,000		
Capital Expenditure		907,953,100	352,667,600	858,571,100		
EBITDA		-861,954,600	-939,258,400	-1,982,741,000		
Return on Assets %						
Return on Equity %						
Debt to Equity						

CONTACT INFORMATION:

Phone: 86 40 0766 6998 Fax:
Toll-Free:
Address: No. 1 Blk B, No. 8 Dongbeiwang W. Rd., Haidian District, Beijing, 100000 China

STOCK TICKER/OTHER:

Stock Ticker: DIDI Exchange: NYS
Employees: 15,914 Fiscal Year Ends: 12/31
Parent Company:

SALARIES/BONUSES:

Top Exec. Salary: $ Bonus: $
Second Exec. Salary: $ Bonus: $

OTHER THOUGHTS:

Estimated Female Officers or Directors:
Hot Spot for Advancement for Women/Minorities:

Digi International Inc

NAIC Code: 334210A

www.digi.com

TYPES OF BUSINESS:

Networking Equipment
Data Communications Hardware & Software
Local Area Networking Products
Wireless & Cellular Products-Backup Connectivity
Internet of Things

BRANDS/DIVISIONS/AFFILIATES:

SmartSense by Digi

GROWTH PLANS/SPECIAL FEATURES:

Digi International Inc is a Minnesota corporation. The company provides business and mission-critical and Internet of Things (IoT) connectivity products and services. It has two segments: IoT Products and Services and IoT Solutions. The IoT Products and Services segment consists primarily of distinct communications products and communication product development services. IoT Solutions segment offers wireless temperature and other environmental condition monitoring services as well as employee task management services.

CONTACTS: *Note: Officers with more than one job title may be intentionally listed here more than once.*

Ronald Konezny, CEO
James Loch, CFO
Satbir Khanuja, Chairman of the Board
David Sampsell, General Counsel
Kevin Riley, President, Divisional
Tracy Roberts, Vice President, Divisional
Terrence Schneider, Vice President, Divisional

FINANCIAL DATA: *Note: Data for latest year may not have been available at press time.*

In U.S. $	2021	2020	2019	2018	2017	2016
Revenue	308,632,000	279,271,000	254,203,000	228,366,000	181,634,000	203,005,000
R&D Expense	46,623,000	43,765,000	37,564,000	33,178,000	28,566,000	30,955,000
Operating Income	11,523,000	11,434,000	9,985,000	2,623,000	11,322,000	17,852,000
Operating Margin %						
SGA Expense	108,511,000	88,773,000	71,486,000	73,082,000	47,286,000	50,873,000
Net Income	10,366,000	8,411,000	9,958,000	1,303,000	9,366,000	16,708,000
Operating Cash Flow	57,723,000	34,478,000	28,964,000	-2,778,000	2,475,000	27,089,000
Capital Expenditure	2,257,000	899,000	9,335,000	1,842,000	1,773,000	2,729,000
EBITDA	31,271,000	30,354,000	24,643,000	15,085,000	15,036,000	21,595,000
Return on Assets %						
Return on Equity %						
Debt to Equity						

CONTACT INFORMATION:

Phone: 952 912-3444 Fax: 952 912-4952
Toll-Free: 877-912-3444
Address: 11001 Bren Rd. E., Minnetonka, MN 55343 United States

STOCK TICKER/OTHER:

Stock Ticker: DGII Exchange: NAS
Employees: 656 Fiscal Year Ends: 09/30
Parent Company:

SALARIES/BONUSES:

Top Exec. Salary: $454,962 Bonus: $
Second Exec. Salary: $307,315 Bonus: $

OTHER THOUGHTS:

Estimated Female Officers or Directors: 1
Hot Spot for Advancement for Women/Minorities:

Diodes Incorporated

www.diodes.com

NAIC Code: 334413

TYPES OF BUSINESS:

Semiconductor Manufacturing
Semiconductor Design
Semiconductor Marketing

BRANDS/DIVISIONS/AFFILIATES:

Diodes FabTech Inc
Shanghai Kaihong Technology Electronic Co Ltd
Diodes Hong Kong Holding Company Limited
Lite-On Semiconductor Corporation

GROWTH PLANS/SPECIAL FEATURES:

Diodes Inc is a global manufacturer and supplier of application-specific products within the broad discrete, logic, analog, and mixed-signal semiconductor markets. It serves the customer electronics, computing, communications, industrial, and automotive markets. Semiconductors are designed for the diverse end-use application and provide signal amplification and switching functions that serve as vital components of nearly every electronic device. The company focuses on low pin count semiconductor devices with few active or passive components and offers these products throughout Asia, North America, and Europe. Diodes' global customer base includes original equipment manufacturers and electronic manufacturing services, providers.

CONTACTS: *Note: Officers with more than one job title may be intentionally listed here more than once.*

Keh-Shew Lu, CEO
Brett Whitmire, CFO
Richard White, Secretary
Julie Holland, Senior VP, Divisional
Emily Yang, Senior VP, Divisional
Evan Yu, Senior VP, Divisional
Francis Tang, Senior VP, Divisional
Gary Yu, Senior VP, Divisional
C.H. Chen, Vice Chairman of the Board
Jin Zhao, Vice President, Divisional

FINANCIAL DATA: *Note: Data for latest year may not have been available at press time.*

In U.S. $	2021	2020	2019	2018	2017	2016
Revenue		1,229,215,000	1,249,130,000	1,213,989,000	1,054,204,000	942,162,000
R&D Expense		94,288,000	88,517,000	86,286,000	77,877,000	69,937,000
Operating Income		134,438,000	176,179,000	155,078,000	92,708,000	38,056,000
Operating Margin %						
SGA Expense		185,067,000	181,343,000	176,197,000	167,639,000	158,256,000
Net Income		98,088,000	153,250,000	104,021,000	-1,805,000	15,935,000
Operating Cash Flow		187,220,000	229,772,000	185,566,000	181,123,000	124,742,000
Capital Expenditure		75,813,000	98,505,000	87,507,000	111,161,000	58,549,000
EBITDA		240,010,000	315,723,000	264,507,000	171,720,000	137,257,000
Return on Assets %						
Return on Equity %						
Debt to Equity						

CONTACT INFORMATION:

Phone: 972 987-3900 Fax: 972 731-3510
Toll-Free:
Address: 4949 Hedgcoxe Rd., Ste. 200, Plano, TX 75024 United States

STOCK TICKER/OTHER:

Stock Ticker: DIOD
Exchange: NAS
Employees: 7,271
Fiscal Year Ends: 12/31
Parent Company:

SALARIES/BONUSES:

Top Exec. Salary: $728,250 Bonus: $
Second Exec. Salary: $390,500 Bonus: $

OTHER THOUGHTS:

Estimated Female Officers or Directors: 1
Hot Spot for Advancement for Women/Minorities:

D-Link Corporation

NAIC Code: 334210A

www.dlinktw.com.tw

TYPES OF BUSINESS:

Networking Equipment Manufacturing & Distribution
Broadband Products
Unified Network Solutions
Switching Products
Cloud-base Network Management Solutions
Software
IP Surveillance Products
Network Security Solutions

BRANDS/DIVISIONS/AFFILIATES:

GROWTH PLANS/SPECIAL FEATURES:

D-Link Corporation is a leading global designer, developer, manufacturer and distributor of networking, broadband, digital, voice and data communications products for homes and businesses, as well as service providers. D-Link implements and supports unified network solutions that integrate capabilities in switching, wireless, broadband, internet protocol (IP) surveillance and cloud-based network management. Consumer products include smart home ecosystems, Wi-Fi devices and cloud platforms along with related tools, apps and services by D-Link. Business products span edge and cloud solutions, connectivity solutions, surveillance products, network security solutions, network infrastructure products, Wi-Fi products, along with view-cam, network assistant, content management system software and other management solutions. D-Link is a global brand with employees in 60 countries.

CONTACTS: *Note: Officers with more than one job title may be intentionally listed here more than once.*

An-Ping Chen, Pres.
Benedict Lee, VP-Oper.
Jui-Hsu Chen, Exec. VP
John Lee, Chmn.
Bendict Lee, Pres., Latin America

FINANCIAL DATA: *Note: Data for latest year may not have been available at press time.*

In U.S. $	2021	2020	2019	2018	2017	2016
Revenue		536,339,000	549,600,000	632,998,000	650,070,000	758,781,167
R&D Expense						
Operating Income						
Operating Margin %						
SGA Expense						
Net Income		44,097,900	4,892,572	4,750,070	-15,380,000	-31,585,848
Operating Cash Flow						
Capital Expenditure						
EBITDA						
Return on Assets %						
Return on Equity %						
Debt to Equity						

CONTACT INFORMATION:

Phone: 886-2-6600-0123 Fax: 886-2-6600-9898
Toll-Free:
Address: No. 289, Xinhu Third Rd., Neihu Dist., Taipei, 114 Taiwan

STOCK TICKER/OTHER:

Stock Ticker: 2332 Exchange: TWSE
Employees: 2,725 Fiscal Year Ends: 12/31
Parent Company:

SALARIES/BONUSES:

Top Exec. Salary: $ Bonus: $
Second Exec. Salary: $ Bonus: $

OTHER THOUGHTS:

Estimated Female Officers or Directors: 1
Hot Spot for Advancement for Women/Minorities:

DSP Group Inc

www.dspg.com

NAIC Code: 334413

TYPES OF BUSINESS:

Integrated Circuits-Digital Signal Processors
Wireless Chipsets
Voice Recognition

BRANDS/DIVISIONS/AFFILIATES:

HDClear
DBM10

CONTACTS:
Note: Officers with more than one job title may be intentionally listed here more than once.

Ofer Elyakim, CEO
Dror Levy, CFO
Kenneth Traub, Chairman of the Board

GROWTH PLANS/SPECIAL FEATURES:

DSP Group, Inc. produces wireless chipsets for a wide range of smart-enabled devices. Founded in 1987 on the principles of experience, insight and continuous advancement enables DSP to consistently deliver next-generation solutions in the areas of voice, audio, video and data connectivity across diverse mobile, consumer and enterprise products. The group delivers semiconductor system solutions with software and hardware reference designs, enabling original equipment manufacturers (OEMs), original design manufacturers (ODMs), consumer electronics manufacturers and service providers to cost-effectively develop new revenue-generating products with fast time-to-market. DSP's broad portfolio of wireless chipsets integrate digital enhanced cordless telecommunications (DECT), cordless advanced technology-internet and quality (CAT-iq), ultra-low energy (ULE), WiFi, public switched telephone network (PSTN), HDClear, video and voice-over-internet-protocol (VoIP) technologies. HDClear is DSP's own technology and is incorporated into its smart voice product line for mobile, wearables and always-one Internet of Things (IoT) devices. HDClear capitalizes on the voice user interface by incorporating voice command, voice activation, proprietary noise cancellation, acoustic echo cancellation and beam-forming algorithms for the purpose of improving user experience and delivering voice and speech recognition. Recently (2021), DSP Group launched its DBM10 low-power Edge artificial intelligence/machine learning (AI/ML) system on chip (SoC), which comprises a digital signal processor (DSP) and the company's nNetLite neural network processor, both optimized for low-power voice and sensor processing in battery-operated devices. Based in California, USA, the firm has international offices in Israel, Germany, the U.K., Hong Kong, China, Japan, South Korea and India. Export sales account for the majority (approximately 95%) of DSP's total annual revenues.

FINANCIAL DATA:
Note: Data for latest year may not have been available at press time.

In U.S. $	2021	2020	2019	2018	2017	2016
Revenue	118,000,000	114,480,000	117,613,000	117,438,000	124,753,000	137,868,992
R&D Expense						
Operating Income						
Operating Margin %						
SGA Expense						
Net Income		-6,790,000	-1,190,000	-1,957,000	-3,003,000	4,813,000
Operating Cash Flow						
Capital Expenditure						
EBITDA						
Return on Assets %						
Return on Equity %						
Debt to Equity						

CONTACT INFORMATION:

Phone: 408 986-4300 Fax: 408 986-4323
Toll-Free:
Address: 2055 Gateway Pl., Ste. 480, San Jose, CA 95110 United States

STOCK TICKER/OTHER:

Stock Ticker: Subsidiary
Employees: 352
Parent Company: Synaptics Incorporated
Exchange:
Fiscal Year Ends: 12/31

SALARIES/BONUSES:

Top Exec. Salary: $ Bonus: $
Second Exec. Salary: $ Bonus: $

OTHER THOUGHTS:

Estimated Female Officers or Directors: 2
Hot Spot for Advancement for Women/Minorities:

Dyson Singapore Pte Ltd

NAIC Code: 335210

www.dyson.com.sg

TYPES OF BUSINESS:

Vacuum Cleaner Manufacturing
Artificial Intelligence
Hair Dryers and Air Filters
Robotics
Advanced, Solid-State Battery Technologies
Research and Development
Consumer and Household Goods

BRANDS/DIVISIONS/AFFILIATES:

Dyson Airblade
Dyson Lightcycle Morph
Dyson Technology Limited

CONTACTS: *Note: Officers with more than one job title may be intentionally listed here more than once.*

Steven Wichary, Global Pres.
James Dyson, Chmn.

GROWTH PLANS/SPECIAL FEATURES:

Dyson Singapore Pte Ltd. designs and manufactures vacuum cleaners, as well as hair care, air treatment and lighting products. Owner and inventor James Dyson built an industrial cyclone tower that separated particles from the air using centrifugal force. More than 5,000 prototypes later, the Dyson bagless vacuum cleaner was invented. Today, there are Dyson machines in over 65 countries worldwide, and more than one-third of Dyson employees are engineers and scientists engaged in research, design and development. Vacuum cleaner products include uprights, cylinders, cordless, handheld and robots, along with related parts. Hair care products include dryers, straighteners, stylers and related accessories. Air treatment products include purifiers, fans, heaters, humidifiers and related filters and other accessories. Dyson's commercial hand dryers are primarily used in bathrooms and replace the need for towels after washing one's hands. Dyson Airblade hand dryers are hygienic, quiet and use 430-miles-per-hour sheets of air to scrape water from hands, drying them in just 10-12 seconds. Room fans are therefore bladeless, safe and clean; bladeless purifiers remove allergens and pollutants; bladeless heaters provide fast, even room heating; and bladeless humidifiers provide hygienic humidification with even room coverage. Lighting products include the Dyson Lightcycle Morph line of lamps, which intelligently tracks local daylight to automatically adjust lighting for visibility and reading purposes. Dyson Technology Limited is a separate company that operates Dyson's website, apps and connected products. Dyson recently moved its corporate headquarters to Singapore, keeping its British facility as an R&D center. In early-2022, Dyson announced the expansion of its retail footprint in VivoCity, Singapore, offering an immersive demo space to grow its direct-to-consumer retail business strategy.

FINANCIAL DATA: *Note: Data for latest year may not have been available at press time.*

In U.S. $	2021	2020	2019	2018	2017	2016
Revenue	500,000,000	498,419,012	467,194,000	480,833,000	504,572,000	546,437,000
R&D Expense						
Operating Income						
Operating Margin %						
SGA Expense						
Net Income		7,739,004	53,141,000	334,007,000	236,232,000	110,099,000
Operating Cash Flow						
Capital Expenditure						
EBITDA						
Return on Assets %						
Return on Equity %						
Debt to Equity						

CONTACT INFORMATION:

Phone: Fax: 01666 827 200
Toll-Free: 0800-298-0298
Address: 2 Science Park Dr., 03-13/26, Singapore, 118222 Singapore

STOCK TICKER/OTHER:

Stock Ticker: Private
Employees: 785
Parent Company:
Exchange:
Fiscal Year Ends: 12/31

SALARIES/BONUSES:

Top Exec. Salary: $ Bonus: $
Second Exec. Salary: $ Bonus: $

OTHER THOUGHTS:

Estimated Female Officers or Directors:
Hot Spot for Advancement for Women/Minorities:

EAG Global Tech Services Ltd (Eastern Peak)

easternpeak.com

NAIC Code: 511210M

TYPES OF BUSINESS:

Computer Software, e-Commerce, Web Analytics & Applications Management
Software Development
Mobile Applications
Website Creation

BRANDS/DIVISIONS/AFFILIATES:

CONTACTS:

Note: Officers with more than one job title may be intentionally listed here more than once.

Alexey Chalimov, CEO

GROWTH PLANS/SPECIAL FEATURES:

EAG Global Tech Services, Ltd. operates as Eastern Peak, a global software development company based in Israel. The firm builds complex software solutions, intuitive mobile apps and creative websites for startups, mid-size businesses and large enterprises, helping them reach their full potential and increase profits. Eastern Peak keeps ideas safe, with intellectual property rights fully protected. The company shares timely updates on the progress of its client's work, and sets up regular skype meetings, demonstration sessions and feedback sessions to ensure they are meeting demands. How the software development lifecycle works: product definition and specification development is the first process, then the user integration/experience and graphic design process is next, then onto software development, quality assurance and bug-fixing, and the provision of technical and marketing support. Transparency is provided throughout the entire process. Eastern Peak's principles of software development include: continuous delivery of software, technical excellence, intuitive design, constant communication with the customers, short sprints to deliver working software frequently, simplicity in structure and function and 100% customer satisfaction. Costs are fixed in accordance with an agreement, but estimates are free. Services offered by the firm include web development, mobile development, software testing, creative design, digital marketing and video production. The company has global locations in the U.K., Cyprus and eastern Europe.

FINANCIAL DATA:

Note: Data for latest year may not have been available at press time.

In U.S. $	2021	2020	2019	2018	2017	2016
Revenue						
R&D Expense						
Operating Income						
Operating Margin %						
SGA Expense						
Net Income						
Operating Cash Flow						
Capital Expenditure						
EBITDA						
Return on Assets %						
Return on Equity %						
Debt to Equity						

CONTACT INFORMATION:

Phone: 972-9-374-0318 Fax:
Toll-Free:
Address: 1 Shankar St., Herzliya, 4672501 Israel

STOCK TICKER/OTHER:

Stock Ticker: Private
Employees: 200
Parent Company:
Exchange:
Fiscal Year Ends:

SALARIES/BONUSES:

Top Exec. Salary: $ Bonus: $
Second Exec. Salary: $ Bonus: $

OTHER THOUGHTS:

Estimated Female Officers or Directors:
Hot Spot for Advancement for Women/Minorities:

eClinicalWorks

NAIC Code: 511210D

www.eclinicalworks.com

TYPES OF BUSINESS:

Computer Software, Healthcare & Biotechnology
Electronic Prescription Filing
Patient Flow Management
Claims Submission & Management Software
Business Optimization Software

BRANDS/DIVISIONS/AFFILIATES:

healow TeleVisits

CONTACTS:

Note: Officers with more than one job title may be intentionally listed here more than once.

Girish Kumar Navani, CEO

GROWTH PLANS/SPECIAL FEATURES:

eClinicalWorks is a private company operating in the ambulatory clinical systems market. The company primarily provides electronic health record (EHR) and practice management tools for its clients, including physicians; large and small health systems; large and medium medical group practices, including federally qualified health centers and community health centers; and small, solo provider practices. The firm's customer base consists of more than 130,000 physicians and over 850,000 medical professionals in all 50 states and 24 countries. eClinicalWorks' EHR cloud solution provides patient flow management, patient record access, registry reporting, electronic prescription request, referring physician communication and clinical data transfers, all while keeping the data private. When used with the firm's patient management system, the solution enables clients to: review patient history, current medications, allergies and diagnostic tests; streamline medical billing management; check patient insurance eligibility; electronically submit and manage claims; and perform clinical and financial analyses through its patient engagement and enterprise business optimizing tools. Healow TeleVisits delivers an in-office experience via online devices, and offer pre-op consultations, post-op checkups and routine-based encounters. TeleVisits are secure and fully integrated into EHR and patient records. eClincialWorks's population health solution covers the population health across all functional accountable care organization (ACO) categories; and the revenue cycle management console assists in processing claims, financial analytics, reimbursement evaluation and six levels of clearinghouse integrations. The company's cloud platform keeps private data private, and each client's database cannot be affected by another practice's upgrades.

eClinicalWorks offers its employees health, dental, vision, life and disability insurance; flexible spending accounts; and a 401(k) plan.

FINANCIAL DATA:

Note: Data for latest year may not have been available at press time.

In U.S. $	2021	2020	2019	2018	2017	2016
Revenue	670,000,000	646,000,000	600,000,000	490,000,000	462,000,000	440,000,000
R&D Expense						
Operating Income						
Operating Margin %						
SGA Expense						
Net Income						
Operating Cash Flow						
Capital Expenditure						
EBITDA						
Return on Assets %						
Return on Equity %						
Debt to Equity						

CONTACT INFORMATION:

Phone: 508-836-2700 Fax: 508-836-4466
Toll-Free: 866-888-6929
Address: 2 Technology Dr., Westborough, MA 01581 United States

STOCK TICKER/OTHER:

Stock Ticker: Private
Employees: 5,000
Parent Company:
Exchange:
Fiscal Year Ends: 12/31

SALARIES/BONUSES:

Top Exec. Salary: $ Bonus: $
Second Exec. Salary: $ Bonus: $

OTHER THOUGHTS:

Estimated Female Officers or Directors:
Hot Spot for Advancement for Women/Minorities:

ECSI International Inc

www.anti-terrorism.com

NAIC Code: 334290

TYPES OF BUSINESS:

Alarm Systems and Equipment Manufacturing
Integrated Security Systems
Entry Control Technology

BRANDS/DIVISIONS/AFFILIATES:

CONTACTS:

Note: Officers with more than one job title may be intentionally listed here more than once.

Arthur Barchenko, CEO
Natalie Barchenko, Director
Phillip Bower, President, Subsidiary
Richard Stern, Vice President, Divisional
Eldon Moberg, Vice President, Divisional
Thomas Isdanavich, Vice President, Divisional
Robert Oliver, Vice President, Divisional

GROWTH PLANS/SPECIAL FEATURES:

ECSI International, Inc. is a leading manufacturer and global provider of entry control technology solutions for the U.S. Departments of Defense, Energy, Homeland Security and Justice. The company provides systems to protect nuclear power stations, prisons, military bases, seaports and airports, as well as chemical, petrochemical, border protection and commercial facilities of all sizes. ECSI offers U.S. Air Force-certified technology and a comprehensive services portfolio that includes site survey/risk assessment, design and engineering, systems manufacturing and integration, factory acceptance testing, installation supervision, commissioning, operations and maintenance training. Systems that ECSI manufactures and deploys include automated entry control systems, infrared perimeter intrusion detection, fiber optic intelligence detection systems, day/night and thermal imaging cameras, intelligent video motion detection, water infrastructure sensing equipment, interoperable device management systems, local control centers, and central command, control and communication centers. Additional technology solutions by ECSI include long-range infrared camera, small target radar, long-range acoustic device, fiber optic/wireless communications, and observation tower, among others.

FINANCIAL DATA:

Note: Data for latest year may not have been available at press time.

In U.S. $	2021	2020	2019	2018	2017	2016
Revenue						
R&D Expense						
Operating Income						
Operating Margin %						
SGA Expense						
Net Income						
Operating Cash Flow						
Capital Expenditure						
EBITDA						
Return on Assets %						
Return on Equity %						
Debt to Equity						

CONTACT INFORMATION:

Phone: 973 574-8555 Fax: 973 574-8562
Toll-Free:
Address: 65 Kingsland Ave., Clifton, NJ 07014 United States

STOCK TICKER/OTHER:

Stock Ticker: Private
Employees: 15
Parent Company:
Exchange:
Fiscal Year Ends: 06/30

SALARIES/BONUSES:

Top Exec. Salary: $ Bonus: $
Second Exec. Salary: $ Bonus: $

OTHER THOUGHTS:

Estimated Female Officers or Directors:
Hot Spot for Advancement for Women/Minorities:

Electro Optic Systems Holdings Limited

NAIC Code: 334511

www.eos-aus.com

TYPES OF BUSINESS:

Search, Detection, Navigation, Guidance, Aeronautical, and Nautical System and Instrument Manufacturing
Electro-Optic Technologies
Technology Development
Software
Laser Applications
Telescopes
Beam Directors
Precision Mechanisms

BRANDS/DIVISIONS/AFFILIATES:

EOS Space Systems

GROWTH PLANS/SPECIAL FEATURES:

Electro Optic Systems Hldgs Ltd is an Australian technology company. It develops and produces electro-optic technologies for the aerospace market. The group's reportable segments are Communication, Defence and Space. It generates maximum revenue from the Defence segment. The Defence segment develops, manufactures and markets advanced fire control, surveillance, and weapon systems to approved military customers. Geographically, it derives a majority of revenue from North America.

CONTACTS: *Note: Officers with more than one job title may be intentionally listed here more than once.*

Benny Allan Greene, CEO
Pete Short, COO
Michael Lock, CFO
Peter Leahy, Chmn.

FINANCIAL DATA: *Note: Data for latest year may not have been available at press time.*

In U.S. $	2021	2020	2019	2018	2017	2016
Revenue		128,754,700	118,180,800	61,696,360	16,480,940	18,231,460
R&D Expense						
Operating Income		-16,126,170	15,109,030	4,726,938	-5,496,625	-2,704,553
Operating Margin %						
SGA Expense		53,376,040	34,553,680	25,075,290	13,587,730	12,971,870
Net Income		-17,437,670	13,173,590	10,934,660	-6,717,002	-633,612
Operating Cash Flow						
Capital Expenditure		21,238,090	3,286,955	2,278,734	815,298	287,959
EBITDA		-14,251,120	18,061,960	11,255,710	-6,553,856	-1,995,075
Return on Assets %						
Return on Equity %						
Debt to Equity						

CONTACT INFORMATION:

Phone: 61 2-6222-7900 Fax: 61 2-6288-2853
Toll-Free:
Address: 18 Wormald St., Symonston, ACT 2609 Australia

STOCK TICKER/OTHER:

Stock Ticker: EOPSY
Employees: 548
Parent Company:
Exchange: PINX
Fiscal Year Ends: 12/31

SALARIES/BONUSES:

Top Exec. Salary: $ Bonus: $
Second Exec. Salary: $ Bonus: $

OTHER THOUGHTS:

Estimated Female Officers or Directors:
Hot Spot for Advancement for Women/Minorities:

Electro-Sensors Inc

www.electro-sensors.com

NAIC Code: 334513

TYPES OF BUSINESS:

Instruments and Related Products Manufacturing for Measuring, Displaying, and Controlling Industrial Process Variables
Monitoring Systems
Process Control Systems

BRANDS/DIVISIONS/AFFILIATES:

Electro-Sentry
HazardPRO
Motrona

GROWTH PLANS/SPECIAL FEATURES:

Electro-Sensors Inc is engaged in manufacturing and selling a variety of monitoring systems that measure actual machine production and operation rates, as well as systems that regulate the speed of related machines in production processes. Its speed monitoring systems compare revolutions per minute or speed against acceptable rates as determined by a customer. It also includes a line of products that measure production counts or rates, such as parts, gallons, or board feet, alarm systems, tachometers, and other devices that translate impulses from the sensors into alarm signals, computer inputs, or digital displays that are usable by the customer.

CONTACTS: *Note: Officers with more than one job title may be intentionally listed here more than once.*

David Klenk, CEO
Joseph Marino, Chairman of the Board
Gloria Grundhoefer, Controller

FINANCIAL DATA: *Note: Data for latest year may not have been available at press time.*

In U.S. $	2021	2020	2019	2018	2017	2016
Revenue		7,621,000	8,258,000	7,495,000	7,840,000	7,087,000
R&D Expense		836,000	811,000	813,000	812,000	767,000
Operating Income		-204,000	-31,000	-145,000	410,000	170,000
Operating Margin %						
SGA Expense		3,298,000	3,586,000	3,379,000	3,077,000	2,947,000
Net Income		-124,000	187,000	-10,000	295,000	202,000
Operating Cash Flow		331,000	152,000	130,000	468,000	196,000
Capital Expenditure		25,000	257,000	32,000	114,000	8,000
EBITDA		191,000	508,000	304,000	766,000	518,000
Return on Assets %						
Return on Equity %						
Debt to Equity						

CONTACT INFORMATION:

Phone: 952 930-0100 Fax: 952 930-0130
Toll-Free:
Address: 6111 Blue Circle Dr., Minnetonka, MN 55343-9108 United States

STOCK TICKER/OTHER:

Stock Ticker: ELSE
Employees: 37
Parent Company:
Exchange: NAS
Fiscal Year Ends: 12/31

SALARIES/BONUSES:

Top Exec. Salary: $238,847 Bonus: $
Second Exec. Salary: $ Bonus: $

OTHER THOUGHTS:

Estimated Female Officers or Directors:
Hot Spot for Advancement for Women/Minorities:

Embarcadero Technologies Inc

www.embarcadero.com

NAIC Code: 511210J

TYPES OF BUSINESS:

Software, Application & Database Management Technology
Application Development Tools
Embedded Structural Query Language
Mobile Enterprise Application Platform
Creating and Testing Code
App Deployment Tools

BRANDS/DIVISIONS/AFFILIATES:

Idera Inc
RESTful MEAP
RAD Studio
Delphi
C++ Builder
INterBase

CONTACTS: *Note: Officers with more than one job title may be intentionally listed here more than once.*

Michael Swindell, Sr. VP-Prod. Mgmt.
Tony de la Lama, Sr. VP-Eng.
Michael Swindell, Sr. VP-Strategy
David Intersimone, VP-Developer Rel.
Steve Young, Chmn.-Corp.
Nigel Brown, Gen. Mgr.-Int'l

GROWTH PLANS/SPECIAL FEATURES:

Embarcadero Technologies, Inc. is a technology company that designs and produces tools for elite developers who build and maintain critical applications. The company's products are grouped into three categories: development tools, embedded structural query language (SQL) database and RESTful MEAP. Development tools include: RAD Studio, an integrated development environment (IDE) for coding, debugging, testing and designing for cross-platform mobile and desktop deployment; Delphi, for Object Pascal developers worldwide to create apps across devices; and C++ Builder, for creating and testing code in order to deploy apps. The embedded SQL database category offers InterBase, an ultrafast, scalable, embedded SQL database equipped with commercial-grade data security, disaster recovery and change synchronization. The RESTful MEAP (mobile enterprise application platform) is a turnkey application server that provides an out-of-the-box backend platform on which to build and deploy Delphi and C++ Builder application services. Free development tools offered by Embarcadero include C++ compiler, community education platforms, REST debugger, InterBase developer edition, FMX stencils, PyScripter and more. Embarcadero Technologies is a subsidiary of Idera, Inc., an application and server management software provider.

FINANCIAL DATA: *Note: Data for latest year may not have been available at press time.*

In U.S. $	2021	2020	2019	2018	2017	2016
Revenue	180,000,000	174,636,000	176,400,000	168,000,000	160,000,000	150,000,000
R&D Expense						
Operating Income						
Operating Margin %						
SGA Expense						
Net Income						
Operating Cash Flow						
Capital Expenditure						
EBITDA						
Return on Assets %						
Return on Equity %						
Debt to Equity						

CONTACT INFORMATION:

Phone: 512-226-8080 Fax: 415-434-1721
Toll-Free:
Address: 10801 North Mopac Expressway, Bldg. 1, Ste. 100, Austin, TX 78759 United States

STOCK TICKER/OTHER:

Stock Ticker: Private
Employees: 222
Parent Company: Idera Inc
Exchange:
Fiscal Year Ends: 12/31

SALARIES/BONUSES:

Top Exec. Salary: $ Bonus: $
Second Exec. Salary: $ Bonus: $

OTHER THOUGHTS:

Estimated Female Officers or Directors: 1
Hot Spot for Advancement for Women/Minorities:

Emerson Electric Co

NAIC Code: 334513

www.emerson.com

TYPES OF BUSINESS:

Engineering & Technology Products & Services
Industrial Automation Products
Power Products
Air Conditioning & Refrigeration Products
Appliances & Tools

BRANDS/DIVISIONS/AFFILIATES:

Mita-Teknik

GROWTH PLANS/SPECIAL FEATURES:

Emerson Electric is a multi-industrial conglomerate that operates under two business platforms: automation solutions and commercial and residential solutions. The latter is further subdivided into two operating segments: climate technologies, which sells HVAC and refrigeration products and services, as well as tools and home products, which sells tools and compressors, among other products and services. Commercial and residential solutions boasts several household brands, including Copeland, InSinkErator, and RIDGID. Automation solutions is most known for its process manufacturing solutions, which consists of measurement instrumentation, as well as valves and actuators, among other products and services. About half of the firm's geographic sales take place in the United States.

CONTACTS: *Note: Officers with more than one job title may be intentionally listed here more than once.*

Surendralal Karsanbhai, CEO
Frank Dellaquila, CFO
James Turley, Chairman of the Board
Michael Baughman, Chief Accounting Officer
Lisa Flavin, Chief Compliance Officer
Katherine Bell, Chief Marketing Officer
Ram Krishnan, COO
Mark Bulanda, Executive VP, Divisional
Sara Bosco, General Counsel
Elizabeth Adefioye, Other Executive Officer
Michael Train, Other Executive Officer
James Froedge, President, Divisional

FINANCIAL DATA: *Note: Data for latest year may not have been available at press time.*

In U.S. $	2021	2020	2019	2018	2017	2016
Revenue	18,236,000,000	16,785,000,000	18,372,000,000	17,408,000,000	15,264,000,000	14,522,000,000
R&D Expense						
Operating Income	3,084,000,000	2,771,000,000	3,120,000,000	2,991,000,000	2,650,000,000	2,714,000,000
Operating Margin %						
SGA Expense	4,179,000,000	3,999,000,000	4,457,000,000	4,258,000,000	3,618,000,000	3,464,000,000
Net Income	2,303,000,000	1,965,000,000	2,306,000,000	2,203,000,000	1,518,000,000	1,635,000,000
Operating Cash Flow	3,575,000,000	3,083,000,000	3,006,000,000	2,892,000,000	1,912,000,000	2,881,000,000
Capital Expenditure	581,000,000	538,000,000	594,000,000	617,000,000	476,000,000	447,000,000
EBITDA	4,047,000,000	3,364,000,000	3,882,000,000	3,627,000,000	3,172,000,000	3,099,000,000
Return on Assets %						
Return on Equity %						
Debt to Equity						

CONTACT INFORMATION:

Phone: 314 553-2000 Fax: 314 553-3527
Toll-Free:
Address: 8000 W. Florissant Ave., (PO Box 4100), St. Louis, MO 63136 United States

STOCK TICKER/OTHER:

Stock Ticker: EMR
Employees: 86,700
Parent Company:
Exchange: NYS
Fiscal Year Ends: 09/30

SALARIES/BONUSES:

Top Exec. Salary: $1,303,750 Bonus: $2,050,000
Second Exec. Salary: $709,613 Bonus: $1,050,000

OTHER THOUGHTS:

Estimated Female Officers or Directors: 2
Hot Spot for Advancement for Women/Minorities: Y

Entrust Corporation

www.entrust.com

NAIC Code: 511210E

TYPES OF BUSINESS:

Computer Software, Network Security, Managed Access, Digital ID,
Cybersecurity & Anti-Virus
Digital Identification & Certificates
Digital Security

BRANDS/DIVISIONS/AFFILIATES:

Entrust

CONTACTS:

Note: Officers with more than one job title may be intentionally listed here more than once.

Todd Wilkinson, CEO
Jeff Smolinksi, Sr. VP-Operations
Kurt Ishaug, CFO
Karen Kaukol, CMO
Beth Klehr, Chief Human Resources Officer
Anudeep Parhar, CIO
Robert (Bob) VanKirk, Sr. VP-American Sales
Mike Baxter, Sr. VP-Product Dev.
Mark Reeves, Sr. VP-Int'l Sales

GROWTH PLANS/SPECIAL FEATURES:

Entrust Corporation is a global provider of security applications that protect and secure digital identities and information. The firm designs, produces and sells security, policy and access management software products and related services. Solutions include financial cards, passports, identification cards, authentication solutions (cloud-based, mobile, hybrid), digital certificates, border control, credential lifecycle management and transaction technologies. Entrust products consist of categories such as secure socket layer (SSL) certificates, qualified certificates, digital signing certificates, passport systems, identification card printers, financial card printers, central card issuance, software, short message service (SMS) passcode, authentication, Internet of Things (IoT) security, public key infrastructure, nCipher hardware security modules, related supplies and related accessories. Supplies include print ribbons, overlays, laminates, tactile impression solutions, cleaning supplies, topping foils, card delivery stickers/labels and more. Accessories include devices such as pin pads, magnetic strip encoders and digital signature pads. Entrust serves financial, corporate, government, education, healthcare, and retail clients located throughout the world. The company is based in Minnesota, USA, and has additional office locations in the U.S., Asia Pacific, Canada, Europe, Latin America, the Caribbean and the Middle East.

FINANCIAL DATA:

Note: Data for latest year may not have been available at press time.

In U.S. $	2021	2020	2019	2018	2017	2016
Revenue	880,000,000	840,000,000	800,000,000	700,000,000	600,000,000	570,000,000
R&D Expense						
Operating Income						
Operating Margin %						
SGA Expense						
Net Income						
Operating Cash Flow						
Capital Expenditure						
EBITDA						
Return on Assets %						
Return on Equity %						
Debt to Equity						

CONTACT INFORMATION:

Phone: 952-933-1223 Fax:
Toll-Free: 800-621-6972
Address: 1187 Park Pl., Shakopee, MN 55379 United States

STOCK TICKER/OTHER:

Stock Ticker: Private
Employees: 2,500
Parent Company:
Exchange:
Fiscal Year Ends: 12/31

SALARIES/BONUSES:

Top Exec. Salary: $ Bonus: $
Second Exec. Salary: $ Bonus: $

OTHER THOUGHTS:

Estimated Female Officers or Directors:
Hot Spot for Advancement for Women/Minorities:

Epic Systems Corporation

www.epic.com

NAIC Code: 511210D

TYPES OF BUSINESS:

Computer Software, Healthcare & Biotechnology
Information Networks
Support Services
Software
Clinical Software
Health Records Management

BRANDS/DIVISIONS/AFFILIATES:

Epicenter
EpicCare
Lucy
Community Library Exchange

CONTACTS: *Note: Officers with more than one job title may be intentionally listed here more than once.*

Judy Faulkner, CEO
Carl Dvorak, Exec. VP

GROWTH PLANS/SPECIAL FEATURES:

Epic Systems Corporation is a developer of health industry clinical, access and revenue software for mid-and large-sized medical groups, hospitals, academic facilities, children's organizations, multi-hospital systems and integrated health care organizations. All Epic software applications are designed to share a single database, called Epicenter, so that each viewer can access available patient data through a single interface from anywhere in the organization. The firm's clinical software products include integrated inpatient and ambulatory systems under the EpicCare brand as well as health information management tools and specialty information systems. The firm's interoperability service, Lucy, personal health record that allows patients to organize and access their medical history independently of any one facility. Other products offer access services, including scheduling, inpatient and ambulatory registration, call management and nurse triage; revenue cycle services, such as hospital and professional billing; health plan and managed care administration systems; clinical and financial data repositories; enterprise reporting; patient medical record access systems; and connectivity tools, including voice recognition, interfacing and patient monitoring devices. In conjunction with its software applications, the company provides extensive client services, including training, process engineering, tailoring of applications to the client's situation and access to network specialists who plan and implement client systems. In addition, Epic hosts Community Library Exchange, an online collection of application tools and pre-made content that allows clients to share report and registration templates, custom forms, enterprise report formats and documentation shortcuts. Epic is headquartered in Wisconsin, USA, with international offices in the Netherlands, Australia, Denmark, Norway, United Arab Emirates, the U.K., Saudi Arabia, Finland and Singapore.

FINANCIAL DATA: *Note: Data for latest year may not have been available at press time.*

In U.S. $	2021	2020	2019	2018	2017	2016
Revenue	3,500,000,000	3,300,000,000	3,200,000,000	2,890,000,000	2,740,000,000	2,550,000,000
R&D Expense						
Operating Income						
Operating Margin %						
SGA Expense						
Net Income						
Operating Cash Flow						
Capital Expenditure						
EBITDA						
Return on Assets %						
Return on Equity %						
Debt to Equity						

CONTACT INFORMATION:

Phone: 608-271-9000 Fax: 608-271-7237
Toll-Free:
Address: 1979 Milky Way, Verona, WI 53593 United States

STOCK TICKER/OTHER:

Stock Ticker: Private
Exchange:
Employees: 10,000
Fiscal Year Ends: 12/31
Parent Company:

SALARIES/BONUSES:

Top Exec. Salary: $ Bonus: $
Second Exec. Salary: $ Bonus: $

OTHER THOUGHTS:

Estimated Female Officers or Directors: 1
Hot Spot for Advancement for Women/Minorities:

Extreme Networks Inc

www.extremenetworks.com

NAIC Code: 334210A

TYPES OF BUSINESS:

Computer Networking & Related Equipment, Manufacturing
Network Solutions
Cloud Solutions
Internet of Things
Wired and Wireless Infrastructure Equipment
Cloud Networking Platform

BRANDS/DIVISIONS/AFFILIATES:

Ipanema

GROWTH PLANS/SPECIAL FEATURES:

Extreme Networks provides software-driven networking services for enterprise customers. Its products include wired and wireless network infrastructure equipment and software for network management, policy, analytics, and access controls. It offers high-density Wi-Fi, centralized management, cloud-based network management, and application analytics capabilities. Roughly half of the firm's revenue is generated in the Americas, with the rest coming from Europe, the Middle East, Africa, and Asia-Pacific.

CONTACTS: *Note: Officers with more than one job title may be intentionally listed here more than once.*

Edward Meyercord, CEO
Remi Thomas, CFO
John Shoemaker, Chairman of the Board
Joseph Vitalone, Other Executive Officer

FINANCIAL DATA: *Note: Data for latest year may not have been available at press time.*

In U.S. $	2021	2020	2019	2018	2017	2016
Revenue	1,009,418,000	948,019,000	995,789,000	983,142,000	598,118,000	528,389,000
R&D Expense	196,995,000	209,606,000	210,132,000	183,877,000	93,724,000	78,721,000
Operating Income	38,976,000	-44,815,000	-6,192,000	23,830,000	21,268,000	-13,415,000
Operating Margin %						
SGA Expense	343,042,000	344,623,000	340,949,000	318,095,000	200,791,000	188,481,000
Net Income	1,936,000	-126,845,000	-25,853,000	-46,792,000	-8,517,000	-31,884,000
Operating Cash Flow	144,535,000	35,884,000	104,945,000	19,043,000	59,283,000	30,366,000
Capital Expenditure	17,176,000	15,268,000	22,730,000	40,411,000	10,425,000	5,327,000
EBITDA	88,358,000	-32,921,000	39,596,000	16,332,000	26,249,000	18,722,000
Return on Assets %						
Return on Equity %						
Debt to Equity						

CONTACT INFORMATION:

Phone: 408 579-2800 Fax: 408 579-3000
Toll-Free: 888-257-3000
Address: 2121 RDU Center Dr., Ste. 300, Morrisville, NC 27560 United States

STOCK TICKER/OTHER:

Stock Ticker: EXTR Exchange: NAS
Employees: 2,584 Fiscal Year Ends: 06/30
Parent Company:

SALARIES/BONUSES:

Top Exec. Salary: $725,000 Bonus: $
Second Exec. Salary: $400,000 Bonus: $100,000

OTHER THOUGHTS:

Estimated Female Officers or Directors: 1
Hot Spot for Advancement for Women/Minorities: Y

F5 Networks Inc

www.f5.com

NAIC Code: 511210B

TYPES OF BUSINESS:

Computer Software: Network Management (IT), System Testing & Storage
Multi-Cloud
Security
Managed Services
Software
Hardware

BRANDS/DIVISIONS/AFFILIATES:

Volterra

GROWTH PLANS/SPECIAL FEATURES:

F5 is a market leader in the application delivery controller market. The company sells products for networking traffic, security, and policy management. Its products ensure applications are safely routed in efficient manners within on-premises data centers and across cloud environments. More than half of its revenue is based on providing services, and its three customer verticals are enterprises, service providers, and government entities. The Seattle-based firm was incorporated in 1996 and generates sales globally.

F5 Networks offers its employees comprehensive health benefits and a variety of assistance programs.

CONTACTS: *Note: Officers with more than one job title may be intentionally listed here more than once.*

Francis Pelzer, CFO
Mika Yamamoto, Chief Marketing Officer
Tom Fountain, Chief Strategy Officer
Geng Lin, Chief Technology Officer
Alan Higginson, Director
Francois Locoh-Donou, Director
Chad Whalen, Executive VP, Divisional
Scot Rogers, Executive VP
Kara Sprague, Executive VP
Haiyan Song, Executive VP
Ana White, Executive VP

FINANCIAL DATA: *Note: Data for latest year may not have been available at press time.*

In U.S. $	2021	2020	2019	2018	2017	2016
Revenue	2,603,416,000	2,350,822,000	2,242,447,000	2,161,407,000	2,090,041,000	1,995,034,000
R&D Expense	512,627,000	441,324,000	408,058,000	366,084,000	350,365,000	334,227,000
Operating Income	394,025,000	400,067,000	518,463,000	609,325,000	577,065,000	556,428,000
Operating Margin %						
SGA Expense	1,203,618,000	1,101,544,000	959,349,000	824,517,000	809,126,000	767,174,000
Net Income	331,241,000	307,441,000	427,734,000	453,689,000	420,761,000	365,855,000
Operating Cash Flow	645,196,000	660,898,000	747,841,000	761,068,000	740,281,000	711,535,000
Capital Expenditure	30,651,000	59,940,000	103,542,000	53,465,000	42,681,000	68,238,000
EBITDA	509,449,000	495,924,000	586,970,000	668,816,000	638,213,000	613,204,000
Return on Assets %						
Return on Equity %						
Debt to Equity						

CONTACT INFORMATION:

Phone: 206 272-5555 Fax: 206 272-5556
Toll-Free: 888-882-4447
Address: 801 5th Ave., Seattle, WA 98104 United States

STOCK TICKER/OTHER:

Stock Ticker: FFIV
Exchange: NAS
Employees: 6,461
Fiscal Year Ends: 09/30
Parent Company:

SALARIES/BONUSES:

Top Exec. Salary: $875,000 Bonus: $
Second Exec. Salary: $528,273 Bonus: $

OTHER THOUGHTS:

Estimated Female Officers or Directors: 3
Hot Spot for Advancement for Women/Minorities: Y

Fanuc Corporation

www.fanuc.co.jp

NAIC Code: 333517

TYPES OF BUSINESS:

Machine Tool Manufacturing
Robotics
Factory Automation
Robot Manufacturing
Equipment Manufacturing
Machines
Motors
Lasers

BRANDS/DIVISIONS/AFFILIATES:

ROBOMACHINE
ROBODRILL
ROBOSHOT
ROBOCUT
ROBONANO
FANUC Robot i
FANUC Intelligent Edge Link & Drive
FANUC MT-LINKi

GROWTH PLANS/SPECIAL FEATURES:

Fanuc Corporation provides factory automation products, such as industrial robots, computerized numerical control (CNC) systems, and compact machining centers (Robodrills) to mainly manufacturing companies globally. Fanuc had its beginnings as part of Fujitsu developing early numerical control (NC) systems, and now commands the top global market share with its CNC systems and industrial robots. Fanuc has approximately 260 service stations across the world and currently has more than 4 million CNC controls and 550,000 robots installed globally.

CONTACTS:

Note: Officers with more than one job title may be intentionally listed here more than once.

Kenji Yamaguchi, CEO
Yoshiharu Inaba, Chmn.

FINANCIAL DATA:

Note: Data for latest year may not have been available at press time.

In U.S. $	2021	2020	2019	2018	2017	2016
Revenue	4,844,179,000	4,466,029,000	5,584,759,000	6,384,626,000	4,718,129,000	5,477,997,000
R&D Expense						
Operating Income	988,664,600	776,334,700	1,434,897,000	2,017,539,000	1,346,323,000	1,894,195,000
Operating Margin %						
SGA Expense						
Net Income	826,086,900	644,713,700	1,354,636,000	1,598,863,000	1,122,078,000	1,403,290,000
Operating Cash Flow	1,036,835,000	1,272,996,000	1,561,790,000	1,546,431,000	1,069,497,000	1,235,747,000
Capital Expenditure	191,276,200	662,797,400	1,101,227,000	905,205,400	768,944,800	896,348,000
EBITDA	1,384,978,000	1,179,774,000	1,783,821,000	2,317,968,000	1,579,443,000	2,079,654,000
Return on Assets %						
Return on Equity %						
Debt to Equity						

CONTACT INFORMATION:

Phone: 81 555845555 Fax: 81 555845512
Toll-Free:
Address: 3580 Furubaba, Shibokusa Oshinomura, Minamitsuru-gun, 401-0597 Japan

STOCK TICKER/OTHER:

Stock Ticker: FANUY
Exchange: PINX
Employees: 10,210
Fiscal Year Ends: 03/31
Parent Company:

SALARIES/BONUSES:

Top Exec. Salary: $ Bonus: $
Second Exec. Salary: $ Bonus: $

OTHER THOUGHTS:

Estimated Female Officers or Directors:
Hot Spot for Advancement for Women/Minorities:

Faro Technologies Inc

www.faro.com

NAIC Code: 334513

TYPES OF BUSINESS:

Instruments and Related Products Manufacturing for Measuring, Displaying, and Controlling Industrial Process Variables
Measurement Solutions
Imaging Solutions
Three-Dimensional

GROWTH PLANS/SPECIAL FEATURES:

Faro Technologies Inc is a global technology company. It designs, develops, manufactures, markets and supports software driven, three-dimensional (3-D) measurement, imaging, and realization systems. The operating segments of the company are 3D Manufacturing, Construction BIM, and Emerging Verticals.

BRANDS/DIVISIONS/AFFILIATES:

FaroArm
FARO ScanArm
FARO Laser Tracker
FARO Laser Projector
FARO Focus
FARO SCENE
FARO As-Built
BuildIT

CONTACTS: *Note: Officers with more than one job title may be intentionally listed here more than once.*

Michael Burger, CEO
Allen Muhich, CFO
John Donofrio, Chairman of the Board
Kevin Beadle, Senior VP, Divisional

FINANCIAL DATA: *Note: Data for latest year may not have been available at press time.*

In U.S. $	2021	2020	2019	2018	2017	2016
Revenue		303,768,000	381,765,000	403,627,000	360,917,000	325,584,000
R&D Expense		42,896,000	44,175,000	39,706,000	35,376,000	30,125,000
Operating Income		-14,876,000	-23,421,000	5,754,000	5,322,000	13,284,000
Operating Margin %						
SGA Expense		131,827,000	177,378,000	164,572,000	147,351,000	120,683,000
Net Income		629,000	-62,147,000	4,930,000	-14,516,000	11,107,000
Operating Cash Flow		21,394,000	32,468,000	6,323,000	10,355,000	37,583,000
Capital Expenditure		6,072,000	8,793,000	12,921,000	11,347,000	9,377,000
EBITDA		-16,534,000	-41,717,000	23,357,000	22,419,000	26,542,000
Return on Assets %						
Return on Equity %						
Debt to Equity						

CONTACT INFORMATION:

Phone: 407 333-9911 Fax: 407 333-4181
Toll-Free:
Address: 250 Technology Park, Lake Mary, FL 32746 United States

STOCK TICKER/OTHER:

Stock Ticker: FARO
Employees: 1,818
Parent Company:
Exchange: NAS
Fiscal Year Ends: 12/31

SALARIES/BONUSES:

Top Exec. Salary: $700,000 Bonus: $
Second Exec. Salary: $376,223 Bonus: $

OTHER THOUGHTS:

Estimated Female Officers or Directors:
Hot Spot for Advancement for Women/Minorities:

FAW Group Corporation (First Automotive Works) www.faw.com

NAIC Code: 336111

TYPES OF BUSINESS:

Automobile Manufacturing
Parts Manufacturing
Truck Manufacturing
Passenger Vehicle Manufacturing
All-Electric Vehicles

BRANDS/DIVISIONS/AFFILIATES:

First Automotive Works
China FAW Group Import & Export Co Ltd
Hongqi
Besturne
Junpai
Senia
Advanced Technical Innovation Center
New Energy Vehicle R&D Center

CONTACTS: *Note: Officers with more than one job title may be intentionally listed here more than once.*

Xiandong Qiu, Pres.
Tieqi Teng, Chief Acct.
Xianping Xu, Chmn.

GROWTH PLANS/SPECIAL FEATURES:

FAW Group Corporation is a state-owned Chinese vehicle manufacturer. Founded in 1953 as First Automotive Works, the firm became one of the first vehicle producers in China, starting with the 1956 rollout of Jiefang trucks and the 1958 launch of Hongqi cars. Since then, FAW has grown to produce millions of vehicles annually, including light-, medium- and heavy-duty trucks; automobiles; municipal buses; luxury tourist coaches; custom bus chassis; and mini-vehicles. Passenger vehicle models include the Hongqi, Besturne, Junpai and Senia lines; commercial trucks such as long-distance trucks, construction trucks and distribution trucks; and buses and coaches such as municipal transit buses, urban buses, luxury tourist coaches and school buses. FAW Group offers all-electric vehicles, including the Hongqi line of passenger models. Headquartered in Changchun, Jilin Province, the firm's domestic production facilities, subsidiaries and engineering development/test centers are located throughout China. FAW's Advanced Technical Innovation Center is located in Beijing, China; its New Energy Vehicle Research and Development (R&D) Center and Exterior/Interior Design Center are located in Shanghai; its forward-looking technology R&D center is located in Munich, Germany; and its artificial-intelligence (AI) R&D center is located in California, USA. Subsidiary China FAW Group Import & Export Co., Ltd. provides global marketing services and solutions for the group's passenger and commercial vehicles.

FINANCIAL DATA: *Note: Data for latest year may not have been available at press time.*

In U.S. $	2021	2020	2019	2018	2017	2016
Revenue		106,848,000,000	88,723,900,000	69,524,000,000	68,174,700,000	62,852,000,000
R&D Expense						
Operating Income						
Operating Margin %						
SGA Expense						
Net Income			2,907,032,000	2,855,800,000	2,330,332,800	3,253,000,000
Operating Cash Flow						
Capital Expenditure						
EBITDA						
Return on Assets %						
Return on Equity %						
Debt to Equity						

CONTACT INFORMATION:

Phone: 86-431-8590-0715 Fax: 86-431-8761-4780
Toll-Free:
Address: Dongfeng St., No. 3025, Changchun, 130011 China

STOCK TICKER/OTHER:

Stock Ticker: Government-Owned
Employees: 130,000
Parent Company:
Exchange:
Fiscal Year Ends: 12/31

SALARIES/BONUSES:

Top Exec. Salary: $ Bonus: $
Second Exec. Salary: $ Bonus: $

OTHER THOUGHTS:

Estimated Female Officers or Directors:
Hot Spot for Advancement for Women/Minorities:

Flex Ltd

NAIC Code: 334418

www.flextronics.com

TYPES OF BUSINESS:

Printed Circuit Assembly (Electronic Assembly) Manufacturing
Telecommunications Equipment Manufacturing
Engineering, Design & Testing Services
Logistics Services
Camera Modules
Medical Devices
LCD Displays
Original Design Manufacturing (ODM)

BRANDS/DIVISIONS/AFFILIATES:

GROWTH PLANS/SPECIAL FEATURES:

Flex Ltd is a contract manufacturing companies, providing comprehensive electronics design, manufacturing, and product management services to global electronics and technology companies. The company's operating segments include Flex Agility Solutions (FAS) and Flex Reliability Solutions (FRS). It generates maximum revenue from Flex Agility Solutions. Flex Agility Solutions segment includes Communications, Enterprise and Cloud; Lifestyle and Consumer Devices markets.

CONTACTS: *Note: Officers with more than one job title may be intentionally listed here more than once.*

Revathi Advaithi, CEO
Francois Barbier, Pres.
Christopher Collier, CFO
Phil Ulrich, Chief Human Resources Officer
Mark Kemp, Pres., Medical
Gus Shahin, CIO
Erik Volkerink, CTO
Christopher Obey, Pres., Automotive
Christopher Cook, Pres., Power Solutions
Jeannine Sargent, Pres., Energy
Jonathan Hoak, General Counsel
Francois Barbier, Pres., Global Oper. & Components
David Mark, Chief Strategy Officer
Renee Brotherton, VP-Corp. Comm.
Christopher Collier, Chief Accounting Officer
Paul Humphries, Pres., High Reliability Solutions
Caroline Dowling, Pres., Integrated Network Solutions
Doug Britt, Pres., Industrial & Emerging Solutions
Mike Dennison, Pres., High Velocity Solutions
Tom Linton, Chief Procurement & Supply Chain Officer

FINANCIAL DATA: *Note: Data for latest year may not have been available at press time.*

In U.S. $	2021	2020	2019	2018	2017	2016
Revenue	24,124,000,000	24,209,870,000	26,210,510,000	25,441,130,000	23,862,930,000	24,418,890,000
R&D Expense						
Operating Income	808,000,000	439,745,000	490,302,000	497,843,000	502,210,000	587,206,000
Operating Margin %						
SGA Expense	817,000,000	834,105,000	953,077,000	1,019,399,000	937,339,000	954,890,000
Net Income	613,000,000	87,579,000	93,399,000	428,534,000	319,564,000	444,081,000
Operating Cash Flow	144,000,000	-1,533,276,000	-2,971,024,000	753,598,000	1,149,909,000	1,136,445,000
Capital Expenditure	351,000,000	461,745,000	725,606,000	561,997,000	525,111,000	510,634,000
EBITDA	1,433,000,000	1,052,513,000	1,092,736,000	1,199,080,000	1,080,040,000	1,054,835,000
Return on Assets %						
Return on Equity %						
Debt to Equity						

CONTACT INFORMATION:

Phone: 65 6890-7188 Fax: 65 6543-1888
Toll-Free:
Address: 2 Changi South Ln., Singapore, 486123 Singapore

STOCK TICKER/OTHER:

Stock Ticker: FLEX
Employees: 167,201
Parent Company:
Exchange: NAS
Fiscal Year Ends: 03/31

SALARIES/BONUSES:

Top Exec. Salary: $390,833 Bonus: $500,000
Second Exec. Salary: $862,500 Bonus: $

OTHER THOUGHTS:

Estimated Female Officers or Directors: 4
Hot Spot for Advancement for Women/Minorities: Y

FogHorn Systems

NAIC Code: 511210I

www.foghorn.io

TYPES OF BUSINESS:

Computer Software, Operating Systems, Languages & Development Tools

BRANDS/DIVISIONS/AFFILIATES:

Johnson Controls

GROWTH PLANS/SPECIAL FEATURES:

FogHorn is a leading developer of edge AI software for industrial and commercial IoT application solutions. FogHorn's software platform brings the power of advanced analytics and machine learning to the on-premises edge environment enabling a new class of applications for advanced monitoring and diagnostics, machine performance optimization, proactive maintenance and operational intelligence use cases. The firm's technology is ideally designed for OEMs, systems integrators and end customers in manufacturing, power and water, oil and gas, renewable energy, mining, transportation, healthcare, retail, as well as smart grid, smart city, smart building and connected vehicle applications. In January 2022, FogHorn was acquired by Johnson Controls, a developer of smart and sustainable buildings.

CONTACTS:

Note: Officers with more than one job title may be intentionally listed here more than once.

Sastry Malladi, VP-OpenBlue Artificial Intelligence

FINANCIAL DATA:

Note: Data for latest year may not have been available at press time.

In U.S. $	2021	2020	2019	2018	2017	2016
Revenue						
R&D Expense						
Operating Income						
Operating Margin %						
SGA Expense						
Net Income						
Operating Cash Flow						
Capital Expenditure						
EBITDA						
Return on Assets %						
Return on Equity %						
Debt to Equity						

CONTACT INFORMATION:

Phone: 408-906-0700 Fax:

Toll-Free:

Address: 150 Mathilda Pl., Ste. 600, Sunnyvale, CA 94086 United States

STOCK TICKER/OTHER:

Stock Ticker: Subsidiary Exchange:

Employees: Fiscal Year Ends:

Parent Company: Johnson Controls

SALARIES/BONUSES:

Top Exec. Salary: $ Bonus: $

Second Exec. Salary: $ Bonus: $

OTHER THOUGHTS:

Estimated Female Officers or Directors:

Hot Spot for Advancement for Women/Minorities:

Forcepoint LLC

www.forcepoint.com

NAIC Code: 511210E

TYPES OF BUSINESS:

Computer Software, Network Security, Managed Access, Digital ID,
Cybersecurity & Anti-Virus
Network & Internet Security Software
Data Protection
Cloud Security
Artificial Intelligence
Machine Learning
Edge Protection
Remote Security Protection

BRANDS/DIVISIONS/AFFILIATES:

Francisco Partners
Cyberinc
Bitglass

CONTACTS:

Note: Officers with more than one job title may be intentionally listed here more than once.

Manny Rivelo, CEO
Matthew T. Santangelo, CFO
Karen Clark, Chief Human Resources Officer
Rees Johnson, Chief Product Officer
JT Taylor, VP

GROWTH PLANS/SPECIAL FEATURES:

Forcepoint, LLC is focused on protecting organizations from advanced cyberattacks and data theft. Forcepoint's cloud platform solutions provide user protection and monitoring services, risk-adaptive data production, and human-centric edge protection for web, cloud, private apps. Its hybrid products include cloud security gateways, private access, data loss prevention, next-generation firewall, cross domain security, cloud access security brokering, remote browser isolation, secure web gateway, email security, insider threats, behavior analytics and data protection. Artificial Intelligence and machine learning are utilized for behavioral understanding, causing Forcepoint's solutions to adapt in real-time to how people interact with data. Primary products include data loss prevention, next-generation firewall and secure web gateway. Industries served by Forcepoint primarily include government, finance, critical infrastructure and healthcare. Forcepoint is owned by Francisco Partners, a global investment firm that specializes in partnering with technology and technology-enabled businesses. During 2021, Forcepoint acquired Cyberinc, which delivers intelligent remote browser isolation technology; and acquired Bitglass, a leader in security service edge, making security easier to deploy and operate by consolidating technologies for protecting people everywhere as they access and use business data in cloud applications, on the web, and in private apps.

FINANCIAL DATA:

Note: Data for latest year may not have been available at press time.

In U.S. $	2021	2020	2019	2018	2017	2016
Revenue	735,000,000	700,000,000	658,000,000	634,000,000	608,000,000	586,000,000
R&D Expense						
Operating Income						
Operating Margin %						
SGA Expense						
Net Income			8,000,000	50,000,000	33,000,000	90,000,000
Operating Cash Flow						
Capital Expenditure						
EBITDA						
Return on Assets %						
Return on Equity %						
Debt to Equity						

CONTACT INFORMATION:

Phone: 858 320-8000 Fax: 858 458-2950
Toll-Free: 800-723-1166
Address: 10900-A Stonelake Blvd., Quarry Oaks 1, Ste. 350, Austin, TX 78759 United States

STOCK TICKER/OTHER:

Stock Ticker: Private
Employees: 2,592
Parent Company: Francisco Partners
Exchange:
Fiscal Year Ends: 12/31

SALARIES/BONUSES:

Top Exec. Salary: $ Bonus: $
Second Exec. Salary: $ Bonus: $

OTHER THOUGHTS:

Estimated Female Officers or Directors: 2
Hot Spot for Advancement for Women/Minorities: Y

Ford Motor Company

www.ford.com

NAIC Code: 336111

TYPES OF BUSINESS:

Automobile Manufacturing
Automobile Design
Automobile Manufacture
Automobile Distribution
Autonomous Vehicles
Automotive Parts
Automotive Financing Services
Artificial Intelligence

BRANDS/DIVISIONS/AFFILIATES:

Ford
Lincoln
Ford Credit
Argo AI
Spin
BlueOvalSK

GROWTH PLANS/SPECIAL FEATURES:

Ford Motor Co. manufactures automobiles under its Ford and Lincoln brands. The company has about 14% market share in the United States and about 7% share in Europe. Sales in North America and Europe made up 69% and 19.5% of 2020 auto revenue, respectively. Ford has about 186,000 employees, including about 58,000 UAW employees, and is based in Dearborn, Michigan.

CONTACTS: *Note: Officers with more than one job title may be intentionally listed here more than once.*

Anning Chen, CEO, Geographical
James Farley, CEO
John Lawler, CFO
William Ford, Chairman of the Board
Cathy OCallaghan, Chief Accounting Officer
John Mellen, General Counsel
Hau Thai-Tang, Other Executive Officer
Kiersten Robinson, Other Executive Officer
Stuart Rowley, President, Geographical
Kumar Galhotra, President, Geographical

FINANCIAL DATA: *Note: Data for latest year may not have been available at press time.*

In U.S. $	2021	2020	2019	2018	2017	2016
Revenue		127,144,000,000	155,900,000,000	160,338,000,000	156,776,000,000	151,800,000,000
R&D Expense						
Operating Income		4,199,000,000	10,046,000,000	12,666,000,000	13,917,000,000	13,020,000,000
Operating Margin %						
SGA Expense		10,193,000,000	11,161,000,000	11,403,000,000	11,527,000,000	12,196,000,000
Net Income		-1,279,000,000	47,000,000	3,677,000,000	7,602,000,000	4,596,000,000
Operating Cash Flow		24,269,000,000	17,639,000,000	15,022,000,000	18,096,000,000	19,792,000,000
Capital Expenditure		5,742,000,000	7,632,000,000	7,785,000,000	7,049,000,000	6,992,000,000
EBITDA		16,597,000,000	18,371,000,000	23,344,000,000	26,838,000,000	25,311,000,000
Return on Assets %						
Return on Equity %						
Debt to Equity						

CONTACT INFORMATION:

Phone: 313 322-3000 Fax: 313 222-4177
Toll-Free: 800-392-3673
Address: 1 American Rd., Dearborn, MI 48126 United States

STOCK TICKER/OTHER:

Stock Ticker: F Exchange: NYS
Employees: 183,000 Fiscal Year Ends: 12/31
Parent Company:

SALARIES/BONUSES:

Top Exec. Salary: $1,800,000 Bonus: $
Second Exec. Salary: $1,700,000 Bonus: $

OTHER THOUGHTS:

Estimated Female Officers or Directors: 4
Hot Spot for Advancement for Women/Minorities: Y

Forrester Research Inc

www.forrester.com

NAIC Code: 541910

TYPES OF BUSINESS:

Market Research
Consulting & Advisory
Workshops & Events

BRANDS/DIVISIONS/AFFILIATES:

Research
Forrester Wave (The)
Age of the Customer Research
Forrester Connect
Leadership Boards
ForecastView
FeedbackNow

CONTACTS: *Note: Officers with more than one job title may be intentionally listed here more than once.*

George Colony, CEO
Michael Doyle, CFO
Scott Chouinard, Chief Accounting Officer
Mike Kasparian, Chief Information Officer
Ryan Darrah, Chief Legal Officer
Shirley Macbeth, Chief Marketing Officer
Kelley Hippler, Other Executive Officer
Carrie Fanlo, Other Executive Officer
Sherri Kottmann, Other Executive Officer
Steven Peltzman, Other Executive Officer

GROWTH PLANS/SPECIAL FEATURES:

Forrester Research Inc is a United-States-based company that provides independent research, data, and advisory services. It operates through the following segments: The Research segment develops and delivers research, connect, and analytics products; The consulting segment includes the revenues and the related costs of the company's consulting organization, and the Events segment is engaged in developing and hosting in-person and virtual events.

Forrester employees receive medical and dental insurance, retirement savings and employee perks, which may be differentiated by location.

FINANCIAL DATA: *Note: Data for latest year may not have been available at press time.*

In U.S. $	2021	2020	2019	2018	2017	2016
Revenue		448,984,000	461,697,000	357,575,000	337,673,000	326,095,000
R&D Expense						
Operating Income		21,954,000	7,873,000	26,212,000	27,549,000	31,800,000
Operating Margin %						
SGA Expense		216,569,000	225,907,000	175,744,000	165,823,000	157,477,000
Net Income		9,990,000	-9,570,000	15,380,000	15,140,000	17,651,000
Operating Cash Flow		47,754,000	48,406,000	38,418,000	37,493,000	41,858,000
Capital Expenditure		8,905,000	11,890,000	5,049,000	7,861,000	4,140,000
EBITDA		61,232,000	42,238,000	35,329,000	34,978,000	40,443,000
Return on Assets %						
Return on Equity %						
Debt to Equity						

CONTACT INFORMATION:

Phone: 617 613-5730 Fax:
Toll-Free:
Address: 60 Acorn Park Dr., Cambridge, MA 02140 United States

STOCK TICKER/OTHER:

Stock Ticker: FORR Exchange: NAS
Employees: 1,798 Fiscal Year Ends: 12/31
Parent Company:

SALARIES/BONUSES:

Top Exec. Salary: $425,000 Bonus: $237,500
Second Exec. Salary: $410,712 Bonus: $127,500

OTHER THOUGHTS:

Estimated Female Officers or Directors: 3
Hot Spot for Advancement for Women/Minorities: Y

Fortinet Inc

www.fortinet.com

NAIC Code: 334210A

TYPES OF BUSINESS:

Network Security Products
ASIC Network Security Appliances
Security Subscription Services
Threat Management Security Systems
Artificial Intelligence
Internet of Things Solutions

GROWTH PLANS/SPECIAL FEATURES:

Fortinet is a cybersecurity vendor that sells products, support, and services to small and midsize businesses, enterprises, and government entities. Its products include unified threat management appliances, firewalls, network security, and its security platform, Security Fabric. Services revenue is primarily from FortiGuard security subscriptions and FortiCare technical support. At the end of 2019, products were 37% of revenue and services were 63% of sales. The California-based company sells products worldwide, with the Americas representing 43% of sales in 2019.

BRANDS/DIVISIONS/AFFILIATES:

FortiOS
FortiASIC
FortiGuard
Fortinet Security Fabric
Fabric Ready Partners
Client Access Security Broker Solution
FortiCASB

CONTACTS: *Note: Officers with more than one job title may be intentionally listed here more than once.*

Ken Xie, CEO
Keith Jensen, CFO
Michael Xie, Chief Technology Officer
John Whittle, Executive VP, Divisional

FINANCIAL DATA: *Note: Data for latest year may not have been available at press time.*

In U.S. $	2021	2020	2019	2018	2017	2016
Revenue		2,594,400,000	2,156,200,000	1,801,200,000	1,494,930,000	1,275,443,000
R&D Expense		341,400,000	277,100,000	244,500,000	210,614,000	183,084,000
Operating Income		491,600,000	344,200,000	231,000,000	110,144,000	46,941,000
Operating Margin %						
SGA Expense		1,191,400,000	1,029,000,000	875,300,000	788,888,000	707,581,000
Net Income		488,500,000	326,500,000	332,200,000	31,399,000	32,187,000
Operating Cash Flow		1,083,700,000	808,000,000	638,900,000	594,405,000	345,708,000
Capital Expenditure		125,900,000	92,200,000	53,000,000	135,312,000	67,182,000
EBITDA		560,400,000	405,800,000	286,700,000	165,620,000	95,461,000
Return on Assets %						
Return on Equity %						
Debt to Equity						

CONTACT INFORMATION:

Phone: 866-789-9001 Fax: 408 235-7737
Toll-Free:
Address: 899 Kifer Rd., Sunnyvale, CA 94086 United States

STOCK TICKER/OTHER:

Stock Ticker: FTNT
Employees: 7,082
Parent Company:
Exchange: NAS
Fiscal Year Ends: 12/31

SALARIES/BONUSES:

Top Exec. Salary: $797,000 Bonus: $
Second Exec. Salary: $490,000 Bonus: $

OTHER THOUGHTS:

Estimated Female Officers or Directors: 3
Hot Spot for Advancement for Women/Minorities: Y

Foxconn Technology Co Ltd

www.foxconntech.com.tw

NAIC Code: 334418

TYPES OF BUSINESS:

Contract Electronics Manufacturing
Original Design Manufacturer (ODM)
Electronics Manufacturing & Design
Research and Engineering Services
Outsourcing

BRANDS/DIVISIONS/AFFILIATES:

Future Mobility Corporation
Belkin International Inc

GROWTH PLANS/SPECIAL FEATURES:

Foxconn Technology Co Ltd along with its subsidiaries is engaged in manufacturing, processing, and sales of case, heat dissipation modules, and consumer electronics products. The firm's operating segments include Trading services of electronic products and Manufacturing and sales of mechanical components. It generates a majority of its revenue from the Electronic product trading segment. Geographically, the company operates in China, Japan, Taiwan, USA, and others. It generates a majority of its revenue from Japan followed by China.

CONTACTS: *Note: Officers with more than one job title may be intentionally listed here more than once.*

Han-Ming Li, Pres.
Tzu-Hung Li, Dir.-Finance
Guangyao Li, Chmn.

FINANCIAL DATA: *Note: Data for latest year may not have been available at press time.*

In U.S. $	2021	2020	2019	2018	2017	2016
Revenue		3,776,801,000	3,597,043,000	5,119,999,000	5,327,534,000	2,887,321,000
R&D Expense		62,789,200	80,134,000	63,368,280	53,103,920	35,162,690
Operating Income		94,372,620	190,815,600	310,189,200	379,380,600	408,144,200
Operating Margin %						
SGA Expense		76,012,920	87,679,780	112,744,600	81,445,890	83,011,720
Net Income		170,057,300	256,970,500	329,661,600	359,170,000	386,407,500
Operating Cash Flow		87,692,570	454,616,900	423,488,400	301,112,400	522,980,000
Capital Expenditure		16,401,850	42,213,760	69,071,420	51,974,660	51,137,120
EBITDA		261,026,200	394,211,100	497,174,100	505,940,000	597,314,100
Return on Assets %						
Return on Equity %						
Debt to Equity						

CONTACT INFORMATION:

Phone: 886 222680970 Fax: 886 222687176
Toll-Free:
Address: No. 3-2, Zhongshan Road, Taipei, 236 Taiwan

STOCK TICKER/OTHER:

Stock Ticker: FXCOF
Exchange: PINX
Employees: 700,000
Fiscal Year Ends: 12/31
Parent Company:

SALARIES/BONUSES:

Top Exec. Salary: $ Bonus: $
Second Exec. Salary: $ Bonus: $

OTHER THOUGHTS:

Estimated Female Officers or Directors:
Hot Spot for Advancement for Women/Minorities:

FPT Software Company Limited

www.fpt-software.com

NAIC Code: 541511

TYPES OF BUSINESS:

Custom Computer Programming Services
Software Development
Developer Tools
Digital Tools
Robotic Process Automation
Artificial Intelligence
DevOps
Platforms

BRANDS/DIVISIONS/AFFILIATES:

FPT Corporation
akaSuite
akaBot
akaWork
akaDev
akaLink
akaChain
akaminds

CONTACTS: *Note: Officers with more than one job title may be intentionally listed here more than once.*

Pham Minh Tuan, CEO
Tran Dang Hoa, COO
Nguyen Khai Hoan, CFO
Chu Thi Thanh Ha, Chairperson

GROWTH PLANS/SPECIAL FEATURES:

FPT Software Company Limited is part of FPT Corporation, and is a global technology and information technology (IT) services group based in Vietnam. The firm's akaSuite offers innovative digital tools for organizations, including the ability to develop an enterprise-level blockchain platform and data container platform. The suite's akaBot product offers robotic process automation; akaTrans offers an artificial intelligent (AI)-powered translation solution; akaWork is a DevOps solution; akaDev is a low-code platform; akaMES is a MOM/MES platform; akaAT is an all-in-one automation test solution; akaNOX is a comprehensive data migration toolset; akaLink is an employee engagement platform, akaCoola is a smart home product; akaDrive is an autonomous driving solution; akaInsights is a customer data platform; akaMeet is a video collaboration platform; akaChain, an enterprise blockchain platform, akaminds, a data container platform, and CloudSuite, an accelerator for the cloud. FPT Software comprises development and delivery centers across the U.S., Japan, Europe, United Arab Emirates, Australia, New Zealand, Vietnam and Asia Pacific.

FINANCIAL DATA: *Note: Data for latest year may not have been available at press time.*

In U.S. $	2021	2020	2019	2018	2017	2016
Revenue	750,000,000	726,777,000	527,608,600	363,868,000	274,082,000	225,853,000
R&D Expense						
Operating Income						
Operating Margin %						
SGA Expense						
Net Income						
Operating Cash Flow						
Capital Expenditure						
EBITDA						
Return on Assets %						
Return on Equity %						
Debt to Equity						

CONTACT INFORMATION:

Phone: 84-3-768-9048 Fax: 84-3-768-9049
Toll-Free:
Address: FPT Cau Giay Bldg., Duy Tan St., Cau Giay Distr., Hanoi, Vietnam

STOCK TICKER/OTHER:

Stock Ticker: Subsidiary
Employees: 17,628
Parent Company: FPT Corporation
Exchange:
Fiscal Year Ends: 12/31

SALARIES/BONUSES:

Top Exec. Salary: $ Bonus: $
Second Exec. Salary: $ Bonus: $

OTHER THOUGHTS:

Estimated Female Officers or Directors:
Hot Spot for Advancement for Women/Minorities:

Fujitsu Laboratories Ltd

www.fujitsu.com/global/about/research

NAIC Code: 541712

TYPES OF BUSINESS:

Research & Development
Computing Research
RFID Technology
Semiconductors
Security & Encryption Technology
Robotics Research
Nanotechnology Research

BRANDS/DIVISIONS/AFFILIATES:

Fujitsu Limited
Fujitsu Laboratories of America Inc
Fujitsu Laboratories of Europe Limited
Fujitsu Research and Development Center Co Ltd

CONTACTS: *Note: Officers with more than one job title may be intentionally listed here more than once.*

Shigeru Sasaki, CEO

GROWTH PLANS/SPECIAL FEATURES:

Fujitsu Laboratories Ltd. is Fujitsu Limited's central research and development unit. Fujitsu Lab's stated goal is to make ubiquitous networking a reality, meaning that communication would be possible anytime, anywhere and with anyone. To this end, the firm divides its research into four target areas. The people, which focuses on developing a system of sensors, interactive interfaces and surveillance programs designed to anticipate and assist user needs. These technologies include cloud devices, sensing and actuation, human-friendly interfaces, front-end systems, and personal-area networks and body-area networks. Information via creative intelligence, which includes social intelligence, intelligent optimization, digital transformation and social innovation-oriented technologies. This target area is dedicated to creating widespread systems for easily-accessible and secure information. The connected infrastructure target area aims to develop technologies that provide information and communication technology environments that are capable of quickly adapting to change. Its technologies include platform-as-a-service (PaaS) environments, network services, cloud services and flexible storage systems. The common foundation target area supports Fujitsu Lab's other business units, as well as client needs, through the development of various technologies as product bases, manufacturing technologies for product formations, energy management technologies, networking technologies and green solutions technologies. Global research and development subsidiaries include Fujitsu Laboratories of America, Inc.; Fujitsu Laboratories of Europe Limited; and Fujitsu Research and Development Center Co. Ltd. The firm's various laboratory niches include computer systems, software, information systems technologies, Internet of Things (IoT) systems, network systems, front technologies, artificial intelligence, security research, devices and materials, applied innovation research and R&D strategy and planning.

FINANCIAL DATA: *Note: Data for latest year may not have been available at press time.*

In U.S. $	2021	2020	2019	2018	2017	2016
Revenue						
R&D Expense						
Operating Income						
Operating Margin %						
SGA Expense						
Net Income						
Operating Cash Flow						
Capital Expenditure						
EBITDA						
Return on Assets %						
Return on Equity %						
Debt to Equity						

CONTACT INFORMATION:

Phone: 81-44-754-2613 Fax:
Toll-Free:
Address: 4-1-1, Kamikodanaka, Nakahara-ku, Kawasaki-shi, 211-8588 Japan

STOCK TICKER/OTHER:

Stock Ticker: Subsidiary
Exchange:
Employees: 1,200
Fiscal Year Ends: 03/31
Parent Company: Fujitsu Limited

SALARIES/BONUSES:

Top Exec. Salary: $ Bonus: $
Second Exec. Salary: $ Bonus: $

OTHER THOUGHTS:

Estimated Female Officers or Directors:
Hot Spot for Advancement for Women/Minorities:

Fujitsu Limited

www.fujitsu.com

NAIC Code: 334111

TYPES OF BUSINESS:

Computer Manufacturing
Information Technology
Internet of Things
Artificial Intelligence
Cyber Security
Digital Workplace
Hybrid IT
Digital Transformation

BRANDS/DIVISIONS/AFFILIATES:

GROWTH PLANS/SPECIAL FEATURES:

Fujitsu Ltd delivers total solutions in the field of information and communication technology. The company provides solutions/system integration services focused on information system consulting and construction, and infrastructure services centered on outsourcing services. Fujitsu provides services across a wide range of countries and regions, including Europe, the Americas, Asia, and Oceania. It operates in three segments namely, Technology Solutions; Ubiqitous Solutions and Device Solutions. Ubiquitous Solutions consists of PCs, mobile phones, and mobilewear. In PCs, Fujitsu's lineup includes desktop and laptop PCs known for energy efficiency, security, and other enhanced features, as well as water- and dust-resistant tablets.

CONTACTS: *Note: Officers with more than one job title may be intentionally listed here more than once.*

Takahito Tokita, Pres.
Masami Fujita, Sr. Exec. VP
Hideyuki Saso, Sr. Exec. VP
Masahiro Koezuka, Vice Chmn.
Kazuhiko Kato, Exec. VP

FINANCIAL DATA: *Note: Data for latest year may not have been available at press time.*

In U.S. $	2021	2020	2019	2018	2017	2016
Revenue	31,542,840,000	33,898,600,000	34,730,210,000	36,012,610,000	39,626,850,000	41,644,350,000
R&D Expense						
Operating Income	2,340,199,000	1,858,309,000	1,144,310,000	1,603,538,000	1,132,306,000	1,059,822,000
Operating Margin %						
SGA Expense	7,332,949,000	7,598,019,000	8,201,522,000	8,871,287,000	9,239,762,000	9,552,581,000
Net Income	1,781,132,000	1,406,295,000	918,790,100	1,487,997,000	777,556,100	762,389,700
Operating Cash Flow	2,705,942,000	3,051,413,000	873,572,000	1,761,054,000	2,199,668,000	2,223,929,000
Capital Expenditure	1,131,516,000	1,168,412,000	1,060,042,000	1,186,294,000	1,744,200,000	1,667,516,000
EBITDA	4,144,652,000	3,933,912,000	2,856,815,000	3,706,038,000	2,905,618,000	3,074,321,000
Return on Assets %						
Return on Equity %						
Debt to Equity						

CONTACT INFORMATION:

Phone: 81 362522220 Fax:
Toll-Free:
Address: Shiodome City Center, 1-5-2 Higashi-Shimbashi, Tokyo, 105-7123 Japan

STOCK TICKER/OTHER:

Stock Ticker: FJTSY
Employees: 145,845
Parent Company:
Exchange: PINX
Fiscal Year Ends: 03/31

SALARIES/BONUSES:

Top Exec. Salary: $ Bonus: $
Second Exec. Salary: $ Bonus: $

OTHER THOUGHTS:

Estimated Female Officers or Directors: 1
Hot Spot for Advancement for Women/Minorities:

Fujitsu Network Communications Inc

www.fujitsu.com/us/products/network

NAIC Code: 334210

TYPES OF BUSINESS:

Telecommunications Equipment & Software
Digital Transformation Solutions
Optical Network Solutions
5G Network Solutions
Network Automation Services
Network Deployment Solutions
Open RAN Solutions
Consultancy Services

BRANDS/DIVISIONS/AFFILIATES:

Fujitsu Limited

GROWTH PLANS/SPECIAL FEATURES:

Fujitsu Network Communications, Inc. is a subsidiary of Fujitsu Limited and a provider of network products and services that drive digital transformation. The company's network solutions span optical networks, 5G networks, 5G transport, network services, network automation, rural broadband networks, network deployment solutions and open radio access networks (RAN). Fujitsu Networks' products and services help customers achieve goals such as reducing expenses, stretching capital, speeding up deployment time and modernizing legacy networks. Services include cybersecurity, network automation and operational efficiency consultancy; network design, build and integration solutions; supply chain optimization and program management solutions; network operations and maintenance; digital transformation; and managed network services.

CONTACTS: *Note: Officers with more than one job title may be intentionally listed here more than once.*

Doug Moore, CEO

FINANCIAL DATA: *Note: Data for latest year may not have been available at press time.*

In U.S. $	2021	2020	2019	2018	2017	2016
Revenue						
R&D Expense						
Operating Income						
Operating Margin %						
SGA Expense						
Net Income						
Operating Cash Flow						
Capital Expenditure						
EBITDA						
Return on Assets %						
Return on Equity %						
Debt to Equity						

CONTACT INFORMATION:

Phone: 972-690-6000 Fax: 972-479-4647
Toll-Free: 800-873-3822
Address: 2801 Telecom Pkwy., Richardson, TX 75082 United States

STOCK TICKER/OTHER:

Stock Ticker: Subsidiary
Employees: 1,358
Parent Company: Fujitsu Limited
Exchange:
Fiscal Year Ends: 03/31

SALARIES/BONUSES:

Top Exec. Salary: $ Bonus: $
Second Exec. Salary: $ Bonus: $

OTHER THOUGHTS:

Estimated Female Officers or Directors:
Hot Spot for Advancement for Women/Minorities:

Garmin Ltd

NAIC Code: 334511

www.garmin.com

TYPES OF BUSINESS:

Communications Equipment-GPS-Based
Aviation Electronics
Marine Electronics
Automotive Electronics
Recreation & Fitness Electronics
Navigational Equipment

BRANDS/DIVISIONS/AFFILIATES:

Garmin Connect
Connect IQ
Vesper Marine

GROWTH PLANS/SPECIAL FEATURES:

Garmin produces GPS-enabled hardware and software for five verticals: fitness, outdoors, auto, aviation, and marine. The company relies on licensing mapping data to enable its hardware specialized for often niche activities like scuba diving or sailing. Garmin operates in 100 countries and sells its products via distributors as well as relationships with original equipment manufacturers.

CONTACTS: *Note: Officers with more than one job title may be intentionally listed here more than once.*

Clifton Pemble, CEO
Andrew Etkind, VP-Gen. Counsel
Doug Boessen, CFO
Frank McLoughlin, VP-Aviation Eng.
Andrew Etkind, General Counsel
Brian J. Pokorny, VP-Oper.
Dawn Iddings, VP-Bus. Dev. & Customer Care
Jon Cassat, VP-Comm. Affairs
Patrick Desbois, VP-Exec. Office
Matthew Munn, VP
Philip Straub, VP
Michael Wiegers, VP-Consumer Eng.
Min Kao, Exec. Chmn.

FINANCIAL DATA: *Note: Data for latest year may not have been available at press time.*

In U.S. $	2021	2020	2019	2018	2017	2016
Revenue		4,186,573,000	3,757,505,000	3,347,444,000	3,087,004,000	3,018,665,000
R&D Expense		705,685,000	605,366,000	567,805,000	511,634,000	467,960,000
Operating Income		1,054,240,000	945,586,000	778,343,000	668,860,000	623,909,000
Operating Margin %						
SGA Expense		721,411,000	683,024,000	633,571,000	602,670,000	587,701,000
Net Income		992,324,000	952,486,000	694,080,000	694,955,000	510,814,000
Operating Cash Flow		1,135,267,000	698,549,000	919,520,000	660,842,000	705,682,000
Capital Expenditure		187,466,000	120,408,000	160,355,000	151,928,000	96,675,000
EBITDA		1,180,955,000	1,051,761,000	874,537,000	755,112,000	710,249,000
Return on Assets %						
Return on Equity %						
Debt to Equity						

CONTACT INFORMATION:

Phone: 41 526301600 Fax:
Toll-Free:
Address: Muhlentalstrasse 2, Schaffhausen, 8200 Switzerland

STOCK TICKER/OTHER:

Stock Ticker: GRMN
Employees: 16,000
Parent Company:
Exchange: NAS
Fiscal Year Ends: 12/31

SALARIES/BONUSES:

Top Exec. Salary: $900,000 Bonus: $ 307
Second Exec. Salary: $600,000 Bonus: $3,846

OTHER THOUGHTS:

Estimated Female Officers or Directors: 2
Hot Spot for Advancement for Women/Minorities: Y

Gartner Inc

www.gartner.com

NAIC Code: 541910

TYPES OF BUSINESS:

Research-Computer Hardware & Software
Industry Research
IT Symposia & Conferences
Measurement & Advisory Services

BRANDS/DIVISIONS/AFFILIATES:

Symposium/Xpo

GROWTH PLANS/SPECIAL FEATURES:

Based in Stamford, Conn., Gartner provides independent research and analysis on information technology and other related technology industries. Its research is delivered to clients' desktops in the form of reports, briefings, and updates. Typical clients are chief information officers and other business executives who help plan companies' IT budgets. Gartner also provides consulting services and hosted nearly 80 IT conferences across the globe in 2007.

CONTACTS: *Note: Officers with more than one job title may be intentionally listed here more than once.*

Eugene Hall, CEO
Craig Safian, CFO
James Smith, Chairman of the Board
Michael Diliberto, Chief Information Officer
Kenneth Allard, Chief Marketing Officer
Yvonne Genovese, Executive VP, Divisional
Joe Beck, Executive VP, Divisional
Alwyn Dawkins, Executive VP, Divisional
Scott Hensel, Executive VP, Divisional
Michael Harris, Executive VP, Divisional
Claire Herkes, Executive VP, Divisional
Jules Kaufman, Executive VP
Robin Kranich, Executive VP
Akhil Jain, Senior VP, Divisional

FINANCIAL DATA: *Note: Data for latest year may not have been available at press time.*

In U.S. $	2021	2020	2019	2018	2017	2016
Revenue		4,099,403,000	4,245,321,000	3,975,454,000	3,311,494,000	2,444,540,000
R&D Expense						
Operating Income		496,432,000	379,550,000	366,912,000	152,121,000	347,739,000
Operating Margin %						
SGA Expense		2,038,963,000	2,103,424,000	1,884,141,000	1,599,004,000	1,089,184,000
Net Income		266,745,000	233,290,000	122,456,000	3,279,000	193,582,000
Operating Cash Flow		903,278,000	565,436,000	471,158,000	254,517,000	365,632,000
Capital Expenditure		83,888,000	149,016,000	126,873,000	110,765,000	49,863,000
EBITDA		660,753,000	590,349,000	563,496,000	240,301,000	377,965,000
Return on Assets %						
Return on Equity %						
Debt to Equity						

CONTACT INFORMATION:

Phone: 203 316-1111 Fax:
Toll-Free:
Address: 56 Top Gallant Rd., Stamford, CT 06902-7700 United States

STOCK TICKER/OTHER:

Stock Ticker: IT
Employees: 16,724
Parent Company:
Exchange: NYS
Fiscal Year Ends: 12/31

SALARIES/BONUSES:

Top Exec. Salary: $908,197 Bonus: $
Second Exec. Salary: $600,000 Bonus: $

OTHER THOUGHTS:

Estimated Female Officers or Directors: 3
Hot Spot for Advancement for Women/Minorities: Y

Sales, profits and employees may be estimates. Financial information, benefits and other data can change quickly and may vary from those stated here.

GE Aviation

www.geaviation.com

NAIC Code: 336412

TYPES OF BUSINESS:

Aircraft Engine and Engine Parts Manufacturing
Gas Turbine Manufacturing
Marine Engines
Engine Maintenance & Parts
Engine Leasing

BRANDS/DIVISIONS/AFFILIATES:

General Electric Company
GE90
F110
CF34
Passport
LM6000
Avionics
Dowty

CONTACTS:

Note: Officers with more than one job title may be intentionally listed here more than once.

John S. Slattery, CEO
Shane M. Wright, CFO
Jason Tonich, VP-Mktg. & Sales
Kathleen T. McCarthy, Chief Human Resources Officer
David Burns, CIO
Mohammad Ehteshami, VP-New Prod. Introduction Oper.
Gary Mercer, Chief Engineer
Michael McAlevey, General Counsel
Bill Fitzgerald, VP
Michael R. McAlevey, VP-Bus. Dev.
Jamie Regg, Sr. Exec.-Global Comm. & GE Advantage
Peter Prowitt, Exec. Dir.-Global Gov't Rel.
Jean Lydon-Rodgers, VP
Paul McElhinney, VP
Jeanne M. Rosario, VP
Chris S. Beaufait, Sr. Exec.-China
Colleen Athans, VP

GROWTH PLANS/SPECIAL FEATURES:

GE Aviation, a subsidiary of General Electric Company, produces jet, turboprop and turbo shaft engines, components and integrated systems. The company manufactures its products for commercial, military, business and general aviation aircraft (B&GA), digital and manufactures marine gas turbines. GE Aviation has a global service network to support these offerings. Commercial engines include GE90, GE9X, GEnx, GP7200, CF6, CFM56, LEAP, CF34 and CT7; and its commercial systems include Avionics computing systems, electrical power components, silicon carbines, structures, Avio Aero-branded components and systems, Dowty-branded propellers and Unison-branded solid-state ignition systems. Military engines include B-52 re-engining, adaptive cycle, F110, F404, F414, T408, T700, T901, F108 and F103/138; and military systems include Avionics computer systems, electrical power components, silicon carbides, structures, Avio Aero-branded components and systems, Dowty propellers and Unison ignition systems. B&GA engines include advanced turboprop GE Catalyst and H-Series, and turbofan CF34, Passport, LEAP, CF700, CFE738, CJ610 and HF120; and B&GA systems include Avionics computer systems, electrical power components, silicon carbides, structures, Avio Aero-branded components and systems, Dowty propellers and Unison ignition systems. Digital solutions span network operations, technical operations, flight operations, connected aircraft, data integration and digital transformations, all of which also enables digital mission-ready solutions for the government and defense sector. For the marine industry, military gas turbine products include the LM500, LM2500, LM2500+, LM2500+G4 and LM6000; commercial gas turbine products include the 4.6 MW, 25.1 MW, 30.2 MW, 35.3 MW and 46.1 MW; and systems for the marine industry include propulsion systems, exhaust energy recovery systems and the firm's optional dry low emissions combustor system.

FINANCIAL DATA:

Note: Data for latest year may not have been available at press time.

In U.S. $	2021	2020	2019	2018	2017	2016
Revenue	21,310,000,000	22,042,000,000	32,875,000,000	30,566,000,000	27,013,000,000	26,261,000,000
R&D Expense						
Operating Income						
Operating Margin %						
SGA Expense						
Net Income	2,882,000,000	1,229,000,000	6,812,000,000	6,466,000,000	5,370,000,000	6,115,000,000
Operating Cash Flow						
Capital Expenditure						
EBITDA						
Return on Assets %						
Return on Equity %						
Debt to Equity						

CONTACT INFORMATION:

Phone: 513-243-2000 Fax:
Toll-Free:
Address: 1 Neumann Way, Cincinnati, OH 45215-6301 United States

STOCK TICKER/OTHER:

Stock Ticker: Subsidiary Exchange:
Employees: 40,000 Fiscal Year Ends: 12/31
Parent Company: General Electric Company (GE)

SALARIES/BONUSES:

Top Exec. Salary: $ Bonus: $
Second Exec. Salary: $ Bonus: $

OTHER THOUGHTS:

Estimated Female Officers or Directors: 4
Hot Spot for Advancement for Women/Minorities: Y

General Dynamics Corporation

www.generaldynamics.com

NAIC Code: 336411

TYPES OF BUSINESS:

Aircraft Manufacturing
Combat Vehicles & Systems
Telecommunications Systems
Naval Vessels & Submarines
Ship Management Services
Information Systems & Technology
Defense Systems & Services
Business Jets

BRANDS/DIVISIONS/AFFILIATES:

Bath Iron Works
Electric Boat Corporation
General Dynamics NASSCO
Jet Aviation
Gulfstream Aerospace Corporation

CONTACTS: *Note: Officers with more than one job title may be intentionally listed here more than once.*

Phebe Novakovic, CEO
Kimberly Kuryea, Sr. VP, Divisional
Jason Aiken, CFO
William Moss, Chief Accounting Officer
Christopher Marzilli, Executive VP, Divisional
Mark Roualet, Executive VP, Divisional
Robert Smith, Executive VP, Divisional
Gregory Gallopoulos, General Counsel
Marguerite Gilliland, President, Subsidiary
Mark Burns, President, Subsidiary
Kevin Graney, President, Subsidiary
Danny Deep, President, Subsidiary
Christopher Brady, President, Subsidiary

GROWTH PLANS/SPECIAL FEATURES:

General Dynamics is a defense contractor and business jet manufacturer. The firm's segments include aerospace, combat systems, marine, and technologies. The company's aerospace segment creates Gulfstream business jets. Combat systems mostly produces land-based combat vehicles, such as the M1 Abrams tank. The marine subsegment creates nuclear-powered submarines, among other things. The technologies segment contains two business units, an IT business that primarily serves the government market and a mission systems business that focuses on products that provide command, control, computers, intelligence, surveillance, and reconnaissance capabilities to the military.

FINANCIAL DATA: *Note: Data for latest year may not have been available at press time.*

In U.S. $	2021	2020	2019	2018	2017	2016
Revenue		37,925,000,000	39,350,000,000	36,193,000,000	30,973,000,000	31,353,000,000
R&D Expense						
Operating Income		4,133,000,000	4,648,000,000	4,457,000,000	4,177,000,000	4,309,000,000
Operating Margin %						
SGA Expense		2,192,000,000	2,411,000,000	2,258,000,000	2,010,000,000	1,940,000,000
Net Income		3,167,000,000	3,484,000,000	3,345,000,000	2,912,000,000	2,955,000,000
Operating Cash Flow		3,858,000,000	2,981,000,000	3,148,000,000	3,879,000,000	2,198,000,000
Capital Expenditure		967,000,000	987,000,000	690,000,000	428,000,000	392,000,000
EBITDA		5,105,000,000	5,503,000,000	5,222,000,000	4,635,000,000	4,784,000,000
Return on Assets %						
Return on Equity %						
Debt to Equity						

CONTACT INFORMATION:

Phone: 703 876-3000 Fax: 703 876-3125
Toll-Free:
Address: 11011 Sunset Hills Rd., Renton, VA 20190 United States

STOCK TICKER/OTHER:

Stock Ticker: GD
Employees: 103,100
Parent Company:
Exchange: NYS
Fiscal Year Ends: 12/31

SALARIES/BONUSES:

Top Exec. Salary: $1,585,000 Bonus: $
Second Exec. Salary: $887,500 Bonus: $

OTHER THOUGHTS:

Estimated Female Officers or Directors: 3
Hot Spot for Advancement for Women/Minorities: Y

General Motors Company (GM)

NAIC Code: 336111

www.gm.com

TYPES OF BUSINESS:

Automobile Manufacturing
Security & Information Services
Automotive Electronics
Financing & Insurance
Parts & Service
Transmissions
Engines
Locomotives

BRANDS/DIVISIONS/AFFILIATES:

Cruise
Buick
Cadillac
Chevrolet
GMC
Baojun
Wuling
Ultium Cells LLC

GROWTH PLANS/SPECIAL FEATURES:

General Motors Co. emerged from the bankruptcy of General Motors Corp. (old GM) in July 2009. GM has eight brands and operates under four segments: GM North America, GM International, Cruise, and GM Financial. The United States now has four brands instead of eight under old GM. The company remains the market leader in the U.S. with 17.3% share in 2020. GM Financial became the company's captive finance arm in October 2010 via the purchase of AmeriCredit.

CONTACTS: *Note: Officers with more than one job title may be intentionally listed here more than once.*

Mary Barra, CEO
Paul Jacobson, CFO
Christopher Hatto, Chief Accounting Officer
Randall Mott, Chief Information Officer
Matthew Tsien, Chief Technology Officer
Gerald Johnson, Executive VP, Divisional
Douglas Parks, Executive VP, Divisional
Craig Glidden, Executive VP
Julian Blissett, Executive VP
Stephen Carlisle, Executive VP
Mark Reuss, President

FINANCIAL DATA: *Note: Data for latest year may not have been available at press time.*

In U.S. $	2021	2020	2019	2018	2017	2016
Revenue		122,485,000,000	137,237,000,000	147,049,000,000	145,588,000,000	166,380,000,000
R&D Expense						
Operating Income		6,634,000,000	5,481,000,000	4,445,000,000	10,016,000,000	9,545,000,000
Operating Margin %						
SGA Expense		7,038,000,000	8,491,000,000	9,650,000,000	9,575,000,000	11,710,000,000
Net Income		6,427,000,000	6,732,000,000	8,014,000,000	-3,864,000,000	9,427,000,000
Operating Cash Flow		16,670,000,000	15,021,000,000	15,256,000,000	17,328,000,000	16,545,000,000
Capital Expenditure		20,533,000,000	23,996,000,000	25,497,000,000	27,633,000,000	29,166,000,000
EBITDA		22,008,000,000	22,336,000,000	22,873,000,000	24,699,000,000	22,664,000,000
Return on Assets %						
Return on Equity %						
Debt to Equity						

CONTACT INFORMATION:

Phone: 313 556-5000 Fax:
Toll-Free:
Address: 300 Renaissance Ctr., Detroit, MI 48265-3000 United States

STOCK TICKER/OTHER:

Stock Ticker: GM
Employees: 135,000
Parent Company:
Exchange: NYS
Fiscal Year Ends: 12/31

SALARIES/BONUSES:

Top Exec. Salary: $1,995,000 Bonus: $
Second Exec. Salary: $1,235,000 Bonus: $

OTHER THOUGHTS:

Estimated Female Officers or Directors: 8
Hot Spot for Advancement for Women/Minorities: Y

George Risk Industries Inc

www.grisk.com

NAIC Code: 334290

TYPES OF BUSINESS:

Motion Detectors, Security System, Manufacturing
Manufacture
Computer Keyboards
Switches
Alarm Components
Hydro Sensors

BRANDS/DIVISIONS/AFFILIATES:

GROWTH PLANS/SPECIAL FEATURES:

George Risk Industries Inc manufactures security products. The company is engaged in the designing, manufacturing, and sale of various products which include magnetic reed switches as well as keyboards, keypads, pushbutton and keyboard switches, proximity sensors and engraved keycaps. These security products are used in alarm system installations in the residential, commercial, industrial, and government sectors.

CONTACTS: *Note: Officers with more than one job title may be intentionally listed here more than once.*

Ken Risk, CEO
Stephanie Risk, CFO
Sharon Westby, Treasurer

FINANCIAL DATA: *Note: Data for latest year may not have been available at press time.*

In U.S. $	2021	2020	2019	2018	2017	2016
Revenue	18,505,000	14,809,000	14,126,000	11,931,000	10,904,000	11,240,000
R&D Expense					73,000	92,000
Operating Income	5,306,000	3,730,000	3,306,000	2,492,000	2,783,000	3,362,000
Operating Margin %						
SGA Expense	4,023,000	3,675,000	3,494,000	3,123,000	2,824,000	2,809,000
Net Income	10,822,000	2,104,000	3,284,000	2,546,000	2,401,000	3,086,000
Operating Cash Flow	3,792,000	3,320,000	2,735,000	370,000	3,184,000	2,894,000
Capital Expenditure	517,000	731,000	154,000	2,157,000	115,000	276,000
EBITDA	14,847,000	3,039,000	4,703,000	2,749,000	2,970,000	4,499,000
Return on Assets %						
Return on Equity %						
Debt to Equity						

CONTACT INFORMATION:

Phone: 308 235-4645 Fax:
Toll-Free: 800-445-5218
Address: 802 South Elm St., Kimball, NE 69145-1599 United States

STOCK TICKER/OTHER:

Stock Ticker: RSKIA
Employees: 172
Parent Company:
Exchange: PINX
Fiscal Year Ends: 04/30

SALARIES/BONUSES:

Top Exec. Salary: $ Bonus: $
Second Exec. Salary: $ Bonus: $

OTHER THOUGHTS:

Estimated Female Officers or Directors:
Hot Spot for Advancement for Women/Minorities:

Getronics NV

www.getronics.com

NAIC Code: 541512

TYPES OF BUSINESS:

IT Consulting
Digital Solutions
Workplace
Smart Spaces
Business Applications
Security
Compliance
Network

BRANDS/DIVISIONS/AFFILIATES:

GSH Private Capital

GROWTH PLANS/SPECIAL FEATURES:

Getronics NV provides end-to-end digital solutions that drive business outcomes. The firm's services include digital workplace, cloud (private, public and on-premise), smart spaces, business applications, security, field support, service desk and network services. Getronics has a team of thousands in 20 countries across Europe, Asia Pacific and Latin America, serving more than 2,000 customers globally. GSH Private Capital is the owner and manager of Getronics NV.

CONTACTS: *Note: Officers with more than one job title may be intentionally listed here more than once.*

Rogier Bronsgeet, COO
Mike Field, CFO
Tom Regent, CCO
Harsha Gowda, CTO
Matthias Taubl, Exec. Dir.-Process Standardization
Pom Burie, Exec. Dir.-Legal
Thomas Fetten, Exec. Dir.-Delivery Oper.
Christian Schmehl, Exec. Dir.-Corp. Dev.
Pom Burie, Exec. Dir.-Finance
Matthias Taubl, Exec. Dir.-Hungary
Kenton Fine, Chmn.
Thomas Fetten, Exec. Dir.-Asia Pacific
Pom Burie, Exec. Dir.-Procurement

FINANCIAL DATA: *Note: Data for latest year may not have been available at press time.*

In U.S. $	2021	2020	2019	2018	2017	2016
Revenue	610,000,000	569,400,000	584,000,000	571,896,000	530,000,000	526,780,000
R&D Expense						
Operating Income						
Operating Margin %						
SGA Expense						
Net Income						
Operating Cash Flow						
Capital Expenditure						
EBITDA						
Return on Assets %						
Return on Equity %						
Debt to Equity						

CONTACT INFORMATION:

Phone: 31707-703905 Fax:
Toll-Free:
Address: Gustav Mahlerplain 23A, Amsterdam, 1082MA Netherlands

STOCK TICKER/OTHER:

Stock Ticker: Private
Employees: 3,700
Parent Company: GSH Private Capital
Exchange:
Fiscal Year Ends: 12/31

SALARIES/BONUSES:

Top Exec. Salary: $ Bonus: $
Second Exec. Salary: $ Bonus: $

OTHER THOUGHTS:

Estimated Female Officers or Directors:
Hot Spot for Advancement for Women/Minorities: Y

Gilat Satellite Networks Ltd

www.gilat.com

NAIC Code: 517410

TYPES OF BUSINESS:

Satellite-Based Internet Service
Satellite-Based Communication Services
VSAT Technology
Cloud-Based Satellite Network

BRANDS/DIVISIONS/AFFILIATES:

CONTACTS: *Note: Officers with more than one job title may be intentionally listed here more than once.*

Adi Sfadia, CEO
Yuval Shani, COO
Bosmat Halpern-Levy, CFO
Ron Levin, VP-Global Accounts & Mobility
Lior Moyal, VP-Human Resources
Gai Berkovich, VP-R&D
Alik Shimelmits, CTO
Alon Levy, General Counsel
Yair Shahrabany, VP-Global Oper. & Customer Svcs.
Doron Elinav, VP-Strategic Accounts
Ari Krashin, VP-Finance
Glenn Katz, CEO-Spacenet, Inc.
Assaf Eyal, VP-Commercial Div.
Moshe Tamir, VP-Defense & Homeland Security
Isaac Angel, Chmn.
Danny Fridman, CEO-Gilat Peru & Colombia

GROWTH PLANS/SPECIAL FEATURES:

Gilat Satellite Networks Ltd is a provider of satellite-based broadband communications. The company designs and manufactures ground-based satellite communications equipment and provides comprehensive solutions and end-to-end services. Its portfolio includes a cloud-based satellite network platform, very small aperture terminals (VSATs), amplifiers, high-speed modems, on-the-move antennas and high-power solid-state power amplifiers (SSPAs), block up converters (BUCs) and Trancievers. The company's solutions support multiple applications with a full portfolio of products to address key applications including broadband access, cellular backhaul, enterprise, in-flight connectivity, maritime, trains, defense and public safety.

FINANCIAL DATA: *Note: Data for latest year may not have been available at press time.*

In U.S. $	2021	2020	2019	2018	2017	2016
Revenue		165,885,000	263,492,000	266,391,000	282,756,000	279,551,000
R&D Expense		26,303,000	30,184,000	33,023,000	28,014,000	24,853,000
Operating Income		-16,022,000	25,572,000	21,284,000	10,861,000	755,000
Operating Margin %						
SGA Expense		30,934,000	40,121,000	39,730,000	43,620,000	49,882,000
Net Income		34,911,000	36,538,000	18,409,000	6,801,000	-5,340,000
Operating Cash Flow		43,160,000	34,782,000	32,017,000	20,800,000	10,778,000
Capital Expenditure		4,716,000	7,982,000	10,759,000	3,692,000	4,307,000
EBITDA		46,190,000	34,328,000	30,749,000	20,538,000	10,118,000
Return on Assets %						
Return on Equity %						
Debt to Equity						

CONTACT INFORMATION:

Phone: 972 39252000 Fax:
Toll-Free:
Address: 21 Yegia Kapayim St., Kiryat Arie, Petah Tikva, 49130 Israel

STOCK TICKER/OTHER:

Stock Ticker: GILT
Employees: 780
Parent Company:
Exchange: NAS
Fiscal Year Ends: 12/31

SALARIES/BONUSES:

Top Exec. Salary: $366,510 Bonus: $
Second Exec. Salary: $211,010 Bonus: $45,850

OTHER THOUGHTS:

Estimated Female Officers or Directors: 3
Hot Spot for Advancement for Women/Minorities: Y

GLOBALFOUNDRIES Inc

NAIC Code: 334413

gf.com

TYPES OF BUSINESS:

Semiconductors
Contract Manufacturing
Semiconductor Wafers
Wafer Fabrication

BRANDS/DIVISIONS/AFFILIATES:

FDXcelerator
Rfwave
GLOBALSOLUTIONS
Multi Project Wafer
Mask Services
Post-Fab Services
Avera Semiconductor LLC

GROWTH PLANS/SPECIAL FEATURES:

GLOBALFOUNDRIES Inc. is a semiconductor foundry. It manufactures complex ICs that enable electronic devices that are pervasive in every sector of the economy. It derives revenue primarily from fabricating semiconductor wafers using the company's manufacturing processes for the company's customers based on their proprietary integrated circuit designs and, from design, mask making, bumping, probing, assembly, and testing services.

CONTACTS: *Note: Officers with more than one job title may be intentionally listed here more than once.*

Thomas Caulfield, CEO
David Reeder, CFO
Ahmed Al Idrissi, Chairman of the Board
Saam Azar, Chief Legal Officer
Amir Faintuch, General Manager, Divisional
Michael Hogan, General Manager, Divisional
Bamdad Bastani, General Manager, Divisional
Kay Chai Ang, Senior VP, Divisional
Juan Cordovez, Senior VP, Divisional
Emily Reilly, Senior VP, Divisional
Gregg Bartlett, Senior VP, Divisional
Michael Cadigan, Senior VP, Divisional
Thomas Weber, Senior VP, Divisional
Americo Lemos, Senior VP, Geographical

FINANCIAL DATA: *Note: Data for latest year may not have been available at press time.*

In U.S. $	2021	2020	2019	2018	2017	2016
Revenue		4,850,505,000	5,812,788,000	6,196,039,000		
R&D Expense		475,769,000	582,974,000	926,220,000		
Operating Income		-1,633,349,000	-1,560,846,000	-1,829,018,000		
Operating Margin %						
SGA Expense		287,641,000	308,089,000	325,269,000		
Net Income		-1,347,571,000	-1,371,186,000	-2,701,603,000		
Operating Cash Flow		1,005,897,000	496,819,000	279,309,000		
Capital Expenditure		592,488,000	772,818,000	1,328,636,000		
EBITDA		1,292,049,000	1,733,547,000	475,852,000		
Return on Assets %						
Return on Equity %						
Debt to Equity						

CONTACT INFORMATION:

Phone: 518-305-9013 Fax:
Toll-Free:
Address: 400 Stonebreak Rd., Malta, NY 12020 United States

STOCK TICKER/OTHER:

Stock Ticker: GFS Exchange: NAS
Employees: 16,000 Fiscal Year Ends: 12/31
Parent Company: Mubadala Investment Company PJSC

SALARIES/BONUSES:

Top Exec. Salary: $ Bonus: $
Second Exec. Salary: $ Bonus: $

OTHER THOUGHTS:

Estimated Female Officers or Directors: 1
Hot Spot for Advancement for Women/Minorities:

Globalstar Inc

www.globalstar.com

NAIC Code: 517410

TYPES OF BUSINESS:

Satellite Phone & Data Service
Satellite Network Operations
Satellite Communications Equipment
Logistics & Transportation Data Services
Shipping Container Data Services

BRANDS/DIVISIONS/AFFILIATES:

Thermo Capital Partners LLC
Globalstar System
SPOT
SmartOne
STX-3
STINGR

CONTACTS: *Note: Officers with more than one job title may be intentionally listed here more than once.*

David Kagan, CEO
Rebecca Clary, CFO
James Monroe, Chairman of the Board
L. Ponder, General Counsel

GROWTH PLANS/SPECIAL FEATURES:

Globalstar Inc is a telecommunications company that derives revenue from the provision of mobile satellite services. Mobile satellite services are typically used by customers where existing terrestrial wireline and wireless communications networks are impaired or do not exist. The company provides communications services such as two-way voice and data transmission. In addition, one-way data transmission is also offered. Both services are offered using mobile or fixed devices. The company is an owner of satellite assets. The company generates the vast majority of its revenue within the United States.

FINANCIAL DATA: *Note: Data for latest year may not have been available at press time.*

In U.S. $	2021	2020	2019	2018	2017	2016
Revenue		128,487,000	131,718,000	130,113,000	112,660,000	96,861,000
R&D Expense						
Operating Income		-58,747,000	-62,922,000	-67,857,000	-51,746,000	-63,326,000
Operating Margin %						
SGA Expense		41,738,000	45,233,000	55,443,000	39,099,000	40,982,000
Net Income		-109,639,000	15,324,000	-6,516,000	-89,074,000	-132,646,000
Operating Cash Flow		22,215,000	3,048,000	5,920,000	13,857,000	8,813,000
Capital Expenditure		7,219,000	8,149,000	10,369,000	9,321,000	11,381,000
EBITDA		38,068,000	174,105,000	127,659,000	23,385,000	-25,847,000
Return on Assets %						
Return on Equity %						
Debt to Equity						

CONTACT INFORMATION:

Phone: 408 933-4000 Fax: 409 933-4100
Toll-Free:
Address: 1351 Holiday Sqare Blvd., Covington, CA 70433 United States

STOCK TICKER/OTHER:

Stock Ticker: GSAT
Employees: 329
Parent Company:
Exchange: ASE
Fiscal Year Ends: 12/31

SALARIES/BONUSES:

Top Exec. Salary: $534,808 Bonus: $
Second Exec. Salary: $305,132 Bonus: $

OTHER THOUGHTS:

Estimated Female Officers or Directors: 1
Hot Spot for Advancement for Women/Minorities:

GlobeRanger Corporation

NAIC Code: 511210I

www.globeranger.com

TYPES OF BUSINESS:

RFID Software
Internet of Things
Automated Identification Technology
IoT Enablement
Supply Chain Data
Personnel Date and Tracking Solutions
Asset Tracking Solutions
Software Integration

BRANDS/DIVISIONS/AFFILIATES:

Fujitsu Limited
iMotion IoT Enablement Platform
AIT Personnel Tracking
Edge Data Orchestration

CONTACTS: *Note: Officers with more than one job title may be intentionally listed here more than once.*

George Brody, Pres.
Eric Pearson, Dir.-Eng.
David South, VP-Solutions & Support

GROWTH PLANS/SPECIAL FEATURES:

GlobeRanger Corporation develops and operates Internet of Things (IoT) and automated identification technology (AIT) platforms. The company's iMotion IoT Enablement Platform identifies points of value within businesses and delivers near real-time business-critical information. It connects various components of the supply chain, such as equipment, inventory stock, tools and other assets, with their associated processes so that businesses can act on the insights, enhance productivity and reduce costs. The IoT platform also enables organizations to rapidly develop, configure and deploy a solution. GlobeRanger's asset tracking solutions automates data capture from a wide range of AIT readers and sensors, including barcodes, radio frequency identification (RFID) and Bluetooth Low Energy (BLE) tags or IoT devices associated with each individual asset. The company can implement readers and devices from a supplier matching the business' requirements without the need to change existing information management systems or back-end infrastructure. All devices, objects and data work together and integrate into existing software systems, transforming the raw data into business intelligence. In addition, the GlobeRanger AIT Personnel Tracking solution is an integrated tracking solution that can monitor personnel in near real-time, including time, attendance and movements. AIT Personnel Tracking captures data from a wide range of identification technology readers and sensors and can be applied to ID cards, wrist bands, clothing or protective equipment. Parameters can be applied to areas of the site or to individuals in order to monitor and control movement and access. Last, GlobeRanger's Edge Data Orchestration offers full integration with Microsoft Azure IoT to turn raw edge data into actionable information by orchestrating, monitoring and filtering data. It collects data from site-wide connected devices and enables device management, operational efficiency and more. GlobeRanger operates as a subsidiary of Fujitsu Limited.

FINANCIAL DATA: *Note: Data for latest year may not have been available at press time.*

In U.S. $	2021	2020	2019	2018	2017	2016
Revenue						
R&D Expense						
Operating Income						
Operating Margin %						
SGA Expense						
Net Income						
Operating Cash Flow						
Capital Expenditure						
EBITDA						
Return on Assets %						
Return on Equity %						
Debt to Equity						

CONTACT INFORMATION:

Phone: 469-330-5500 Fax:
Toll-Free:
Address: 1130 E. Arapaho Rd., Ste. 450, Richardson, TX 75081 United States

STOCK TICKER/OTHER:

Stock Ticker: Subsidiary
Employees: 23
Parent Company: Fujitsu Limited
Exchange:
Fiscal Year Ends: 12/31

SALARIES/BONUSES:

Top Exec. Salary: $ Bonus: $
Second Exec. Salary: $ Bonus: $

OTHER THOUGHTS:

Estimated Female Officers or Directors:
Hot Spot for Advancement for Women/Minorities:

Happiest Minds Technologies Private Limited

www.happiestminds.com

NAIC Code: 541512

TYPES OF BUSINESS:

Computer Systems Design Services
Digital Transformation Solutions
Infrastructure Services
Online Security Solutions
Product Engineering Services
Internet of Things
Big Data Analytics
Mobility Technologies

BRANDS/DIVISIONS/AFFILIATES:

GROWTH PLANS/SPECIAL FEATURES:

Happiest Minds Technologies Private Limited is a next-generation digital transformation, infrastructure, security and product engineering services company. The firm enables digital transformation for enterprises and technology providers. It does this by delivering an integrated set of technologies, including big data analytics, agile infrastructure, Internet of Things (IoT), mobility, cloud, security, unified communications and more. Happiest Minds offers domain-centric solutions, intellectual property in IT services, product engineering, infrastructure management and security. These services have applicability across industry sectors such as retail, consumer packaged goods, ecommerce, banking, insurance, hi-tech, engineering R&D, manufacturing, automotive, travel, transportation and hospitality. Based in Bangalore, India, the company has operations in the U.S., the U.K., Canada, Australia and the Middle East.

CONTACTS: *Note: Officers with more than one job title may be intentionally listed here more than once.*

Joseph Anantharaju, CEO
Venkatraman Narayanan, CFO
Ashok Soota, Chmn.

FINANCIAL DATA: *Note: Data for latest year may not have been available at press time.*

In U.S. $	2021	2020	2019	2018	2017	2016
Revenue	108,701,845	94,930,500	86,501,800	74,453,800	75,000,000	62,000,000
R&D Expense						
Operating Income						
Operating Margin %						
SGA Expense						
Net Income	22,142,161	9,531,200	2,042,490	-3,037,610		
Operating Cash Flow						
Capital Expenditure						
EBITDA						
Return on Assets %						
Return on Equity %						
Debt to Equity						

CONTACT INFORMATION:

Phone: 91-80-3320-3333 Fax: 91-80-3320-3000
Toll-Free:
Address: Fl. 3&4, SJR Equinox, Sy.No. 47/8, Doddathogur Vill, Bengaluru, 560-100 India

STOCK TICKER/OTHER:

Stock Ticker: 543227
Employees: 2,818
Parent Company:
Exchange: Bombay
Fiscal Year Ends: 03/31

SALARIES/BONUSES:

Top Exec. Salary: $ Bonus: $
Second Exec. Salary: $ Bonus: $

OTHER THOUGHTS:

Estimated Female Officers or Directors:
Hot Spot for Advancement for Women/Minorities:

Hewlett Packard Enterprise Company

www.hpe.com

NAIC Code: 334111

TYPES OF BUSINESS:

Computer Manufacturing
Hybrid IT
Intelligent Edge
Financial Services
Computer Servers
Artificial Intelligence
Hardware and Software
Storage

BRANDS/DIVISIONS/AFFILIATES:

HPE Apollo
HPE Cray
HPE Superdome
HPE Nonstop
HPE Integrity
HPE Edgeline
Aruba
Hewlett Packard Labs

CONTACTS: *Note: Officers with more than one job title may be intentionally listed here more than once.*

Irv Rothman, CEO, Divisional
Antonio Neri, CEO
Tarek Robbiati, CFO
Patricia Russo, Chairman of the Board
John Schultz, Chief Legal Officer
Alan May, Executive VP
Neil MacDonald, General Manager, Divisional
Thomas Black, General Manager, Divisional
Kirt Karros, Senior VP, Divisional
Jeff Ricci, Senior VP

GROWTH PLANS/SPECIAL FEATURES:

Hewlett Packard Enterprise is a supplier of IT infrastructure products and services. The company operates as three major segments. Its hybrid IT division primarily sells computer servers, storage arrays, and Pointnext technical services. The intelligent edge group sells Aruba networking products and services. HPE's financial services division offers financing and leasing plans for customers. The Palo Alto, California-based company sells on a global scale and has approximately 66,000 employees.

FINANCIAL DATA: *Note: Data for latest year may not have been available at press time.*

In U.S. $	2021	2020	2019	2018	2017	2016
Revenue		26,982,000,000	29,135,000,000	30,852,000,000	28,871,000,000	50,123,000,000
R&D Expense		1,874,000,000	1,842,000,000	1,663,000,000	1,486,000,000	2,298,000,000
Operating Income		1,491,000,000	2,854,000,000	1,130,000,000	1,878,000,000	4,059,000,000
Operating Margin %						
SGA Expense		4,624,000,000	4,907,000,000	4,851,000,000	5,006,000,000	7,821,000,000
Net Income		-322,000,000	1,049,000,000	1,908,000,000	344,000,000	3,161,000,000
Operating Cash Flow		2,240,000,000	3,997,000,000	2,964,000,000	889,000,000	4,958,000,000
Capital Expenditure		2,383,000,000	2,856,000,000	2,956,000,000	3,137,000,000	3,280,000,000
EBITDA		4,116,000,000	5,389,000,000	3,706,000,000	4,929,000,000	7,834,000,000
Return on Assets %						
Return on Equity %						
Debt to Equity						

CONTACT INFORMATION:

Phone: 650-687-5817 Fax:
Toll-Free:
Address: 11445 Compaq Center West Dr., Houston, TX 77070 United States

STOCK TICKER/OTHER:

Stock Ticker: HPE
Employees: 59,400
Parent Company:
Exchange: NYS
Fiscal Year Ends: 10/31

SALARIES/BONUSES:

Top Exec. Salary: $460,000 Bonus: $7,689,111
Second Exec. Salary: $1,077,083 Bonus: $

OTHER THOUGHTS:

Estimated Female Officers or Directors:
Hot Spot for Advancement for Women/Minorities:

Hewlett Packard Laboratories (HP Labs) www8.hp.com/us/en/hp-labs/index.html

NAIC Code: 541712

TYPES OF BUSINESS:

Electronics Research
Innovation
Research and Development
3D Printing
Microfluidics
Cyber Security
Digital Manufacturing

BRANDS/DIVISIONS/AFFILIATES:

Hewlett Packard Enterprise Company

CONTACTS: *Note: Officers with more than one job title may be intentionally listed here more than once.*

John Sontag, Dir.-Systems Research
Martin Sadler, Dir.-Security & Cloud Lab
Chandrakant D. Patel, Chief Engineer
Jaap Suermondt, Dir.-Analytics Lab
Laurel Krieger, VP-Strategy & Oper.
Ruth Bergman, Head-HP Labs Israel
David Lee, Dir.-Networking & Mobility
David Lee, Head-HP Labs China
Eric Hanson, Dir.-Printing & Content Lab
Tolga Kurtoglu, Chmn.

GROWTH PLANS/SPECIAL FEATURES:

Hewlett-Packard Laboratories (HP Labs) is the innovation and research arm of Hewlett Packard Enterprise Company. HP Labs' current areas of research include: 3D, microfluidics and systems technology, security and digital manufacturing. Within 3D, HP Labs builds its expertise in 3D printing to drive innovation at scale in industries such as medicine, dentistry and manufacturing. The microfluidics and systems technology division invents printing, imaging and microfluidics technologies that open new applications in sensing, smart packaging and life sciences. The security division looks at emerging security concerns that may arise as users integrate new connected products and services and works to develop solutions that will ensure cyber resilience all the way to the enterprise edge. Last, the digital marketing division researches and develops technologies to accelerate the fourth industrial revolution and impact customers' product design, fulfillment and lifetime use. This division works across additive manufacturing, artificial intelligence (AI), machine learning, data science and security to advance digital manufacturing processes.

FINANCIAL DATA: *Note: Data for latest year may not have been available at press time.*

In U.S. $	2021	2020	2019	2018	2017	2016
Revenue						
R&D Expense						
Operating Income						
Operating Margin %						
SGA Expense						
Net Income						
Operating Cash Flow						
Capital Expenditure						
EBITDA						
Return on Assets %						
Return on Equity %						
Debt to Equity						

CONTACT INFORMATION:

Phone: 650-857-1501 Fax: 650-857-5518
Toll-Free: 800-752-0900
Address: 1501 Page Mill Rd., Palo Alto, CA 94304 United States

STOCK TICKER/OTHER:

Stock Ticker: Subsidiary Exchange:
Employees: 155 Fiscal Year Ends: 10/31
Parent Company: Hewlett Packard Enterprise Company

SALARIES/BONUSES:

Top Exec. Salary: $ Bonus: $
Second Exec. Salary: $ Bonus: $

OTHER THOUGHTS:

Estimated Female Officers or Directors: 2
Hot Spot for Advancement for Women/Minorities: Y

Hitachi High Technologies America Inc www.hitachi-hightech.com/us

NAIC Code: 541712

TYPES OF BUSINESS:

Research & Development
Semiconductor Manufacturing Equipment
Nano-Technology Solutions
Analytical Solutions and Systems
Medical and Laboratory Systems
Factory Automation Solutions and Systems
Internet of Things
Thin-Film Equipment

BRANDS/DIVISIONS/AFFILIATES:

Hitachi Limited

CONTACTS: *Note: Officers with more than one job title may be intentionally listed here more than once.*

Craig Kerkove, CEO
Masahiro Miyazaki, Pres.
Greg Rigby, VP
Tom Grossi, Asst. Dir.-Corp. Business. Dev.
Steve Keough, Head-Media, Central & Eastern U.S.
Monica Degnan, Head-Media, Western U.S.
Phil Bryson, Gen. Mgr.-Nanotechnology Systems Division

GROWTH PLANS/SPECIAL FEATURES:

Hitachi High Technologies America, Inc. (Hitachi Hi-Tech), a subsidiary of Hitachi Limited of Japan, specializes in electronics. Hitachi Hi-Tech operates through three business fields: nano-technology solutions, analytical and medical solutions, and industrial solutions. The nano-technology solutions business unit integrates and strengthens electron beam technologies to provide semiconductor integration solutions and to create new materials and new biological applications. This division's primary products include dry etch systems, critical dimension scanning electron microscope (CD-SEM) and defect inspection equipment, electron microscopes and atomic force microscopes. The analytical and medical solutions business segment builds on a foundation of analytical technology to create new value in fields such as biomedicine and safety and security. This division's primary products consist of: thermal analysis systems, chromatography systems, spectrophotometers, atomic absorption spectrometers, thickness gauges, silicon drift detectors, titrators, mercury analyzers, and medical systems, clinical analyzers and laboratory automatic systems. Last, the industrial solutions business unit provides added value through solutions focused on operational technologies such as factory automation, Internet of Things (IoT) and full value-chain solutions. This division's primary products include: information and communication technologies (ICT) solutions such as equipment monitoring devices, raw data visualization intelligence tools, wide-area network (WAN) accelerators and computer-integrated manufacturing (CIM) systems; industrial solutions such as thin film equipment, power train testing systems, inspection and diagnostic systems, ion beam etching machines, processing machines for MEMS devices, railway infrastructure inspection systems and micro-electro-mechanical systems; and advanced industrial products such as automotive sensors and control devices, industrial materials, electronic components, functional chemicals and battery lifecycle management solutions.

Hitachi Hi-Tech offers its employees comprehensive health, income protection, retirement and savings protection benefits and plans.

FINANCIAL DATA: *Note: Data for latest year may not have been available at press time.*

In U.S. $	2021	2020	2019	2018	2017	2016
Revenue						
R&D Expense						
Operating Income						
Operating Margin %						
SGA Expense						
Net Income						
Operating Cash Flow						
Capital Expenditure						
EBITDA						
Return on Assets %						
Return on Equity %						
Debt to Equity						

CONTACT INFORMATION:

Phone: 847-273-4141 Fax: 847-273-4407
Toll-Free:
Address: 10 N. Martingale Rd., Ste. 500, Schaumburg, IL 60173-2295 United States

STOCK TICKER/OTHER:

Stock Ticker: Subsidiary
Employees: 802
Parent Company: Hitachi Limited
Exchange:
Fiscal Year Ends: 03/31

SALARIES/BONUSES:

Top Exec. Salary: $ Bonus: $
Second Exec. Salary: $ Bonus: $

OTHER THOUGHTS:

Estimated Female Officers or Directors: 1
Hot Spot for Advancement for Women/Minorities:

Hitachi Limited

www.hitachi.com

NAIC Code: 334111

TYPES OF BUSINESS:

Computer & Electronics Manufacturing
Information Technology
Nuclear Energy
Industrial Manufacturing
Transportation Mobility
Smart Life Products and Solutions
Automotive Systems
Automotive Components

BRANDS/DIVISIONS/AFFILIATES:

Hitachi Astemo Ltd
Hitachi Solutions Technology Ltd
Hitachi GE Nuclear Ltd
Hitachi Industry & Control Solutions Ltd
Hitachi Rail STS Mobilinx Hurontario GP Inc
Hitachi High-tech Amata Smart Services Co Ltd

GROWTH PLANS/SPECIAL FEATURES:

Hitachi Ltd provides IT services and has an expertise in the range of business fields, including financial services. The company's main products and services include system integration, consulting, cloud services, servers, storage, software, telecommunications and networks, and ATMs. Hitachi operates in various segments namely, Information and Telecommunication Systems; Social Infrastructure and Industrial Systems; Electronic Systems and Equipment; Construction Machinery; High Functional Materials and Components; Automotive Systems; Smart Life and Ecofriendly Systems; Financial Services; and Others.

CONTACTS: *Note: Officers with more than one job title may be intentionally listed here more than once.*

Toshiaki Higashihara, CEO
Shigeru Azuhata, Gen. Mgr.-R&D
Toyoaki Nakamura, Gen. Mgr.-Consumer Bus.
Koji Tanaka, Exec. VP-Power Systems Bus.
Nobuo Mochida, Exec. VP-Prod. Eng.
Tatsuro Ishizuka, CEO-Power Systems Group
Junzo Nakajima, CEO-Asia Pacific

FINANCIAL DATA: *Note: Data for latest year may not have been available at press time.*

In U.S. $	2021	2020	2019	2018	2017	2016
Revenue	76,703,770,000	77,038,260,000	83,306,550,000	82,322,360,000	80,509,150,000	88,171,810,000
R&D Expense						
Operating Income	4,351,165,000	5,815,990,000	6,634,002,000	6,279,480,000	5,160,706,000	5,578,617,000
Operating Margin %						
SGA Expense	14,939,070,000	15,012,520,000	15,474,040,000	15,706,490,000	15,748,810,000	17,050,040,000
Net Income	4,407,692,000	769,709,200	1,955,520,000	3,189,589,000	2,032,099,000	1,512,732,000
Operating Cash Flow	6,969,245,000	4,928,825,000	5,360,312,000	6,389,652,000	5,532,161,000	7,137,060,000
Capital Expenditure	3,277,081,000	3,701,768,000	4,149,669,000	3,897,710,000	6,239,613,000	9,009,806,000
EBITDA	11,940,560,000	5,600,945,000	7,952,901,000	8,994,560,000	7,937,225,000	9,233,603,000
Return on Assets %						
Return on Equity %						
Debt to Equity						

CONTACT INFORMATION:

Phone: 81 332581111 Fax: 81 332582375
Toll-Free:
Address: 6-6, Marunouchi 1-chome, Chiyoda-ku, Tokyo, 100-8280 Japan

STOCK TICKER/OTHER:

Stock Ticker: HTHIF Exchange: PINX
Employees: 295,941 Fiscal Year Ends: 03/31
Parent Company:

SALARIES/BONUSES:

Top Exec. Salary: $ Bonus: $
Second Exec. Salary: $ Bonus: $

OTHER THOUGHTS:

Estimated Female Officers or Directors: 1
Hot Spot for Advancement for Women/Minorities:

Hon Hai Precision Industry Company Ltd

www.foxconn.com

NAIC Code: 334418

TYPES OF BUSINESS:

Contract Manufacturing of Electronics
Technology Solutions
Cloud Computing
Mobile Devices
Internet of Things
Artificial Intelligence
Smart Networks
Robotics

BRANDS/DIVISIONS/AFFILIATES:

Foxconn Technology Group
Foxconn Industrial Internet
Foxconn Interconnect Technology Limited
FIH Mobile Limited

GROWTH PLANS/SPECIAL FEATURES:

Hon Hai Precision is the world's largest contract manufacturer of consumer electronics, communications, and computer products. It is the biggest supplier to Apple, whose business accounts for 50% of overall revenue. Hon Hai is also involved in the production of upstream components such as electronic connectors, semiconductor packaging, industrial robots, and metal casings for smartphones. These upstream activities are mainly conducted through its listed majority-owned subsidiaries Foxconn Industrial Internet, FIH Mobile, Foxconn Interconnect Technology, and ShunSin Technology.

CONTACTS: *Note: Officers with more than one job title may be intentionally listed here more than once.*

Young-Way Liu, Pres.

FINANCIAL DATA: *Note: Data for latest year may not have been available at press time.*

In U.S. $	2021	2020	2019	2018	2017	2016
Revenue		193,112,500,000	192,564,300,000	190,797,900,000	169,639,000,000	157,096,400,000
R&D Expense		3,391,908,000	3,299,556,000	3,043,008,000	2,947,536,000	1,843,185,000
Operating Income		3,994,415,000	4,141,085,000	4,906,972,000	4,057,236,000	6,305,126,000
Operating Margin %						
SGA Expense		3,531,398,000	3,943,811,000	4,016,959,000	3,916,130,000	3,442,175,000
Net Income		3,668,863,000	4,155,929,000	4,651,732,000	5,000,231,000	5,358,074,000
Operating Cash Flow		13,610,230,000	8,938,994,000	-1,447,301,000	-1,417,930,000	6,272,012,000
Capital Expenditure		2,434,129,000	2,811,696,000	2,361,917,000	2,176,376,000	1,917,578,000
EBITDA		9,042,983,000	10,721,970,000	10,297,930,000	10,195,040,000	10,373,070,000
Return on Assets %						
Return on Equity %						
Debt to Equity						

CONTACT INFORMATION:

Phone: 886 222683466 Fax: 886 222686204
Toll-Free:
Address: 66 Zhonngshan Rd., Tu-Chen Industrial Zone, Tu-Chen City, Taipei, 236 Taiwan

STOCK TICKER/OTHER:

Stock Ticker: HNHAY
Employees: 1,100,000
Parent Company:
Exchange: PINX
Fiscal Year Ends: 12/31

SALARIES/BONUSES:

Top Exec. Salary: $ Bonus: $
Second Exec. Salary: $ Bonus: $

OTHER THOUGHTS:

Estimated Female Officers or Directors:
Hot Spot for Advancement for Women/Minorities:

Honda Motor Co Ltd

global.honda

NAIC Code: 336111

TYPES OF BUSINESS:

Automobile Manufacturing
Motorcycles
ATVs & Personal Watercraft
Generators
Marine Engines
Lawn & Garden Equipment
Fuel Cell & Hybrid Vehicles
Airplanes

BRANDS/DIVISIONS/AFFILIATES:

Fit/Jazz
Civic
Accord
CR-V
HR-V
NSX
Clarity Fuel Cell
HondaJet

GROWTH PLANS/SPECIAL FEATURES:

Incorporated in 1948, Honda Motor was originally a motorcycle manufacturer. Today, the firm makes automobiles, motorcycles, and power products such as boat engines, generators, and lawnmowers. Honda sold 19.7 million cars and motorcycles in fiscal 2021 (4.5 million of which were autos), and consolidated sales were JPY 13.2 trillion. Automobiles constitute 65% of revenue and motorcycles 14%, with the rest split between power products and financial services. Honda also makes robots and private jets.

Employee benefits vary by location.

CONTACTS: *Note: Officers with more than one job title may be intentionally listed here more than once.*

Toshihiro Mibe, CEO

FINANCIAL DATA: *Note: Data for latest year may not have been available at press time.*

In U.S. $	2021	2020	2019	2018	2017	2016
Revenue	115,729,800,000	131,199,300,000	139,613,900,000	134,979,000,000	123,011,500,000	128,300,900,000
R&D Expense	6,492,689,000	7,065,859,000	7,090,304,000	6,606,586,000	6,075,612,000	5,768,708,000
Operating Income	5,801,272,000	5,567,792,000	6,382,640,000	7,324,505,000	7,387,359,000	4,423,183,000
Operating Margin %						
SGA Expense	11,701,940,000	14,424,710,000	15,591,660,000	15,598,320,000	14,069,910,000	18,530,750,000
Net Income	5,776,818,000	4,004,657,000	5,362,869,000	9,308,433,000	5,417,815,000	3,027,407,000
Operating Cash Flow	9,423,033,000	8,606,156,000	6,818,635,000	8,678,701,000	7,777,169,000	12,222,730,000
Capital Expenditure	4,842,861,000	5,283,276,000	5,340,823,000	5,030,491,000	5,601,314,000	7,661,936,000
EBITDA	13,638,970,000	13,307,830,000	15,063,500,000	16,177,250,000	14,883,360,000	11,548,890,000
Return on Assets %						
Return on Equity %						
Debt to Equity						

CONTACT INFORMATION:

Phone: 81 3 3423 1111 Fax:
Toll-Free:
Address: 2-1-1, Minami-Aoyama, Minato-ku, Tokyo, 107-8556 Japan

STOCK TICKER/OTHER:

Stock Ticker: HMC
Employees: 211,374
Parent Company:
Exchange: NYS
Fiscal Year Ends: 03/31

SALARIES/BONUSES:

Top Exec. Salary: $896,278 Bonus: $465,713
Second Exec. Salary: $ Bonus: $

OTHER THOUGHTS:

Estimated Female Officers or Directors:
Hot Spot for Advancement for Women/Minorities:

Honeywell International Inc

www.honeywell.com

NAIC Code: 336412

TYPES OF BUSINESS:

Aircraft Engine and Engine Parts Manufacturing
Automation & Control Systems
Turboprop Engines
Performance Polymers
Specialty Chemicals
Nuclear Services
Warehouse Automation
Quantum Computing

BRANDS/DIVISIONS/AFFILIATES:

Sparta Systems

GROWTH PLANS/SPECIAL FEATURES:

Honeywell traces its roots to 1885 with Albert Butz's firm, Butz-Thermo Electric Regulator, which produced a predecessor to the modern thermostat. Today, Honeywell is a global multi-industry behemoth with one of the largest installed bases of equipment. The firm operates through four business segments, including aerospace, building technologies, performance materials and technologies, and safety and productivity solutions. In recent years, the firm has made several portfolio changes, including the addition of Intelligrated in 2016, as well as the spins of Garrett Technologies and Resideo in 2018. In 2019, the firm launched Honeywell Forge, its enterprise performance management software solution that leverages the firm's domain expertise in buildings, airlines, and critical infrastructure.

CONTACTS: *Note: Officers with more than one job title may be intentionally listed here more than once.*

Rajeev Gautam, CEO, Divisional
Vimal Kapur, CEO, Divisional
John Waldron, CEO, Divisional
Que Dallara, CEO, Divisional
Michael Madsen, CEO, Divisional
Darius Adamczyk, CEO
Gregory Lewis, CFO
Robert Mailloux, Chief Accounting Officer
Anne Madden, General Counsel
Karen Mattimore, Other Executive Officer
Doug Wright, President, Divisional

FINANCIAL DATA: *Note: Data for latest year may not have been available at press time.*

In U.S. $	2021	2020	2019	2018	2017	2016
Revenue		32,637,000,000	36,709,000,000	41,802,000,000	40,534,000,000	39,302,000,000
R&D Expense						
Operating Income		5,696,000,000	6,851,000,000	6,705,000,000	7,151,000,000	6,683,000,000
Operating Margin %						
SGA Expense		4,772,000,000	5,519,000,000	6,051,000,000	5,808,000,000	5,469,000,000
Net Income		4,779,000,000	6,143,000,000	6,765,000,000	1,655,000,000	4,809,000,000
Operating Cash Flow		6,208,000,000	6,897,000,000	6,434,000,000	5,966,000,000	5,498,000,000
Capital Expenditure		906,000,000	839,000,000	828,000,000	1,031,000,000	1,095,000,000
EBITDA		7,373,000,000	9,004,000,000	8,970,000,000	8,333,000,000	7,815,000,000
Return on Assets %						
Return on Equity %						
Debt to Equity						

CONTACT INFORMATION:

Phone: 704-627-6200 Fax:
Toll-Free:
Address: 300 S. Tryon St., Charlotte, NC 28202 United States

STOCK TICKER/OTHER:

Stock Ticker: HON
Employees: 103,000
Parent Company:
Exchange: NAS
Fiscal Year Ends: 12/31

SALARIES/BONUSES:

Top Exec. Salary: $1,566,154 Bonus: $
Second Exec. Salary: $825,529 Bonus: $

OTHER THOUGHTS:

Estimated Female Officers or Directors: 2
Hot Spot for Advancement for Women/Minorities: Y

Hoya Corporation

www.hoya.co.jp

NAIC Code: 334413

TYPES OF BUSINESS:

Semiconductor Manufacturing Equipment
Glass Semiconductor Components
Medical Equipment
Eyeglass Lenses
Optical Glass
Bio-Compatible Bone Replacement
Laser & UV Light Sources
Nanoimprint Technology

BRANDS/DIVISIONS/AFFILIATES:

ViXion Inc

GROWTH PLANS/SPECIAL FEATURES:

Hoya Corp is a diversified, multinational company and supplier of innovative and indispensable high-tech and healthcare products. HOYA is active in two core business segments: The Life Care segment and Information Technology segment. The Life Care segment encompasses health care areas such as eyeglass lenses and the operation of contact lens retail stores, as well as medical endoscopes, surgical equipment and artificial bones and implants. Information Technology segment focuses on electronics products for the semiconductor industry and LCD panels, glass disks for HDDs and optical lenses for digital cameras and smartphones.

CONTACTS: *Note: Officers with more than one job title may be intentionally listed here more than once.*

Hiroshi Suzuki, CEO
Ryo Hirooka, CFO
Eiichiro Ikeda, CTO
Mitsudo Urano, Chmn.

FINANCIAL DATA: *Note: Data for latest year may not have been available at press time.*

In U.S. $	2021	2020	2019	2018	2017	2016
Revenue	4,905,486,000	5,118,185,000	5,029,331,000	4,755,307,000	4,303,267,000	4,526,949,000
R&D Expense						
Operating Income	2,676,136,000	2,663,412,000	2,738,278,000	2,479,526,000	2,199,545,000	2,236,529,000
Operating Margin %						
SGA Expense	87,861,580	107,324,900	111,762,300	114,978,400	113,458,200	114,908,100
Net Income	1,102,299,000	1,005,290,000	1,072,924,000	874,257,500	762,187,600	818,732,200
Operating Cash Flow	1,333,978,000	1,435,503,000	1,288,074,000	1,190,635,000	946,030,000	1,158,914,000
Capital Expenditure	274,559,700	396,972,000	234,367,900	157,938,200	189,167,300	159,783,500
EBITDA	1,736,002,000	1,603,046,000	1,506,660,000	1,350,831,000	1,245,141,000	1,349,680,000
Return on Assets %						
Return on Equity %						
Debt to Equity						

CONTACT INFORMATION:

Phone: 81339521151 Fax: 81339520726
Toll-Free:
Address: Fl. 20, Nittochi Nishishinjuku Bldg, 6-10-1 Nishi-S, Tokyo, 160-8347 Japan

STOCK TICKER/OTHER:

Stock Ticker: HOCPF
Employees: 37,412
Parent Company:
Exchange: PINX
Fiscal Year Ends: 03/31

SALARIES/BONUSES:

Top Exec. Salary: $ Bonus: $
Second Exec. Salary: $ Bonus: $

OTHER THOUGHTS:

Estimated Female Officers or Directors:
Hot Spot for Advancement for Women/Minorities:

HP Inc

NAIC Code: 334111

www.hp.com

TYPES OF BUSINESS:

Computer Manufacturing
Computer Software
Printers & Supplies
Scanners
Computing Devices

BRANDS/DIVISIONS/AFFILIATES:

HP Labs

GROWTH PLANS/SPECIAL FEATURES:

HP Inc. is a leading provider of computers, printers, and printer supplies. The company's three operating business segments are its personal systems, containing notebooks, desktops, and workstations; and its printing segment which contains supplies, consumer hardware, and commercial hardware; and corporate investments. In 2015, Hewlett-Packard was separated into HP Inc. and Hewlett Packard Enterprise and the Palo Alto, California-based company sells on a global scale.

CONTACTS: *Note: Officers with more than one job title may be intentionally listed here more than once.*

Enrique Lores, CEO
Marie Myers, CFO
Charles Bergh, Chairman of the Board
Harvey Anderson, Chief Legal Officer
Sarabjit Singh Baveja, Chief Strategy Officer
Tolga Kurtoglu, Chief Technology Officer
Barb Weiszhaar, Other Corporate Officer
Tracy Keogh, Other Executive Officer
Christoph Schell, Other Executive Officer
Tuan Tran, President, Divisional
Alex Cho, President, Divisional

FINANCIAL DATA: *Note: Data for latest year may not have been available at press time.*

In U.S. $	2021	2020	2019	2018	2017	2016
Revenue		56,639,000,000	58,756,000,000	58,472,000,000	52,056,000,000	48,238,000,000
R&D Expense		1,478,000,000	1,499,000,000	1,404,000,000	1,190,000,000	1,209,000,000
Operating Income		3,727,000,000	3,001,000,000	3,664,000,000	4,058,000,000	3,933,000,000
Operating Margin %						
SGA Expense		5,120,000,000	5,368,000,000	4,859,000,000	4,376,000,000	3,840,000,000
Net Income		2,844,000,000	3,152,000,000	5,327,000,000	2,526,000,000	2,496,000,000
Operating Cash Flow		4,316,000,000	4,654,000,000	4,528,000,000	3,677,000,000	3,230,000,000
Capital Expenditure		580,000,000	671,000,000	546,000,000	402,000,000	433,000,000
EBITDA		4,259,000,000	3,509,000,000	3,853,000,000	3,939,000,000	4,265,000,000
Return on Assets %						
Return on Equity %						
Debt to Equity						

CONTACT INFORMATION:

Phone: 650 857-1501 Fax:
Toll-Free:
Address: 1501 Page Mill Rd., Palo Alto, CA 94304 United States

STOCK TICKER/OTHER:

Stock Ticker: HPQ
Employees: 53,000
Parent Company:
Exchange: NYS
Fiscal Year Ends: 10/31

SALARIES/BONUSES:

Top Exec. Salary: $1,100,000 Bonus: $
Second Exec. Salary: $764,166 Bonus: $

OTHER THOUGHTS:

Estimated Female Officers or Directors: 6
Hot Spot for Advancement for Women/Minorities: Y

HQSoftware

NAIC Code: 511210B

hqsoftwarelab.com

TYPES OF BUSINESS:

Computer Software: Network Management (IT), System Testing & Storage
Mobile App Development
Web Application Development
Internet of Things
Augmented Reality
Virtual Reality
Video
Enterprise Software

BRANDS/DIVISIONS/AFFILIATES:

CONTACTS: *Note: Officers with more than one job title may be intentionally listed here more than once.*

Alexei Lemeshev, CEO

GROWTH PLANS/SPECIAL FEATURES:

HQSoftware creates tailored software for enterprise customers across a wide range of industries. The firm offers full-cycle custom software development to help enterprises power their customers, employees and partners via multiple channels. These customers are primarily based in the U.S. and Europe, and include the top 10 companies in the Fortune 500. HQSoftware specializes in Internet of Things (IoT), augmented reality (AR) and virtual reality (VR), where it partners with hardware producers to provide enterprise adopters with complete ecosystems. IoT ecosystem solutions include IoT consulting, programming for IoT devices, customizing existing IoT platforms, building IoT platforms from scratch, creating smart device networks, big data, analytics, artificial intelligence, machine learning, user interface (UI), user experience (UX), and IoT web and mobile app development. AR/VR solutions include consultancy, full-stack development, prototyping or a minimum viable product, maintenance and enhancement services. The company specializes in sensor-based AR/VR, data visualization and computer vision, AR/VR hardware integration and IoT + AR/VR. Primary industries that HQSoftware currently serves include industrial, agriculture, automotive, healthcare, smart city, data analytics, AR/VR, insurance, finance, eLearning, marketing/advertising and video/media. The firm offers several types of business models, including flexible with no deadlines and hourly rates, fixed priced with deadlines, and outsourced with an evolving scope. The entire project can be carried out/delivered off-site, on-site or in hybrid format. HQSoftware is based in New York City, USA, with global offices in Estonia and Georgia.

FINANCIAL DATA: *Note: Data for latest year may not have been available at press time.*

In U.S. $	2021	2020	2019	2018	2017	2016
Revenue						
R&D Expense						
Operating Income						
Operating Margin %						
SGA Expense						
Net Income						
Operating Cash Flow						
Capital Expenditure						
EBITDA						
Return on Assets %						
Return on Equity %						
Debt to Equity						

CONTACT INFORMATION:

Phone: 917-720-3806 Fax:
Toll-Free:
Address: 315 Madison Ave., Ste. 3045, New York, NY 10017 United States

STOCK TICKER/OTHER:

Stock Ticker: Private
Employees: 90
Parent Company:
Exchange:
Fiscal Year Ends:

SALARIES/BONUSES:

Top Exec. Salary: $ Bonus: $
Second Exec. Salary: $ Bonus: $

OTHER THOUGHTS:

Estimated Female Officers or Directors:
Hot Spot for Advancement for Women/Minorities:

HTC Corporation

www.htc.com

NAIC Code: 334418

TYPES OF BUSINESS:

Contract Electronics Manufacturing
Innovative Technology
Virtual Reality Products
Augmented Reality Products
5G
Artificial Intelligence
Blockchain Solutions
Security Solutions

BRANDS/DIVISIONS/AFFILIATES:

VIVE
HTC 5G
EXODUX

GROWTH PLANS/SPECIAL FEATURES:

HTC Corporation is an innovation company that creates products, solutions and platforms in mobile and immersive technologies. HTC's technologies include virtual reality (VR), augmented reality (AR), 5G, artificial intelligence (AI) and blockchain, which are marketed under the VIVE and other brand names and can be embedded to support, develop and deploy products and solutions for customers across a range of industries. VIVE VR is the firm's virtual reality headset, VIVEPORT Infinity offers hundreds of VR games and apps, and VIVE Business offers solutions for businesses. The HTC 5G hub is a connectivity device for home and office environments, enabling 4K video streaming, low-latency gaming and fast networks. EXODUS is a security technology solution for blockchain and cryptocurrency environments.

CONTACTS: *Note: Officers with more than one job title may be intentionally listed here more than once.*

Fred Liu, Pres., Eng.
Fred Liu, Pres., Oper.
Cher Wang, Chairwoman

FINANCIAL DATA: *Note: Data for latest year may not have been available at press time.*

In U.S. $	2021	2020	2019	2018	2017	2016
Revenue		206,480,000	350,381,888	830,584,960	2,078,141,696	2,678,586,624
R&D Expense						
Operating Income						
Operating Margin %						
SGA Expense						
Net Income		-214,194,000	-327,400,128	422,216,064	-565,559,744	-361,895,264
Operating Cash Flow						
Capital Expenditure						
EBITDA						
Return on Assets %						
Return on Equity %						
Debt to Equity						

CONTACT INFORMATION:

Phone: 886 33753252 Fax: 886 33753251
Toll-Free:
Address: NO. 23, Xinghua Rd., Taoyuan, 330 Taiwan

STOCK TICKER/OTHER:

Stock Ticker: 2498 Exchange: TWSE
Employees: 2,605 Fiscal Year Ends: 12/31
Parent Company:

SALARIES/BONUSES:

Top Exec. Salary: $ Bonus: $
Second Exec. Salary: $ Bonus: $

OTHER THOUGHTS:

Estimated Female Officers or Directors: 2
Hot Spot for Advancement for Women/Minorities:

Huawei Technologies Co Ltd

www.huawei.com

NAIC Code: 334210

TYPES OF BUSINESS:

Telecommunications Equipment Manufacturing
Network Equipment
Software
Wireless Technology
Smartphones
5G Wireless Technology
Watches

BRANDS/DIVISIONS/AFFILIATES:

Union of Huawei Investment & Holding Co
Huaewi

CONTACTS:

Note: Officers with more than one job title may be intentionally listed here more than once.

Ren Zhengfei, Pres.
Ding Yun (Ryan Ding), Chief Prod. & Solutions Officer
Yu Chengdong (Richard Yu), Chief Strategy Officer
Chen Lifang, Corp. Sr. VP-Public Affairs & Comm. Dept.
Guo Ping, Chmn.-Finance Committee
Zhang Ping'an (Alex Zhang), CEO-Huawei Symantec
Hu Houkun (Ken Hu), Chmn.-Huawei USA
Liang Hua, Chmn.
Wan Biao, Pres., Russia

GROWTH PLANS/SPECIAL FEATURES:

Huawei Technologies Co., Ltd., founded in 1987, is a leading global information and communications technology (ICT) solutions provider. Huawei is one of the world's leading manufacturers of smartphones. The company's ICT portfolio of end-to-end solutions in telecom, enterprise networks, and consumers are used in more than 170 countries and regions, serving more than one-third of the world's population. Huawei's consumer products include the Huawei brand of mobile smart phones, the laptops, tablets, watches, ear buds, speakers, Wi-Fi connection devices and more. The company's business products include switches, routers, WLAN (wireless local area network), servers, storage, cloud computing, network energy services and more. Its carrier products include cloud data centers, wireless network, fixed network, cloud core network, carrier software, IT infrastructure and network energy global services. Huawei Technologies has rolled out 53 NB-IoT city-aware network using a one network/one platform/N-tier applications model. NB-IoT stands for NarrowBand Internet of Things, and is a low-power, wide-area network radio technology standard that enables a wide range of devices and services to be connected using cellular telecommunications bands. Huawei's smart city solutions senses, processes and delivers informed decisions for improving the environment for citizens, with recent information and communications technology (ICT) offering real-time situation reporting and analysis, empowered by a combination of cloud computing, IoT technologies, big data analytics and artificial intelligence (AI). The company has global joint innovation centers and research and development centers and offices. It has invested very heavily in 5G wireless technologies. Huawei Technologies operates as a subsidiary of the Union of Huawei Investment & Holding Co., Ltd.

FINANCIAL DATA:

Note: Data for latest year may not have been available at press time.

In U.S. $	2021	2020	2019	2018	2017	2016
Revenue						
R&D Expense						
Operating Income						
Operating Margin %						
SGA Expense						
Net Income						
Operating Cash Flow						
Capital Expenditure						
EBITDA						
Return on Assets %						
Return on Equity %						
Debt to Equity						

CONTACT INFORMATION:

Phone: 86-755-28780808 Fax: 86-755-28789251
Toll-Free:
Address: Section H, Bantian, Longgang Distr., Shenzhen, Guangdong 518129 China

STOCK TICKER/OTHER:

Stock Ticker: Subsidiary
Exchange:
Employees: 200,000
Fiscal Year Ends: 12/31
Parent Company: Union of Huawei Investment & Holding Co Ltd

SALARIES/BONUSES:

Top Exec. Salary: $ Bonus: $
Second Exec. Salary: $ Bonus: $

OTHER THOUGHTS:

Estimated Female Officers or Directors: 3
Hot Spot for Advancement for Women/Minorities: Y

Hyundai Motor Company

worldwide.hyundai.com

NAIC Code: 336111

TYPES OF BUSINESS:

Automobile Manufacturing
Trucks
Buses
Light Commercial Vehicles
Machine Tools
Factory Automation Equipment
Material Handling Equipment
Specialty Vehicle Manufacturing

BRANDS/DIVISIONS/AFFILIATES:

Accent
Sonata
Elantra
Xcient
Kia Motors Corporation
Hyundai Capital
Hyundai Mobis
Boston Dynamics

GROWTH PLANS/SPECIAL FEATURES:

Hyundai Motor Co is engaged in the manufacturing and distribution of motor vehicles and parts. The business of the group is operated through a vehicle, finance, and other segments. Its vehicle segment is engaged in the manufacturing and sale of motor vehicles. The finance segment operates vehicle financing, credit card processing, and other financing activities. Others segment includes the research and development, train manufacturing and other activities. The company derives most of the revenue from vehicle segment.

CONTACTS: *Note: Officers with more than one job title may be intentionally listed here more than once.*

Mong-Koo Chung, Pres.
Choong Ho Kim, Co-CEO

FINANCIAL DATA: *Note: Data for latest year may not have been available at press time.*

In U.S. $	2021	2020	2019	2018	2017	2016
Revenue		87,338,630,000	88,807,320,000	81,304,580,000	80,937,980,000	78,647,750,000
R&D Expense		1,123,564,000	1,083,121,000	945,297,000	872,785,000	855,928,300
Operating Income		2,011,078,000	3,027,953,000	2,034,168,000	3,841,869,000	4,361,573,000
Operating Margin %						
SGA Expense		9,584,487,000	7,923,312,000	7,042,559,000	7,424,455,000	6,994,431,000
Net Income		1,196,261,000	2,502,687,000	1,266,510,000	3,386,822,000	4,540,399,000
Operating Cash Flow		-344,161,600	352,540,400	3,161,282,000	3,294,104,000	837,264,200
Capital Expenditure		5,365,949,000	4,453,865,000	4,080,821,000	3,794,385,000	3,676,296,000
EBITDA		5,577,209,000	6,981,051,000	5,541,194,000	6,971,277,000	9,185,911,000
Return on Assets %						
Return on Equity %						
Debt to Equity						

CONTACT INFORMATION:

Phone: 82 234641114 Fax: 82 234643477
Toll-Free:
Address: 12 Heolleung-ro Seocho-gu, Seoul, 06797 South Korea

STOCK TICKER/OTHER:

Stock Ticker: HYMLF
Exchange: PINX
Employees: 62,000
Fiscal Year Ends: 12/31
Parent Company: Hyundai Motor Group

SALARIES/BONUSES:

Top Exec. Salary: $ Bonus: $
Second Exec. Salary: $ Bonus: $

OTHER THOUGHTS:

Estimated Female Officers or Directors:
Hot Spot for Advancement for Women/Minorities:

IBM Research

www.research.ibm.com

NAIC Code: 541712

TYPES OF BUSINESS:

Research & Development
Hybrid Cloud
Artificial Intelligence
Quantum Computing
Science Innovation
Research and Development

BRANDS/DIVISIONS/AFFILIATES:

International Business Machines Corporation (IBM)

CONTACTS:

Note: Officers with more than one job title may be intentionally listed here more than once.

T.C. Chen, VP-Science

GROWTH PLANS/SPECIAL FEATURES:

IBM Research is the R&D arm of International Business Machines Corporation (IBM). The company often works with private customers and academic and government research centers. Featured research areas include: hybrid cloud, artificial intelligence (AI), quantum computing and science. Hybrid cloud focuses on open standards and opensource code to build a seamless hybrid cloud platform, encompassing security, compliance and reliability for the enterprise. AI focuses on providing enterprises with AI that is adaptable to new challenges and domains, and therefore engages in algorithm development and improving AI engineering tools and hardware. Quantum computing is engaged in innovating across the entire stack to make quantum frictionless, and is therefore building libraries of circuits to empower researchers, developers and businesses to tap into quantum-as-a-service through the cloud via easy-to-use coding language. The science research area is engaged in developing new technologies, making processes scalable, and deploying new models of collaborative innovation.

FINANCIAL DATA:

Note: Data for latest year may not have been available at press time.

In U.S. $	2021	2020	2019	2018	2017	2016
Revenue						
R&D Expense						
Operating Income						
Operating Margin %						
SGA Expense						
Net Income						
Operating Cash Flow						
Capital Expenditure						
EBITDA						
Return on Assets %						
Return on Equity %						
Debt to Equity						

CONTACT INFORMATION:

Phone: 914-945-3000 Fax: 914-945-2141
Toll-Free:
Address: 1101 Kitchawan Rd., Rte. 134, Yorktown Heights, NY 10598 United States

STOCK TICKER/OTHER:

Stock Ticker: Subsidiary
Exchange:
Employees: 3,000
Fiscal Year Ends: 12/31
Parent Company: International Business Machines Corporation (IBM)

SALARIES/BONUSES:

Top Exec. Salary: $ Bonus: $
Second Exec. Salary: $ Bonus: $

OTHER THOUGHTS:

Estimated Female Officers or Directors:
Hot Spot for Advancement for Women/Minorities: Y

Ideal Power Inc

www.idealpower.com

NAIC Code: 334513

TYPES OF BUSINESS:

Instruments and Related Products Manufacturing for Measuring, Displaying, and Controlling Industrial Process Variables
Bi-directional Power Switches
Semiconductors
Alternative Energy
Technology

GROWTH PLANS/SPECIAL FEATURES:

Ideal Power Inc is engaged in the development of its broadly patented bi-directional power switches. The firm is focused on its patented Bi-directional, Bi-polar Junction Transistor (B-TRAN) semiconductor technology. B-TRAN is a unique double-sided bi-directional AC switchable to deliver substantial performance improvements over today's conventional power semiconductors.

BRANDS/DIVISIONS/AFFILIATES:

B-TRAN

CONTACTS: *Note: Officers with more than one job title may be intentionally listed here more than once.*

R. Brdar, CEO
Timothy Burns, CFO

FINANCIAL DATA: *Note: Data for latest year may not have been available at press time.*

In U.S. $	2021	2020	2019	2018	2017	2016
Revenue		428,129			1,212,270	1,628,740
R&D Expense		1,720,893	1,050,151	871,742	4,184,905	5,224,992
Operating Income		-4,067,982	-3,115,263	-4,311,624	-10,452,690	-11,017,140
Operating Margin %						
SGA Expense		2,347,089	2,065,112	3,439,882	5,238,369	5,481,173
Net Income		-7,793,897	-3,927,662	-7,904,989	-10,435,100	-10,981,090
Operating Cash Flow		-3,019,032	-3,218,657	-3,832,259	-7,415,539	-10,098,650
Capital Expenditure		67,160	104,098	134,149	434,030	750,992
EBITDA		-7,666,696	-3,004,800	-4,174,115	-10,001,140	-10,610,500
Return on Assets %						
Return on Equity %						
Debt to Equity						

CONTACT INFORMATION:

Phone: 512 264-1542 Fax:
Toll-Free:
Address: 4120 Freidrich Ln., Ste. 100, Austin, TX 78744 United States

STOCK TICKER/OTHER:

Stock Ticker: IPWR
Exchange: NAS
Employees: 5
Fiscal Year Ends: 12/31
Parent Company:

SALARIES/BONUSES:

Top Exec. Salary: $285,332 Bonus: $247,500
Second Exec. Salary: $214,754 Bonus: $112,500

OTHER THOUGHTS:

Estimated Female Officers or Directors:
Hot Spot for Advancement for Women/Minorities:

II-VI Incorporated

www.ii-vi.com

NAIC Code: 334513

TYPES OF BUSINESS:

Infrared Instruments, Industrial Process-Type, Manufacturing
Engineered Materials Manufacturing
Optoelectronic Components Manufacturing

BRANDS/DIVISIONS/AFFILIATES:

Ascatron AB
INNOViON Corporation

GROWTH PLANS/SPECIAL FEATURES:

II-VI Inc manufactures engineered materials, optoelectronic components and products used in industrial, optical communications, military, semiconductor, consumer, and life science applications. The firm operates in two segments Photonic Solutions Segment and Compound Semiconductors Segment. The Photonic Solutions Segment leverages II-VI's compound semiconductor technology platforms to deliver components and subsystems. The Compound Semiconductors Segment is a market leader in differentiated materials and devices.

CONTACTS: *Note: Officers with more than one job title may be intentionally listed here more than once.*

Vincent Mattera, CEO
Mary Raymond, CFO
Francis Kramer, Chairman Emeritus
Giovanni Barbarossa, Chief Strategy Officer
Christopher Koeppen, Chief Technology Officer
Walter Bashaw, President

FINANCIAL DATA: *Note: Data for latest year may not have been available at press time.*

In U.S. $	2021	2020	2019	2018	2017	2016
Revenue	3,105,891,000	2,380,071,000	1,362,496,000	1,158,794,000	972,046,000	827,216,000
R&D Expense	330,105,000	339,073,000	139,163,000	117,244,000	96,810,000	60,354,000
Operating Income	402,119,000	39,479,000	148,668,000	135,287,000	115,541,000	91,813,000
Operating Margin %						
SGA Expense	483,989,000	440,998,000	233,518,000	208,757,000	176,002,000	160,646,000
Net Income	297,552,000	-67,029,000	107,517,000	88,002,000	95,274,000	65,486,000
Operating Cash Flow	574,353,000	297,292,000	178,475,000	161,014,000	118,616,000	122,970,000
Capital Expenditure	146,337,000	140,627,000	137,122,000	153,438,000	138,517,000	58,170,000
EBITDA	682,558,000	246,363,000	243,595,000	221,316,000	189,234,000	149,699,000
Return on Assets %						
Return on Equity %						
Debt to Equity						

CONTACT INFORMATION:

Phone: 724 352-4455 Fax: 724 352-4980
Toll-Free:
Address: 375 Saxonburg Blvd., Saxonburg, PA 16056 United States

STOCK TICKER/OTHER:

Stock Ticker: IIVI
Employees: 22,969
Parent Company:
Exchange: NAS
Fiscal Year Ends: 06/30

SALARIES/BONUSES:

Top Exec. Salary: $950,833 Bonus: $
Second Exec. Salary: $515,000 Bonus: $

OTHER THOUGHTS:

Estimated Female Officers or Directors:
Hot Spot for Advancement for Women/Minorities:

Illumio

NAIC Code: 511210E

www.illumio.com

TYPES OF BUSINESS:

Computer Software: Network Security, Managed Access, Digital ID, Cybersecurity & Anti-Virus
Zero Trust Segmentation Products
Cyber Attack Solutions
Workload Security
Cloud Security
Endpoint Security

BRANDS/DIVISIONS/AFFILIATES:

Illumio Core
Illumio CloudSecure
Illumio Edge

GROWTH PLANS/SPECIAL FEATURES:

Illumio provides Zero Trust segmentation products and solutions against cyber attacks. The company's offerings protect critical applications and digital assets by identifying risks, isolating attacks and securing data across cloud-native apps, hybrid and multi-clouds, data centers and endpoints. Illumio's products span workload security, cloud security and endpoint security through its Illumio Core, Illumio CloudSecure and Illumio Edge product lines. Solutions include visibility and ransomware containment, Zero Trust segmentation and Zero Trust security. Industries served by Illumio include airlines, federal, financial services, healthcare, law firms and retail.

CONTACTS: *Note: Officers with more than one job title may be intentionally listed here more than once.*

Andrew Rubin, CEO
Joel Bauman, Sr. VP-Business & Corporate Development
Anup Singh, CFO
Shay Mowlem, CMO
Kathleen Swift, Chief People Officer
PJ Kirner, CTO
Ben Verghese, Sr. VP-Engineering

FINANCIAL DATA: *Note: Data for latest year may not have been available at press time.*

In U.S. $	2021	2020	2019	2018	2017	2016
Revenue						
R&D Expense						
Operating Income						
Operating Margin %						
SGA Expense						
Net Income						
Operating Cash Flow						
Capital Expenditure						
EBITDA						
Return on Assets %						
Return on Equity %						
Debt to Equity						

CONTACT INFORMATION:

Phone: 669-800-5000 Fax:
Toll-Free:
Address: 920 De Guigne Dr., Sunnyvale, CA 94085 United States

STOCK TICKER/OTHER:

Stock Ticker: Private
Employees: 160
Parent Company:
Exchange:
Fiscal Year Ends:

SALARIES/BONUSES:

Top Exec. Salary: $ Bonus: $
Second Exec. Salary: $ Bonus: $

OTHER THOUGHTS:

Estimated Female Officers or Directors:
Hot Spot for Advancement for Women/Minorities:

Infineon Technologies AG

www.infineon.com

NAIC Code: 334413

TYPES OF BUSINESS:

Semiconductor Manufacturing
Semiconductors
Automotive
Power Systems
Sensors
Security Systems
Mobility
Internet of Things

BRANDS/DIVISIONS/AFFILIATES:

Syntronixs Asia Sdn Bhd

GROWTH PLANS/SPECIAL FEATURES:

Infineon was spun off from German industrial conglomerate Siemens in 2000 and today is one of Europe's largest chipmakers. The company is a leader in the automotive and industrial chip markets and has also focused on ID cards and security solutions that include semiconductor content. Infineon has divested itself of some less profitable businesses in recent years, most notably the sale of its wireless chip division to Intel in 2010.

CONTACTS: *Note: Officers with more than one job title may be intentionally listed here more than once.*

Reinhard Ploss, CEO
Jochen Hanebeck, COO
Sven Schneider, CFO
Helmut Gassel, CMO
Constanze Hufenbecker, CTO
Arunjai Mittal, Exec. VP-Strategy Dev.
Klaus Walther, Corp. VP-Comm. & Public Authorities & Associations

FINANCIAL DATA: *Note: Data for latest year may not have been available at press time.*

In U.S. $	2021	2020	2019	2018	2017	2016
Revenue	12,490,541,056	9,675,087,872	9,067,501,568	8,581,883,392	7,634,685,440	7,640,372,736
R&D Expense						
Operating Income						
Operating Margin %						
SGA Expense						
Net Income	1,320,202,752	415,598,496	982,529,088	1,214,044,544	853,943,296	878,176,640
Operating Cash Flow						
Capital Expenditure						
EBITDA						
Return on Assets %						
Return on Equity %						
Debt to Equity						

CONTACT INFORMATION:

Phone: 49-89-234-0 Fax: 49-89-2349553431
Toll-Free: 49-800-951-951-951
Address: Am Campeon 1-15, Munich, 85579 Germany

STOCK TICKER/OTHER:

Stock Ticker: IFNNY
Employees: 46,665
Parent Company:
Exchange: OTC
Fiscal Year Ends: 09/30

SALARIES/BONUSES:

Top Exec. Salary: $ Bonus: $
Second Exec. Salary: $ Bonus: $

OTHER THOUGHTS:

Estimated Female Officers or Directors:
Hot Spot for Advancement for Women/Minorities:

Infosys Limited

NAIC Code: 541512

www.infosys.com

TYPES OF BUSINESS:

IT Consulting
Software Development & Services
Business Process Outsourcing

BRANDS/DIVISIONS/AFFILIATES:

Finacle
Global Delivery Model
EdgeVerve Systems Limited
Infosys BPM
Infosys Consulting
Infosys Public Services

CONTACTS:

Note: Officers with more than one job title may be intentionally listed here more than once.

Salil Parekh, CEO
Mohit Joshi, Co-Pres.
Nilnajan Roy, CFO
Inderpreet Sawhney, Chief Compliance Officer
Krishnamurthy Shankar, Exec. VP-Human Resources
Subrahmanyan Goparaju, Sr. VP-Infosys Labs
Ravi Kumar S., Co-Pres.
Sanjay Purohit, Sr. VP-Prod., Platforms & Solutions
Sanjay Jalona, Sr. VP-Mfg. & Eng. Svcs.
Nithyanandan Radhakrishnan, Sr. VP
K. Murali Krishna, Sr. VP-Computers & Comm.
N.R. Narayana Murthy, Co-Chmn.
V. Balakrishnan, Head-Infosys BPO, Fin. & India Bus. Unit
Srinath Batni, Head-Delivery Excellence
Nandita Gurjar, Sr. VP-Education & Research
Nandan Nilekani, Chmn.
Dheeshjith V.G., Sr. VP-Asia Pacific, Middle East & Africa
Chandrashekar Kakal, Sr. VP-Global Delivery

GROWTH PLANS/SPECIAL FEATURES:

Infosys is a leading global IT services provider, with nearly 250,000 employees. Based in Bangalore, the Indian IT services firm leverages its offshore outsourcing model to derive 60% of its revenue from North America. The company offers traditional IT services offerings: consulting, managed services and cloud infrastructure services, and business process outsourcing as a service (BPaaS).

FINANCIAL DATA:

Note: Data for latest year may not have been available at press time.

In U.S. $	2021	2020	2019	2018	2017	2016
Revenue	13,561,000,000	12,780,000,000	11,799,000,000	10,939,000,000	10,208,000,000	9,501,000,000
R&D Expense						
Operating Income	3,350,000,000	2,748,000,000	2,731,000,000	2,670,000,000	2,575,000,000	2,375,000,000
Operating Margin %						
SGA Expense	1,223,000,000	1,302,000,000	1,220,000,000	1,116,000,000	1,020,000,000	1,176,000,000
Net Income	2,613,000,000	2,331,000,000	2,199,000,000	2,486,000,000	2,140,000,000	2,052,000,000
Operating Cash Flow	3,258,000,000	2,611,000,000	2,262,000,000	2,257,000,000	2,099,000,000	1,862,000,000
Capital Expenditure	285,000,000	465,000,000	349,000,000	310,000,000	411,000,000	413,000,000
EBITDA	4,063,000,000	3,526,000,000	3,018,000,000	2,959,000,000	2,829,000,000	2,597,000,000
Return on Assets %						
Return on Equity %						
Debt to Equity						

CONTACT INFORMATION:

Phone: 91 8028520261 Fax: 91 8028520362
Toll-Free:
Address: Hosur Rd., Electronics City, Bengaluru, Karnataka 560 100 India

STOCK TICKER/OTHER:

Stock Ticker: INFY
Exchange: NYS
Employees: 259,619
Fiscal Year Ends: 03/31
Parent Company:

SALARIES/BONUSES:

Top Exec. Salary: $768,536 Bonus: $1,710,006
Second Exec. Salary: $737,457 Bonus: $735,219

OTHER THOUGHTS:

Estimated Female Officers or Directors: 2
Hot Spot for Advancement for Women/Minorities: Y

Inmarsat Global Limited

www.inmarsat.com

NAIC Code: 517410

TYPES OF BUSINESS:

Satellite Carrier & Equipment
Mobile Satellite Communications
Broadband
Satellite Launch Operations
Remote Connectivity
Satellites
Internet of Things
Low Earth Orbit Satellite

BRANDS/DIVISIONS/AFFILIATES:

Connect Bidco Limited
Global Xpress
European Aviation Network
ORCHESTRA

CONTACTS: *Note: Officers with more than one job title may be intentionally listed here more than once.*

Rajeev Suri, CEO
Jason Smith, COO
Tony Bates, CFO
Barry French, CMO
Natasha Dillon, Chief People Officer
Peter Hadinger, CTO
Richard Denny, Sr. VP-Eng. & Global Networks
Alison Horrocks, Corp. Sec.
Diane Cornell, VP-Govt Affairs
Jat Brainch, Chief Product Officer & Chief Commercial Officer

GROWTH PLANS/SPECIAL FEATURES:

Inmarsat Global Limited is a world-leading provider of global mobile satellite communications solutions and services. The firm's broadband global area network (BGAN) offers seamless global coverage, and satellite and ground network availability 99.9% of the time. Through its L-band services, Inmarsat connects people and machines in remote locations (on ships and in airplanes), enabling the global Internet of Things (IoT), voice calls and internet access. L-band service capabilities span email and web browsing to high bandwidth applications such as live streaming and telemedicine. The company's Global Xpress (GX) is a mobile high-speed broadband network from a single provider. Its Ka-band service offers content-rich applications from certified developers. Inmarsat's European Aviation Network (EAN) is an integrated satellite and air-to-ground connectivity network, developed to meet the particular requirements of European skies. The EAN combines S-band satellite coverage with a long-term evolution (LTE)-based terrestrial network to deliver cost-effective, scalable capacity across all 28 member states of the European Union, as well as Switzerland and Norway. Developed in partnership with Deutsche Telekom, EAN gives European aviation cutting-edge inflight connectivity. Inmarsat's sixth generation (I-6) of satellites feature dual-payload satellites, each supporting L-band and Ka-band services. The I-6 satellites support advanced global safety services, very low cost mobile services and Internet of Things (IoT) applications. The Ka-band payload will further extend GX capacity in regions of greatest demand. Inmarsat has locations across every continent, offering 24/7/365 customer support. In Inmarsat is a private company owned by Connect Bidco Limited, a consortium consisting of Apax Partners, Warburg Pincus, the CPP Investment Board and the Ontario Teachers' Pension Plan. During 2021, Inmarsat launched ORCHESTRA, a communications network for global mobility and government communications. ORCHESTRA successfully activated a low-earth orbit (LEO) satellite payload in December 2021.

FINANCIAL DATA: *Note: Data for latest year may not have been available at press time.*

In U.S. $	2021	2020	2019	2018	2017	2016
Revenue	1,195,000,000	1,137,300,000	1,091,500,000	1,465,200,000	1,400,199,936	1,328,999,936
R&D Expense						
Operating Income						
Operating Margin %						
SGA Expense						
Net Income		218,400,000	126,200,000	124,200,000	181,700,000	242,800,000
Operating Cash Flow						
Capital Expenditure						
EBITDA						
Return on Assets %						
Return on Equity %						
Debt to Equity						

CONTACT INFORMATION:

Phone: 44 2077281000 Fax: 44 2077281044
Toll-Free:
Address: 99 City Rd., London, EC1Y 1AX United Kingdom

STOCK TICKER/OTHER:

Stock Ticker: Private
Employees: 1,842
Parent Company: Connect Bidco Limited
Exchange:
Fiscal Year Ends: 12/31

SALARIES/BONUSES:

Top Exec. Salary: $ Bonus: $
Second Exec. Salary: $ Bonus: $

OTHER THOUGHTS:

Estimated Female Officers or Directors: 3
Hot Spot for Advancement for Women/Minorities: Y

Intel Corporation

www.intel.com

NAIC Code: 334413

TYPES OF BUSINESS:

Microprocessors
Processors
Chipsets
Technologies
Graphics Processing Units
Memory and Storage Products
Programmable Devices
Internet of Things

BRANDS/DIVISIONS/AFFILIATES:

Mobileye

GROWTH PLANS/SPECIAL FEATURES:

Intel is the world's largest chipmaker. It designs and manufactures microprocessors for the global personal computer and data center markets. Intel pioneered the x86 architecture for microprocessors. It was the prime proponent of Moore's law for advances in semiconductor manufacturing, though the firm has recently faced manufacturing delays. While Intel's server processor business has benefited from the shift to the cloud, the firm has also been expanding into new adjacencies as the personal computer market has stagnated. These include areas such as the Internet of Things, artificial intelligence, and automotive. Intel has been active on the merger and acquisitions front, acquiring Altera, Mobileye, and Habana Labs in order to bolster these efforts in non-PC arenas.

CONTACTS: *Note: Officers with more than one job title may be intentionally listed here more than once.*

Patrick Gelsinger, CEO
George Davis, CFO
Omar Ishrak, Chairman of the Board
Kevin McBride, Chief Accounting Officer
Greg Lavender, Chief Technology Officer
Steven Rodgers, Executive VP
Gregory Bryant, Executive VP
Sandra Rivera, Executive VP
Nick McKeown, Managing Director, Divisional
Raja Koduri, Other Corporate Officer

FINANCIAL DATA: *Note: Data for latest year may not have been available at press time.*

In U.S. $	2021	2020	2019	2018	2017	2016
Revenue		77,867,000,000	71,965,000,000	70,848,000,000	62,761,000,000	59,387,000,000
R&D Expense		13,556,000,000	13,362,000,000	13,543,000,000	13,098,000,000	12,740,000,000
Operating Income		23,876,000,000	22,428,000,000	23,244,000,000	18,320,000,000	14,760,000,000
Operating Margin %						
SGA Expense		6,180,000,000	6,150,000,000	6,750,000,000	7,474,000,000	8,397,000,000
Net Income		20,899,000,000	21,048,000,000	21,053,000,000	9,601,000,000	10,316,000,000
Operating Cash Flow		35,384,000,000	33,145,000,000	29,432,000,000	22,110,000,000	21,808,000,000
Capital Expenditure		14,453,000,000	16,213,000,000	15,181,000,000	11,778,000,000	9,625,000,000
EBITDA		37,946,000,000	35,373,000,000	32,870,000,000	29,127,000,000	21,459,000,000
Return on Assets %						
Return on Equity %						
Debt to Equity						

CONTACT INFORMATION:

Phone: 408 765-8080 Fax: 408 765-2633
Toll-Free: 800-628-8686
Address: 2200 Mission College Blvd., Santa Clara, CA 95054-1549 United States

STOCK TICKER/OTHER:

Stock Ticker: INTC
Employees: 110,600
Parent Company:
Exchange: NAS
Fiscal Year Ends: 12/31

SALARIES/BONUSES:

Top Exec. Salary: $900,000 Bonus: $1,000,000
Second Exec. Salary: $1,250,000 Bonus: $

OTHER THOUGHTS:

Estimated Female Officers or Directors: 10
Hot Spot for Advancement for Women/Minorities: Y

Intelsat SA

www.intelsat.com

NAIC Code: 517410

TYPES OF BUSINESS:

Satellite Carrier
Global Network
Broadband
Satellites
Terrestrial Infrastructure
Video Broadcasting
Mobility
Communications

BRANDS/DIVISIONS/AFFILIATES:

Intelsat General Communications LLC
IntelsatOne

GROWTH PLANS/SPECIAL FEATURES:

Intelsat SA is a Luxembourg-based company which operates satellite services business. It is engaged in providing diversified communications services to the media companies, fixed and wireless telecommunications operators, data networking service providers for enterprise and mobile applications in the air and on the seas, and a multinational corporation. In addition, it provides commercial satellite communication services to the United States government and other select military organizations and their contractors. Intelsat operates through a single segment being Providing satellite services. The company earns the majority of its revenue from North America.

CONTACTS: *Note: Officers with more than one job title may be intentionally listed here more than once.*

Stephen Spengler, CEO
David Tolley, CFO
Samer Halawi, CCO
Bruno Fromont, CTO
Michelle Bryan, Chief Admin. Officer
Michelle Bryan, General Counsel
David McGlade, Chmn.

FINANCIAL DATA: *Note: Data for latest year may not have been available at press time.*

In U.S. $	2021	2020	2019	2018	2017	2016
Revenue		1,913,080,000	2,061,465,000	2,161,190,000	2,148,612,000	2,188,047,000
R&D Expense						
Operating Income		460,939,000	770,161,000	941,870,000	914,557,000	920,612,000
Operating Margin %						
SGA Expense		314,229,000	226,918,000	200,857,000	204,015,000	231,397,000
Net Income		-911,664,000	-913,595,000	-599,605,000	-178,728,000	990,197,000
Operating Cash Flow		331,302,000	255,539,000	344,173,000	464,230,000	683,506,000
Capital Expenditure		607,103,000	229,818,000	255,696,000	461,627,000	714,570,000
EBITDA		550,724,000	1,012,751,000	1,434,342,000	1,624,910,000	2,643,490,000
Return on Assets %						
Return on Equity %						
Debt to Equity						

CONTACT INFORMATION:

Phone: 352-27-84-1600 Fax: 352-27-84-1690
Toll-Free:
Address: 4 rue Albert Borschette, Luxembourg, L-1246 Luxembourg

STOCK TICKER/OTHER:

Stock Ticker: INTEQ
Employees: 1,774
Parent Company:
Exchange: PINX
Fiscal Year Ends: 12/31

SALARIES/BONUSES:

Top Exec. Salary: $ Bonus: $
Second Exec. Salary: $ Bonus: $

OTHER THOUGHTS:

Estimated Female Officers or Directors: 1
Hot Spot for Advancement for Women/Minorities:

InterDigital Inc

www.interdigital.com

NAIC Code: 334220

TYPES OF BUSINESS:

Technologies Engineering for Wireless Communications
Research and Development
Connected Technologies
Communications
Wireless
Video Coding
Artificial Intelligence

BRANDS/DIVISIONS/AFFILIATES:

GROWTH PLANS/SPECIAL FEATURES:

InterDigital designs and develops technologies that enable and enhance wireless communications and capabilities. The company derives revenue primarily from patent licensing and sales, with contributions from technology solutions licensing and sales and engineering services. However, the majority of revenue is recurring in nature as they are from current patent royalties and sales as well as technology solutions revenue. Interdigital is focused on two technology areas: cellular wireless technology and "Internet of Things" technology.

CONTACTS: *Note: Officers with more than one job title may be intentionally listed here more than once.*

Lawrence Chen, CEO
Richard Brezski, CFO
S. Hutcheson, Chairman of the Board
Joshua Schmidt, Chief Legal Officer

FINANCIAL DATA: *Note: Data for latest year may not have been available at press time.*

In U.S. $	2021	2020	2019	2018	2017	2016
Revenue		358,991,000	318,924,000	307,404,000	532,938,000	665,854,000
R&D Expense		84,646,000	74,860,000	69,698,000	70,708,000	68,733,000
Operating Income		55,168,000	37,835,000	62,595,000	301,495,000	437,306,000
Operating Margin %						
SGA Expense		48,999,000	51,289,000	51,030,000	49,578,000	46,271,000
Net Income		44,801,000	20,928,000	63,868,000	174,293,000	309,001,000
Operating Cash Flow		163,467,000	89,433,000	146,792,000	315,800,000	430,778,000
Capital Expenditure		42,408,000	37,990,000	36,895,000	37,004,000	43,440,000
EBITDA		153,133,000	143,991,000	134,122,000	367,288,000	496,150,000
Return on Assets %						
Return on Equity %						
Debt to Equity						

CONTACT INFORMATION:

Phone: 302 281-3600 Fax: 302 281-3763
Toll-Free:
Address: 200 Bellevue Pkwy., Ste. 300, Wilmington, DE 19809 United States

STOCK TICKER/OTHER:

Stock Ticker: IDCC
Exchange: NAS
Employees: 487
Fiscal Year Ends: 12/31
Parent Company:

SALARIES/BONUSES:

Top Exec. Salary: $690,000 Bonus: $
Second Exec. Salary: $463,777 Bonus: $

OTHER THOUGHTS:

Estimated Female Officers or Directors: 1
Hot Spot for Advancement for Women/Minorities:

International Business Machines Corporation (IBM)

www.ibm.com

NAIC Code: 541513

TYPES OF BUSINESS:

Computer Facilities and Business Process Outsourcing
Computer Facilities Management
Business Process Outsourcing
Software & Hardware
Cloud-Based Computer Services
IT Consulting & Outsourcing
Financial Services
Data Analytics and Health Care Analytics

BRANDS/DIVISIONS/AFFILIATES:

Aspera
Cognos
IBM
Red Hat OpenShift
Watson
Kyndryl Holdings Inc

GROWTH PLANS/SPECIAL FEATURES:

IBM looks to be a part of every aspect of an enterprise's IT needs. The company primarily sells software, IT services, consulting, and hardware. IBM operates in 175 countries and employs approximately 350,000 people. The company has a robust roster of 80,000 business partners to service 5,200 clients--which includes 95% of all Fortune 500. While IBM is a B2B company, IBM's outward impact is substantial. For example, IBM manages 90% of all credit card transactions globally and is responsible for 50% of all wireless connections in the world.

IBM offers employees medical, vision, dental and disability insurance; a flexible spending account; and 401(k) and stock purchase options.

CONTACTS: *Note: Officers with more than one job title may be intentionally listed here more than once.*

Arvind Krishna, CEO
James Kavanaugh, CFO, Divisional
Robert Del Bene, Chief Accounting Officer
Nickle Lamoreaux, Other Executive Officer
Michelle Browdy, Senior VP, Divisional
Gary Cohn, Vice Chairman

FINANCIAL DATA: *Note: Data for latest year may not have been available at press time.*

In U.S. $	2021	2020	2019	2018	2017	2016
Revenue		73,621,000,000	77,147,000,000	79,590,000,000	79,139,000,000	79,920,000,000
R&D Expense		6,333,000,000	5,989,000,000	5,379,000,000	5,787,000,000	5,751,000,000
Operating Income		6,895,000,000	10,631,000,000	13,285,000,000	11,855,000,000	13,192,000,000
Operating Margin %						
SGA Expense		21,850,000,000	19,754,000,000	18,863,000,000	19,555,000,000	20,479,000,000
Net Income		5,590,000,000	9,431,000,000	8,728,001,000	5,753,000,000	11,872,000,000
Operating Cash Flow		18,197,000,000	14,770,000,000	15,247,000,000	16,724,000,000	16,958,000,000
Capital Expenditure		3,230,000,000	2,907,000,000	3,964,000,000	3,773,000,000	4,150,000,000
EBITDA		12,620,000,000	17,569,000,000	16,545,000,000	16,556,000,000	17,341,000,000
Return on Assets %						
Return on Equity %						
Debt to Equity						

CONTACT INFORMATION:

Phone: 914-499-1900 Fax: 800-314-1092
Toll-Free: 800-426-4968
Address: 1 New Orchard Rd., Armonk, NY 10504 United States

STOCK TICKER/OTHER:

Stock Ticker: IBM
Employees: 365,000
Parent Company:
Exchange: NYS
Fiscal Year Ends: 12/31

SALARIES/BONUSES:

Top Exec. Salary: $1,173,864 Bonus: $2,000,000
Second Exec. Salary: $1,600,000 Bonus: $

OTHER THOUGHTS:

Estimated Female Officers or Directors: 6
Hot Spot for Advancement for Women/Minorities: Y

Inventec Corporation

NAIC Code: 334418

www.inventec.com

TYPES OF BUSINESS:

Contract Electronics Manufacturing
Computers & Laptops
Servers
Cloud Computing
Wireless
Internet of Things
Network Devices
Artificial Intelligence

BRANDS/DIVISIONS/AFFILIATES:

Inventec Appliances Corporation
AIMobile Company Limited
Inventec Besta Company Limited

CONTACTS:

Note: Officers with more than one job title may be intentionally listed here more than once.

Kou-I Yeh, Pres.
Chuikuan Qiu, Sr. Deputy Gen. Mgr.
Qinwen Lin, Sr. Deputy Gen. Mgr.
Zhian Cai, Sr. Deputy Gen. Mgr.
Guifen Jian, Deputy Gen. Mgr.
Tom Cho, Chmn.

GROWTH PLANS/SPECIAL FEATURES:

Inventec Corporation was founded in 1975, and manufactures computers and servers. In recent years, the firm has become active in industries such as cloud computing, wireless communication, intelligent devices and Internet of Things (IoT). Inventec's personal computer division produces enterprise and personal class computers, notebook and gaming laptops, as well desktop, thin client, small-form-factor and cloud computer products. The company's enterprise systems division specializes in the development and manufacturing of servers, blade servers, network switches, storage equipment, rack solutions and server management software. Inventec comprises global operation centers in Taiwan, Shanghai, Mexico and the Czech Republic, all of which are equipped with built-to-order and configure-to-order capabilities and offer customers technology support through a variety of models and channels. The firm's networking products include a range of switches that can be deployed in large-scale layer 2 and layer 3 networks. Networking solutions include access, campus, carrier, data center, enterprise 5G, orchestration, telemetry, software-defined networking (SDN) and more. Networking artificial intelligence (AI) solutions include field-programmable gate arrays (FPGAs) and graphics processing units (GPUs). Group companies of Inventec include: Inventec Appliances Corporation, AIMobile Company Limited, and Inventec Besta Company Limited. Headquartered in Taipei City, Inventec also has a research and development facility in Taoyuan City.

Inventec offers its employees health benefits and other insurance coverage.

FINANCIAL DATA:

Note: Data for latest year may not have been available at press time.

In U.S. $	2021	2020	2019	2018	2017	2016
Revenue		14,490,420,369	11,886,685,615	17,293,893,632	15,640,049,664	14,294,111,232
R&D Expense						
Operating Income						
Operating Margin %						
SGA Expense						
Net Income		268,444,087	183,156,194	221,762,400	225,977,248	188,060,704
Operating Cash Flow						
Capital Expenditure						
EBITDA						
Return on Assets %						
Return on Equity %						
Debt to Equity						

CONTACT INFORMATION:

Phone: 886-2-2881-0721 Fax: 886-2-2883-8006
Toll-Free:
Address: No. 66, Hougang St., Shilin Dist., Taipei, 11170 Taiwan

STOCK TICKER/OTHER:

Stock Ticker: 2356 Exchange: TWSE
Employees: 31,589 Fiscal Year Ends: 12/31
Parent Company:

SALARIES/BONUSES:

Top Exec. Salary: $ Bonus: $
Second Exec. Salary: $ Bonus: $

OTHER THOUGHTS:

Estimated Female Officers or Directors:
Hot Spot for Advancement for Women/Minorities:

Invoxia

www.invoxia.com

NAIC Code: 334310

TYPES OF BUSINESS:

Audio and Video Equipment Manufacturing
GPS Sensors
Fleet Tracking
Innovative Technologies
Product Manufacturing
Product Design

BRANDS/DIVISIONS/AFFILIATES:

CONTACTS:

Note: Officers with more than one job title may be intentionally listed here more than once.

Amelie Caudron, CEO
Eric Carreel, Pres.

GROWTH PLANS/SPECIAL FEATURES:

Invoxia is an innovative France-based firm that designs and markets a range of sensors that integrate embedded artificial intelligence (AI) for the general public and professionals. The company has developed geo-positioning system (GPS) trackers dedicated to vehicles, pets and bicycles, as well as for monitoring and optimizing industrial production chains. For example, the GPS tracker is a small, low-power system often used by or leased to third parties for tracking routes. It can be placed in a vehicle (even a motorcycle or scooter), in luggage or elsewhere, for keeping an eye on the vehicle when parked, for tracking suitcases during national airport flights and transfers, for knowing if a child is home from school and other purposes. The company's sensors identify key behaviors and sends real-time notifications concerning them to the customer's server. The sensors collect data such as sounds, vibrations, movements, temperatures and more. Invoxia also offers a geolocation and optimization solution for tracking and monitoring fleet assets. Invoxia has global offices throughout Europe and North America. The firm, founded in 2010, has more than 10 patents.

FINANCIAL DATA:

Note: Data for latest year may not have been available at press time.

In U.S. $	2021	2020	2019	2018	2017	2016
Revenue						
R&D Expense						
Operating Income						
Operating Margin %						
SGA Expense						
Net Income						
Operating Cash Flow						
Capital Expenditure						
EBITDA						
Return on Assets %						
Return on Equity %						
Debt to Equity						

CONTACT INFORMATION:

Phone: 331-4644-7288 Fax:
Toll-Free:
Address: 8 Espl. de la Manufacture, Issy les Moulineaux, 92130 France

STOCK TICKER/OTHER:

Stock Ticker: Private
Exchange:
Employees:
Fiscal Year Ends:
Parent Company:

SALARIES/BONUSES:

Top Exec. Salary: $ Bonus: $
Second Exec. Salary: $ Bonus: $

OTHER THOUGHTS:

Estimated Female Officers or Directors:
Hot Spot for Advancement for Women/Minorities:

Iridium Communications Inc

www.iridium.com

NAIC Code: 517410

TYPES OF BUSINESS:

Satellite Communications Services
Satellites
Mobile Voice
Data Communications
Surveillance
Telecommunications

BRANDS/DIVISIONS/AFFILIATES:

Iridium NEXT

GROWTH PLANS/SPECIAL FEATURES:

Iridium Communications Inc offers voice and data communications services and products to businesses, U.S. and international government agencies, and other customers on a global basis. It is a provider of mobile voice and data communications services through a constellation of low earth-orbiting satellites. Reaching across land, sea, and air, including the polar regions, Iridium's solutions are ideally suited for industries such as maritime, aviation, government/military, emergency/humanitarian services, mining, forestry, oil and gas, heavy equipment, transportation, and utilities. Iridium also provides service to subscribers from the U.S. Department of Defense, as well as other civil and government agencies around the world.

Employee benefits include medical, dental and vision coverage, and a 401(k).

CONTACTS: *Note: Officers with more than one job title may be intentionally listed here more than once.*

Matthew Desch, CEO
Thomas Fitzpatrick, CFO
Robert Niehaus, Chairman of the Board
Timothy Kapalka, Chief Accounting Officer
Thomas Hickey, Chief Legal Officer
Suzanne McBride, COO
Bryan Hartin, Executive VP, Divisional
Scott Scheimreif, Executive VP, Divisional

FINANCIAL DATA: *Note: Data for latest year may not have been available at press time.*

In U.S. $	2021	2020	2019	2018	2017	2016
Revenue		583,439,000	560,444,000	523,008,000	448,046,000	433,640,000
R&D Expense		12,037,000	14,310,000	22,429,000	15,247,000	16,079,000
Operating Income		35,483,000	10,120,000	41,653,000	115,476,000	176,371,000
Operating Margin %						
SGA Expense		90,052,000	93,165,000	97,846,000	84,405,000	82,552,000
Net Income		-56,054,000	-161,999,000	-13,384,000	233,856,000	111,032,000
Operating Cash Flow		249,767,000	198,143,000	263,709,000	259,621,000	225,199,000
Capital Expenditure		38,689,000	117,819,000	391,390,000	400,107,000	405,687,000
EBITDA		308,481,000	307,825,000	259,860,000	237,742,000	225,765,000
Return on Assets %						
Return on Equity %						
Debt to Equity						

CONTACT INFORMATION:

Phone: 703 287-7400 Fax: 703 287-7450
Toll-Free:
Address: 1750 Tysons Blvd., Ste. 1400, McLean, VA 22102 United States

STOCK TICKER/OTHER:

Stock Ticker: IRDM Exchange: NAS
Employees: 543 Fiscal Year Ends: 12/31
Parent Company:

SALARIES/BONUSES:

Top Exec. Salary: $956,733 Bonus: $
Second Exec. Salary: $574,039 Bonus: $

OTHER THOUGHTS:

Estimated Female Officers or Directors:
Hot Spot for Advancement for Women/Minorities:

Isuzu Motors Limited

www.isuzu.co.jp

NAIC Code: 336111

TYPES OF BUSINESS:

Automobile Manufacturing
Trucks & Buses
Diesel Engines
Logistics Services
Sport Utility Vehicles
Passenger Pickup Trucks
Commercial Trucks

BRANDS/DIVISIONS/AFFILIATES:

D-MAX
TRAGA
Erga
GALA
UD Trucks Corporation

GROWTH PLANS/SPECIAL FEATURES:

Isuzu Motors is a Japanese automobile manufacturing company focused on the production of commercial vehicles, passenger vehicles, and diesel engines. The company primarily manufactures light- to heavy-duty trucks, buses, pickup trucks, and industrial diesel engines. Isuzu derives the vast majority of revenue from vehicle sales. While Isuzu conducts sales across the globe, by individual country, Japan contributes the largest portion of consolidated revenue, followed by Thailand. The company mainly conducts manufacturing operations domestically.

CONTACTS: *Note: Officers with more than one job title may be intentionally listed here more than once.*

Masanori Katayama, Pres.

FINANCIAL DATA: *Note: Data for latest year may not have been available at press time.*

In U.S. $	2021	2020	2019	2018	2017	2016
Revenue	16,766,980,000	18,276,470,000	18,884,820,000	18,192,320,000	17,162,720,000	16,932,330,000
R&D Expense						
Operating Income	841,244,600	1,235,343,000	1,553,451,000	1,465,405,000	1,286,853,000	1,507,530,000
Operating Margin %						
SGA Expense	397,745,200	485,668,300	504,859,200	478,963,800	426,988,500	457,611,300
Net Income	375,276,800	713,788,600	996,836,700	928,464,600	824,733,700	1,007,662,000
Operating Cash Flow	1,958,789,000	1,086,965,000	1,375,576,000	1,553,583,000	1,329,936,000	1,168,430,000
Capital Expenditure						
EBITDA	1,531,132,000	1,977,268,000	2,292,503,000	2,169,265,000	1,892,297,000	2,178,271,000
Return on Assets %						
Return on Equity %						
Debt to Equity						

CONTACT INFORMATION:

Phone: 81 354711141 Fax: 81 354711043
Toll-Free:
Address: 6-26-1 Minami-Oi, Shinagawa-Ku, Tokyo, 140-8722 Japan

STOCK TICKER/OTHER:

Stock Ticker: ISUZF
Employees: 44,773
Parent Company:
Exchange: PINX
Fiscal Year Ends: 03/31

SALARIES/BONUSES:

Top Exec. Salary: $ Bonus: $
Second Exec. Salary: $ Bonus: $

OTHER THOUGHTS:

Estimated Female Officers or Directors:
Hot Spot for Advancement for Women/Minorities:

Iteris Inc

NAIC Code: 334290

www.iteris.com

TYPES OF BUSINESS:

Intelligent Transportation Systems
Smart Transportation
Intelligent Systems
Roadway Sensors
Traffic Engineering

GROWTH PLANS/SPECIAL FEATURES:

Iteris Inc is engaged in the technology sector as a provider of mobility infrastructure management. The company operates through two segments: Roadway Sensors and Transportation Systems. The Roadway Sensors segment provides various advanced detection sensors and systems for traffic intersection management, communication systems, and roadway traffic data collection applications. The Transportation Systems segment provides traffic engineering and consulting services, as well as performance measurement, traffic analytics, traveler information, and commercial vehicle operating software solutions. Its products include Vantage, VantagePegasus, VantageRadius, SmartCycle, SmartCycle Bike Indicator, SmartSpan, VersiCam, PedTrax, P-Series products, and other products.

BRANDS/DIVISIONS/AFFILIATES:

ClearAg Inc
Albeck Gerken Inc
Vantage
VersiCam
ClearFleet
CheckPoint
CVIEW-Plus

CONTACTS: *Note: Officers with more than one job title may be intentionally listed here more than once.*

J. Bergera, CEO
Douglas Groves, CFO
Thomas Thomas, Chairman of the Board
Ramin Massoumi, General Manager, Divisional
Todd Kreter, General Manager, Divisional

FINANCIAL DATA: *Note: Data for latest year may not have been available at press time.*

In U.S. $	2021	2020	2019	2018	2017	2016
Revenue	117,138,000	114,117,000	99,123,000	103,729,000	95,982,000	77,748,000
R&D Expense	5,130,000	8,597,000	7,819,000	7,945,000	6,877,000	6,933,000
Operating Income	1,058,000	-5,976,000	-7,959,000	-5,602,000	-3,069,000	-3,470,000
Operating Margin %						
SGA Expense	39,164,000	44,383,000	38,471,000	37,400,000	33,313,000	26,846,000
Net Income	10,134,000	-5,610,000	-7,816,000	-3,526,000	-4,826,000	-12,321,000
Operating Cash Flow	6,490,000	-3,827,000	-5,828,000	-268,000	2,903,000	-4,110,000
Capital Expenditure	1,368,000	1,101,000	1,146,000	4,015,000	1,838,000	1,346,000
EBITDA	3,828,000	-3,636,000	-5,980,000	-4,057,000	-1,717,000	-2,295,000
Return on Assets %						
Return on Equity %						
Debt to Equity						

CONTACT INFORMATION:

Phone: 949 270-9400 Fax: 949 270-9401
Toll-Free:
Address: 1700 Carnegie Ave., Santa Ana, CA 92705 United States

STOCK TICKER/OTHER:

Stock Ticker: ITI
Employees: 439
Parent Company:
Exchange: NAS
Fiscal Year Ends: 03/31

SALARIES/BONUSES:

Top Exec. Salary: $432,030 Bonus: $
Second Exec. Salary: $401,947 Bonus: $

OTHER THOUGHTS:

Estimated Female Officers or Directors:
Hot Spot for Advancement for Women/Minorities:

Itron Inc

www.itron.com

NAIC Code: 334515

TYPES OF BUSINESS:

Wireless Meter Reading Transmitters
Data Collection Systems & Software
Industrial Internet of Things
Meters
Sensors
Software

BRANDS/DIVISIONS/AFFILIATES:

CONTACTS:
Note: Officers with more than one job title may be intentionally listed here more than once.

Thomas Deitrich, CEO
Joan Hooper, CFO
Lynda Ziegler, Chairman of the Board
Sarah Hlavinka, General Counsel
Michel Cadieux, Senior VP, Divisional
Justin Patrick, Senior VP, Divisional
John Marcolini, Senior VP, Divisional
Donald Reeves, Senior VP, Divisional

GROWTH PLANS/SPECIAL FEATURES:

Itron Inc provides solutions that measure, manage, and analyze energy and water use. The company's metering systems fall into three categories: standard, advanced, and smart metering systems. Standard metering systems measure electricity, natural gas, water, or thermal energy and require manual reading by a utility representative or service provider. These meters contribute the majority of Itron's sales. Advanced metering systems use a meter with a communication module that can collect, store, and transmit data. Smart metering systems can collect and send data, remotely connect and disconnect service to the meter, receive commands, and interact with other devices, including smart thermostats and appliances. Itron generates the majority of its revenue outside of the United States.

Itron offers its employees retirement and health benefits as well as access to the Itron Employee Emergency Foundation.

FINANCIAL DATA:
Note: Data for latest year may not have been available at press time.

In U.S. $	2021	2020	2019	2018	2017	2016
Revenue		2,173,350,000	2,502,470,000	2,376,117,000	2,018,197,000	2,013,186,000
R&D Expense		194,101,000	202,200,000	207,905,000	169,977,000	168,209,000
Operating Income		86,435,000	138,961,000	27,491,000	157,844,000	145,301,000
Operating Margin %						
SGA Expense		276,920,000	346,872,000	423,210,000	326,548,000	321,698,000
Net Income		-57,955,000	49,006,000	-99,250,000	57,298,000	31,770,000
Operating Cash Flow		109,514,000	172,840,000	109,755,000	191,354,000	115,842,000
Capital Expenditure		46,208,000	60,749,000	59,952,000	49,495,000	43,543,000
EBITDA		84,652,000	239,885,000	71,549,000	209,371,000	163,893,000
Return on Assets %						
Return on Equity %						
Debt to Equity						

CONTACT INFORMATION:

Phone: 509 924-9900 Fax:
Toll-Free: 800 635-5641
Address: 2111 N. Molter Rd., Liberty Lake, WA 99019 United States

STOCK TICKER/OTHER:

Stock Ticker: ITRI
Employees: 6,065
Parent Company:
Exchange: NAS
Fiscal Year Ends: 12/31

SALARIES/BONUSES:

Top Exec. Salary: $800,000 Bonus: $
Second Exec. Salary: $511,298 Bonus: $

OTHER THOUGHTS:

Estimated Female Officers or Directors: 6
Hot Spot for Advancement for Women/Minorities: Y

Jabil Inc

NAIC Code: 334418

www.jabil.com

TYPES OF BUSINESS:

Contract Electronics Manufacturing
Electronic Manufacturing Services
Engineering Solutions

BRANDS/DIVISIONS/AFFILIATES:

GROWTH PLANS/SPECIAL FEATURES:

Jabil Inc is a United States-based company engaged in providing manufacturing services and solutions. It provides comprehensive electronics design, production and product management services to companies in various industries and end markets. It operates in two segments. The Electronics Manufacturing Services (EMS) segment, which is the key revenue driver, is focused on leveraging IT, supply chain design and engineering, technologies largely centered on core electronics. The Diversified Manufacturing Services (DMS) segment is focused on providing engineering solutions, with an emphasis on material sciences, technologies, and healthcare.

CONTACTS: *Note: Officers with more than one job title may be intentionally listed here more than once.*

Michael Loparco, CEO, Divisional
Steven Borges, CEO, Divisional
Kenneth Wilson, CEO, Divisional
Mark Mondello, CEO
Meheryar Dastoor, CFO
Timothy Main, Chairman of the Board
Thomas Sansone, Director
Robert Katz, Executive VP
Bruce Johnson, Executive VP
Daryn Smith, Senior VP, Divisional

FINANCIAL DATA: *Note: Data for latest year may not have been available at press time.*

In U.S. $	2021	2020	2019	2018	2017	2016
Revenue	29,285,000,000	27,266,440,000	25,282,320,000	22,095,420,000	19,063,120,000	18,353,090,000
R&D Expense	34,000,000	44,143,000	42,861,000	38,531,000	29,680,000	31,954,000
Operating Income	1,065,000,000	656,432,000	727,270,000	579,055,000	572,737,000	534,202,000
Operating Margin %						
SGA Expense	1,213,000,000	1,174,694,000	1,111,347,000	1,050,716,000	907,702,000	924,427,000
Net Income	696,000,000	53,912,000	287,111,000	86,330,000	129,090,000	254,095,000
Operating Cash Flow	1,433,000,000	1,257,275,000	1,193,066,000	933,850,000	1,256,643,000	916,207,000
Capital Expenditure	1,159,000,000	983,035,000	1,005,480,000	1,036,651,000	716,485,000	924,239,000
EBITDA	1,950,000,000	1,229,196,000	1,411,267,000	1,296,107,000	1,154,712,000	1,220,333,000
Return on Assets %						
Return on Equity %						
Debt to Equity						

CONTACT INFORMATION:

Phone: 727 577-9749 Fax: 727 579-8529
Toll-Free:
Address: 10560 Dr. Martin Luther King Jr. St. N., St. Petersburg, FL 33716 United States

STOCK TICKER/OTHER:

Stock Ticker: JBL
Employees: 240,000
Parent Company:
Exchange: NYS
Fiscal Year Ends: 08/31

SALARIES/BONUSES:

Top Exec. Salary: $1,144,904 Bonus: $
Second Exec. Salary: $591,827 Bonus: $

OTHER THOUGHTS:

Estimated Female Officers or Directors:
Hot Spot for Advancement for Women/Minorities: Y

Jaguar Land Rover Limited

www.jaguarlandrover.com

NAIC Code: 336111

TYPES OF BUSINESS:

Automobile Manufacturing
Vehicle Design and Manufacture
Vehicle Distribution
Sedans
Sports Cars
Electric and Hybrid Vehicles
Sport Utility Vehicles

BRANDS/DIVISIONS/AFFILIATES:

Tata Group
Tata Motors Limited
XE
XF
F-Type
Range Rover
Defender
Discovery

CONTACTS:

Note: Officers with more than one job title may be intentionally listed here more than once.

Thierry Bollore Thierry Bollore, CEO
Ian Callum, Dir.-Jaguar Design

GROWTH PLANS/SPECIAL FEATURES:

Jaguar Land Rover Limited, founded in 1922 and based in the U.K., manufactures a distinctive line of luxury sedans, sports cars, electric/hybrid vehicles and sports utility vehicles (SUV). The company is part of India-based Tata Motors Limited, itself part of the Tata Group. Jaguar's current line includes six models: the XE, XF, F-Type, I-Pace, E-Pace and F-Pace. The XE, XF and F-Type are all luxury sports cars with various differing characteristics such as a lightweight aluminum intensive architecture, a supercharged engine, a monocoque alloy body shell or is a convertible. The I-Pace is an all-electric performance sport utility vehicle (SUV). The E-Pace is a compact SUV. The F-Pace is a sports car based on the C-X17 crossover concept vehicle, and also includes the lightweight aluminum intensive architecture. Land Rovers' current line includes the Range Rover, Range Rover Sport, Range Rover Velar, Range Rover Evoque, Land Rover Defender, Land Rover Discovery and Land Rover Discovery Sport. All of Land Rovers' models are SUVs of varying sizes and interior packages, and available as plug-in hybrids. The firm operates research, engineering and/or production facilities in the U.S., Brazil, The U.K., Austria, Hungary, Slovakia, India and China. During 2021, Jaguar Land Rover announced that it canceled the development of its all-electric XJ saloon due to poor sales. That same year, the company announced that the entire Jaguar range will become all-electric for the 2025 model year.

FINANCIAL DATA:

Note: Data for latest year may not have been available at press time.

In U.S. $	2021	2020	2019	2018	2017	2016
Revenue	23,110,900,000	22,170,100,000	31,759,200,000	32,723,100,000	32,836,300,000	25,605,600,000
R&D Expense						
Operating Income						
Operating Margin %						
SGA Expense						
Net Income	-2,317,910,000	-6,176,680,000	-4,355,840,000	1,413,690,000	1,675,610,000	1,613,970,000
Operating Cash Flow						
Capital Expenditure						
EBITDA						
Return on Assets %						
Return on Equity %						
Debt to Equity						

CONTACT INFORMATION:

Phone: 44-24-7640-2121 Fax:
Toll-Free:
Address: Abbey Rd., Whitley, Coventry, CV3 4LF United Kingdom

STOCK TICKER/OTHER:

Stock Ticker: Subsidiary
Employees: 33,048
Parent Company: Tata Group
Exchange:
Fiscal Year Ends: 03/31

SALARIES/BONUSES:

Top Exec. Salary: $ Bonus: $
Second Exec. Salary: $ Bonus: $

OTHER THOUGHTS:

Estimated Female Officers or Directors:
Hot Spot for Advancement for Women/Minorities:

Jio (Reliance Jio Infocomm Limited)

www.jio.com

NAIC Code: 517210

TYPES OF BUSINESS:

Wireless Telecommunications Carriers (except Satellite)
LTE Network
Mobile Network Operations
Fiber-to-the-Home
Internet Services
Communication Technologies
Payment Solutions
Mobile Apps

BRANDS/DIVISIONS/AFFILIATES:

Reliance Industries Limited
Jio
JioFi
JioFiber

CONTACTS:

Note: Officers with more than one job title may be intentionally listed here more than once.

Mukesh D. Ambani, Chmn.

GROWTH PLANS/SPECIAL FEATURES:

Reliance Jio Infocomm Limited (popularly known as Jio), a subsidiary of Reliance Industries Limited, is an Indian mobile network operator and fiber-to-the-home (FTTH) provider serving the India market. Jio operates a national long-term evolution (LTE) network with coverage across all telecommunication circles. The firm has built a world-class, all-IP data network with next-generation LTE technology, which utilizes voice over LTE (VoLTE) to provide voice service on its network. The company's future-ready network can be easily upgraded to support even more data as technologies advance on to 5G, 6G and beyond. Its data routers and phones are marketed under the JioFi and Jio brand names. Jio apps enable users to manage their Jio accounts and related devices, connect to Wi-Fi, chat, watch entertainment, listen to music, read online magazines and news, browse the web, secure data, file into the cloud, make payments, make calls, make online purchases, and connect with doctors and health test results. Devices can be purchased in-store (in the Mumbai area), as well as online at www.jio.com or via mobile app. Jio has the ability to offer free calls and very cheap internet access by relying on advertising and content revenues. JioFiber offers FTTH broadband throughout a home or business, separate Wi-Fi identifications for guests, Norton's mobile security for a select number of devices, high-definition (HD) voice calls throughout India, TV video calling and conferencing, integrated TV, home networking, security and surveillance solutions, a multi-player platform and more.

FINANCIAL DATA:

Note: Data for latest year may not have been available at press time.

In U.S. $	2021	2020	2019	2018	2017	2016
Revenue	9,599,828,802	8,504,180,000	6,889,980,000	3,645,450,000	17,797,100	5,699,870
R&D Expense						
Operating Income						
Operating Margin %						
SGA Expense						
Net Income	1,637,569,936	734,478,000	426,095,000	111,143,000	-5,235,450	-6,276,040
Operating Cash Flow						
Capital Expenditure						
EBITDA						
Return on Assets %						
Return on Equity %						
Debt to Equity						

CONTACT INFORMATION:

Phone: 91-79-3503-1200 Fax:
Toll-Free:
Address: 101, Saffron, Nr. Cntr. Point Panchwati 5 Rast, Ambawadi, Ahmedabad 380006 India

STOCK TICKER/OTHER:

Stock Ticker: Subsidiary
Exchange:
Employees:
Fiscal Year Ends: 03/31
Parent Company: Reliance Industries Limited

SALARIES/BONUSES:

Top Exec. Salary: $ Bonus: $
Second Exec. Salary: $ Bonus: $

OTHER THOUGHTS:

Estimated Female Officers or Directors:
Hot Spot for Advancement for Women/Minorities:

Johnson Controls International plc

www.johnsoncontrols.com

NAIC Code: 561600

TYPES OF BUSINESS:

Fire & Security Systems & Services
Security Monitoring Services
Fire Detection Systems
Raw Materials
Intelligent Buildings

BRANDS/DIVISIONS/AFFILIATES:

GROWTH PLANS/SPECIAL FEATURES:

Johnson Controls manufactures, installs, and services HVAC systems, building management systems and controls, industrial refrigeration systems, and fire and security solutions. Commercial HVAC accounts for about 40% of sales, fire and security represents another 40% of sales, and residential HVAC, industrial refrigeration, and other solutions account for the remaining 20% of revenue. In fiscal 2021, Johnson Controls generated over $23.5 billion in revenue.

CONTACTS: *Note: Officers with more than one job title may be intentionally listed here more than once.*

George Oliver, CEO
Olivier Leonetti, CFO
Lynn Minella, Exec. VP-Human Resources
Scott Clements, CTO
Judith A. Reinsdorf, General Counsel
Chris Brown, VP-Strategy
Juan Mogollon, Pres., Growth Markets
Colleen Repplier, Pres., Fire & Protection Products
Mike Ryan, Pres., Life Safety & Security Products
George Oliver, Chmn.
Vivek Kamath, Chief Procurement Officer

FINANCIAL DATA: *Note: Data for latest year may not have been available at press time.*

In U.S. $	2021	2020	2019	2018	2017	2016
Revenue	23,668,000,000	22,317,000,000	23,968,000,000	31,400,000,000	30,172,000,000	37,674,000,000
R&D Expense						
Operating Income	2,801,000,000	1,746,000,000	1,449,000,000	3,370,000,000	3,181,000,000	1,989,000,000
Operating Margin %						
SGA Expense	5,258,000,000	5,665,000,000	6,244,000,000	6,010,000,000	6,158,000,000	5,325,000,000
Net Income	1,637,000,000	631,000,000	5,674,000,000	2,162,000,000	1,611,000,000	-868,000,000
Operating Cash Flow	2,487,000,000	2,219,000,000	1,202,000,000	2,513,000,000	12,000,000	1,895,000,000
Capital Expenditure	552,000,000	443,000,000	586,000,000	1,030,000,000	1,343,000,000	1,249,000,000
EBITDA	3,678,000,000	1,965,000,000	2,216,000,000	4,423,000,000	4,212,000,000	2,848,000,000
Return on Assets %						
Return on Equity %						
Debt to Equity						

CONTACT INFORMATION:

Phone: 353-21735-5800 Fax:
Toll-Free:
Address: One Albert Quay, Cork, T12 X8N6 Ireland

STOCK TICKER/OTHER:

Stock Ticker: JCI
Employees: 101,000
Parent Company:
Exchange: NYS
Fiscal Year Ends: 09/30

SALARIES/BONUSES:

Top Exec. Salary: $580,000 Bonus: $775,000
Second Exec. Salary: $1,348,846 Bonus: $

OTHER THOUGHTS:

Estimated Female Officers or Directors: 2
Hot Spot for Advancement for Women/Minorities: Y

Juniper Networks Inc

NAIC Code: 334210A

www.juniper.net

TYPES OF BUSINESS:

Networking Equipment
Network Product Development
Network Security Solutions
Artificial Intelligence
Machine Learning
Automated WAN Solutions
Cloud-Based Data Center Solutions

BRANDS/DIVISIONS/AFFILIATES:

Mist
EX
128 Technology
SRX
MX
PTX
ACX
Apstra

CONTACTS: *Note: Officers with more than one job title may be intentionally listed here more than once.*

Rami Rahim, CEO
Kenneth Miller, CFO
Scott Kriens, Chairman of the Board
Thomas Austin, Chief Accounting Officer
Manoj Leelanivas, COO
Anand Athreya, Executive VP
Brian Martin, Senior VP

GROWTH PLANS/SPECIAL FEATURES:

Juniper Networks develops and sells switching, routing, security, related software products, and services for the networking industry. The company operates as one segment and its primary selling verticals are communication service providers, cloud, and enterprise. The California-based company was incorporated in 1996, employs over 9,000 individuals, and sells worldwide, with over half of its sales from the Americas region.

Juniper Networks offers medical, dental, prescription and vision insurance; paid time off; and stock/savings plans.

FINANCIAL DATA: *Note: Data for latest year may not have been available at press time.*

In U.S. $	2021	2020	2019	2018	2017	2016
Revenue		4,445,100,000	4,445,400,000	4,647,500,000	5,027,200,000	4,990,100,000
R&D Expense		958,400,000	955,700,000	1,003,200,000	980,700,000	1,013,700,000
Operating Income		421,100,000	477,500,000	579,500,000	913,700,000	893,000,000
Operating Margin %						
SGA Expense		1,194,200,000	1,183,600,000	1,158,500,000	1,177,700,000	1,197,800,000
Net Income		257,800,000	345,000,000	566,900,000	306,200,000	592,700,000
Operating Cash Flow		612,000,000	528,900,000	861,100,000	1,260,100,000	1,106,000,000
Capital Expenditure		100,400,000	109,600,000	147,400,000	151,200,000	214,700,000
EBITDA		554,600,000	713,400,000	846,400,000	1,138,600,000	1,131,800,000
Return on Assets %						
Return on Equity %						
Debt to Equity						

CONTACT INFORMATION:

Phone: 408 745-2000 Fax: 408 745-2100
Toll-Free: 888-586-4737
Address: 1133 Innovation Way, Sunnyvale, CA 94089 United States

STOCK TICKER/OTHER:

Stock Ticker: JNPR Exchange: NYS
Employees: 9,950 Fiscal Year Ends: 12/31
Parent Company:

SALARIES/BONUSES:

Top Exec. Salary: $1,000,000 Bonus: $350,000
Second Exec. Salary: $600,000 Bonus: $120,000

OTHER THOUGHTS:

Estimated Female Officers or Directors: 3
Hot Spot for Advancement for Women/Minorities: Y

KDDI Corporation

www.kddi.com

NAIC Code: 517210

TYPES OF BUSINESS:

Wireless Telecommunications Carriers (except Satellite)
Telecommunications
Communication Technology
Internet of Things
Business Services
Internet Service

BRANDS/DIVISIONS/AFFILIATES:

GROWTH PLANS/SPECIAL FEATURES:

KDDI is Japan's second-largest wireless operator (31% market share), the largest pay-TV operator (53% market share) and the second-largest provider of fibre-to-the-home broadband (12% market share). It has grown through acquisition and is focusing on increasing the number of customers who subscribe to more than one telecommunication service. It is also looking to grow its Life Design business which includes commerce, energy, and finance and had over 18 million IOT connections by the end of March 2021.

CONTACTS: *Note: Officers with more than one job title may be intentionally listed here more than once.*

Makoto Takahashi, CEO
Makoto Takahashi, Sr. VP
Kanichiro Aritomi, Vice Chmn.
Hirofumi Morozumi, Exec. VP
Hideo Yuasa, Associate Sr. VP

FINANCIAL DATA: *Note: Data for latest year may not have been available at press time.*

In U.S. $	2021	2020	2019	2018	2017	2016
Revenue	46,682,000,000	46,019,650,000	44,641,250,000	44,304,050,000	41,723,130,000	39,244,090,000
R&D Expense						
Operating Income	9,072,713,000	8,980,185,000	8,865,672,000	8,419,739,000	7,998,154,000	7,277,319,000
Operating Margin %						
SGA Expense	11,987,570,000	11,418,790,000	10,636,440,000	11,170,210,000	10,312,130,000	9,725,475,000
Net Income	5,724,719,000	5,621,657,000	5,427,480,000	5,030,824,000	4,803,504,000	4,344,882,000
Operating Cash Flow	14,781,250,000	11,628,380,000	9,047,195,000	9,326,605,000	10,202,400,000	7,772,468,000
Capital Expenditure	5,488,699,000	5,441,847,000	5,291,009,000	4,928,456,000	4,565,498,000	4,708,094,000
EBITDA	15,589,190,000	15,131,310,000	13,907,150,000	13,303,110,000	12,779,550,000	12,046,020,000
Return on Assets %						
Return on Equity %						
Debt to Equity						

CONTACT INFORMATION:

Phone: 81 333470077 Fax:
Toll-Free:
Address: Garden Air Tower, 3-10-10, Iidabashi, Chiyoda-ku, Tokyo, 102-8460 Japan

STOCK TICKER/OTHER:

Stock Ticker: KDDIY
Employees: 78,337
Parent Company:
Exchange: PINX
Fiscal Year Ends: 03/31

SALARIES/BONUSES:

Top Exec. Salary: $ Bonus: $
Second Exec. Salary: $ Bonus: $

OTHER THOUGHTS:

Estimated Female Officers or Directors:
Hot Spot for Advancement for Women/Minorities:

Keyence Corporation

www.keyence.com

NAIC Code: 334513

TYPES OF BUSINESS:

Instruments and Related Products Manufacturing for Measuring, Displaying, and Controlling Industrial Process Variables
Automatic Controlling Equipment
Measurement Instruments

BRANDS/DIVISIONS/AFFILIATES:

GROWTH PLANS/SPECIAL FEATURES:

Keyence Corporation develops and sells factory automation sensors, machine vision systems, barcode readers, laser markers, measuring instruments, and digital microscopes. The company has a fabless business model where manufacturing of its products is outsourced to qualified contract manufacturing companies, while it focuses on product planning and development of its products. It serves customers in automotive, metals/machining, semiconductor/electronics, food, pharmaceutical, and other industries. Keyence was founded in 1972 and is headquartered in Osaka, Japan.

CONTACTS: *Note: Officers with more than one job title may be intentionally listed here more than once.*

Tamotsu Nakata, Pres.

FINANCIAL DATA: *Note: Data for latest year may not have been available at press time.*

In U.S. $	2021	2020	2019	2018	2017	2016
Revenue	4,728,603,000	4,849,065,000	5,158,825,000	4,629,424,000	2,779,753,000	2,559,066,000
R&D Expense						
Operating Income	2,431,891,000	2,439,554,000	2,793,118,000	2,573,644,000	1,491,599,000	1,366,103,000
Operating Margin %						
SGA Expense						
Net Income	1,733,586,000	1,740,923,000	1,987,162,000	1,850,506,000	1,060,420,000	928,306,500
Operating Cash Flow	1,692,840,000	1,787,582,000	1,839,830,000	1,783,188,000	1,069,031,000	931,162,300
Capital Expenditure	38,293,910	72,431,540	64,681,380	59,488,240	31,545,460	21,563,390
EBITDA	2,498,278,000	2,509,806,000	2,848,371,000	2,613,862,000	1,515,799,000	1,391,796,000
Return on Assets %						
Return on Equity %						
Debt to Equity						

CONTACT INFORMATION:

Phone: 81 663791111 Fax: 81 663792222
Toll-Free:
Address: 1-3-14, Higashi-nakajima, Higashi-Yodogawa-ku, Osaka, 533-8555 Japan

STOCK TICKER/OTHER:

Stock Ticker: KYCCF
Exchange: PINX
Employees: 7,941
Fiscal Year Ends: 03/20
Parent Company:

SALARIES/BONUSES:

Top Exec. Salary: $ Bonus: $
Second Exec. Salary: $ Bonus: $

OTHER THOUGHTS:

Estimated Female Officers or Directors:
Hot Spot for Advancement for Women/Minorities:

Kia Corporation

www.kia.com

NAIC Code: 336111

TYPES OF BUSINESS:

Automobile Manufacturing
Automobile Manufacture
Mobility Solutions
Electric Vehicles
Augmented Reality Technology
Driver Assistance Systems

BRANDS/DIVISIONS/AFFILIATES:

Hyundai Motor Group
Hyundai Motor Company
Kia EV6
Kia Sportage
Kia Niro
LX
GT
Kia Motor Corporation

CONTACTS: *Note: Officers with more than one job title may be intentionally listed here more than once.*

Ho-sung Song, Pres.
Eui-sun Chung, Chmn.

GROWTH PLANS/SPECIAL FEATURES:

Kia Corp is a Korean motor-vehicle manufacturer. While the company has factories in several countries, the majority of vehicles are manufactured domestically. The company's consolidated revenue is principally derived from the manufacture of passenger vehicles, with another third from recreational vehicles, and a small footprint in commercial vehicles. The three largest individual countries together constitute more than half of total retail sales, with the United States contributing the largest portion, followed closely by China and then Korea.

FINANCIAL DATA: *Note: Data for latest year may not have been available at press time.*

In U.S. $	2021	2020	2019	2018	2017	2016
Revenue		49,690,190,000	48,831,790,000	45,492,560,000	44,960,010,000	44,269,030,000
R&D Expense		752,952,000	767,599,200	725,609,300	648,844,400	665,498,000
Operating Income		1,736,352,000	1,687,844,000	972,063,600	556,146,600	2,067,185,000
Operating Margin %						
SGA Expense		4,525,251,000	4,016,843,000	3,709,809,000	4,929,203,000	4,727,830,000
Net Income		1,249,295,000	1,534,054,000	970,777,000	812,954,900	2,313,385,000
Operating Cash Flow		4,555,063,000	3,032,281,000	3,754,610,000	2,178,637,000	2,751,131,000
Capital Expenditure		1,948,218,000	2,023,832,000	2,588,063,000	2,008,580,000	1,992,968,000
EBITDA		3,607,340,000	4,072,468,000	3,029,434,000	2,700,865,000	4,423,989,000
Return on Assets %						
Return on Equity %						
Debt to Equity						

CONTACT INFORMATION:

Phone: 82 234641114 Fax: 82 234646816
Toll-Free:
Address: 12 Heolleung-ro Seocho-gu, Seoul, 06797 South Korea

STOCK TICKER/OTHER:

Stock Ticker: KIMTF
Employees: 51,899
Parent Company: Hyundai Motor Group
Exchange: PINX
Fiscal Year Ends: 12/31

SALARIES/BONUSES:

Top Exec. Salary: $ Bonus: $
Second Exec. Salary: $ Bonus: $

OTHER THOUGHTS:

Estimated Female Officers or Directors:
Hot Spot for Advancement for Women/Minorities:

Kongsberg Gruppen ASA

www.kongsberg.com

NAIC Code: 336410

TYPES OF BUSINESS:

Aerospace and Defense Manufacturing
Oil and Gas Drilling Equipment
Offshore Drilling Equipment
Energy Industry Software
Information Systems and Software
Marine Systems

BRANDS/DIVISIONS/AFFILIATES:

GROWTH PLANS/SPECIAL FEATURES:

Kongsberg Gruppen ASA is an international technology company that supplies products and services to defense, maritime, oil, gas, and aerospace industries. The company is divided into two business segments: the maritime segment and defense and aerospace systems. Maritime, which earns most of the company revenue, creates navigation, automation, monitoring, and positioning products for commercial ships and offshore industries. The defense and aerospace segment provides defense and space-related products and systems. Outside of the two main segments, the firm operates Kongsberg Digital, which produces digital solutions for oil, gas, wind, and merchant marine markets. Products are delivered globally, with North America accounting for about a third of total revenue.

CONTACTS: *Note: Officers with more than one job title may be intentionally listed here more than once.*

Geir Haoy, CEO
Gyrid Skalleberg Ingero, CFO

FINANCIAL DATA: *Note: Data for latest year may not have been available at press time.*

In U.S. $	2021	2020	2019	2018	2017	2016
Revenue		2,842,272,000	2,672,371,000	1,595,921,000	1,608,017,000	1,758,387,000
R&D Expense						
Operating Income		224,168,000	130,838,600	85,450,170	69,358,900	54,044,460
Operating Margin %						
SGA Expense						
Net Income		320,826,600	77,681,970	77,792,940	61,479,730	72,466,180
Operating Cash Flow		311,615,700	222,614,300	242,922,600	321,714,300	89,778,170
Capital Expenditure		84,229,450	79,901,460	41,171,440	58,594,400	100,653,600
EBITDA		381,751,400	257,238,300	155,031,000	141,381,200	146,042,100
Return on Assets %						
Return on Equity %						
Debt to Equity						

CONTACT INFORMATION:

Phone: 47 32288200 Fax: 47 32288201
Toll-Free:
Address: Kirkegardsveien 45 (PO Box 1000), Kongsberg, 3601 Norway

STOCK TICKER/OTHER:

Stock Ticker: NSKFF
Employees: 11,122
Parent Company:
Exchange: PINX
Fiscal Year Ends: 12/31

SALARIES/BONUSES:

Top Exec. Salary: $ Bonus: $
Second Exec. Salary: $ Bonus: $

OTHER THOUGHTS:

Estimated Female Officers or Directors:
Hot Spot for Advancement for Women/Minorities:

Koninklijke Philips NV (Royal Philips)

www.philips.com

NAIC Code: 334310

TYPES OF BUSINESS:

Manufacturing-Electrical & Electronic Equipment
Consumer Electronics & Appliances
Lighting Systems
Medical Imaging Equipment
Semiconductors
Consulting Services
Nanotech Research
MEMS

BRANDS/DIVISIONS/AFFILIATES:

BioTelemetry Inc

GROWTH PLANS/SPECIAL FEATURES:

Philips is a diversified global healthcare company operating in three segments: diagnosis and treatment, connected care, and personal health. About 44% of the company's revenue comes from the diagnosis and treatment segment, which features imaging systems, ultrasound equipment, image-guided therapy solutions and healthcare informatics. The connected care segment (24% of revenue) encompasses monitoring and analytics systems for hospitals and sleep and respiratory care devices, whereas the personal health business (remainder of revenue) includes electric toothbrushes and men's grooming and personal-care products. In 2020, Philips generated EUR 19.5 billion of sales and had 80,000 employees in over 100 countries.

CONTACTS: *Note: Officers with more than one job title may be intentionally listed here more than once.*

Frans van Houten, CEO
Sophie Bechu, COO
Abhijit Bhattacharya, CFO
Daniela Seabrook, Chief Human Resources Officer
Shez Partovi, Exec. VP-Innovation & Strategy
Eric Coutinho, Chief Legal Officer
Jim Andrew, Chief Strategy & Innovation Officer
Deborah DiSanzo, Exec. VP
Pieter Nota, CEO-Phillips Consumer Lifestyle
Eric Rondolat, Exec. VP
Jeroen van der Veer, Chmn.
Patrick Kung, CEO-Greater China

FINANCIAL DATA: *Note: Data for latest year may not have been available at press time.*

In U.S. $	2021	2020	2019	2018	2017	2016
Revenue		22,061,730,000	22,000,750,000	20,464,840,000	20,079,730,000	27,686,990,000
R&D Expense		2,162,693,000	2,127,684,000	1,986,516,000	1,992,162,000	2,282,404,000
Operating Income		1,875,840,000	1,862,288,000	1,852,124,000	1,628,514,000	2,098,321,000
Operating Margin %						
SGA Expense		5,956,159,000	6,000,203,000	5,794,662,000	5,618,485,000	7,603,872,000
Net Income		1,340,531,000	1,317,944,000	1,230,985,000	1,871,322,000	1,635,290,000
Operating Cash Flow		3,136,187,000	2,293,697,000	2,010,232,000	2,111,873,000	2,150,270,000
Capital Expenditure		1,063,842,000	1,144,025,000	952,036,800	970,106,300	981,399,700
EBITDA		3,594,701,000	3,530,329,000	3,139,576,000	3,009,701,000	3,642,134,000
Return on Assets %						
Return on Equity %						
Debt to Equity						

CONTACT INFORMATION:

Phone: 31 402791111 Fax:
Toll-Free: 877-248-4237
Address: Breitner Ctr., Amstelplein 2, Amsterdam, 1096 BC Netherlands

STOCK TICKER/OTHER:

Stock Ticker: PHG
Employees: 78,392
Parent Company:
Exchange: NYS
Fiscal Year Ends: 12/31

SALARIES/BONUSES:

Top Exec. Salary: $1,496,381 Bonus: $1,466,453
Second Exec. Salary: $886,535 Bonus: $673,767

OTHER THOUGHTS:

Estimated Female Officers or Directors: 3
Hot Spot for Advancement for Women/Minorities: Y

KT Corporation

NAIC Code: 517110

www.kt.com

TYPES OF BUSINESS:

Local Telephone Service
Mobile Phone Service
Internet Access & Portal Services
Undersea Cable Construction, Maintenance & Repair
IT Consulting & Outsourcing
Online Billing Services
Security Services
e-Commerce Services

BRANDS/DIVISIONS/AFFILIATES:

BC Card Co Ltd

GROWTH PLANS/SPECIAL FEATURES:

KT is South Korea's largest fixed-line telecom operator, with around 15 million customers. It is the largest broadband firm in the country, with 9.1 million customers, and the second-largest wireless operator with 22.3 million subscribers; the company also has 8.7 million pay-television customers. Additionally, it has about 30 nontelecom businesses. These nontelecom businesses, IPTV and wireless data are the focus of its growth strategy.

CONTACTS: *Note: Officers with more than one job title may be intentionally listed here more than once.*

Hyeon-Mo Ky, CEO
Sang-Bong Nam, Exec. VP-Group Legal & Ethics
Young-Soo Woo, Sr. VP-Corp. Center Strategy & Planning Office
Eun-Hye Kim, Exec. VP-Comm. Office
Hyun-Myung Pyo, Pres., Telecom & Convergence Group
Il Yung Kim, Pres., KT Corp. Center
Seong-Mok Oh, Exec. VP-Network Group
Se-Hyun Oh, Exec. VP-New Bus. Unit

FINANCIAL DATA: *Note: Data for latest year may not have been available at press time.*

In U.S. $	2021	2020	2019	2018	2017	2016
Revenue		20,525,600,000	20,910,690,000	19,681,920,000	19,775,040,000	
R&D Expense		131,800,400	138,592,800	148,443,800	141,622,000	
Operating Income		858,569,500	856,756,300	924,517,500	897,838,300	
Operating Margin %						
SGA Expense		6,522,085,000	6,576,892,000	6,349,461,000	6,358,541,000	
Net Income		588,616,300	545,130,800	542,159,500	387,623,700	
Operating Cash Flow		3,980,573,000	3,145,248,000	3,368,044,000	3,256,588,000	
Capital Expenditure		3,127,874,000	3,191,586,000	2,525,398,000	2,566,286,000	
EBITDA		4,167,844,000	4,172,258,000	3,943,590,000	3,827,151,000	
Return on Assets %						
Return on Equity %						
Debt to Equity						

CONTACT INFORMATION:

Phone: 82-31-727-0114 Fax:
Toll-Free:
Address: 90, Buljeong-ro, Gundang-gu, Seongnam-si, Gyeonggi-do, 03155 South Korea

STOCK TICKER/OTHER:

Stock Ticker: KT
Employees: 23,000
Parent Company:
Exchange: NYS
Fiscal Year Ends:

SALARIES/BONUSES:

Top Exec. Salary: $442,582 Bonus: $384,635
Second Exec. Salary: $363,639 Bonus: $305,692

OTHER THOUGHTS:

Estimated Female Officers or Directors:
Hot Spot for Advancement for Women/Minorities:

KUKA AG

www.kuka.com

NAIC Code: 333519

TYPES OF BUSINESS:

Industrial Robotics
Intelligent Automation
Robots
Software
Production Machines
Mobility Products
Mobile Platforms
Automated Guided Vehicle Systems

BRANDS/DIVISIONS/AFFILIATES:

Midea Group

GROWTH PLANS/SPECIAL FEATURES:

KUKA AG supplies industrial robotics and offers support to plant and systems engineering. Its product portfolio ranges from intelligent automation solutions and individual components to complete production lines. The company integrates mechatronics know-how with cloud technologies and mobile platforms. Solutions may be customized for customers and vary from heavy-duty robots to small models. Kuka operates five business segments: Robotics, Systems, Swisslog, Swisslog Healthcare, and China.

CONTACTS: *Note: Officers with more than one job title may be intentionally listed here more than once.*

Peter Mohnen, CEO
Alexander Liong Hauw Tan, CFO

FINANCIAL DATA: *Note: Data for latest year may not have been available at press time.*

In U.S. $	2021	2020	2019	2018	2017	2016
Revenue		2,906,366,000	3,605,543,000	3,661,445,000	3,929,100,000	3,330,322,000
R&D Expense		201,023,200	181,259,700	171,547,300	145,346,500	142,974,900
Operating Income		-124,340,700	58,048,270	41,333,980	118,468,200	147,605,200
Operating Margin %						
SGA Expense		95,429,540	130,213,300	241,114,900	207,347,500	190,520,300
Net Income		-116,435,300	10,954,630	14,342,670	99,946,920	97,801,170
Operating Cash Flow		87,411,210	242,244,200	-54,434,370	103,899,600	-10,841,700
Capital Expenditure		91,250,980	170,643,800	297,695,000	158,221,100	111,692,100
EBITDA		62,791,510	227,336,900	150,654,400	202,265,500	236,258,700
Return on Assets %						
Return on Equity %						
Debt to Equity						

CONTACT INFORMATION:

Phone: 49 8217970 Fax: 49 8217975252
Toll-Free:
Address: Zugspitzstrasse 140, Augsburg, BY 86165 Germany

STOCK TICKER/OTHER:

Stock Ticker: KUKAY
Employees: 14,128
Parent Company: Midea Group
Exchange: PINX
Fiscal Year Ends: 12/31

SALARIES/BONUSES:

Top Exec. Salary: $ Bonus: $
Second Exec. Salary: $ Bonus: $

OTHER THOUGHTS:

Estimated Female Officers or Directors:
Hot Spot for Advancement for Women/Minorities:

L3Harris Technologies Inc

www.l3harris.com

NAIC Code: 334220

TYPES OF BUSINESS:

Communications Equipment Manufacturing
Aerospace and Defense Technology
Communication Systems
Electronic Systems
Space Systems
Intelligence Systems
Command and Control Systems
Signals Intelligence Systems

BRANDS/DIVISIONS/AFFILIATES:

GROWTH PLANS/SPECIAL FEATURES:

L3Harris Technologies was created in 2019 from the merger of L3 Technologies and Harris, two defense contractors that provide products for the command, control, communications, computers, intelligence, surveillance, and reconnaissance (C4ISR) market. The firm also has smaller operations serving the civil government, particularly the Federal Aviation Administration's communication infrastructure, and produces various avionics for defense and commercial aviation.

CONTACTS: *Note: Officers with more than one job title may be intentionally listed here more than once.*

Christopher Kubasik, CEO
Jesus Malave, CFO
William Brown, Chairman of the Board
Corliss Montesi, Chief Accounting Officer
Scott Mikuen, General Counsel
James Girard, Other Executive Officer
Edward Zoiss, President, Divisional
Todd Gautier, President, Divisional
Sean Stackley, President, Divisional
Dana Mehnert, President, Divisional

FINANCIAL DATA: *Note: Data for latest year may not have been available at press time.*

In U.S. $	2021	2020	2019	2018	2017	2016
Revenue		18,194,000,000	9,263,000,000	6,182,000,000	5,900,000,000	7,467,000,000
R&D Expense						
Operating Income		1,993,000,000	610,000,000	1,122,000,000	1,073,000,000	1,149,000,000
Operating Margin %						
SGA Expense		3,315,000,000	1,927,000,000	1,129,000,000	1,016,000,000	1,186,000,000
Net Income		1,119,000,000	822,000,000	718,000,000	553,000,000	324,000,000
Operating Cash Flow		2,790,000,000	939,000,000	751,000,000	569,000,000	924,000,000
Capital Expenditure		368,000,000	173,000,000	136,000,000	119,000,000	152,000,000
EBITDA		2,624,000,000	1,485,000,000	1,355,000,000	1,388,000,000	1,155,000,000
Return on Assets %						
Return on Equity %						
Debt to Equity						

CONTACT INFORMATION:

Phone: 321 727-9100 Fax: 321 724-3973
Toll-Free: 800-442-7747
Address: 1025 West NASA Blvd., Melbourne, FL 32919 United States

STOCK TICKER/OTHER:

Stock Ticker: LHX
Employees: 48,000
Parent Company:
Exchange: NYS
Fiscal Year Ends: 06/30

SALARIES/BONUSES:

Top Exec. Salary: $1,492,308 Bonus: $
Second Exec. Salary: $1,492,308 Bonus: $

OTHER THOUGHTS:

Estimated Female Officers or Directors: 2
Hot Spot for Advancement for Women/Minorities: Y

LaQuest Inc

www.laquest.net

NAIC Code: 511210B

TYPES OF BUSINESS:

Computer Software: Network Management (IT), System Testing & Storage
Digital Business Solutions
Internet of Things
Blockchain Platform Development

BRANDS/DIVISIONS/AFFILIATES:

GROWTH PLANS/SPECIAL FEATURES:

LaQuest, Inc. is a global business solutions company that helps customers transform from a traditional business to a connected digital one. LaQuest offers strategic consulting and advising in improving business operations via enhanced efficiency and customer/business satisfaction. The firm specializes in web application development, mobile application development, custom application development, Internet of Things (IoT) and platform development in the blockchain, application program interface (API) integration/support, systems, software development, user experience design, user interface design, cloud, healthcare technology systems, accounting management systems, inventory management systems and much more.

CONTACTS: *Note: Officers with more than one job title may be intentionally listed here more than once.*

Anoop Lakhera, CEO

FINANCIAL DATA: *Note: Data for latest year may not have been available at press time.*

In U.S. $	2021	2020	2019	2018	2017	2016
Revenue						
R&D Expense						
Operating Income						
Operating Margin %						
SGA Expense						
Net Income						
Operating Cash Flow						
Capital Expenditure						
EBITDA						
Return on Assets %						
Return on Equity %						
Debt to Equity						

CONTACT INFORMATION:

Phone: 63946-012-9717 Fax:
Toll-Free:
Address: Fl. 1-10, One Global Pl., 25th St., Corner 5th Ave., Taguig, Metro Manila 1632 Philippines

STOCK TICKER/OTHER:

Stock Ticker: Private
Employees:
Parent Company:
Exchange:
Fiscal Year Ends:

SALARIES/BONUSES:

Top Exec. Salary: $ Bonus: $
Second Exec. Salary: $ Bonus: $

OTHER THOUGHTS:

Estimated Female Officers or Directors:
Hot Spot for Advancement for Women/Minorities:

Lattice Semiconductor Corporation

www.latticesemi.com

NAIC Code: 334413

TYPES OF BUSINESS:

Integrated Circuits-Programmable Logic Devices
Semiconductors
Technology
Low-Power Solutions
Design Solutions
Application Services
Lattice Semiconductors
Artificial Intelligence

BRANDS/DIVISIONS/AFFILIATES:

Mirametrix Inc

GROWTH PLANS/SPECIAL FEATURES:

Lattice Semiconductor Corp is a developer of semiconductor technology that it distributes through products, solutions, and licenses. The company reaches its customers through consumer, communications, and industrial markets. Lattice's product lines consist of programmable logic devices, video connectivity application-specific standard products, and wave devices. Product offerings enable customers in the consumer market to build technology that utilizes more computing power, higher resolution video, and reduced energy consumption. Customers in the industrial and communication market are aided with data gathering, higher bandwidth, and increased reliability for their products. Lattice's products are offered globally; however, the majority of sales are derived from customers in Asia.

LSC offers its employees health, retirement and savings plans.

CONTACTS: *Note: Officers with more than one job title may be intentionally listed here more than once.*

James Anderson, CEO
Sherri Luther, CFO
D. Richardson, Chairman of the Board
Esam Elashmawi, Chief Marketing Officer
Byron Milstead, General Counsel
Mark Nelson, Vice President, Divisional
Stephen Douglass, Vice President, Divisional

FINANCIAL DATA: *Note: Data for latest year may not have been available at press time.*

In U.S. $	2021	2020	2019	2018	2017	2016
Revenue		408,120,000	404,093,000	398,799,000	385,961,000	427,054,000
R&D Expense		89,223,000	78,617,000	82,449,000	103,357,000	117,518,000
Operating Income		56,303,000	63,705,000	28,246,000	-8,836,000	-3,261,000
Operating Margin %						
SGA Expense		95,331,000	82,542,000	91,054,000	90,718,000	98,602,000
Net Income		47,392,000	43,493,000	-26,322,000	-70,562,000	-54,099,000
Operating Cash Flow		91,687,000	124,137,000	51,458,000	38,514,000	41,734,000
Capital Expenditure		20,868,000	25,191,000	16,507,000	22,391,000	25,752,000
EBITDA		83,258,000	89,852,000	35,892,000	6,955,000	39,410,000
Return on Assets %						
Return on Equity %						
Debt to Equity						

CONTACT INFORMATION:

Phone: 503 268-8000 Fax: 503 268-8347
Toll-Free:
Address: 5555 NE Moore Ct., Hillsboro, OR 97124-6421 United States

STOCK TICKER/OTHER:

Stock Ticker: LSCC
Employees: 746
Parent Company:
Exchange: NAS
Fiscal Year Ends: 12/31

SALARIES/BONUSES:

Top Exec. Salary: $598,077 Bonus: $
Second Exec. Salary: $416,692 Bonus: $

OTHER THOUGHTS:

Estimated Female Officers or Directors: 1
Hot Spot for Advancement for Women/Minorities:

LG Corporation

www.lgcorp.com

NAIC Code: 551114

TYPES OF BUSINESS:

Corporate, Subsidiary, and Regional Managing Offices
Electronics
Technology
Mobile Communications
Vehicle Components
Commercial Displays
Energy Storage
Network Materials

BRANDS/DIVISIONS/AFFILIATES:

LG Electronics
LG Display
LG Innotek
LG Chem
LG Household & Health Care
LG Energy Solution
LG U+
LX Holdings Corp

CONTACTS: *Note: Officers with more than one job title may be intentionally listed here more than once.*

Kwang-mo Koo, Chmn.

GROWTH PLANS/SPECIAL FEATURES:

LG Corporation is a South Korean firm that operates in the electronics, chemicals and communication & services segments. The electronics division consists of three subsidiaries: LG Electronics, which manufactures and markets home appliances, TVs and mobile communications for consumers, and manufactures and markets commercial air conditioners and car parts for businesses; LG Display, a manufacturer of innovative displays, utilizing technologies such as organic light-emitting diodes (OLEDs) and in-plane switching (IPS); and LG Innotek, a developer and producer of materials parts in the fields of vehicles, mobile devices, Internet of Things (IoT), displays, semiconductors and LEDs. The chemicals division consists of three subsidiaries: LG Chem, a chemical, business-to-business company that produces basic materials and chemicals, battery solutions, IT materials, electronics materials, advanced materials, pharmaceuticals and fine chemicals; LG Household & Health Care, a consumer goods company that manages cosmetics, household goods and beverages businesses; and LG Energy Solution, a battery company whose business covers advanced automotive batteries, mobility and IT batteries, energy storage system batteries and next-generation battery technology. Last, the communication & services segment comprises seven subsidiaries: LG U+, a telecommunications service company; GIIR, an advertising and marketing holding company; LG HelloVision Corp., a cable TV company that provides cable TV, internet services, and operates a mobile virtual network; LG CNS, a global IT service company; S&I Corporation, a space solution company for construction, leisure and other industry clients; LG Management Development Institute, which specializes in management consulting and research for future LG businesses; and LG Sports, a professional sports management company in Korea. In addition, LX Holdings Corp. is a 2021 spinoff company that provides global network materials, components and services through subsidiaries: LX International, LX Pantos, LX Hausys, LX Semicon and LX MMA.

FINANCIAL DATA: *Note: Data for latest year may not have been available at press time.*

In U.S. $	2021	2020	2019	2018	2017	2016
Revenue		6,206,060,000	5,494,190,000	6,862,430,000	11,088,100,000	8,018,680,000
R&D Expense						
Operating Income						
Operating Margin %						
SGA Expense						
Net Income		1,524,570,000	955,782,000	1,685,530,000	2,280,680,000	904,544,000
Operating Cash Flow						
Capital Expenditure						
EBITDA						
Return on Assets %						
Return on Equity %						
Debt to Equity						

CONTACT INFORMATION:

Phone: 822-3773-1114 Fax: 822-3773-2292
Toll-Free:
Address: LG Twin Towers, 128 Yeoui-daero, Yeongdeungpo-gu, Seoul, 150-721 South Korea

STOCK TICKER/OTHER:

Stock Ticker: 3550
Employees: 222,000
Parent Company:
Exchange: Seoul
Fiscal Year Ends: 12/31

SALARIES/BONUSES:

Top Exec. Salary: $ Bonus: $
Second Exec. Salary: $ Bonus: $

OTHER THOUGHTS:

Estimated Female Officers or Directors:
Hot Spot for Advancement for Women/Minorities:

LG Electronics Inc

NAIC Code: 334220

www.lg.com

TYPES OF BUSINESS:

Manufacturing-Electronics
Technology
Home Appliances
Home Entertainment
Mobile Communications
Vehicle Component Solutions
Commercial Displays
Energy Management

BRANDS/DIVISIONS/AFFILIATES:

LG Corporation
LG Signature
LG ThinQ

GROWTH PLANS/SPECIAL FEATURES:

LG Electronics Inc is a South Korea-based company that produces a broad range of electronic products. Its businesses are the home entertainment segment, which produces and sells TVs and digital media products; the mobile communications segment, which produces and sells mobile communications equipment; the home appliance and air solutions segment, which produces and sells washing machines, refrigerators, and other products; the vehicle components segment, which designs and produces vehicle parts; the business solutions segment, which manufactures and sells PCs, solar panels, and other products; and Innotek, which sells substrates, sensors, and other items. The company generates the majority of total revenue from the home entertainment and home appliance and air solutions segments.

CONTACTS: *Note: Officers with more than one job title may be intentionally listed here more than once.*

William Cho, CEO
Hyun-Hoi Ha, Pres.

FINANCIAL DATA: *Note: Data for latest year may not have been available at press time.*

In U.S. $	2021	2020	2019	2018	2017	2016
Revenue		53,128,340,000	52,325,590,000	51,515,580,000	51,561,460,000	46,498,000,000
R&D Expense		424,656,900	2,085,599,000	310,050,000	229,074,400	297,636,800
Operating Income		2,683,194,000	2,045,903,000	2,270,262,000	2,073,122,000	1,123,472,000
Operating Margin %						
SGA Expense		6,383,295,000	8,747,522,000	6,195,662,000	6,033,339,000	6,280,949,000
Net Income		1,653,033,000	26,273,580	1,041,486,000	1,449,329,000	64,564,060
Operating Cash Flow		3,887,142,000	3,098,211,000	3,814,071,000	1,819,264,000	2,652,124,000
Capital Expenditure		2,589,181,000	2,136,990,000	3,228,556,000	2,703,625,000	2,079,456,000
EBITDA		4,590,181,000	2,890,812,000	3,714,674,000	3,941,208,000	2,421,193,000
Return on Assets %						
Return on Equity %						
Debt to Equity						

CONTACT INFORMATION:

Phone: 82 237771114 Fax:
Toll-Free: 800-243-0000
Address: LG Twin Towers, 20 Yoido Dong, Seoul, 150-721 South Korea

STOCK TICKER/OTHER:

Stock Ticker: LGEJY
Employees: 100,000
Parent Company: LG Corporation
Exchange: PINX
Fiscal Year Ends: 12/31

SALARIES/BONUSES:

Top Exec. Salary: $ Bonus: $
Second Exec. Salary: $ Bonus: $

OTHER THOUGHTS:

Estimated Female Officers or Directors:
Hot Spot for Advancement for Women/Minorities:

LG Electronics USA Inc

www.lg.com/us

NAIC Code: 334220

TYPES OF BUSINESS:

Consumer Electronics
Mobile Phones & Accessories
Home Appliances
Computer Products

BRANDS/DIVISIONS/AFFILIATES:

LG Corporation
LG Electronics Inc

CONTACTS: *Note: Officers with more than one job title may be intentionally listed here more than once.*

Thomas Yoon, CEO

GROWTH PLANS/SPECIAL FEATURES:

LG Electronics USA, Inc., a subsidiary of South Korea-based LG Electronics, Inc., sells consumer electronics, home appliances, mobile phones and digital applications in the U.S., Canada and Mexico. Products are grouped into five categories: mobile phones; television, audio and video; appliances; computer products; and solar. The mobile phone segment works in conjunction with service providers, developing a wide range of phones including Android powered smartphones, quad core processors, 4G, 5G, touch screens and more. Additionally, the company sells an array of mobile phone accessories including batteries, cables, chargers, hands-free headsets and Bluetooth products. The television, audio and video category includes organic light-emitting diode (OLED) and nanocell TVs, sound bars, projectors, Blu-ray players, speakers and more. The appliances segment sells washers, dryers, refrigerators, built-in ovens, cooktops, dishwashers, microwave ovens, air conditioners, vacuums, dehumidifiers and accessories. The computer products segment offers consumer and commercial laptops, monitors, burners/drives and related accessories. Last, the solar segment manufactures and installs solar cells and solar panels, which come with a 25-year guarantee. Headquartered in Englewood Cliffs, New Jersey, the firm operates additional training facilities in California and Georgia and a R&D center in Illinois. LG Electronics is itself a subsidiary of holding company LG Corporation.

FINANCIAL DATA: *Note: Data for latest year may not have been available at press time.*

In U.S. $	2021	2020	2019	2018	2017	2016
Revenue	14,500,000,000	12,429,400,000	8,941,270,432	8,515,495,650	8,473,130,000	6,984,197,082
R&D Expense						
Operating Income						
Operating Margin %						
SGA Expense						
Net Income		152,231,000	-74,658,681	-78,588,085	-82,724,300	-105,207,004
Operating Cash Flow						
Capital Expenditure						
EBITDA						
Return on Assets %						
Return on Equity %						
Debt to Equity						

CONTACT INFORMATION:

Phone: 201-816-2000 Fax: 201-816-0636
Toll-Free: 800-243-0000
Address: 1000 Sylvan Ave., Englewood Cliffs, NJ 60654 United States

STOCK TICKER/OTHER:

Stock Ticker: Subsidiary
Employees: 3,000
Parent Company: LG Corporation
Exchange:
Fiscal Year Ends: 12/31

SALARIES/BONUSES:

Top Exec. Salary: $ Bonus: $
Second Exec. Salary: $ Bonus: $

OTHER THOUGHTS:

Estimated Female Officers or Directors:
Hot Spot for Advancement for Women/Minorities:

LG Uplus Corp

www.uplus.co.kr

NAIC Code: 517210

TYPES OF BUSINESS:

Mobile Telephone Services
Wireless Internet Service
Mobile Commerce Services
Consulting Services
Internet Data Center Services

BRANDS/DIVISIONS/AFFILIATES:

LG Corporation
LG U+
U+ homeBoy

GROWTH PLANS/SPECIAL FEATURES:

LG Uplus Corp is a telecommunications company that sells cellular-related products. The firm is a subsidiary of the LG Corporation. The company operates four business segments that include fixed-line communications, Internet services, mobile voice, and mobile data. The company's terminal distribution segment sells both wireless and wired terminals. LG Uplus also offers Uplus TV and develops both hardware and software. The company generates the vast majority of its revenue in South Korea. The firm sells its products to both individuals and businesses.

CONTACTS: *Note: Officers with more than one job title may be intentionally listed here more than once.*

Hyun-sik Hwang, CEO

FINANCIAL DATA: *Note: Data for latest year may not have been available at press time.*

In U.S. $	2021	2020	2019	2018	2017	2016
Revenue		11,268,308,992	10,398,550,016	10,182,787,072	11,498,500,000	10,202,652,290
R&D Expense						
Operating Income						
Operating Margin %						
SGA Expense						
Net Income		391,994,912	368,556,544	404,485,440	512,216,000	438,126,013
Operating Cash Flow						
Capital Expenditure						
EBITDA						
Return on Assets %						
Return on Equity %						
Debt to Equity						

CONTACT INFORMATION:

Phone: 82-070-4080-1114 Fax:
Toll-Free:
Address: LG Uplus Tower, 82, Seoul, 100-095 South Korea

STOCK TICKER/OTHER:

Stock Ticker: 32640
Employees: 10,221
Parent Company: LG Corporation
Exchange: Seoul
Fiscal Year Ends: 12/31

SALARIES/BONUSES:

Top Exec. Salary: $ Bonus: $
Second Exec. Salary: $ Bonus: $

OTHER THOUGHTS:

Estimated Female Officers or Directors:
Hot Spot for Advancement for Women/Minorities:

LiveRamp Holdings Inc

liveramp.com/about-us

NAIC Code: 511210K

TYPES OF BUSINESS:

Consumer Data Management
Consumer Databases
Consulting and Analytics
Risk Mitigation Services
CDI Technology
Consumer Privacy Solutions
Data Marketplace

GROWTH PLANS/SPECIAL FEATURES:

LiveRamp Holdings Inc is a United States based technology company. The company provides the identity platform leveraged by brands and their partners. LiveRamp's IdentityLink connects people, data, and devices across the digital and physical world, powering the people-based marketing revolution and allowing consumers to safely connect with the brands and products.

BRANDS/DIVISIONS/AFFILIATES:

LiveRamp Safe Haven

CONTACTS: *Note: Officers with more than one job title may be intentionally listed here more than once.*

Gerald Jones, Assistant Secretary
Scott Howe, CEO
Warren Jenson, CFO
Clark Kokich, Chairman of the Board
Anneka Gupta, Co-President

FINANCIAL DATA: *Note: Data for latest year may not have been available at press time.*

In U.S. $	2021	2020	2019	2018	2017	2016
Revenue	443,026,000	380,572,000	285,620,000	917,406,000	880,247,000	850,088,000
R&D Expense	135,111,000	105,981,000	85,697,000	94,873,000	82,109,000	74,247,000
Operating Income	-117,833,000	-175,921,000	-178,213,000	16,972,000	24,062,000	5,898,000
Operating Margin %						
SGA Expense	281,744,000	297,808,000	257,418,000	339,125,000	296,390,000	281,561,000
Net Income	-90,268,000	-124,511,000	1,028,547,000	23,480,000	4,108,000	6,703,000
Operating Cash Flow	-20,560,000	-28,782,000	-460,503,000	112,153,000	115,830,000	119,965,000
Capital Expenditure	2,182,000	11,711,000	8,642,000	57,936,000	62,470,000	62,303,000
EBITDA	-90,092,000	-140,020,000	-144,431,000	97,211,000	98,713,000	72,852,000
Return on Assets %						
Return on Equity %						
Debt to Equity						

CONTACT INFORMATION:

Phone: 866-352-3267 Fax:
Toll-Free:
Address: 225 Bush St., Fl. 17, San Francisco, CA 94104 United States

STOCK TICKER/OTHER:

Stock Ticker: RAMP
Employees: 1,200
Parent Company:
Exchange: NYS
Fiscal Year Ends: 03/31

SALARIES/BONUSES:

Top Exec. Salary: $690,000 Bonus: $
Second Exec. Salary: $550,000 Bonus: $

OTHER THOUGHTS:

Estimated Female Officers or Directors: 4
Hot Spot for Advancement for Women/Minorities: Y

LM Ericsson Telephone Company (Ericsson)

www.ericsson.com

NAIC Code: 334220

TYPES OF BUSINESS:

Wireless Telecommunications Equipment
Information Technology
Communications
Networks
Digital
Internet of Things
Telecommunications
Artificial Intelligence

BRANDS/DIVISIONS/AFFILIATES:

GROWTH PLANS/SPECIAL FEATURES:

Ericsson is leading supplier in the telecommunications equipment sector. The company's three major operating segments are networks, digital services, and managed services. Ericsson sells hardware, software, and services primarily to communications service providers while licensing patents to handset manufacturers. The Stockholm-based company derives sales worldwide and had 95,000 employees as of June.

CONTACTS: *Note: Officers with more than one job title may be intentionally listed here more than once.*

Borje Ekholm, CEO
Carl Mellander, Sr. VP
Stella Medlicott, Sr. VP
MajBritt Arfert, Chief People Officer
Erik Ekudden, Sr. VP
Nina Macpherson, General Counsel
Douglas L. Gilstrap, Sr. VP-Function Strategy
Helena Norrman, Sr. VP-Comm..
Jan Frykhammar, Head-Group Function Finance
Angel Ruiz, Head-North America
Magnus Mandersson, Head-Global Svcs.
Rima Qureshi, Sr. VP-Strategic Projects
Johan Wibergh, Exec. VP-Networks
Ronnie Leten, Chmn.
Mats H. Olsson, Head-Asia Pacific

FINANCIAL DATA: *Note: Data for latest year may not have been available at press time.*

In U.S. $	2021	2020	2019	2018	2017	2016
Revenue		25,646,320,000	25,075,320,000	23,267,860,000	22,215,590,000	24,566,780,000
R&D Expense		4,382,795,000	4,283,582,000	4,293,956,000	4,181,169,000	3,491,205,000
Operating Income		3,097,224,000	1,031,856,000	230,760,600	-2,797,710,000	687,646,600
Operating Margin %						
SGA Expense		2,944,818,000	2,884,452,000	3,036,968,000	3,606,089,000	3,185,622,000
Net Income		1,929,405,000	245,328,000	-720,643,900	-3,885,297,000	189,376,000
Operating Cash Flow		3,193,015,000	1,862,087,000	1,030,973,000	1,059,556,000	1,546,129,000
Capital Expenditure		586,006,000	735,321,700	540,758,800	587,220,000	1,171,129,000
EBITDA		4,059,443,000	2,130,369,000	796,350,100	-3,286,158,000	1,574,491,000
Return on Assets %						
Return on Equity %						
Debt to Equity						

CONTACT INFORMATION:

Phone: 46 87190000 Fax: 46 87191976
Toll-Free:
Address: Torshamnsgatan 21, Kista, Stockholm, 164 83 Sweden

STOCK TICKER/OTHER:

Stock Ticker: ERIC Exchange: NAS
Employees: 100,824 Fiscal Year Ends: 12/31
Parent Company:

SALARIES/BONUSES:

Top Exec. Salary: $1,695,400 Bonus: $2,025,226
Second Exec. Salary: $ Bonus: $

OTHER THOUGHTS:

Estimated Female Officers or Directors: 10
Hot Spot for Advancement for Women/Minorities: Y

Location Labs Inc

www.location-labs.com

NAIC Code: 511210C

TYPES OF BUSINESS:

Computer Software: Telecom, Communications & VOIP
GPS-Based Cell Phone Services
City Directories & Mapping Applications
Privacy Software
Apps

BRANDS/DIVISIONS/AFFILIATES:

Avast plx
AVG Technologies Inc

CONTACTS: *Note: Officers with more than one job title may be intentionally listed here more than once.*

Gagan Singh, Managing Dir.
Jarret Cuisinier, VP-Mktg. & Operations
Jesse Myers, Chief Scientist
Andy Ruff, VP-Prod.
Scott A. Hotes, VP-Eng.
Justin Safdie, VP-Oper.
Ryo Kawaoka, VP-Project Mgmt.

GROWTH PLANS/SPECIAL FEATURES:

Location Labs, Inc. is a location-based services firm near San Francisco in Emeryville, California. The company utilizes location-based techniques to provide a full spectrum of services for mobile devices. Location Labs' universal location service partners with wireless companies such as AT&T, Sprint and Verizon to locate and communicate with smart devices. The firm is engaged in geofencing, the practice of setting virtual boundaries around a physical location and targeting mobile device users within those areas. Moreover, Location Labs offers a mobile phone software that allows parents to set their children's phones to automatically lockout at pre-designated times, such as while they are at school, late at night or dinner time. Family phone use can also be retrieved and managed, including seeing all activity such as texts, calls and apps. Alerts can inform parents of questionable activities or contacts. Location Labs' on-demand location feature enables users to see where their important people are on a map, with no app necessary, and offers a track record history of where they've been. Location Labs operates as a subsidiary of online security company AVG Technologies, Inc., itself is a subsidiary of Avast plc.

FINANCIAL DATA: *Note: Data for latest year may not have been available at press time.*

In U.S. $	2021	2020	2019	2018	2017	2016
Revenue	55,000,000	52,093,125	49,612,500	47,250,000	45,000,000	44,000,000
R&D Expense						
Operating Income						
Operating Margin %						
SGA Expense						
Net Income						
Operating Cash Flow						
Capital Expenditure						
EBITDA						
Return on Assets %						
Return on Equity %						
Debt to Equity						

CONTACT INFORMATION:

Phone: 510-601-7012 Fax:
Toll-Free:
Address: 2100 Powell St., 14/Fl, Emeryville, CA 94608 United States

STOCK TICKER/OTHER:

Stock Ticker: Subsidiary
Employees: 150
Parent Company: Avast plc
Exchange:
Fiscal Year Ends: 12/31

SALARIES/BONUSES:

Top Exec. Salary: $ Bonus: $
Second Exec. Salary: $ Bonus: $

OTHER THOUGHTS:

Estimated Female Officers or Directors:
Hot Spot for Advancement for Women/Minorities:

Lockheed Martin Corporation

www.lockheedmartin.com

NAIC Code: 336411

TYPES OF BUSINESS:

Aircraft Manufacturing
Military Aircraft
Defense Electronics
Systems Integration & Technology Services
Communications Satellites & Launch Services
Undersea, Shipboard, Land & Airborne Systems & Subsystems
Cyber Resilient Systems

BRANDS/DIVISIONS/AFFILIATES:

F-35 Lightning
F-22
F-16
C-130

GROWTH PLANS/SPECIAL FEATURES:

Lockheed Martin is the largest defense contractor globally and has dominated the Western market for high-end fighter aircraft since being awarded the F-35 program in 2001. Lockheed's largest segment is Aeronautics, which is dominated by the massive F-35 program. Lockheed's remaining segments are rotary & mission systems, which is mainly the Sikorsky helicopter business; missiles and fire control, which creates missiles and missile defense systems; and space systems, which produces satellites and receives equity income from the United Launch Alliance joint venture.

CONTACTS: *Note: Officers with more than one job title may be intentionally listed here more than once.*

James Taiclet, CEO
John Mollard, CFO
Brian Colan, Chief Accounting Officer
Frank St John, COO
Richard Ambrose, Executive VP, Divisional
Gregory Ulmer, Executive VP, Divisional
Stephanie Hill, Executive VP, Divisional
Scott Greene, Executive VP, Divisional
Maryanne Lavan, General Counsel

FINANCIAL DATA: *Note: Data for latest year may not have been available at press time.*

In U.S. $	2021	2020	2019	2018	2017	2016
Revenue		65,398,000,000	59,812,000,000	53,762,000,000	51,048,000,000	47,248,000,000
R&D Expense						
Operating Income		8,644,000,000	8,367,000,000	7,370,000,000	5,548,000,000	5,142,000,000
Operating Margin %						
SGA Expense						
Net Income		6,833,000,000	6,230,000,000	5,046,000,000	2,002,000,000	5,302,000,000
Operating Cash Flow		8,183,000,000	7,311,000,000	3,138,000,000	6,476,000,000	5,189,000,000
Capital Expenditure		1,766,000,000	1,484,000,000	1,278,000,000	1,177,000,000	1,063,000,000
EBITDA		10,116,000,000	9,083,000,000	7,667,000,000	7,115,000,000	6,764,000,000
Return on Assets %						
Return on Equity %						
Debt to Equity						

CONTACT INFORMATION:

Phone: 301 897-6000   Fax: 301 897-6083
Toll-Free:
Address: 6801 Rockledge Dr., Bethesda, MD 20817 United States

STOCK TICKER/OTHER:

Stock Ticker: LMT   Exchange: NYS
Employees: 114,000   Fiscal Year Ends: 12/31
Parent Company:

SALARIES/BONUSES:

Top Exec. Salary: $1,877,519   Bonus: $
Second Exec. Salary: $1,000,769   Bonus: $

OTHER THOUGHTS:

Estimated Female Officers or Directors: 5
Hot Spot for Advancement for Women/Minorities: Y

Long View Systems

www.longviewsystems.com

NAIC Code: 541512

TYPES OF BUSINESS:

Computer Systems Design Services
IT Services
Data Insights
Business Transformation
Networks
Cybersecurity
Technology Licensing

BRANDS/DIVISIONS/AFFILIATES:

GROWTH PLANS/SPECIAL FEATURES:

Long View Systems is an information technology (IT) and services company active in the North American region. The firm combines business and technology through a hybrid IT methodology. Long View's wide range of solutions span end-user experience for empowering the workforce, data insights, business transformation, data modernization, applications, cloud management, managed infrastructure services, SD-WAN and SD-ACCESS networks, cybersecurity and technology licensing and procurement. Primary partners of Long View include Cisco and Microsoft, with others including Adobe, BlackBerry, Duo, Lenovo, Oracle, Red Hat and VMware. The firm is based in Calgary, Canada, with additional domestic offices in Edmonton, Toronto, Vancouver and Victoria, as well as U.S. offices in Dallas, Denver and Houston.

CONTACTS: *Note: Officers with more than one job title may be intentionally listed here more than once.*

Brent Allison, CEO
Keith Howe, Exec. VP-Strategy
Neil Smith, CFO
Dave Frederickson, Exec. VP-Sales
Tasha Westerman, Exec. VP-People Svcs.
Michael Kochorek, VP-Mktg. & Bus. Dev.
Don Bialik, Chmn.

FINANCIAL DATA: *Note: Data for latest year may not have been available at press time.*

In U.S. $	2021	2020	2019	2018	2017	2016
Revenue	300,000,000	275,500,000	290,000,000	293,189,000	312,863,040	302,705,000
R&D Expense						
Operating Income						
Operating Margin %						
SGA Expense						
Net Income						
Operating Cash Flow						
Capital Expenditure						
EBITDA						
Return on Assets %						
Return on Equity %						
Debt to Equity						

CONTACT INFORMATION:

Phone: 403-515-6900 Fax: 403-515-6919
Toll-Free: 866-515-6900
Address: Ste. 2100, 250 - 2 St. SW, Calgary, ALB T2P 0C1 Canada

STOCK TICKER/OTHER:

Stock Ticker: Private
Employees:
Parent Company:
Exchange:
Fiscal Year Ends:

SALARIES/BONUSES:

Top Exec. Salary: $ Bonus: $
Second Exec. Salary: $ Bonus: $

OTHER THOUGHTS:

Estimated Female Officers or Directors:
Hot Spot for Advancement for Women/Minorities:

Lookout Inc

www.lookout.com

NAIC Code: 511210E

TYPES OF BUSINESS:

Computer Software: Network Security, Managed Access, Digital ID, Cybersecurity & Anti-Virus

BRANDS/DIVISIONS/AFFILIATES:

Lookout Security Cloud
Lookout for Small Business
Lookout App Defense
Lookout Personal
CipherCloud

CONTACTS: *Note: Officers with more than one job title may be intentionally listed here more than once.*

Jim Dolce, CEO
Mark Nasiff, COO
Mike Banic, CMO
Missy Ballew, Chief Human Resources Officer

GROWTH PLANS/SPECIAL FEATURES:

Lookout, Inc. is a cybersecurity company that predicts and stops mobile attacks before harm is done to an individual or an enterprise. The company's cloud-based technology is generated by a global network of millions of endpoints and analyzed applications. Within this data, Lookout identifies connections that would otherwise go unseen and stop cybercriminals from attacking mobile devices. Lookout produces mobile security applications for iOS and Android devices. A highly scalable cloud-first, mobile-first platform, only Lookout Security Cloud provides a privacy-centric approach that continuously protects users and cloud data from the latest phishing, application, device, and network threats. The platform comes with easy to use cloud modules for security detection, visibility, response and remediation. Products of the firm include: mobile endpoint security, which provides comprehensive and continuous assessment of risk across iOS and Android devices to secure against app, device, and network-based threats; phishing and content protection, protects end users from new and emerging phishing attacks beyond a company's existing perimeter solutions; Lookout for Small Business has fixed configurations and a more simplified console; Lookout App Defense leverages the power of the Lookout Security Cloud to offer the most secure and easy to deploy solution to protect individuals and organizations from data compromise when conducting transactions via mobile apps; and Lookout Personal provides protection against mobile threats such as malware, device compromises, unsafe wireless networks and malicious websites. Partners of the company include Google, Microsoft and VMware, as well as AT&T, NTT Docomo, Orange, Telefonica, Telstra, T-Mobile, Verizon and Vodafone. Based in San Francisco, California, Lookout has office locations in Boston, Washington DC, Bengaluru, Dubai, London, Netherlands, Sydney, Toronto, and Tokyo. In March 2021, Lookout acquired CipherCloud, a cloud-native security company that operates in the emerging Secure Access Service Edge market.

FINANCIAL DATA: *Note: Data for latest year may not have been available at press time.*

In U.S. $	2021	2020	2019	2018	2017	2016
Revenue						
R&D Expense						
Operating Income						
Operating Margin %						
SGA Expense						
Net Income						
Operating Cash Flow						
Capital Expenditure						
EBITDA						
Return on Assets %						
Return on Equity %						
Debt to Equity						

CONTACT INFORMATION:

Phone: 415-281-2820 Fax:
Toll-Free:
Address: 275 Battery St., Ste. 200, San Francisco, CA 94111 United States

STOCK TICKER/OTHER:

Stock Ticker: Private
Employees: 347
Parent Company:
Exchange:
Fiscal Year Ends:

SALARIES/BONUSES:

Top Exec. Salary: $ Bonus: $
Second Exec. Salary: $ Bonus: $

OTHER THOUGHTS:

Estimated Female Officers or Directors:
Hot Spot for Advancement for Women/Minorities:

Lyft Inc

NAIC Code: 561599

www.lyft.me

TYPES OF BUSINESS:

Car Ride Dispatch Service, Mobile App-Based
Bicycle Rental & Sharing Systems
Augmented Reality Technology
Rental Cars
Vehicle Sharing

BRANDS/DIVISIONS/AFFILIATES:

Lyft
Lyft Rental

GROWTH PLANS/SPECIAL FEATURES:

Lyft is the second- largest ride-sharing service provider in the U.S., connecting riders and drivers over the Lyft app. Lyft recently entered the Canadian market in an effort to expand its market outside the U.S. Incorporated in 2013, Lyft offers a variety of rides via private vehicles, including traditional private rides, shared rides, and luxury ones. Besides ride-share, Lyft also has entered the bike- and scooter-share market to bring multimodal transportation options to users.

CONTACTS: *Note: Officers with more than one job title may be intentionally listed here more than once.*

Logan Green, CEO
Brian Roberts, CFO
Prashant Aggarwal, Chairman of the Board
Lisa Blackwood-Kapral, Chief Accounting Officer
John Zimmer, Co-Founder
Eisar Lipkovitz, Executive VP, Divisional
Lindsay Llewellyn, General Counsel
Ashwin Raj, Other Corporate Officer
Kristin Sverchek, President, Divisional

FINANCIAL DATA: *Note: Data for latest year may not have been available at press time.*

In U.S. $	2021	2020	2019	2018	2017	2016
Revenue		2,364,681,000	3,615,960,000	2,156,616,000	1,059,881,000	343,298,000
R&D Expense		909,126,000	1,505,640,000	300,836,000	136,646,000	64,704,000
Operating Income		-1,808,382,000	-2,702,480,000	-977,711,000	-708,272,000	-692,603,000
Operating Margin %						
SGA Expense		1,362,458,000	2,000,215,000	1,251,689,000	788,461,000	594,306,000
Net Income		-1,752,857,000	-2,602,241,000	-911,335,000	-688,301,000	-682,794,000
Operating Cash Flow		-1,378,899,000	-105,702,000	-280,673,000	-393,526,000	-487,163,000
Capital Expenditure		93,639,000	178,088,000	70,868,000	12,023,000	8,819,000
EBITDA		-1,607,360,000	-2,594,051,000	-958,959,000	-705,661,000	-692,076,000
Return on Assets %						
Return on Equity %						
Debt to Equity						

CONTACT INFORMATION:

Phone: 855-946-7433 Fax:
Toll-Free:
Address: 185 Berry St., Ste. 5000, San Francisco, CA 94107 United States

STOCK TICKER/OTHER:

Stock Ticker: LYFT
Employees: 4,675
Parent Company:
Exchange: NAS
Fiscal Year Ends:

SALARIES/BONUSES:

Top Exec. Salary: $418,846 Bonus: $
Second Exec. Salary: $418,846 Bonus: $

OTHER THOUGHTS:

Estimated Female Officers or Directors: 2
Hot Spot for Advancement for Women/Minorities:

Macronix International Co Ltd

www.macronix.com

NAIC Code: 334413

TYPES OF BUSINESS:

Semiconductors-Memory Chips
Flash Memory Cards
Digital Voice Recorders
Digital Cameras
Flat Panel Displays
Design Services

BRANDS/DIVISIONS/AFFILIATES:

Serial NOR Flash
Parallel NOR Flash
OctaFlash
OctaBus
1.2V Serial NOR Flash
NBIT/Nbit
e-MMC
ArmorFlash

CONTACTS: *Note: Officers with more than one job title may be intentionally listed here more than once.*

Miin Chyou Wu, CEO
Chih-Yuan Lu, Pres.
Dang-Hsing Yiu, Sr. VP
Ful-Long Ni, VP
Wen-Sen Pan, VP
Pei-Fu Yeh, VP
Yen-Hie Chao, VP
Miin Chyou Wu, Chmn.

GROWTH PLANS/SPECIAL FEATURES:

Macronix International Co., Ltd. designs, produces and supplies non-volatile memory (NVM) semiconductor products. The company's offerings include flash memory cards, digital voice recorders, sound generators, digital answering machines, digital still cameras and flat panel displays. Macronix's family of flash products includes: Serial NOR Flash, which range in densities from 512 kilobytes to 2 gigabytes; Parallel NOR Flash, which range from 2 megabytes to 1Gb in densities ; OctaFlash, including the new-generation OctaBus built on serial peripheral interface and command protocol for extended I/O capability; 1.2V Serial NOR Flash, for low power applications such as health monitoring, Bluetooth connection, Internet of Things (IoT), wearables and mobile internet devices; and ultra-low power/wide range Vcc memory products. Macronix's broad NAND flash portfolio covers a wide range of customer requirements, including both SLC NAND and Serial NAND designed for demanding applications. Macronix's ROM (read-only memory) business division includes products such as ASIC XtraROM and NBIT/Nbit. The e-MMC family of memory meets the needs of high-capacity storage and high reliability applications. ArmorFlash supports standard SPI, QSPI and OctaBus interface, which are based on highly configurable security technologies to support secure ID, authentication and encrypted links for various flash. LybraFlash is a solution for gigabit flash memory. Multichip packages (MCP) are offered for power saving and space constraint needs and include NOR-based MCP and NAND-based MCP. The company owns more than 7,400 patents and reinvests an average of 20% of its annual revenue to research and development. Macronix treats clients as strategic partners, working closely with them from the early stages of product development to designing silicon chips that meet their specific needs.

FINANCIAL DATA: *Note: Data for latest year may not have been available at press time.*

In U.S. $	2021	2020	2019	2018	2017	2016
Revenue		1,415,520,680	1,228,800,000	1,221,709,056	1,130,588,800	797,598,912
R&D Expense						
Operating Income						
Operating Margin %						
SGA Expense						
Net Income		186,204,541	299,039,000	297,318,944	182,426,272	-8,034,284
Operating Cash Flow						
Capital Expenditure						
EBITDA						
Return on Assets %						
Return on Equity %						
Debt to Equity						

CONTACT INFORMATION:

Phone: 886-3-578-6688 Fax: 886-3-563-2888
Toll-Free:
Address: 16 Li-Hsin Rd., Science Park, Hsinchu City, 30078 Taiwan

STOCK TICKER/OTHER:

Stock Ticker: 2337
Exchange: TWSE
Employees: 3,892
Fiscal Year Ends: 12/31
Parent Company:

SALARIES/BONUSES:

Top Exec. Salary: $ Bonus: $
Second Exec. Salary: $ Bonus: $

OTHER THOUGHTS:

Estimated Female Officers or Directors:
Hot Spot for Advancement for Women/Minorities:

Magneto IT Solutions LLC

magnetoitsolutions.com

NAIC Code: 511210M

TYPES OF BUSINESS:

Computer Software, e-Commerce, Web Analytics & Applications Management
IT Solutions
Internet of Things
Ecommerce Solutions
Application Development
Digital Transformation

BRANDS/DIVISIONS/AFFILIATES:

CONTACTS:

Note: Officers with more than one job title may be intentionally listed here more than once.

Ronak Meghani, Managing Dir.

GROWTH PLANS/SPECIAL FEATURES:

Magneto IT Solutions, LLC is a software, information technology (IT) solutions provider based in New York, USA, with global offices in India. Magneto specializes in Internet of Things (IoT), digital transformation, ecommerce, web applications and mobile applications in order to help clients turn their ideas into business applications. In regards to IoT, Magneto offers product engineering, application development and connected application. Regarding ecommerce, the firm offers consulting services, strategy, marketplace solutions, support, development, migration, integration, online market management, content marketing, conversion rate optimization, email marketing, affiliate marketing, social media optimization, user interface (UI) and user experience (UX) apps, and business-to-business solutions. Ecommerce industries served by Magneto include furniture, home decor, fashion, bridal, gems/jewelry, health, beauty, computer, electronics, automotive, floristry, grocery and wholesale. Web applications include the development of Laravel, AngularJS, Yii, NodeJS, WordPress and/or PHP platforms. Mobile applications' services include: iOS and Android app consulting, development, support, maintenance and UI/UX; hire developer apps, including iOS, Android, SWIFT, REST application program interface, iBeacon, Ionic and PhoneGap; and Chatbot consulting, development and support. This division primarily serves the FinTech, real estate and utility industries. Magneto operates in more than 20 countries and serves over 650 customers.

FINANCIAL DATA:

Note: Data for latest year may not have been available at press time.

In U.S. $	2021	2020	2019	2018	2017	2016
Revenue						
R&D Expense						
Operating Income						
Operating Margin %						
SGA Expense						
Net Income						
Operating Cash Flow						
Capital Expenditure						
EBITDA						
Return on Assets %						
Return on Equity %						
Debt to Equity						

CONTACT INFORMATION:

Phone: 646-205-8151 Fax:
Toll-Free:
Address: 347 Fifth Ave., Ste. 1402-182, New York, NY 10016 United States

STOCK TICKER/OTHER:

Stock Ticker: Private
Exchange:
Employees:
Fiscal Year Ends:
Parent Company:

SALARIES/BONUSES:

Top Exec. Salary: $ Bonus: $
Second Exec. Salary: $ Bonus: $

OTHER THOUGHTS:

Estimated Female Officers or Directors:
Hot Spot for Advancement for Women/Minorities:

Mandiant Inc

NAIC Code: 511210E

www.mandiant.com

TYPES OF BUSINESS:

Computer Software, Network Security, Managed Access, Digital ID,
Cybersecurity & Anti-Virus
Cybersecurity Solutions
Software-as-a-Service Platform
Automated Alerts
Security Validation Solutions

GROWTH PLANS/SPECIAL FEATURES:

Mandiant (formally FireEye,) is a pure-play cybersecurity firm that focuses on incident response, threat intelligence, automated response, and managed security. Mandiant's security experts can be used on demand or customers can outsource their security to Mandiant. The California-based company sells solutions security solutions worldwide, and sold its FireEye products division in October 2021.

BRANDS/DIVISIONS/AFFILIATES:

Mandiant Advantage SaaS
FireEye Inc

CONTACTS: *Note: Officers with more than one job title may be intentionally listed here more than once.*

Kevin Mandia, CEO
Frank Verdecanna, CFO
Enrique Salem, Chairman of the Board
John Watters, COO
Peter Bailey, Executive VP, Divisional
Alexa King, Executive VP, Divisional
William Robbins, Executive VP
Richard Meamber, General Counsel

FINANCIAL DATA: *Note: Data for latest year may not have been available at press time.*

In U.S. $	2021	2020	2019	2018	2017	2016
Revenue		940,584,000	889,152,000	830,950,000	751,086,000	714,114,000
R&D Expense		252,771,000	271,326,000	254,142,000	243,273,000	279,594,000
Operating Income		-128,664,000	-199,769,000	-182,402,000	-258,606,000	-416,686,000
Operating Margin %						
SGA Expense		482,450,000	508,703,000	486,735,000	497,532,000	579,338,000
Net Income		-207,303,000	-257,409,000	-243,123,000	-303,691,000	-480,129,000
Operating Cash Flow		94,895,000	67,537,000	17,381,000	17,640,000	-14,585,000
Capital Expenditure		26,326,000	45,605,000	50,831,000	43,779,000	36,314,000
EBITDA		-47,959,000	-86,487,000	-94,668,000	-145,876,000	-321,714,000
Return on Assets %						
Return on Equity %						
Debt to Equity						

CONTACT INFORMATION:

Phone: 408-321-6300 Fax: 408-321-9818
Toll-Free:
Address: 601 McCarthy Blvd., Milpitas, CA 95035 United States

STOCK TICKER/OTHER:

Stock Ticker: MNDT
Employees: 3,400
Parent Company:
Exchange: NAS
Fiscal Year Ends: 12/31

SALARIES/BONUSES:

Top Exec. Salary: $475,000 Bonus: $
Second Exec. Salary: $440,000 Bonus: $

OTHER THOUGHTS:

Estimated Female Officers or Directors: 4
Hot Spot for Advancement for Women/Minorities: Y

Manhattan Associates Inc

www.manh.com

NAIC Code: 511210A

TYPES OF BUSINESS:

Computer Software, Supply Chain & Logistics
Consulting & Support
RFID System Integration
Consulting Services

BRANDS/DIVISIONS/AFFILIATES:

CONTACTS:
Note: Officers with more than one job title may be intentionally listed here more than once.

Eddie Capel, CEO
Dennis Story, CFO
John Huntz, Chairman of the Board
Linda Pinne, Chief Accounting Officer
Bruce Richards, Chief Legal Officer
Deepak Raghavan, Co-Founder
Robert Howell, Senior VP, Geographical

GROWTH PLANS/SPECIAL FEATURES:

Manhattan Associates provides software that helps users manage their supply chains, inventory, and omnichannel operations. Customers are generally retailers, wholesalers, manufacturers, and logistics providers. The company was founded in 1990 and serves more than 1,200 customers around the world.

FINANCIAL DATA:
Note: Data for latest year may not have been available at press time.

In U.S. $	2021	2020	2019	2018	2017	2016
Revenue		586,372,000	617,949,000	559,157,000	594,599,000	604,557,000
R&D Expense		84,276,000	87,608,000	71,896,000	57,704,000	54,736,000
Operating Income		114,061,000	115,924,000	133,887,000	188,566,000	194,307,000
Operating Margin %						
SGA Expense		109,202,000	121,463,000	103,880,000	93,536,000	96,545,000
Net Income		87,240,000	85,762,000	104,690,000	116,481,000	124,234,000
Operating Cash Flow		140,885,000	146,908,000	137,349,000	164,066,000	139,346,000
Capital Expenditure		2,730,000	15,193,000	7,306,000	6,199,000	6,843,000
EBITDA		123,007,000	123,911,000	142,500,000	197,626,000	203,397,000
Return on Assets %						
Return on Equity %						
Debt to Equity						

CONTACT INFORMATION:

Phone: 770 955-7070 Fax: 770 995-0302
Toll-Free:
Address: 2300 Windy Ridge Pkwy., 10/Fl, Atlanta, GA 30339 United States

STOCK TICKER/OTHER:

Stock Ticker: MANH
Employees: 3,400
Parent Company:
Exchange: NAS
Fiscal Year Ends: 12/31

SALARIES/BONUSES:

Top Exec. Salary: $503,750 Bonus: $
Second Exec. Salary: $380,738 Bonus: $

OTHER THOUGHTS:

Estimated Female Officers or Directors:
Hot Spot for Advancement for Women/Minorities:

Marketo

NAIC Code: 541810E

www.marketo.com

TYPES OF BUSINESS:

Advertising Agency
Marketing Automation Software
Email Marketing Solutions
Lead Management Solutions
Revenue Attribution Solutions
Experience Automation
Data and Analytic Technology
Cross-channel Engagement

BRANDS/DIVISIONS/AFFILIATES:

Adobe Inc
Adobe Marketo Engage

GROWTH PLANS/SPECIAL FEATURES:

Marketo is a software-as-a-service (SaaS)-based marketing automation software owned by Adobe, Inc. The Adobe Marketo Engage platform offers measurable results from acquisition to advocacy with experiences that engage customers. It comprises marketing automation, email marketing, lead management and revenue attribution solutions. Marketo Engage powers experiences for customers such as Fujitsu, Roche, Cloudera, CenturyLink, RingCentral, Panasonic, BetterCloud, Mitel, Citrix and others. Marketo Engage enables content personalization, experience automation, marketing impact analytics, marketing data environment, sales partnership and cross-channel engagement.

CONTACTS: *Note: Officers with more than one job title may be intentionally listed here more than once.*

Steven Winter, Executive VP, Divisional
Shantanu Narayen, Chmn.-Adobe

FINANCIAL DATA: *Note: Data for latest year may not have been available at press time.*

In U.S. $	2021	2020	2019	2018	2017	2016
Revenue	380,000,000	355,000,000	330,000,000	321,000,000	288,000,000	248,000,000
R&D Expense						
Operating Income						
Operating Margin %						
SGA Expense						
Net Income						
Operating Cash Flow						
Capital Expenditure						
EBITDA						
Return on Assets %						
Return on Equity %						
Debt to Equity						

CONTACT INFORMATION:

Phone: 650-376-2300 Fax: 650-376-2331
Toll-Free: 877-260-6586
Address: 901 Mariners Island Blvd., Ste. 200, San Mateo, CA 94404 United States

STOCK TICKER/OTHER:

Stock Ticker: Subsidiary
Employees: 720
Parent Company: Adobe Inc
Exchange:
Fiscal Year Ends:

SALARIES/BONUSES:

Top Exec. Salary: $ Bonus: $
Second Exec. Salary: $ Bonus: $

OTHER THOUGHTS:

Estimated Female Officers or Directors: 2
Hot Spot for Advancement for Women/Minorities: Y

Marvell Technology Group Ltd

www.marvell.com

NAIC Code: 334413

TYPES OF BUSINESS:

Semiconductor Manufacturing
Storage Technology
Broadband Technology
Wireless Technology
Power Management Technology
Switching Technology

GROWTH PLANS/SPECIAL FEATURES:

Marvell Technology is a leading fabless chipmaker focused on networking and storage applications. Marvell serves the data center, carrier, enterprise, automotive, and consumer end markets with processors, optical interconnections, application-specific integrated circuits (ASICs), and merchant silicon for Ethernet applications. The firm is an active acquirer, with five large acquisitions since 2017 helping it pivot out of legacy consumer applications to focus on the cloud and 5G markets.

BRANDS/DIVISIONS/AFFILIATES:

OCTEON
OCTEON Fusion-M
NITROX
LiquidIO Server Adapter
ThunderX
Inphi Corporation
Innovium Inc

CONTACTS: *Note: Officers with more than one job title may be intentionally listed here more than once.*

Matt Murphy, CEO
Andy Micallef, COO
Jean Hu, CFO
Dean Jarnac, Sr. VP-Global Sales
Janice Hall, Sr. VP-Human Resources
Pantas Sutardja, Chief R&D Officer
Chris Koopmans, Exec. VP-Mktg.& Bus. Oper.
Gani Jusuf, VP-Prod. Dev., Comm., & Consumer Bus. Group
Yosef Meyouhas, VP-Enterprise Bus. Unit Eng., Marvell Israel
Tom Savage, VP-Worldwide Legal Affairs
James Laufman, General Counsel
Albert Wu, VP-Oper.
Sukhi Nagesh, VP-Investor Rel.
Chris Chang, VP-Greater China Bus.
Bouchung Lin, VP
Renu Bhatia, VP-Sales, Strategic Partnerships
Gaurav Shah, Gen. Mgr.-Digital Entertainment Bus.
Hoo Kuong, VP

FINANCIAL DATA: *Note: Data for latest year may not have been available at press time.*

In U.S. $	2021	2020	2019	2018	2017	2016
Revenue	2,968,900,000	2,699,161,000	2,865,791,000	2,409,170,000	2,317,674,000	2,725,828,000
R&D Expense	1,072,740,000	1,080,391,000	914,009,000	714,444,000	831,398,000	1,054,257,000
Operating Income	-51,630,000	-188,030,000	120,023,000	509,330,000	205,180,000	-108,821,000
Operating Margin %						
SGA Expense	467,240,000	464,580,000	424,360,000	238,166,000	243,193,000	274,908,000
Net Income	-277,298,000	1,584,391,000	-179,094,000	520,831,000	21,151,000	-811,400,000
Operating Cash Flow	817,287,000	360,297,000	596,744,000	571,113,000	-358,435,000	205,352,000
Capital Expenditure	119,506,000	86,633,000	87,461,000	45,138,000	54,819,000	55,731,000
EBITDA	388,624,000	1,408,753,000	363,016,000	538,946,000	235,876,000	-685,484,000
Return on Assets %						
Return on Equity %						
Debt to Equity						

CONTACT INFORMATION:

Phone: 441 2966395 Fax: 441 2924720
Toll-Free:
Address: Victoria Place, 5/Fl, 31 Victoria St., Hamilton, HM 10 Bermuda

STOCK TICKER/OTHER:

Stock Ticker: MRVL
Employees: 5,340
Parent Company:
Exchange: NAS
Fiscal Year Ends: 01/31

SALARIES/BONUSES:

Top Exec. Salary: $934,615 Bonus: $
Second Exec. Salary: $567,308 Bonus: $

OTHER THOUGHTS:

Estimated Female Officers or Directors: 2
Hot Spot for Advancement for Women/Minorities:

Maxar Technologies Inc

NAIC Code: 334220

www.maxar.com

TYPES OF BUSINESS:

Radio and Television Broadcasting and Wireless Communications Equipment Manufacturing
Earth Intelligence
Space Infrastructure
Geospatial Applications
Surveillance Solutions
Communications
Robotics

BRANDS/DIVISIONS/AFFILIATES:

GROWTH PLANS/SPECIAL FEATURES:

Maxar Technologies Inc is an integrated space and geospatial intelligence company with a full range of space technology solutions for commercial and government customers including satellites, Earth imagery, geospatial data and analytics.

Maxar offers its employees comprehensive health coverage, 401(k) and reimbursement programs.

CONTACTS: *Note: Officers with more than one job title may be intentionally listed here more than once.*

Daniel Jablonsky, CEO
Biggs Porter, CFO
Howell Estes, Chairman of the Board
Carolyn Pittman, Chief Accounting Officer
Nancy Coleman, Chief Marketing Officer
Walter Scott, Chief Technology Officer
Leon Frazier, Executive VP, Divisional
James Lee, General Counsel
Elizabeth Andora, Other Executive Officer
Jeffrey Culwell, Other Executive Officer
E. Robertson, Other Executive Officer

FINANCIAL DATA: *Note: Data for latest year may not have been available at press time.*

In U.S. $	2021	2020	2019	2018	2017	2016
Revenue		1,723,000,000	1,666,000,000	2,141,000,000	1,631,200,000	1,535,439,000
R&D Expense						
Operating Income		50,000,000	-10,000,000	-95,000,000	151,700,000	171,333,200
Operating Margin %						
SGA Expense		332,000,000	325,000,000	507,000,000	650,700,000	572,964,800
Net Income		303,000,000	109,000,000	-1,264,000,000	100,400,000	103,880,700
Operating Cash Flow		189,000,000	317,000,000	139,000,000	205,900,000	128,530,600
Capital Expenditure		308,000,000	314,000,000	218,000,000	126,600,000	99,228,480
EBITDA		447,000,000	650,000,000	-677,000,000	214,200,000	240,924,000
Return on Assets %						
Return on Equity %						
Debt to Equity						

CONTACT INFORMATION:

Phone: 303 684-2207 Fax:
Toll-Free:
Address: 1300 W. 120th Ave., Westminster, CO 80234 United States

STOCK TICKER/OTHER:

Stock Ticker: MAXR
Employees: 5,800
Parent Company:
Exchange: NYS
Fiscal Year Ends: 12/31

SALARIES/BONUSES:

Top Exec. Salary: $750,000 Bonus: $
Second Exec. Salary: $612,501 Bonus: $

OTHER THOUGHTS:

Estimated Female Officers or Directors:
Hot Spot for Advancement for Women/Minorities:

Maxim Integrated Products Inc

www.maximintegrated.com

NAIC Code: 334413

TYPES OF BUSINESS:

Integrated Circuits-Analog & Mixed Signal
High-Frequency Design Processes
Custom Manufacturing
Power Conversion Chips
Environmental Management & Monitoring Systems
Data Interface and Interconnection
Wireless & RF Receivers and Transmitters
Data Storage

BRANDS/DIVISIONS/AFFILIATES:

Analog Devices Inc

CONTACTS: *Note: Officers with more than one job title may be intentionally listed here more than once.*

TunÃ§ Doluca, CEO
Bruce Kiddoo, CFO
William Sullivan, Chairman of the Board
Edwin Medlin, General Counsel
Vivek Jain, Senior VP, Divisional
Christopher Neil, Senior VP, Divisional
Bryan Preeshl, Senior VP, Divisional
David Loftus, Vice President, Divisional

GROWTH PLANS/SPECIAL FEATURES:

Maxim Integrated Products, Inc. designs, develops, manufactures and markets analog and mixed-signal integrated circuits (ICs). Maxim's ICs connect the analog and digital world by detecting, measuring, amplifying and converting real-world signals into the digital signals necessary for computer processing. It produces electronic interface products to interact with people, through audio, video, touchpad, key pad and security devices; the physical world, through motion, time, temperature and humidity sensors; power sources, via conversion, charging, supervision and regulation systems; and other digital systems, including wireless, storage and fiber optic systems. Its products serve five major end-markets: automotive, which includes infotainment, powertrain, body electronics and safety/security products; communications and data center, which includes base station, data center, data storage, network/Datacom, server, telecom and other communications products; computing, including desktop computers, notebook computers, as well as peripherals and other computer products; consumer, including smartphones, digital cameras, handheld computers, home entertainment, appliances, mobility/fitness wearables and other consumer products; and industrial, including automatic test equipment, control/automation, electrical instrumentation, financial terminals, medical, military/aerospace, security, utility/meters and other industrial products. In August 2021, Analog Devices, Inc. completed its acquisition of Maxim Integrated Products.

FINANCIAL DATA: *Note: Data for latest year may not have been available at press time.*

In U.S. $	2021	2020	2019	2018	2017	2016
Revenue	2,279,050,874	2,191,395,072	2,314,329,088	2,480,066,048	2,295,614,976	2,194,718,976
R&D Expense						
Operating Income						
Operating Margin %						
SGA Expense						
Net Income		654,694,016	827,486,016	467,318,016	571,612,992	227,475,008
Operating Cash Flow						
Capital Expenditure						
EBITDA						
Return on Assets %						
Return on Equity %						
Debt to Equity						

CONTACT INFORMATION:

Phone: 408 601-1000 Fax: 408 737-7194
Toll-Free:
Address: 160 Rio Robles, San Jose, CA 95134 United States

STOCK TICKER/OTHER:

Stock Ticker: Subsidiary
Exchange:
Employees: 7,115
Fiscal Year Ends: 06/30
Parent Company: Analog Devices Inc

SALARIES/BONUSES:

Top Exec. Salary: $ Bonus: $
Second Exec. Salary: $ Bonus: $

OTHER THOUGHTS:

Estimated Female Officers or Directors: 1
Hot Spot for Advancement for Women/Minorities:

Mazda Motor Corporation

www.mazda.com

NAIC Code: 336111

TYPES OF BUSINESS:

Automobile Manufacturing
Commercial Vans & Trucks
Hydrogen Engine Technology

BRANDS/DIVISIONS/AFFILIATES:

Mazda
CX
Flair
Scrum
Carol
Bongo
Titan
Mazda BT-50

GROWTH PLANS/SPECIAL FEATURES:

Mazda Motor Corp is a Japanese automobile manufacturer. The company primarily manufactures passenger cars and commercial vehicles. Also, Mazda manufactures diesel and petroleum gasoline engines, along with manual and automatic transmissions for vehicles. The vast majority of Mazda's production is manufactured locally. The company segments itself across four geographic areas: Japan, North America, Europe, and other markets. The company derives more than half its consolidated revenue from operations in Japan, followed by North America, and then Europe.

CONTACTS: *Note: Officers with more than one job title may be intentionally listed here more than once.*

Akira Marumoto, CEO
Masamichi Kogai, Pres.
Kiyoshi Fujiwara, Gen. Mgr.-R&D
Masafumi Nakano, Managing Exec. Officer-Prod. & Brand Quality
Kiyotaka Shobuda, Gen. Mgr.-Eng.
Koji Kurosawa, Sec.
Akira Marumoto, Exec. VP-Corp. Planning & American Oper.
Yuji Nakamine, Sr. Managing Exec. Officer-Corp. Comm.
Seita Kanai, Vice Chmn.
Nobuhide Inamoto, Sr. Managing Exec. Officer-China & Domestic Sales
Koji Kurosawa, Pres.
Keishi Egawa, Managing Exec. Officer-Latin America
Yuji Nakamine, Sr. Managing Exec. Officer-EMEA, Asia & Oceania
Kazuki Imai, Managing Exec. Officer-Purchasing

FINANCIAL DATA: *Note: Data for latest year may not have been available at press time.*

In U.S. $	2021	2020	2019	2018	2017	2016
Revenue	25,324,820,000	30,142,040,000	31,323,120,000	30,526,380,000	28,244,730,000	29,933,940,000
R&D Expense						
Operating Income	77,501,660	383,141,200	729,438,300	1,286,607,000	1,104,416,000	1,992,680,000
Operating Margin %						
SGA Expense						
Net Income	-278,118,500	106,595,500	557,766,000	984,649,000	824,048,300	1,181,145,000
Operating Cash Flow	1,054,954,000	306,087,600	1,288,970,000	1,825,902,000	1,415,565,000	2,308,970,000
Capital Expenditure	756,027,900	1,075,164,000	1,060,182,000	871,524,700	788,258,800	773,953,400
EBITDA	878,712,400	1,297,696,000	1,780,790,000	2,213,279,000	1,935,011,000	2,274,235,000
Return on Assets %						
Return on Equity %						
Debt to Equity						

CONTACT INFORMATION:

Phone: 81 822821111 Fax:
Toll-Free:
Address: 3-1 Shinchi, Fuchu-cho, Aki-gun, Hiroshima, 100-0011 Japan

STOCK TICKER/OTHER:

Stock Ticker: MZDAF
Employees: 49,998
Parent Company:
Exchange: PINX
Fiscal Year Ends: 03/31

SALARIES/BONUSES:

Top Exec. Salary: $ Bonus: $
Second Exec. Salary: $ Bonus: $

OTHER THOUGHTS:

Estimated Female Officers or Directors:
Hot Spot for Advancement for Women/Minorities:

McAfee Corp

www.mcafee.com

NAIC Code: 511210E

TYPES OF BUSINESS:

Computer Software: Network Security, Managed Access, Digital ID, Cybersecurity & Anti-Virus
Virus Protection Software
Network Management Software
Cybersecurity
Malware Protection

BRANDS/DIVISIONS/AFFILIATES:

Foundation Technology Worldwide LLC
McAfee LLC
McAfee Global Threat Intelligence
MVISION Device

GROWTH PLANS/SPECIAL FEATURES:

McAfee Corp is a device-to-cloud cybersecurity company. It is engaged in protecting consumers, enterprises, and governments from cyberattacks with integrated security, privacy, and trust solutions. The company's Personal Protection Service provides holistic digital protection for an individual or family at home, on the go, and on the web. Its platform includes device security, privacy and safe Wi-Fi, online protection, and identity protection, creating a seamless and integrated digital moat. It operating segment include Consumer and Enterprise of which consumer derives a majority revenue to the company.

CONTACTS: *Note: Officers with more than one job title may be intentionally listed here more than once.*

Peter Leav, CEO
Venkat Bhamidipati, CFO
Christine Kornegay, Chief Accounting Officer
Lynne Doherty McDonald, Executive VP, Divisional
Gagan Singh, Executive VP
Ashish Agarwal, Senior VP, Divisional

FINANCIAL DATA: *Note: Data for latest year may not have been available at press time.*

In U.S. $	2021	2020	2019	2018	2017	2016
Revenue	1,920,000,000	1,558,000,000	1,303,000,000	2,408,999,936	2,076,000,000	2,387,000,000
R&D Expense						
Operating Income						
Operating Margin %						
SGA Expense						
Net Income	2,688,000,000	-289,000,000	-236,000,000	-512,000,000	-686,000,000	-95,000,000
Operating Cash Flow						
Capital Expenditure						
EBITDA						
Return on Assets %						
Return on Equity %						
Debt to Equity						

CONTACT INFORMATION:

Phone: 866-622-3911 Fax:
Toll-Free:
Address: 6220 America Center Dr., San Jose, CA 95002 United States

STOCK TICKER/OTHER:

Stock Ticker: Private
Employees: 6,916
Parent Company: Advent International Corp
Exchange:
Fiscal Year Ends: 12/31

SALARIES/BONUSES:

Top Exec. Salary: $ Bonus: $
Second Exec. Salary: $ Bonus: $

OTHER THOUGHTS:

Estimated Female Officers or Directors: 3
Hot Spot for Advancement for Women/Minorities: Y

MediaTek Inc

NAIC Code: 334413

www.mediatek.com

TYPES OF BUSINESS:

Semiconductor Manufacturing
Digital Media Products
IC Design & Engineering Services

BRANDS/DIVISIONS/AFFILIATES:

MediaTek Helio
MediaTek MiraVision Pro
Dimensity 5G
MediaTek Labs
AOMedia Video 1
mmWAVE

GROWTH PLANS/SPECIAL FEATURES:

MediaTek is a fabless semiconductor designer focusing on solutions for smartphones, digital televisions, and connectivity products. The business is divided into four segments. The first is "mobile," which accounts for half of sales, where MediaTek is the second- largest third-party supplier of smartphone SoCs to the likes of Xiaomi and Vivo. The second is the "Internet of Things, ASIC, computing segment" that includes chips for a wide product line ranging from gaming to data centers. The third is "smart home" that mainly includes SoCs for TVs. The fourth is "power IC" that includes power management products for mobile devices, data centers, connectivity devices and more. Mediatek is headquartered in Hsinchu, Taiwan.

CONTACTS: *Note: Officers with more than one job title may be intentionally listed here more than once.*

Ming-Kai Tsai, CEO
Kuan-Chou Chen, Pres.
Wei-Fu Hsu, General Counsel
Oliver Chow, Chief Strategy Officer
Sophia Liang, Dir.-Investor Rel.
Jyh-Jer Cho, Vice Chmn.
Ping-Hsing Lu, VP
Chwei-Huang Chang, VP
Kou-Hung Loh, VP
Ming-Kai Tsai, Chmn.

FINANCIAL DATA: *Note: Data for latest year may not have been available at press time.*

In U.S. $	2021	2020	2019	2018	2017	2016
Revenue		11,610,700,000	8,874,263,000	8,580,003,000	8,585,733,000	9,929,925,000
R&D Expense		2,786,922,000	2,270,681,000	2,074,158,000	2,060,535,000	2,006,994,000
Operating Income		1,557,989,000	812,803,500	574,985,500	353,899,100	831,691,300
Operating Margin %						
SGA Expense		756,276,900	630,456,300	656,738,300	645,001,900	700,248,400
Net Income		1,474,713,000	830,139,600	748,244,700	876,989,600	854,211,100
Operating Cash Flow		2,867,415,000	1,535,593,000	733,191,600	769,435,000	1,173,077,000
Capital Expenditure		369,169,900	286,470,600	245,202,100	210,818,300	253,668,600
EBITDA		2,093,260,000	1,335,069,000	1,188,874,000	1,275,415,000	1,249,491,000
Return on Assets %						
Return on Equity %						
Debt to Equity						

CONTACT INFORMATION:

Phone: 886-3-567-0766 Fax: 886-3-578-7610
Toll-Free:
Address: No. 1, Dusing 1st Rd., Hsinchu Science Park, Hsinchu City, 30078 Taiwan

STOCK TICKER/OTHER:

Stock Ticker: MDTKF
Employees: 3,237
Parent Company:
Exchange: PINX
Fiscal Year Ends: 12/31

SALARIES/BONUSES:

Top Exec. Salary: $ Bonus: $
Second Exec. Salary: $ Bonus: $

OTHER THOUGHTS:

Estimated Female Officers or Directors: 1
Hot Spot for Advancement for Women/Minorities:

Medical Information Technology Inc (MEDITECH)

www.meditech.com

NAIC Code: 511210D

TYPES OF BUSINESS:

Computer Software, Healthcare & Biotechnology

BRANDS/DIVISIONS/AFFILIATES:

Web EHR
Expanse

CONTACTS:

Note: Officers with more than one job title may be intentionally listed here more than once.

Michelle O'Connor, CEO
Barbara Manzolillo, CFO
Chris Anschuetz, VP-Tech.
Michelle O'Connor, Exec. VP-Prod. Dev.
Hoda Sayed-Friel, Exec. VP-Strategy & Mktg.
Barbara A. Manzolillo, Treas.
Robert Gale, Sr. VP-Prod. Dev.
Leah Farina, VP-Client Svcs. & Int'l
Scott Radner, VP-Advanced Tech.
A. Neil Pappalardo, Chmn.
Steven Koretz, Sr. VP- Int'l & Client Svcs.

GROWTH PLANS/SPECIAL FEATURES:

Medical Information Technology, Inc. (MEDITECH) develops and markets information system software for the health care industry. MEDITECH's software products automate a variety of hospital functions, and offer various solutions for long-term care facilities, ambulatory care centers, acute-care hospitals, emergency rooms and pharmacies, as well as imaging, therapeutic service and behavioral health facilities. The company specifies aggregate components for each hospital and suggests typical configurations from selected hardware vendors pertaining to software needs. The firm's solutions are accessible via desktop and mobile devices anywhere, any time. MEDITECH'S Web EHR (electronic health record) product offers a cohesive set of software designed to work in conjunction with the overall operation of the hospital. Web EHR facilitates over 300 billion data transactions per year. MEDITECH as a Services (MaaS) is a cloud-based subscription model that powers the firm's Expanse next-generation EHR web platform. The firm's software products will automate clinical laboratory departments, which perform diagnostic tests; and automate hospital billing, accounts receivable and general accounting. MEDITECH's primary international subsidiary locations are based in Canada, Asia Pacific, South Africa, the U.K. and Ireland.

MEDITECH offers its employees health and dental insurance, group life and accidental insurance, short- and long-term disability insurance, as well as a variety of company incentives and perks.

FINANCIAL DATA:

Note: Data for latest year may not have been available at press time.

In U.S. $	2021	2020	2019	2018	2017	2016
Revenue	515,000,000	502,851,197	493,844,632	488,188,746	480,256,468	462,256,468
R&D Expense						
Operating Income						
Operating Margin %						
SGA Expense						
Net Income		74,542,923	180,157,193	56,205,796	77,428,576	72,890,198
Operating Cash Flow						
Capital Expenditure						
EBITDA						
Return on Assets %						
Return on Equity %						
Debt to Equity						

CONTACT INFORMATION:

Phone: 781-821-3000 Fax: 781-821-2199
Toll-Free:
Address: Meditech Circle, Westwood, MA 02090 United States

STOCK TICKER/OTHER:

Stock Ticker: Private
Employees: 3,700
Parent Company:
Exchange:
Fiscal Year Ends: 12/31

SALARIES/BONUSES:

Top Exec. Salary: $ Bonus: $
Second Exec. Salary: $ Bonus: $

OTHER THOUGHTS:

Estimated Female Officers or Directors: 10
Hot Spot for Advancement for Women/Minorities: Y

Mercedes-Benz Group AG

group.mercedes-benz.com/en

NAIC Code: 336111

TYPES OF BUSINESS:

Automobile Manufacturing
Financial Services & Insurance
Commercial Vehicles, Trucks & Buses
Aerospace & Defense Technology
Automotive Manufacture
Vehicle Distribution
Vehicle Development

BRANDS/DIVISIONS/AFFILIATES:

Mercedes-Benz
Daimler
Maybach
Freightliner
BharatBenz
car2go
Citan
eActros

GROWTH PLANS/SPECIAL FEATURES:

Based in Stuttgart, Germany, Mercedes-Benz Group AG makes premium passenger vehicles, commercial trucks and vans, and buses. Brands include Mercedes-Benz, AMG, Maybach, Freightliner, Western Star, Fuso, Thomas Built, BharatBenz, Setra, and Orion. Daimler Mobility provides the company's dealers and its customers with vehicle financing as well as mobility services in ride hailing, car sharing, and charging. Daimler owns 3.0% each of Renault and Nissan, 11.9% of Aston Martin, 15.0% of Russian truck maker Kamaz, and 9.6% of Beijing Automotive Group. Li Shufu, chairman of Chinese automaker Geely Automobile, owns 9.7% of Daimler. Other major shareholders include Kuwait Investment Authority at 6.8%, Beijing Automotive group at 5.0%, and Nissan at 1.5%.

CONTACTS: *Note: Officers with more than one job title may be intentionally listed here more than once.*

Thomas Weber, Dir.-Group Research
Andreas Renschler, Dir.-Mfg.
Cristine Hohmann-Dennhardt, Dir.-Legal Affairs & Integrity
Bodo Uebber, Dir.-Controlling
Thomas Weber, Dir.-Mercedes-Benz Cars Dev.
Wolfgang Bernhard, Dir.-Trucks
Bernd Pischetsrieder, Chmn.
Andreas Renschler, Dir.-Procurement

FINANCIAL DATA: *Note: Data for latest year may not have been available at press time.*

In U.S. $	2021	2020	2019	2018	2017	2016
Revenue		174,267,900,000	195,088,500,000	189,009,200,000	185,585,100,000	173,084,300,000
R&D Expense		6,907,066,000	7,437,858,000	7,432,211,000	6,706,043,000	5,936,960,000
Operating Income		6,945,464,000	4,548,997,000	11,358,940,000	14,663,400,000	13,635,700,000
Operating Margin %						
SGA Expense		16,479,380,000	19,030,570,000	19,315,170,000	18,943,610,000	17,668,580,000
Net Income		4,096,130,000	2,684,450,000	8,186,613,000	11,886,340,000	9,628,785,000
Operating Cash Flow		25,220,510,000	8,908,263,000	387,364,900	-1,865,676,000	4,190,995,000
Capital Expenditure		9,667,183,000	12,236,440,000	12,085,110,000	11,471,870,000	9,975,494,000
EBITDA		17,821,040,000	14,072,750,000	19,981,480,000	23,218,180,000	21,003,540,000
Return on Assets %						
Return on Equity %						
Debt to Equity						

CONTACT INFORMATION:

Phone: 49 7111792543 Fax: 49 7111794116
Toll-Free:
Address: Mercedesstrasse 137, Stuttgart, 70372 Germany

STOCK TICKER/OTHER:

Stock Ticker: DMLRY
Employees: 298,655
Parent Company:
Exchange: PINX
Fiscal Year Ends: 12/31

SALARIES/BONUSES:

Top Exec. Salary: $ Bonus: $
Second Exec. Salary: $ Bonus: $

OTHER THOUGHTS:

Estimated Female Officers or Directors: 6
Hot Spot for Advancement for Women/Minorities: Y

Mesa Laboratories Inc

www.mesalabs.com

NAIC Code: 334513

TYPES OF BUSINESS:

Instruments and Related Products Manufacturing for Measuring, Displaying, and Controlling Industrial Process Variables
Manufacturing
Hygiene
Quality Control Products
Sterilization
Disposable Products
Biopharmaceutical Development

BRANDS/DIVISIONS/AFFILIATES:

GROWTH PLANS/SPECIAL FEATURES:

Mesa Laboratories Inc provides control products and services. Its Instruments division manufactures quality-control instruments and disposable products for the pharmaceutical, food and beverage, medical device, industrial hygiene, air sampling, and semiconductor industries. The Sterilization and disinfection control division provides testing services, as well as biological and chemical indicators used to assess the efficacy of sterilization and disinfection processes. The Continuous monitoring division designs, develops and markets systems used to monitor environmental parameters, such as temperature and humidity. The biopharmaceutical development division develops and manufactures automated systems for protein analysis. The company generates most of the revenue from the United States.

CONTACTS: *Note: Officers with more than one job title may be intentionally listed here more than once.*

Gary Owens, CEO
John Sakys, CFO
John Sullivan, Chairman of the Board
Greg DiNoia, Senior VP, Divisional
Brian Archbold, Senior VP, Divisional

FINANCIAL DATA: *Note: Data for latest year may not have been available at press time.*

In U.S. $	2021	2020	2019	2018	2017	2016
Revenue	133,937,000	117,687,000	103,135,000	96,179,000	93,665,000	84,659,000
R&D Expense	10,388,000	6,355,000	3,506,000	3,539,000	4,157,000	3,972,000
Operating Income	12,449,000	7,842,000	17,855,000	16,002,000	16,313,000	16,323,000
Operating Margin %						
SGA Expense	64,177,000	50,736,000	39,555,000	35,078,000	32,769,000	31,118,000
Net Income	3,274,000	1,349,000	7,484,000	-2,962,000	11,183,000	11,169,000
Operating Cash Flow	37,073,000	26,559,000	30,554,000	24,814,000	7,750,000	16,903,000
Capital Expenditure	1,992,000	1,498,000	1,262,000	2,799,000	11,605,000	7,729,000
EBITDA	27,987,000	21,927,000	27,283,000	25,473,000	25,050,000	23,497,000
Return on Assets %						
Return on Equity %						
Debt to Equity						

CONTACT INFORMATION:

Phone: 303 987-8000 Fax: 303 987-8989
Toll-Free:
Address: 12100 W. Sixth Ave., Lakewood, CO 80228 United States

STOCK TICKER/OTHER:

Stock Ticker: MLAB
Employees: 506
Parent Company:
Exchange: NAS
Fiscal Year Ends: 03/31

SALARIES/BONUSES:

Top Exec. Salary: $523,846 Bonus: $
Second Exec. Salary: $342,354 Bonus: $

OTHER THOUGHTS:

Estimated Female Officers or Directors:
Hot Spot for Advancement for Women/Minorities:

Micro Focus International Plc

www.microfocus.com

NAIC Code: 511210H

TYPES OF BUSINESS:

Computer Software, Business Management & ERP
Enterprise Software
Mission-Critical
Digital Transformation
Big Data
Analytics
Application Management
Team Collaboration

BRANDS/DIVISIONS/AFFILIATES:

GROWTH PLANS/SPECIAL FEATURES:

Micro Focus International PLC is a United Kingdom-based provider of software solutions. Its software portfolio includes identity access and security solutions, COBOL development and mainframe solutions, development and IT operations management tools, host connectivity solutions, collaboration and networking solutions, software-defined storage, and enterprise Linux solutions. The firm helps organizations install, operate, and improve IT infrastructure and business applications. Its clients span a variety of industries, including healthcare, airlines, and the public sector.

CONTACTS: *Note: Officers with more than one job title may be intentionally listed here more than once.*

Stephen Murdock, CEO
Paul Rodgers, COO
Matt Ashley, CFO
Eric Varness, CMO
Susan Ferguson, Chief Human Resources Officer
Greg Lock, Chmn.

FINANCIAL DATA: *Note: Data for latest year may not have been available at press time.*

In U.S. $	2021	2020	2019	2018	2017	2016
Revenue		3,001,000,000	3,348,400,000	3,208,676,000	1,380,702,000	1,245,049,000
R&D Expense		513,600,000	491,200,000	458,362,000	180,104,000	259,388,000
Operating Income		-2,661,400,000	221,700,000	578,774,000	293,443,000	294,934,000
Operating Margin %						
SGA Expense		4,446,100,000	1,845,600,000	1,470,713,000	669,986,000	555,295,000
Net Income		-2,969,500,000	1,468,800,000	726,234,000	157,906,000	162,894,000
Operating Cash Flow		678,200,000	661,800,000	364,426,000	452,379,000	284,641,000
Capital Expenditure		86,900,000	85,600,000	122,500,000	43,165,000	44,769,000
EBITDA		-1,956,300,000	978,700,000	872,893,000	526,294,000	493,489,000
Return on Assets %						
Return on Equity %						
Debt to Equity						

CONTACT INFORMATION:

Phone: 44 1635565200 Fax: 44 163533966
Toll-Free:
Address: The Lawn, 22-30 Old Bath Rd., Newbury, Berkshire RG14 1QN United Kingdom

STOCK TICKER/OTHER:

Stock Ticker: MFGP
Employees: 12,100
Parent Company:
Exchange: NYS
Fiscal Year Ends: 04/30

SALARIES/BONUSES:

Top Exec. Salary: $1,131,779 Bonus: $376,816
Second Exec. Salary: $798,903 Bonus: $264,969

OTHER THOUGHTS:

Estimated Female Officers or Directors:
Hot Spot for Advancement for Women/Minorities:

Microchip Technology Incorporated

www.microchip.com

NAIC Code: 334413

TYPES OF BUSINESS:

Semiconductors-Specialized
Microcontrollers
Battery Management & Interface Devices
Development Tools
Memory Products

BRANDS/DIVISIONS/AFFILIATES:

SuperFlash
Smartbits

GROWTH PLANS/SPECIAL FEATURES:

Microchip became an independent company in 1989 when it was spun off from General Instrument. More than half of revenue comes from MCUs, which are used in a wide array of electronic devices from remote controls to garage door openers to power windows in autos. The company's strength lies in lower-end 8-bit MCUs that are suitable for a wider range of less technologically advanced devices, but the firm has expanded its presence in higher-end MCUs and analog chips as well.

Microchip offers its employees health benefits, and shared profit and training opportunities.

CONTACTS: *Note: Officers with more than one job title may be intentionally listed here more than once.*

Ganesh Moorthy, CEO
J. Bjornholt, CFO
Steve Sanghi, Chairman of the Board
Mitchell Little, Senior VP, Divisional
Richard Simoncic, Senior VP, Divisional
Stephen Drehobl, Senior VP, Divisional

FINANCIAL DATA: *Note: Data for latest year may not have been available at press time.*

In U.S. $	2021	2020	2019	2018	2017	2016
Revenue	5,438,400,000	5,274,200,000	5,349,500,000	3,980,800,000	3,407,807,000	2,173,334,000
R&D Expense	836,400,000	877,800,000	826,300,000	529,300,000	545,293,000	372,596,000
Operating Income	999,800,000	693,800,000	748,000,000	953,800,000	374,425,000	356,302,000
Operating Margin %						
SGA Expense	610,300,000	676,600,000	682,900,000	452,100,000	499,811,000	301,670,000
Net Income	349,400,000	570,600,000	355,900,000	255,400,000	164,639,000	324,132,000
Operating Cash Flow	1,916,500,000	1,543,800,000	1,674,800,000	1,419,600,000	1,059,452,000	744,483,000
Capital Expenditure	92,600,000	67,600,000	228,900,000	206,800,000	75,310,000	97,895,000
EBITDA	1,849,700,000	1,863,300,000	1,583,800,000	1,552,200,000	705,341,000	668,482,000
Return on Assets %						
Return on Equity %						
Debt to Equity						

CONTACT INFORMATION:

Phone: 480 792-7200 Fax: 480 899-9210
Toll-Free:
Address: 2355 W. Chandler Blvd., Chandler, AZ 85224-6199 United States

STOCK TICKER/OTHER:

Stock Ticker: MCHP
Employees: 19,500
Parent Company:
Exchange: NAS
Fiscal Year Ends: 02/28

SALARIES/BONUSES:

Top Exec. Salary: $702,087 Bonus: $22,086
Second Exec. Salary: $421,014 Bonus: $12,792

OTHER THOUGHTS:

Estimated Female Officers or Directors: 3
Hot Spot for Advancement for Women/Minorities: Y

Micron Technology Inc

NAIC Code: 334413

www.micron.com

TYPES OF BUSINESS:

Components-Semiconductor Memory
Storage
Memory
Artificial Intelligence
5G
Machine Learning
Autonomous
Security

BRANDS/DIVISIONS/AFFILIATES:

3D Xpoint
Authenta

GROWTH PLANS/SPECIAL FEATURES:

Micron historically focused on designing and manufacturing DRAM for PCs and servers. The firm then expanded into the NAND flash memory market. It increased its DRAM scale with the purchase of Elpida (completed in mid-2013) and Inotera (completed in December 2016). The firm's DRAM and NAND products tailored to PCs, data centers, smartphones, game consoles, automotives, and other computing devices.

Micron offers its employees health insurance, a retirement plan, a stock purchase program, tuition support, training and more.

CONTACTS: *Note: Officers with more than one job title may be intentionally listed here more than once.*

Sanjay Mehrotra, CEO
David Zinsner, CFO
Robert Switz, Chairman of the Board
Scott Allen, Chief Accounting Officer
Scott Deboer, Executive VP, Divisional
Manish Bhatia, Executive VP, Divisional
Sumit Sadana, Executive VP
April Arnzen, Other Executive Officer
Michael Bokan, Senior VP, Divisional
Joel Poppen, Senior VP, Divisional

FINANCIAL DATA: *Note: Data for latest year may not have been available at press time.*

In U.S. $	2021	2020	2019	2018	2017	2016
Revenue	27,705,000,000	21,435,000,000	23,406,000,000	30,391,000,000	20,322,000,000	12,399,000,000
R&D Expense	2,663,000,000	2,600,000,000	2,441,000,000	2,141,000,000	1,824,000,000	1,617,000,000
Operating Income	6,747,000,000	3,060,000,000	7,390,000,000	14,926,000,000	5,864,000,000	231,000,000
Operating Margin %						
SGA Expense	894,000,000	881,000,000	836,000,000	813,000,000	743,000,000	659,000,000
Net Income	5,861,000,000	2,687,000,000	6,313,000,000	14,135,000,000	5,089,000,000	-276,000,000
Operating Cash Flow	12,468,000,000	8,306,000,000	13,189,000,000	17,400,000,000	8,153,000,000	3,168,000,000
Capital Expenditure	10,030,000,000	8,223,000,000	9,780,000,000	8,879,000,000	4,734,000,000	5,817,000,000
EBITDA	12,615,000,000	8,827,000,000	12,600,000,000	19,408,000,000	9,658,000,000	3,136,000,000
Return on Assets %						
Return on Equity %						
Debt to Equity						

CONTACT INFORMATION:

Phone: 208 368-4000 Fax: 208 368-4435
Toll-Free:
Address: 8000 S. Federal Way, Boise, ID 83716-9632 United States

STOCK TICKER/OTHER:

Stock Ticker: MU
Employees: 40,000
Parent Company:
Exchange: NAS
Fiscal Year Ends: 08/31

SALARIES/BONUSES:

Top Exec. Salary: $1,369,039 Bonus: $
Second Exec. Salary: $755,173 Bonus: $

OTHER THOUGHTS:

Estimated Female Officers or Directors: 2
Hot Spot for Advancement for Women/Minorities:

Microsoft Corporation

www.microsoft.com

NAIC Code: 511210H

TYPES OF BUSINESS:

Computer Software, Operating Systems, Languages & Development Tools
Enterprise Software
Game Consoles
Operating Systems
Software as a Service (SAAS)
Search Engine and Advertising
E-Mail Services
Instant Messaging

BRANDS/DIVISIONS/AFFILIATES:

Office 365
Exchange
SharePoint
Microsoft Teams
Skype for Business
Outlook.com
OneDrive
LinkedIn

GROWTH PLANS/SPECIAL FEATURES:

Microsoft develops and licenses consumer and enterprise software. It is known for its Windows operating systems and Office productivity suite. The company is organized into three equally sized broad segments: productivity and business processes (legacy Microsoft Office, cloud-based Office 365, Exchange, SharePoint, Skype, LinkedIn, Dynamics), intelligence cloud (infrastructure- and platform-as-a-service offerings Azure, Windows Server OS, SQL Server), and more personal computing (Windows Client, Xbox, Bing search, display advertising, and Surface laptops, tablets, and desktops).

Microsoft offers its employees comprehensive benefits, a 401(k) and employee stock purchase plans; and employee assistance programs.

CONTACTS: *Note: Officers with more than one job title may be intentionally listed here more than once.*

Satya Nadella, CEO
Amy Hood, CFO
Alice Jolla, Chief Accounting Officer
Bradford Smith, Chief Legal Officer
Christopher Capossela, Chief Marketing Officer
Christopher Young, Executive VP, Divisional
Kathleen Hogan, Executive VP, Divisional
Judson Althoff, Executive VP
Jean-Philippe Courtois, Executive VP

FINANCIAL DATA: *Note: Data for latest year may not have been available at press time.*

In U.S. $	2021	2020	2019	2018	2017	2016
Revenue	168,088,000,000	143,015,000,000	125,843,000,000	110,360,000,000	89,950,000,000	85,320,000,000
R&D Expense	20,716,000,000	19,269,000,000	16,876,000,000	14,726,000,000	13,037,000,000	11,988,000,000
Operating Income	69,916,000,000	52,959,000,000	42,959,000,000	35,058,000,000	22,632,000,000	21,292,000,000
Operating Margin %						
SGA Expense	25,224,000,000	24,709,000,000	23,098,000,000	22,223,000,000	20,020,000,000	19,260,000,000
Net Income	61,271,000,000	44,281,000,000	39,240,000,000	16,571,000,000	21,204,000,000	16,798,000,000
Operating Cash Flow	76,740,000,000	60,675,000,000	52,185,000,000	43,884,000,000	39,507,000,000	33,325,000,000
Capital Expenditure	20,622,000,000	15,441,000,000	13,925,000,000	11,632,000,000	8,129,000,000	8,343,000,000
EBITDA	85,134,000,000	68,423,000,000	58,056,000,000	49,468,000,000	34,149,000,000	27,616,000,000
Return on Assets %						
Return on Equity %						
Debt to Equity						

CONTACT INFORMATION:

Phone: 425 882-8080 Fax: 425 936-7329
Toll-Free: 800-642-7676
Address: One Microsoft Way, Redmond, WA 98052 United States

STOCK TICKER/OTHER:

Stock Ticker: MSFT
Employees: 163,000
Parent Company:
Exchange: NAS
Fiscal Year Ends: 06/30

SALARIES/BONUSES:

Top Exec. Salary: $541,875 Bonus: $3,500,000
Second Exec. Salary: $2,500,000 Bonus: $

OTHER THOUGHTS:

Estimated Female Officers or Directors: 4
Hot Spot for Advancement for Women/Minorities: Y

Mitsubishi Electric Corporation

www.mitsubishielectric.com

NAIC Code: 335311

TYPES OF BUSINESS:

Electrical and Electronic Equipment Manufacturer
Power Plant Manufacturing, Nuclear & Fossil
Wind & Solar Generation Systems
Consumer Electronics
Telecommunications & Computer Equipment
Industrial Automation Systems
Chips & Memory Devices
Semiconductors

BRANDS/DIVISIONS/AFFILIATES:

Mitsubishi Corporation

GROWTH PLANS/SPECIAL FEATURES:

Mitsubishi Electric Corporation is a general electric industrials conglomerate that develops, manufactures, distributes, and sells electrical equipment worldwide. The company's core segments include: industrial automation systems, energy and electric systems, electric devices, information and communication systems, and home appliances (which includes commercial A/C). Mitsubishi Electric was founded in 1921 and is headquartered in Tokyo, Japan.

CONTACTS: *Note: Officers with more than one job title may be intentionally listed here more than once.*

Kei Uruma, CEO
Tadashi Kawagoishi, CFO
Kuniaki Masuda, General Affairs and Human Resources
Kazuhiko Tsutsumi, Exec. Officer-R&D
Eiichiro Mitani, CIO
Masaharu Moriyaso, Exec. Officer-Total Productivity Mgmt.
Tsuyoshi Nakamura, Exec. Officer-Legal Affairs & Compliance
Noritomo Hashimoto, Sr. VP-Corp. Strategic Planning & Oper.
Takayuki Sueki, Exec. Officer-Global Strategic Planning & Mktg.
Masayuki Ichige, Exec. Officer-Govt & External & Public Rel.
Masayuki Ichige, Exec. Officer-Auditing
Yoshiaki Nakatani, Exec. Officer-Energy & Industrial Systems
Takashi Sasakawa, Exec. Officer-Electronic Systems
Mitsuo Muneyuki, Exec. VP-Export Control & Building Systems
Masaki Sakuyama, Exec. VP-Semiconductors & Device
Mitoji Yabunaka, Chmn.

FINANCIAL DATA: *Note: Data for latest year may not have been available at press time.*

In U.S. $	2021	2020	2019	2018	2017	2016
Revenue	36,830,280,000	39,212,230,000	39,716,710,000	38,937,100,000	37,245,320,000	38,613,340,000
R&D Expense				1,695,599,000	1,625,286,000	1,643,457,000
Operating Income	2,022,732,000	2,281,651,000	2,552,432,000	2,974,570,000	2,403,676,000	2,720,941,000
Operating Margin %						
SGA Expense	8,379,336,000	8,937,076,000	9,167,462,000	7,634,283,000	7,288,188,000	7,260,131,000
Net Income	1,697,058,000	1,949,264,000	1,991,564,000	2,389,020,000	1,849,610,000	2,007,785,000
Operating Cash Flow	4,763,620,000	3,478,208,000	2,107,281,000	2,112,843,000	3,215,616,000	3,222,004,000
Capital Expenditure	1,655,117,000	1,908,518,000	1,915,811,000	1,641,348,000	1,468,885,000	1,601,446,000
EBITDA	4,172,982,000	4,390,707,000	4,363,528,000	4,585,638,000	3,875,593,000	4,105,479,000
Return on Assets %						
Return on Equity %						
Debt to Equity						

CONTACT INFORMATION:

Phone: 81 332182111 Fax: 81 332182431
Toll-Free:
Address: Tokyo Bldg. 2-7-3 Marunouchi, Chiyoda-ku, Tokyo, 100-8310 Japan

STOCK TICKER/OTHER:

Stock Ticker: MIELY
Exchange: PINX
Employees: 146,518
Fiscal Year Ends: 03/31
Parent Company: Mitsubishi Corporation

SALARIES/BONUSES:

Top Exec. Salary: $ Bonus: $
Second Exec. Salary: $ Bonus: $

OTHER THOUGHTS:

Estimated Female Officers or Directors:
Hot Spot for Advancement for Women/Minorities:

Mitsubishi Motors Corporation

www.mitsubishi-motors.co.jp

NAIC Code: 336111

TYPES OF BUSINESS:

Automobile Manufacturing
Automobile Parts
Agricultural Machinery & Industrial Engines
Automotive Sales
Financial Services
Plug-In Hybrid Electric Vehicles
Electric Vehicles

BRANDS/DIVISIONS/AFFILIATES:

Nissan Motor Co Ltd
Mitsubishi Corporation
Renault-Nissan
Eclipse Cross
Xpander
Outlander
i-MiEV
eK

CONTACTS: *Note: Officers with more than one job title may be intentionally listed here more than once.*

Takao Kato, CEO
Ryugo Nakao, Managing Dir.-Prod. Projects & Strategy
Hiizu Ichikawa, Exec. VP-Corp. Planning
Shuichi Aoto, Managing Dir.-Corp. Affairs
Hiizu Ichikawa, Exec. VP-Finance
Shuichi Aoto, Chief Bus. Ethics Officer
Seiji Izumisawa, Head-Quality Affairs Group
Tomofumi Hiraku, Chmn.
Hiroshi Harunari, Exec. VP-Overseas Oper.
Shuichi Aoto, Head-Procurement Group

GROWTH PLANS/SPECIAL FEATURES:

Mitsubishi Motors is a Japanese automobile manufacturer. The company principally produces small passenger vehicles, electric and hybrid vehicles, and sport utility vehicles, or SUVs. Mitsubishi Motors is organised into two business segments: automobile business and automobile financing business. The company derives the vast majority of company revenue from the automotive business. Geographically, the company is separated into five regions: Japan, North America, Europe, Asia (excluding Japan), and other. With more than half of its products manufactures in Japan where it also generates the majority of its consolidated revenue, followed by Asia, and North America.

FINANCIAL DATA: *Note: Data for latest year may not have been available at press time.*

In U.S. $	2021	2020	2019	2018	2017	2016
Revenue	12,789,320,000	19,949,000,000	22,095,830,000	19,264,600,000	16,753,650,000	19,927,670,000
R&D Expense	491,986,200	648,711,800	579,241,500	492,654,000	506,827,500	395,522,100
Operating Income	-837,571,600	112,395,000	982,557,600	862,930,900	44,998,420	1,215,959,000
Operating Margin %						
SGA Expense	562,396,700	874,002,600	1,114,820,000	1,338,819,000	1,132,043,000	1,293,188,000
Net Income	-2,744,341,000	-226,521,000	1,167,542,000	945,652,100	-1,744,438,000	637,719,200
Operating Cash Flow	-364,987,100	165,073,300	1,283,373,000	1,051,140,000	-402,701,100	1,737,118,000
Capital Expenditure	807,177,200	1,136,858,000	1,217,558,000	735,896,800	597,553,700	606,305,600
EBITDA	-1,994,631,000	724,746,000	1,618,924,000	1,398,009,000	-972,856,800	1,486,160,000
Return on Assets %						
Return on Equity %						
Debt to Equity						

CONTACT INFORMATION:

Phone: 81 334561111 Fax:
Toll-Free:
Address: 1-21, Shibaura 3 chome, Minato-ku, Tokyo, 108-8410 Japan

STOCK TICKER/OTHER:

Stock Ticker: MMTOF
Employees: 44,042
Parent Company: Nissan Motor Co Ltd
Exchange: PINX
Fiscal Year Ends: 03/31

SALARIES/BONUSES:

Top Exec. Salary: $ Bonus: $
Second Exec. Salary: $ Bonus: $

OTHER THOUGHTS:

Estimated Female Officers or Directors:
Hot Spot for Advancement for Women/Minorities:

MKS Instruments Inc

www.mksinst.com

NAIC Code: 334513

TYPES OF BUSINESS:

Instruments and Related Products Manufacturing for Measuring, Displaying, and Controlling Industrial Process Variables
Power Instruments
Subsystems
Process Control
Laser Systems
Interconnect Solutions

BRANDS/DIVISIONS/AFFILIATES:

Newport Corporation
Photon Control Inc

GROWTH PLANS/SPECIAL FEATURES:

MKS Instruments Inc is engaged in providing instruments, subsystems, and process control systems used to measure, monitor, deliver, and control parameters of manufacturing processes. The company's product portfolio includes instruments, components, and systems required in manufacturing products such as flat panel displays, medical devices, and electronic materials, among others used in industrial technologies, semiconductor, life and health sciences, and research and defense markets. The company organizes itself into three reportable business segments: vacuum and analysis, light and motion, and equipment and solutions. The vacuum and analysis segment contributes to roughly half of the company's revenue, and the majority of its revenue is earned in the United States.

CONTACTS: *Note: Officers with more than one job title may be intentionally listed here more than once.*

John Lee, CEO
Seth Bagshaw, CFO
Gerald Colella, Chairman of the Board
James Schreiner, COO, Divisional
Kathleen Burke, General Counsel
Mark Gitin, General Manager, Divisional
Eric Taranto, General Manager, Divisional
David Henry, Senior VP, Divisional

FINANCIAL DATA: *Note: Data for latest year may not have been available at press time.*

In U.S. $	2021	2020	2019	2018	2017	2016
Revenue		2,330,000,000	1,899,773,000	2,075,108,000	1,915,977,000	1,295,342,000
R&D Expense		173,100,000	164,061,000	135,720,000	132,555,000	110,579,000
Operating Income		468,100,000	268,622,000	501,117,000	422,605,000	190,188,000
Operating Margin %						
SGA Expense		353,100,000	330,346,000	298,118,000	290,548,000	229,171,000
Net Income		350,100,000	140,386,000	392,896,000	339,132,000	104,809,000
Operating Cash Flow		513,200,000	244,509,000	413,781,000	355,222,000	180,098,000
Capital Expenditure		84,900,000	63,904,000	62,941,000	31,287,000	19,123,000
EBITDA		551,300,000	332,005,000	577,745,000	561,171,000	224,514,000
Return on Assets %						
Return on Equity %						
Debt to Equity						

CONTACT INFORMATION:

Phone: 978 645-5500 Fax: 978 975-0093
Toll-Free:
Address: 2 Tech Dr., Ste. 201, Andover, MA 01810 United States

STOCK TICKER/OTHER:

Stock Ticker: MKSI
Exchange: NAS
Employees: 560
Fiscal Year Ends: 12/31
Parent Company:

SALARIES/BONUSES:

Top Exec. Salary: $850,000 Bonus: $30,921
Second Exec. Salary: $555,736 Bonus: $19,715

OTHER THOUGHTS:

Estimated Female Officers or Directors:
Hot Spot for Advancement for Women/Minorities:

MongoDB Inc

www.mongodb.com

NAIC Code: 511210J

TYPES OF BUSINESS:

Computer Software, Data Base & File Management
Database Platform
Applications
Cloud Data
Application Development Solutions
Software
Consulting Services

BRANDS/DIVISIONS/AFFILIATES:

MongoDB

GROWTH PLANS/SPECIAL FEATURES:

Founded in 2007, MongoDB is a document-oriented database with nearly 25,000 paying customers and well past 1.5 million free users. MongoDB provides both licenses as well as subscriptions as a service for its NoSQL database. MongoDB's database is compatible with all major programming languages and is capable of being deployed for a variety of use cases.

CONTACTS: *Note: Officers with more than one job title may be intentionally listed here more than once.*

Dev Ittycheria, CEO
Michael Gordon, CFO
Peter Killalea, Chairman of the Board
Thomas Bull, Chief Accounting Officer
Mark Porter, Chief Technology Officer
Dwight Merriman, Co-Founder
Cedric Pech, Other Executive Officer

FINANCIAL DATA: *Note: Data for latest year may not have been available at press time.*

In U.S. $	2021	2020	2019	2018	2017	2016
Revenue	590,380,000	421,720,000	267,016,000	154,519,000	101,358,000	65,271,000
R&D Expense	205,161,000	149,033,000	89,854,000	62,202,000	51,772,000	43,465,000
Operating Income	-209,304,000	-147,866,000	-97,765,000	-97,267,000	-85,947,000	-72,738,000
Operating Margin %						
SGA Expense	417,447,000	295,197,000	201,359,000	146,725,000	105,666,000	73,683,000
Net Income	-266,944,000	-175,522,000	-99,011,000	-96,359,000	-86,681,000	-73,486,000
Operating Cash Flow	-42,673,000	-29,540,000	-41,989,000	-44,881,000	-38,078,000	-46,961,000
Capital Expenditure	11,773,000	3,564,000	6,848,000	2,135,000	1,683,000	468,000
EBITDA	-182,054,000	-135,421,000	-86,247,000	-91,361,000	-82,202,000	-68,958,000
Return on Assets %						
Return on Equity %						
Debt to Equity						

CONTACT INFORMATION:

Phone: 646-727-4092 Fax:
Toll-Free:
Address: 1633 Broadway, Fl. 38, New York, NY 10019 United States

STOCK TICKER/OTHER:

Stock Ticker: MDB
Employees: 2,539
Parent Company:
Exchange: NAS
Fiscal Year Ends: 01/31

SALARIES/BONUSES:

Top Exec. Salary: $400,000 Bonus: $
Second Exec. Salary: $325,000 Bonus: $

OTHER THOUGHTS:

Estimated Female Officers or Directors: 2
Hot Spot for Advancement for Women/Minorities:

Motorola Mobility LLC

www.motorola.com

NAIC Code: 334220

TYPES OF BUSINESS:

Smartphone Manufacturing
Set-Top Box Manufacturing
Computer Technology
Wireless Technology
Tablet Manufacturing
Apps

BRANDS/DIVISIONS/AFFILIATES:

Lenovo Group Limited
Moto
Razr
Motorola Edge
Motorola One
Moto 360
Motorola Home

CONTACTS: *Note: Officers with more than one job title may be intentionally listed here more than once.*

Sergio Buniac, Pres.
Ken Russell, CFO
Francois LaFlamme, CMO
Annabelle Wang, Exec. Dir.-Human Resources
Jason Ruger, CIO
Iqbal Arshad, Sr. VP-Global Prod. Dev.
Steve Horowitz, Sr. VP-Software Eng.
Scott Offer, General Counsel
Adrienne Hayes, Sr. VP-Comm.
John Carney, Sr. VP-Global Go-to-Market
Jim Wicks, Sr. VP-Consumer Express Design
Sergio Buniac, Chmn.
Mark Randall, Sr. VP-Supply Chain & Oper.

GROWTH PLANS/SPECIAL FEATURES:

Motorola Mobility, LLC designs and develops technologies, products and services used for digital communication, information and entertainment purposes. Motorola Mobility operates in two primary segments: the mobile devices segment and Motorola Home. The mobile devices segment designs and manufactures products such as smartphones, feature phones, voice-centric phones and media tablet devices. The division includes mobile software, services, accessories and intellectual property licenses. The current product lineup includes smartphones under the Moto brand, which operates on the Android OS; cordless phones; and baby monitors with remote wireless video capabilities. Moto smartphones include Razr, Motorola Edge, Motorola One and Moto G. Moto360 is a smartwatch crafted from premium materials, scratch-resistant glass, heart rate monitor, stainless steel body, sealed with titanium screws and coated with an ultra-hard scratch resistant PVD coating. The Motorola Home segment designs and manufactures baby monitors, home monitors, cable modems, Wi-Fi routers and range extenders, pet monitors and training supplies, wireless headphones, Bluetooth devices, power and charging accessories and car speakerphones. The company primarily sells its products through wireless carriers, such as Verizon and AT&T; Amazon; network and cable operators; distributors; and directly to end customers. The company is owned by Lenovo Group Limited, a provider of innovative consumer, commercial and enterprise technology.

FINANCIAL DATA: *Note: Data for latest year may not have been available at press time.*

In U.S. $	2021	2020	2019	2018	2017	2016
Revenue	5,000,000,000	5,218,000,000	6,460,000,000	7,240,927,000	4,575,375,000	4,357,500,000
R&D Expense						
Operating Income						
Operating Margin %						
SGA Expense						
Net Income						
Operating Cash Flow						
Capital Expenditure						
EBITDA						
Return on Assets %						
Return on Equity %						
Debt to Equity						

CONTACT INFORMATION:

Phone: 312-595-1758 Fax: 847-523-4818
Toll-Free:
Address: 222 W. Merchandise Mart Plaza, Ste. 1800, Chicago, IL 60654 United States

STOCK TICKER/OTHER:

Stock Ticker: Subsidiary
Employees: 39,000
Parent Company: Lenovo Group Limited
Exchange:
Fiscal Year Ends: 12/31

SALARIES/BONUSES:

Top Exec. Salary: $ Bonus: $
Second Exec. Salary: $ Bonus: $

OTHER THOUGHTS:

Estimated Female Officers or Directors: 2
Hot Spot for Advancement for Women/Minorities:

Motorola Solutions Inc

www.motorolasolutions.com

NAIC Code: 334220

TYPES OF BUSINESS:

Communications Equipment
Handheld Computers
Mission Critical Communications
Public Safety

BRANDS/DIVISIONS/AFFILIATES:

911 Datamaster Inc

GROWTH PLANS/SPECIAL FEATURES:

Motorola Solutions is a leading provider of communications and analytics, primarily serving public safety departments as well as schools, hospitals, and businesses. The bulk of the firm's revenue comes from sales of land mobile radios and radio network infrastructure, but the firm also sells surveillance equipment and dispatch software. Seventy-five percent of Motorola's revenue comes from government agencies, while 25% comes from its commercial customers. Motorola has customers in over 100 countries and in every state in the United States.

CONTACTS: *Note: Officers with more than one job title may be intentionally listed here more than once.*

Gregory Brown, CEO
Jason Winkler, CFO
Daniel Pekofske, Chief Accounting Officer
Mark Hacker, Chief Administrative Officer
Kelly Mark, Executive VP
John Molloy, Executive VP, Divisional
Cynthia Yazdi, Other Executive Officer
Rajan Naik, Senior VP, Divisional

FINANCIAL DATA: *Note: Data for latest year may not have been available at press time.*

In U.S. $	2021	2020	2019	2018	2017	2016
Revenue		7,414,000,000	7,887,000,000	7,343,000,000	6,380,000,000	6,038,000,000
R&D Expense		686,000,000	687,000,000	637,000,000	568,000,000	553,000,000
Operating Income		1,414,000,000	1,633,000,000	1,344,000,000	1,326,000,000	1,203,000,000
Operating Margin %						
SGA Expense		1,293,000,000	1,403,000,000	1,254,000,000	979,000,000	1,000,000,000
Net Income		949,000,000	868,000,000	966,000,000	-155,000,000	560,000,000
Operating Cash Flow		1,613,000,000	1,823,000,000	1,075,000,000	1,346,000,000	1,165,000,000
Capital Expenditure		217,000,000	248,000,000	197,000,000	227,000,000	271,000,000
EBITDA		1,816,000,000	1,632,000,000	1,702,000,000	1,634,000,000	1,364,000,000
Return on Assets %						
Return on Equity %						
Debt to Equity						

CONTACT INFORMATION:

Phone: 847 576-5000 Fax: 847 576-3477
Toll-Free:
Address: 500 West Monroe St., Chicago, IL 60661 United States

STOCK TICKER/OTHER:

Stock Ticker: MSI
Employees: 18,000
Parent Company:
Exchange: NYS
Fiscal Year Ends: 12/31

SALARIES/BONUSES:

Top Exec. Salary: $937,500 Bonus: $1,421,875
Second Exec. Salary: $584,827 Bonus: $871,134

OTHER THOUGHTS:

Estimated Female Officers or Directors: 3
Hot Spot for Advancement for Women/Minorities: Y

Nachi-Fujikoshi Corporation

www.nachi-fujikoshi.co.jp

NAIC Code: 333517

TYPES OF BUSINESS:

Machine Tool Manufacturing
Robotics
Factory Automation
Tool Manufacturing
Equipment Manufacturing

BRANDS/DIVISIONS/AFFILIATES:

CONTACTS:

Note: Officers with more than one job title may be intentionally listed here more than once.

Jun Sakamoto, Pres.
Yukihiko Tanaka, Managing. Dir.-Prod. Mfg. & Quality Assurance
Kenji Susukida, Gen. Mgr.-Legal Affairs & Admin. Improvement
Kenji Susukida, Gen. Mgr.-Bus. Oper., Tokyo
Noriyasu Shiba, Managing Dir.-Corp. Planning
Noriyasu Shiba, Managing Dir.-Corp. Comm.
Naoshi Katayama, Managing Dir.-Finance, Gen. Affairs & Risk Mgmt.
Kazuhito Yoshida, Gen. Mgr.-Hydraulic Div.
Katsumi Nishijima, Gen. Mgr.-Material Div.
Isao Hori, Gen. Mgr.-Cutting Tool Div.
Hidenori Hayashi, Gen. Mgr.-Eastern Japan Main Branch
Hiroo Honma, Chmn.
Nishiki Seto, Gen. Mgr.-Int'l Trade Headquarters
Yukihiko Tanaka, Managing. Dir.-Procurement & Logistics

GROWTH PLANS/SPECIAL FEATURES:

Nachi-Fujikoshi Corporation (NACHI) is a Tokyo-based company involved in the manufacture of tools, systems and equipment for various applications and industries. The group is comprised of 54 companies, 22 of which are domestic and 32 are international. Offices can be found in Europe, the Middle East, the Americas, Asia and Australia. NACHI's products are divided into five categories: machining, robots, components, materials and engineering. Machining products include cutting tools, forming tools, cutting saws, machine tools, precision machinery and machining systems. Robot products include robots, robot systems and electronic equipment. Robots are manufactured for applications such as arc welding, painting, handling and automation. Component products include bearings, hydraulic equipment, automotive parts, seismic isolation system and filtration system. Products in this segment can be found in automobiles, railroads, construction machinery, machine tools, electric equipment and other devices. The materials category consists of products such as special steels, coating and industrial furnaces. The focus in this division is steel tools for high-speed use as well as providing the material for precision machining. Last, the engineering category offers a combination of products as well as services, including robots, machining equipment, heat instrument equipment, bearings, hydraulic equipment and special steels, as well as regrinding and recoating tools. Half (50%) of NACHI's 2021 net sales were derived from the automotive industry, 26% from the machinery retail industry and 24% from the energy infrastructure industry.

FINANCIAL DATA:

Note: Data for latest year may not have been available at press time.

In U.S. $	2021	2020	2019	2018	2017	2016
Revenue	2,078,936,632	1,930,330,000	2,273,430,000	2,292,000,000	2,119,241,000	1,908,676,204
R&D Expense						
Operating Income						
Operating Margin %						
SGA Expense						
Net Income	90,673,384	23,599,300	75,255,000	78,890,300	86,987,000	35,212,778
Operating Cash Flow						
Capital Expenditure						
EBITDA						
Return on Assets %						
Return on Equity %						
Debt to Equity						

CONTACT INFORMATION:

Phone: 81-3-5568-5240 Fax: 81-3-5568-5236
Toll-Free:
Address: 1-9-2 Higashi-Shinbashi, Minato-ku, Tokyo, 105-0021 Japan

STOCK TICKER/OTHER:

Stock Ticker: 6474
Employees: 7,240
Parent Company:
Exchange: Tokyo
Fiscal Year Ends: 11/30

SALARIES/BONUSES:

Top Exec. Salary: $ Bonus: $
Second Exec. Salary: $ Bonus: $

OTHER THOUGHTS:

Estimated Female Officers or Directors:
Hot Spot for Advancement for Women/Minorities:

Sales, profits and employees may be estimates. Financial information, benefits and other data can change quickly and may vary from those stated here.

Navistar International Corporation

www.navistar.com

NAIC Code: 336120

TYPES OF BUSINESS:

Truck Manufacturing
Truck Design
Commercial Truck Manufacturing
Bus Manufacturing
Engines
GenSets
Automotive Parts
Finance Services

BRANDS/DIVISIONS/AFFILIATES:

Volkswagen AG
TRATON SE
International
IC Bus
OnCommand
MWM Motores Diesel e Geradores

GROWTH PLANS/SPECIAL FEATURES:

Navistar International Corporation is an international manufacturer of commercial trucks and parts. The firm is the parent company of the International brand of commercial trucks and engines, the IC Bus brand of school and commercial buses, the OnCommand brand of advanced connectivity services, and the Fleetrite/ReNEWed/Diamond Advantage brands of aftermarket parts. Navistar is also the parent of MWM Motores Diesel e Geradores, a manufacturer of engines and gensets (generator and engine combinations). Navistar also provides and manages retail, wholesale and lease financing of products sold by its operating truck and parts segments, as well as their associated dealers within the U.S., Canada and Mexico. During 2021, Navistar was acquired by TRATON SE, a world-leading commercial vehicle manufacturer, itself a subsidiary of Volkswagen AG.

CONTACTS: *Note: Officers with more than one job title may be intentionally listed here more than once.*

Matthias Carlbaum, CEO
Michael G. Grahe, Exec. VP-Oper.
Troy Clarke, CEO
Do Young Kim, CFO
Friedrich W. Baumann, Exec. VP-Mktg. & Sales
Donna G. Dorsey, Chief People Officer
Julie Ragland, CIO
Persio Lisboa, Executive VP
Curt Kramer, General Counsel
William McMenamin, President, Divisional

FINANCIAL DATA: *Note: Data for latest year may not have been available at press time.*

In U.S. $	2021	2020	2019	2018	2017	2016
Revenue	7,878,150,067	7,503,000,064	11,251,000,320	10,250,000,384	8,569,999,872	8,111,000,064
R&D Expense						
Operating Income						
Operating Margin %						
SGA Expense						
Net Income		-347,000,000	221,000,000	340,000,000	30,000,000	-97,000,000
Operating Cash Flow						
Capital Expenditure						
EBITDA						
Return on Assets %						
Return on Equity %						
Debt to Equity						

CONTACT INFORMATION:

Phone: 630 753-5000 Fax: 630 753-3982
Toll-Free: 800-448-7825
Address: 2701 Navistar Dr., Lisle, IL 60532 United States

STOCK TICKER/OTHER:

Stock Ticker: Subsidiary
Exchange:
Employees: 11,000
Fiscal Year Ends: 10/31
Parent Company: Volkswagen AG

SALARIES/BONUSES:

Top Exec. Salary: $ Bonus: $
Second Exec. Salary: $ Bonus: $

OTHER THOUGHTS:

Estimated Female Officers or Directors: 1
Hot Spot for Advancement for Women/Minorities:

NEC Corporation

www.nec.com

NAIC Code: 334111

TYPES OF BUSINESS:

Computer Manufacturing
Computer Integration
Network Technology
Security
5G
Big Data
Analytics
Smart City

BRANDS/DIVISIONS/AFFILIATES:

GROWTH PLANS/SPECIAL FEATURES:

NEC Corporation is a global provider of computer integration and network technology products and solutions. Operating through approximately 300 subsidiaries, the firm serves the aviation, aerospace, agriculture, broadcasting, finance, government, healthcare, hospitality, logistics, manufacturing, retail, telecommunications and transportation industries. NEC enables businesses and communities to adapt to rapid changes in society and the marketplace, providing safety, security, communications and efficiency. NEC's products include computers, data storage, embedded systems, integrated IT infrastructure, network products, software and unified communications. Solutions and services by NEC include 5G, big data analytics, biometric authentication, cloud, display and digital signage, energy, safety, smart city and smart connectivity. NEC has operations throughout the world, including North America, Latin America, Europe, the Middle East, Africa, Asia and Oceania.

CONTACTS: *Note: Officers with more than one job title may be intentionally listed here more than once.*

Takayuki Morita, CEO
Hajime Matsukura, Chief Human Resources Officer
Motoo Nishihara, CTO
Takashi Niino, Chief Strategy Officer
Toshiyuki Mineno, Exec. VP
Kuniaki Okada, Exec. VP
Manabu Kinoshita, Exec. VP
Tomonori Nishimura, Exec. VP
Nobuhiro Endo, Chmn.
Junji Yasui, Chief Supply Chain Officer

FINANCIAL DATA: *Note: Data for latest year may not have been available at press time.*

In U.S. $	2021	2020	2019	2018	2017	2016
Revenue	27,166,836,555	28,703,776,308	27,528,448,000	26,876,493,824	24,775,811,072	25,751,980,032
R&D Expense						
Operating Income						
Operating Margin %						
SGA Expense						
Net Income	1,357,478,466	927,047,973	379,792,864	433,414,560	253,890,624	627,546,752
Operating Cash Flow						
Capital Expenditure						
EBITDA						
Return on Assets %						
Return on Equity %						
Debt to Equity						

CONTACT INFORMATION:

Phone: 81 334541111 Fax:
Toll-Free: 800-268-3997
Address: 7-1, Shiba 5-Chome, Minato-ku, Tokyo, 108-8001 Japan

STOCK TICKER/OTHER:

Stock Ticker: 6701 Exchange: Tokyo
Employees: 114,714 Fiscal Year Ends: 03/31
Parent Company:

SALARIES/BONUSES:

Top Exec. Salary: $ Bonus: $
Second Exec. Salary: $ Bonus: $

OTHER THOUGHTS:

Estimated Female Officers or Directors:
Hot Spot for Advancement for Women/Minorities:

NEC Laboratories America Inc

www.nec-labs.com

NAIC Code: 541712

TYPES OF BUSINESS:

Communications Technology
Electronics
Broadband & Mobile Networking
Internet of Things
Software
Storage Technologies
Security Systems
Quantum Computing

BRANDS/DIVISIONS/AFFILIATES:

NEC Corporation

CONTACTS: *Note: Officers with more than one job title may be intentionally listed here more than once.*

Christopher White, Pres.
Kaoru Yano, Chmn.-NEC Corp.

GROWTH PLANS/SPECIAL FEATURES:

NEC Laboratories America, Inc. is the U.S.-based facility in NEC Corporation's global network of research laboratories. Operating through two laboratories, located in Princeton, New Jersey and San Jose, California, the company focuses on six areas of research. The data science and system security department focuses on building novel big data solutions and service platforms to support complex computer systems management, and to develop new information technology that supports innovative applications, from big data analytics to the Internet of Things (IoT). The integrated systems department focuses on accelerating enterprise workloads on computing clusters that include various types of heterogeneity in computing, interconnect, networking and storage units. The machine learning department develops solutions such as deep learning, support vector machines and semantic analysis in order to interpret multi-modal data and complex situations. The media analytics department aims to solve challenges in computer vision, including image-based recognition, object detection, tracking, segmentation and 3D reconstruction. The mobile communications and networking department focuses on two areas: technologies for improving the capacity, coverage and scalability of next-generation 5G cellular networks; and end-to-end solution creation via wireless sensing formats and communication technologies. Last, the optical networking and sensing department researches into the next-generation of optical networks and sensing systems that will power ICT-based (information and communication technologies) social solutions for the future. These solutions include optics, photonics, multi-dimensional optical processing, optical transmission systems and software. Other current areas of research include big data analytics, deep learning and agile digital signal processing (DSP)-based optical transmission systems.

NEC Labs offers employees medical, dental, vision, life, AD&D and disability insurance; 401(k); and various employee-assistance programs.

FINANCIAL DATA: *Note: Data for latest year may not have been available at press time.*

In U.S. $	2021	2020	2019	2018	2017	2016
Revenue						
R&D Expense						
Operating Income						
Operating Margin %						
SGA Expense						
Net Income						
Operating Cash Flow						
Capital Expenditure						
EBITDA						
Return on Assets %						
Return on Equity %						
Debt to Equity						

CONTACT INFORMATION:

Phone: 609-520-1555 Fax: 609-951-2481
Toll-Free:
Address: 4 Independence Way, Ste. 200, Princeton, NJ 08540 United States

STOCK TICKER/OTHER:

Stock Ticker: Subsidiary
Employees: 2,769
Parent Company: NEC Corporation
Exchange:
Fiscal Year Ends: 03/31

SALARIES/BONUSES:

Top Exec. Salary: $ Bonus: $
Second Exec. Salary: $ Bonus: $

OTHER THOUGHTS:

Estimated Female Officers or Directors:
Hot Spot for Advancement for Women/Minorities:

NETGEAR Inc

NAIC Code: 334210A

www.netgear.com

TYPES OF BUSINESS:

Networking Equipment
Wireless Networking Products
Broadband Products
Entertainment Management Software
Security Products
Wi-Fi Phones
Gaming Router

BRANDS/DIVISIONS/AFFILIATES:

Orbi Voice
Meural
Nighthawk

GROWTH PLANS/SPECIAL FEATURES:

Netgear Inc is a provider of networking solutions. The reportable segments of the company are connected home, and Small and Medium Business (SMB). The Connected Home segment focuses on consumers and consists of high-performance, dependable and easy-to-use 4G/5G mobile, Wi-Fi internet networking solutions and smart devices such as Orbi Voice smart speakers and Meural digital canvas; and SMB focused on small and medium-sized businesses and consists of business networking, storage, wireless LAN and security solutions that bring enterprise-class functionality to small and medium-sized businesses at an affordable price.

CONTACTS: *Note: Officers with more than one job title may be intentionally listed here more than once.*

Patrick Lo, CEO
Bryan Murray, CFO
Andrew Kim, Chief Legal Officer
Mark Merrill, Co-Founder
Michael Falcon, COO
David Henry, Director
Martin Westhead, Other Executive Officer
Vikram Mehta, Senior VP, Divisional
Michael Werdann, Senior VP, Divisional
Tamesa Rogers, Senior VP, Divisional
Heidi Cormack, Senior VP, Divisional

FINANCIAL DATA: *Note: Data for latest year may not have been available at press time.*

In U.S. $	2021	2020	2019	2018	2017	2016
Revenue		1,255,202,000	998,763,000	1,058,816,000	1,406,920,000	1,328,298,000
R&D Expense		88,788,000	77,982,000	82,416,000	94,603,000	89,367,000
Operating Income		75,544,000	26,188,000	41,856,000	86,850,000	117,981,000
Operating Margin %						
SGA Expense		209,002,000	187,582,000	217,426,000	214,589,000	204,837,000
Net Income		58,293,000	25,791,000	-9,162,000	19,436,000	75,851,000
Operating Cash Flow		181,150,000	13,525,000	-103,211,000	87,524,000	115,173,000
Capital Expenditure		10,296,000	14,230,000	12,251,000	13,674,000	10,972,000
EBITDA		94,475,000	45,594,000	60,707,000	112,944,000	149,974,000
Return on Assets %						
Return on Equity %						
Debt to Equity						

CONTACT INFORMATION:

Phone: 408 907-8000 Fax: 408 907-8097
Toll-Free: 888-638-4327
Address: 350 E. Plumeria Dr., San Jose, CA 95134 United States

STOCK TICKER/OTHER:

Stock Ticker: NTGR
Employees: 809
Parent Company:
Exchange: NAS
Fiscal Year Ends: 12/31

SALARIES/BONUSES:

Top Exec. Salary: $895,000 Bonus: $
Second Exec. Salary: $556,691 Bonus: $62,823

OTHER THOUGHTS:

Estimated Female Officers or Directors: 4
Hot Spot for Advancement for Women/Minorities: Y

NetScout Systems Inc

www.netscout.com

NAIC Code: 511210B

TYPES OF BUSINESS:

Computer Software, Network Management (IT), System Testing & Storage
Digital Cyber Security
Digital Business Network Security Solutions
Cyber Threat Solutions
Technologies
Business Transformation Solutions
Digital Transformation Solutions
Software Security Solutions

BRANDS/DIVISIONS/AFFILIATES:

Ngenius
Omnis
Arbor
Spectra

GROWTH PLANS/SPECIAL FEATURES:

NetScout Systems Inc is a provider of service assurance and cybersecurity solutions to enterprise and government networks. It bases its solutions on proprietary adaptive service intelligence technology, which helps customers monitor and identify performance issues and provides insight into network-based security threats. These solutions also deliver real-time and historical information, which provides insight to restore service and understand the quality of user experience. The company derives revenue primarily from the sale of network management tools and security solutions. The firm generates its revenue in the Americas, Europe, Middle East, India, Africa, and Asia-Pacific regions.

CONTACTS: *Note: Officers with more than one job title may be intentionally listed here more than once.*

Anil Singhal, CEO
Jean Bua, CFO
Michael Szabados, COO
John Downing, Executive VP, Divisional

FINANCIAL DATA: *Note: Data for latest year may not have been available at press time.*

In U.S. $	2021	2020	2019	2018	2017	2016
Revenue	831,282,000	891,820,000	909,918,000	986,787,000	1,162,112,000	955,419,000
R&D Expense	179,163,000	188,294,000	203,588,000	215,076,000	232,701,000	208,630,000
Operating Income	37,192,000	20,312,000	-7,544,000	1,151,000	66,065,000	-25,082,000
Operating Margin %						
SGA Expense	331,699,000	376,517,000	385,442,000	422,015,000	447,066,000	411,049,000
Net Income	19,352,000	-2,754,000	-73,324,000	79,812,000	33,291,000	-28,369,000
Operating Cash Flow	213,921,000	225,023,000	149,838,000	222,454,000	227,809,000	95,285,000
Capital Expenditure	16,523,000	19,922,000	23,526,000	16,594,000	32,148,000	30,370,000
EBITDA	139,011,000	138,625,000	71,109,000	147,477,000	222,232,000	113,961,000
Return on Assets %						
Return on Equity %						
Debt to Equity						

CONTACT INFORMATION:

Phone: 978 614-4000 Fax: 978 614-4004
Toll-Free: 800-357-7666
Address: 310 Littleton Rd., Westford, MA 01886 United States

STOCK TICKER/OTHER:

Stock Ticker: NTCT
Employees: 2,421
Parent Company:
Exchange: NAS
Fiscal Year Ends: 03/31

SALARIES/BONUSES:

Top Exec. Salary: $525,000 Bonus: $
Second Exec. Salary: $385,000 Bonus: $

OTHER THOUGHTS:

Estimated Female Officers or Directors: 2
Hot Spot for Advancement for Women/Minorities:

Nexient

NAIC Code: 541511

www.nexient.com

TYPES OF BUSINESS:

Custom Computer Programming Services
Software Development Solutions
Product Strategy Solutions

BRANDS/DIVISIONS/AFFILIATES:

Nippon Telegraph and Telephone Corporation (NTT)
NTT DATA Corporation

CONTACTS: *Note: Officers with more than one job title may be intentionally listed here more than once.*

Mark Orttung, CEO
Tanmoy Chowdhury, CFO
Dan Broekhuizen, VP-People

GROWTH PLANS/SPECIAL FEATURES:

Nexient is a software product development company that serves tech businesses in the U.S. Nexient's services are grouped into three categories: product development strategy, product design & development and product operations. Product development strategy services include agile transformation, co-building, applied innovation, creative strategy, product roadmaps, technical architecture and technology business management. Product design & development services consist of two units: engineering, offering digital products and applications, integrations, platforms, quality engineering, core technologies and artificial intelligence (AI); and experience design, offering creative services, digital accessibility and user experience. Product operations services include DevOps, support engineering and cloud. Nexient specializes in a myriad of technology stacks, including: platforms such as Pivotal Cloud Foundry, Salesforce and SharePoint; mobile such as iOS, Android, Flutter, Ionic, React Native and Xamarin; frontend such as Angular, AngularJS, Backbone, Ember.js, JavaScript, jQuery, React, Redux, RxJS, Microsoft WPF, Sass/LESS, Vue and Webpack; backend such as Java, .NET, C#/C++, ASP, Node.js, Go, Ruby on Rails, PHP, Python, Scala, Rust and Erlang; test and automation such as Selenium, Cypress, Storybook, SoapUI, Appium, Coded UI, Device Anywhere, HP UFT, Jasmine, Mocha, Chai, JMeter, Junit, TestNG, Load Runner, LoadUI and Perfecto Mobile, among others; DevOps and cloud, such as Ansible, Artifactory, AWS, Azure, Chef, CloudFormation, Docker, Google Cloud, Jenkins, Kubernetes, OpenShift, Terraform and Puppet; and data, such as Cassandra, Hadoop, Microsoft SSIS, MongoDB, Kafka, Oracle, Pentaho, Redis, Spark, SQL Server, MySQL, Tableau and Qlik. Based in Newark California, Nexient has a product delivery center based in Ann Arbor, Michigan; Columbus, Ohio; and Kokomo, Indiana. During 2021, Nexient was acquired by NTT Data Corporation, itself a subsidiary of Nippon Telegraph and Telephone Corporation (NTT).

FINANCIAL DATA: *Note: Data for latest year may not have been available at press time.*

In U.S. $	2021	2020	2019	2018	2017	2016
Revenue						
R&D Expense						
Operating Income						
Operating Margin %						
SGA Expense						
Net Income						
Operating Cash Flow						
Capital Expenditure						
EBITDA						
Return on Assets %						
Return on Equity %						
Debt to Equity						

CONTACT INFORMATION:

Phone: 415-992-7277 Fax:
Toll-Free:
Address: 8000 Jarvis Ave., Newark, CA 94560 United States

STOCK TICKER/OTHER:

Stock Ticker: Subsidiary Exchange:
Employees: 300 Fiscal Year Ends:
Parent Company: Nippon Telegraph and Telephone Corporation (NTT)

SALARIES/BONUSES:

Top Exec. Salary: $ Bonus: $
Second Exec. Salary: $ Bonus: $

OTHER THOUGHTS:

Estimated Female Officers or Directors:
Hot Spot for Advancement for Women/Minorities:

NIO Inc

NAIC Code: 336111

www.nio.io

TYPES OF BUSINESS:

Automobile Manufacturing, All-Electric
Self-Driving Cars

BRANDS/DIVISIONS/AFFILIATES:

EP9
ES8
ES6
NIO Pilot
EC6
ES3
ET5
ET7

CONTACTS: *Note: Officers with more than one job title may be intentionally listed here more than once.*

Bin Li, CEO
Lihong Qin, Pres.
Wei Feng, CFO
Ganesh V. Iyer, CIO
Bin Li, Chmn.

GROWTH PLANS/SPECIAL FEATURES:

NIO Inc operates in China's premium electric vehicle market. The company designs and jointly manufactures, and sells smart and connected premium electric vehicles, driving innovations in next-generation technologies in connectivity, autonomous driving, and artificial intelligence. Its model includes EP9 supercar, ES8, ES6, and EC6. The company sells vehicles through its own sales network, including NIO Houses, NIO Spaces, and their mobile application. The majority of the revenue is earned from selling vehicles.

FINANCIAL DATA: *Note: Data for latest year may not have been available at press time.*

In U.S. $	2021	2020	2019	2018	2017	2016
Revenue		2,545,473,000	1,225,130,000	775,195,100		
R&D Expense		389,505,200	693,374,000	625,949,900	407,529,200	229,427,400
Operating Income		-721,409,900	-1,734,647,000	-1,502,365,000	-775,574,700	-407,474,500
Operating Margin %						
SGA Expense		563,196,900	764,985,700	797,248,300	347,861,100	172,055,600
Net Income		-829,672,800	-1,767,107,000	-1,502,626,000	-780,450,000	-397,106,000
Operating Cash Flow		305,447,600	-1,365,540,000	-1,238,730,000	-716,254,700	-344,694,500
Capital Expenditure		176,559,600	267,228,300	413,960,200	174,400,000	102,466,700
EBITDA		-520,741,800	-1,471,153,000	-1,412,098,000	-755,804,900	-394,989,500
Return on Assets %						
Return on Equity %						
Debt to Equity						

CONTACT INFORMATION:

Phone: 86-21-6908-3306 Fax:
Toll-Free:
Address: No. 56 AnTuo Rd., Bldg 20, AnTing Town, JiaDing Di, Shanghai, Shanghai 201804 China

STOCK TICKER/OTHER:

Stock Ticker: NIO
Employees: 7,800
Parent Company:
Exchange: NYS
Fiscal Year Ends: 12/31

SALARIES/BONUSES:

Top Exec. Salary: $ Bonus: $
Second Exec. Salary: $ Bonus: $

OTHER THOUGHTS:

Estimated Female Officers or Directors:
Hot Spot for Advancement for Women/Minorities:

Nippon Telegraph and Telephone Corporation (NTT) group.ntt

NAIC Code: 517110

TYPES OF BUSINESS:

Local Telephone Service
Long-Distance Service
Internet Service
Information Technology Services
Cellular Phone Service
Wireless Internet

GROWTH PLANS/SPECIAL FEATURES:

NTT owns NTT DoCoMo, the largest wireless operator in Japan, with 80.3 million subscribers. It also owns NTT East and NTT West, the two regional incumbent fixed-line operators in Japan, with about 15 million traditional fixed-line and 22 million broadband lines (around 56% of which are wholesaled). The firm also provides IT and communications systems integration via NTT Communications and 52.4%-owned NTT Data.

BRANDS/DIVISIONS/AFFILIATES:

NTT East
NTT West
NTT Communications Corporation
NTT Ltd
NTT Data Corporation
NTT DoCoMo Inc
NTT Urban Solutions Inc
NTT Anode Energy Corporation

CONTACTS: *Note: Officers with more than one job title may be intentionally listed here more than once.*

Jun Sawada, CEO
Akira Shimada, CFO
Hiromichi Shinohara, Dir.-R&D Planning
Hiroki Watanabe, Chief Compliance Officer
Mitsuyoshi Kobayashi, Sr. VP-Strategic Bus. Dev. Div.
Yoshikiyo Sakai, Sr. VP-Finance & Acct.
Akira Shimada, Sr. VP-Gen. Affairs & Internal Control
Hiroshi Tsujigami, Sr. VP-Corp. Strategy
Hiromichi Shinohara, Chmn.
Tsunehisa Okuno, Sr. VP-Global Bus. Office

FINANCIAL DATA: *Note: Data for latest year may not have been available at press time.*

In U.S. $	2021	2020	2019	2018	2017	2016
Revenue	104,952,100,000	104,560,600,000	104,388,600,000	103,683,400,000	100,093,300,000	101,411,200,000
R&D Expense						
Operating Income	14,912,390,000	13,873,030,000	15,994,440,000	15,860,710,000	14,179,120,000	12,133,760,000
Operating Margin %						
SGA Expense				25,655,720,000	24,487,890,000	24,320,420,000
Net Income	8,050,516,000	7,515,606,000	7,509,059,000	7,993,523,000	7,030,763,000	6,482,531,000
Operating Cash Flow	26,440,760,000	26,319,030,000	21,142,990,000	23,176,220,000	25,634,920,000	23,829,080,000
Capital Expenditure	15,774,170,000	16,311,820,000	14,695,000,000	15,032,180,000	14,953,840,000	14,389,180,000
EBITDA	28,211,290,000	27,114,190,000	26,729,020,000	27,479,130,000	26,605,080,000	27,567,170,000
Return on Assets %						
Return on Equity %						
Debt to Equity						

CONTACT INFORMATION:

Phone: 81 352055581 Fax: 81 352055589
Toll-Free:
Address: 5-1 Otemachi 1-Chome, Chiyoda-ku, Tokyo, 100-8116 Japan

STOCK TICKER/OTHER:

Stock Ticker: NPPXF
Exchange: PINX
Employees: 324,650
Fiscal Year Ends: 03/31
Parent Company:

SALARIES/BONUSES:

Top Exec. Salary: $ Bonus: $
Second Exec. Salary: $ Bonus: $

OTHER THOUGHTS:

Estimated Female Officers or Directors:
Hot Spot for Advancement for Women/Minorities:

Nissan Motor Co Ltd

www.nissan-global.com

NAIC Code: 336111

TYPES OF BUSINESS:

Automobile Manufacturing
Research & Development
Industrial Machinery
Marine Equipment
Logistics Services
Alternative Fuels Research
Financial Services

GROWTH PLANS/SPECIAL FEATURES:

While Nissan annually sells about 4 million vehicles, total 2020 Renault-Nissan-Mitsubishi alliance sales volume of 7.8 million vehicles makes the alliance the third largest vehicle group in the world, behind Toyota at 9.5 million and Volkswagen at 9.3 million vehicles sold. Nissan's financial services subsidiary provides consumers with auto loans and leases. In addition, the subsidiary also finances Nissan's sales to its dealerships (known as floor-plan financing). Nissan is 43.4% owned by French automaker Renault, while Nissan in turn owns 15% of Renault. The Alliance also has controlling interests in AvtoVAZ (Lada) in Russia and Mitsubishi Motors in Japan.

BRANDS/DIVISIONS/AFFILIATES:

Nissan
Infiniti
Datsun
Nissan Motorsport International Limited
Renault SA
Versa
Q50
QX55

CONTACTS: *Note: Officers with more than one job title may be intentionally listed here more than once.*

Makoto Uchida, CEO
Ashwanti Gupta, COO
Stephen Ma, CFO
Yasushi Kimura, Chmn.

FINANCIAL DATA: *Note: Data for latest year may not have been available at press time.*

In U.S. $	2021	2020	2019	2018	2017	2016
Revenue	69,088,710,000	86,805,960,000	101,703,300,000	105,015,400,000	102,984,400,000	107,109,800,000
R&D Expense						
Operating Income	-1,323,776,000	-355,602,600	2,796,246,000	5,050,438,000	6,521,985,000	6,970,563,000
Operating Margin %						
SGA Expense	3,951,610,000	5,014,226,000	5,919,290,000	5,578,916,000	5,693,929,000	6,248,462,000
Net Income	-3,942,717,000	-5,897,999,000	2,804,278,000	6,562,967,000	5,830,190,000	4,603,010,000
Operating Cash Flow	11,623,400,000	10,420,140,000	12,749,010,000	9,413,114,000	11,734,850,000	8,145,697,000
Capital Expenditure	7,204,738,000	9,796,227,000	11,411,740,000	12,570,390,000	11,369,020,000	12,178,750,000
EBITDA	3,099,408,000	2,288,636,000	11,922,020,000	13,895,640,000	15,794,100,000	13,812,870,000
Return on Assets %						
Return on Equity %						
Debt to Equity						

CONTACT INFORMATION:

Phone: 81 455235523 Fax:
Toll-Free:
Address: 1-1, Takashima 1-chome, Nishi-ku, Yokohama-shi, Kanagawa, 220-8686 Japan

STOCK TICKER/OTHER:

Stock Ticker: NSANY
Employees: 158,133
Parent Company:
Exchange: PINX
Fiscal Year Ends: 03/31

SALARIES/BONUSES:

Top Exec. Salary: $ Bonus: $
Second Exec. Salary: $ Bonus: $

OTHER THOUGHTS:

Estimated Female Officers or Directors:
Hot Spot for Advancement for Women/Minorities:

Nissan North America Inc

www.nissanusa.com

NAIC Code: 336111

TYPES OF BUSINESS:

Automobile Manufacturing
Vehicle Manufacturing
Automobile Engineering
Manufacturing Facilities
Powertrain Assembly
Automobile Design
Automobile Financing Solutions
Technologies

BRANDS/DIVISIONS/AFFILIATES:

Nissan Motor Co Ltd
Nissan Design America
Nissan Motor Acceptance Company
Nissan Technical Center North America
Nissan Rouge
Pathfinder
TITAN
INFINITI

CONTACTS: *Note: Officers with more than one job title may be intentionally listed here more than once.*

Makoto Uchida, CEO
Bill Krueger, Sr. VP-Mfg.
Scott E. Becker, Sr. VP-Admin.
Alan J. Buddendeck, VP-Corp. Comm.
Scott E. Becker, Sr. VP-Finance
Victor Nacif, VP-Design Bus. Aspects, Nissan Design America
Bill Krueger, Sr. VP-Supply Chain & Purchasing

GROWTH PLANS/SPECIAL FEATURES:

Nissan North America, Inc. (Nissan NA), a subsidiary of Nissan Motor Co., Ltd., specializes in the research and development of vehicles, as well as the design, engineering, marketing and sales of automobiles. Nissan NA also offers related consumer and corporate financing and the distribution of vehicles. The company has four manufacturing facilities in Tennessee and Mississippi. The Smyrna vehicle assembly plant has an annual production capacity of 640,000 vehicles and produces the Nissan Rogue, Pathfinder, Murano, Maxima, LEAF and INFINITI QX60. The Canton vehicle assembly plant has an annual production capacity of 410,000 vehicles and produces the Nissan Altima, Frontier and TITAN. The Decherd powertrain assembly plant manufactures all engines for the complete lineup of Nissan and INFINITI vehicles produced in the U.S., and also forges crankshafts and cylinder block castings. The Decher INFINITI powertrain assembly plant assembles 2.0-liter 4-cylinder gasoline engines for the INFINITI Q50 sports sedan and Mercedes-Benz C-class and their derivatives. The facility was developed as a collaboration between the Renault-Nissan Alliance and Daimler AG. Nissan Design America is a full-service design studio capable of handling all phases of automotive design development, from exploratory to production. Nissan Motor Acceptance Company (NMAC) is the automotive financial services arm of Nissan North America, and specializes in providing purchase and lease financing for the group's line of Nissan and INFINITI vehicles to consumers throughout the U.S. Last, Nissan Technical Center North America blends technology and engineering to create cars, and is engaged in all technical departments of Nissan.

FINANCIAL DATA: *Note: Data for latest year may not have been available at press time.*

In U.S. $	2021	2020	2019	2018	2017	2016
Revenue	49,577,944,000	47,671,100,000	54,986,100,000	60,441,000,000	57,079,700,000	57,790,000,000
R&D Expense						
Operating Income						
Operating Margin %						
SGA Expense						
Net Income		-147,792,000	649,872,000	1,882,780,000	2,585,520,000	3,547,930,000
Operating Cash Flow						
Capital Expenditure						
EBITDA						
Return on Assets %						
Return on Equity %						
Debt to Equity						

CONTACT INFORMATION:

Phone: 615-725-1000 Fax: 615-725-8535
Toll-Free: 800-647-7261
Address: 1 Nissan Way, Franklin, TN 37067 United States

STOCK TICKER/OTHER:

Stock Ticker: Subsidiary
Employees: 22,000
Parent Company: Nissan Motor Co Ltd
Exchange:
Fiscal Year Ends: 03/31

SALARIES/BONUSES:

Top Exec. Salary: $ Bonus: $
Second Exec. Salary: $ Bonus: $

OTHER THOUGHTS:

Estimated Female Officers or Directors: 1
Hot Spot for Advancement for Women/Minorities:

Nokia Bell Labs

www.bell-labs.com

NAIC Code: 541712

TYPES OF BUSINESS:

Research & Development-Communications
Science Development
Computer Science & Software
Vectoring
Photonic Service Engine
Internet of Things
Artificial Intelligence
Machine Learning

BRANDS/DIVISIONS/AFFILIATES:

Nokia Corporation

CONTACTS: *Note: Officers with more than one job title may be intentionally listed here more than once.*

Thierry Klein, Pres.

GROWTH PLANS/SPECIAL FEATURES:

Nokia Bell Labs is a research and scientific development company headquartered in Murray Hill, New Jersey, with global locations throughout Europe as well as in China and Israel. Winner of Nobel prizes, U.S. Medals of Science and U.S. Medals of Technology & Innovation, the firm designs products and services at the forefront of communications technology and conducts fundamental research in fields such as physical technologies, computer science and software, mathematical/algorithmic sciences, optical and wireless networking, security solutions and government research. Nokia Bell Labs offers consulting services in relation to business strategy, digitizing and transforming organizations, network evolution and industrial disruption. Current research (early-2022) by Nokia Bell Labs includes 6G innovation, network integration systems, autonomous systems, and physical and cognitive human augmentation. Recent innovations include: Vectoring, demonstrating how vectoring could cancel cross-talk between lines in a twisted-pair DSL cable; Photonic Service Engine, a chipset to implement probabilistic constellation shaping, which pushes fiber-optic performance close to its theoretical limited over any distance; World Wide Streams, , where tens of billions Internet of Things (IoT) sensors worldwide each continuously collect and transmit mixed types of streaming data; Integrated Optical Coherence Tomography (OCT), which leverages photonic integration technologies pioneered for telecom networks; Cognitive Cloud Control, offering related software that uses artificial intelligence (AI) and machine learning to manage cloud services intelligently; and KNIX, which is serverless computing developed for short-transactional applications such as web transactions and IoT functions. Nokia Bell Labs operates as a subsidiary of Nokia Corporation.

FINANCIAL DATA: *Note: Data for latest year may not have been available at press time.*

In U.S. $	2021	2020	2019	2018	2017	2016
Revenue						
R&D Expense						
Operating Income						
Operating Margin %						
SGA Expense						
Net Income						
Operating Cash Flow						
Capital Expenditure						
EBITDA						
Return on Assets %						
Return on Equity %						
Debt to Equity						

CONTACT INFORMATION:

Phone: 908-582-3000 Fax: 908-508-2576
Toll-Free:
Address: 600 Mountain Ave., Murray Hill, NJ 07974-0636 United States

STOCK TICKER/OTHER:

Stock Ticker: Subsidiary
Employees: 748
Parent Company: Nokia Corporation
Exchange:
Fiscal Year Ends: 12/31

SALARIES/BONUSES:

Top Exec. Salary: $ Bonus: $
Second Exec. Salary: $ Bonus: $

OTHER THOUGHTS:

Estimated Female Officers or Directors:
Hot Spot for Advancement for Women/Minorities:

Nokia Corporation

NAIC Code: 334220

www.nokia.com

TYPES OF BUSINESS:

Smartphones and Cellphones
Network Systems & Services
Internet Software & Services
Multimedia Equipment
Brand Licensing
Collaboration Devices
5G
Innovation

BRANDS/DIVISIONS/AFFILIATES:

Nokia Bell Labs

GROWTH PLANS/SPECIAL FEATURES:

Nokia is a leading vendor in the telecommunications equipment industry. The company's network business derives revenue from selling wireless and fixed-line hardware, software, and services. Nokia's technology segment licenses its patent portfolio to handset manufacturers and makes royalties from Nokia-branded cellphones. The company, headquartered in Espoo, Finland, operates on a global scale, with most of its revenue from communication service providers.

CONTACTS: *Note: Officers with more than one job title may be intentionally listed here more than once.*

Pekka Lundmark, CEO
Marco Wiren, CFO
Stephanie Werner-Dietz, Chief People Officer
Nishant Batra, CTO
Louise Pentland, Chief Legal Officer
Juha Rutkiranta, Exec. VP-Oper.
Kai Oistamo, Chief Dev. Officer
Stephen Elop, Exec. VP-Devices & Svcs.
Timo Toikkanen, Exec. VP-Mobile Phones
Jo Harlow, Exec. VP-Smart Devices

FINANCIAL DATA: *Note: Data for latest year may not have been available at press time.*

In U.S. $	2021	2020	2019	2018	2017	2016
Revenue		24,678,420,000	26,330,650,000	25,481,380,000	26,140,920,000	26,668,320,000
R&D Expense		4,615,628,000	4,981,535,000	5,217,568,000	5,551,854,000	5,538,302,000
Operating Income		1,158,707,000	1,084,170,000	377,200,800	738,590,800	-329,768,400
Operating Margin %						
SGA Expense		3,272,838,000	3,502,095,000	3,910,917,000	4,082,578,000	4,312,964,000
Net Income		-2,841,429,000	7,905,406	-383,976,900	-1,687,240,000	-865,077,300
Operating Cash Flow		1,986,516,000	440,444,100	406,563,700	2,045,242,000	-1,642,066,000
Capital Expenditure		540,955,600	779,247,200	758,919,000	678,735,600	538,697,000
EBITDA		2,382,915,000	2,398,726,000	1,555,106,000	1,795,657,000	612,104,300
Return on Assets %						
Return on Equity %						
Debt to Equity						

CONTACT INFORMATION:

Phone: 358-10-44-88-000 Fax: 358-10-44-81-002
Toll-Free:
Address: Karakaari 7A, Espoo, FI-02610 Finland

STOCK TICKER/OTHER:

Stock Ticker: NOK
Employees: 92,039
Parent Company:
Exchange: NYS
Fiscal Year Ends: 12/31

SALARIES/BONUSES:

Top Exec. Salary: $857,584 Bonus: $
Second Exec. Salary: $611,728 Bonus: $

OTHER THOUGHTS:

Estimated Female Officers or Directors: 4
Hot Spot for Advancement for Women/Minorities: Y

Northrop Grumman Corporation

www.northropgrumman.com

NAIC Code: 336411

TYPES OF BUSINESS:

Aircraft Manufacturing
Aeronautics Systems
Defense Systems
Mission Systems
Space Systems
Product Design and Engineering
System Production
System Integration Services

BRANDS/DIVISIONS/AFFILIATES:

GROWTH PLANS/SPECIAL FEATURES:

Northrop Grumman is a defense contractor that is diversified across short-cycle and long-cycle businesses. The firm's segments include aeronautics, mission systems, defense services, and space systems. The company's aerospace segment creates the fuselage for the massive F-35 program and produces various piloted and autonomous flight systems. Mission systems creates a variety of sensors and processors for defense hardware. The defense systems segment is a mix between a long-range missile manufacturer and a defense IT service provider. Finally, the company's space systems segment produces various space structures, sensors, and satellites.

CONTACTS: *Note: Officers with more than one job title may be intentionally listed here more than once.*

Kathy Warden, CEO
Blake Larson, Pres., Divisional
David Keffer, CFO
Michael Hardesty, Chief Accounting Officer
Lesley Kalan, Chief Strategy Officer
Sheila Cheston, General Counsel
Thomas Wilson, General Manager, Divisional
David Perry, Other Executive Officer
Ann Addison, Other Executive Officer
Shawn Purvis, President, Divisional
Mary Petryszyn, President, Divisional
Thomas Jones, President, Divisional
Mark Caylor, President, Divisional
Jennifer McGarey, Secretary
Lucy Ryan, Vice President, Divisional

FINANCIAL DATA: *Note: Data for latest year may not have been available at press time.*

In U.S. $	2021	2020	2019	2018	2017	2016
Revenue		36,799,000,000	33,841,000,000	30,095,000,000	25,803,000,000	24,508,000,000
R&D Expense						
Operating Income		4,065,000,000	3,969,000,000	3,780,000,000	3,299,000,000	3,193,000,000
Operating Margin %						
SGA Expense		3,413,000,000	3,290,000,000	3,011,000,000	2,655,000,000	2,584,000,000
Net Income		3,189,000,000	2,248,000,000	3,229,000,000	2,015,000,000	2,200,000,000
Operating Cash Flow		4,305,000,000	4,297,000,000	3,827,000,000	2,613,000,000	2,813,000,000
Capital Expenditure		1,420,000,000	1,264,000,000	1,249,000,000	928,000,000	920,000,000
EBITDA		5,588,000,000	4,094,000,000	5,104,000,000	3,884,000,000	3,680,000,000
Return on Assets %						
Return on Equity %						
Debt to Equity						

CONTACT INFORMATION:

Phone: 703 280-2900 Fax: 310 201-3023
Toll-Free:
Address: 2980 Fairview Park Dr., Falls Church, VA 22042 United States

STOCK TICKER/OTHER:

Stock Ticker: NOC
Employees: 88,000
Parent Company:
Exchange: NYS
Fiscal Year Ends: 12/31

SALARIES/BONUSES:

Top Exec. Salary: $1,536,346 Bonus: $
Second Exec. Salary: $855,000 Bonus: $

OTHER THOUGHTS:

Estimated Female Officers or Directors: 9
Hot Spot for Advancement for Women/Minorities: Y

Sales, profits and employees may be estimates. Financial information, benefits and other data can change quickly and may vary from those stated here.

NortonLifeLock Inc

NAIC Code: 511210E

www.nortonlifelock.com

TYPES OF BUSINESS:

Computer Software: Network Security, Managed Access, Digital ID, Cybersecurity & Anti-Virus
Cybersecurity
Identity Security

BRANDS/DIVISIONS/AFFILIATES:

NortonLifeLock
Norton 360

GROWTH PLANS/SPECIAL FEATURES:

NortonLifeLock sells cybersecurity and identity protection for individual consumers through its Norton antivirus and LifeLock brands. The company divested the Symantec enterprise security business to Broadcom in 2019. The Arizona-based company was founded in 1982, went public in 1989, and sells its solutions worldwide.

NortonLifeLock offers its employees health and financial benefits, including medical/dental/vision insurance and an employee stock purchase program.

CONTACTS: *Note: Officers with more than one job title may be intentionally listed here more than once.*

Vincent Pilette, CEO
Natalie Derse, CFO
Frank Dangeard, Chairman of the Board
Bryan Ko, Chief Legal Officer

FINANCIAL DATA: *Note: Data for latest year may not have been available at press time.*

In U.S. $	2021	2020	2019	2018	2017	2016
Revenue	2,551,000,000	2,490,000,000	4,731,000,000	4,834,000,000	4,019,000,000	3,600,000,000
R&D Expense	267,000,000	328,000,000	913,000,000	956,000,000	823,000,000	748,000,000
Operating Income	1,057,000,000	621,000,000	621,000,000	459,000,000	173,000,000	593,000,000
Operating Margin %						
SGA Expense	791,000,000	1,069,000,000	1,940,000,000	2,167,000,000	2,023,000,000	1,587,000,000
Net Income	554,000,000	3,887,000,000	31,000,000	1,138,000,000	-106,000,000	2,488,000,000
Operating Cash Flow	706,000,000	-861,000,000	1,495,000,000	950,000,000	-220,000,000	796,000,000
Capital Expenditure	6,000,000	89,000,000	207,000,000	142,000,000	70,000,000	272,000,000
EBITDA	1,166,000,000	1,376,000,000	931,000,000	1,333,000,000	476,000,000	766,000,000
Return on Assets %						
Return on Equity %						
Debt to Equity						

CONTACT INFORMATION:

Phone: 650 527-8000 Fax:
Toll-Free:
Address: 60 E. Rio Salado Pkwy, Ste. 1000, Tempe, AZ 85281 United States

STOCK TICKER/OTHER:

Stock Ticker: NLOK
Employees: 2,800
Parent Company:
Exchange: NAS
Fiscal Year Ends: 03/31

SALARIES/BONUSES:

Top Exec. Salary: $753,974 Bonus: $1,300,000
Second Exec. Salary: $472,615 Bonus: $

OTHER THOUGHTS:

Estimated Female Officers or Directors: 3
Hot Spot for Advancement for Women/Minorities: Y

Novatek Microelectronics Corp

www.novatek.com.tw

NAIC Code: 334413

TYPES OF BUSINESS:

Manufacturing-Semiconductors
Integrated Circuits
Products Design
Research & Development

BRANDS/DIVISIONS/AFFILIATES:

Cheertek International Inc

CONTACTS:

Note: Officers with more than one job title may be intentionally listed here more than once.

Steve Wang, Pres.
David Chen, Dir.-Media Rel.
David Chen, Dir.-Investor Rel.
Tai-Shung Ho, Chmn.

GROWTH PLANS/SPECIAL FEATURES:

Novatek Microelectronics Corp. is based in Taiwan, and designs, manufactures and markets integrated circuits (ICs) used in telecommunication, computer peripherals and liquid crystal display (LED) drivers. Novatek sorts its products in two categories: display driver ICs and SoC (system-on-chip) solutions. Display driver ICs manufactured by the company provide high performance, lower electromagnetic interference, low power consumption and are highly integrated. Novatek's full range of display driver IC solutions are provided for diverse applications and displays with a variety of panel sizes and technologies. The firm's SoC solutions are used in multi-media devices, internet infrastructures, as well as wireless communication and interactive devices. They offer high integration capabilities, powerful features and value-added functions for applications in TVs, DVD players, digital cameras, set top boxes and iDTVs. During 2021, Novatek acquired Cheertek International, Inc., a provider of digital video and audio multi-media IC solutions.

Novatek offers its employees welfare and retirement benefits, and a variety of insurance plans.

FINANCIAL DATA:

Note: Data for latest year may not have been available at press time.

In U.S. $	2021	2020	2019	2018	2017	2016
Revenue		2,843,618,069	2,140,570,000	1,790,710,000	1,584,230,000	1,511,735,546
R&D Expense						
Operating Income						
Operating Margin %						
SGA Expense						
Net Income		420,280,105	265,107,000	208,699,000	169,082,000	165,652,558
Operating Cash Flow						
Capital Expenditure						
EBITDA						
Return on Assets %						
Return on Equity %						
Debt to Equity						

CONTACT INFORMATION:

Phone: 886-3-567-0889 Fax: 886-3-577-0132
Toll-Free:
Address: Innovation Rd I, Hsinchu Science Park, No. 13, Fl. 2, Hsinchu, 300 Taiwan

STOCK TICKER/OTHER:

Stock Ticker: 3034
Employees: 2,699
Parent Company:
Exchange: TWSE
Fiscal Year Ends: 12/31

SALARIES/BONUSES:

Top Exec. Salary: $ Bonus: $
Second Exec. Salary: $ Bonus: $

OTHER THOUGHTS:

Estimated Female Officers or Directors:
Hot Spot for Advancement for Women/Minorities:

NTT DATA Corporation

www.nttdata.com/global/en/about-us

NAIC Code: 541512

TYPES OF BUSINESS:

IT Services
Information Technology Solutions
IT Services
Business Services
Consulting Services
Business Process Services
IT Modernization
System and Software Development

BRANDS/DIVISIONS/AFFILIATES:

Nippon Telegraph and Telephone Corporation (NTT)

GROWTH PLANS/SPECIAL FEATURES:

NTT Data Corp provides IT services to a wide range of business fields. The company's operations are divided into three segments: global, public and social infrastructure; enterprise and solutions; and financial. Each segment contributes approximately an even proportion of the company's revenue. The services the company provides include system integration by constructing systems tailored to individual customer needs, multiple Internet and computer network-based information and processing services, consulting that evaluates customers' management issues, system support for large-scale systems, and new IT-based business models. The company is based in Japan but has a global presence.

CONTACTS: *Note: Officers with more than one job title may be intentionally listed here more than once.*

Yo Honma, CEO
Toru Yamashita, Counselor
Masanori Shiina, Exec. VP
Hironobu Sagae, Sr. VP

FINANCIAL DATA: *Note: Data for latest year may not have been available at press time.*

In U.S. $	2021	2020	2019	2018	2017	2016
Revenue	20,374,130,000	19,918,520,000	19,011,850,000			
R&D Expense						
Operating Income	1,222,918,000	1,150,548,000	1,297,986,000			
Operating Margin %						
SGA Expense	3,913,764,000	3,877,667,000	3,490,844,000			
Net Income	675,222,300	660,328,300	822,607,200			
Operating Cash Flow	3,097,360,000	2,460,625,000	2,126,542,000			
Capital Expenditure	1,433,289,000	1,680,907,000	1,581,544,000			
EBITDA	3,109,372,000	2,956,434,000	2,748,383,000			
Return on Assets %						
Return on Equity %						
Debt to Equity						

CONTACT INFORMATION:

Phone: 81 355468202 Fax: 81 355462405
Toll-Free:
Address: Toyosu Ctr. Bldg., 3-3 Toyosu 3-chome, Koto-ku, Tokyo, 135-6033 Japan

STOCK TICKER/OTHER:

Stock Ticker: NTDTY Exchange: PINX
Employees: 126,953 Fiscal Year Ends: 03/31
Parent Company: Nippon Telegraph and Telephone Corporation (NTT)

SALARIES/BONUSES:

Top Exec. Salary: $ Bonus: $
Second Exec. Salary: $ Bonus: $

OTHER THOUGHTS:

Estimated Female Officers or Directors:
Hot Spot for Advancement for Women/Minorities:

NTT DOCOMO Inc

www.nttdocomo.co.jp/english

NAIC Code: 517210

TYPES OF BUSINESS:

Mobile Telephone Service
Mobile
5G
Telecommunications
Tablets
Data Communication
Advanced Wireless Networks
LTE Networks

BRANDS/DIVISIONS/AFFILIATES:

Nippon Telegraph and Telephone Corporation (NTT)
docomo

GROWTH PLANS/SPECIAL FEATURES:

NTT DOCOMO, Inc. is a leading telecommunications company in Japan. The firm serves more than 73 million customers in Japan via advanced wireless networks, including long-term evolution (LTE) and LTE-advanced networks. NTT DOCOMO is a world-leading developer of 5G networks, deploying the network and network function virtualization (NFV) and other related technologies during the 2020s. Outside Japan, NTT DOCOMO provides technical and operational expertise to mobile operators and other partner companies, and contributes to the global standardization of new mobile technologies. Products by NTT DOCOMO include iPhones, iPads, docomo 4G and 5G smartphones, docomo tablets and other phones, watches, data communications products, drivers support products and more. The parent company of the firm is Nippon Telegraph and Telephone Corporation (NTT).

CONTACTS: *Note: Officers with more than one job title may be intentionally listed here more than once.*

Motoyuki Ii, CEO
Seizo Onoe, CTO
Fumio Iwasaki, Sr. Exec. VP
Tsutomu Shindou, Exec. VP
Takashi Tanaka, Exec. VP
Kazuhiro Yoshizawa, Exec. VP

FINANCIAL DATA: *Note: Data for latest year may not have been available at press time.*

In U.S. $	2021	2020	2019	2018	2017	2016
Revenue	42,874,999,988	43,134,016,602	46,076,108,800	45,396,140,032	42,620,825,600	43,089,641,472
R&D Expense						
Operating Income						
Operating Margin %						
SGA Expense						
Net Income	8,286,093,708	5,485,300,000	6,339,808,768	7,086,691,328	6,066,396,160	5,219,565,568
Operating Cash Flow						
Capital Expenditure						
EBITDA						
Return on Assets %						
Return on Equity %						
Debt to Equity						

CONTACT INFORMATION:

Phone: 81 351561111 Fax: 81 351560271
Toll-Free:
Address: 2-11-1, Nagata-cho, Chiyoda-ku, Tokyo, 100-6150 Japan

STOCK TICKER/OTHER:

Stock Ticker: Subsidiary
Exchange:
Employees: 38,000
Fiscal Year Ends: 03/31
Parent Company: Nippon Telegraph and Telephone Corporation (NTT)

SALARIES/BONUSES:

Top Exec. Salary: $ Bonus: $
Second Exec. Salary: $ Bonus: $

OTHER THOUGHTS:

Estimated Female Officers or Directors:
Hot Spot for Advancement for Women/Minorities:

Nutanix Inc

www.nutanix.com

NAIC Code: 511210B

TYPES OF BUSINESS:

Computer Software: Network Management (IT), System Testing & Storage
Enterprise Cloud Platform
Software Solutions
Cloud Services
Multi-Cloud Solutions
Cloud Infrastructure
Cloud Management
Storage

BRANDS/DIVISIONS/AFFILIATES:

GROWTH PLANS/SPECIAL FEATURES:

Nutanix Inc provides native hybrid cloud capabilities for businesses. The company offers Enterprise Cloud Platform to businesses for various uses such as web-scale engineering and consumer-grade design, virtualization, and storage into a resilient, and software-defined solution. Geographically, it derives a majority of revenue from the United States and also has a presence in Europe, the Middle East, Asia Pacific, Africa, and other regions.

CONTACTS: *Note: Officers with more than one job title may be intentionally listed here more than once.*

Rajiv Ramaswami, CEO
Duston Williams, CFO
Virginia Gambale, Chairman of the Board
Aaron Boynton, Chief Accounting Officer
Tyler Wall, Chief Legal Officer
David Sangster, COO
Christopher Kaddaras, Other Executive Officer

FINANCIAL DATA: *Note: Data for latest year may not have been available at press time.*

In U.S. $	2021	2020	2019	2018	2017	2016
Revenue	1,394,364,000	1,307,682,000	1,236,143,000	1,155,457,000	766,869,000	444,928,000
R&D Expense	556,950,000	553,978,000	500,719,000	313,777,000	288,619,000	116,400,000
Operating Income	-660,782,000	-828,921,000	-598,041,000	-280,408,000	-426,951,000	-165,017,000
Operating Margin %						
SGA Expense	1,206,290,000	1,295,936,000	1,029,337,000	736,058,000	577,870,000	322,758,000
Net Income	-1,034,260,000	-872,883,000	-621,179,000	-297,161,000	-458,011,000	-168,499,000
Operating Cash Flow	-99,810,000	-159,885,000	42,168,000	92,555,000	13,822,000	3,636,000
Capital Expenditure	58,647,000	89,488,000	118,452,000	62,372,000	50,181,000	42,294,000
EBITDA	-841,468,000	-735,148,000	-520,429,000	-230,106,000	-388,552,000	-138,609,000
Return on Assets %						
Return on Equity %						
Debt to Equity						

CONTACT INFORMATION:

Phone: 855-688-2649 Fax: 408-916-4039
Toll-Free:
Address: 1740 Technology Dr., Ste. 150, San Jose, CA 95110 United States

STOCK TICKER/OTHER:

Stock Ticker: NTNX Exchange: NAS
Employees: 6,080 Fiscal Year Ends: 07/31
Parent Company:

SALARIES/BONUSES:

Top Exec. Salary: $586,250 Bonus: $
Second Exec. Salary: $515,151 Bonus: $

OTHER THOUGHTS:

Estimated Female Officers or Directors:
Hot Spot for Advancement for Women/Minorities:

NVIDIA Corporation

www.nvidia.com

NAIC Code: 334413

TYPES OF BUSINESS:

Printed Circuit & Chips Manufacturing
Graphics Processors
Graphics Software
Artificial Intelligence
Compute
Networking
Data Center
Robotics

BRANDS/DIVISIONS/AFFILIATES:

GeForce
Quadro
NVIDIA RTX
AI Cockpit
Jetson

GROWTH PLANS/SPECIAL FEATURES:

Nvidia is the top designer of discrete graphics processing units that enhance the experience on computing platforms. The firm's chips are used in a variety of end markets, including high-end PCs for gaming, data centers, and automotive infotainment systems. In recent years, the firm has broadened its focus from traditional PC graphics applications such as gaming to more complex and favorable opportunities, including artificial intelligence and autonomous driving, which leverage the high-performance capabilities of the firm's graphics processing units.

NVIDIA offers its employees medical benefits, an employee stock purchase plan and flexible paid leave of absence.

CONTACTS: *Note: Officers with more than one job title may be intentionally listed here more than once.*

Jen-Hsun Huang, CEO
Colette Kress, CFO
Michael Mccaffery, Chairman of the Board
Donald Robertson, Chief Accounting Officer
Ajay Puri, Executive VP, Divisional
Debora Shoquist, Executive VP, Divisional
Timothy Teter, Executive VP

FINANCIAL DATA: *Note: Data for latest year may not have been available at press time.*

In U.S. $	2021	2020	2019	2018	2017	2016
Revenue	16,675,000,000	10,918,000,000	11,716,000,000	9,714,000,000	6,910,000,000	5,010,000,000
R&D Expense	3,924,000,000	2,829,000,000	2,376,000,000	1,797,000,000	1,463,000,000	1,331,000,000
Operating Income	4,532,000,000	2,846,000,000	3,804,000,000	3,210,000,000	1,937,000,000	878,000,000
Operating Margin %						
SGA Expense	1,940,000,000	1,093,000,000	991,000,000	815,000,000	663,000,000	602,000,000
Net Income	4,332,000,000	2,796,000,000	4,141,000,000	3,047,000,000	1,666,000,000	614,000,000
Operating Cash Flow	5,822,000,000	4,761,000,000	3,743,000,000	3,502,000,000	1,672,000,000	1,175,000,000
Capital Expenditure	1,128,000,000	489,000,000	600,000,000	593,000,000	176,000,000	86,000,000
EBITDA	5,691,000,000	3,403,000,000	4,216,000,000	3,456,000,000	2,150,000,000	987,000,000
Return on Assets %						
Return on Equity %						
Debt to Equity						

CONTACT INFORMATION:

Phone: 408 486-2000 Fax: 408 486-2200
Toll-Free:
Address: 2788 San Tomas Expressway, Santa Clara, CA 95051 United States

STOCK TICKER/OTHER:

Stock Ticker: NVDA
Employees: 18,975
Parent Company:
Exchange: NAS
Fiscal Year Ends: 01/31

SALARIES/BONUSES:

Top Exec. Salary: $1,017,355 Bonus: $
Second Exec. Salary: $966,487 Bonus: $

OTHER THOUGHTS:

Estimated Female Officers or Directors: 3
Hot Spot for Advancement for Women/Minorities: Y

NXP Semiconductors NV

www.nxp.com

NAIC Code: 334413

TYPES OF BUSINESS:

Semiconductor Research, Development & Manufacturing
Semiconductor Production
Mixed-Signal Products
Power Management Products
Digital Processing
Security Products

BRANDS/DIVISIONS/AFFILIATES:

GROWTH PLANS/SPECIAL FEATURES:

NXP Semiconductors is a leading supplier of high-performance mixed-signal products. The firm acquired Freescale Semiconductor in 2015 and now has significant market share in the automotive market, where it supplies microcontrollers and analog chips into automotive clusters, powertrains, infotainment systems, and radars. NXP Semiconductors also serves industrial and Internet of Things, mobile, and communications infrastructure.

CONTACTS: *Note: Officers with more than one job title may be intentionally listed here more than once.*

Kurt Sievers, CEO
Andy Micallef, Exec. VP-Global Oper.
Bill Betz, CFO
Steve Owen, Exec. VP-Mktg. & Sales
Chris Jensen, Chief Human Resources Officer
Dave French, Exec. VP-R&D
Lars Reger, CTO
Frans Scheper, Sr. VP
Guido Dierick, General Counsel
Chris Belden, Exec. VP
Alexander Everke, Exec. VP
Kurt Sievers, Sr. VP
Sean Hunkler, Exec. VP
Peter Bonfield, Chmn.

FINANCIAL DATA: *Note: Data for latest year may not have been available at press time.*

In U.S. $	2021	2020	2019	2018	2017	2016
Revenue		8,612,000,000	8,877,000,000	9,407,000,000	9,255,999,000	9,498,000,000
R&D Expense		1,725,000,000	1,643,000,000	1,700,000,000	1,554,000,000	1,560,000,000
Operating Income		304,000,000	616,000,000	709,000,000	527,000,000	-159,000,000
Operating Margin %						
SGA Expense		879,000,000	924,000,000	993,000,000	1,090,000,000	1,141,000,000
Net Income		52,000,000	243,000,000	2,208,000,000	2,215,000,000	200,000,000
Operating Cash Flow		2,482,000,000	2,373,000,000	4,369,000,000	2,447,000,000	2,303,000,000
Capital Expenditure		522,000,000	628,000,000	661,000,000	618,000,000	448,000,000
EBITDA		2,351,000,000	2,708,000,000	4,635,000,000	4,219,000,000	2,010,000,000
Return on Assets %						
Return on Equity %						
Debt to Equity						

CONTACT INFORMATION:

Phone: 31 402729233 Fax:
Toll-Free:
Address: 60 High Tech Campus, Eindhoven, 5656 AG Netherlands

STOCK TICKER/OTHER:

Stock Ticker: NXPI
Employees: 29,000
Parent Company:
Exchange: NAS
Fiscal Year Ends: 12/31

SALARIES/BONUSES:

Top Exec. Salary: $1,275,311 Bonus: $
Second Exec. Salary: $759,968 Bonus: $

OTHER THOUGHTS:

Estimated Female Officers or Directors:
Hot Spot for Advancement for Women/Minorities:

Okta Inc

www.okta.com

NAIC Code: 511210E

TYPES OF BUSINESS:

Computer Software: Network Security, Managed Access, Digital ID, Cybersecurity & Anti-Virus
Identity Software
Identity Management
Cloud
Information Technology
Multifactor Authentication

BRANDS/DIVISIONS/AFFILIATES:

Okta Identity Cloud
Auth0

GROWTH PLANS/SPECIAL FEATURES:

Okta, Inc. addresses two primary security concerns via its workforce identity and customer identity solutions. The pureplay cybersecurity firm sells products to protect employees, contractors, and partners as well as its customers' end users. Okta's software solutions are cloud-delivered, and its integration network gives customers security protection across a wide variety of applications that are critical to business and government needs. The California-based company went public in 2017 and had over 2,100 employees at the end of the third quarter of fiscal 2020.

CONTACTS: *Note: Officers with more than one job title may be intentionally listed here more than once.*

Todd McKinnon, CEO
Michael Kourey, CFO
Christopher Kramer, Chief Accounting Officer
Jacques Frederic Kerrest, Co-Founder
Jonathan Runyan, General Counsel
Susan St. Ledger, President, Divisional
Brett Tighe, Senior VP, Divisional

FINANCIAL DATA: *Note: Data for latest year may not have been available at press time.*

In U.S. $	2021	2020	2019	2018	2017	2016
Revenue	835,424,000	586,067,000	399,254,000	259,990,000	160,326,000	85,907,000
R&D Expense	222,826,000	159,269,000	102,385,000	70,821,000	38,659,000	28,761,000
Operating Income	-204,159,000	-185,832,000	-119,622,000	-116,362,000	-83,123,000	-75,988,000
Operating Margin %						
SGA Expense	599,076,000	453,248,000	303,070,000	224,776,000	148,841,000	97,110,000
Net Income	-266,332,000	-208,913,000	-125,497,000	-114,359,000	-83,509,000	-76,302,000
Operating Cash Flow	127,962,000	55,603,000	15,172,000	-25,240,000	-42,101,000	-41,536,000
Capital Expenditure	17,368,000	27,919,000	22,662,000	11,981,000	11,742,000	6,701,000
EBITDA	-156,666,000	-165,500,000	-102,441,000	-109,361,000	-78,555,000	-73,099,000
Return on Assets %						
Return on Equity %						
Debt to Equity						

CONTACT INFORMATION:

Phone: 415-494-8029 Fax:
Toll-Free: 888-722-7871
Address: 100 First St., Ste. 600, San Francisco, CA 94105 United States

STOCK TICKER/OTHER:

Stock Ticker: OKTA
Employees: 2,806
Parent Company:
Exchange: NAS
Fiscal Year Ends: 01/31

SALARIES/BONUSES:

Top Exec. Salary: $362,585 Bonus: $
Second Exec. Salary: $350,900 Bonus: $

OTHER THOUGHTS:

Estimated Female Officers or Directors:
Hot Spot for Advancement for Women/Minorities:

Sales, profits and employees may be estimates. Financial information, benefits and other data can change quickly and may vary from those stated here.

OmniVision Technologies Inc

www.ovt.com

NAIC Code: 334413

TYPES OF BUSINESS:

Semiconductor and Related Device Manufacturing
Fabless Semiconductors
Advanced Digital Imaging Solutions
Analog Solutions
Touch Screen Solutions
Display Solutions
Integrated Circuit Chips
Extended Reality Shutter Sensors

BRANDS/DIVISIONS/AFFILIATES:

Nyxel
PureCel
Omni
CameraCubeChip

CONTACTS: *Note: Officers with more than one job title may be intentionally listed here more than once.*

Renrong Yu, CEO
Henry Yang, Pres.
Anson Chan, CFO
Michael Wu, Sr. VP-Mktg. & Sales
Cooper Wu, COO
Boyd Fowler, CTO
Y. Chou, General Counsel
Ray Cisneros, Senior VP, Divisional
John Li, Vice President, Divisional
Zille Hasnain, Vice President, Divisional
Shaw Hong, Chmn.

GROWTH PLANS/SPECIAL FEATURES:

OmniVision Technologies, Inc. is a global fabless semiconductor organization that develops advanced digital imaging, analog and touch/display solutions for a wide range of applications and industries. The company's products include image sensors, application-specific integrated circuit (ASIC) chips, camera chips, liquid crystal on silicon (LCOS) layers and displays, power management applications, and touch screen/display solutions. OmniVision primarily serves the automotive, medical, mobile, surveillance, Internet of Things (IoT), emerging technology and computing industries. The firm's technology brands include Nyxel, PureCel, Omni and CameraCubeChip. Headquartered in the U.S., OmniVision has operations throughout North America, Europe and the Asia-Pacific. In January 2022, OmniVision and Tobii announced a partnership to advance solutions for vision in the metaverse. The jointly-developed eye-tracking reference design is based on OmniVision's shutter sensor family and helps extended reality (XR) original equipment manufacturer speed time to market for high demand XR consumer electronics products.

OmniVision offers its employees health, vision, dental and life insurance plans; savings and retirement plans; flexible spending accounts; and paid time off.

FINANCIAL DATA: *Note: Data for latest year may not have been available at press time.*

In U.S. $	2021	2020	2019	2018	2017	2016
Revenue	1,984,500,000	1,890,000,000	1,680,000,000	1,600,000,000	1,520,099,482	1,447,713,792
R&D Expense						
Operating Income						
Operating Margin %						
SGA Expense						
Net Income						
Operating Cash Flow						
Capital Expenditure						
EBITDA						
Return on Assets %						
Return on Equity %						
Debt to Equity						

CONTACT INFORMATION:

Phone: 408 567-3000 Fax: 408 733-3061
Toll-Free:
Address: 4275 Burton Dr., Santa Clara, CA 95054 United States

STOCK TICKER/OTHER:

Stock Ticker: Private
Exchange:
Employees: 2,176
Fiscal Year Ends: 04/30
Parent Company:

SALARIES/BONUSES:

Top Exec. Salary: $ Bonus: $
Second Exec. Salary: $ Bonus: $

OTHER THOUGHTS:

Estimated Female Officers or Directors:
Hot Spot for Advancement for Women/Minorities:

Omron Automation Americas

automation.omron.com/en/us

NAIC Code: 334111

TYPES OF BUSINESS:

Computer Manufacturing
Industrial Automation Solutions
Sensors
Motion Control Systems
Power Drives
Software
Laser Marking
Robotics

BRANDS/DIVISIONS/AFFILIATES:

OMRON Corporation

CONTACTS:

Note: Officers with more than one job title may be intentionally listed here more than once.

Robb Black, CEO
Seth Halio, CFO
Michael Kelly, Director

GROWTH PLANS/SPECIAL FEATURES:

Omron Automation America is part of the global Omron Corporation and a leading provider of technology advanced industrial automation solutions that include sensing, control, safety, vision, motion, robotics and more. Omron Automation's products provide operator safety and serves to enhance wellbeing in the workplace as well as in everyday life. The company's products span categories such as automation systems, sensors, motion control, power drives, software, identification, fiber laser marking, machine safety technology, robotics, serial peripheral interface (SPI), automated optical inspection (AOI), advanced extensible interface (AXI), industrial control panel products, machine vision, and sensing. Omron Automation solutions include automation, predictive maintenance, flexible manufacturing, traceability, safety, robotics, fault detection, condition monitoring, Industrial Internet of Things (IIoT), panel building, visualization and 3D solder joint inspection. Industries served by Omron Automation primarily include automotive, food and beverage packaging, semiconductor, electronics, life sciences, logistics, warehouse automation, machine tool, oil and gas, security, detention, entertainment, water and wastewater, among others. In late-2021, Omron Automation Americas announced the opening of a new proof-of-concept center in Dallas/For Worth, Texas. The facility provides customers with a low-risk approach to validating solutions ahead of major manufacturing investments.

FINANCIAL DATA:

Note: Data for latest year may not have been available at press time.

In U.S. $	2021	2020	2019	2018	2017	2016
Revenue	62,045,392	59,659,031	61,188,750	58,275,000	55,500,000	54,000,000
R&D Expense						
Operating Income						
Operating Margin %						
SGA Expense						
Net Income						
Operating Cash Flow						
Capital Expenditure						
EBITDA						
Return on Assets %						
Return on Equity %						
Debt to Equity						

CONTACT INFORMATION:

Phone: 847 843-7900 Fax:
Toll-Free: 800-556-6766
Address: 2895 Greenspoint Pkwy, Ste. 200, Hoffman Estates, IL 60169 United States

STOCK TICKER/OTHER:

Stock Ticker: Subsidiary
Exchange:
Employees: 170
Fiscal Year Ends: 03/31
Parent Company: OMRON Corporation

SALARIES/BONUSES:

Top Exec. Salary: $ Bonus: $
Second Exec. Salary: $ Bonus: $

OTHER THOUGHTS:

Estimated Female Officers or Directors:
Hot Spot for Advancement for Women/Minorities:

ON Semiconductor Corporation

www.onsemi.com

NAIC Code: 334413

TYPES OF BUSINESS:

Semiconductor devices manufacturing
Power Technologies
Sensing Technologies
Power Solutions
Semiconductor Products
Signal Solutions
Integrated Circuits
Imaging Sensors

BRANDS/DIVISIONS/AFFILIATES:

onsemi

GROWTH PLANS/SPECIAL FEATURES:

Onsemi is a leading supplier of power and analog semiconductors, as well as sensors. Onsemi is the second-largest global supplier of discrete transistors like insulated gate bipolar transistors, or IGBTs, and metal oxide semiconductor field-effect transistors, or MOSFETs, and also has a significant integrated power chip business. Onsemi is also the largest supplier of image sensors to the automotive market, targeting autonomous driving applications. The firm is concentrated in and focused on the automotive, industrial, and communications markets, and is reducing its exposure to the consumer and computing markets.

CONTACTS: *Note: Officers with more than one job title may be intentionally listed here more than once.*

Hassane El-Khoury, CEO
Thad Trent, CFO
Alan Campbell, Chairman of the Board
Bernard Colpitts, Chief Accounting Officer
George Cave, Chief Compliance Officer
William Schromm, COO
Paul Rolls, Executive VP, Divisional
Simon Keeton, Executive VP
Vincent Hopkin, Executive VP
Ross Jatou, General Manager, Divisional

FINANCIAL DATA: *Note: Data for latest year may not have been available at press time.*

In U.S. $	2021	2020	2019	2018	2017	2016
Revenue		5,255,000,000	5,517,900,000	5,878,300,000	5,543,100,000	3,906,900,000
R&D Expense		642,900,000	640,900,000	650,700,000	594,400,000	452,300,000
Operating Income		415,200,000	632,500,000	858,300,000	714,800,000	271,500,000
Operating Margin %						
SGA Expense		537,400,000	585,000,000	618,000,000	600,800,000	468,300,000
Net Income		234,200,000	211,700,000	627,400,000	810,700,000	182,100,000
Operating Cash Flow		884,300,000	694,700,000	1,274,200,000	1,094,200,000	581,200,000
Capital Expenditure		483,600,000	634,600,000	514,800,000	395,700,000	212,900,000
EBITDA		970,100,000	1,018,000,000	1,391,900,000	1,170,600,000	690,000,000
Return on Assets %						
Return on Equity %						
Debt to Equity						

CONTACT INFORMATION:

Phone: 602 244-6600 Fax: 602 244-6071
Toll-Free:
Address: 5005 E. McDowell Rd., Phoenix, AZ 85008 United States

STOCK TICKER/OTHER:

Stock Ticker: ON
Employees: 34,800
Parent Company:
Exchange: NAS
Fiscal Year Ends: 12/31

SALARIES/BONUSES:

Top Exec. Salary: $1,021,018 Bonus: $
Second Exec. Salary: $531,954 Bonus: $

OTHER THOUGHTS:

Estimated Female Officers or Directors:
Hot Spot for Advancement for Women/Minorities:

OneSpan Inc

NAIC Code: 511210E

www.onespan.com

TYPES OF BUSINESS:

Computer Software: Network Security, Managed Access, Digital ID, Cybersecurity & Anti-Virus
Identity Security
Authentication
Anti-Fraud Services
Agreement Automation

BRANDS/DIVISIONS/AFFILIATES:

GROWTH PLANS/SPECIAL FEATURES:

OneSpan Inc is a provider of information technology security solutions for banking and financial services and application security markets. Its solutions secure and manage access to digital assets and protect online transactions, via mobile devices and in-person. Authentication and anti-fraud solutions are the organization's primary product offerings and include multifactor authentication and virtual private network access capabilities. The company derives revenues from hardware and license fees, maintenance and support fees, and subscription fees. A large majority of the firm's revenue is generated in Europe, Middle East and Africa, and the rest in the United States and Asia-Pacific region.

CONTACTS: *Note: Officers with more than one job title may be intentionally listed here more than once.*

Steven Worth, CEO
Jan van Gaalen, CFO
Alfred Nietzel, Chairman of the Board
John Bosshart, Chief Accounting Officer

FINANCIAL DATA: *Note: Data for latest year may not have been available at press time.*

In U.S. $	2021	2020	2019	2018	2017	2016
Revenue		215,691,000	254,570,000	212,280,000	193,291,000	192,304,000
R&D Expense		41,194,000	42,463,000	32,197,000	23,119,000	23,214,000
Operating Income		-5,258,000	15,275,000	24,000	6,192,000	9,599,000
Operating Margin %						
SGA Expense		107,194,000	105,400,000	105,394,000	96,394,000	88,995,000
Net Income		-5,455,000	8,789,000	3,846,000	-22,399,000	10,514,000
Operating Cash Flow		14,922,000	18,244,000	1,226,000	17,627,000	28,415,000
Capital Expenditure		3,101,000	7,453,000	3,685,000	3,195,000	2,187,000
EBITDA		6,745,000	26,820,000	12,162,000	16,793,000	20,376,000
Return on Assets %						
Return on Equity %						
Debt to Equity						

CONTACT INFORMATION:

Phone: 312-766-4001 Fax:
Toll-Free:
Address: 121 West Wacker Dr., Ste. 2050, Chicago, IL 60601 United States

STOCK TICKER/OTHER:

Stock Ticker: OSPN
Employees: 870
Parent Company:
Exchange: NAS
Fiscal Year Ends: 12/31

SALARIES/BONUSES:

Top Exec. Salary: $480,000 Bonus: $
Second Exec. Salary: $380,000 Bonus: $

OTHER THOUGHTS:

Estimated Female Officers or Directors:
Hot Spot for Advancement for Women/Minorities:

OneWeb Ltd

NAIC Code: 517410

www.oneweb.world

TYPES OF BUSINESS:

Satellite Internet Access Services
Satellites
Global Communications Network
Internet Connectivity Services
User Terminals
5G

BRANDS/DIVISIONS/AFFILIATES:

UK Department for Business Energy and Industrial
Bharthi Group
Eutelsat

CONTACTS: *Note: Officers with more than one job title may be intentionally listed here more than once.*

Neil Masterson, CEO
Michele Franci, COO
Srikanth Balackandran, CFO
Kate Roddy, Chief People Officer
Massimiliano Ladovaz, CTO

GROWTH PLANS/SPECIAL FEATURES:

OneWeb Ltd. is building a global communications network in space for the delivery of high-throughput, high-speed services capable of connecting everywhere and to everyone. The firm has designed an advanced, low-Earth-orbit satellite constellation referred to as OneWeb. OneWeb's 5G-ready network enables connectivity solutions for maritime, aviation, enterprise and government entities, and will cover cell site backhaul. The company powers digital transformation and offers tailored networking solutions for any need, at any level. OneWeb satellites orbit relatively close to the Earth, allowing for better internet access speeds. As they orbit, they interlock with each other electronically to create coverage over the entire planet. Small, low-cost user terminals communicate with the satellite network and provide wireless internet access. The terminals provide connectivity with no change in latency (speed) during satellite handovers in order to ensure continuous quality of voice, gaming and web surfing experience. User terminals consist of a satellite antenna, a receiver and a customer network exchange unit (CNX). The CNX connects the user terminal to the customer's network which in turn connects to end-user devices such as laptops, smartphones, sensors and more. Compared to traditional satellites, OneWeb units have fewer components, are lighter in weight, easier to manufacture and cheaper to launch. They contain on-board propulsion and state-of-the-art positioning GPS sensors that ground-track their placement within meters. The propulsion systems perform maneuvers for steering clear of space debris. When a OneWeb satellite nears the end of its service life, it will de-orbit automatically. Headquartered in London, UK, OneWeb has an international office in Virginia, USA. The firm is owned by the UK government, Bharti Group and Eutelsat, with additional investments from SoftBank and Hughes Network Group. In January 2022, OneWeb and Hughes Network Systems LLC announced a strategic six-year distribution partner agreement to provide low-Earth orbit connectivity services across India.

FINANCIAL DATA: *Note: Data for latest year may not have been available at press time.*

In U.S. $	2021	2020	2019	2018	2017	2016
Revenue	3,000,000	26,520,760	75,773,600	216,496,000	81,254,000	
R&D Expense						
Operating Income						
Operating Margin %						
SGA Expense						
Net Income	370,800,000			-213,184,000	-73,857,000	
Operating Cash Flow						
Capital Expenditure						
EBITDA						
Return on Assets %						
Return on Equity %						
Debt to Equity						

CONTACT INFORMATION:

Phone: 4420 3727 1160 Fax:
Toll-Free:
Address: 195 Wood Ln., W., Works Bldg., Fl.3, London, W12 7FQ United Kingdom

STOCK TICKER/OTHER:

Stock Ticker: Subsidiary
Employees: 400
Parent Company: UK Department for Business Energy and Industrial
Exchange:
Fiscal Year Ends:

SALARIES/BONUSES:

Top Exec. Salary: $ Bonus: $
Second Exec. Salary: $ Bonus: $

OTHER THOUGHTS:

Estimated Female Officers or Directors:
Hot Spot for Advancement for Women/Minorities:

OnStar LLC

www.onstar.com

NAIC Code: 517210

TYPES OF BUSINESS:

Wireless Telecommunications Carriers (except Satellite)
Vehicle Safety Solutions
Vehicle Accident Assistance
Travel Connectivity Solutions
In-Vehicle Solutions
Out-of-Vehicle Solutions
Connected Vehicle Solutions
Mobile App

BRANDS/DIVISIONS/AFFILIATES:

General Motors Company (GM)
Premium Plan
Safety and Security Plan
Guardian App
Essentials Plan
Connected Vehicle

GROWTH PLANS/SPECIAL FEATURES:

OnStar Corporation, a subsidiary of General Motors Company, provides in- and out-of-vehicle safety and security services. These services include 24-hour-a-day access to trained service advisors to assist in a crash, crisis or emergency. OnStar plans include: the Premium Plan, offering safety, security and seamless connectivity; Safety and Security Plan, offering safety and security services when in the vehicle; Guardian App, offering safety services via smartphone app for anyone, in any vehicle; Essentials Plan, offering connectivity and essential services when traveling; and Connected Vehicle, offering connected services such as remote key fob, voice services, vehicle status/location, remote personalization and more. A la carte and add-ons include in-vehicle unlimited data access, remote access via mobile app, embedded app access, travel safety and driver attention system connection (on over 200,000 miles of compatible roads in the U.S. and Canada).

Parent GM offers employees a comprehensive benefits package, including health and retirement plans.

CONTACTS: *Note: Officers with more than one job title may be intentionally listed here more than once.*

Santiago Chamorro, VP
Greg Ross, Dir.-Prod. Strategy
Phil Abram, Exec. Dir.

FINANCIAL DATA: *Note: Data for latest year may not have been available at press time.*

In U.S. $	2021	2020	2019	2018	2017	2016
Revenue	1,900,000,000	1,874,250,000	2,205,000,000	2,100,000,000	2,021,250,000	1,925,000,000
R&D Expense						
Operating Income						
Operating Margin %						
SGA Expense						
Net Income						
Operating Cash Flow						
Capital Expenditure						
EBITDA						
Return on Assets %						
Return on Equity %						
Debt to Equity						

CONTACT INFORMATION:

Phone: Fax:
Toll-Free: 888-466-7827
Address: PO Box 1027, Warren, MI 48090-1027 United States

STOCK TICKER/OTHER:

Stock Ticker: Subsidiary Exchange:
Employees: Fiscal Year Ends: 12/31
Parent Company: General Motors Company (GM)

SALARIES/BONUSES:

Top Exec. Salary: $ Bonus: $
Second Exec. Salary: $ Bonus: $

OTHER THOUGHTS:

Estimated Female Officers or Directors: 1
Hot Spot for Advancement for Women/Minorities:

Onto Innovation Inc

ontoinnovation.com

NAIC Code: 334513

TYPES OF BUSINESS:

Instruments and Related Products Manufacturing for Measuring, Displaying, and Controlling Industrial Process Variables
Process Control Tool Manufacturer
Process Control Software
Lithograph Systems

BRANDS/DIVISIONS/AFFILIATES:

Inspectrology LLC

GROWTH PLANS/SPECIAL FEATURES:

Onto Innovation designs, develops, and manufactures process control tools and software and lithography systems. Its products are used in the manufacture of semiconductors and other solid-state devices. The company has three reportable segments: systems and software; parts; and services. The segment of systems and software is the largest contributor to the company's total revenue and sales volume. The company mainly operates in the United States, Asia, and Europe, with China and South Korea the largest sources of total revenue.

CONTACTS: *Note: Officers with more than one job title may be intentionally listed here more than once.*

Michael Plisinski, CEO
Steven Roth, CFO
David Miller, Chairman of the Board
James Harlow, COO
Robert Koch, General Counsel
Jin Ju, General Manager, Divisional
Rodney Smedt, General Manager, Divisional
Robert Fiordalice, General Manager, Divisional
Elvino da Silveira, General Manager, Divisional
Danielle Baptiste, General Manager, Divisional
Kevin Heidrich, Senior VP, Divisional
Dean Iacopetti, Senior VP, Divisional
Rollin Kocher, Senior VP, Divisional
Barry Hartunian, Vice President, Divisional

FINANCIAL DATA: *Note: Data for latest year may not have been available at press time.*

In U.S. $	2021	2020	2019	2018	2017	2016
Revenue		556,496,000	305,896,000	273,784,000	255,098,000	232,780,000
R&D Expense		84,584,000	48,358,000	49,053,000	46,986,000	44,964,000
Operating Income		26,677,000	-5,043,000	51,084,000	46,288,000	37,705,000
Operating Margin %						
SGA Expense		113,446,000	81,268,000	46,608,000	39,381,000	38,562,000
Net Income		31,025,000	1,910,000	45,096,000	32,909,000	36,952,000
Operating Cash Flow		105,984,000	18,146,000	35,094,000	64,371,000	46,633,000
Capital Expenditure		3,829,000	6,802,000	7,542,000	11,210,000	5,291,000
EBITDA		94,255,000	11,367,000	57,466,000	52,218,000	43,702,000
Return on Assets %						
Return on Equity %						
Debt to Equity						

CONTACT INFORMATION:

Phone: 978-253-6200 Fax:
Toll-Free:
Address: 16 Jonspin Rd., Wilmington, MA 01887 United States

STOCK TICKER/OTHER:

Stock Ticker: ONTO
Employees: 1,411
Parent Company:
Exchange: NYS
Fiscal Year Ends: 12/31

SALARIES/BONUSES:

Top Exec. Salary: $592,089 Bonus: $
Second Exec. Salary: $400,975 Bonus: $

OTHER THOUGHTS:

Estimated Female Officers or Directors:
Hot Spot for Advancement for Women/Minorities:

OPPO Electronics Corporation

www.oppo.com

NAIC Code: 334220

TYPES OF BUSINESS:

Cellular Telephones Manufacturing
Smart Electronics
Technology
Smartphones
Modems
Smart Watches

BRANDS/DIVISIONS/AFFILIATES:

BKK Electronics Corporation
Find X
Reno
A
OPPO 5G CPE Omni
OPPO Watch

CONTACTS: *Note: Officers with more than one job title may be intentionally listed here more than once.*

Tony Chen, CEO

GROWTH PLANS/SPECIAL FEATURES:

OPPO Electronics Corporation, a subsidiary of BBK Electronics Corporation, is a global electronics and technology service provider that manufactures and sells smart devices. OPPO's smartphones include the Find X, Reno and A models, as well as the OPPO Watch. Some phones include features such as a camera in the front and the back, vivid mode, scroll-like display, augmented reality (AR), LED flash, artificial intelligence (AI) such as intelligent subject and scene detection, a dual SIM slot, rear fingerprint scanner, facial recognition unlocking, 4G, 5G-ready, voice over long-term evolution (VoLTE), Bluetooth and a proprietary mobile operating system called ColorOS. OPPO's 10x lossless zoom lens (for its most recent and next-gen smartphones) enables ultra-wide-angle capabilities as well as telephoto shots, all within a slim phone design. Lossless zoom means that no loss in the quality of the image will occur when scaling it up. OPPO engages in 5G technology development for enhanced data speeds, especially for AR processing, cloud-based gaming and the seamless connection of smart devices. Its OPPO 5G CPE Omni connectivity modem is able to convert 5G signals into Wi-Fi signals, providing a high-speed network for mobile devices. It also supports BLE and ZigBee to connect and control all devices from a single platform. The OPPO Watch features eSIM standalone communication capabilities, a hyperboloid flexible screen, dual engine power, sports health assistance and a ColorOS watch smart system. The firm is based in China, and operates in more than 40 countries and regions. It has over 400,000 sales outlets, six research institutes, four R&D centers and a global design center worldwide.

FINANCIAL DATA: *Note: Data for latest year may not have been available at press time.*

In U.S. $	2021	2020	2019	2018	2017	2016
Revenue						
R&D Expense						
Operating Income						
Operating Margin %						
SGA Expense						
Net Income						
Operating Cash Flow						
Capital Expenditure						
EBITDA						
Return on Assets %						
Return on Equity %						
Debt to Equity						

CONTACT INFORMATION:

Phone: 86-0769-85545555 Fax: 86-0769-85540007
Toll-Free:
Address: Terra 8th Rd., Shenzhen, Guangdong, 518000 China

STOCK TICKER/OTHER:

Stock Ticker: Subsidiary Exchange:
Employees: Fiscal Year Ends:
Parent Company: BBK Electronics Corporation

SALARIES/BONUSES:

Top Exec. Salary: $ Bonus: $
Second Exec. Salary: $ Bonus: $

OTHER THOUGHTS:

Estimated Female Officers or Directors:
Hot Spot for Advancement for Women/Minorities:

Oracle Corporation

NAIC Code: 511210H

www.oracle.com

TYPES OF BUSINESS:

Computer Software, Data Base & File Management
Enterprise Software
Servers
Operating Systems
Infrastructure Technologies
Software
Cloud Deployment

BRANDS/DIVISIONS/AFFILIATES:

GROWTH PLANS/SPECIAL FEATURES:

Oracle provides database technology and enterprise resource planning, or ERP, software to enterprises around the world. Founded in 1977, Oracle pioneered the first commercial SQL-based relational database management system. Today, Oracle has 430,000 customers in 175 countries, supported by its base of 136,000 employees.

Oracle offers employees health, life and disability benefits, a 401(k) plan and an employee stock purchase plan.

CONTACTS: *Note: Officers with more than one job title may be intentionally listed here more than once.*

Safra Catz, CEO
Lawrence Ellison, Chairman of the Board
William West, Chief Accounting Officer
Jeffrey Henley, Director
Dorian Daley, Executive VP
Edward Screven, Executive VP

FINANCIAL DATA: *Note: Data for latest year may not have been available at press time.*

In U.S. $	2021	2020	2019	2018	2017	2016
Revenue	40,479,000,000	39,068,000,000	39,506,000,000	39,831,000,000	37,728,000,000	37,047,000,000
R&D Expense	6,527,000,000	6,067,000,000	6,026,000,000	6,091,000,000	6,159,000,000	5,787,000,000
Operating Income	15,653,000,000	14,202,000,000	14,022,000,000	14,319,000,000	13,276,000,000	13,104,000,000
Operating Margin %						
SGA Expense	8,935,999,000	9,275,000,000	9,774,000,000	9,720,001,000	9,373,000,000	9,039,000,000
Net Income	13,746,000,000	10,135,000,000	11,083,000,000	3,825,000,000	9,335,000,000	8,901,000,000
Operating Cash Flow	15,887,000,000	13,139,000,000	14,551,000,000	15,386,000,000	14,126,000,000	13,561,000,000
Capital Expenditure	2,135,000,000	1,564,000,000	1,660,000,000	1,736,000,000	2,021,000,000	1,189,000,000
EBITDA	18,411,000,000	17,026,000,000	17,269,000,000	17,701,000,000	15,766,000,000	15,418,000,000
Return on Assets %						
Return on Equity %						
Debt to Equity						

CONTACT INFORMATION:

Phone: 737-867-1000 Fax:
Toll-Free:
Address: 2300 Oracle Way, Austin, TX 78741 United States

STOCK TICKER/OTHER:

Stock Ticker: ORCL
Employees: 132,000
Parent Company:
Exchange: NYS
Fiscal Year Ends: 05/31

SALARIES/BONUSES:

Top Exec. Salary: $875,000 Bonus: $1,000,000
Second Exec. Salary: $950,000 Bonus: $

OTHER THOUGHTS:

Estimated Female Officers or Directors: 6
Hot Spot for Advancement for Women/Minorities: Y

Oracle NetSuite

www.netsuite.com

NAIC Code: 511210H

TYPES OF BUSINESS:

Business Management Application Suites
Enterprise Resource Planning
Customer Relationship Management
Ecommerce
Automation
Marketing
Analytics
Business Intelligence

BRANDS/DIVISIONS/AFFILIATES:

Oracle Corporation
FarApp

CONTACTS:

Note: Officers with more than one job title may be intentionally listed here more than once.

Evan Goldberg, Exec. VP
Jason Maynard, Sr. VP-Field Oper.
Sam Levy, Sr. VP-Sales
Douglas Solomon, General Counsel
Marc Huffman, President, Divisional

GROWTH PLANS/SPECIAL FEATURES:

Oracle NetSuite is a global business unit of Oracle Corporation and a leading vendor of cloud-based financials, enterprise resource planning (ERP) and omnichannel commerce software. The firm's solutions are used by more than 28,000 business customers worldwide. Oracle NetSuite's cloud ERP, customer relationship management (CRM) and ecommerce products enable customers to manage their back-office, front-office and web operations in a single application. Products by the company also include global business management, human capital management, professional services automation, omnichannel commerce, accounting software, infrastructure, email marketing, analytics, business intelligence and user experience. Industries served by the company include advertising and digital marketing agencies, apparel/footwear/accessories, campus store, education, energy, financial services, food and beverage, health and beauty, IT services, manufacturing, media and publishing, nonprofit, professional services, restaurants, hospitality, retail, software and technology companies, transportation, logistics and wholesale distribution. During 2021, Oracle NetSuite acquired FarApp, a provider of ecommerce, logistics, retail and hospitality connectors for Oracle NetSuite. The acquisition enables a more seamless and unified experience for NetSuite customers.

FINANCIAL DATA:

Note: Data for latest year may not have been available at press time.

In U.S. $	2021	2020	2019	2018	2017	2016
Revenue	1,100,000,000	1,008,291,375	960,277,500	914,550,000	871,000,000	855,000,000
R&D Expense						
Operating Income						
Operating Margin %						
SGA Expense						
Net Income						
Operating Cash Flow						
Capital Expenditure						
EBITDA						
Return on Assets %						
Return on Equity %						
Debt to Equity						

CONTACT INFORMATION:

Phone: 877-638-7848 Fax:
Toll-Free:
Address: 2300 Oracle Way, Austin, TX 78741 United States

STOCK TICKER/OTHER:

Stock Ticker: Subsidiary
Exchange:
Employees: 3,357
Fiscal Year Ends: 12/31
Parent Company: Oracle Corporation

SALARIES/BONUSES:

Top Exec. Salary: $ Bonus: $
Second Exec. Salary: $ Bonus: $

OTHER THOUGHTS:

Estimated Female Officers or Directors: 3
Hot Spot for Advancement for Women/Minorities: Y

Orange

NAIC Code: 517110

www.orange.com

TYPES OF BUSINESS:

Telephone, Internet Access, Broadband, Data Networks, Server Facilities and Telecommunications Services Industry
Telecommunications Solutions and Services
Mobile Solutions
Fixed Broadband Solutions
Business Services
Artificial Intelligence
Telecommunications Networks
Cybersecurity

BRANDS/DIVISIONS/AFFILIATES:

Orange Business Services
Code School
Solidarity FabLab
Orang Fab
Orange Ventures

GROWTH PLANS/SPECIAL FEATURES:

Orange is the incumbent telecom operator in France, formerly known as France Telecom. The company operates fixed and wireless businesses in France, where it is the market leader ahead of Iliad, Bouygues and SFR. Orange also has fixed and wireless (convergent) operations in Spain, Poland, Belgium, Luxembourg and Central Europe (Romania, Slovakia, Moldova). Around 15% of revenue comes from emerging African markets, where the company only operates wireless networks and 20% comes from the enterprise segment, which serves companies with more than 50 employees in France and internationally.

CONTACTS: *Note: Officers with more than one job title may be intentionally listed here more than once.*

Stephane Richard, CEO
Pierre Louette, Deputy CEO
Benoit Scheen, Sr. Exec. VP-Oper., Europe
Elie Girard, Sr.-Strategy & Dev.
Beatrice Mandine, Sr. Exec. VP-Comm. & Brand
Delphine Ernotte Cunci, Deputy CEO-Orange France
Christine Albanel, Sr. Exec. VP-Corp. Social Responsibility & Events
Thierry Bonhomme, Sr. Exec. VP-Orange Bus. Svcs.
Marc Rennard, Sr. Exec. VP-Oper., Africa, Middle East & Asia
Pierre Louette, Deputy CEO-Group Sourcing & Supply Chain

FINANCIAL DATA: *Note: Data for latest year may not have been available at press time.*

In U.S. $	2021	2020	2019	2018	2017	2016
Revenue		47,737,360,000	47,700,090,000	46,733,370,000	46,411,510,000	46,210,490,000
R&D Expense						
Operating Income		6,437,259,000	6,685,715,000	5,577,828,000	6,231,719,000	6,088,292,000
Operating Margin %						
SGA Expense		9,588,129,000	9,592,646,000	10,247,660,000	9,680,735,000	10,012,760,000
Net Income		5,445,695,000	3,394,808,000	2,206,738,000	2,152,529,000	3,314,624,000
Operating Cash Flow		14,339,280,000	11,473,000,000	10,735,540,000	11,489,940,000	9,881,758,000
Capital Expenditure		9,651,372,000	9,511,333,000	8,630,445,000	8,500,571,000	9,590,388,000
EBITDA		15,813,070,000	16,098,790,000	13,388,370,000	12,786,430,000	11,423,310,000
Return on Assets %						
Return on Equity %						
Debt to Equity						

CONTACT INFORMATION:

Phone: 33 144442222 Fax: 33 144448034
Toll-Free:
Address: 78 rue Olivier de Serres, Paris, 75015 France

STOCK TICKER/OTHER:

Stock Ticker: ORAN
Exchange: NYS
Employees: 139,698
Fiscal Year Ends: 12/31
Parent Company:

SALARIES/BONUSES:

Top Exec. Salary: $1,072,877 Bonus: $739,856
Second Exec. Salary: $677,606 Bonus: $314,274

OTHER THOUGHTS:

Estimated Female Officers or Directors: 5
Hot Spot for Advancement for Women/Minorities: Y

Orbital Insight

orbitalinsight.com

NAIC Code: 511210J

TYPES OF BUSINESS:

Computer Software, Data Base & File Management
Geospatial Analytics
Artificial Intelligence
Software

BRANDS/DIVISIONS/AFFILIATES:

Orbital Insight GO

CONTACTS:

Note: Officers with more than one job title may be intentionally listed here more than once.

Kevin E. O'Brien, CEO
Jens Tellefsen, Sr. VP-Product & Mktg.
Jim Cook, CFO
Jim Demetros, Sr. VP-Sales
Matt Falk, VP-Engineering
James Crawford, CTO
James Crawford, Chmn.

GROWTH PLANS/SPECIAL FEATURES:

Orbital Insight has developed a geospatial analytics platform that turns millions of images of Earth into data. The firm's artificial intelligence (AI) combines with data science to provide insight and knowledge about socio-economic trends so that organizations can make informed decisions. The Orbital Insight GO platform is designed to simplify the use of location data, allowing users to search for types of activity, where and when. The AI-powered platform automates data to offer insights. The platform allows users to select what they want to measure from a proprietary set of algorithms. Object detection includes vehicles, aircraft, ships and railcars; land use includes roads, buildings, water, forests and grass; and geolocation includes foot traffic, car traffic and ship traffic. Therefore, movement analysis encompasses movement tracking, traceability and heatmaps. Industries served by Orbital Insight includes defense, intelligence, law enforcement, consumer goods, supply chain intelligence, energy, industrials, real estate and financial services. Based in California, USA, the firm has additional domestic offices in New York and Washington DC, as well as international offices in London and Tokyo.

FINANCIAL DATA:

Note: Data for latest year may not have been available at press time.

In U.S. $	2021	2020	2019	2018	2017	2016
Revenue						
R&D Expense						
Operating Income						
Operating Margin %						
SGA Expense						
Net Income						
Operating Cash Flow						
Capital Expenditure						
EBITDA						
Return on Assets %						
Return on Equity %						
Debt to Equity						

CONTACT INFORMATION:

Phone: 650-353-2060 Fax:
Toll-Free:
Address: 3000 El Camino Real, Bldg. 2, Fl. 4, Palo Alto, CA 94306 United States

STOCK TICKER/OTHER:

Stock Ticker: Private
Employees:
Parent Company:
Exchange:
Fiscal Year Ends:

SALARIES/BONUSES:

Top Exec. Salary: $ Bonus: $
Second Exec. Salary: $ Bonus: $

OTHER THOUGHTS:

Estimated Female Officers or Directors:
Hot Spot for Advancement for Women/Minorities:

Sales, profits and employees may be estimates. Financial information, benefits and other data can change quickly and may vary from those stated here.

OSDB Ltd

osdb.io

NAIC Code: 511210B

TYPES OF BUSINESS:

Computer Software: Network Management (IT), System Testing & Storage
Internet of Things
Software Development
Open Source Database Benchmarking
Web Development
Software as a Service
Payment Gateway Integration
User Experience

BRANDS/DIVISIONS/AFFILIATES:

GROWTH PLANS/SPECIAL FEATURES:

OSDB, Ltd. is an Internet of Things (IoT) software development company based in Ukraine. OSDB stands for open source database benchmark, which encompasses software expertise across a variety of skills in the arts of coding, databases and benchmarks. The firm's core competency is in JavaScript and Java, but also has full expertise in React, Node.js, Firebase and Typescript. OSDB helps companies with their IoT prototypes for developing software infrastructure, connecting their devices to the world and retrieving crucial data. The company's services include end-to-end platform development, web development, software-as-a-service (SaaS) development, marketplace development, prototype development, progressive web application, payment gateway integration, user interface/user experience (UI/UX) development, user management and AWS development. All OSDB specialists are trained to fit very specific needs, and are assigned to customers accordingly.

CONTACTS: *Note: Officers with more than one job title may be intentionally listed here more than once.*

David Berchiyan, CTO

FINANCIAL DATA: *Note: Data for latest year may not have been available at press time.*

In U.S. $	2021	2020	2019	2018	2017	2016
Revenue						
R&D Expense						
Operating Income						
Operating Margin %						
SGA Expense						
Net Income						
Operating Cash Flow						
Capital Expenditure						
EBITDA						
Return on Assets %						
Return on Equity %						
Debt to Equity						

CONTACT INFORMATION:

Phone: 380 98-472-9822 Fax:
Toll-Free:
Address: Chervonoshkilna Embaresmant, 24, Kharkiv, 61000 Ukraine

STOCK TICKER/OTHER:

Stock Ticker: Private
Employees:
Parent Company:
Exchange:
Fiscal Year Ends:

SALARIES/BONUSES:

Top Exec. Salary: $ Bonus: $
Second Exec. Salary: $ Bonus: $

OTHER THOUGHTS:

Estimated Female Officers or Directors:
Hot Spot for Advancement for Women/Minorities:

PACCAR Inc

www.paccar.com

NAIC Code: 336120

TYPES OF BUSINESS:

Truck Manufacturing
Premium Truck Manufacturer
Parts Distribution
Finance, Lease and Insurance Services

GROWTH PLANS/SPECIAL FEATURES:

Paccar is a leading manufacturer of medium- and heavy-duty trucks under the premium brands Kenworth and Peterbilt, which are primarily sold in the NAFTA region and Australia, and DAF trucks, which are sold in Europe and South America. Its trucks are sold through over 2,200 independent dealers globally. Paccar Financial Services provides retail and wholesale financing for customers and dealers, respectively. The company commands approximately 30% of the Class 8 market share in North America and 16% of the heavy-duty market share in Europe.

BRANDS/DIVISIONS/AFFILIATES:

Kenworth Truck Company
Peterbilt Motors
DAF Trucks
PACCAR Financial Services
Braden
Carco
Gearmatic

CONTACTS: *Note: Officers with more than one job title may be intentionally listed here more than once.*

Preston Feight, CEO
Jack LeVier, VP-Divisional
Harrie Schippers, CFO
Mark Pigott, Chairman of the Board
Michael Barkley, Chief Accounting Officer
A Ley, Chief Information Officer
John Rich, Chief Technology Officer
Michael Walton, General Counsel
Kevin Baney, General Manager, Subsidiary
David Danforth, General Manager, Subsidiary
Jason Skoog, General Manager, Subsidiary
Harry Wolters, President, Subsidiary
Darrin Siver, Senior VP
Michael Dozier, Senior VP
T. Quinn, Senior VP
Todd Hubbard, Vice President, Divisional

FINANCIAL DATA: *Note: Data for latest year may not have been available at press time.*

In U.S. $	2021	2020	2019	2018	2017	2016
Revenue		18,728,500,000	25,599,700,000	23,495,700,000	19,456,400,000	17,033,300,000
R&D Expense		273,900,000	326,600,000	306,100,000	264,700,000	247,200,000
Operating Income		1,567,900,000	2,974,900,000	2,688,500,000	2,143,600,000	1,947,400,000
Operating Margin %						
SGA Expense		581,400,000	698,500,000	644,700,000	555,000,000	540,200,000
Net Income		1,298,400,000	2,387,900,000	2,195,100,000	1,675,200,000	521,700,000
Operating Cash Flow		2,987,200,000	2,860,300,000	2,992,300,000	2,715,800,000	2,300,800,000
Capital Expenditure		1,638,400,000	1,970,800,000	1,952,300,000	1,846,600,000	1,964,900,000
EBITDA		2,616,900,000	4,052,200,000	3,742,600,000	3,251,100,000	2,940,500,000
Return on Assets %						
Return on Equity %						
Debt to Equity						

CONTACT INFORMATION:

Phone: 425 468-7400 Fax: 425 468-8216
Toll-Free:
Address: 777 106th Ave. NE, Bellevue, WA 98004 United States

STOCK TICKER/OTHER:

Stock Ticker: PCAR
Employees: 27,000
Parent Company:
Exchange: NAS
Fiscal Year Ends: 12/31

SALARIES/BONUSES:

Top Exec. Salary: $1,200,000 Bonus: $
Second Exec. Salary: $856,731 Bonus: $

OTHER THOUGHTS:

Estimated Female Officers or Directors:
Hot Spot for Advancement for Women/Minorities:

Palantir Technologies Inc

www.palantir.com

NAIC Code: 511210J

TYPES OF BUSINESS:

Computer Software, Data Base & File Management
Software Development
Software Deployment
Data Management
Data Security
Data Analytics
Business Operating System

BRANDS/DIVISIONS/AFFILIATES:

Palantir Gotham
Palantir Foundry
Palantir Apollo

GROWTH PLANS/SPECIAL FEATURES:

Palantir Technologies provides organizations with solutions to manage large disparate data sets in an attempt to gain insight and drive operational outcomes. Founded in 2003, Palantir released its Gotham software platform in 2008, which focuses on the government intelligence and defense sectors. Palantir expanded into various commercial markets with its Foundry software platform in 2016 with the intent of becoming the data operating system for companies and industries. The Denver company had 125 customers as of its initial public offering and roughly splits its revenue between commercial and government customers.

CONTACTS: *Note: Officers with more than one job title may be intentionally listed here more than once.*

Alexander Karp, CEO
David Glazer, CFO
Peter Thiel, Chairman of the Board
Jeffrey Buckley, Chief Accounting Officer
Ryan Taylor, Chief Legal Officer
Stephen Cohen, Co-Founder
William Ho, Controller
Shyam Sankar, COO
Matthew Long, General Counsel

FINANCIAL DATA: *Note: Data for latest year may not have been available at press time.*

In U.S. $	2021	2020	2019	2018	2017	2016
Revenue		1,092,673,000	742,555,000	595,409,000		
R&D Expense		560,660,000	305,563,000	285,451,000		
Operating Income		-1,173,679,000	-576,444,000	-623,440,000		
Operating Margin %						
SGA Expense		1,353,145,000	771,063,000	767,997,000		
Net Income		-1,166,391,000	-579,646,000	-580,027,000		
Operating Cash Flow		-296,608,000	-165,215,000	-39,012,000		
Capital Expenditure		12,236,000	13,096,000	13,004,000		
EBITDA		-1,151,017,000	-551,955,000	-553,575,000		
Return on Assets %						
Return on Equity %						
Debt to Equity						

CONTACT INFORMATION:

Phone: 720-358-3679 Fax:
Toll-Free:
Address: 1555 Blake St., Ste. 250, Denver, CO 80202 United States

STOCK TICKER/OTHER:

Stock Ticker: PLTR
Employees: 2,439
Parent Company:
Exchange: NYS
Fiscal Year Ends:

SALARIES/BONUSES:

Top Exec. Salary: $2,175,610 Bonus: $28,081
Second Exec. Salary: $1,101,637 Bonus: $28,081

OTHER THOUGHTS:

Estimated Female Officers or Directors:
Hot Spot for Advancement for Women/Minorities:

Palo Alto Networks Inc

www.paloaltonetworks.com

NAIC Code: 511210E

TYPES OF BUSINESS:

Computer Software: Network Security, Managed Access, Digital ID, Cybersecurity & Anti-Virus
Cybersecurity Products
Cloud Security
Security Operation Center Solutions
Network Security
Access Security
Analytics and Automation
Artificial Intelligence

BRANDS/DIVISIONS/AFFILIATES:

Palo Alto Networks
Prisma

GROWTH PLANS/SPECIAL FEATURES:

Palo Alto Networks is a pure-play cybersecurity vendor that sells security appliances, subscriptions, and support into enterprises, government entities, and service providers. The company's product portfolio includes firewall appliances, virtual firewalls, endpoint protection, cloud security, and cybersecurity analytics. The Santa Clara, California, firm was established in 2005 and sells its products worldwide.

CONTACTS: *Note: Officers with more than one job title may be intentionally listed here more than once.*

Nikesh Arora, CEO
Kathleen Bonanno, CFO
Jean Compeau, Chief Accounting Officer
Rene Bonvanie, Chief Marketing Officer
Nir Zuk, Chief Technology Officer
Mark McLaughlin, Director
Lee Klarich, Other Executive Officer
Amit Singh, President

FINANCIAL DATA: *Note: Data for latest year may not have been available at press time.*

In U.S. $	2021	2020	2019	2018	2017	2016
Revenue	4,256,100,000	3,408,400,000	2,899,600,000	2,273,100,000	1,761,600,000	1,378,500,000
R&D Expense	1,140,400,000	768,100,000	539,500,000	400,700,000	347,400,000	284,200,000
Operating Income	-304,100,000	-179,000,000	-54,100,000	-129,100,000	-179,800,000	-190,100,000
Operating Margin %						
SGA Expense	2,144,900,000	1,819,800,000	1,605,800,000	1,356,200,000	1,117,400,000	914,400,000
Net Income	-498,900,000	-267,000,000	-81,900,000	-147,900,000	-216,600,000	-225,900,000
Operating Cash Flow	1,503,000,000	1,035,700,000	1,055,600,000	1,037,000,000	868,500,000	658,100,000
Capital Expenditure	116,000,000	214,400,000	131,200,000	112,000,000	163,400,000	72,500,000
EBITDA	3,200,000	110,400,000	163,100,000	-4,200,000	-109,800,000	-138,900,000
Return on Assets %						
Return on Equity %						
Debt to Equity						

CONTACT INFORMATION:

Phone: 408 753-4000 Fax: 408 753-4001
Toll-Free:
Address: 3000 Tannery Way, Santa Clara, CA 95054 United States

STOCK TICKER/OTHER:

Stock Ticker: PANW
Exchange: NAS
Employees: 8,014
Fiscal Year Ends: 07/31
Parent Company:

SALARIES/BONUSES:

Top Exec. Salary: $750,000 Bonus: $
Second Exec. Salary: $550,000 Bonus: $

OTHER THOUGHTS:

Estimated Female Officers or Directors:
Hot Spot for Advancement for Women/Minorities:

Panasonic Corporation

www.panasonic.com/global/home.html

NAIC Code: 334310

TYPES OF BUSINESS:

Audio & Video Equipment, Manufacturing
Appliances
Automotive Systems
Digital Cameras
Housing Construction Systems
Industrial Connected Systems
Batteries
Business-to-Business Solutions

BRANDS/DIVISIONS/AFFILIATES:

Blue Yonder

GROWTH PLANS/SPECIAL FEATURES:

Panasonic is a conglomerate that has diversified from its consumer electronics roots. It has five main business units: appliances (air conditioners, refrigerators, laundry machines, and TVs); life solutions (LED lighting, housing systems, and solar panels; connected solutions (PCs, factory automations, and in-flight entertainment systems); automotive (infotainment systems and rechargeable batteries); and industrial solutions (electronic devices). After the crisis in 2012, former president Kazuhiro Tsuga has focused on shifting the business portfolio to increase the proportion of B2B businesses to mitigate the tough competition in consumer electronics products.

CONTACTS: *Note: Officers with more than one job title may be intentionally listed here more than once.*

Yuki Kusumi, CEO
Kazuhiro Tsuga, Chmn.

FINANCIAL DATA: *Note: Data for latest year may not have been available at press time.*

In U.S. $	2021	2020	2019	2018	2017	2016
Revenue	58,862,550,000	65,820,190,000	70,320,310,000	70,139,570,000	64,529,430,000	66,374,790,000
R&D Expense						
Operating Income	2,454,685,000	2,534,647,000	3,520,482,000	3,255,290,000	2,358,493,000	3,652,850,000
Operating Margin %						
SGA Expense	14,654,110,000	16,382,380,000	17,042,170,000	17,029,370,000	16,193,880,000	15,799,170,000
Net Income	1,450,538,000	1,983,296,000	2,496,828,000	2,074,092,000	1,312,432,000	1,698,148,000
Operating Cash Flow	4,429,001,000	3,781,088,000	1,789,717,000	3,718,516,000	3,386,612,000	3,503,216,000
Capital Expenditure	2,604,715,000	3,034,058,000	3,504,824,000	4,179,141,000	3,003,532,000	2,125,022,000
EBITDA	5,246,020,000	6,134,108,000	6,442,146,000	6,072,414,000	5,003,189,000	4,470,985,000
Return on Assets %						
Return on Equity %						
Debt to Equity						

CONTACT INFORMATION:

Phone: 81 669081121 Fax:
Toll-Free:
Address: 1006 Oaza Kadoma, Kadoma City, Osaka, 571-8501 Japan

STOCK TICKER/OTHER:

Stock Ticker: PCRFF
Employees: 271,869
Parent Company:
Exchange: PINX
Fiscal Year Ends: 03/31

SALARIES/BONUSES:

Top Exec. Salary: $ Bonus: $
Second Exec. Salary: $ Bonus: $

OTHER THOUGHTS:

Estimated Female Officers or Directors:
Hot Spot for Advancement for Women/Minorities:

PAR Technology Corporation

www.partech.com

NAIC Code: 511210H

TYPES OF BUSINESS:

Point-of-Sale Systems
Technical Services
System Design & Engineering
Hospitality IT Services
Government Contract Services

BRANDS/DIVISIONS/AFFILIATES:

Brink POS
PixelPoint
EverServ POS

GROWTH PLANS/SPECIAL FEATURES:

PAR Technology Corp together with its subsidiaries provides management technology solutions including software, hardware, and related services, integral to the point-of-sale infrastructure and task management, information gathering, assimilation and communication services. It has two segments. Restaurant/ Retail segment provides point-of-sale and management technology solutions such as hardware, software and integrated technical solutions to the restaurant and retail industries. Government segment provides intelligence, surveillance, and reconnaissance solutions and mission systems support. The company derives the majority of its revenues from the Restaurant/ Retail segment.

CONTACTS: *Note: Officers with more than one job title may be intentionally listed here more than once.*

Savneet Singh, CEO
Bryan Menar, CFO
Matthew Cicchinelli, President, Subsidiary

FINANCIAL DATA: *Note: Data for latest year may not have been available at press time.*

In U.S. $	2021	2020	2019	2018	2017	2016
Revenue		213,786,000	187,232,000	201,246,000	232,605,000	229,653,000
R&D Expense		19,252,000	13,372,000	12,412,000	13,814,000	11,581,000
Operating Income		-27,286,000	-14,127,000	-10,763,000	-121,000	1,551,000
Operating Margin %						
SGA Expense		46,196,000	38,010,000	35,848,000	38,171,000	32,102,000
Net Income		-36,562,000	-15,571,000	-24,122,000	-3,386,000	1,783,000
Operating Cash Flow		-20,243,000	-16,129,000	-3,849,000	314,000	10,996,000
Capital Expenditure		9,231,000	6,530,000	7,840,000	8,857,000	6,118,000
EBITDA		-16,809,000	-6,872,000	-6,033,000	3,912,000	6,175,000
Return on Assets %						
Return on Equity %						
Debt to Equity						

CONTACT INFORMATION:

Phone: 315 738-0600 Fax: 315 738-0411
Toll-Free: 800-448-6505
Address: 8383 Seneca Turnpike, New Hartford, NY 13413-4991 United States

STOCK TICKER/OTHER:

Stock Ticker: PAR
Employees: 1,000
Parent Company:
Exchange: NYS
Fiscal Year Ends: 12/31

SALARIES/BONUSES:

Top Exec. Salary: $493,510 Bonus: $
Second Exec. Salary: $268,138 Bonus: $12,490

OTHER THOUGHTS:

Estimated Female Officers or Directors: 1
Hot Spot for Advancement for Women/Minorities:

Particle Industries Inc

www.particle.io

NAIC Code: 511210B

TYPES OF BUSINESS:

Computer Software: Network Management (IT), System Testing & Storage
Internet of Things Hardware
Internet of Things Software
IoT Product Development
Unified Connectivity Solution
IoT Cellular Management Solution
Network Connectivity Solution

BRANDS/DIVISIONS/AFFILIATES:

Device OS
Device Cloud
Device Management Console
EtherSIM

CONTACTS: *Note: Officers with more than one job title may be intentionally listed here more than once.*

Zach Supalla, CEO

GROWTH PLANS/SPECIAL FEATURES:

Particle Industries, Inc. provides hardware and software solutions to help customers prototype, scale and manage their Internet of Things (IoT) products. IoT products are about connecting everything seamlessly; therefore, Particle has developed an all-in-one IoT platform encompassing everything needed to power an IoT product, from device to edge to cloud. This platform includes solutions covering IoT hardware, connectivity, IoT device cloud and IoT applications. How it works: first, the customer begins to build IoT product by getting the device online via an opensource hardware development kit developed by Particle. Kits include cloud-connected microcontrollers powered by a lightweight operating system (OS) for embedded IoT devices, enabling the customer to get the prototype up and running swiftly and easily. Networking, protocols, security and SIM cards are built into the Device OS; so, there is no need to build one's own network stack. Every Particle device connects to its Device Cloud, a secure and scalable gateway between the customer's devices and the web. The customer can then manage and control the device (or devices) through the Device Management Console. Every device is exposed through a secure application program interface (API). Through the console, devices can be re-programmed and new software can be pushed to an entire fleet of devices with a click of a button. Particle's EtherSIM product is a unified connectivity solution designed to make IoT cellular management simple, automatically connecting to networks and seamlessly working with Particle's IoT platform. Particle Industries supports clients across agriculture, automotive, smart city and other industries. The firm is headquartered in California, USA and has additional domestic and global offices.

FINANCIAL DATA: *Note: Data for latest year may not have been available at press time.*

In U.S. $	2021	2020	2019	2018	2017	2016
Revenue	11,000,000	10,197,000	10,300,000	5,150,000		
R&D Expense						
Operating Income						
Operating Margin %						
SGA Expense						
Net Income						
Operating Cash Flow						
Capital Expenditure						
EBITDA						
Return on Assets %						
Return on Equity %						
Debt to Equity						

CONTACT INFORMATION:

Phone: 415-316-1024 Fax:
Toll-Free:
Address: 548 Market St., PMB 34833, San Francisco, CA 94105 United States

STOCK TICKER/OTHER:

Stock Ticker: Private
Employees:
Parent Company:
Exchange:
Fiscal Year Ends:

SALARIES/BONUSES:

Top Exec. Salary: $ Bonus: $
Second Exec. Salary: $ Bonus: $

OTHER THOUGHTS:

Estimated Female Officers or Directors:
Hot Spot for Advancement for Women/Minorities:

Pegasystems Inc

www.pega.com

NAIC Code: 511210H

TYPES OF BUSINESS:

Business Process Management Software
Consulting
Robotic-Process Automation
Software Development
Software Distribution
Artificial Intelligence
Cloud Services
Enterprise Connectivity

BRANDS/DIVISIONS/AFFILIATES:

Pega Platform
Pega Cloud Services
Pega Infinity

GROWTH PLANS/SPECIAL FEATURES:

Founded in 1983, Pegasystems provides a suite of solutions for customer engagement and business process automation. The company's key offering is the Pega Infinity platform, which combines business process automation with customer engagement applications.

Pegasystems offers its employees health care coverage, additional training and certification programs and retirement savings/pension plans.

CONTACTS: *Note: Officers with more than one job title may be intentionally listed here more than once.*

Alan Trefler, CEO
Kenneth Stillwell, CFO
Judy Buchholz, Other Corporate Officer
Joaquin Reixa, Other Corporate Officer
John Higgins, Other Corporate Officer
Kerim Akgonul, Other Executive Officer
Hayden Stafford, President, Divisional
Michael Pyle, Senior VP, Divisional
Douglas Kra, Senior VP, Divisional
Efstathios Kouninis, Treasurer

FINANCIAL DATA: *Note: Data for latest year may not have been available at press time.*

In U.S. $	2021	2020	2019	2018	2017	2016
Revenue		1,017,517,000	911,383,000	891,581,000	840,582,000	750,266,000
R&D Expense		236,986,000	205,210,000	181,710,000	162,886,000	145,548,000
Operating Income		-143,527,000	-134,878,000	-17,032,000	38,660,000	40,662,000
Operating Margin %						
SGA Expense		613,145,000	531,029,000	425,138,000	359,363,000	324,800,000
Net Income		-61,373,000	-90,433,000	10,617,000	32,934,000	26,986,000
Operating Cash Flow		-563,000	-42,165,000	104,356,000	158,235,000	39,874,000
Capital Expenditure		25,369,000	10,608,000	11,893,000	13,741,000	19,088,000
EBITDA		-84,185,000	-113,482,000	8,263,000	63,373,000	64,799,000
Return on Assets %						
Return on Equity %						
Debt to Equity						

CONTACT INFORMATION:

Phone: 617 374-9600 Fax: 617 374-9620
Toll-Free:
Address: One Main St., Cambridge, MA 02142 United States

STOCK TICKER/OTHER:

Stock Ticker: PEGA
Employees: 3,908
Parent Company:
Exchange: NAS
Fiscal Year Ends: 12/31

SALARIES/BONUSES:

Top Exec. Salary: $248,077 Bonus: $923,307
Second Exec. Salary: $365,000 Bonus: $312,890

OTHER THOUGHTS:

Estimated Female Officers or Directors:
Hot Spot for Advancement for Women/Minorities:

Perceptron Inc

NAIC Code: 334513

www.perceptron.com

TYPES OF BUSINESS:

Optical Instrument and Lens Manufacturing
Automated Industrial Metrology
Robotic Guidance Systems
Software Solutions
Product Development
Product Manufacture
Material Bonding and Adhesive
Fit and Finish Part Assembly Solution

BRANDS/DIVISIONS/AFFILIATES:

Atlas Copco AB
Atlas Copco North America LLC
AutoGauge
AccuSite Optical Tracking
AutoFit
QUISS
AutoGuide

CONTACTS: *Note: Officers with more than one job title may be intentionally listed here more than once.*

Anders Hoberg, CEO
Jay Freeland, Chairman of the Board
Bill Roeschlein, CFO
Rick Van Valkenburg, VP-Global Sales & Mktg.
Richard Van Valkenburg, Vice President, Divisional

GROWTH PLANS/SPECIAL FEATURES:

Perceptron, Inc. develops, produces and sells automated industrial metrology products and solutions to manufacturing organizations. The company's solutions are grouped into two primary categories: automated metrology and robot guidance. AutoGauge is an automated metrology solution that enables manufacturers to contain, correct, verify and control manufacturing quality immediately, without touching the part. The software solution accumulates data on every part so that manufacturers can proactively detect and monitor production trends before a crisis occurs or production stops. For high-accuracy coordinate manufacturing machine (CMM) needs, AccuSite Optical Tracking complements the system and turns the robot into a simple mover by eliminating all of its mechanical drift and temperature influence from the measurement results. Automated metrology with AccuSite is a robotic measurement solution available for the factory floor, can be mounted in multiple configurations and ships pre-configured to ensure optimal part coverage. AutoFit is a fit and finish optimization solution for assembly lines. The fully-automated, non-contact gap and flush solution measures mating parts and directs personnel where to adjust or what to correct in the manufacturing process as needed. AutoFit comprises laser technology suitable for measurement on all materials. Its measurement results can be presented on large displays above or around the AutoFit system and provide guidance to the operator for analysis and accurate adjustments. Perceptron's QUISS adhesive and bead inspection systems for the automotive industry ensure structural, safety-critical bonds. QUISS offers 2D and 3D solutions for bonding and dispensing applications. Last, AutoGuide is a solution for 3D robot guidance needs, and capable of handling materials or complex operations. Whether unloading a pallet, automating and optimizing critical applications or loading closures and verifying build quality, AutoGuide is a flexible guidance solution. Perceptron operates as a subsidiary of Atlas Copco North America, LLC, itself a subsidiary of Atlas Copco AB.

FINANCIAL DATA: *Note: Data for latest year may not have been available at press time.*

In U.S. $	2021	2020	2019	2018	2017	2016
Revenue	65,000,000	62,262,000	76,822,000	84,693,000	77,947,000	69,135,000
R&D Expense						
Operating Income						
Operating Margin %						
SGA Expense						
Net Income		-3,971,000	-6,791,000	3,716,000	-168,000	-22,113,000
Operating Cash Flow						
Capital Expenditure						
EBITDA						
Return on Assets %						
Return on Equity %						
Debt to Equity						

CONTACT INFORMATION:

Phone: 734 414-6100 Fax: 734 414-4700
Toll-Free:
Address: 47827 Halyard Dr., Plymouth, MI 48170 United States

STOCK TICKER/OTHER:

Stock Ticker: Subsidiary
Employees: 295
Parent Company: Atlas Copco AB
Exchange:
Fiscal Year Ends: 12/31

SALARIES/BONUSES:

Top Exec. Salary: $ Bonus: $
Second Exec. Salary: $ Bonus: $

OTHER THOUGHTS:

Estimated Female Officers or Directors:
Hot Spot for Advancement for Women/Minorities:

Phazar Antenna Corp

phazar.com

NAIC Code: 334220

TYPES OF BUSINESS:

Antenna Systems & Towers
Wireless Equipment
Contract Manufacturing

BRANDS/DIVISIONS/AFFILIATES:

Antenna Products Corporation
TACSAT-214-SATCOM

CONTACTS: *Note: Officers with more than one job title may be intentionally listed here more than once.*

Robert Fitzgerald, Pres.

GROWTH PLANS/SPECIAL FEATURES:

Phazar Antenna Corp. is the wireless infrastructure antenna division of Antenna Products Corporation (ACP). The firm offers a complete line of distributed antenna system (DAS) and small cell antenna solutions built to meet the needs of wireless service, WiMAX, Wi-Fi and broadband internet system suppliers for the purpose of increasing network data capacity and speed via densification. The DAS antennas for cellular, sensorimotor rhythm (SMR), advanced wireless service (AWS) and personal communication service (PCS) frequencies are installed on utility poles, streetlights, rooftops and lamp posts in urban and remote areas to increase wireless carrier services. These product lines complement APC's existing product lines of cellular, PCS, paging, industrial, scientific, medical, automated meter reading (AMR), omni-directional and sector wireless antennas. The firm's TACSAT-214-SATCOM antenna is custom engineered for special operations soldiers. The antenna is a holster-worn, lightweight mobile system that allows for quick deployment and reliable performance during mission-critical operations. All of Phazar's DAS, oDAS and small cell antennas are designed in-house using state-of-the-art design tools and software. They are available in single, dual, triple, quad and multi-band configurations and in combinations of a plethora of frequencies. Phazar provides fully integrated antenna services, with research and development, engineering, testing, manufacturing, production and tech support housed within its 100,000+ square foot facility located in Texas. Phazar Antenna is utilized by every major U. S. wireless carrier, including Verizon, AT&T, Sprint and T-Mobile.

FINANCIAL DATA: *Note: Data for latest year may not have been available at press time.*

In U.S. $	2021	2020	2019	2018	2017	2016
Revenue	14,391,000	13,837,500	13,500,000	13,125,000	12,500,000	12,000,000
R&D Expense						
Operating Income						
Operating Margin %						
SGA Expense						
Net Income						
Operating Cash Flow						
Capital Expenditure						
EBITDA						
Return on Assets %						
Return on Equity %						
Debt to Equity						

CONTACT INFORMATION:

Phone: 940 325-3301 Fax: 940 325-0716
Toll-Free:
Address: 6300 Columbia Rd., Mineral Wells, TX 76067 United States

STOCK TICKER/OTHER:

Stock Ticker: Subsidiary
Exchange:
Employees: 66
Fiscal Year Ends: 06/30
Parent Company: Antenna Products Corporation

SALARIES/BONUSES:

Top Exec. Salary: $ Bonus: $
Second Exec. Salary: $ Bonus: $

OTHER THOUGHTS:

Estimated Female Officers or Directors: 1
Hot Spot for Advancement for Women/Minorities:

Pioneer Corporation

NAIC Code: 334310

global.pioneer/en

TYPES OF BUSINESS:

Consumer Electronics
Audio/Video Equipment
CD/DVD Players
Automotive Electronics
Telecommunications Equipment
Research & Development
Software Development

BRANDS/DIVISIONS/AFFILIATES:

CONTACTS:

Note: Officers with more than one job title may be intentionally listed here more than once.

Shiro Yahara, CEO
Masanori Koshoubu, Gen. Mgr.-R&D
Hideki Okayasu, Sr. Mgr. Dir.-Gen. Admin. Div.
Masanori Koshoubu, Mgr. Dir.-Legal & Intellectual Property Div.
Mikio Ono, Gen. Mgr.-Corp. Planning Div.
Hideki Okayasu, Sr. Mgr. Dir.-Corp. Comm.
Hideki Okayasu, Sr. Mgr. Dir.-Finance & Acct. Div.
Satoshi Matsumoto, Mgr. Dir.-Quality Assurance Div.
Mikio Ono, Gen. Mgr.-Home Audiovisual Bus.
Tatsuo Takeuchi, Gen. Mgr.-Intl Bus. Div.

GROWTH PLANS/SPECIAL FEATURES:

Pioneer Corporation, headquartered in Japan, is a leading manufacturer of consumer electronics. The firm operates primarily in two segments: car electronics business and others. The car electronics business is divided into four subsections: consumer, OEM, map and autonomous driving. The consumer subsection provides a lineup of in-vehicle hardware for car entertainment, such as car navigation, car Audio/Visual and car speakers. The OEM subsection sells high-quality in-vehicle hardware for automakers. For next-generation vehicles, Pioneer also provides proposals for comfort and safety in vehicles using Pioneer's advanced technologies. The map business creates and sells maps for navigation systems, smartphones and PCs. This business also sells maps in the corporate and GIS markets, as well as creating maps for autonomous driving. The autonomous driving field consists of Pioneer's telematic services and its 3D-LiDAR sensors that measure distances to objects accurately and capture information on distances and surroundings in real time and in three dimensions. The other segment manufactures home theater components, such as Blu-ray disc players, surround sound systems, audiovisual components, Blu-ray and DVD drives for computers, professional disc jockey equipment and professional speakers. Additionally, the segment produces bicycle GPS systems; organic electroluminescent lighting, electronics manufacturing services and components; medical and healthcare equipment; electric and autonomous vehicle products; and horizontal vertical transforming (HVT) speakers.

FINANCIAL DATA:

Note: Data for latest year may not have been available at press time.

In U.S. $	2021	2020	2019	2018	2017	2016
Revenue	2,548,509,163	3,193,021,383	3,433,356,326	3,269,863,168	3,460,148,736	4,023,426,816
R&D Expense						
Operating Income						
Operating Margin %						
SGA Expense						
Net Income				-63,738,780	-45,224,736	6,541,212
Operating Cash Flow						
Capital Expenditure						
EBITDA						
Return on Assets %						
Return on Equity %						
Debt to Equity						

CONTACT INFORMATION:

Phone: 81-3-6634-8777 Fax:
Toll-Free:
Address: 28-8, Honkomagome 2-chome, Bunkyo-ku, Tokyo, 113-0021 Japan

STOCK TICKER/OTHER:

Stock Ticker: Private
Employees: 11,027
Parent Company:
Exchange:
Fiscal Year Ends: 03/31

SALARIES/BONUSES:

Top Exec. Salary: $ Bonus: $
Second Exec. Salary: $ Bonus: $

OTHER THOUGHTS:

Estimated Female Officers or Directors:
Hot Spot for Advancement for Women/Minorities:

Placemeter Inc

www.placemeter.com

NAIC Code: 511210M

TYPES OF BUSINESS:

Computer Software, e-Commerce, Web Analytics & Applications Management
Computer Vision Algorithms
Machine Learning Technology

BRANDS/DIVISIONS/AFFILIATES:

Netgear Inc
Arlo Technologies Inc

CONTACTS:

Note: Officers with more than one job title may be intentionally listed here more than once.

Alexandre Winter, CEO

GROWTH PLANS/SPECIAL FEATURES:

Placemeter, Inc. is a New York-based company that has developed a platform utilizing public video feeds and computer vision algorithms to create a real-time data layer about places, streets and neighborhoods. The video feeds reveal what is going on in the physical world, such as how busy places are, what people are doing, how fast cars are going and more. Developers, citizens, cities and retailers primarily use the data for decision-making purposes. Placemeter operates as a subsidiary of Arlo Technologies, Inc., (itself a subsidiary of Netgear, Inc.), a home automation company that produces wireless security cameras. Placemeter's platform either works with Arlo's line of cameras or with the customer's existing security camera system. Within the platform, a series of algorithms separate the moving objects from the video's background, and the computer vision cascade then classifies those objects as pedestrians, bicycles, motorcycles, vehicles and large vehicles. This process is made possible due to Placemeter's machine learning technology. Within smart cities, Placementer's proprietary computer vision algorithms can measure multi-modal traffic trends, identify opportunities for infrastructure improvement, discover crowded areas versus under-used areas, analyze the use of public features (such as park benches, recycling bins, playground equipment), determine the impact of temporary events and special programming, and process multiple activities all from a single video feed. Out-of-home advertisers can utilize Placemeter's solutions to estimate how well their clients' media investments are performing. Retailers can obtain measurements about what is happening in their stores in order to maximize revenue. Measurements can include store door counts, pedestrian traffic in front of the store, street-to-purchase conversion rates and the impact of Black Friday and other high-peak sales seasons. Placemeter was incorporated in 2012.

FINANCIAL DATA:

Note: Data for latest year may not have been available at press time.

In U.S. $	2021	2020	2019	2018	2017	2016
Revenue						
R&D Expense						
Operating Income						
Operating Margin %						
SGA Expense						
Net Income						
Operating Cash Flow						
Capital Expenditure						
EBITDA						
Return on Assets %						
Return on Equity %						
Debt to Equity						

CONTACT INFORMATION:

Phone: 212-226-6984 Fax: 270-912-9818
Toll-Free:
Address: 425 Broadway, 4/Fl, New York, NY 10013 United States

STOCK TICKER/OTHER:

Stock Ticker: Subsidiary
Employees:
Parent Company: Netgear Inc
Exchange:
Fiscal Year Ends:

SALARIES/BONUSES:

Top Exec. Salary: $ Bonus: $
Second Exec. Salary: $ Bonus: $

OTHER THOUGHTS:

Estimated Female Officers or Directors:
Hot Spot for Advancement for Women/Minorities:

Potevio Corporation

NAIC Code: 334220

www.cccme.org.cn/shop/cccme3055/index.aspx

TYPES OF BUSINESS:

Communications Equipment-Telecom & Mobile
Information Technology
Telecommunications
Equipment
Electronics
Automotive Parts
Terminal Products
Storage

BRANDS/DIVISIONS/AFFILIATES:

Potevio Capitel
Potevio Eastcom
Ningbo Electronics
Beijing Ericsson Potevio
Nanjing Ericsson Panda
Potevio Taili
Potevio Designing & Planning Institute

CONTACTS:

Note: Officers with more than one job title may be intentionally listed here more than once.

Liang Sun, Gen. Mgr.-Broadcasting Dept.
Xu Mingwen, VP
Lv Weiping, Chmn.

GROWTH PLANS/SPECIAL FEATURES:

Potevio Corporation is an information technology (IT) products and service provider for the telecommunication industry. Based in China, the company consists of seven subsidiaries: Potevio Capitel, Potevio Eastcom, Ningbo Electronics, Biejing Ericsson Potevio, Nanjing Ericsson Panda, Potevio Taili, and Potevio Designing & Planning Institute for Engineering. Together, these businesses cover both fixed and mobile communications. The firm's product categories consist of communication devices, computer products, electronic apparatus, office supplies, machinery equipment, automotive and motorcycle parts, electrical wire and other electrical parts and components. Products include communication equipment and terminal products include mobile communication network equipment and handsets, optical transmission equipment, communication cables, power connectors, power supplies, microwave communication equipment, telecommunication network operation support systems (OSS), stored program control (SPC) switches, videophones, integrated circuit card payphones, personal handyphone system (PHS) handsets, logistics information systems, ITS series products, office information equipment and much more.

FINANCIAL DATA:

Note: Data for latest year may not have been available at press time.

In U.S. $	2021	2020	2019	2018	2017	2016
Revenue		12,618,112,500	12,017,250,000	11,445,000,000	10,900,000,000	10,732,293,749
R&D Expense						
Operating Income						
Operating Margin %						
SGA Expense						
Net Income						
Operating Cash Flow						
Capital Expenditure						
EBITDA						
Return on Assets %						
Return on Equity %						
Debt to Equity						

CONTACT INFORMATION:

Phone: 86-10-6268-3863 Fax: 86-10-62683898
Toll-Free:
Address: 6 Beier St., Haidian Distr., Beijing, 100080 China

STOCK TICKER/OTHER:

Stock Ticker: Government-Owned
Employees: 22,000
Parent Company: SASAC
Exchange:
Fiscal Year Ends: 12/31

SALARIES/BONUSES:

Top Exec. Salary: $ Bonus: $
Second Exec. Salary: $ Bonus: $

OTHER THOUGHTS:

Estimated Female Officers or Directors: 1
Hot Spot for Advancement for Women/Minorities:

Powell Industries Inc

www.powellind.com

NAIC Code: 334513

TYPES OF BUSINESS:

Electrical Sensors, Microelectronics, Optomechanicals Manufacturer
Engineered Equipment
Electrical Energy Flow
Motor Protection
Power Control
Modules
Switches

BRANDS/DIVISIONS/AFFILIATES:

Powell Electrical Systems Inc
Powell (UK) Limited
Powell Canada Inc
Power Industries International BV

GROWTH PLANS/SPECIAL FEATURES:

Powell Industries Inc is a United States-based company that develops, designs, manufactures, and services custom-engineered equipment and systems for electrical energy distribution, control, and monitoring. The company's principal products comprise integrated power control room substations, custom-engineered modules, electrical houses, traditional and arc-resistant distribution switchgear and control gear, and so on. These products are applied in oil and gas refining, offshore oil and gas production, petrochemical, pipeline, terminal, mining and metals, light-rail traction power, electric utility, pulp and paper, and other heavy industrial markets. The company generates the majority of its sales from the United States.

Power Industries offers employees medical, dental, vision, life, AD&D and short/long-term disability insurance; flexible spending accounts, annual incentive programs; 401(k); and various employee assistance programs.

CONTACTS: *Note: Officers with more than one job title may be intentionally listed here more than once.*

Brett Cope, CEO
Michael Metcalf, CFO
Thomas Powell, Chairman Emeritus
Milburn Honeycutt, Chief Accounting Officer

FINANCIAL DATA: *Note: Data for latest year may not have been available at press time.*

In U.S. $	2021	2020	2019	2018	2017	2016
Revenue		518,499,000	517,180,000	448,716,000	395,911,000	565,243,000
R&D Expense		6,265,000	6,327,000	6,717,000	6,906,000	6,731,000
Operating Income		20,471,000	10,522,000	-8,335,000	-18,016,000	24,198,000
Operating Margin %						
SGA Expense		67,662,000	69,950,000	66,768,000	61,524,000	74,924,000
Net Income		16,660,000	9,890,000	-7,152,000	-9,486,000	15,510,000
Operating Cash Flow		72,394,000	68,759,000	-28,543,000	36,815,000	74,906,000
Capital Expenditure		5,130,000	4,255,000	4,502,000	3,636,000	3,044,000
EBITDA		31,096,000	24,596,000	5,411,000	-3,996,000	31,273,000
Return on Assets %						
Return on Equity %						
Debt to Equity						

CONTACT INFORMATION:

Phone: 713 944-6900 Fax: 713 947-4435
Toll-Free:
Address: 8550 Mosley Rd., Houston, TX 77075-1180 United States

STOCK TICKER/OTHER:

Stock Ticker: POWL
Employees: 2,073
Parent Company:
Exchange: NAS
Fiscal Year Ends: 09/30

SALARIES/BONUSES:

Top Exec. Salary: $331,500 Bonus: $215,045
Second Exec. Salary: $510,000 Bonus: $

OTHER THOUGHTS:

Estimated Female Officers or Directors:
Hot Spot for Advancement for Women/Minorities:

PowerFleet Inc

www.powerfleet.com

NAIC Code: 334220

TYPES OF BUSINESS:

Wireless Asset Security Systems
Wireless Technology
Mobile Tracking
Internet of Things
Asset Management
Telematics
ELD System

BRANDS/DIVISIONS/AFFILIATES:

PowerFleet
Pointer
Cellocator

GROWTH PLANS/SPECIAL FEATURES:

PowerFleet Inc provides subscription-based wireless Internet-of-Things (IoT) and machine-to-machine (M2M) solutions for securing, controlling, tracking, and managing high-value enterprise assets such as industrial trucks, trailers, containers, cargo, and light vehicles and heavy truck fleets. The firm's systems utilize radio frequency identification, Wi-fi, satellite communications and sensor technology to manage their assets. It operates in the segment of Wireless IoT asset management. The company has a business presence in the US, Israel and other countries, of which key revenue is derived from the US.

CONTACTS: *Note: Officers with more than one job title may be intentionally listed here more than once.*

Chris Wolfe, CEO
Ned Mavrommatis, CFO
Michael Brodsky, Chairman of the Board
Elizabeth Elkins, Other Executive Officer

FINANCIAL DATA: *Note: Data for latest year may not have been available at press time.*

In U.S. $	2021	2020	2019	2018	2017	2016
Revenue		113,593,000	81,915,000	53,064,000	40,958,000	36,822,000
R&D Expense		10,597,000	8,540,000	6,863,000	3,965,000	4,536,000
Operating Income		-3,458,000	-5,048,000	-5,736,000	-4,091,000	-6,368,000
Operating Margin %						
SGA Expense		51,878,000	34,872,000	24,671,000	21,053,000	20,126,000
Net Income		-9,007,000	-10,963,000	-5,812,000	-3,870,000	-6,370,000
Operating Cash Flow		8,848,000	-7,269,000	-1,702,000	3,918,000	-2,484,000
Capital Expenditure		3,373,000	1,042,000	251,000	386,000	505,000
EBITDA		4,920,000	-6,761,000	-4,078,000	-2,707,000	-5,392,000
Return on Assets %						
Return on Equity %						
Debt to Equity						

CONTACT INFORMATION:

Phone: 201 996-9000 Fax: 201 670-9222
Toll-Free:
Address: 123 Tice Blvd., Woodcliff Lake, NJ 07677 United States

STOCK TICKER/OTHER:

Stock Ticker: PWFL Exchange: NAS
Employees: 669 Fiscal Year Ends: 12/31
Parent Company:

SALARIES/BONUSES:

Top Exec. Salary: $424,675 Bonus: $
Second Exec. Salary: $299,704 Bonus: $

OTHER THOUGHTS:

Estimated Female Officers or Directors:
Hot Spot for Advancement for Women/Minorities:

Preferred Networks Inc

NAIC Code: 511210I

www.preferred-networks.jp/en

TYPES OF BUSINESS:

Computer Software, Operating Systems, Languages & Development Tools
Personal Robots
Automated Cleaning Equipment
Deep Learning
Artificial Intelligence
Software Development
Technologies

BRANDS/DIVISIONS/AFFILIATES:

PFDeNA Inc
Preferred Medicine Inc
Preferred Robotics Inc

CONTACTS: *Note: Officers with more than one job title may be intentionally listed here more than once.*

Toru Nishikawa, CEO

GROWTH PLANS/SPECIAL FEATURES:

Preferred Networks, Inc. (PFN) is an artificial intelligence (AI) computer software startup that develops practical applications of cutting-edge technologies to solve real-world problems. PFN's deep learning strategy encompasses new information technology and is therefore a flexible solution for: developing state-of-the-art technologies such as frameworks; and for building large-scale compute clusters. PFN's business is divided into four core segments: transportation, manufacturing, bio & healthcare, and personal robots. The transportation business encompasses a joint research and development project with Toyota in the field of object recognition technologies and vehicle information analysis, which are required for the development of autonomous driving and connected cars. The manufacturing business aims to innovate manufacturing processes by combining manufacturing technology and know-how from companies with machine learning technology. It has a collaboration with FANUC, and is applying technologies such as vision, control, anomaly detection and parameter optimization to robots and machine tools. Products released to market by this division include: an AI thermal displacement compensation function, an AI backflow monitor, AI servo tuning, AI bin picking, an AI servo monitor and an AI error proof solution. The bio & healthcare business focuses on omics analysis, medical image analysis and compound analysis using deep learning. This division has two joint ventures: PFDeNA Inc. (with DeNA Inc.) in Japan, and Preferred Medicine Inc. (with Mitsui & Co. Ltd.) in the U.S., each to develop new blood tests for early cancer detection. Last, the personal robot business develops technology to support daily living activities, primarily for use in the home such as cleaning activities. The technologies will enable the robot to recognize objects and understand spoken language. During 2021, PFN established Preferred Robotics Inc., to develop and produce autonomous mobile robots.

FINANCIAL DATA: *Note: Data for latest year may not have been available at press time.*

In U.S. $	2021	2020	2019	2018	2017	2016
Revenue						
R&D Expense						
Operating Income						
Operating Margin %						
SGA Expense						
Net Income						
Operating Cash Flow						
Capital Expenditure						
EBITDA						
Return on Assets %						
Return on Equity %						
Debt to Equity						

CONTACT INFORMATION:

Phone: Fax:
Toll-Free:
Address: Otemachi Bldg., Fl. 2, 1-6-1 Otemachi, Chiyoda-ku, Tokyo, 100-0004 Japan

STOCK TICKER/OTHER:

Stock Ticker: Private
Employees: 305
Parent Company:
Exchange:
Fiscal Year Ends:

SALARIES/BONUSES:

Top Exec. Salary: $ Bonus: $
Second Exec. Salary: $ Bonus: $

OTHER THOUGHTS:

Estimated Female Officers or Directors:
Hot Spot for Advancement for Women/Minorities:

Program-Ace

NAIC Code: 541511

program-ace.com

TYPES OF BUSINESS:

Custom Computer Programming Services
Software Development
Software Engineering
Mobile Applications
Business Intelligence
Artificial Intelligence
Machine Learning
Internet of Things

BRANDS/DIVISIONS/AFFILIATES:

CONTACTS:

Note: Officers with more than one job title may be intentionally listed here more than once.

Oleg Fonarov, CEO
Svetlana Lobazeva, Head-Mktg.
Denis Potapenko, CTO

GROWTH PLANS/SPECIAL FEATURES:

Program-Ace is a European R&D company that offers custom software development services for a broad spectrum of verticals. Industries the firm serves include agriculture, education, manufacturing, media, entertainment, marketing, advertising, healthcare, retail, fintech (financial technology), insurance technology, energy and utilities. Program-Ace's services are categorized into four groups: software engineering, encompassing mobile applications, web-based software, business intelligence (BI), artificial intelligence (AI), machine learning (ML), Internet of Things (IoT), integration and interactive applications; IT consulting, spanning industry analysis, competitor research, IT modernization, software solution design, architecture assessment and digital transformation; quality assurance, including QA consulting, quality control, security testing, performance testing, independent testing and test automation; and R&D and innovation, providing technology research, proof of concept (PoC), prototyping, full-cycle R&D and minimum viable product (MVP) development. Solutions offered by Program-Ace include remote augmented reality (AR) assistance, mixed reality (MR) assistance, virtual product configurator, business process gamification, augmented marketing and AR-enabled user interfaces. Program-Ace's technological stack utilized to deliver its core offerings include the web, mobile, unity, engine development via multi-platform custom-tailored solutions, IoT and blockchain. The company's expertise also includes interactive 3D manuals, 3D visualization and experience design.

FINANCIAL DATA:

Note: Data for latest year may not have been available at press time.

In U.S. $	2021	2020	2019	2018	2017	2016
Revenue						
R&D Expense						
Operating Income						
Operating Margin %						
SGA Expense						
Net Income						
Operating Cash Flow						
Capital Expenditure						
EBITDA						
Return on Assets %						
Return on Equity %						
Debt to Equity						

CONTACT INFORMATION:

Phone: 38 095 752 9838 Fax: 28 057 712 2180
Toll-Free:
Address: 3 Prodolna St., Apt. 47, Kharkiv, 61052 Ukraine

STOCK TICKER/OTHER:

Stock Ticker: Private
Employees: 120
Parent Company:
Exchange:
Fiscal Year Ends:

SALARIES/BONUSES:

Top Exec. Salary: $ Bonus: $
Second Exec. Salary: $ Bonus: $

OTHER THOUGHTS:

Estimated Female Officers or Directors:
Hot Spot for Advancement for Women/Minorities:

Progress Software Corporation

web.progress.com

NAIC Code: 511210I

TYPES OF BUSINESS:

Software, Application Development & Integration
Consulting & Technical Support Services
Data Connectivity Products
Data Management Software

BRANDS/DIVISIONS/AFFILIATES:

Progress OpenEdge
Progress DataDirect
Progress DataDirect Hybrid Data Pipeline
NativeChat
NativeScript
Telerik
Corticon
Kemp

CONTACTS: *Note: Officers with more than one job title may be intentionally listed here more than once.*

Yogesh Gupta, CEO
Anthony Folger, CFO
John Egan, Chairman of the Board
Tony Murphy, Chief Information Officer
Stephen Faberman, Chief Legal Officer
Loren Jarrett, General Manager, Divisional
Sundar Subramanian, General Manager, Divisional
Kathryn Kulikoski, Other Corporate Officer
Jeremy Segal, Senior VP, Divisional
John Ainsworth, Senior VP, Divisional
Gary Quinn, Senior VP, Divisional
Jennifer Ortiz, Vice President, Divisional

GROWTH PLANS/SPECIAL FEATURES:

Progress Software Corporation is a provider of cloud-based security solutions to large- and mid-sized organizations in a wide range of industries. The firm operates in three segments: OpenEdge, which offers development software for building multi-language applications; Data Connectivity and Integration, which focuses on data integration components of its cloud offerings; and Application Development and Deployment, which focuses on growing application development assets for customers. The company derives revenue from perpetual licenses to its products, but some products also use term licensing models. Its cloud-based offerings use a subscription-based model. A majority of the firm's revenue is generated in the United States, Europe, the Middle East, and Africa (EMEA).

FINANCIAL DATA: *Note: Data for latest year may not have been available at press time.*

In U.S. $	2021	2020	2019	2018	2017	2016
Revenue		442,150,000	413,298,000	397,165,000	397,572,000	405,341,000
R&D Expense		88,599,000	88,572,000	79,739,000	76,988,000	88,587,000
Operating Income		117,271,000	72,169,000	93,654,000	94,282,000	70,274,000
Operating Margin %						
SGA Expense		154,117,000	155,061,000	143,558,000	144,104,000	168,033,000
Net Income		79,722,000	26,400,000	63,491,000	37,417,000	-55,726,000
Operating Cash Flow		144,847,000	128,484,000	121,352,000	105,686,000	102,845,000
Capital Expenditure		6,517,000	3,998,000	7,250,000	3,377,000	5,786,000
EBITDA		141,570,000	95,087,000	128,631,000	113,114,000	8,219,000
Return on Assets %						
Return on Equity %						
Debt to Equity						

CONTACT INFORMATION:

Phone: 781 280-4000 Fax: 781 280-4095
Toll-Free: 800-477-6473
Address: 14 Oak Park, Bedford, MA 01730 United States

STOCK TICKER/OTHER:

Stock Ticker: PRGS
Exchange: NAS
Employees: 1,796
Fiscal Year Ends: 11/30
Parent Company:

SALARIES/BONUSES:

Top Exec. Salary: $575,000 Bonus: $
Second Exec. Salary: $365,192 Bonus: $

OTHER THOUGHTS:

Estimated Female Officers or Directors: 2
Hot Spot for Advancement for Women/Minorities: Y

ProofPoint Inc

NAIC Code: 511210E

www.proofpoint.com

TYPES OF BUSINESS:

Computer Software, Network Security, Managed Access, Digital ID, Cybersecurity & Anti-Virus
Cybersecurity
Software
On-Demand Protection Solutions
Secure Communication Solutions

BRANDS/DIVISIONS/AFFILIATES:

proofpoint
Dathena

CONTACTS:

Note: Officers with more than one job title may be intentionally listed here more than once.

Gary Steele, CEO
Paul Auvil, CFO
Blake Salle, Executive VP, Divisional
Bhagwat Swaroop, Executive VP, Divisional
Robert Lee, Executive VP
David Knight, Executive VP

GROWTH PLANS/SPECIAL FEATURES:

Proofpoint is a security service vendor that enables large- and mid-sized organizations worldwide to defend, protect, archive and govern their sensitive data. The company's platform comprises an integrated suite of on-demand data protection solutions, including threat protection, regulatory compliance, archiving and governance, and secure communication. Its solutions are built on a flexible, cloud-based architecture and leverage a number of proprietary technologies, including data analytics, machine learning, deep content inspection, secure storage and advanced encryption, to address today's rapidly changing threat landscape. Proofpoint derives its revenue primarily from two sources: subscription revenue for rights related to the use of security-as-a-service platform; and hardware, training, and professional services revenue provided to customers related to their use of its platform. Subscription revenue is derived from a subscription-based enterprise licensing model with contract terms typically ranging from one to three years and consists of subscription fees for the licensing of security-as-a-service platform; for access to the on-demand elements of its platform and subscription fees for the right to access customer support services. Proofpoint markets and sells its solutions worldwide both directly through sales teams and indirectly through a hybrid model where the sales organization actively assists its network of distributors and resellers. The company also distributes its solutions through strategic partners. The company's registered trademark in the U.S. is proofpoint (all lowercase), as well as the proofpoint logo and all its product names. In January 2022, Proofpoint acquired Dathena, an innovator in artificial intelligence (AI)-powered data protection.

FINANCIAL DATA:

Note: Data for latest year may not have been available at press time.

In U.S. $	2021	2020	2019	2018	2017	2016
Revenue	1,100,000,000	1,050,009,984	888,190,016	716,993,984	515,288,992	375,496,000
R&D Expense						
Operating Income						
Operating Margin %						
SGA Expense						
Net Income		-163,808,992	-130,265,000	-103,749,000	-84,337,000	-111,208,000
Operating Cash Flow						
Capital Expenditure						
EBITDA						
Return on Assets %						
Return on Equity %						
Debt to Equity						

CONTACT INFORMATION:

Phone: 408 517-4710 Fax: 408 517-4711
Toll-Free:
Address: 925 W. Maude Ave., Sunnyvale, CA 94085 United States

STOCK TICKER/OTHER:

Stock Ticker: Private
Employees: 3,368
Parent Company: Thoma Bravo LP
Exchange:
Fiscal Year Ends: 12/31

SALARIES/BONUSES:

Top Exec. Salary: $ Bonus: $
Second Exec. Salary: $ Bonus: $

OTHER THOUGHTS:

Estimated Female Officers or Directors:
Hot Spot for Advancement for Women/Minorities:

Proxim Wireless Corporation

www.proxim.com

NAIC Code: 334220

TYPES OF BUSINESS:

Wireless Networking Equipment
Home & Office Networking Equipment
Millimeter Wave Products
Wireless Systems
Product Manufacturing
Multi-Point Wireless Systems

BRANDS/DIVISIONS/AFFILIATES:

SRA Holdings Inc
Proxim SmartConnect
Proxim ClearConnect
WORP
Proxim FastConnect

CONTACTS: *Note: Officers with more than one job title may be intentionally listed here more than once.*

Fred Huey, CEO
Lee Gopadze, Pres.
David L. Renauld, General Counsel
David L. Renauld, VP-Corp. Affairs
Yoram Rubin, VP-Customer Support & Quality Mgmt.

GROWTH PLANS/SPECIAL FEATURES:

Proxim Wireless Corporation produces and sells advanced Wi-Fi, point-to-point and point-to-multipoint outdoor wireless systems. These systems are primarily built for mission-critical and high-availability communications environments. The company's products serve a wide variety of markets, including enterprises, service providers, carriers, governments, municipalities, Wi-Fi operators, hot spot operators and other organizations that need high-performance, secure scalable wireless solutions. Proxim's solutions include smart city, mobility, video surveillance, backhaul, wireless broadband, internet service provider (ISP) and Wi-Fi. Technology-wise, Proxim's proprietary products include: Proxim SmartConnect, an intelligent interface avoidance technology designed to deliver high-performance in high-density environments and under challenging radio frequency interference conditions; Proxim ClearConnect, a suite of interference mitigation technologies ensuring robust and reliable communications in high-density wireless deployments via continuous analysis and automatic link tuning; WORP, a wireless outdoor router protocol that optimizes the performance of multi-stream voice, video and data over wireless networks; and Proxim FastConnect, offering high-speed mobility technology for use on public transportation systems such as buses, trains, metros and ferries. Based in California, USA, the firm serves customers all over the world, with offices in over 15 countries and a partner network in 105 countries. Proxim is majority-held by SRA Holdings, Inc., a Japan-based IT holding company.

Proxim offers its employees medical, dental and vision insurance; short- and long-term disability coverage; flexible spending accounts; and a 401(k) plan.

FINANCIAL DATA: *Note: Data for latest year may not have been available at press time.*

In U.S. $	2021	2020	2019	2018	2017	2016
Revenue						
R&D Expense						
Operating Income						
Operating Margin %						
SGA Expense						
Net Income						
Operating Cash Flow						
Capital Expenditure						
EBITDA						
Return on Assets %						
Return on Equity %						
Debt to Equity						

CONTACT INFORMATION:

Phone: 408 383-7600 Fax: 408 383-7680
Toll-Free: 800-229-1630
Address: 2114 Ringwood Ave., San Jose, CA 95131 United States

STOCK TICKER/OTHER:

Stock Ticker: Subsidiary
Employees: 353
Parent Company: SRA Holdings Inc
Exchange:
Fiscal Year Ends: 12/31

SALARIES/BONUSES:

Top Exec. Salary: $ Bonus: $
Second Exec. Salary: $ Bonus: $

OTHER THOUGHTS:

Estimated Female Officers or Directors:
Hot Spot for Advancement for Women/Minorities:

Publicis Sapient

www.publicissapient.com

NAIC Code: 541512

TYPES OF BUSINESS:

IT Consulting
Internet Strategy Consulting
Interactive Marketing Software
Business Consulting
Technology Services
Digital Transformation

BRANDS/DIVISIONS/AFFILIATES:

Publicis Groupe SA
Publicis.Sapient
Tremend

CONTACTS:

Note: Officers with more than one job title may be intentionally listed here more than once.

Nigel Vaz, CEO
Nathalie Le Bos, CFO
Teresa Barreira, CMO
Kameshwari Rao, Chief Talent Officer
Alan Wexler, Executive VP
J. Moore, Founder
Joseph LaSala, General Counsel
Harry Register, Managing Director, Divisional
Christian Oversohl, Managing Director, Geographical
Laurie MacLaren, Senior VP, Divisional

GROWTH PLANS/SPECIAL FEATURES:

Publicis Sapient, a subsidiary of Publicis Groupe SA, is a business consulting and technology services firm focused on digital transformation and the dynamics of an always-on world. The firm's Publicis.Sapient platform is designed to help clients reimagine core business activities via transformation in order to drive growth and improve operating efficiency. The platform's digital transformation technology helps businesses in three keyways: creates business opportunities by rapidly reaching, meeting and/or changing customer expectations and behavior; creates new value via ongoing technological advances in marketing, sales, service, supply chain, IT and more; and stays ahead of competitors through smart/connected products and an enterprise-wide open ecosystem. According to Publicis Sapient, digital is at the core of transformation because the entire business eventually needs to be wired for the digital world, primarily change-sensitive technology architectures and rapid development methods. The Publicis.Sapient platform's data and analytics on customers provide strategy and direction to Sapient Corporation's business consulting services to its clients. Therefore, Sapient combines these technology capabilities with consulting expertise for the best outcomes for its business clients. Publicis Sapient serves financial services, retail, technology, communications, consumer packaged goods, travel/leisure, automotive, energy services, government, health and education sectors, among others. Based in the USA, the firm has operations worldwide, including the Americas, Europe, the Middle East, the U.K. and Asia-Pacific. In January 2022, Publicis acquired Tremend, an independent software engineering company based in Europe.

FINANCIAL DATA:

Note: Data for latest year may not have been available at press time.

In U.S. $	2021	2020	2019	2018	2017	2016
Revenue	1,950,000,000	1,877,871,996	1,805,646,150	1,765,050,000	1,681,000,000	1,625,000,000
R&D Expense						
Operating Income						
Operating Margin %						
SGA Expense						
Net Income						
Operating Cash Flow						
Capital Expenditure						
EBITDA						
Return on Assets %						
Return on Equity %						
Debt to Equity						

CONTACT INFORMATION:

Phone: 617 621-0200 Fax: 617 621-1300
Toll-Free: 877-454-9860
Address: 40 Water St., Boston, MA 02109 United States

STOCK TICKER/OTHER:

Stock Ticker: Subsidiary
Exchange:
Employees: 20,000
Fiscal Year Ends: 12/31
Parent Company: Publicis Groupe SA

SALARIES/BONUSES:

Top Exec. Salary: $ Bonus: $
Second Exec. Salary: $ Bonus: $

OTHER THOUGHTS:

Estimated Female Officers or Directors: 2
Hot Spot for Advancement for Women/Minorities:

Qualcomm Incorporated

www.qualcomm.com

NAIC Code: 334413

TYPES OF BUSINESS:

Telecommunications Equipment
Digital Wireless Communications Products
Integrated Circuits
Mobile Communications Systems
Wireless Software & Services
E-Mail Software
Code Division Multiple Access

BRANDS/DIVISIONS/AFFILIATES:

GROWTH PLANS/SPECIAL FEATURES:

Qualcomm develops and licenses wireless technology and designs chips for smartphones. The company's key patents revolve around CDMA and OFDMA technologies, which are standards in wireless communications that are the backbone of all 3G and 4G networks. The firm is a leader in 5G network technology as well. Qualcomm's IP is licensed by virtually all wireless device makers. The firm is also the world's largest wireless chip vendor, supplying nearly every premier handset maker with leading-edge processors. Qualcomm also sells RF-front end modules into smartphones and chips into automotive and Internet of Things markets.

U.S. employees of the company receive medical, dental and vision insurance; dependent/health care reimbursement accounts; tuition reimbursement; a 401(k); and an employee stock purchase plan.

CONTACTS: *Note: Officers with more than one job title may be intentionally listed here more than once.*

Cristiano Amon, CEO
Akash Palkhiwala, CFO
Mark McLaughlin, Chairman of the Board
Erin Polek, Chief Accounting Officer
James Thompson, Chief Technology Officer
Ann Cathcart Chaplin, General Counsel
Heather Ace, Other Executive Officer
Alexander Rogers, President, Subsidiary
Rogerio Amon, Vice President, Subsidiary

FINANCIAL DATA: *Note: Data for latest year may not have been available at press time.*

In U.S. $	2021	2020	2019	2018	2017	2016
Revenue	33,566,000,000	23,531,000,000	24,273,000,000	22,732,000,000	22,291,000,000	23,554,000,000
R&D Expense	7,176,000,000	5,975,000,000	5,398,000,000	5,625,000,000	5,485,000,000	5,151,000,000
Operating Income	9,789,000,000	6,255,000,000	7,667,000,000	742,000,000	2,614,000,000	6,495,000,000
Operating Margin %						
SGA Expense	2,339,000,000	2,074,000,000	2,195,000,000	2,986,000,000	2,658,000,000	2,385,000,000
Net Income	9,043,000,000	5,198,000,000	4,386,000,000	-4,864,000,000	2,466,000,000	5,705,000,000
Operating Cash Flow	10,536,000,000	5,814,000,000	7,286,000,000	3,895,000,000	4,693,000,000	7,400,000,000
Capital Expenditure	1,888,000,000	1,407,000,000	887,000,000	784,000,000	690,000,000	539,000,000
EBITDA	12,415,000,000	7,714,000,000	9,509,000,000	2,842,000,000	4,975,000,000	8,558,000,000
Return on Assets %						
Return on Equity %						
Debt to Equity						

CONTACT INFORMATION:

Phone: 858 587-1121 Fax: 858 658-2100
Toll-Free:
Address: 5775 Morehouse Dr., San Diego, CA 92121-1714 United States

STOCK TICKER/OTHER:

Stock Ticker: QCOM
Employees: 41,000
Parent Company:
Exchange: NAS
Fiscal Year Ends: 09/30

SALARIES/BONUSES:

Top Exec. Salary: $1,528,659 Bonus: $
Second Exec. Salary: $928,654 Bonus: $250,000

OTHER THOUGHTS:

Estimated Female Officers or Directors: 2
Hot Spot for Advancement for Women/Minorities: Y

Qualtrics International Inc

NAIC Code: 511210J

www.qualtrics.com

TYPES OF BUSINESS:

Computer Software, Data Base & File Management
Software Development
Experience Management Solutions
Behavior Analysis
Predictive Intelligence Engine
Machine Learning
Artificial Intelligence

BRANDS/DIVISIONS/AFFILIATES:

SAP SE
XM
Qualtrics IQ

GROWTH PLANS/SPECIAL FEATURES:

Qualtrics International Inc is a software technology company based in the United States. It develops software for organizations. Its XM Platform is purpose-built to help organizations collect feedback and data across the four vital signs of a business: Customers, Employees, Brand, and Product. The firm derives revenue from sales of subscriptions to access its XM Platform; research services and professional services.

CONTACTS: *Note: Officers with more than one job title may be intentionally listed here more than once.*

Zig Serafin, CEO
Robert Bachman, CFO
Ryan Smith, Chairman of the Board
John Thimsen, Chief Technology Officer
Bill McMurray, Other Executive Officer
Chris Beckstead, President
Brad Anderson, President, Divisional

FINANCIAL DATA: *Note: Data for latest year may not have been available at press time.*

In U.S. $	2021	2020	2019	2018	2017	2016
Revenue		763,522,000	591,155,000	401,908,000	289,903,000	190,603,000
R&D Expense		212,795,000	242,124,000	65,925,000	40,680,000	22,303,000
Operating Income		-255,053,000	-994,148,000	-33,121,000	3,093,000	-10,508,000
Operating Margin %						
SGA Expense		607,293,000	1,157,688,000	266,390,000	167,046,000	117,828,000
Net Income		-272,502,000	-1,007,633,000	-37,308,000	2,556,000	-12,034,000
Operating Cash Flow		-410,722,000	-370,904,000	36,404,000	39,618,000	17,806,000
Capital Expenditure		89,518,000	33,181,000	22,821,000	18,272,000	14,372,000
EBITDA		-228,596,000	-974,433,000	-18,334,000	13,880,000	-1,536,000
Return on Assets %						
Return on Equity %						
Debt to Equity						

CONTACT INFORMATION:

Phone: 385-203-4999 Fax:
Toll-Free: 800-340-9194
Address: 333 W. River Park Dr., Provo, UT 84604 United States

STOCK TICKER/OTHER:

Stock Ticker: XM
Employees: 3,455
Parent Company: SAP SE
Exchange: NAS
Fiscal Year Ends:

SALARIES/BONUSES:

Top Exec. Salary: $500,000 Bonus: $
Second Exec. Salary: $500,000 Bonus: $

OTHER THOUGHTS:

Estimated Female Officers or Directors:
Hot Spot for Advancement for Women/Minorities:

Quanta Computer Inc

www.quantatw.com

NAIC Code: 334418

TYPES OF BUSINESS:

Contract Electronics Manufacturing
Server Systems
Optical Storage Hardware
LCD Displays
Smart Phones
Automotive Electronics
Notebook Computers
Internet of Things

BRANDS/DIVISIONS/AFFILIATES:

GROWTH PLANS/SPECIAL FEATURES:

Quanta Computer Inc is a Taiwan-based original design manufacturer of notebook computers and electronic hardware for use in communication, networking, consumer electronics, auto electronics, and cloud computing solutions. Its products include enterprise network systems, home entertainment systems, rack-mount servers, data center networking switches, high-density storage solutions, encoding cameras, and smart home devices. A majority of the firm's revenue is generated in the America region, with the rest coming from countries across the world.

CONTACTS: *Note: Officers with more than one job title may be intentionally listed here more than once.*

CC Leung, Pres.
Barry Lam, Chmn.

FINANCIAL DATA: *Note: Data for latest year may not have been available at press time.*

In U.S. $	2021	2020	2019	2018	2017	2016
Revenue		39,316,460,000	37,109,000,000	37,050,600,000	36,805,220,000	32,220,690,000
R&D Expense		603,791,400	543,975,800	496,577,300	458,840,100	403,864,700
Operating Income		1,169,573,000	684,465,500	515,234,700	634,549,800	688,586,800
Operating Margin %						
SGA Expense		532,204,700	543,647,200	569,410,300	552,030,800	586,887,300
Net Income		912,852,200	574,603,300	544,899,100	517,815,100	545,606,000
Operating Cash Flow		2,811,436,000	1,360,023,000	613,186,400	-311,197,600	1,693,734,000
Capital Expenditure		390,419,200	264,059,300	480,697,700	214,685,600	179,844,900
EBITDA		1,609,288,000	1,320,883,000	1,190,333,000	1,116,392,000	1,079,087,000
Return on Assets %						
Return on Equity %						
Debt to Equity						

CONTACT INFORMATION:

Phone: 886 3 3272345 Fax: 886 3 3271511
Toll-Free:
Address: 211, Wenhua 2nd Rd., Guishan District, Taoyuan City, 33377 Taiwan

STOCK TICKER/OTHER:

Stock Ticker: QUCPY
Employees: 90,895
Parent Company:
Exchange: GREY
Fiscal Year Ends: 12/31

SALARIES/BONUSES:

Top Exec. Salary: $ Bonus: $
Second Exec. Salary: $ Bonus: $

OTHER THOUGHTS:

Estimated Female Officers or Directors:
Hot Spot for Advancement for Women/Minorities:

Radware Ltd

NAIC Code: 511210B

www.radware.com

TYPES OF BUSINESS:

Computer Software: Network Management (IT), System Testing & Storage
Internet Security Software
Ecommerce Software
Connectivity Software
Cloud Solutions

BRANDS/DIVISIONS/AFFILIATES:

RAD Group
Application Delivery Controller
DefensePro
AppWall
DefenseFlow
Alteon
LinkProof
FastView

GROWTH PLANS/SPECIAL FEATURES:

Radware Ltd develops and sells a broad portfolio of network products including physical and virtual application delivery controllers, web application firewalls, intrusion prevention systems, and other security products geared toward large enterprise and service provider segments. It offers an infrastructure that supports our DDoS scrubbing center services, WAF and bot management cloud-based services. In addition, It provides other services through the cloud, such as Cloud Workload Protect (CWP) and Content Delivery Network (CDN).

CONTACTS:

Note: Officers with more than one job title may be intentionally listed here more than once.

Roy Zisapel, CEO
Gabi Malka, COO
Yoav Gazelle, VP-Int'l Sales
Riki Goldriech, VP-Global Human Resources
David Aviv, CTO
Gadi Meroz, General Counsel
David Aviv, VP-Advanced Svcs.
Gilad Zlotkin, VP-Virtualization & Management
Terence Ying, VP-Asia Pacific
Yehuda Zisapel, Chmn.
Yoav Gazelle, VP-EMEA, Central & Latin America
Christina Aruza, VP-Corporate Mktg.

FINANCIAL DATA:

Note: Data for latest year may not have been available at press time.

In U.S. $	2021	2020	2019	2018	2017	2016
Revenue		250,027,000	252,072,000	234,404,000	211,369,000	196,585,000
R&D Expense		66,836,000	61,841,000	57,674,000	59,003,000	51,732,000
Operating Income		6,168,000	16,917,000	7,524,000	-6,671,000	-12,749,000
Operating Margin %						
SGA Expense		131,939,000	128,140,000	127,531,000	126,321,000	121,907,000
Net Income		9,636,000	22,566,000	11,735,000	-7,493,000	-8,659,000
Operating Cash Flow		63,865,000	52,852,000	49,251,000	31,462,000	38,480,000
Capital Expenditure		8,671,000	8,155,000	8,869,000	7,216,000	9,404,000
EBITDA		16,727,000	28,200,000	17,306,000	4,561,000	-2,377,000
Return on Assets %						
Return on Equity %						
Debt to Equity						

CONTACT INFORMATION:

Phone: 972 37668666 Fax: 972-3-7668982
Toll-Free:
Address: 22 Raoul Wallenberg St., Tel Aviv, 6971917 Israel

STOCK TICKER/OTHER:

Stock Ticker: RDWR
Exchange: NAS
Employees: 1,094
Fiscal Year Ends: 12/31
Parent Company:

SALARIES/BONUSES:

Top Exec. Salary: $421,000 Bonus: $393,000
Second Exec. Salary: $214,000 Bonus: $215,000

OTHER THOUGHTS:

Estimated Female Officers or Directors: 3
Hot Spot for Advancement for Women/Minorities: Y

Raytheon Technologies Corporation

www.rtx.com

NAIC Code: 336412

TYPES OF BUSINESS:

Aircraft Engine and Engine Parts Manufacturing
Advanced Aerospace Products
Defense Products
Aftermarket Aircraft Solutions
Avionic Systems
Aircraft Engines
Sensors
Communication Systems

BRANDS/DIVISIONS/AFFILIATES:

Collins Aerospace Systems
Pratt & Whitney
Raytheon Intelligence & Space
Raytheon Missiles & Defense

GROWTH PLANS/SPECIAL FEATURES:

Raytheon Technologies is a diversified aerospace and defense industrial company formed from the merger of United Technologies and Raytheon, with roughly equal exposure as a supplier to the commercial aerospace manufactures and to the defense market as a prime and subprime contractor. The company operates in four segments: Pratt & Whitney, an engine manufacturer, Collins Aerospace, which is a diversified aerospace supplier, and intelligence, space and airborne systems, a mix between a sensors business and a government IT contractor, and integrated defense and missile systems, a defense prime contractor focusing on missiles and missile defense hardware.

CONTACTS: *Note: Officers with more than one job title may be intentionally listed here more than once.*

Gregory Hayes, CEO
Wesley Kremer, Pres., Divisional
Neil Mitchill, CFO
Thomas Kennedy, Chairman of the Board
Amy Johnson, Chief Accounting Officer
Steven Forrest, Controller
Frank Jimenez, Executive VP
Michael Dumais, Executive VP
Dantaya Williams, Executive VP
Stephen Timm, President, Divisional
Roy Azevedo, President, Divisional
Christopher Calio, President, Subsidiary
Kevin DaSilva, Treasurer

FINANCIAL DATA: *Note: Data for latest year may not have been available at press time.*

In U.S. $	2021	2020	2019	2018	2017	2016
Revenue		56,587,000,000	77,046,000,000	66,501,000,000	59,837,000,000	57,244,000,000
R&D Expense		2,582,000,000	3,015,000,000	2,462,000,000	2,387,000,000	2,337,000,000
Operating Income		1,294,000,000	8,966,000,000	8,553,000,000	8,672,000,000	8,172,000,000
Operating Margin %						
SGA Expense		5,540,000,000	8,521,000,000	7,066,000,000	6,183,000,000	6,060,000,000
Net Income		-3,519,000,000	5,537,000,000	5,269,000,000	4,552,000,000	5,055,000,000
Operating Cash Flow		3,606,000,000	8,883,000,000	6,322,000,000	5,631,000,000	3,880,000,000
Capital Expenditure		1,967,000,000	2,607,000,000	2,302,000,000	2,394,000,000	2,087,000,000
EBITDA		3,211,000,000	13,799,000,000	11,938,000,000	10,920,000,000	10,256,000,000
Return on Assets %						
Return on Equity %						
Debt to Equity						

CONTACT INFORMATION:

Phone: 781-522-3000 Fax:
Toll-Free:
Address: 870 Winter St., Waltham, MA 02451 United States

STOCK TICKER/OTHER:

Stock Ticker: RTX
Employees: 181,000
Parent Company:
Exchange: NYS
Fiscal Year Ends: 12/31

SALARIES/BONUSES:

Top Exec. Salary: $1,413,333 Bonus: $2,500,000
Second Exec. Salary: $1,140,192 Bonus: $1,600,000

OTHER THOUGHTS:

Estimated Female Officers or Directors: 2
Hot Spot for Advancement for Women/Minorities: Y

Reliance Communications Ltd

NAIC Code: 517110

www.rcom.co.in

TYPES OF BUSINESS:

Telecommunications
Fixed-Line Communications
Data Center
Enterprise Solutions
Subsea Cable Networks

BRANDS/DIVISIONS/AFFILIATES:

Reliance Anil Dhirubhai Ambani Group

GROWTH PLANS/SPECIAL FEATURES:

Reliance Communications Ltd., a member of the Reliance Anil Dhirubhai Ambani Group, is a provider of fixed-line communications, data center services, enterprise solutions and subsea cable networks. The firm's solutions include business internet, network services, cloud networking, data center, enterprise IT infrastructure, voice, access number services, cloud telephone, wholesale voice, and collaboration. Reliance communications offers its services and solutions to enterprises and over-the-top (OTT) providers throughout India and globally.

CONTACTS: *Note: Officers with more than one job title may be intentionally listed here more than once.*

Prakash Shenoy, Corp. Sec.
Anil D. Ambani, Chmn.

FINANCIAL DATA: *Note: Data for latest year may not have been available at press time.*

In U.S. $	2021	2020	2019	2018	2017	2016
Revenue		230,471,000	602,829,000	661,767,936	2,808,587,264	3,128,161,024
R&D Expense						
Operating Income						
Operating Margin %						
SGA Expense						
Net Income		-5,675,650,000	-1,035,760,000	-3,434,767,104	-202,146,832	98,119,736
Operating Cash Flow						
Capital Expenditure						
EBITDA						
Return on Assets %						
Return on Equity %						
Debt to Equity						

CONTACT INFORMATION:

Phone: 91 2230386010 Fax: 91 2230386010
Toll-Free:
Address: DAKC, Kopar Khairane, H Block, Thane Belapur Rd., Navi Mumbai, 400 710 India

STOCK TICKER/OTHER:

Stock Ticker: 532712
Employees: 3,038
Parent Company: Reliance Anil Dhirubhai Ambani Group
Exchange: Bombay
Fiscal Year Ends: 03/31

SALARIES/BONUSES:

Top Exec. Salary: $ Bonus: $
Second Exec. Salary: $ Bonus: $

OTHER THOUGHTS:

Estimated Female Officers or Directors:
Hot Spot for Advancement for Women/Minorities:

Renault SA

www.renault.com

NAIC Code: 336111

TYPES OF BUSINESS:

Automobile Manufacturing
Automobile
Manufacture
Electric Vehicles
Mobility
Sport Cars

GROWTH PLANS/SPECIAL FEATURES:

Renault possesses a global alliance of automotive manufacturing, financing, and sales operations. The company's alliance partners consist of AvtoVAZ (61.09%), Dacia (99.4%), Nissan (43.7%), Renault Samsung Motors (80.0%), Mitsubishi (Nissan owns 34%) and Daimler (1.55% owned by Nissan). Total 2020 Renault-Nissan-Mitsubishi alliance sales volume of 7.8 million vehicles makes the alliance the third largest vehicle group in the world, behind Toyota at 9.5 million and Volkswagen at 9.3 million vehicles sold.

BRANDS/DIVISIONS/AFFILIATES:

Renault
Dacia
LADA
Alpine
Mobilize
Twingo
Sandero
Mobilize EZ-1

CONTACTS: *Note: Officers with more than one job title may be intentionally listed here more than once.*

Luca de Meo, CEO
Clotilde Delbos, CFO
Philippe Klein, Exec. VP-Prod. Planning, Plan & Programs
Jean-Michel Billig, Exec. VP-Eng. & Quality
Jose Vicente de los Mosoz Obispo, Exec. VP-Mfg.
Philippe Klein, Exec. VP-Corp. Planning
Mouna Sepehri, Exec. VP-Office of CEO
Stefan Mueller, Exec. VP
Jean-Dominique Senard, Chmn.
Gerard Leclercq, Exec. VP-Supply Chain

FINANCIAL DATA: *Note: Data for latest year may not have been available at press time.*

In U.S. $	2021	2020	2019	2018	2017	2016
Revenue		49,098,220,000	62,720,360,000	64,845,790,000	66,371,530,000	57,870,960,000
R&D Expense		2,901,284,000	3,001,796,000	2,934,035,000	2,925,000,000	2,676,545,000
Operating Income		-620,009,700	2,919,354,000	4,006,912,000	4,307,317,000	3,705,377,000
Operating Margin %						
SGA Expense		5,629,778,000	6,270,116,000	6,541,159,000	6,605,532,000	6,025,049,000
Net Income		-9,043,785,000	-158,108,100	3,729,093,000	5,775,464,000	3,861,226,000
Operating Cash Flow		6,497,115,000	6,323,196,000	7,097,926,000	6,439,518,000	4,956,690,000
Capital Expenditure		4,752,279,000	5,671,564,000	4,977,018,000	4,066,767,000	3,497,577,000
EBITDA		-2,829,006,000	6,432,742,000	8,919,557,000	10,867,680,000	8,918,428,000
Return on Assets %						
Return on Equity %						
Debt to Equity						

CONTACT INFORMATION:

Phone: 33 176840404 Fax:
Toll-Free:
Address: 13-15, quai Le Gallo, Billancourt, 92100 France

STOCK TICKER/OTHER:

Stock Ticker: RNLSY
Employees: 183,002
Parent Company:
Exchange: PINX
Fiscal Year Ends: 12/31

SALARIES/BONUSES:

Top Exec. Salary: $ Bonus: $
Second Exec. Salary: $ Bonus: $

OTHER THOUGHTS:

Estimated Female Officers or Directors: 7
Hot Spot for Advancement for Women/Minorities: Y

Renesas Electronics America Inc

www.renesas.com/us/en

NAIC Code: 334413

TYPES OF BUSINESS:

Semiconductor Systems
System in Package Technology
Microcontrollers
Smartcard Products
Semiconductors
Manufacturing
Sensors
Memory Devices

BRANDS/DIVISIONS/AFFILIATES:

Renesas Electronics Corporation

GROWTH PLANS/SPECIAL FEATURES:

Renesas Electronics America, Inc., a subsidiary of Renesas Electronics Corporation, manufactures semiconductors. The firm offers diodes, microprocessors, integrated chips and transistors, as well as timing and digital logic devices, sensors, optoelectronics, memory devices, and power management devices. Renesas Electronics America' product portfolios of analog + power + embedded processing work together to deliver comprehensive solutions, and primarily serve the automotive, healthcare, office automation, building automation, home appliance, energy management, technology and industrial automation sectors, among many others.

CONTACTS: *Note: Officers with more than one job title may be intentionally listed here more than once.*

Hidetoshi Shibata, Chmn.

FINANCIAL DATA: *Note: Data for latest year may not have been available at press time.*

In U.S. $	2021	2020	2019	2018	2017	2016
Revenue	642,000,000	629,955,000	607,243,000	609,400,000	681,837,000	943,327,000
R&D Expense						
Operating Income						
Operating Margin %						
SGA Expense						
Net Income						
Operating Cash Flow						
Capital Expenditure						
EBITDA						
Return on Assets %						
Return on Equity %						
Debt to Equity						

CONTACT INFORMATION:

Phone: 408-432-8888 Fax: 408-434-5351
Toll-Free:
Address: 1001 Murphy Ranch Rd., Milpitas, CA 95035 United States

STOCK TICKER/OTHER:

Stock Ticker: Subsidiary Exchange:
Employees: 33,500 Fiscal Year Ends: 12/31
Parent Company: Renesas Electronics Corporation

SALARIES/BONUSES:

Top Exec. Salary: $ Bonus: $
Second Exec. Salary: $ Bonus: $

OTHER THOUGHTS:

Estimated Female Officers or Directors:
Hot Spot for Advancement for Women/Minorities:

Renesas Electronics Corporation

www.renesas.com

NAIC Code: 334413

TYPES OF BUSINESS:

Semiconductor and Related Device Manufacturing
Semiconductors
Manufacturing

GROWTH PLANS/SPECIAL FEATURES:

Renesas Electronics Corp is a Japan-based company that manufactures and distributes semiconductor components and other products for use in automotive, healthcare, computer peripheral, connectivity, home appliance, and industrial end markets. Its product portfolio includes microcontrollers and microprocessors, embedded systems platform, insulated-gate bipolar transistors, intelligent power devices, thrysistors, transistors, diodes, analog integrated circuits, and optoelectronics products. The firm has operations in Japan, the Americas, Europe, Middle East and Africa, and Asia.

BRANDS/DIVISIONS/AFFILIATES:

CONTACTS: *Note: Officers with more than one job title may be intentionally listed here more than once.*

Hidetoshi Shibata, CEO
Tetsuya Tsurumaru, Chmn.

FINANCIAL DATA: *Note: Data for latest year may not have been available at press time.*

In U.S. $	2021	2020	2019	2018	2017	2016
Revenue		6,288,645,000	6,311,227,000	6,647,420,000	6,856,182,000	6,091,956,000
R&D Expense						
Operating Income		572,405,200	60,147,270	599,240,800	688,903,700	911,936,300
Operating Margin %						
SGA Expense		2,339,707,000	2,469,228,000	2,205,731,000		
Net Income		400,917,300	-51,966,540	448,042,200	678,324,100	758,250,900
Operating Cash Flow		1,967,321,000	1,774,630,000	1,498,207,000	1,443,025,000	1,109,768,000
Capital Expenditure		335,541,800	495,307,700	763,365,000	1,086,403,000	416,075,000
EBITDA		1,882,992,000	1,380,066,000	1,604,487,000	1,587,932,000	1,259,420,000
Return on Assets %						
Return on Equity %						
Debt to Equity						

CONTACT INFORMATION:

Phone: 81 352015111 Fax:
Toll-Free:
Address: 3-2-24 Toyosu, Koto-ku, Tokyo, 135-0061 Japan

STOCK TICKER/OTHER:

Stock Ticker: RNECY
Employees: 20,962
Parent Company:
Exchange: PINX
Fiscal Year Ends: 03/31

SALARIES/BONUSES:

Top Exec. Salary: $ Bonus: $
Second Exec. Salary: $ Bonus: $

OTHER THOUGHTS:

Estimated Female Officers or Directors:
Hot Spot for Advancement for Women/Minorities:

Ring Protect Inc

ring.com

NAIC Code: 334310

TYPES OF BUSINESS:

Audio and Video Equipment Manufacturing
Video Equipped Doorbell
Home Security Cameras
Smart Lighting

BRANDS/DIVISIONS/AFFILIATES:

Amazon.com Inc

CONTACTS:

Note: Officers with more than one job title may be intentionally listed here more than once.

Jamie Siminoff, CEO

GROWTH PLANS/SPECIAL FEATURES:

Ring Protect, Inc. develops video doorbells, allowing users to safely and securely answer the door from anywhere, anytime. How it works: the doorbells encompass motion detection capabilities that send notifications to the property owner's phone, tablet and/or personal computer. Through these devices, the user can see, hear and speak to visitors in real-time from anywhere in the world. Ring offers a variety of doorbells that comprise a range of power options and color combinations so consumers can choose which model would work best for the premises. The doorbells are compatible with Alexa, iOS, Android and Mac devices. Doorbell features include high-definition video, two-way talk and weather resistance. Ring offers protection plans for a monthly fee, which include the recording, reviewing and/or sharing of videos from the devices. Additional products include security cameras, such as stickup cameras, floodlight cameras, spotlight cameras, as well as smart lighting and accessories. Based in the U.S., Ring has operations in Latin America, the U.S., Asia-Pacific, Europe, the Middle East and Africa. The firm holds U.S. patent rights associated with its doorbell, camera and alert/notification products. Ring operates as a subsidiary of Amazon.com, Inc.

FINANCIAL DATA:

Note: Data for latest year may not have been available at press time.

In U.S. $	2021	2020	2019	2018	2017	2016
Revenue						
R&D Expense						
Operating Income						
Operating Margin %						
SGA Expense						
Net Income						
Operating Cash Flow						
Capital Expenditure						
EBITDA						
Return on Assets %						
Return on Equity %						
Debt to Equity						

CONTACT INFORMATION:

Phone: 310 929-7085 Fax:
Toll-Free: 800-656-1918
Address: 1523 26th St., Santa Monca, CA 90404 United States

STOCK TICKER/OTHER:

Stock Ticker: Subsidiary
Employees:
Parent Company: Amazon.com Inc
Exchange:
Fiscal Year Ends: 12/31

SALARIES/BONUSES:

Top Exec. Salary: $ Bonus: $
Second Exec. Salary: $ Bonus: $

OTHER THOUGHTS:

Estimated Female Officers or Directors:
Hot Spot for Advancement for Women/Minorities:

Robert Bosch GmbH

www.bosch.com

NAIC Code: 336300

TYPES OF BUSINESS:

Automobile Components Manufacturing
Software and Machine to Machine Data
Motor, Control & Motion Products
Mobility Solutions
Industrial Technology
Smart Home Products and Solutions
Connected Apps
Power Tools

BRANDS/DIVISIONS/AFFILIATES:

GROWTH PLANS/SPECIAL FEATURES:

Robert Bosch GmbH is a global supplier of technology and services, with operations divided into four business sectors: mobility solutions, industrial technology, consumer goods, and energy and building technology. Mobility products and solutions span keyless entry, connected mobility gateways, connected mobility apps, wrong-way driver warning, secure truck parking, visual sensors, connectivity control and more. Industrial technology and energy/building products and solutions include sensors, track and trace solutions, energy consumption software solutions, Internet of Things (IoT) gateway software solutions, field-level energy/power equipment, connected factory and machine automation solutions. Consumer goods products and solutions include home appliances with connected features and apps, home heating system apps and connectivity, security cameras and solutions, connected smoke detectors, smart home solutions, as well as garden tools with innovative tools, apps and accessories. Bosch's objective is to facilitate connected living with products and solutions that either contain artificial intelligence (AI) or have been developed or manufactured with its help. Bosch has approximately 440 subsidiaries and regional companies in approximately 60 countries worldwide, including 129 engineering locations. During 2021, Bosch announced plans to invest more than 400 million euros in expanding its wafer fabs in Dresden and Reutlingen, Germany, and its semiconductor operations in Penang, Malaysia.

CONTACTS: *Note: Officers with more than one job title may be intentionally listed here more than once.*

Volkmar Denner, Dir.-Research
Volkmar Denner, Dir.-Prod. Planning
Volkmar Denner, Dir.-Eng.
Stefan Asenkerschbaumer, Dir.-Bus. Admin.
Christoph Kubel, Dir.-Legal Svcs., Taxes & Internal Auditing
Stefan Asenkerschbaumer, Dir.-Corp. Planning
Volkmar Denner, Dir.-Corp. Comm.
Stefan Asenkerschbaumer, Dir.-Finance & Controlling
Wolf-Henning Scheider, Dir.-Coordination Automotive Tech.
Uwe Raschke, Dir.-Consumer Goods & User Experience
Werner Struth, Dir.-North & South America
Stefan Hartung, Chmn.
Peter Tyroller, Dir.-Asia Pacific
Stefan Asenkerschbaumer, Dir.-Purchasing & Logistics

FINANCIAL DATA: *Note: Data for latest year may not have been available at press time.*

In U.S. $	2021	2020	2019	2018	2017	2016
Revenue	85,056,714,000	87,812,100,000	84,327,290,000	88,321,400,000	93,512,400,000	77,058,200,000
R&D Expense						
Operating Income						
Operating Margin %						
SGA Expense						
Net Income	3,650,000,000	2,158,862,000	2,235,170,000	3,877,660,000	3,921,810,000	2,805,000,000
Operating Cash Flow						
Capital Expenditure						
EBITDA						
Return on Assets %						
Return on Equity %						
Debt to Equity						

CONTACT INFORMATION:

Phone: 49-711-400-40990 Fax: 49-711-400-40999
Toll-Free:
Address: Robert-Bosch-Platz 1, Gerlingen-Schillerhohe, 70839 Germany

STOCK TICKER/OTHER:

Stock Ticker: Private
Employees: 401,300
Parent Company:
Exchange:
Fiscal Year Ends: 12/31

SALARIES/BONUSES:

Top Exec. Salary: $ Bonus: $
Second Exec. Salary: $ Bonus: $

OTHER THOUGHTS:

Estimated Female Officers or Directors: 3
Hot Spot for Advancement for Women/Minorities: Y

Rocket Software Inc

www.rocketsoftware.com

NAIC Code: 511210B

TYPES OF BUSINESS:

Computer Software, Network Management (IT), System Testing & Storage
Data & Network Management Products
Security Software
Mobile & Wireless Software
Training & Maintenance Services

BRANDS/DIVISIONS/AFFILIATES:

Rocket Aldon
Rocket BlueZone
Rocke LegaSuite
Rocket Mainstar
Rocket Servergraph
Rocket UniVerse
Rocket API
Rocket iCluster

CONTACTS: *Note: Officers with more than one job title may be intentionally listed here more than once.*

Milan Shetti, CEO
Barbara Goose, CMO
Tracey Leahy, Chief People Officer
Bryan Smith, VP-R&D
Bryan Smith, CTO
David Reibel, General Counsel
Marcus Hatfield, VP-Corp. Dev.
Sam Elias, VP-Application Dev., Integration & Modernization
Susie Siegesmund, VP
Claudia Franco, VP
Brian Starr, VP

GROWTH PLANS/SPECIAL FEATURES:

Rocket Software, Inc. is a global developer of software products that help corporations, government agencies and other organizations run their critical infrastructure, business processes and data. The firm's products can also help them extend the value of their assets via the cloud, mobile computing, advanced analytics and other innovative channels and technologies. Rocket Software products are grouped into the following categories: modernization, terminal emulation, application lifecycle management, DevOps, storage monitoring, capacity planning, compliance solutions and business-to-business (B2B) supply chain integration. Its brands include Rocket Aldon, Rocket BlueZone, Rocket LegaSuite, Rocket Mainstar, Rocket Servergraph, Rocket UniVerse, Rocket API, Rocket D3, Rocket iCluster, Rocket OpenTech, Rocket TRUfusion Enterprise, Rocket UniData and z/OS open source languages and tools. The company's core platforms include: IBM, which narrows the z/OS skills gap for developers, improves user/customer experiences, keeps mainframe data safe and secure, optimizes mainframe performance and integrity and provides mainframe access across devices; and Multi-Value, for simplifying the delivery of digital transformation projects, narrowing the multi-value skills gap, improves user/customer experiences, ensures 24/7 availability for multi-value apps and protects critical data and applications. More than 10 million IT and business professionals rely on Rocket to run their most critical applications, business process and data, including more than 40 of the Fortune 50 companies. Markets served by the company include aerospace, defense, auto manufacturing, banking, finance, chemicals, education, energy, government, healthcare, insurance, manufacturing, retail, technology, telecommunications and transportation. Bain Capital holds a majority stake in the firm. In late-2021, Rocket Software acquired the database and tools products of Zumasys Inc., a provider of multi-value database software, known as PICK.

Rocket Software offers its employees health coverage, retirement savings, life and disability coverage, and a variety of employee assistant programs and perks.

FINANCIAL DATA: *Note: Data for latest year may not have been available at press time.*

In U.S. $	2021	2020	2019	2018	2017	2016
Revenue	510,000,000	500,000,000	496,125,000	472,500,000	450,000,000	
R&D Expense						
Operating Income						
Operating Margin %						
SGA Expense						
Net Income						
Operating Cash Flow						
Capital Expenditure						
EBITDA						
Return on Assets %						
Return on Equity %						
Debt to Equity						

CONTACT INFORMATION:

Phone: 781-577-4321 Fax:
Toll-Free: 855-577-4323
Address: 77 4th Ave., Waltham, MA 02451 United States

STOCK TICKER/OTHER:

Stock Ticker: Private
Employees: 1,400
Parent Company: Bain Capital
Exchange:
Fiscal Year Ends: 12/31

SALARIES/BONUSES:

Top Exec. Salary: $ Bonus: $
Second Exec. Salary: $ Bonus: $

OTHER THOUGHTS:

Estimated Female Officers or Directors: 2
Hot Spot for Advancement for Women/Minorities:

Rolls-Royce plc

www.rolls-royce.com

NAIC Code: 336412

TYPES OF BUSINESS:

Aircraft Engine and Engine Parts Manufacturing
Engines
Power Systems
Nuclear
Artificial Intelligence Technology
Machine Learning

GROWTH PLANS/SPECIAL FEATURES:

Rolls-Royce operates three core business segments: civil aerospace, power systems, and defense. The civil aerospace segment builds engines powering wide-body aircraft, regional and business jets, and offers aftermarket services. Twenty years ago, the firm pioneered full-service flight hour contracts with the TotalCare package. Power systems provides power solutions to multiple end markets (defense, agriculture, marine, and power generation) while the defense business provides military, ground vehicle and naval propulsion solutions.

BRANDS/DIVISIONS/AFFILIATES:

CONTACTS: *Note: Officers with more than one job title may be intentionally listed here more than once.*

Warren East, CEO
Stephen Daintith, CFO
Ben Story, Dir.-Mktg.
Harry Holt, Chief People Officer
Paul Stein, CTO
Rob Webb, General Counsel
Alain Michaelis, Dir.-Oper.
Miles Cowdry, Dir.-Corp. Dev.
Lawrie Haynes, Pres., Nuclear & Marine
Andrew Heath, Pres., Energy
John Paterson, Pres., Marine & Industrial Power Systems
Ian Davis, Chmn.
James M. Guyette, CEO
Tony Wood, Pres., Aerospace

FINANCIAL DATA: *Note: Data for latest year may not have been available at press time.*

In U.S. $	2021	2020	2019	2018	2017	2016
Revenue		15,743,710,000	22,085,670,000	20,943,240,000	21,712,850,000	19,912,650,000
R&D Expense		888,113,700	1,025,259,000	1,022,596,000	1,058,546,000	1,222,321,000
Operating Income		-3,025,179,000	-1,272,919,000	-1,551,203,000	1,539,219,000	-97,199,840
Operating Margin %						
SGA Expense		1,075,856,000	1,501,937,000	2,123,750,000	1,627,099,000	2,939,962,000
Net Income		-4,220,870,000	-1,750,929,000	-3,196,943,000	5,601,640,000	-5,368,627,000
Operating Cash Flow		-4,006,498,000	3,058,466,000	2,963,929,000	2,410,023,000	1,878,753,000
Capital Expenditure		1,264,929,000	1,846,797,000	2,110,435,000	2,324,807,000	1,619,110,000
EBITDA		-366,163,800	806,891,800	-2,335,459,000	7,781,313,000	-4,666,924,000
Return on Assets %						
Return on Equity %						
Debt to Equity						

CONTACT INFORMATION:

Phone: 44 2072229020 Fax: 44 2072279170
Toll-Free:
Address: 90 York Way, London, N1C 4 United Kingdom

STOCK TICKER/OTHER:

Stock Ticker: RYCEF Exchange: PINX
Employees: 50,000 Fiscal Year Ends: 12/31
Parent Company:

SALARIES/BONUSES:

Top Exec. Salary: $1,162,404 Bonus: $
Second Exec. Salary: $837,516 Bonus: $

OTHER THOUGHTS:

Estimated Female Officers or Directors: 4
Hot Spot for Advancement for Women/Minorities: Y

Roper Technologies Inc

NAIC Code: 334513

www.ropertech.com

TYPES OF BUSINESS:

Controls Manufacturing
Energy Controls
Medical Systems
Flow Controls

BRANDS/DIVISIONS/AFFILIATES:

Aderant
Strata
ConstructConnect
TransCore
Alpha
Verathon
AMOT
Zetec

CONTACTS: *Note: Officers with more than one job title may be intentionally listed here more than once.*

L. Neil Hunn, CEO
Robert Crisci, CFO
Jason Conley, Chief Accounting Officer
John Stipancich, Executive VP

GROWTH PLANS/SPECIAL FEATURES:

Roper is a diversified technology company that operates out of four segments: application software; network software and systems; measurement and analytical solutions; and process technologies. The firm's culture emphasizes acquiring asset-light, cash-generative businesses. Roper then reinvests this excess cash in businesses that yield incrementally higher rates of return. While the firm's businesses are managed in a decentralized manner, Roper does not passively manage its portfolio. Instead, Roper manages its businesses through the Socratic method and empowers decision-makers through group executive coaching. Roper has now rotated a clear majority of its business from legacy industrial products into technology software in mature, niche markets with large quantities of deferred revenue.

FINANCIAL DATA: *Note: Data for latest year may not have been available at press time.*

In U.S. $	2021	2020	2019	2018	2017	2016
Revenue		5,527,100,000	5,366,800,000	5,191,200,000	4,607,471,000	3,789,925,000
R&D Expense						
Operating Income		1,431,100,000	1,498,400,000	1,396,400,000	1,210,244,000	1,054,563,000
Operating Margin %						
SGA Expense		2,111,900,000	1,928,700,000	1,883,100,000	1,654,552,000	1,277,847,000
Net Income		949,700,000	1,767,900,000	944,400,000	971,772,000	658,645,000
Operating Cash Flow		1,525,100,000	1,461,800,000	1,430,100,000	1,234,482,000	963,785,000
Capital Expenditure		48,900,000	62,900,000	58,600,000	59,536,000	40,106,000
EBITDA		1,949,000,000	2,830,000,000	1,747,500,000	1,560,254,000	1,292,664,000
Return on Assets %						
Return on Equity %						
Debt to Equity						

CONTACT INFORMATION:

Phone: 941 556-2601 Fax: 941 556-2670
Toll-Free:
Address: 6901 Professional Parkway East, Sarasota, FL 34240 United States

STOCK TICKER/OTHER:

Stock Ticker: ROP
Employees: 19,300
Parent Company:
Exchange: NYS
Fiscal Year Ends: 12/31

SALARIES/BONUSES:

Top Exec. Salary: $895,833 Bonus: $
Second Exec. Salary: $660,000 Bonus: $

OTHER THOUGHTS:

Estimated Female Officers or Directors:
Hot Spot for Advancement for Women/Minorities:

R-STYLE LAB Company (R-Style Lab)

r-stylelab.com

NAIC Code: 511210B

TYPES OF BUSINESS:

Computer Software: Network Management (IT), System Testing & Storage
Software Development

BRANDS/DIVISIONS/AFFILIATES:

CONTACTS:

Note: Officers with more than one job title may be intentionally listed here more than once.

Pavel Shylenok, CTO

GROWTH PLANS/SPECIAL FEATURES:

R-STYLE LAB Company operates as R-Style Lab, a software development company founded in 2006, in San Francisco, USA. Today, the firm has a research and development center in Eastern Europe, and serves more than 100 customers worldwide. R-Style Lab helps hardware manufacturers, software vendors (with limited in-house resources) and non-technology companies create entire software ecosystems for their connected devices. The company's software also helps to reduce time-to-market by scaling up internal teams and transforming business requirements into fully-functional software solutions. R-Style Lab's software solutions span smart home, healthcare Internet of Things (IoT), industrial IoT (IIoT), smart retail, social networking and eCommerce. Its services include IoT development, electronics prototyping, cloud application development, startup development services, dedicated development center, digital transformation, mobile applications development and web applications development. How the process works: a roadmap is developed, then software is developed, then the project is delivered. In the roadmap development phase, R-Style Lab receives and processes the client's request within 12 hours' time, signs a non-disclosure agreement, discusses the project between the client and R-Style's development manager and software architect, and then provides an estimate, vision of phases and project management methodology. Within the software development phase, a contract is signed, the project is broken down into iterations with detailed software requirement specifications, prototypes and/or features, and the client works with selected R-Style managers to review the deliverables. Last, the project delivery phase consists of R-Style's quality assurance tools for ensuring software quality, provides comprehensive consulting services to maximize product success, and helps the startup with pitching. The company offers an exclusive warranty on its software solution, which guarantees the system will work as described in the specification. All internet protocol (IP) rights and the source code belong to the client.

FINANCIAL DATA:

Note: Data for latest year may not have been available at press time.

In U.S. $	2021	2020	2019	2018	2017	2016
Revenue						
R&D Expense						
Operating Income						
Operating Margin %						
SGA Expense						
Net Income						
Operating Cash Flow						
Capital Expenditure						
EBITDA						
Return on Assets %						
Return on Equity %						
Debt to Equity						

CONTACT INFORMATION:

Phone: Fax:
Toll-Free: 888-252-3073
Address: 425 Market St., San Francisco, CA 94105 United States

STOCK TICKER/OTHER:

Stock Ticker: Private
Employees: 120
Parent Company:
Exchange:
Fiscal Year Ends:

SALARIES/BONUSES:

Top Exec. Salary: $ Bonus: $
Second Exec. Salary: $ Bonus: $

OTHER THOUGHTS:

Estimated Female Officers or Directors:
Hot Spot for Advancement for Women/Minorities:

SAIC Motor Corporation Limited

www.saicmotor.com

NAIC Code: 336111

TYPES OF BUSINESS:

Automobile Manufacturing
Motorcycle Manufacturing
Bus Manufacturing
Car Rental Services
Tractor & Heavy Equipment Manufacturing
Parts Manufacturing, Distribution & Retailing
Consumer Finance & Leasing
Insurance

BRANDS/DIVISIONS/AFFILIATES:

SAIC Passenger Vehicle Branch
SAIC Maxus
SAIC Volkswagen
SAIC General Motors
SAIC-GM-Wuling
NAVECO
SAIC-IVECO Hongyan
SAIC Mobility Robotaxi

CONTACTS:

Note: Officers with more than one job title may be intentionally listed here more than once.

Xiaoqiu Wang, Pres.
Wei Yong, CFO
Wang Jianzhang, Sec.
Chen Demei, VP
Chen Zhixin, Exec. VP
Xiao Guopu, Exec. VP
Yu Jianwei, VP-Nanjing Automotive Group
Zhu Genlin, VP
Chen Hong, Chmn.

GROWTH PLANS/SPECIAL FEATURES:

SAIC Motor Corporation Limited is a state-owned entity and one of China's largest automotive companies. The group operates manufacturing facilities, mainly near Shanghai, which produce passenger cars, trucks, buses and automotive parts. SAIC has branches in Korea, Japan, Hong Kong, the U.S. and Europe. SAIC Motor's business covers the research, production and vehicle sales of both passenger cars and commercial vehicles. The company actively promotes new energy vehicles, the commercialization of internet-connected cars and is exploring intelligent driving technology. SAIC is engaged in the research and development, production and sales of parts for motor drive systems, chassis systems, interior/exterior decoration, battery, electric drive and power electronics, as well as auto-related services such as logistics, ecommerce, travel, energy saving/charging services, finance, insurance and investments. SAIC Motor's affiliated original equipment manufacturers (OEMs) include SAIC Passenger Vehicle Branch, SAIC Maxus, SAIC Volkswagen, SAIC General Motors, SAIC-GM-Wuling, NAVECO, SAIC-IVECO Hongyan and Sunwin. In December 2021, SAIC Motor announced the official operation of SAIC Mobility Robotaxi, an L4 self-driving platform launched in Shanghai. Robotaxi vehicles can be hailed on the SAIC Mobility app, and primarily serve urban areas. The company expected to have approximately 200 Robotaxi vehicles nationwide during the year 2022.

FINANCIAL DATA:

Note: Data for latest year may not have been available at press time.

In U.S. $	2021	2020	2019	2018	2017	2016
Revenue		113,698,000,000	188,775,450,000	198,711,000,000	132,474,000,000	108,846,000,000
R&D Expense						
Operating Income						
Operating Margin %						
SGA Expense						
Net Income		4,471,750,000	4,972,243,000	5,233,940,000	5,283,550,000	46,048,000
Operating Cash Flow						
Capital Expenditure						
EBITDA						
Return on Assets %						
Return on Equity %						
Debt to Equity						

CONTACT INFORMATION:

Phone: 86-21-2201-1888 Fax: 86-21-2201-1777
Toll-Free:
Address: 489 WeiHai Rd., Shanghai, Shanghai 200041 China

STOCK TICKER/OTHER:

Stock Ticker: 600104.SS
Employees: 204,815
Parent Company:
Exchange: Shanghai
Fiscal Year Ends: 12/31

SALARIES/BONUSES:

Top Exec. Salary: $ Bonus: $
Second Exec. Salary: $ Bonus: $

OTHER THOUGHTS:

Estimated Female Officers or Directors: 1
Hot Spot for Advancement for Women/Minorities:

salesforce.com inc

www.salesforce.com

NAIC Code: 511210K

TYPES OF BUSINESS:

Software, Sales & Marketing Automation
Customer Relationship Management Software
Software Subscription Services

GROWTH PLANS/SPECIAL FEATURES:

Salesforce.com provides enterprise cloud computing solutions, including Sales Cloud, the company's main customer relationship management software-as-a-service product. Salesforce.com also offers Service Cloud for customer support, Marketing Cloud for digital marketing campaigns, Commerce Cloud as an e-commerce engine, the Salesforce Platform, which allows enterprises to build applications, and other solutions, such as MuleSoft for data integration.

BRANDS/DIVISIONS/AFFILIATES:

Sales Cloud
Service Cloud
Marketing Cloud
Community Cloud
Industries
IoT Cloud
Tableau Software Inc
myTrailhead

CONTACTS: *Note: Officers with more than one job title may be intentionally listed here more than once.*

Marc Benioff, CEO
Amy Weaver, CFO
Joe Allanson, Chief Accounting Officer
Parker Harris, Chief Technology Officer
Bret Taylor, Co-President
Brent Hyder, Co-President
Srinivas Tallapragada, Co-President
Gavin Patterson, Co-President

FINANCIAL DATA: *Note: Data for latest year may not have been available at press time.*

In U.S. $	2021	2020	2019	2018	2017	2016
Revenue	21,252,000,000	17,098,000,000	13,282,000,000	10,480,010,000	8,391,984,000	6,667,216,000
R&D Expense	3,598,000,000	2,766,000,000	1,886,000,000	1,553,073,000	1,208,127,000	946,300,000
Operating Income	455,000,000	463,000,000	535,000,000	235,768,000	64,228,000	114,923,000
Operating Margin %						
SGA Expense	11,761,000,000	9,634,000,000	7,410,000,000	5,917,649,000	4,885,590,000	3,951,445,000
Net Income	4,072,000,000	126,000,000	1,110,000,000	127,478,000	179,632,000	-47,426,000
Operating Cash Flow	4,801,000,000	4,331,000,000	3,398,000,000	2,737,965,000	2,162,198,000	1,612,585,000
Capital Expenditure	710,000,000	643,000,000	595,000,000	534,027,000	463,958,000	709,852,000
EBITDA	3,301,000,000	2,598,000,000	2,099,000,000	1,041,651,000	746,616,000	662,514,000
Return on Assets %						
Return on Equity %						
Debt to Equity						

CONTACT INFORMATION:

Phone: 415 901-7000 Fax: 415 901-7040
Toll-Free:
Address: Salesforce Tower, 415 Mission St., 3/Fl, San Francisco, CA 94105 United States

STOCK TICKER/OTHER:

Stock Ticker: CRM Exchange: NYS
Employees: 49,000 Fiscal Year Ends: 01/31
Parent Company:

SALARIES/BONUSES:

Top Exec. Salary: $947,032 Bonus: $1,373,200
Second Exec. Salary: $1,550,000 Bonus: $

OTHER THOUGHTS:

Estimated Female Officers or Directors: 4
Hot Spot for Advancement for Women/Minorities: Y

Samsara Inc

www.samsara.com

NAIC Code: 511210A

TYPES OF BUSINESS:

Computer Software: Supply Chain & Logistics
Software Development
Internet of Things
Cloud-based Software

BRANDS/DIVISIONS/AFFILIATES:

CONTACTS:

Note: Officers with more than one job title may be intentionally listed here more than once.

Sanjit Biswas, CEO
Dominic Phillips, CFO
Brion O'Connor, VP-Mktg. & Sales
Melissa Yeh, VP-Human Resources
John Bicket, CTO

GROWTH PLANS/SPECIAL FEATURES:

Samsara, Inc. designs, develops and markets connected sensors and software that improve the safety, efficiency and quality of its customers' operations. The firm, founded in 2015, serves more than 10,000 customers worldwide, and therefore has emerged as a fast-growing Internet of Things (IoT) entity. Samsara's products are divided into three groups: fleet management, factory and industrial. The fleet management product consists of a unified system that covers fleet management, driver safety and compliance. The platform includes: cellular gateways, offering real-time telematics with global positioning system (GPS) tracking, Wi-Fi and diagnostics; dash cameras, which are internet-connected and encompass high-definition with computer vision; wireless sensors, offering live and historical temperature, cargo and equipment tracking and monitoring; and a driver mobile app, which forms with any Android or iOS mobile device and provides electronic logging, routing, dispatch and messaging capabilities. In addition, the fleet management solution offers reporting, alerts and seamless document capture/management options in real-time. Samsara's factory division offers solutions in regards to consumer goods, pharmaceuticals, automotive and food and beverage industries, with products including manufacturing analytics, process monitoring, condition monitoring and quality inspection. The infrastructure group serves the oil and gas and water industries, with products offering remote monitoring and condition monitoring. Headquartered in San Francisco, California, USA, the firm has an engineering facility in San Francisco, as well as domestic offices in San Jose and Atlanta, and European headquarters in London, U.K. Its investors include Andreessen Horowitz, General Catalyst, Tiger Global and Dragoneer.

Samsara offers employees comprehensive health benefits, 401(k) and company perks.

FINANCIAL DATA:

Note: Data for latest year may not have been available at press time.

In U.S. $	2021	2020	2019	2018	2017	2016
Revenue	249,905,000	119,865,000				
R&D Expense						
Operating Income						
Operating Margin %						
SGA Expense						
Net Income	-210,208,000	-225,224,000				
Operating Cash Flow						
Capital Expenditure						
EBITDA						
Return on Assets %						
Return on Equity %						
Debt to Equity						

CONTACT INFORMATION:

Phone: 415-985-2400 Fax:
Toll-Free:
Address: 350 Rhode Island St., Fl. 4, S. Bldg., San Francisco, CA 94103 United States

STOCK TICKER/OTHER:

Stock Ticker: IOT
Employees: 1,490
Parent Company:
Exchange: NYS
Fiscal Year Ends: 01/31

SALARIES/BONUSES:

Top Exec. Salary: $ Bonus: $
Second Exec. Salary: $ Bonus: $

OTHER THOUGHTS:

Estimated Female Officers or Directors:
Hot Spot for Advancement for Women/Minorities:

Samsung Electro-Mechanics Co Ltd

www.samsungsem.com

NAIC Code: 334418

TYPES OF BUSINESS:

Electronic Components Manufacturing
Printed Circuit Boards
Capacitors
LED Products
Tuners
Network Modules
Crystal Devices

BRANDS/DIVISIONS/AFFILIATES:

Samsung Group

CONTACTS: *Note: Officers with more than one job title may be intentionally listed here more than once.*

Duckhyun Chang, CEO

GROWTH PLANS/SPECIAL FEATURES:

Samsung Electro-Mechanics Co., Ltd. (SEM) is a South Korean-based manufacturer of electronic parts and components that are incorporated into televisions, PCs, game systems, digital cameras, navigation systems, mobile devices, audio players and portable movie players. The company, part of the Samsung Group, offers products in three categories: passive components, module and substrate. The firm's passive components, which store electrical charges to reduce noise in electronic circuits, are sold in a variety of sizes and charge capacities for use in mobile technology, computers, television and automobiles. Its products include multi-layer ceramic capacitors inductors, chip resistors, tantalum capacitors and filters. Module products include camera modules for quality low illumination and swift autofocusing in small devices, vibration to support small linear actuators for applicability in smartphones and tablets, wireless LAN for short-distance data transmission and reception systems, wireless power transfer for wireless charging products and cellular FEM for transmission and reception of signals. The substrate category includes: package substrates, which transmit electrical signals between semiconductors and the main board; high-density interconnection (HDI) substrates, which make it possible for electronic parts mounted on a printed circuit board (PCB) to send and receive electrical signals between themselves; and radio frequency PCB substrates, which do not require connectors between modules and come in rigid and flexible formats. The company maintains production and sales subsidiaries, R&D centers and other offices in the U.S., Europe, Japan, China and Southeast Asia.

SEM offers its employees an in-house hospital for health care needs, a day care center and other employee assistance programs.

FINANCIAL DATA: *Note: Data for latest year may not have been available at press time.*

In U.S. $	2021	2020	2019	2018	2017	2016
Revenue		7,541,537,908	6,943,950,000	7,215,852,544	6,022,858,240	5,313,487,360
R&D Expense						
Operating Income						
Operating Margin %						
SGA Expense						
Net Income		5,731,006,550	456,062,000	577,972,608	142,448,704	12,953,238
Operating Cash Flow						
Capital Expenditure						
EBITDA						
Return on Assets %						
Return on Equity %						
Debt to Equity						

CONTACT INFORMATION:

Phone: 82-31-210-5114 Fax: 82-31-210-6363
Toll-Free:
Address: 150 Maeyoung-ro Yeongtong-gu, Suwon, 16674 South Korea

STOCK TICKER/OTHER:

Stock Ticker: 9150
Exchange: Seoul
Employees:
Fiscal Year Ends: 12/31
Parent Company: Samsung Group

SALARIES/BONUSES:

Top Exec. Salary: $ Bonus: $
Second Exec. Salary: $ Bonus: $

OTHER THOUGHTS:

Estimated Female Officers or Directors:
Hot Spot for Advancement for Women/Minorities:

Samsung Electronics Co Ltd

NAIC Code: 334310

www.samsung.com

TYPES OF BUSINESS:

Consumer Electronics
Semiconductors and Memory Products
Smartphones
Computers & Accessories
Digital Cameras
Fuel-Cell Technology
LCD Displays
Solar Energy Panels

BRANDS/DIVISIONS/AFFILIATES:

Samsung Group

GROWTH PLANS/SPECIAL FEATURES:

Samsung Electronics is a diversified electronics conglomerate that manufactures and sells a wide range of products, including smartphones, semiconductor chips, printers, home appliances, medical equipment, and telecom network equipment. About 52% of its profit is generated from semiconductor business, and a further 30%-35% is generated from its mobile handset business, although these percentages vary with the fortunes of each of these businesses. It is the largest smartphone and television manufacturer in the world, which helps provide a base demand for its component businesses, such as memory chips and displays, and is also the largest manufacturer of these globally.

CONTACTS: *Note: Officers with more than one job title may be intentionally listed here more than once.*

Ki Nam Kim, CEO
Oh-Hyun Kwon, Vice Chmn.

FINANCIAL DATA: *Note: Data for latest year may not have been available at press time.*

In U.S. $	2021	2020	2019	2018	2017	2016
Revenue		198,873,800,000	193,493,900,000	204,722,600,000	201,198,700,000	169,530,500,000
R&D Expense		17,729,720,000	16,718,370,000	15,414,010,000	13,735,670,000	11,850,930,000
Operating Income		30,228,160,000	23,320,380,000	49,453,840,000	45,051,850,000	24,556,720,000
Operating Margin %						
SGA Expense		21,906,370,000	22,693,600,000	22,034,340,000	27,000,250,000	26,251,660,000
Net Income		21,911,460,000	18,060,240,000	36,860,170,000	34,721,740,000	18,824,980,000
Operating Cash Flow		54,828,940,000	38,113,200,000	56,294,290,000	52,204,540,000	39,795,120,000
Capital Expenditure		33,820,830,000	24,033,520,000	25,678,930,000	36,763,670,000	21,155,450,000
EBITDA		56,489,030,000	50,990,290,000	74,169,520,000	66,319,070,000	43,682,460,000
Return on Assets %						
Return on Equity %						
Debt to Equity						

CONTACT INFORMATION:

Phone: 82-31-200-1114 Fax: 82-31-200-7538
Toll-Free:
Address: 129, Samsung-ro, Suwon-si, 443-742 South Korea

STOCK TICKER/OTHER:

Stock Ticker: SSNHZ
Exchange: PINX
Employees: 95,798
Fiscal Year Ends: 12/31
Parent Company: Samsung Group

SALARIES/BONUSES:

Top Exec. Salary: $ Bonus: $
Second Exec. Salary: $ Bonus: $

OTHER THOUGHTS:

Estimated Female Officers or Directors:
Hot Spot for Advancement for Women/Minorities:

Sanmina Corporation

www.sanmina.com

NAIC Code: 334418

TYPES OF BUSINESS:

Printed Circuit Assembly (Electronic Assembly) Manufacturing
Assembly & Testing
Logistics Services
Support Services
Product Design & Engineering
Repair & Maintenance Services
Printed Circuit Boards

BRANDS/DIVISIONS/AFFILIATES:

GROWTH PLANS/SPECIAL FEATURES:

Sanmina Corp is a provider of integrated manufacturing solutions, components, and after-market services to original equipment manufacturers in the communications networks, storage, industrial, defense and aerospace end markets. The company operates in two business segments: Integrated Manufacturing Solutions, which consists of printed circuit board assembly and represents a majority of the firm's revenue; and Components, Products, and Services, which includes interconnect systems and mechanical systems. The firm generates revenue primarily in the United States, China, and Mexico, but has a presence around the world.

CONTACTS: *Note: Officers with more than one job title may be intentionally listed here more than once.*

Jure Sola, CEO
Kurt Adzema, CFO
Brent Billinger, Chief Accounting Officer
Dennis Young, Executive VP, Divisional
Alan Reid, Executive VP, Divisional

FINANCIAL DATA: *Note: Data for latest year may not have been available at press time.*

In U.S. $	2021	2020	2019	2018	2017	2016
Revenue	6,756,643,000	6,960,370,000	8,233,859,000	7,110,130,000	6,868,619,000	6,481,181,000
R&D Expense	20,911,000	22,564,000	27,552,000	30,754,000	33,716,000	37,746,000
Operating Income	296,357,000	262,212,000	299,870,000	179,197,000	230,955,000	228,486,000
Operating Margin %						
SGA Expense	234,537,000	240,931,000	260,032,000	250,924,000	251,568,000	244,604,000
Net Income	268,998,000	139,713,000	141,515,000	-95,533,000	138,833,000	187,838,000
Operating Cash Flow	338,342,000	300,555,000	382,965,000	156,424,000	250,961,000	390,116,000
Capital Expenditure	73,296,000	65,982,000	134,674,000	118,881,000	111,833,000	120,400,000
EBITDA	436,212,000	343,879,000	393,331,000	244,093,000	354,165,000	341,438,000
Return on Assets %						
Return on Equity %						
Debt to Equity						

CONTACT INFORMATION:

Phone: 408-964-3500 Fax: 408-964-3636
Toll-Free:
Address: 2700 N. First St., San Jose, CA 95134 United States

STOCK TICKER/OTHER:

Stock Ticker: SANM
Employees: 37,000
Parent Company:
Exchange: NAS
Fiscal Year Ends: 09/30

SALARIES/BONUSES:

Top Exec. Salary: $928,606 Bonus: $
Second Exec. Salary: $850,057 Bonus: $

OTHER THOUGHTS:

Estimated Female Officers or Directors:
Hot Spot for Advancement for Women/Minorities:

SAP SE

NAIC Code: 511210H

www.sap.com

TYPES OF BUSINESS:

Computer Software, Business Management & ERP
Consulting & Training Services
Hosting Services
Software Licensing
Software Development

BRANDS/DIVISIONS/AFFILIATES:

SAP HANA

GROWTH PLANS/SPECIAL FEATURES:

Founded in 1972 by former IBM employees, SAP provides database technology and enterprise resource planning software to enterprises around the world. Across more than 180 countries, the company serves 440,000 customers, approximately 80% of which are small to medium-size enterprises.

SAP offers medical, dental, vision and life insurance; a 401(k) and spending/saving accounts.

CONTACTS: *Note: Officers with more than one job title may be intentionally listed here more than once.*

Christian Klein, CEO
Luka Mucic, CFO
Sabine Bendiek, Chief People Officer
Juergen Mueller, CTO
Luca Mucic, Head-Global Finance
Jim Hagemann Snabe, Co-CEO
Bernd Leukert, Head- Application Innovation

FINANCIAL DATA: *Note: Data for latest year may not have been available at press time.*

In U.S. $	2021	2020	2019	2018	2017	2016
Revenue		30,874,000,000	31,116,810,000	27,903,830,000	26,494,400,000	24,915,580,000
R&D Expense		5,030,097,000	4,847,143,000	4,092,742,000	3,785,560,000	3,437,722,000
Operating Income		7,477,385,000	6,327,713,000	6,463,234,000	5,714,479,000	5,829,672,000
Operating Margin %						
SGA Expense		9,556,507,000	10,527,740,000	8,898,099,000	9,033,620,000	8,210,329,000
Net Income		5,810,473,000	3,750,551,000	4,611,110,000	4,537,703,000	4,117,587,000
Operating Cash Flow		8,124,499,000	3,948,186,000	4,859,566,000	5,697,540,000	5,226,602,000
Capital Expenditure		921,544,500	922,673,900	1,646,583,000	1,439,913,000	1,130,473,000
EBITDA		11,008,840,000	7,969,779,000	8,334,557,000	7,426,565,000	7,226,671,000
Return on Assets %						
Return on Equity %						
Debt to Equity						

CONTACT INFORMATION:

Phone: 49 6227747474 Fax: 49 6227757575
Toll-Free: 800-872-1727
Address: Dietmar-Hopp-Allee 16, Walldorf, 69190 Germany

STOCK TICKER/OTHER:

Stock Ticker: SAP
Employees: 101,476
Parent Company:
Exchange: NYS
Fiscal Year Ends: 12/31

SALARIES/BONUSES:

Top Exec. Salary: $1,298,745 Bonus: $
Second Exec. Salary: $790,541 Bonus: $

OTHER THOUGHTS:

Estimated Female Officers or Directors: 4
Hot Spot for Advancement for Women/Minorities: Y

SAS Institute Inc

www.sas.com

NAIC Code: 511210H

TYPES OF BUSINESS:

Computer Software, Statistical Analysis
Business Intelligence Software
Data Warehousing
Online Bookstore
Consulting
Artificial Intelligence
Internet of Things
Cloud Analytics

BRANDS/DIVISIONS/AFFILIATES:

Boemska
SAS Viya

CONTACTS: *Note: Officers with more than one job title may be intentionally listed here more than once.*

James Goodnight, CEO
John Sall, Exec. VP-Oper.
Wm. David Davis, CFO
Jennifer Chase, CMO
Jenn Mann, Chief Human Resources Officer
Jay Upchurch, CIO
John Boswell, Chief Legal Officer
Carl Farrell, Exec. VP-SAS Americas
John Sall, Exec. VP
Bryan Harris, CTO
Mikael Hagstrom, Exec. VP-EMEA & Asia Pacific

GROWTH PLANS/SPECIAL FEATURES:

SAS Institute, Inc. provides statistical analysis software. The company's products are designed to extract, manage and analyze large volumes of data, often assisting in financial reporting and credit analysis. Individual contracts can be tailored to specific global and local industries, such as banking, manufacturing and government. SAS' advanced analytics software is infused with cutting-edge, innovative algorithms that help clients solve intractable problems, make informed decisions and capture new opportunities. The software comprises data mining, statistical analysis, forecasting, text analysis, optimization and stimulation features. Other products that provide enterprise solutions include artificial intelligence, Internet of Things (IoT), business intelligence, cloud analytics, customer intelligence, data management, fraud and security intelligence, in-memory analytics, performance management, risk management, solutions for Hadoop and supply chain intelligence. Industries that utilize SAS products and solutions include banking, capital markets, casinos, communications, consumer goods, defense/security, government, healthcare, P-12 education, higher education, hotels, insurance, life science, manufacturing, media, oil and gas, retail, small/midsize business, sports, travel, transportation and utilities. SAS serves more than 82,000 business, government and university sites in 145 different countries, including 91 of the top 100 companies on the 2020 Fortune Global 500 list. In early-2021, SAS institute acquired Boemska, a technology company specializing in low-code/no-code application development and analytics workload management. Boemska was integrated with SAS Viya, a cloud-native, advanced analytics platform.

FINANCIAL DATA: *Note: Data for latest year may not have been available at press time.*

In U.S. $	2021	2020	2019	2018	2017	2016
Revenue	3,200,000,000	3,000,000,000	3,100,000,000	3,270,000,000	3,240,000,000	3,200,000,000
R&D Expense						
Operating Income						
Operating Margin %						
SGA Expense						
Net Income						
Operating Cash Flow						
Capital Expenditure						
EBITDA						
Return on Assets %						
Return on Equity %						
Debt to Equity						

CONTACT INFORMATION:

Phone: 919-677-8000 Fax: 919-677-4444
Toll-Free: 800-727-0025
Address: 100 SAS Campus Dr., Cary, NC 27513 United States

STOCK TICKER/OTHER:

Stock Ticker: Private
Employees: 13,939
Parent Company:
Exchange:
Fiscal Year Ends: 12/31

SALARIES/BONUSES:

Top Exec. Salary: $ Bonus: $
Second Exec. Salary: $ Bonus: $

OTHER THOUGHTS:

Estimated Female Officers or Directors: 1
Hot Spot for Advancement for Women/Minorities: Y

Schmitt Industries Inc

www.schmittindustries.com

NAIC Code: 334513

TYPES OF BUSINESS:

Instruments and Related Products Manufacturing for Measuring, Displaying, and Controlling Industrial Process Variables
Process Control Systems
Manufacture
Laser Sensors
Tank Monitoring Systems

BRANDS/DIVISIONS/AFFILIATES:

Acuity
Xact
Ample Hills Acquisition LLC
Ample Hills Creamery

GROWTH PLANS/SPECIAL FEATURES:

Schmitt Industries Inc is engaged in propane tank monitoring solutions, precision measurement solutions, and ice cream production and distribution. The Company operates as two reportable segments: the Measurement Segment and the Ice Cream Segment. Xact product line includes satellite-focused remote tank monitoring products and related monitoring services for markets in the IoT environment. The Company also manufactures, wholesales, and retails ice cream and related products.

CONTACTS: *Note: Officers with more than one job title may be intentionally listed here more than once.*

Michael Zapata, CEO
Philip Bosco, CFO

FINANCIAL DATA: *Note: Data for latest year may not have been available at press time.*

In U.S. $	2021	2020	2019	2018	2017	2016
Revenue	7,864,350	4,189,924	13,810,160	13,888,060	12,397,640	11,685,350
R&D Expense	83,130	68,849	129,040	327,317	256,164	287,672
Operating Income	-8,857,542	-2,179,922	-1,107,500	155,372	-988,684	-1,436,474
Operating Margin %						
SGA Expense	12,045,170	4,061,621	5,951,765	5,582,625	5,618,327	6,016,097
Net Income	-8,089,672	3,880,575	-1,210,990	210,639	-1,073,364	-1,515,189
Operating Cash Flow	-6,939,962	28,741	-716,613	-1,002,849	-148,288	-819,808
Capital Expenditure	1,404,830	32,982	6,473	8,467	52,633	3,520
EBITDA	-7,925,077	-1,693,370	-919,152	360,611	-769,602	-1,190,650
Return on Assets %						
Return on Equity %						
Debt to Equity						

CONTACT INFORMATION:

Phone: 503 227-7908 Fax: 503 223-1258
Toll-Free:
Address: 2765 NW Nicolai St., Portland, OR 97210-1818 United States

STOCK TICKER/OTHER:

Stock Ticker: SMIT
Employees: 18
Parent Company:
Exchange: NAS
Fiscal Year Ends: 05/31

SALARIES/BONUSES:

Top Exec. Salary: $222,667 Bonus: $
Second Exec. Salary: $121,875 Bonus: $

OTHER THOUGHTS:

Estimated Female Officers or Directors:
Hot Spot for Advancement for Women/Minorities:

Schneider Electric SA

www.se.com/ww/en

NAIC Code: 335311

TYPES OF BUSINESS:

Electrical Distribution Products
Infrastructure Products
Building Automation & Control Products

BRANDS/DIVISIONS/AFFILIATES:

EcoStruxure
DC Systems BV

GROWTH PLANS/SPECIAL FEATURES:

France-based Schneider Electric is a leading global supplier to industrial, utility, data center, and energy customers. The company's products span from ground-level equipment to top-level analytics and execution software. Roughly 75% of its revenue comes from its low- and medium-voltage, while revenue from its automation division drives the remaining 25%. The company is the number-two and number-four supplier, respectively, in discrete (for example, manufacturing) and process (for example, fluid processing) automation. However, it holds the leading position in process safety systems.At the group level, software and services contribute about 10% of sales, integrated systems another 30%, and individual products (components and equipment) the final 60%.

CONTACTS: *Note: Officers with more than one job title may be intentionally listed here more than once.*

Jean-Pascal Tricoire, CEO
Emmanuel Babeau, Deputy CEO-Legal Affairs
Julio Rodriguez, Exec. VP-Global Oper.
Michael Crochon, Exec. VP-Strategy
Emmanuel Babeau, Deputy CEO-Finance
Clemens Blum, Exec. VP-Industry Bus.
Philippe Delorme, Exec. VP-Partner Bus.
Zhu Hai, Exec. VP-China Oper.
Danille Doime, Exec VP-IT
Laurent Vernerey, Exec. VP-North America Oper. & End User Bus. Group
Annette Clayton, Exec. VP-Global Supply Chain

FINANCIAL DATA: *Note: Data for latest year may not have been available at press time.*

In U.S. $	2021	2020	2019	2018	2017	2016
Revenue		28,413,160,000	30,670,720,000	29,046,720,000	27,943,350,000	27,886,880,000
R&D Expense		810,868,800	741,978,800	674,218,200	565,801,200	604,198,900
Operating Income		4,172,925,000	4,564,807,000	4,181,960,000	3,991,101,000	3,757,327,000
Operating Margin %						
SGA Expense		6,224,943,000	6,595,367,000	6,292,703,000	6,037,472,000	6,070,223,000
Net Income		2,400,985,000	2,725,106,000	2,635,888,000	2,428,089,000	1,976,352,000
Operating Cash Flow		5,008,639,000	4,835,850,000	3,243,475,000	3,321,400,000	3,354,151,000
Capital Expenditure		922,673,900	953,166,100	930,579,300	845,878,500	970,106,300
EBITDA		4,682,259,000	5,060,589,000	4,721,786,000	4,403,311,000	4,115,329,000
Return on Assets %						
Return on Equity %						
Debt to Equity						

CONTACT INFORMATION:

Phone: 33 141297000 Fax: 33 141297100
Toll-Free:
Address: 35 rue Joseph Monier, Rueil Malmaison, 92500 France

STOCK TICKER/OTHER:

Stock Ticker: SBGSF
Employees: 135,000
Parent Company:
Exchange: PINX
Fiscal Year Ends: 12/31

SALARIES/BONUSES:

Top Exec. Salary: $ Bonus: $
Second Exec. Salary: $ Bonus: $

OTHER THOUGHTS:

Estimated Female Officers or Directors: 2
Hot Spot for Advancement for Women/Minorities:

Science Applications International Corporation (SAIC)

www.saic.com

NAIC Code: 541512

TYPES OF BUSINESS:

IT Consulting
IT Infrastructure Management
Research & Development
Software Development
Engineering

BRANDS/DIVISIONS/AFFILIATES:

GROWTH PLANS/SPECIAL FEATURES:

Science Applications International Corp provides technical, engineering and enterprise IT services primarily to the U.S. government. Specifically, the company offers engineering, systems integration and information technology for large government projects and a broad range of services with an emphasis on higher-end technology services. The company's end-to-end enterprise IT offerings span the entire spectrum of our customers' IT infrastructure.

CONTACTS: *Note: Officers with more than one job title may be intentionally listed here more than once.*

Nazzic Keene, CEO
Prabu Natarajan, CFO
Donna Morea, Chairman of the Board
Michael LaRouche, Executive VP
Robert Genter, Executive VP
Steven Mahon, General Counsel
Michelle O'Hara, Other Executive Officer

FINANCIAL DATA: *Note: Data for latest year may not have been available at press time.*

In U.S. $	2021	2020	2019	2018	2017	2016
Revenue	7,056,000,000	6,379,000,000	4,659,000,000	4,454,000,000	4,450,000,000	4,315,000,000
R&D Expense						
Operating Income	444,000,000	418,000,000	306,000,000	256,000,000	281,000,000	253,000,000
Operating Margin %						
SGA Expense	352,000,000	288,000,000	158,000,000	155,000,000	166,000,000	158,000,000
Net Income	209,000,000	226,000,000	137,000,000	179,000,000	148,000,000	117,000,000
Operating Cash Flow	755,000,000	458,000,000	184,000,000	217,000,000	273,000,000	226,000,000
Capital Expenditure	46,000,000	21,000,000	28,000,000	22,000,000	15,000,000	20,000,000
EBITDA	572,000,000	514,000,000	272,000,000	304,000,000	325,000,000	289,000,000
Return on Assets %						
Return on Equity %						
Debt to Equity						

CONTACT INFORMATION:

Phone: 703 676-4300 Fax:
Toll-Free:
Address: 12010 Sunset Hills Rd., Reston, VA 20190 United States

STOCK TICKER/OTHER:

Stock Ticker: SAIC
Employees: 26,000
Parent Company:
Exchange: NYS
Fiscal Year Ends: 01/31

SALARIES/BONUSES:

Top Exec. Salary: $1,063,462 Bonus: $
Second Exec. Salary: $596,154 Bonus: $

OTHER THOUGHTS:

Estimated Female Officers or Directors: 5
Hot Spot for Advancement for Women/Minorities: Y

ScienceSoft USA Corporation

www.scnsoft.com

NAIC Code: 511210B

TYPES OF BUSINESS:

Computer Software: Network Management (IT), System Testing & Storage
IT Consulting
IoT Consulting
Software Development
Application Services
User Experience
Data Analytics
Cybersecurity

BRANDS/DIVISIONS/AFFILIATES:

CONTACTS:
Note: Officers with more than one job title may be intentionally listed here more than once.

Nikolay Kurayev, CEO
Valentina Borokha, CFO
Ulad Radkevitch, VP-Sales & Bus. Dev.
Boris Shiklo, CTO

GROWTH PLANS/SPECIAL FEATURES:

ScienceSoft USA Corporation provides information technology (IT) consulting services, as well as custom software development services globally. Founded in 1989, the firm offers its custom and platform-based solutions to large- and mid-sized companies across the healthcare, manufacturing, professional services, banking/finance, insurance, retail, transportation, logistics, telecommunications and oil and gas industries. ScienceSoft's solutions include customer relations management, marketing, advertising, human resources, eLearning, supply chain management, fleet management, enterprise resource planning (ERP), data analytics, ecommerce, web portals and content management system (CMS) development. Its services span software development, testing and quality assurance, application services, user interface/user experience (UI/UX) design, infrastructure services, data analytics, managed IT services, IT outsourcing, IT consulting, IT support and cybersecurity. Headquartered in Texas, USA, ScienceSoft has offices and delivery centers in Finland, Latvia and the United Arab Emirates.

FINANCIAL DATA:
Note: Data for latest year may not have been available at press time.

In U.S. $	2021	2020	2019	2018	2017	2016
Revenue						
R&D Expense						
Operating Income						
Operating Margin %						
SGA Expense						
Net Income						
Operating Cash Flow						
Capital Expenditure						
EBITDA						
Return on Assets %						
Return on Equity %						
Debt to Equity						

CONTACT INFORMATION:

Phone: 214-306-6837 Fax:
Toll-Free:
Address: 5900 S. Lake Forest Dr., Ste. 300, McKinney, TX 75070 United States

STOCK TICKER/OTHER:

Stock Ticker: Private
Employees: 700
Parent Company:
Exchange:
Fiscal Year Ends:

SALARIES/BONUSES:

Top Exec. Salary: $ Bonus: $
Second Exec. Salary: $ Bonus: $

OTHER THOUGHTS:

Estimated Female Officers or Directors:
Hot Spot for Advancement for Women/Minorities:

SecureWorks Corporation

www.secureworks.com

NAIC Code: 511210E

TYPES OF BUSINESS:

Computer Software: Network Security, Managed Access, Digital ID, Cybersecurity & Anti-Virus
Cyber Security

GROWTH PLANS/SPECIAL FEATURES:

SecureWorks Corp is a provider of intelligence-driven information security solutions exclusively focused on protecting its clients from cyber-attacks. Its solutions enable organizations to fortify their cyber defenses to prevent security breaches. The company's solutions include managed security, threat intelligence, security and risk consulting, and incident response. Its solutions enable organizations to fortify their cyber defenses to prevent security breaches, detect malicious activity in real time, prioritize and respond to security incidents, and predict emerging threats.

BRANDS/DIVISIONS/AFFILIATES:

Dell Inc
Dell Technologies Inc
SecureWorks Counter Threat Platform
Delve Laboratories Inc

CONTACTS: *Note: Officers with more than one job title may be intentionally listed here more than once.*

Michael Cote, CEO
Paul Parrish, CFO
Michael Dell, Chairman of the Board
Christian Grant, Chief Accounting Officer
Wendy Thomas, President, Divisional

FINANCIAL DATA: *Note: Data for latest year may not have been available at press time.*

In U.S. $	2021	2020	2019	2018	2017	2016
Revenue	561,034,000	552,765,000	518,709,000	467,904,000	429,502,000	339,522,000
R&D Expense	105,008,000	94,964,000	87,608,000	80,164,000	71,030,000	49,747,000
Operating Income	-32,835,000	-52,174,000	-48,732,000	-83,045,000	-65,953,000	-106,008,000
Operating Margin %						
SGA Expense	246,694,000	257,179,000	233,716,000	244,067,000	211,826,000	211,974,000
Net Income	-21,902,000	-31,666,000	-39,101,000	-28,077,000	-38,213,000	-72,381,000
Operating Cash Flow	60,589,000	78,839,000	57,199,000	787,000	-6,838,000	-9,843,000
Capital Expenditure	3,005,000	12,590,000	10,200,000	13,819,000	19,361,000	9,023,000
EBITDA	8,779,000	-9,242,000	-7,525,000	-40,874,000	-26,528,000	-65,370,000
Return on Assets %						
Return on Equity %						
Debt to Equity						

CONTACT INFORMATION:

Phone: 404-327-6339 Fax:
Toll-Free: 877-838-7947
Address: One Concourse Pkwy NE #500, Atlanta, GA 30328 United States

STOCK TICKER/OTHER:

Stock Ticker: SCWX
Employees: 2,696
Parent Company: Dell Inc
Exchange: NAS
Fiscal Year Ends: 02/01

SALARIES/BONUSES:

Top Exec. Salary: $500,000 Bonus: $
Second Exec. Salary: $450,000 Bonus: $

OTHER THOUGHTS:

Estimated Female Officers or Directors:
Hot Spot for Advancement for Women/Minorities:

Semiconductor Manufacturing International Corporation

www.smics.com

NAIC Code: 334413

TYPES OF BUSINESS:

Semiconductor Manufacturing
Intellectual Property Licensing
Semiconductor Production
Semiconductor Foundry
Wafer Fabrication Facilities
Technology
Integrated Circuit Foundry

BRANDS/DIVISIONS/AFFILIATES:

SMIC Advanced Technology R&D (Shanghai) Corp
Semiconductor Manufacturing Electronics (Shaoxing)

CONTACTS: *Note: Officers with more than one job title may be intentionally listed here more than once.*

Liang Mong Song, Co-CEO
Haijun Zhao, Co-CEO
Yonggang Gao, CFO
Jyishyang Liu, VP-Eng. & Svcs.
Gareth Kung, Sec.
Yonggang Gao, Exec. VP
Dong Cui, Exec. VP-Investment & Strategic Bus. Dev.
Zixue Zhou, Chmn.

GROWTH PLANS/SPECIAL FEATURES:

Semiconductor Manufacturing International Corporation (SMIC) is a leading Chinese semiconductor foundry. The firm operates a 12-inch wafer fabrication facility (fab) and an 8-inch mega-fab in Shanghai; an 8-inch wafer fab in Tianjin; a 12-inch wafer fab and a majority-owned 12-inch fab for advanced nodes in Beijing; an 8-inch wafer fab in Shenzhen; a majority-owned 12-inch bumping facility in Jiangyin; and an 8-inch wafer fab in Italy. SMIC provides integrated circuit (IC) foundry and technology services at 0.35-micron to 14-nanometer for logic technologies, including standard logic, mixed-signal, RF (radio frequency) and high voltage circuits; memory technologies, including SRAM (static random access memory), DRAM (dynamic random access memory), Flash and EEPROM (electrically erasable programmable read-only memory). In addition to wafer fabrication, the company owns and licenses intellectual property consisting of libraries and circuit design blocks, design support, mask-making, wafer probing, gold/solder bumping and redistribution layer manufacturing. SMIC also offers assembly and testing services. Majority-owned SMIC Advanced Technology Research and Development (Shanghai) Corporation focuses on R&D toward next-generation CMOS (complementary metal-oxide semiconductor) logic technology. It was designed to build China's most advanced IC development R&D platform. The joint venture includes minority owners Huawei, Qualcomm Global and IMEC International. Semiconductor Manufacturing Electronics (Shaoxing) Corporation is a joint venture between SMIC and the Shaoxing government, and produces micro-electro-mechanical systems (MEMS) technologies and power devices for applications fields such as artificial intelligence (AI), mobile communications, the Internet of Things (IoT), automotive electronics and industrial controls. In addition to its marketing and customers service offices in China, SMIC has international offices in the Americas, Europe, Hong Kong, Taiwan and Japan.

SMIC offers its employees health plans, retirement plans and a wide variety of life and education benefits.

FINANCIAL DATA: *Note: Data for latest year may not have been available at press time.*

In U.S. $	2021	2020	2019	2018	2017	2016
Revenue		3,906,975,000	3,115,672,064	3,359,984,128	3,101,175,040	2,914,180,096
R&D Expense						
Operating Income						
Operating Margin %						
SGA Expense						
Net Income		669,098,000	234,680,992	134,055,000	179,679,008	376,630,016
Operating Cash Flow						
Capital Expenditure						
EBITDA						
Return on Assets %						
Return on Equity %						
Debt to Equity						

CONTACT INFORMATION:

Phone: 86-21-3861-0000 Fax: 86-21-5080-2868
Toll-Free:
Address: No.18 Zhangjiang Rd., Pudong New Area, Shanghai, 201203 China

STOCK TICKER/OTHER:

Stock Ticker: 981
Employees: 17,354
Parent Company:
Exchange: Hong Kong
Fiscal Year Ends: 12/31

SALARIES/BONUSES:

Top Exec. Salary: $ Bonus: $
Second Exec. Salary: $ Bonus: $

OTHER THOUGHTS:

Estimated Female Officers or Directors: 1
Hot Spot for Advancement for Women/Minorities:

SentinelOne Inc

NAIC Code: 511210E

www.sentinelone.com

TYPES OF BUSINESS:

Computer Software: Security & Anti-Virus

GROWTH PLANS/SPECIAL FEATURES:

SentinelOne, Inc. is an autonomous cybersecurity platform developer and service provider. The company's cybersecurity solutions encompass AI-powered prevention, detection, response and hunting across endpoints, containers, cloud workloads and internet of things (IoT) devices in a single, autonomous XDR platform.

BRANDS/DIVISIONS/AFFILIATES:

CONTACTS: *Note: Officers with more than one job title may be intentionally listed here more than once.*

Tomer Weingarten, CEO
Vats Srivatsan, COO
David Bernhardt, CFO
Divya Ghatak, Chief People Officer
Ric Smith, CTO

FINANCIAL DATA: *Note: Data for latest year may not have been available at press time.*

In U.S. $	2021	2020	2019	2018	2017	2016
Revenue						
R&D Expense						
Operating Income						
Operating Margin %						
SGA Expense						
Net Income						
Operating Cash Flow						
Capital Expenditure						
EBITDA						
Return on Assets %						
Return on Equity %						
Debt to Equity						

CONTACT INFORMATION:

Phone: 855-868-3733 Fax:
Toll-Free:
Address: 444 Castro St., Ste. 400, Mountain View, CA 94041 United States

STOCK TICKER/OTHER:

Stock Ticker: S
Exchange: NYSE
Employees:
Fiscal Year Ends:
Parent Company:

SALARIES/BONUSES:

Top Exec. Salary: $ Bonus: $
Second Exec. Salary: $ Bonus: $

OTHER THOUGHTS:

Estimated Female Officers or Directors:
Hot Spot for Advancement for Women/Minorities:

SES SA

www.ses.com

NAIC Code: 517410

TYPES OF BUSINESS:

Satellite Carrier
Satellite Operations
Broadband Internet Service
Secure Communications
Broadcasting Services
Video on Demand
Direct to Home TV

BRANDS/DIVISIONS/AFFILIATES:

QuetzSat
Ciel
GovSat
YahLive
SES Government Solutions
SES Techcom
HD Plus GmbH
Redu Space Services

CONTACTS: *Note: Officers with more than one job title may be intentionally listed here more than once.*

Steve Collar, CEO
Sandeep Jalan, CFO
Evie Ross, Chief Human Resources Officer
Ruy Pinto, CTO
Gerson Souto, Chief Dev. Officer
Patrick Biewer, Managing Dir.-SES Broadband Svcs.
Wilfried Urner, CEO-SES Platform Svcs.
Frank Esser, Chmn.
Tip Osterthaler, CEO-SES Gov't Solutions

GROWTH PLANS/SPECIAL FEATURES:

SES SA is a communications satellite owner and operator and functions in the television broadcasting space. The company has four primary business segments: Video, mobility, fixed data, and government. The largest segment, video, delivers television and radio satellite signals to homes through various media providers such as Comcast, Viacom, M7, and QVC. The company's mobility segment offers high-bandwidth Internet connection to maritime users, and SES SA's government segment offers secure communication links to international institutions and governments. Fixed Data works to bring satellite networks and connectivity to remote areas. Over half of the company's revenue is generated in the United States, Germany, and the United Kingdom.

FINANCIAL DATA: *Note: Data for latest year may not have been available at press time.*

In U.S. $	2021	2020	2019	2018	2017	2016
Revenue		2,073,475,000	2,191,943,000	2,183,586,000	2,298,215,000	2,336,386,000
R&D Expense						
Operating Income		369,295,400	372,005,800	354,952,700	689,577,300	926,400,700
Operating Margin %						
SGA Expense						
Net Income		-97,123,560	334,511,600	330,220,100	673,201,800	1,087,219,000
Operating Cash Flow		1,184,682,000	1,280,789,000	1,345,387,000	1,413,035,000	1,438,897,000
Capital Expenditure		237,162,200	344,788,600	370,650,600	543,440,200	700,193,200
EBITDA		1,149,672,000	1,349,453,000	1,397,224,000	1,458,999,000	2,162,354,000
Return on Assets %						
Return on Equity %						
Debt to Equity						

CONTACT INFORMATION:

Phone: 352 7107251 Fax:
Toll-Free:
Address: Chateau de Betzdorf, Rue Pierre Werner, Luxembourg, L-6815 Luxembourg

STOCK TICKER/OTHER:

Stock Ticker: SGBAF
Employees: 2,037
Parent Company:
Exchange: PINX
Fiscal Year Ends: 12/31

SALARIES/BONUSES:

Top Exec. Salary: $ Bonus: $
Second Exec. Salary: $ Bonus: $

OTHER THOUGHTS:

Estimated Female Officers or Directors:
Hot Spot for Advancement for Women/Minorities:

Sharp Corporation

NAIC Code: 334310

global.sharp

TYPES OF BUSINESS:

Audiovisual & Communications Equipment
Electronic Components
Solar Cells & Advanced Batteries
Home Appliances
Consumer Electronics
Manufacturing
Product Distribution
Communication Equipment

BRANDS/DIVISIONS/AFFILIATES:

Foxconn Technology Co Ltd
Smart Appliances & Solutions BU
Smart Business Solutions BU
Digital Imaging Solutions BU
Mobile Communication BU

GROWTH PLANS/SPECIAL FEATURES:

Sharp Corp is a Japan-based company that is principally engaged in producing and selling a broad range of consumer and industrial electronic products. The company's business segments consist of the consumer electronics segment, the energy solutions segment, the business solutions segment, the electronic components and devices segment, and the display devices segment. The company generates over half of its revenue from the consumer electronics segment and the display devices segment. It has a global business presence, with China, Japan, the Americas, and Europe its four largest markets.

CONTACTS: *Note: Officers with more than one job title may be intentionally listed here more than once.*

Jeng-Wu Tai, CEO
Katsuaki Nomura, Pres.
Mototaka Taneya, Exec. Gen. Mgr.-Corp. R&D Group
Toshihiko Fujimoto, Exec. Gen. Mgr.-Bus. Dev. Group
Shogo Fukahori, Chief Officer-In-House Comm.
Shinichi Niihara, Exec. Officer
Fujikazu Nakayama, Sr. Exec. Managing Officer-Products Bus. Group
Akihiko Imaya, Exec. Group Gen. Mgr.-Display Device Business
Masahiro Okitsu, Exec. Group Gen. Mgr.-Health & Environment
Paul Molyneux, Exec. Gen. Mgr.-Sales & Mktg., Europe

FINANCIAL DATA: *Note: Data for latest year may not have been available at press time.*

In U.S. $	2021	2020	2019	2018	2017	2016
Revenue	21,316,560,000	19,957,540,000	21,089,520,000	21,328,520,000	18,019,040,000	21,630,070,000
R&D Expense						
Operating Income	730,308,200	463,718,300	739,350,100	791,940,500	548,785,600	-1,423,210,000
Operating Margin %						
SGA Expense						
Net Income	468,023,900	184,158,700	652,226,600	617,069,700	-218,595,100	-2,249,235,000
Operating Cash Flow	1,798,197,000	598,274,200	694,553,800	925,011,400	1,117,983,000	-165,776,200
Capital Expenditure	451,495,600	823,688,100	1,255,211,000	896,831,300	680,090,300	407,402,200
EBITDA	1,264,411,000	1,034,761,000	1,395,487,000	1,496,722,000	650,609,800	-1,192,199,000
Return on Assets %						
Return on Equity %						
Debt to Equity						

CONTACT INFORMATION:

Phone: 81 666211221 Fax:
Toll-Free:
Address: 1 Takumi-cho. Sakai-Ku, Sakai City, Osaka, 590-8522 Japan

STOCK TICKER/OTHER:

Stock Ticker: SHCAF Exchange: PINX
Employees: 54,156 Fiscal Year Ends: 03/31
Parent Company: Foxconn Technology Co Ltd

SALARIES/BONUSES:

Top Exec. Salary: $ Bonus: $
Second Exec. Salary: $ Bonus: $

OTHER THOUGHTS:

Estimated Female Officers or Directors:
Hot Spot for Advancement for Women/Minorities:

Siemens AG

www.siemens.com

NAIC Code: 334513

TYPES OF BUSINESS:

Industrial Control Manufacturing
Digitalization
Smart Infrastructure
Mobility
Advanced Technologies
Artificial Intelligence
Internet of Things
Robotics

BRANDS/DIVISIONS/AFFILIATES:

Siemens Advanta
Siemens Healthineers AG
Siemens Financial Services
Siemens Real Estate
Next47

GROWTH PLANS/SPECIAL FEATURES:

Siemens AG is an industrial conglomerate, with businesses selling components and equipment for factory automation, railway equipment, electrical distribution equipment, and medical equipment. Its separately listed business units include Siemens Healthineers, Siemens Energy, and Siemens Gamesa, which supply medical imaging equipment, power generation, and wind turbines, respectively.

CONTACTS: *Note: Officers with more than one job title may be intentionally listed here more than once.*

Joe Kaeser, CEO
Ralf P. Thomas, CFO
Peter Y. Solmssen, Head-Corp. Legal & Compliance
Joe Kaeser, Head-Controlling
Roland Busch, CEO-Infrastructure & Cities Sector
Hermann Requardt, CEO-Health Care Sector
Michael Suess, CEO-Energy Sector
Siegfried Russwurm, CEO-Industry Sector
Jim Hagemenn Snabe, Chmn.
Barbara Kux, Chief Sustainability Officer

FINANCIAL DATA: *Note: Data for latest year may not have been available at press time.*

In U.S. $	2021	2020	2019	2018	2017	2016
Revenue		64,529,570,000	98,082,380,000	93,785,220,000	93,790,860,000	89,945,460,000
R&D Expense		5,196,110,000	6,403,379,000	6,276,893,000	5,831,931,000	5,344,055,000
Operating Income		5,143,031,000	7,557,568,000	6,676,680,000	8,292,771,000	8,064,644,000
Operating Margin %						
SGA Expense		12,167,550,000	15,071,090,000	14,614,840,000	13,806,230,000	13,178,310,000
Net Income		4,551,256,000	5,843,225,000	6,558,099,000	6,828,013,000	6,154,924,000
Operating Cash Flow		10,008,240,000	9,549,731,000	9,514,721,000	8,104,170,000	8,595,436,000
Capital Expenditure		1,755,000,000	2,947,587,000	2,938,552,000	2,717,201,000	2,411,149,000
EBITDA		10,891,390,000	13,711,360,000	14,182,300,000	14,193,590,000	12,600,090,000
Return on Assets %						
Return on Equity %						
Debt to Equity						

CONTACT INFORMATION:

Phone: 49 8963633032 Fax: 49 8932825
Toll-Free:
Address: Werner-von-Siemens-Strabe 1, Munich, BY 80333 Germany

STOCK TICKER/OTHER:

Stock Ticker: SMAWF
Employees: 293,000
Parent Company:
Exchange: PINX
Fiscal Year Ends: 09/30

SALARIES/BONUSES:

Top Exec. Salary: $2,258,688 Bonus: $1,535,795
Second Exec. Salary: $1,535,861 Bonus: $621,997

OTHER THOUGHTS:

Estimated Female Officers or Directors: 5
Hot Spot for Advancement for Women/Minorities: Y

Siemens Limited

NAIC Code: 334513

https://new.siemens.com/in/en.html

TYPES OF BUSINESS:

Electrical & Electronics Engineering
Electrification Solutions
Automation Solutions
Digitalization Solutions
Manufacturing
Software
Steam Turbines
Smart Grid Systems

BRANDS/DIVISIONS/AFFILIATES:

Siemens AG
C&S Electric Limited

CONTACTS: *Note: Officers with more than one job title may be intentionally listed here more than once.*

Sunil Mathur, Managing Dir.
Bhaskar Mandal, Sector Cluster Leader-Industry Sector, South Asia
Tilak Raj Seth, Head-Infrastructure & Cities Sector, South Asia
Richard Guest, Head-Health Care Sector, South Asia
A. K. Dixit, Head-Energy Sector, South Asia

GROWTH PLANS/SPECIAL FEATURES:

Siemens Limited, a subsidiary of Siemens AG, is an India-based company operating in the fields of electrification, automation and digitalization. The company operates more than 20 manufacturing factories, in addition to centers of competence and research and development centers, as well as a nation-wide sales and service network throughout the country. Siemens is one of the leading producers of energy-efficient, resource-saving technologies; combined cycle turbines for power generation; and power transmission solutions. Siemens is a pioneer in infrastructure solutions and automation and software solutions for industry; a supplier of medical imaging equipment such as computed tomography and magnetic resonance imaging systems; and a leader in laboratory diagnostics and clinical information technology. Siemens' factories manufacture steam turbines, switchgear, remote monitoring systems, motors, generators, relays, smart grid systems, transformers, integrated drive systems, railway bogies and X-ray machines. The company's solutions are utilized in smart grids, building technologies, mobility and power distribution. Tailored financial solutions are offered, including project finance, equipment finance/leasing, structured finance, capital loans and advisory services. Market-specific solutions by Siemens spans many industries, including aerospace, automotive, battery manufacturing, campus, chemical industry, cement, cranes, data centers, distributors, food/beverage, machinery and plant construction, marine, mining, oil and gas, panel building, pharmaceutical, power/utilities, tires, transportation/logistics, water, and wind equipment. During 2021, Siemens Limited acquired C&S Electric Limited, which offers low-voltage power distribution in India.

FINANCIAL DATA: *Note: Data for latest year may not have been available at press time.*

In U.S. $	2021	2020	2019	2018	2017	2016
Revenue	1,998,270,000	1,389,970,000	1,909,840,000	1,791,880,000	1,731,490,000	1,682,330,000
R&D Expense						
Operating Income						
Operating Margin %						
SGA Expense						
Net Income	150,332,000	104,112,000	155,736,000	123,164,000	172,961,000	437,020,000
Operating Cash Flow						
Capital Expenditure						
EBITDA						
Return on Assets %						
Return on Equity %						
Debt to Equity						

CONTACT INFORMATION:

Phone: 91-22-3967-7000 Fax: 91-22-3967-7500
Toll-Free:
Address: Birla Aurora, Level 21, Plot No. 1080, Dr. Annie B, Mumbai, 400030 India

STOCK TICKER/OTHER:

Stock Ticker: 500550
Employees: 8,606
Parent Company: Siemens AG
Exchange: Bombay
Fiscal Year Ends: 09/30

SALARIES/BONUSES:

Top Exec. Salary: $ Bonus: $
Second Exec. Salary: $ Bonus: $

OTHER THOUGHTS:

Estimated Female Officers or Directors:
Hot Spot for Advancement for Women/Minorities:

Siemens USA

www.siemens.com/us/en.html

NAIC Code: 541712

TYPES OF BUSINESS:

Research & Development
Engineering Services
Smart Infrastructure
Digital Industry Solutions
Mobility Solutions
Logistics
Flexible Sheet Metal Processing
Medical Diagnostic Systems

BRANDS/DIVISIONS/AFFILIATES:

Siemens AG
Siemens Mobility
Siemens Advanta
Siemens Healthcare
Sykatec

CONTACTS: *Note: Officers with more than one job title may be intentionally listed here more than once.*

Barbara Humpton, CEO
Marsha Smith, CFO
Mike Bokina, VP-Human Resources
Raj Batra, Pres.-Digital Industries
Joe Kaeser, Pres.

GROWTH PLANS/SPECIAL FEATURES:

Siemens USA is the American arm of Siemens AG, offering engineering services in all 50 states and Puerto Rico. The company operates through six businesses: smart infrastructure, digital industries, Siemens Mobility, umbrella companies, Siemens Advanta and Siemens Healthcare. The smart infrastructure business connects energy systems, buildings and industries to intuitively respond to the needs of people and help customers to better use resources. The digital industries business innovates in industrial automation and digitalization for the purpose of enabling manufacturers in the discrete and process industries to become digital enterprises. Siemens Mobility offers transport solutions, and continually innovates in the core areas of rolling stock, rail automation and electrification, turn-key systems, intelligent traffic systems and related services. Umbrella companies within Siemens USA operate independently and include: Large Drives Applications, which develops and produces heavy-duty electrical drive systems for medium- and high-voltage ranges: electrical motors, converters and generators; Siemens Logistics GmbH provides innovative products and solutions in mail and parcel logistics as well as in airport logistics with baggage and cargo handling; Siemens Commercial Vehicles provides innovative systems, solutions and products for a variety of commercial vehicles, including buses, trucks, off-road vehicles, underground equipment and more; and Mechanical Systems and Components provides flexible sheet-metal processing with advanced welding and surface technology, high-precision million, wire harnessing and related solutions, all offered under the Sykatec brand name. Siemens Advanta offers end-to-end support to companies in regards to their digitalization transformation and journey, including strategy and operations consulting, design and prototyping and data services. Last, Siemens Healthcare AG is a medical technology company that provides innovative technologies and services in diagnostic and therapeutic imaging

FINANCIAL DATA: *Note: Data for latest year may not have been available at press time.*

In U.S. $	2021	2020	2019	2018	2017	2016
Revenue	20,437,004,350	17,791,100,000	19,984,500,000	17,776,200,000		
R&D Expense						
Operating Income						
Operating Margin %						
SGA Expense						
Net Income						
Operating Cash Flow						
Capital Expenditure						
EBITDA						
Return on Assets %						
Return on Equity %						
Debt to Equity						

CONTACT INFORMATION:

Phone: 609-734-6500 Fax:
Toll-Free:
Address: 755 College Rd. E., Princeton, NJ 08540 United States

STOCK TICKER/OTHER:

Stock Ticker: Subsidiary
Employees: 7,400
Parent Company: Siemens AG
Exchange:
Fiscal Year Ends: 09/30

SALARIES/BONUSES:

Top Exec. Salary: $ Bonus: $
Second Exec. Salary: $ Bonus: $

OTHER THOUGHTS:

Estimated Female Officers or Directors:
Hot Spot for Advancement for Women/Minorities:

Sigma Software

NAIC Code: 541511

sigma.software

TYPES OF BUSINESS:

Custom Computer Programming Services

BRANDS/DIVISIONS/AFFILIATES:

CONTACTS:

Note: Officers with more than one job title may be intentionally listed here more than once.

Valery Krasovsky, CEO
Dmitry Vartanian, CFO
Julia Ostroukh, Head-HR
Carl Vikingsson, Chmn.

GROWTH PLANS/SPECIAL FEATURES:

Sigma Software provides software development services under the Sigma Group, their parent. These services include the automotive, aviation, construction/real estate, gambling, gaming, telecom, media, advertising, finance, banking, information technology (IT), healthcare and energy industries. Sigma's three primary service areas consist of: software development, including product development, turn-key solutions and related support and maintenance; testing, including software testing, automated testing, quality process and compliance; graphic design, including usability analysis, user interface/user experience (UI/UX) design and motion graphics; and special services such as CTO-as-a-service (chief technology officer) for startups, as well as embedded software, Internet of Things (IoT) and migration from legacy systems. Solutions offered by Sigma include eCommerce, business intelligence, big data, web and intranet portals, mobile solutions, business systems, cloud software-as-a-service (SaaS), advertising solutions, collection solutions, gaming solutions, in-vehicle infotainment, augmented reality (AR), virtual reality (VR), artificial intelligence (AI), business process management, document management and platforms. Sigma specializes in the development of products for technological startups, led by serial entrepreneurs. The firm applies a unique methodology based on 10+ years of helping startups, from the product's initiation phase to successful exit and further development. Based in Ukraine, Sigma Software has global locations in Sweden, the U.S., Poland and Australia.

FINANCIAL DATA:

Note: Data for latest year may not have been available at press time.

In U.S. $	2021	2020	2019	2018	2017	2016
Revenue						
R&D Expense						
Operating Income						
Operating Margin %						
SGA Expense						
Net Income						
Operating Cash Flow						
Capital Expenditure						
EBITDA						
Return on Assets %						
Return on Equity %						
Debt to Equity						

CONTACT INFORMATION:

Phone: 380-95-3777773 Fax:
Toll-Free:
Address: 58 Yaroslavska St., BC Astarta. 7/Fl, Kyiv, 04071 Ukraine

STOCK TICKER/OTHER:

Stock Ticker: Private
Employees: 950
Parent Company: Sigma Group
Exchange:
Fiscal Year Ends:

SALARIES/BONUSES:

Top Exec. Salary: $ Bonus: $
Second Exec. Salary: $ Bonus: $

OTHER THOUGHTS:

Estimated Female Officers or Directors:
Hot Spot for Advancement for Women/Minorities:

Silicon Laboratories Inc

www.silabs.com

NAIC Code: 334413

TYPES OF BUSINESS:

Integrated Circuits
Internet of Things
Silicon Software
Industrial Automation
Smart Home
Smart Industry
Automotive
Data Center

BRANDS/DIVISIONS/AFFILIATES:

GROWTH PLANS/SPECIAL FEATURES:

Silicon Laboratories Inc develops semiconductors, software, and system solutions for the "Internet of Things," Internet infrastructure, industrial control, consumer, and automotive markets. The company operates through one segment, mixed-signal analog intensive products, consisting of diverse product areas, which the company groups into four categories: Internet of Things, broadcast, infrastructure and access. The Internet of Things category is the largest contributor to the company's total revenue. Geographically, the company mainly operates in the United States and China, with the U.S. the largest source of revenue.

CONTACTS: *Note: Officers with more than one job title may be intentionally listed here more than once.*

G. Tuttle, CEO
John Hollister, CFO
Navdeep Sooch, Chairman of the Board
Mark Mauldin, Chief Accounting Officer
Daniel Thompson, General Manager, Divisional
Robert Johnson, President
Brandon Tolany, Senior VP, Divisional
Sandeep Kumar, Senior VP, Divisional

FINANCIAL DATA: *Note: Data for latest year may not have been available at press time.*

In U.S. $	2021	2020	2019	2018	2017	2016
Revenue		886,677,000	837,554,000	868,267,000	768,867,000	697,626,000
R&D Expense		287,887,000	257,150,000	238,347,000	209,491,000	199,744,000
Operating Income		38,300,000	56,697,000	85,208,000	84,974,000	66,277,000
Operating Margin %						
SGA Expense		201,339,000	196,437,000	197,844,000	159,726,000	155,483,000
Net Income		12,531,000	19,265,000	83,591,000	47,092,000	61,494,000
Operating Cash Flow		135,718,000	166,522,000	173,542,000	189,521,000	128,910,000
Capital Expenditure		20,422,000	16,279,000	24,462,000	12,252,000	10,927,000
EBITDA		111,956,000	126,349,000	151,869,000	133,043,000	108,014,000
Return on Assets %						
Return on Equity %						
Debt to Equity						

CONTACT INFORMATION:

Phone: 512 416-8500 Fax: 512 464-9444
Toll-Free: 877-444-3032
Address: 400 W. Cesar Chavez, Austin, TX 78701 United States

STOCK TICKER/OTHER:

Stock Ticker: SLAB
Employees: 1,838
Parent Company:
Exchange: NAS
Fiscal Year Ends: 12/31

SALARIES/BONUSES:

Top Exec. Salary: $671,739 Bonus: $
Second Exec. Salary: $408,720 Bonus: $

OTHER THOUGHTS:

Estimated Female Officers or Directors: 1
Hot Spot for Advancement for Women/Minorities:

Silicon Motion Technology Corporation

www.siliconmotion.com

NAIC Code: 334413

TYPES OF BUSINESS:

Semiconductor and Related Device Manufacturing
NAND Flash
Integrated Circuits

BRANDS/DIVISIONS/AFFILIATES:

SMI
Shanon
Ferri

GROWTH PLANS/SPECIAL FEATURES:

Silicon Motion Technology Corp is active in the semiconductor industry and primarily focuses on designing, developing, and marketing of controllers for managing NAND flash used in embedded storage applications, such as eMMC embedded memory. Its only operating segment of Developing NAND flash controllers and SSDs solutions. The company derives revenue from product categories such as Mobile Storage, Mobile Communications, and others. Silicon earns the majority of the revenue from China and also has a presence in Taiwan, the United States, Japan, Korea, and Other Countries. The company products are used in Personal Computing, Smartphone/Tablet/CE, Flash Card/USB Flash Drive, Industrial and Embedded, Automotive, and Enterprise and Data Center.

CONTACTS: *Note: Officers with more than one job title may be intentionally listed here more than once.*

Wallace C. Kou, CEO
Ken Chen, VP-Operations
Riyadh Lai, CFO
Nelson Duann, Sr. VP-Mktg.
James Chow, Chmn.

FINANCIAL DATA: *Note: Data for latest year may not have been available at press time.*

In U.S. $	2021	2020	2019	2018	2017	2016
Revenue		539,521,000	457,253,000	530,348,000	523,404,000	556,146,000
R&D Expense		121,784,000	110,305,000	102,028,000	102,053,000	92,405,000
Operating Income		97,963,000	68,115,000	108,903,000	103,806,000	137,260,000
Operating Margin %						
SGA Expense		40,409,000	42,986,000	46,912,000	42,801,000	42,837,000
Net Income		79,746,000	64,398,000	98,070,000	74,955,000	110,940,000
Operating Cash Flow		117,229,000	77,695,000	108,242,000	103,881,000	125,568,000
Capital Expenditure		19,545,000	11,015,000	74,853,000	11,683,000	12,220,000
EBITDA		99,131,000	85,290,000	125,035,000	112,557,000	150,342,000
Return on Assets %						
Return on Equity %						
Debt to Equity						

CONTACT INFORMATION:

Phone: 886 35526888 Fax: 886 35526988
Toll-Free:
Address: Unit B, 16/Fl, Center 600, 82 King Lam St., Cheung Sha Wan, Hong Kong, Kowloon 999077 Hong Kong

STOCK TICKER/OTHER:

Stock Ticker: SIMO
Employees: 1,323
Parent Company:
Exchange: NAS
Fiscal Year Ends: 12/31

SALARIES/BONUSES:

Top Exec. Salary: $ Bonus: $
Second Exec. Salary: $ Bonus: $

OTHER THOUGHTS:

Estimated Female Officers or Directors:
Hot Spot for Advancement for Women/Minorities:

Singapore Technologies Telemedia Pte Ltd www.sttelemedia.com

NAIC Code: 517110

TYPES OF BUSINESS:

Telecommunications Services
Cellular Service
Internet Services
Satellite & Broadcasting Services
Wireless Telecommunications Equipment
Data Centers & Internet Exchange
Network Design & Integration Services
Cloud

BRANDS/DIVISIONS/AFFILIATES:

Temasek Holdings Pvt Limited

CONTACTS: *Note: Officers with more than one job title may be intentionally listed here more than once.*

Stephen Miller, CEO
Johnny Ong, CFO
Chan Jen Keet, VP
Nicholas Tan, Sr. VP-Corp. Planning
Melinda Tan, Media Contact
Richard Lim, Exec. VP-Corp. Svcs.
Kek Soon Eng, Sr. VP-Investee Companies Mgmt.
Alvin Oei, Sr. VP-Intl Bus. Dev.
Melinda Tan, VP-Strategic Rel.
Ek Tor Teo, Chmn.
Steven Terrell Clontz, Sr. Exec. VP-North America & Europe

GROWTH PLANS/SPECIAL FEATURES:

Singapore Technologies Telemedia Pte., Ltd. (ST Telemedia) is an active investor in communications, media, data centers and infrastructure technology businesses worldwide. ST Telemedia's team of industry professionals has deep and broad experience in these sectors worldwide, in both developed and emerging markets. The firm has a long-term view on value creation and works with its portfolio companies and business partners to achieve mutual success. ST Telemedia's investments in communications and media companies are primarily located in the Asia-Pacific region. They enable the company to combine data, mobility, voice and content services with state-of-the-art delivery platforms. ST Telemedia's investments in data centers spans a footprint in key global economic hubs, particularly in China, India, Singapore, Thailand and the U.K. This division's agile and multi-tenant business model enables its global data center assets to be differentiated and diversified. Last, ST Telemedia's infrastructure technology investments are in cutting-edge technology companies that are ready to scale up in areas such as cloud computing, system performance, cybersecurity and advanced analytics. They are at the forefront of technology innovation critical for the digital transformation of governments, enterprises and telecommunications companies. ST Telemedia operates as a subsidiary of Temasek Holdings Pvt. Limited.

FINANCIAL DATA: *Note: Data for latest year may not have been available at press time.*

In U.S. $	2021	2020	2019	2018	2017	2016
Revenue	3,000,000,000	2,970,803,015	3,062,386,348	4,909,244,928	4,669,999,616	4,917,730,816
R&D Expense						
Operating Income						
Operating Margin %						
SGA Expense						
Net Income		68,702,179	-158,603,746	362,253,824	361,128,768	356,493,568
Operating Cash Flow						
Capital Expenditure						
EBITDA						
Return on Assets %						
Return on Equity %						
Debt to Equity						

CONTACT INFORMATION:

Phone: 65-6723-8777 Fax: 65-6720-7266
Toll-Free:
Address: 1 Temasek Ave., #33-01 Millenia Twr., Singapore, 567710 Singapore

STOCK TICKER/OTHER:

Stock Ticker: Subsidiary Exchange:
Employees: 5,000 Fiscal Year Ends: 12/31
Parent Company: Temasek Holdings Pvt Limited

SALARIES/BONUSES:

Top Exec. Salary: $ Bonus: $
Second Exec. Salary: $ Bonus: $

OTHER THOUGHTS:

Estimated Female Officers or Directors: 1
Hot Spot for Advancement for Women/Minorities:

Singtel Optus Pty Limited

NAIC Code: 517110

www.optus.com.au

TYPES OF BUSINESS:

Diversified Telecommunications Services
Mobile Phone Service
Digital Television Service
Local & Long-Distance Phone Service
Business Network Services
Satellite Services
Multimedia Services
5G

BRANDS/DIVISIONS/AFFILIATES:

Singapore Telecommunications Limited

CONTACTS:

Note: Officers with more than one job title may be intentionally listed here more than once.

Kelly Bayer Rosmarin, CEO
Michael Venter, CFO
Kate Aitken, VP-People & Culture
Mark Potter, CIO
Martin Mercer, Managing Dir.-Strategy & Fixed
David Epstein, VP-Corp. & Regulatory Affairs
Vicki Brady, Managing Dir.-Customer
John Paitaridis, Managing Dir.-Optus Bus.
Gunther Ottendorfer, Managing Dir.-Optus Networks
Austin R. Bryan, VP-Transformation, Consumer Australia
Paul O'Sullivan, Chmn.

GROWTH PLANS/SPECIAL FEATURES:

Singtel Optus Pty. Limited (Optus), a subsidiary of Singapore Telecommunications Limited (Singtel), provides telecommunications services in Australia. Optus' mobile network reaches 98.5% of the Aussie population through its mobile, satellite and broadband networks. The firm's home and mobile network offers 5G coverage in select locations, which becomes faster, more responsive and has higher capacity than Optus' 3G and 4G networks. The company's 4G+ coverage reaches all of the country's capital cities as well as hundreds of regional towns. Optus owns and operates its own satellite fleet, which provides satellite-based communications services throughout Australia and Asia. The satellites in orbit are tracked by its ground network of domestic and international Earth stations. Over 1 million Australians utilize Optus for internet services, including digital subscriber line (DSL) connectivity. Optus' regional network invests in and builds the company's regional coverage. In addition, Optus has retail stores throughout Australia, which offer mobile phones, office phones, tablets and other communication devices, as well as related accessories and services. For businesses and enterprises, Optus provides digital transformation services and solutions through its managed cloud strategy, which enables firms to build a simple, secure and cost-effective way for driving business outcomes. The company also provides managed security, security technology, cyber security, digital business solutions, mobility solutions and related consultancy services to businesses, enterprises and all tiers of government entities.

FINANCIAL DATA:

Note: Data for latest year may not have been available at press time.

In U.S. $	2021	2020	2019	2018	2017	2016
Revenue	5,400,340,112	4,768,040,000	5,434,520,000	5,478,460,000	5,285,450,000	5,764,390,000
R&D Expense						
Operating Income						
Operating Margin %						
SGA Expense						
Net Income	1,435,417,716	1,570,080,000	1,761,130,000	1,898,400,000	1,851,480,000	1,884,220,000
Operating Cash Flow						
Capital Expenditure						
EBITDA						
Return on Assets %						
Return on Equity %						
Debt to Equity						

CONTACT INFORMATION:

Phone: 61-2-8082-7800 Fax: 61-2-8082-7100
Toll-Free:
Address: 1 Lyonpark Rd., Macquarie Park, NSW 2113 Australia

STOCK TICKER/OTHER:

Stock Ticker: Subsidiary Exchange:
Employees: 8,400 Fiscal Year Ends: 03/31
Parent Company: Singapore Telecommunications Limited

SALARIES/BONUSES:

Top Exec. Salary: $ Bonus: $
Second Exec. Salary: $ Bonus: $

OTHER THOUGHTS:

Estimated Female Officers or Directors: 1
Hot Spot for Advancement for Women/Minorities:

SK Hynix Inc

www.skhynix.com

NAIC Code: 334413

TYPES OF BUSINESS:

Semiconductor Manufacturing
Memory Chips
Imaging Chips

GROWTH PLANS/SPECIAL FEATURES:

SK Hynix is a semiconductor supplier with around 70-75% of its revenue from DRAM and 20-25% of its revenue from NAND flash. SK Hynix is the second-largest DRAM supplier globally with approximately 29% market share and the fourth-largest NAND supplier globally with approximately 10% market share. SK Telecom, the largest telecom carrier in South Korea, became the largest shareholder in 2012 and currently holds 20% of SK Hynix's shares.

BRANDS/DIVISIONS/AFFILIATES:

SK Holdings Co Ltd

CONTACTS: *Note: Officers with more than one job title may be intentionally listed here more than once.*

Seok-Hee Lee, CEO

FINANCIAL DATA: *Note: Data for latest year may not have been available at press time.*

In U.S. $	2021	2020	2019	2018	2017	2016
Revenue		26,790,410,000	22,667,190,000	33,966,330,000	25,286,320,000	14,443,100,000
R&D Expense		2,612,911,000	2,398,209,000	1,918,135,000	1,658,957,000	1,465,233,000
Operating Income		4,209,671,000	2,278,178,000	17,504,870,000	11,523,360,000	2,751,857,000
Operating Margin %						
SGA Expense		701,544,400	755,153,900	659,943,400	519,514,800	436,856,900
Net Income		3,993,401,000	1,690,787,000	13,050,800,000	8,936,890,000	2,480,621,000
Operating Cash Flow		10,341,950,000	5,444,671,000	18,666,710,000	12,337,380,000	4,660,062,000
Capital Expenditure		9,128,266,000	12,255,910,000	14,251,040,000	8,325,255,000	5,447,645,000
EBITDA		13,657,640,000	9,434,999,000	23,400,570,000	15,611,910,000	6,544,696,000
Return on Assets %						
Return on Equity %						
Debt to Equity						

CONTACT INFORMATION:

Phone: 82 31630-4114 Fax: 82 31645-8000
Toll-Free:
Address: 2091, Gyeongchung-daero, Icheon-si, Gyeonggi-do 17336 South Korea

STOCK TICKER/OTHER:

Stock Ticker: HXSCL
Employees: 28,244
Parent Company: SK Holdings Co Ltd
Exchange: PINX
Fiscal Year Ends: 12/31

SALARIES/BONUSES:

Top Exec. Salary: $ Bonus: $
Second Exec. Salary: $ Bonus: $

OTHER THOUGHTS:

Estimated Female Officers or Directors:
Hot Spot for Advancement for Women/Minorities:

SK Telecom Co Ltd

NAIC Code: 517210

www.sktelecom.com

TYPES OF BUSINESS:

Wireless Telecommunications Services
Multimedia Broadcasting
Online Shopping
Internet of Things
Telecommunications

GROWTH PLANS/SPECIAL FEATURES:

SK Telecom is South Korea's largest wireless telecom operator, with 29 million mobile customers. The firm also owns SK Broadband (formerly Hanaro Telecom), which has 6.5 million broadband customers and 8.7 million broadband TV customers. While the firm also purchased stakes in businesses in security and semiconductor memory production as well as developing e-commerce and Internet platform businesses, these were all spun off into the separate, SK Square business in November 2021.

BRANDS/DIVISIONS/AFFILIATES:

Eleven Street
SK Hynix Inc
KEB HanaCard Co Ltd
Content Wavve

CONTACTS: *Note: Officers with more than one job title may be intentionally listed here more than once.*

Jung-Ho Park, CEO
Young Sang Ryu, Dir.-Mobile Network Oper.
Dong Seob Jee, Head-Corp. Vision Dept.
Young Tae Kim, Exec. Dir.
Daesik Cho, Chmn.

FINANCIAL DATA: *Note: Data for latest year may not have been available at press time.*

In U.S. $	2021	2020	2019	2018	2017	2016
Revenue		15,641,240,000	14,901,410,000	14,170,990,000	14,713,550,000	14,353,940,000
R&D Expense		349,736,300	328,641,900	325,574,800	331,958,300	289,556,900
Operating Income		1,171,860,000	980,906,000	1,046,502,000	1,249,330,000	1,329,939,000
Operating Margin %						
SGA Expense		8,163,084,000	7,709,766,000	7,403,181,000	7,551,045,000	7,292,470,000
Net Income		1,263,376,000	747,356,300	2,626,843,000	2,183,373,000	1,407,500,000
Operating Cash Flow		4,889,292,000	3,347,567,000	3,638,561,000	3,238,171,000	3,563,471,000
Capital Expenditure		3,097,046,000	2,953,535,000	2,767,707,000	2,403,211,000	2,625,126,000
EBITDA		5,413,619,000	4,615,941,000	6,355,396,000	5,836,596,000	4,581,311,000
Return on Assets %						
Return on Equity %						
Debt to Equity						

CONTACT INFORMATION:

Phone: 82-2-6100-2114 Fax: 82-2-6110-7830
Toll-Free:
Address: SK T-Tower, 65, Eulji-ro, Jung-gu, Seoul, 100-999 South Korea

STOCK TICKER/OTHER:

Stock Ticker: SKM
Exchange: NYS
Employees: 41,097
Fiscal Year Ends: 12/31
Parent Company:

SALARIES/BONUSES:

Top Exec. Salary: $ Bonus: $
Second Exec. Salary: $ Bonus: $

OTHER THOUGHTS:

Estimated Female Officers or Directors:
Hot Spot for Advancement for Women/Minorities:

SkyBell Technologies Inc

www.skybell.com

NAIC Code: 334310

TYPES OF BUSINESS:

Audio and Video Equipment Manufacturing
Video Equipped Doorbell
Home Automation Solutions
Product Manufacturing
Wi-Fi Connectivity Solutions
Technologies
Product Development
Software Development

BRANDS/DIVISIONS/AFFILIATES:

SkyBell
SkyBell HD
SkyBell Trim Plus
SkyBell Connect

CONTACTS: *Note: Officers with more than one job title may be intentionally listed here more than once.*

Ron Garriques, CEO
Desiree Mejia, COO
Greg Estell, CFO
Michael Tatelman, CMO
Joe Scalisi, CTO

GROWTH PLANS/SPECIAL FEATURES:

SkyBell Technologies, Inc. develops home automation solutions, with its flagship product being a smart video doorbell trademarked under the SkyBell name. The firm offers two Wi-Fi-enabled video doorbell models: SkyBell HD, a round doorbell that features a 1080p high-definition (HD) video with full-color night vision capabilities, free cloud recording (no monthly fees), motion sensor alerts and weather/rain-proof; and SkyBell Trim Plus, a slim rectangular doorbell that offers the same features as SkyBell HD. Owners of the doorbell can keep tabs on their front door anytime, anywhere through the free SkyBell app for iOS and Android. Accessories are provided by the company, and include wedge mounts and a digital adapter, which range in price from about $10 to $18. A third-party security platform can arm the SkyBell doorbell system or go into a vigilant mode. Doors can be locked automatically via the motion sensor or by the user pressing a button, smart lights can be connected and turned on through the doorbell device, an alarm can be heard, the light-emitting diode (LED) color can be changed, the motion sensor can be turned off/on, the doorbell chime can be turned off/on and the doorbells are Alexa compatible. In addition, SkyBell Connect keeps the Wi-Fi connection active at all times, which is possible through the firm's patented power management system. Through this technology, partner products and platforms can receive triggers and send actions to SkyBell HD at any time. Product details, installation/setup, how-to's and troubleshooting information are provided on the company's website. SkyBell has more than 150 issued patents.

FINANCIAL DATA: *Note: Data for latest year may not have been available at press time.*

In U.S. $	2021	2020	2019	2018	2017	2016
Revenue						
R&D Expense						
Operating Income						
Operating Margin %						
SGA Expense						
Net Income						
Operating Cash Flow						
Capital Expenditure						
EBITDA						
Return on Assets %						
Return on Equity %						
Debt to Equity						

CONTACT INFORMATION:

Phone: 949 336-7676 Fax:
Toll-Free: 888-423-9194
Address: 1 Jenner St., Ste. 100, Irvine, CA 92618 United States

STOCK TICKER/OTHER:

Stock Ticker: Private
Exchange:
Employees:
Fiscal Year Ends:
Parent Company:

SALARIES/BONUSES:

Top Exec. Salary: $ Bonus: $
Second Exec. Salary: $ Bonus: $

OTHER THOUGHTS:

Estimated Female Officers or Directors:
Hot Spot for Advancement for Women/Minorities:

Skyworks Solutions Inc

NAIC Code: 334413

www.skyworksinc.com

TYPES OF BUSINESS:

Semiconductor Manufacturing
Radio Frequency & Cellular Systems

BRANDS/DIVISIONS/AFFILIATES:

GROWTH PLANS/SPECIAL FEATURES:

Skyworks Solutions produces semiconductors for wireless handsets and other devices that are used to enable wireless connectivity. Its main products include power amplifiers, filters, switches, and integrated front-end modules that support wireless transmissions. Skyworks' customers are mostly large smartphone manufacturers, but the firm also has a growing presence in nonhandset applications such as wireless routers, medical devices, and automobiles.

Skyworks offers its employees medical, dental and vision insurance; life insurance; disability coverage; flexible spending accounts; an education assistance program; a 401(k) plan; a discount stock purchase plan; and fitness benefits.

CONTACTS: *Note: Officers with more than one job title may be intentionally listed here more than once.*

Liam Griffin, CEO
Kris Sennesael, CFO
David Aldrich, Chairman of the Board
Karilee Durham, Senior VP, Divisional

FINANCIAL DATA: *Note: Data for latest year may not have been available at press time.*

In U.S. $	2021	2020	2019	2018	2017	2016
Revenue	5,109,100,000	3,355,700,000	3,376,800,000	3,868,000,000	3,651,400,000	3,289,000,000
R&D Expense	532,300,000	464,100,000	424,100,000	404,500,000	355,200,000	312,400,000
Operating Income	1,621,600,000	905,600,000	958,800,000	1,320,100,000	1,254,400,000	1,123,500,000
Operating Margin %						
SGA Expense	322,500,000	231,400,000	198,300,000	207,800,000	204,600,000	195,900,000
Net Income	1,498,300,000	814,800,000	853,600,000	918,400,000	1,010,200,000	995,200,000
Operating Cash Flow	1,772,000,000	1,204,500,000	1,367,400,000	1,260,600,000	1,471,300,000	1,095,700,000
Capital Expenditure	652,100,000	398,500,000	423,400,000	430,900,000	315,400,000	195,300,000
EBITDA	2,048,800,000	1,269,900,000	1,330,400,000	1,619,300,000	1,509,200,000	1,371,300,000
Return on Assets %						
Return on Equity %						
Debt to Equity						

CONTACT INFORMATION:

Phone: 949-231-3000 Fax:
Toll-Free:
Address: 5260 California Ave., Irvine, CA 92617 United States

STOCK TICKER/OTHER:

Stock Ticker: SWKS
Employees: 10,000
Parent Company:
Exchange: NAS
Fiscal Year Ends: 09/30

SALARIES/BONUSES:

Top Exec. Salary: $1,043,888 Bonus: $
Second Exec. Salary: $537,192 Bonus: $

OTHER THOUGHTS:

Estimated Female Officers or Directors:
Hot Spot for Advancement for Women/Minorities: Y

Slack Technologies Inc

slack.com

NAIC Code: 511210C

TYPES OF BUSINESS:

Computer Software, Telecom, Communications & VOIP

BRANDS/DIVISIONS/AFFILIATES:

Slack
Slack Enterprise Grid
salesforce.com Inc

CONTACTS: *Note: Officers with more than one job title may be intentionally listed here more than once.*

Stewart Butterfield, CEO
Allen Shim, CFO
Allen Shim, Chief Accounting Officer
Cal Henderson, Chief Technology Officer
Nadia Rawlinson, Chief People Officer
David Schellhase, General Counsel
Tamar Yehoshua, Other Executive Officer
Robert Frati, Senior VP, Divisional

GROWTH PLANS/SPECIAL FEATURES:

Slack Technologies, Inc. is a computer software firm that operates Slack, a platform that enables team communications through a single hub. The platform provides real-time messaging, archiving and searching services primarily for small-to-medium-sized companies or teams. Slack's solutions are divided into two groups: channels and direct messages. Channels provides a way to organize team conversations in open channels and are displayed per subject categories that relate to the project (such as feedback, product, customer service, app, issues, etc.). Direct messages reach colleagues directly and are completely private and secure. Private group features are available for sensitive information, with the ability to invite select team members that no one else can see or join. The direct messages are also categorized by subject for team members to easily see and access. Prices range from free introductory access to $12.50 per month. Free access includes search and browse of 10,000 most recent messages, 10 service integrations, free native apps for iOS/Android/Mac&Windows Desktop and 1:1 voice and video calls, 5GB file storage and two-factor identification. Standard access includes everything in Free, as well as searchable archive with unlimited messages, unlimited service integrations, custom retention policies, guest access, Google Authentication/Apps for Domains sign-on, configurable email ingestion and group voice/video calls, screen sharing, 10GB file storage and custom profiles. Plus access includes everything in Standard, as well as SAML-based single sign-on, compliance exports of all message history, support for external message and archival solutions, 99.99% guaranteed uptime SLA, user provisioning and deprovisioning, real-time active directory sync with OneLogic, Okta and Ping, and 20GB file storage. For enterprise collaboration, Slack offers a communication hub with channels for communication, file-sharing and decision-making purposes, as well as the Slack Enterprise Grid for managing large, complex teams. In July 2021, Slack Technologies was acquired by salesforce.com inc.

FINANCIAL DATA: *Note: Data for latest year may not have been available at press time.*

In U.S. $	2021	2020	2019	2018	2017	2016
Revenue	655,638,896	630,422,016	400,552,000	220,544,000	105,153,000	88,000,000
R&D Expense						
Operating Income						
Operating Margin %						
SGA Expense						
Net Income		-571,057,984	-140,683,008	-140,084,992	-146,864,000	
Operating Cash Flow						
Capital Expenditure						
EBITDA						
Return on Assets %						
Return on Equity %						
Debt to Equity						

CONTACT INFORMATION:

Phone: 415-630-7943 Fax:
Toll-Free:
Address: 500 Howard St., San Francisco, CA 94105 United States

STOCK TICKER/OTHER:

Stock Ticker: Subsidiary
Employees: 2,545
Parent Company: salesforce.com Inc
Exchange:
Fiscal Year Ends: 01/31

SALARIES/BONUSES:

Top Exec. Salary: $ Bonus: $
Second Exec. Salary: $ Bonus: $

OTHER THOUGHTS:

Estimated Female Officers or Directors:
Hot Spot for Advancement for Women/Minorities:

SoftBank Group Corp

NAIC Code: 517110

www.softbank.co.jp

TYPES OF BUSINESS:

Telecommunications Services
Investment
Managed Funds
Technology
Artificial Intelligence
Robotics
Smartphone Payment
Electricity

BRANDS/DIVISIONS/AFFILIATES:

SoftBank Group Capital Limited
SB Northstar LP
SoftBank Investment Advisers
SoftBank Vision Fund LP
Z Holdings
Arm Limited
Fortress Investment Group LLC
PayPay Corporation

GROWTH PLANS/SPECIAL FEATURES:

SoftBank is a Japan-based telecom and e-commerce conglomerate that has expanded mainly through acquisitions, and its key assets include a 28% stake in Chinese e-commerce giant Alibaba and a 40% owned mobile and fixed broadband telecom operator business in Japan. It also owns 75% of semiconductor chip designer ARM Holdings although has agreed to sell this and is waiting on regulatory approvals, and has a vast portfolio of mainly Internet- and e-commerce-focused early stage investments. It is also general partner of the $100 billion SoftBank Vision Fund 1 and sole investor in Softbank Vision Fund 2, both of which primarily invest in pre-IPO Internet companies.

CONTACTS: *Note: Officers with more than one job title may be intentionally listed here more than once.*

Masayoshi Shon, CEO
Marcelo Claure, COO
Ken Miyauchi, COO-SOFTBANK MOBILE Corp.
Ronald D. Fisher, Pres., SOFTBANK Holdings, Inc.
Masayoshi Son, Chmn.

FINANCIAL DATA: *Note: Data for latest year may not have been available at press time.*

In U.S. $	2021	2020	2019	2018	2017	2016
Revenue	49,454,910,000	54,348,640,000	84,375,200,000	80,478,400,000	78,213,450,000	80,432,580,000
R&D Expense						
Operating Income	5,302,380,000	-12,095,460,000	19,135,270,000	11,453,280,000	8,855,681,000	8,260,228,000
Operating Margin %						
SGA Expense	19,959,730,000	17,786,430,000	24,486,610,000	22,430,350,000	20,010,290,000	21,507,130,000
Net Income	43,829,410,000	-8,449,403,000	12,400,260,000	9,129,529,000	12,533,020,000	4,166,567,000
Operating Cash Flow	4,896,576,000	9,822,844,000	10,297,210,000	9,565,771,000	13,186,950,000	8,261,449,000
Capital Expenditure	5,684,229,000	10,830,470,000	11,993,900,000	9,356,745,000	8,114,846,000	11,958,810,000
EBITDA	60,006,870,000	20,982,670,000	35,317,370,000	21,850,160,000	23,307,670,000	25,024,050,000
Return on Assets %						
Return on Equity %						
Debt to Equity						

CONTACT INFORMATION:

Phone: 81-3-6889-2000 Fax:
Toll-Free:
Address: 1-9-1 Higashi-shimbashi, Tokyo, 105-7303 Japan

STOCK TICKER/OTHER:

Stock Ticker: SFTBY
Exchange: PINX
Employees: 92,069
Fiscal Year Ends: 03/31
Parent Company:

SALARIES/BONUSES:

Top Exec. Salary: $ Bonus: $
Second Exec. Salary: $ Bonus: $

OTHER THOUGHTS:

Estimated Female Officers or Directors:
Hot Spot for Advancement for Women/Minorities:

SoftServe Inc

www.softserveinc.com

NAIC Code: 541511

TYPES OF BUSINESS:

Custom Computer Programming Services
Technology solutions
Software
Cloud
DevOps
Big Data
Artificial Intelligence
Internet of Things

BRANDS/DIVISIONS/AFFILIATES:

CONTACTS:

Note: Officers with more than one job title may be intentionally listed here more than once.

Yaroslav Lyubinets, Chmn.

GROWTH PLANS/SPECIAL FEATURES:

SoftServe, Inc. is a leading technology solutions company that specializes in software development and consultancy. SoftServe's services span engineering, cloud, DevOps, big data, analytics, artificial intelligence (AI), machine learning (ML), Internet of Things (IoT), experience design, cybersecurity, experience platforms, extended reality (XR), research and development, robotics and innovation platform. Solutions and services also include software testing, architecture, business analysis, operations support and product management. The firm's solutions and services are primarily utilized by the healthcare, life sciences, financial services, retail, high-tech, energy, oil and gas industries. Partners of SoftServe include Google Cloud, AWS, Microsoft, Salesforce, Apigee, MuleSoft and VMware. Based in Texas, USA, the firm has European headquarters in Lviv, Ukraine. Through a partnership with Ivano-Frankivsk IT cluster members, SoftServe has an IoT Laboratory at King Danylo University in Ivano-Frankivsk, Ukraine. SoftServe has more than 40 offices in 12 countries, with headquarter locations in the U.S. and Ukraine.

SoftServe offers employee benefits.

FINANCIAL DATA:

Note: Data for latest year may not have been available at press time.

In U.S. $	2021	2020	2019	2018	2017	2016
Revenue	280,000,000	261,843,750	275,625,000	262,500,000	250,000,000	
R&D Expense						
Operating Income						
Operating Margin %						
SGA Expense						
Net Income						
Operating Cash Flow						
Capital Expenditure						
EBITDA						
Return on Assets %						
Return on Equity %						
Debt to Equity						

CONTACT INFORMATION:

Phone: 512-516-8880 Fax:
Toll-Free: 866-687-3588
Address: 201 W. 5th St., Ste. 1550, Austin, TX 78701 United States

STOCK TICKER/OTHER:

Stock Ticker: Private
Employees: 12,000
Parent Company:
Exchange:
Fiscal Year Ends:

SALARIES/BONUSES:

Top Exec. Salary: $ Bonus: $
Second Exec. Salary: $ Bonus: $

OTHER THOUGHTS:

Estimated Female Officers or Directors:
Hot Spot for Advancement for Women/Minorities:

SolarWinds Corporation

www.solarwinds.com

NAIC Code: 511210B

TYPES OF BUSINESS:

Computer Software, Network Management (IT), System Testing & Storage

GROWTH PLANS/SPECIAL FEATURES:

SolarWinds Corp is a provider of information technology (IT), and infrastructure management software. Products and services offered by the company include network management, system management, database management, IT security, and IT help desk, among others. Geographically, the firm generates a majority of its revenue from the United States of America.

BRANDS/DIVISIONS/AFFILIATES:

SolarWinds
SolarWinds & Design
Orion
THWACK

CONTACTS: *Note: Officers with more than one job title may be intentionally listed here more than once.*

Sudhakar Ramakrishna, CEO
J. Kalsu, CFO
William Bock, Chairman of the Board
Jason Bliss, Chief Administrative Officer
David Gardiner, Executive VP

FINANCIAL DATA: *Note: Data for latest year may not have been available at press time.*

In U.S. $	2021	2020	2019	2018	2017	2016
Revenue		1,019,241,000	932,525,000	833,089,000	728,017,000	
R&D Expense		126,216,000	110,362,000	96,272,000	86,618,000	
Operating Income		107,443,000	135,173,000	115,185,000	69,654,000	
Operating Margin %						
SGA Expense		435,993,000	361,724,000	308,109,000	272,934,000	
Net Income		158,475,000	18,642,000	-102,066,000	-83,866,000	
Operating Cash Flow		389,094,000	299,907,000	254,142,000	232,693,000	
Capital Expenditure		38,220,000	23,041,000	18,632,000	12,380,000	
EBITDA		384,059,000	398,819,000	278,660,000	359,194,000	
Return on Assets %						
Return on Equity %						
Debt to Equity						

CONTACT INFORMATION:

Phone: 512-682-9300 Fax: 512 682-9301
Toll-Free: 866-530-8100
Address: 7171 Southwest Parkway, Bldg. 400, Austin, TX 78735 United States

STOCK TICKER/OTHER:

Stock Ticker: SWI
Exchange: NYS
Employees: 3,340
Fiscal Year Ends: 12/31
Parent Company:

SALARIES/BONUSES:

Top Exec. Salary: $700,000 Bonus: $
Second Exec. Salary: $440,000 Bonus: $48,000

OTHER THOUGHTS:

Estimated Female Officers or Directors: 1
Hot Spot for Advancement for Women/Minorities:

Sony Electronics Inc

electronics.sony.com

NAIC Code: 334220

TYPES OF BUSINESS:

Smartphones
Consumer Electronics
Mobile Phones
Personal Computers
Monitors
Cameras
Entertainment Products and Digital Technology
Robotics and Artificial Intelligence

BRANDS/DIVISIONS/AFFILIATES:

Sony Group Corporation
Sony Corporation of America
Columbia
RCA
Epic
Sony Music Nashville
Sony Classical
Xperia

CONTACTS: *Note: Officers with more than one job title may be intentionally listed here more than once.*

Neal Manowitz, CEO
Bob Ishida, Deputy CEO

GROWTH PLANS/SPECIAL FEATURES:

Sony Electronics, Inc. is a company with a broad portfolio encompassing electronics, music, motion pictures, mobile, gaming and robotics. The firm's operations include research and development, engineering, sales, marketing, distribution and customer service. Consumer electronic products span TVs, monitors, projectors, cameras, camcorders, audio/video, vehicle entertainment, marine entertainment, personal computers, digital readers, mobile phones and tablets. The music division specializes in recorded music across a range of music artists and types of music, with labels including Columbia, RCA, Epic, Sony Music Nashville and Sony Classical. The motion picture division produces, acquires and distributes motion picture and television content, as well as digital content and related products and technologies. Mobile products include mobile phones and smartphones offered under the Xperia brand name, as well as video monitors and related accessories. The gaming division produces and markets PlayStation game products, including video and digital games, gaming hardware and software, and related connectivity accessories and repair services. Last, the robotics division is engaged in artificial intelligence (AI) and robotics, designing and developing technologies and systems for an array of purposes and industries, including industrial, entertainment, healthcare, consumer, professional and more. Sony Electronics is a subsidiary of Sony Corporation of America and an affiliate of Sony Group Corporation.

FINANCIAL DATA: *Note: Data for latest year may not have been available at press time.*

In U.S. $	2021	2020	2019	2018	2017	2016
Revenue	6,400,000,000	5,995,464,166	4,958,156,878	6,719,170,000	6,764,010,000	9,974,120,000
R&D Expense						
Operating Income						
Operating Margin %						
SGA Expense						
Net Income			787,064,568	-260,102,000	91,338,500	-546,168,000
Operating Cash Flow						
Capital Expenditure						
EBITDA						
Return on Assets %						
Return on Equity %						
Debt to Equity						

CONTACT INFORMATION:

Phone: 858-942-2400 Fax:
Toll-Free:
Address: 16535 Via Esprillo, San Diego, CA 92127 United States

STOCK TICKER/OTHER:

Stock Ticker: Subsidiary
Employees: 5,500
Parent Company: Sony Group Corporation
Exchange:
Fiscal Year Ends: 03/31

SALARIES/BONUSES:

Top Exec. Salary: $ Bonus: $
Second Exec. Salary: $ Bonus: $

OTHER THOUGHTS:

Estimated Female Officers or Directors: 1
Hot Spot for Advancement for Women/Minorities:

Sony Group Corporation

NAIC Code: 334310

www.sony.net

TYPES OF BUSINESS:

Consumer Electronics Manufacturer
Film & Television Production
Music Production
Sensors and Cameras for use in Smartphones
Semiconductors
Technology Research
Video Games
Financial Services

BRANDS/DIVISIONS/AFFILIATES:

Sony Music Entertainment
Sony Pictures Entertainment
Sony Semiconductor Solutions Corporation
Sony Energy Devices Corporation
Sony Financial Holdings Inc
Sony Life Insurance Co Ltd
Sony Bank Inc
Sony Corporation

CONTACTS: *Note: Officers with more than one job title may be intentionally listed here more than once.*

Kimio Maki, CEO
Yuichi Oshima, CFO
Keninchiro Yoshida, Chmn.

GROWTH PLANS/SPECIAL FEATURES:

Sony is a conglomerate with consumer electronics roots, which not only designs, develops, produces, and sells electronic equipment and devices, but also is engaged in content businesses, such as console and mobile games, music, and movies. Sony is a global top company of CMOS image sensors, game consoles, professional broadcasting cameras, and music publishing, and is one of the top players on digital cameras, wireless earphones, recorded music, and movies, and so on. Sony's business portfolio is well diversified with six major business segments. The company fully consolidated Sony Financial in September 2020, which provides life and non-life insurance, banking, and other financial services.

FINANCIAL DATA: *Note: Data for latest year may not have been available at press time.*

In U.S. $	2021	2020	2019	2018	2017	2016
Revenue	79,077,700,000	72,579,920,000	76,145,710,000	75,076,280,000	66,810,040,000	71,225,190,000
R&D Expense						
Operating Income	8,504,499,000	7,312,669,000	7,255,157,000	6,417,726,000	3,814,804,000	2,979,948,000
Operating Margin %						
SGA Expense	12,916,550,000	13,203,620,000	13,855,620,000	13,911,610,000	13,232,890,000	14,867,050,000
Net Income	10,296,440,000	5,115,734,000	8,051,307,000	4,312,625,000	643,993,200	1,298,645,000
Operating Cash Flow	11,863,820,000	11,860,260,000	11,060,580,000	11,027,490,000	7,111,015,000	6,582,273,000
Capital Expenditure	4,501,063,000	3,864,196,000	2,747,214,000	2,310,894,000	2,930,556,000	3,298,750,000
EBITDA	16,416,750,000	13,681,340,000	15,347,740,000	12,594,750,000	7,826,755,000	9,019,612,000
Return on Assets %						
Return on Equity %						
Debt to Equity						

CONTACT INFORMATION:

Phone: 81 367482111 Fax: 81 367482244
Toll-Free:
Address: 1-7-1 Konan, Minato-Ku, Tokyo, 108-0075 Japan

STOCK TICKER/OTHER:

Stock Ticker: SONY
Exchange: NYS
Employees: 111,700
Fiscal Year Ends: 03/31
Parent Company:

SALARIES/BONUSES:

Top Exec. Salary: $56,000,000 Bonus: $57,000,000
Second Exec. Salary: $1,713,472 Bonus: $3,075,463

OTHER THOUGHTS:

Estimated Female Officers or Directors:

Hot Spot for Advancement for Women/Minorities:

Speedcast International Limited

www.speedcast.com

NAIC Code: 517110

TYPES OF BUSINESS:

Satellite Network Service Provider.
Communications Technology
Satellite Network

BRANDS/DIVISIONS/AFFILIATES:

Centerbridge Partners LP

CONTACTS:

Note: Officers with more than one job title may be intentionally listed here more than once.

Joe Spytek, CEO
Mike Neugebauer, COO
Lee Eckert, CFO
Olga Pirogova, Chief Human Resources Officer
Chris Hill, CTO

GROWTH PLANS/SPECIAL FEATURES:

Speedcast International Limited is a communications company. The firm's customers are primarily engaged in the maritime, energy, telecommunication, mining, broadcast media, non-government organization (NGO) and government industries. Speedcast's global satellite network and support infrastructure spans across every region in the world. The company's solutions are categorized into: customer experience management, connectivity, professional services, network management and applications and solutions. The customer experience management division works alongside businesses to deliver communication services and support, from implementation to delivery to field support and solution management. The connectivity division unites its diverse connectivity resources into a single, seamless network experience, from both very small aperture terminal (VSAT) two-way satellite ground station and mobile two-way voice and data communication satellite services (MSS). This division has a satellite network of more than 95 satellites and 35+ Speedcast and partner teleports. The professional services division offers problem-solving solutions, enterprise solutions and 24/7/365 support in any time zone and multiple languages. The network management division utilizes a multi-protocol label switching (MPLS) routing technique that directs data from one node to the next based on short path labels rather than long network addresses. It gives a complete view of the customer's network operations, whether it's microwave, fiber, 4G/LTE, terrestrial or satellite services. Last, the applications and solutions division designs solutions to suit its customer's needs, utilizing solutions for Internet of Things (IoT), automation and more. Its solutions are built to satisfy any market, industry, initiative and challenge. Speedcast is privately owned by Centerbridge Partners LP.

FINANCIAL DATA:

Note: Data for latest year may not have been available at press time.

In U.S. $	2021	2020	2019	2018	2017	2016
Revenue	700,000,000	685,300,000	623,000,000	603,832,256	450,877,312	206,055,248
R&D Expense						
Operating Income						
Operating Margin %						
SGA Expense						
Net Income			1,897,396	1,789,901	4,863,276	5,574,120
Operating Cash Flow						
Capital Expenditure						
EBITDA						
Return on Assets %						
Return on Equity %						
Debt to Equity						

CONTACT INFORMATION:

Phone: 832-668-2300 Fax:
Toll-Free:
Address: 4400 S. Sam Houston Pkwy. E., Houston, TX 77048 United States

STOCK TICKER/OTHER:

Stock Ticker: Subsidiary
Exchange:
Employees:
Fiscal Year Ends: 12/31
Parent Company: Centerbridge Partners LP

SALARIES/BONUSES:

Top Exec. Salary: $ Bonus: $
Second Exec. Salary: $ Bonus: $

OTHER THOUGHTS:

Estimated Female Officers or Directors:
Hot Spot for Advancement for Women/Minorities:

Stellantis North America (FCA US LLC)

www.stellantis.com/en/group/about-us

NAIC Code: 336111

TYPES OF BUSINESS:

Automobile Manufacturing
Research & Development
Nanotechnology-Coatings
Light Truck Manufacturing
Financial Services

BRANDS/DIVISIONS/AFFILIATES:

Stellantis NV
Chrysler
Jeep
Dodge
RAM
Alfa Romeo
Mopar
FCA US LLC

CONTACTS: *Note: Officers with more than one job title may be intentionally listed here more than once.*

Mark Stewart, COO
Ralph V. Gilles, Sr. VP-Prod. Design
Mark M. Chernoby, Sr. VP-Eng.
Mauro Pino, Sr. VP-Mfg. & World Class Mfg.
Peter Grady, VP-Network Dev. & Fleet
Marjorie Loeb, General Counsel
Barbara J. Pilarski, VP-Bus. Dev.
Gualberto Ranieri, Sr. VP-Comm.
Laurie A. Macaddino, VP-Audit
Doug D. Betts, Sr. VP-Quality
Alistair Gardner, Pres.
Reid Bigland, Head-U.S. Sales
Steven G. Beahm, Sr. VP-Supply Chain Mgmt.

GROWTH PLANS/SPECIAL FEATURES:

Stellantis North America (formerly FCA US LLC) is the U.S. automotive division of Stellantis NV. Based in Michigan, Stellantis North America designs, engineers, manufactures and sells vehicles under the Chrysler, Jeep, Dodge and RAM brand. The company also distributes the Alfa Romeo model and Mopar parts and accessories. Stellantis North America operates manufacturing plants throughout the U.S. Engineering breakthroughs made by the company include: Uconnect, which allows drivers to easily adjust seat or cabin temperature, select a new music station or make a call without taking their eyes from the road; various fuel efficiency features in relation to power, transmissions, engines and electrified propulsion systems; and design, development and vehicle integration of technologies in relation to customer safety and security. In early-2021, parent Fiat Chrysler Automobiles merged with Groupe PSA, with the combined entity's new name becoming Stellantis NV, based in the Netherlands. As a result of the merger, FCA US LLC was renamed Stellantis North America.

FINANCIAL DATA: *Note: Data for latest year may not have been available at press time.*

In U.S. $	2021	2020	2019	2018	2017	2016
Revenue	78,969,046,400	74,090,200,000	82,149,600,000	83,960,000,000	80,855,800,000	73,958,900,000
R&D Expense						
Operating Income						
Operating Margin %						
SGA Expense						
Net Income						
Operating Cash Flow						
Capital Expenditure						
EBITDA						
Return on Assets %						
Return on Equity %						
Debt to Equity						

CONTACT INFORMATION:

Phone: 248-576-5741 Fax:
Toll-Free: 800-992-1997
Address: 1000 Chrysler Dr., Auburn Hills, MI 48326-2766 United States

STOCK TICKER/OTHER:

Stock Ticker: Subsidiary
Exchange:
Employees: 91,289
Fiscal Year Ends: 12/31
Parent Company: Stellantis NV

SALARIES/BONUSES:

Top Exec. Salary: $ Bonus: $
Second Exec. Salary: $ Bonus: $

OTHER THOUGHTS:

Estimated Female Officers or Directors: 3
Hot Spot for Advancement for Women/Minorities: Y

Stellantis NV

NAIC Code: 336111

www.stellantis.com/en

TYPES OF BUSINESS:

Automobile Manufacturing
Mobility Solutions
Vehicles
Car Sharing
Vehicle Rental
Vehicle Leasing
Finance

BRANDS/DIVISIONS/AFFILIATES:

PSA Groupe
Fiat Chrysler Automobiles
Chrysler
Fiat
Maserati
Vauxhall
Free2Move
Leasys SpA

CONTACTS: *Note: Officers with more than one job title may be intentionally listed here more than once.*

Richard K. Palmer, CFO
Guillaume Faury, Exec. VP-R&D
Pierre Todorov, Corp. Sec.
Denis Martin, Exec. VP-Industrial Oper.
Yves Bonnefont, Exec. VP-Strategy
Jonathan Goodman, Exec. VP-Corp. Comm.
Olivier Sartoris, Investors Rel. Mgr.
Frederic Saint-Geours, VP-Finance
Frederic Saint Geours, Exec. VP-Brands
Christian Peugeot, Exec. VP- Public Affairs & External Rel.
Carlos Gomes, Sr. VP-Latin America
Bernd Schantz, Sr. VP- Russia, Ukraine & CIS
Gregoire Olivier, Exec. VP-Asia
Yannick Bezard, VP-Purchasing

GROWTH PLANS/SPECIAL FEATURES:

Stellantis NV was formed on Jan. 16, 2021, from the merger of Fiat Chrysler Automobiles and PSA Group. The combination of the two companies created the world's fourth- largest automaker, with 14 automobile brands. For 2020, we calculate that pro forma Stellantis would have had sales volume of 5.9 million vehicles and EUR 132.8 billion in revenue, albeit substantially affected by COVID-19. We see limited geographic overlap as Fiat Chrysler's major markets were North America, Italy, and Brazil, while PSA Group's major markets were France, the United Kingdom, Germany, and Argentina.

FINANCIAL DATA: *Note: Data for latest year may not have been available at press time.*

In U.S. $	2021	2020	2019	2018	2017	2016
Revenue		97,886,990,000	122,180,300,000	124,693,100,000	125,282,600,000	125,377,500,000
R&D Expense		3,364,315,000	4,079,190,000	3,445,628,000	3,647,780,000	3,697,471,000
Operating Income		2,522,954,000	5,597,028,000	5,682,858,000	8,175,320,000	5,512,327,000
Operating Margin %						
SGA Expense		6,212,520,000	7,289,914,000	8,264,538,000	8,340,204,000	8,546,873,000
Net Income		32,750,970	7,478,515,000	4,074,672,000	3,942,539,000	2,036,207,000
Operating Cash Flow		10,370,760,000	11,815,190,000	11,234,710,000	11,728,240,000	11,964,270,000
Capital Expenditure		9,712,356,000	9,469,548,000	6,089,421,000	9,786,893,000	9,955,164,000
EBITDA		8,290,513,000	11,748,560,000	11,939,420,000	15,021,400,000	12,006,050,000
Return on Assets %						
Return on Equity %						
Debt to Equity						

CONTACT INFORMATION:

Phone: 3120-3421707 Fax:
Toll-Free:
Address: Singaporestraat 92-100, Lijnden, 1175 RA Netherlands

STOCK TICKER/OTHER:

Stock Ticker: STLA
Employees: 281,595
Parent Company:
Exchange: NYS
Fiscal Year Ends: 12/31

SALARIES/BONUSES:

Top Exec. Salary: $1,225,709 Bonus: $
Second Exec. Salary: $1,158,076 Bonus: $

OTHER THOUGHTS:

Estimated Female Officers or Directors: 3
Hot Spot for Advancement for Women/Minorities: Y

STMicroelectronics NV

NAIC Code: 334413

www.st.com

TYPES OF BUSINESS:

Semiconductor Manufacturing
Integrated Circuits
Transistors & Diodes

GROWTH PLANS/SPECIAL FEATURES:

A merger between Italian firm SGS Microelettronica and the nonmilitary business of Thomson Semiconductors in France formed STMicroelectronics in 1987. STMicro is a leader in a variety of semiconductor products, including analog chips, discrete power semiconductors, microcontrollers, and sensors. STMicro is an especially prominent chip supplier into the industrial and automotive industries.

BRANDS/DIVISIONS/AFFILIATES:

BeSpoon

CONTACTS: *Note: Officers with more than one job title may be intentionally listed here more than once.*

Jean-Marc Chery, CEO
Lorenzo Grandi, CFO
Marco Cassis, Global Sales, Mktg. & Communications
Rajita D'Souza, Human Resources & Corp. Social Responsibility
Orio Belleza, Exec. VP-Front-End Mfg. & Tech. R&D
Orio Bellezz, Technology & Manufacturing
Pierre Ollivier, General Counsel
Mario Arlati, Exec. VP-Strategies & Bus. Dev.
George Penalver, Chief Strategy Officer
Lorenzo Grandi, Financial Controller
Otto Kosgalwies, Exec. VP-Infrastructure & Svcs.
Fabio Gualandris, Corp. VP-Product Quality Excellence
Bob Krysiak, Pres., Americas
Francois Guibert, Pres., Greater China & South Asia
Paul Grimme, Pres., EMEA
Marco Cassis, Pres., Japan & Korea

FINANCIAL DATA: *Note: Data for latest year may not have been available at press time.*

In U.S. $	2021	2020	2019	2018	2017	2016
Revenue		10,219,000,000	9,556,000,000	9,664,000,000	8,347,000,000	6,973,000,000
R&D Expense		1,548,000,000	1,498,000,000	1,398,000,000	1,302,000,000	1,336,000,000
Operating Income		1,363,000,000	1,237,000,000	1,418,000,000	1,047,000,000	302,000,000
Operating Margin %						
SGA Expense		1,109,000,000	1,093,000,000	1,095,000,000	983,000,000	911,000,000
Net Income		1,106,000,000	1,032,000,000	1,287,000,000	802,000,000	165,000,000
Operating Cash Flow		2,093,000,000	1,869,000,000	1,845,000,000	1,707,000,000	1,039,000,000
Capital Expenditure		1,358,000,000	1,250,000,000	1,313,000,000	1,372,000,000	653,000,000
EBITDA		2,244,000,000	2,097,000,000	2,234,000,000	1,655,000,000	937,000,000
Return on Assets %						
Return on Equity %						
Debt to Equity						

CONTACT INFORMATION:

Phone: 41 229292929 Fax: 41 229292988
Toll-Free:
Address: 39, Chemin du Champ des FillesPlan-Les-Ouates, Geneva, CH1228 Switzerland

STOCK TICKER/OTHER:

Stock Ticker: STM
Exchange: NYS
Employees: 43,480
Fiscal Year Ends: 12/31
Parent Company:

SALARIES/BONUSES:

Top Exec. Salary: $856,837 Bonus: $1,285,378
Second Exec. Salary: $ Bonus: $

OTHER THOUGHTS:

Estimated Female Officers or Directors: 1
Hot Spot for Advancement for Women/Minorities: Y

Subaru Corporation

www.subaru.co.jp/en

NAIC Code: 336111

TYPES OF BUSINESS:

Automobile Manufacturing
Aircraft Manufacturing & Components
Heavy-Duty Engines & Equipment
Sanitation Vehicles
Specialty Vehicles
Waste Treatment, Recycling & Alternative Energy Technologies
Industrial Robotics

BRANDS/DIVISIONS/AFFILIATES:

Legacy
Forester
Boxer Engine
Flying Forward Observation System
T-5
Subaru Bell 412EPX
AH-64D
Ascent

GROWTH PLANS/SPECIAL FEATURES:

Subaru Corp is a Japan-based company engaged in the automobile manufacturing business. The company is split into three segments: Automotive Business Unit, Aerospace Company, and Other Businesses. The Automotive Business, which constitutes the vast majority of the company's revenue, manufactures, repairs, and sells passenger cars and their components under the Subaru brand. The Aerospace Company includes airplanes and aerospace-related machinery and components. The Other Businesses segment consists of Industrial product, and real estate lease, among others. A vast majority of the sales is derived from North America.

CONTACTS: *Note: Officers with more than one job title may be intentionally listed here more than once.*

Tomomi Nakamura, CEO
Yasuyuki Yoshinaga, Chmn.

FINANCIAL DATA: *Note: Data for latest year may not have been available at press time.*

In U.S. $	2021	2020	2019	2018	2017	2016
Revenue	24,869,160,000	29,384,810,000	27,771,550,000	29,921,800,000	29,225,620,000	28,401,970,000
R&D Expense	915,231,400	812,449,400				
Operating Income	901,444,500	1,850,040,000	1,718,121,000	3,334,215,000	3,609,802,000	4,969,851,000
Operating Margin %						
SGA Expense	2,459,202,000	2,708,402,000				
Net Income	672,296,200	1,340,788,000	1,298,830,000	1,936,259,000	2,481,055,000	3,836,895,000
Operating Cash Flow	2,542,758,000	1,846,455,000	1,528,997,000	3,218,674,000	3,035,411,000	5,397,490,000
Capital Expenditure	1,691,707,000	1,881,032,000				
EBITDA	2,897,859,000	3,680,934,000	2,630,127,000	3,522,029,000	4,237,057,000	6,102,070,000
Return on Assets %						
Return on Equity %						
Debt to Equity						

CONTACT INFORMATION:

Phone: 81-3 6447-8000 Fax: 81-3 6447-8184
Toll-Free:
Address: 1-20-8, Ebisu, Shibuya-ku, Tokyo, 150-8554 Japan

STOCK TICKER/OTHER:

Stock Ticker: FUJHF
Employees: 36,070
Parent Company:
Exchange: PINX
Fiscal Year Ends: 03/31

SALARIES/BONUSES:

Top Exec. Salary: $ Bonus: $
Second Exec. Salary: $ Bonus: $

OTHER THOUGHTS:

Estimated Female Officers or Directors:
Hot Spot for Advancement for Women/Minorities:

Sumitomo Electric Industries Ltd

www.sei.co.jp

NAIC Code: 336320

TYPES OF BUSINESS:

Motor Vehicle Electrical and Electronic Equipment Manufacturing
Cable Manufacturing
Insulated Electrical Wiring
Electrical Apparatus and Related Equipment Wholesalers
Internet of Things

BRANDS/DIVISIONS/AFFILIATES:

Sumiden Wire Products Corporation
Sumitomo Electric Device Innovations USA Inc
Sumidenso do Brasil Industrias Eletricas Ltda
SEWS Canada Ltd
Sumitomo Electric Hardmetal de Mexico SA de CV

GROWTH PLANS/SPECIAL FEATURES:

Sumitomo Electric Industries Ltd manufactures and sells electric wires and cables, and other products. The company is engaged in diversified business activities supporting people's daily lives and industry through five business segments: Automotive, Infocommunications, Electronics, Environment and Energy, and Industrial Materials and Others. The Automobile-related segment offers wire harnesses, rubber cushions, hoses for automobiles, automobile electrical parts and others. Sumitomo's Information Communications-related segment offers fiber-optic cables, electrical cables and equipment for communications use, optical communications-related parts and others. It derives most of the revenue from Japan.

CONTACTS: *Note: Officers with more than one job title may be intentionally listed here more than once.*

Masayoshi Matsumoto, CEO
Osamu Inoue, Pres.
Masayoshi Matsumoto, Chmn.

FINANCIAL DATA: *Note: Data for latest year may not have been available at press time.*

In U.S. $	2021	2020	2019	2018	2017	2016
Revenue	25,645,670,000	27,301,560,000	27,925,070,000	27,083,820,000	24,730,970,000	25,773,160,000
R&D Expense						
Operating Income	1,001,072,000	1,117,852,000	1,460,933,000	1,521,379,000	1,322,475,000	1,260,729,000
Operating Margin %						
SGA Expense						
Net Income	495,096,800	638,993,300	1,037,424,000	1,057,327,000	945,151,200	799,629,200
Operating Cash Flow	1,490,774,000	2,325,120,000	1,561,070,000	2,105,137,000	1,838,538,000	2,115,734,000
Capital Expenditure	1,465,950,000	1,694,791,000	1,564,497,000	1,510,940,000	1,539,225,000	1,408,641,000
EBITDA	2,503,708,000	2,682,515,000	2,981,802,000	3,009,516,000	2,681,180,000	2,592,976,000
Return on Assets %						
Return on Equity %						
Debt to Equity						

CONTACT INFORMATION:

Phone: 81 662204141   Fax: 81 662223380
Toll-Free:
Address: 4-5-33, Kitahama, Osaka, 541-0041 Japan

STOCK TICKER/OTHER:

Stock Ticker: SMTOF   Exchange: PINX
Employees: 286,784   Fiscal Year Ends: 03/31
Parent Company:

SALARIES/BONUSES:

Top Exec. Salary: $ Bonus: $
Second Exec. Salary: $ Bonus: $

OTHER THOUGHTS:

Estimated Female Officers or Directors:
Hot Spot for Advancement for Women/Minorities:

Suzuki Motor Corporation

www.globalsuzuki.com

NAIC Code: 336111

TYPES OF BUSINESS:

Automobile Manufacturing
Motorcycles
ATVs
Marine Products
Wheelchairs
Industrial Equipment

BRANDS/DIVISIONS/AFFILIATES:

Suzuki Auto Parts Mfg Co Ltd
Snic Co Ltd
Suzuki Akita Auto Parts Mfg Co Ltd
Celerio
Suzuki Toyama Auto Parts Mgf Co Ltd
Suzuki Transportation & Packing Co Ltd
Suzuki Engineering Co Ltd
Suzuki Finance Co Ltd

GROWTH PLANS/SPECIAL FEATURES:

Suzuki Motor Corp is a Japanese automobile manufacturing company. Suzuki organises itself into three segments based on product type: automobile, motorcycle, and Marine business. The automotive business, which contributes the vast majority of revenue, largely focuses on passenger vehicles. The motorcycle business manufactures on- and off-road motorcycles and scooters, and contributes the next- largest portion of sales. The Marine business business manufactures four-stroke mators for marine use. Nearly half of consolidated revenue is derived from Asian countries excluding Japan, with a third of sales made domestically.

CONTACTS: *Note: Officers with more than one job title may be intentionally listed here more than once.*

Toshihiro Suzuki, CEO
Minoru Tamura, Exec. VP
Osamu Honda, Exec. VP
Toshihiro Suzuki, Exec. VP
Yasuhito Harayama, Exec. VP
Osamu Suzuki, Chmn.

FINANCIAL DATA: *Note: Data for latest year may not have been available at press time.*

In U.S. $	2021	2020	2019	2018	2017	2016
Revenue	27,927,040,000	30,652,990,000	34,018,980,000	33,014,820,000	27,850,880,000	27,948,570,000
R&D Expense						
Operating Income	1,708,490,000	1,889,819,000	2,850,216,000	3,287,951,000	2,343,371,000	1,716,179,000
Operating Margin %						
SGA Expense						
Net Income	1,286,607,000	1,179,414,000	1,570,762,000	1,895,627,000	1,405,539,000	1,025,096,000
Operating Cash Flow	3,650,478,000	1,507,267,000	3,369,275,000	3,911,734,000	3,218,823,000	2,584,223,000
Capital Expenditure	1,508,787,000	2,160,073,000	2,210,001,000	1,808,847,000	1,687,586,000	1,428,544,000
EBITDA	3,361,428,000	3,653,123,000	3,967,848,000	4,771,906,000	4,071,632,000	3,693,429,000
Return on Assets %						
Return on Equity %						
Debt to Equity						

CONTACT INFORMATION:

Phone: 81-53-440-2061 Fax:
Toll-Free:
Address: 300 Takatsuka-cho, Minami-ku, Hamamatsu, 432-8611 Japan

STOCK TICKER/OTHER:

Stock Ticker: SZKMF
Employees: 68,739
Parent Company:
Exchange: PINX
Fiscal Year Ends: 03/31

SALARIES/BONUSES:

Top Exec. Salary: $ Bonus: $
Second Exec. Salary: $ Bonus: $

OTHER THOUGHTS:

Estimated Female Officers or Directors:
Hot Spot for Advancement for Women/Minorities:

Swisscom AG

www.swisscom.ch/en/residential.html

NAIC Code: 517110

TYPES OF BUSINESS:

Integrated Telecommunications Services
Internet Service Provider
Value-added Services
Mobile Phone Service
Local & Long-Distance Service
IT & Outsourcing Services
5G

BRANDS/DIVISIONS/AFFILIATES:

Swisscom Switzerland
Fastweb
www.bluewin.ch
CT Cinetrade AG

GROWTH PLANS/SPECIAL FEATURES:

Swisscom is the incumbent telephone operator in Switzerland. It dominates both the broadband and wireless market segments, with a 58% wireless postpaid share and 53% fixed broadband share, a level that dwarfs other developed countries' incumbent operators. Swisscom has also 37% market share in pay television. The firm owns Fastweb, an alternative telecom operator in Italy, offering fixed-line telephone, broadband, and wireless services. It holds a 16% market share in fixed broadband and 2% mobile market share.

CONTACTS: *Note: Officers with more than one job title may be intentionally listed here more than once.*

Urs Schaeppi, CEO
Eugen Stermetz, CFO
Klementina Pejic, Human Resources
Christoph Aeschlimann, IT
Jurgen Galler, Head-Strategy & Innovation
Bart Morselt, Head-Investor Rel.
Mario Rossi, Head-Group Bus. Steering
Michael Rechsteiner, Chmn.
Urs Schaeppi, Head-Switzerland

FINANCIAL DATA: *Note: Data for latest year may not have been available at press time.*

In U.S. $	2021	2020	2019	2018	2017	2016
Revenue		12,027,700,000	12,410,200,000	12,693,010,000	12,636,670,000	12,616,080,000
R&D Expense						
Operating Income		2,067,463,000	2,060,962,000	2,233,251,000	2,302,599,000	2,325,354,000
Operating Margin %						
SGA Expense		404,173,900	512,531,600	548,289,500	577,546,100	902,619,000
Net Income		1,657,872,000	1,811,739,000	1,654,621,000	1,701,215,000	1,738,056,000
Operating Cash Flow		4,409,072,000	4,313,717,000	4,030,904,000	4,432,910,000	4,184,771,000
Capital Expenditure		2,370,865,000	2,589,747,000	2,604,917,000	2,576,744,000	2,617,920,000
EBITDA		4,720,058,000	4,653,960,000	4,555,354,000	4,653,960,000	4,689,718,000
Return on Assets %						
Return on Equity %						
Debt to Equity						

CONTACT INFORMATION:

Phone: 4.1058221991e+11 Fax:
Toll-Free:
Address: Alte Tiefenaustrasse 6, Bern, CH-3050 Switzerland

STOCK TICKER/OTHER:

Stock Ticker: SWZCF
Employees: 18,905
Parent Company:
Exchange: PINX
Fiscal Year Ends: 12/31

SALARIES/BONUSES:

Top Exec. Salary: $ Bonus: $
Second Exec. Salary: $ Bonus: $

OTHER THOUGHTS:

Estimated Female Officers or Directors: 2
Hot Spot for Advancement for Women/Minorities: Y

Symbio Group (The)

www.symbio.com

NAIC Code: 541512

TYPES OF BUSINESS:

Software Development Outsourcing
Digital Services
Software Product Development
Outsourced Testing
Globalization
Technical Support
Customer Support
Training

BRANDS/DIVISIONS/AFFILIATES:

VXI Global Solutions LLC

CONTACTS:

Note: Officers with more than one job title may be intentionally listed here more than once.

David Zhou, CEO-VXI Global Solutions LLC
Chris Kalaboukis, CTO-US
Rajeev Kumar, VP-Bus. Dev.
Henry Tang, Managing Dir.-Asia Pacific
Baogue Zhou, COO-Asia Pacific
Anders Lindstrom, Managing Dir.-Sweden
Jarkko Kemppainen, CTO-Europe
Jouni Toijala, Managing Dir.-Finland

GROWTH PLANS/SPECIAL FEATURES:

The Symbio Group is a global digital services company that helps businesses build innovative software products and transformative digital services that connect and engage their customers. Symbio's services encompass digital transformation, agile, DevOps, quality assurance, testing, globalization and localization. Digital transformation services include innovation, design thinking, mobile, web, user experience (UX), embedded development, cloud, edge computing, artificial intelligence (AI), Internet of Things (IoT) and customer experience (CX). Products and solutions by Symbio include automotive infotainment, smart safety, smart storage, mobile payments, dashboard reporting, workforce management and workplace training. Symbio primarily serves the automotive, banking, finance, insurance, high-tech, travel, hospitality, media and entertainment industries. Headquartered in California, USA, the firm has domestic locations throughout North America, as well as international locations in Finland, Sweden, China and Taiwan. Symbio is a subsidiary of VXI Global Solutions LLC.

FINANCIAL DATA:

Note: Data for latest year may not have been available at press time.

In U.S. $	2021	2020	2019	2018	2017	2016
Revenue						
R&D Expense						
Operating Income						
Operating Margin %						
SGA Expense						
Net Income						
Operating Cash Flow						
Capital Expenditure						
EBITDA						
Return on Assets %						
Return on Equity %						
Debt to Equity						

CONTACT INFORMATION:

Phone: 408-996-9700 Fax: 408-966-9722
Toll-Free:
Address: 2055 Gateway Place, Ste. 350, San Jose, CA 95110 United States

STOCK TICKER/OTHER:

Stock Ticker: Subsidiary
Exchange:
Employees: 1,400
Fiscal Year Ends:
Parent Company: VXI Global Solutions LLC

SALARIES/BONUSES:

Top Exec. Salary: $ Bonus: $
Second Exec. Salary: $ Bonus: $

OTHER THOUGHTS:

Estimated Female Officers or Directors:
Hot Spot for Advancement for Women/Minorities:

Symphony Technology Group

NAIC Code: 511210H

www.stgpartners.com

TYPES OF BUSINESS:

Enterprise Management Software
Investments
Innovative Software
Data
Analytics

BRANDS/DIVISIONS/AFFILIATES:

Cadmium
Dodge Construction Network
Escalent
JobRapido
Personica
Symphony Talent
STG Exited Investments
Onclusive

CONTACTS:
Note: Officers with more than one job title may be intentionally listed here more than once.

Marc Bala, Managing Dir.
Stephen Henkenmeier, CFO
Ravindar Chahal, Dir.-IT & Security
Chris Langone, VP-Bus. Dev.
Mattias Derynck, VP-Investor Rel.
Stephen Combs, Chief Recruiting Officer
William Chisholm, Managing Dir.
Pallab Chatterjee, Managing Dir.
J.T.Treadwell, Managing Dir.
Mahinder Mathrani, Managing Dir.-STG India

GROWTH PLANS/SPECIAL FEATURES:

Symphony Technology Group (STG) is a private equity firm with a focus on innovative software, data and analytics to mid-market companies. STG seeks to find, transform and build technology companies in partnership with their management teams. STG's global portfolio of companies include Cadmium, Dodge Construction Network, Escalent, ExtendaRetail, JobRapido, Nomis, Personica, Poplicus, Redseal, RSA, I-Sciforma, Symphony Talent, Traceone and STG Exited Investments. In January 2022, STG acquired Kanta Reputation Intelligence, PRgloo and Onclusive, which will merge to form a new standalone company under the Onclusive name and will provide clients with media monitoring, measurement and workflow management solutions.

FINANCIAL DATA:
Note: Data for latest year may not have been available at press time.

In U.S. $	2021	2020	2019	2018	2017	2016
Revenue	3,000,000,000	2,998,125,000	2,925,000,000	2,900,000,000	2,800,000,000	2,750,000,000
R&D Expense						
Operating Income						
Operating Margin %						
SGA Expense						
Net Income						
Operating Cash Flow						
Capital Expenditure						
EBITDA						
Return on Assets %						
Return on Equity %						
Debt to Equity						

CONTACT INFORMATION:

Phone: 650-935-9500 Fax: 650-935-9501
Toll-Free:
Address: 1300 El Camino Real, Ste. 300, Menlo Park, CA 94025 United States

STOCK TICKER/OTHER:

Stock Ticker: Private
Employees: 15,250
Parent Company:
Exchange:
Fiscal Year Ends: 12/31

SALARIES/BONUSES:

Top Exec. Salary: $ Bonus: $
Second Exec. Salary: $ Bonus: $

OTHER THOUGHTS:

Estimated Female Officers or Directors:
Hot Spot for Advancement for Women/Minorities:

Taiwan Semiconductor Manufacturing Co Ltd (TSMC)

www.tsmc.com

NAIC Code: 334413

TYPES OF BUSINESS:

Contract Manufacturing-Semiconductors
Assembly & Testing Services
CAD Software Products

BRANDS/DIVISIONS/AFFILIATES:

WaferTech LLC
TSMC China Company Limited
TSMC Nanjing Company Limited
Global Unichip Corporation
Xintec Inc
Systems on Silicon Manufacturing Co Pty Ltd
Vanguard International Semiconductor Corp
VisEra Technologies Company Ltd

CONTACTS: *Note: Officers with more than one job title may be intentionally listed here more than once.*

C.C. Wei, CEO
Wendell Huang, CFO
Connie Ma, VP-Human Resources
Wei-Jen Lo, VP-R&D
J.K. Lin, CIO
Jack Sun, CTO
Y.P. Chin, VP-Prod. Dev.
Richard Thurston, General Counsel
M.C. Tzeng, VP-Oper.
Irene Sun, VP-Corp. Planning Organization
Rick Tsai, Chmn.
Burn J. Lin, VP-R&D
Y.J. Mii, VP-R&D
N.S. Tsai, VP-Quality & Reliability
Mark Liu, Chmn.
Rick Cassidy, VP

GROWTH PLANS/SPECIAL FEATURES:

Taiwan Semiconductor Manufacturing Company, or TSMC, is the world's largest dedicated chip foundry, with over 58% market share in 2020 per Gartner. TSMC was founded in 1987 as a joint venture of Philips, the government of Taiwan, and private investors. It went public as an ADR in the U.S. in 1997. TSMC's scale and high-quality technology allow the firm to generate solid operating margins, even in the highly competitive foundry business. Furthermore, the shift to the fabless business model has created tailwinds for TSMC. The foundry leader has an illustrious customer base, including Apple and Nvidia, that looks to apply cutting-edge process technologies to its semiconductor designs.

TSMC offers employees health, fitness, incentive and employee assistance plans; and tuition reimbursement.

FINANCIAL DATA: *Note: Data for latest year may not have been available at press time.*

In U.S. $	2021	2020	2019	2018	2017	2016
Revenue		48,268,500,000	38,564,270,000	37,172,080,000	35,228,740,000	34,164,310,000
R&D Expense		3,946,067,000	3,294,890,000	3,095,828,000	2,909,741,000	2,566,450,000
Operating Income		20,427,880,000	13,456,180,000	13,877,970,000	13,935,800,000	13,620,590,000
Operating Margin %						
SGA Expense		1,282,020,000	1,012,261,000	946,229,300	979,225,500	926,143,200
Net Income		18,408,110,000	12,756,910,000	13,085,050,000	12,434,340,000	11,955,540,000
Operating Cash Flow		29,650,330,000	22,170,680,000	20,686,320,000	21,095,890,000	19,456,590,000
Capital Expenditure		18,794,850,000	16,930,690,000	11,630,030,000	12,106,010,000	12,005,280,000
EBITDA		33,106,240,000	24,508,290,000	24,982,000,000	23,774,400,000	22,095,620,000
Return on Assets %						
Return on Equity %						
Debt to Equity						

CONTACT INFORMATION:

Phone: 886 35636688 Fax: 866 35637000
Toll-Free:
Address: No. 8, Li-Hsin Rd. 6, Hsinchu Science Park, Hsinchu, 300 Taiwan

STOCK TICKER/OTHER:

Stock Ticker: TSM
Employees: 44,050
Parent Company:
Exchange: NYS
Fiscal Year Ends: 12/31

SALARIES/BONUSES:

Top Exec. Salary: $3,553,717 Bonus: $55,219,570
Second Exec. Salary: $378,438 Bonus: $14,712,240

OTHER THOUGHTS:

Estimated Female Officers or Directors: 4
Hot Spot for Advancement for Women/Minorities: Y

Tanium Inc

www.tanium.com

NAIC Code: 511210E

TYPES OF BUSINESS:

Computer Software: Network Security, Managed Access, Digital ID, Cybersecurity & Anti-Virus
Security Software
Management Systems Solutions
Endpoint Data
Asset Discovery
Risk and Compliance Management
Threat Detection
Sensitive Data Monitoring

BRANDS/DIVISIONS/AFFILIATES:

GROWTH PLANS/SPECIAL FEATURES:

Tanium, Inc. is a security and management systems provider with a mission to help organizations manage and protect their mission-critical networks. Tanium's solutions are designed for every workflow that relies on endpoint data. These solutions include asset discovery and inventory, risk and compliance management, threat hunting, client management and sensitive data monitoring. With these solutions, teams can manage and protect mission-critical networks in real-time. Industries served by Tanium include the federal government, state and local governments, higher education, financial services, retail and healthcare.

CONTACTS: *Note: Officers with more than one job title may be intentionally listed here more than once.*

Orion Hindawi, CEO
Bina Chaurasia, Chief Admin. Officer
Marc Levin, CFO
Steve Daheb, CMO
Charles Ross, Chief Customer Officer
Christian Hunt, Sr. VP-Engineering
David Hindawi, Chmn.

FINANCIAL DATA: *Note: Data for latest year may not have been available at press time.*

In U.S. $	2021	2020	2019	2018	2017	2016
Revenue	625,000,000	500,000,000	430,000,000	230,000,000	200,000,000	60,000,000
R&D Expense						
Operating Income						
Operating Margin %						
SGA Expense						
Net Income						
Operating Cash Flow						
Capital Expenditure						
EBITDA						
Return on Assets %						
Return on Equity %						
Debt to Equity						

CONTACT INFORMATION:

Phone: 510-704-0202 Fax:
Toll-Free:
Address: 3550 Carillon Point, Kirkland, WA 98033 United States

STOCK TICKER/OTHER:

Stock Ticker: Private
Employees: 1,700
Parent Company:
Exchange:
Fiscal Year Ends: 01/31

SALARIES/BONUSES:

Top Exec. Salary: $ Bonus: $
Second Exec. Salary: $ Bonus: $

OTHER THOUGHTS:

Estimated Female Officers or Directors:
Hot Spot for Advancement for Women/Minorities:

Tata Consultancy Services Limited (TCS)

www.tcs.com

NAIC Code: 541512

TYPES OF BUSINESS:

IT Consulting
Software Engineering
Business Process Outsourcing
Research
Consulting Services
Software Development
Artificial Intelligence
Big Data

BRANDS/DIVISIONS/AFFILIATES:

Tata Group
Tata America International Corporation
Tata Consultancy Services Asia Pacific Pte Ltd
Diligenta Limited
TCS e-Serve International Limited
TCS BaNCS

CONTACTS: *Note: Officers with more than one job title may be intentionally listed here more than once.*

Rajesh Gopinathan, CEO
N.G. Subramaniam, COO
Samir Seksaria, CFO
Milind Lakkad, Exec. VP-Global Human Resources
N. Chandrasekaran, Chmn.

GROWTH PLANS/SPECIAL FEATURES:

Tata Consultancy Services Limited (TCS) is one of India's largest consulting companies and one of Asia's largest independent software and services organizations, with a presence in more than 45 countries. The firm is part of the Tata Group, an Asian conglomerate with interests in energy, telecommunications, financial services, chemicals, engineering and materials. TCS primarily provides IT consulting, services and business process outsourcing (BPO) for international businesses. TCS' services include application development and maintenance, business intelligence, enterprise solutions, assurance services, engineering and industrial services, infrastructure services, consulting, asset leveraged solutions and business process services. The company focuses on software engineering practices and standards as well as research and development in software engineering and technology. Its TCS BaNCS core banking software suite is used by retail banks, and includes functions for universal banking, core banking, payments, wealth management, foreign exchange, compliance and many more operations. Technologies by TCS span the fields of artificial intelligence (AI), automation, blockchain, big data, cloud, cyber security and Internet of Things (IoT). The firm has formed alliances with leading technology companies, academic institutions and consulting firms to provide customers with expertise in technology fields in which it does not specialize. Development of new strategies and technologies occurs in TCS' global centers of excellence, located in several nations. TCS has offices throughout North America (with a regional headquarter in New York City), four of which are development centers and centers of excellence. A few of the company's many subsidiaries include Tata America International Corporation, Tata Consultancy Services Asia Pacific Pte Limited in Singapore, Diligenta Limited in the UK and TCS e-Serve International Limited in India.

FINANCIAL DATA: *Note: Data for latest year may not have been available at press time.*

In U.S. $	2021	2020	2019	2018	2017	2016
Revenue	22,803,318,123	21,470,898,933	23,219,300,000	19,090,000,000	18,094,166,016	16,664,653,824
R&D Expense						
Operating Income						
Operating Margin %						
SGA Expense						
Net Income	4,437,972,666	4,312,628,111	4,663,800,000	4,730,000,000	4,032,327,168	3,725,990,656
Operating Cash Flow						
Capital Expenditure						
EBITDA						
Return on Assets %						
Return on Equity %						
Debt to Equity						

CONTACT INFORMATION:

Phone: 91-22-6778-9595 Fax: 91-22-6630-3672
Toll-Free:
Address: Fl. 9, Nirmal Bldg., Nariman Point, Mumbai, 400 021 India

STOCK TICKER/OTHER:

Stock Ticker: 532540
Employees: 488,000
Parent Company: Tata Group
Exchange: Bombay
Fiscal Year Ends: 03/31

SALARIES/BONUSES:

Top Exec. Salary: $ Bonus: $
Second Exec. Salary: $ Bonus: $

OTHER THOUGHTS:

Estimated Female Officers or Directors:
Hot Spot for Advancement for Women/Minorities:

Tata Motors Limited

NAIC Code: 336111

www.tatamotors.com

TYPES OF BUSINESS:

Automobile Manufacturing
Light & Medium Commercial Vehicles Manufacturing
Heavy Commercial Vehicles Manufacturing
Passenger Vehicles Manufacturing

GROWTH PLANS/SPECIAL FEATURES:

Tata Motors owns iconic brands Jaguar and Land Rover, while offering a broad product line of motor vehicles including compact passenger cars, sport utility vehicles, luxury passenger vehicles and large semi trucks. At 45%, it holds the largest market share of commercial vehicles in India. Tata also operates a financial services business, which supports vehicle sales.

BRANDS/DIVISIONS/AFFILIATES:

Tata Group
Jaguar Land Rover Automotive plc
Tata Motors European Technical Centre plc
Tata Motors Insurance Broking and Advisory
TMF Holdings Limited
TML Distribution Company Limited
Tata Altroz
Tata Safari

CONTACTS: *Note: Officers with more than one job title may be intentionally listed here more than once.*

Guenter Butschek, CEO
P.B. Balaji, CFO
Thomas Flack, Chief Purchasing Officer
Ravindra Kumar, Chief Human Resources Officer
Rajendra Petkar, CTO
Rajesh Bagga, VP-Legal
Ravindra Pisharody, Pres., Commercial Vehicles
S.B. Borwankar, Exec. Dir.
Ravi Kant, Vice Chmn.
N. Chandrasekaran, Chmn.
Venkatram Mamillapalle, Sr. VP

FINANCIAL DATA: *Note: Data for latest year may not have been available at press time.*

In U.S. $	2021	2020	2019	2018	2017	2016
Revenue	33,064,220,000	34,564,710,000	39,886,300,000	38,411,230,000	35,394,030,000	35,939,320,000
R&D Expense	696,372,900	558,056,800	562,864,000	470,571,500	454,809,700	462,164,400
Operating Income	-1,023,930,000	-2,683,669,000	-2,705,908,000	-1,542,038,000	-852,124,200	371,536,000
Operating Margin %						
SGA Expense	4,385,330,000	5,167,601,000	5,823,866,000	5,271,695,000	4,992,292,000	5,056,905,000
Net Income	-1,901,287,000	-1,518,093,000	-3,905,710,000	888,160,400	815,543,000	1,277,510,000
Operating Cash Flow	3,863,906,000	3,548,461,000	2,516,924,000	3,178,662,000	4,038,474,000	4,992,519,000
Capital Expenditure	2,692,082,000	3,957,374,000	4,703,693,000	4,673,768,000	4,084,977,000	4,151,662,000
EBITDA	2,581,461,000	2,276,275,000	-396,633,600	4,822,119,000	4,299,193,000	4,534,979,000
Return on Assets %						
Return on Equity %						
Debt to Equity						

CONTACT INFORMATION:

Phone: 91-22-66658282 Fax:
Toll-Free:
Address: Homi Mody St., Bombay House, 24, Mumbai, 400 001 India

STOCK TICKER/OTHER:

Stock Ticker: TTM
Employees: 75,278
Parent Company: Tata Group
Exchange: NYS
Fiscal Year Ends: 03/31

SALARIES/BONUSES:

Top Exec. Salary: $3,647,930 Bonus: $
Second Exec. Salary: $1,100,368 Bonus: $

OTHER THOUGHTS:

Estimated Female Officers or Directors:
Hot Spot for Advancement for Women/Minorities:

TCI International Inc

www.tcibr.com

NAIC Code: 334220

TYPES OF BUSINESS:

Transmission, Receiving & Test Equipment
Spectrum Monitoring & Management Systems
Broadcast & Communication Antennas
Communication Intelligence
Direction Finding Systems
System Software

BRANDS/DIVISIONS/AFFILIATES:

SPX Corporation
Blackbird

CONTACTS: *Note: Officers with more than one job title may be intentionally listed here more than once.*

Gene Lowe, CEO-SPX Corp

GROWTH PLANS/SPECIAL FEATURES:

TCI International, Inc. is a systems engineering and manufacturing company that specializes in spectrum monitoring, signal collection, radio frequency (RF) solutions and radio direction finding solutions, primarily targeting the government, military, civilian and intelligence markets. The company, a subsidiary of SPX Corporation, designs, manufactures, sells and installs high frequency (HF) and medium frequency (MF) broadcast antennas, HF communications antennas and monitoring antennas. The antennas are designed to capture signals from 9 kilohertz (kHz) to 43 gigahertz (GHz). The firm builds and optimizes its antennas for various applications including spectrum monitoring, direction finding (DF), drone detection, signal interception, radio broadcasting and radio communications. TCI also makes computer-controlled radio frequency (RF) distribution systems that interface between multiple-element antenna arrays and communications receivers; specialized receivers for communications, DF/monitoring and COMINT/SIGINT applications; high-speed 32-bit digital signal processors, which deliver signal analysis by simultaneously scanning, detecting, measuring and analyzing RF signals at rates up to 4 GHz per second; and application-specific software to provide real-time control, data processing, digital signal processing, database structures, graphical user interfaces and network management services. TCI's next-generation Blackbird system combines TCI's modular, scalable RF hardware platform and DF/geolocation technology with second-generation Blackbird software, all designed for NextGen automation, smart recording and ease of use. The firm offers installation, training and services in over 105 countries.

FINANCIAL DATA: *Note: Data for latest year may not have been available at press time.*

In U.S. $	2021	2020	2019	2018	2017	2016
Revenue	1,536,311,000	1,449,350,000	1,414,000,000	1,400,000,000		
R&D Expense						
Operating Income						
Operating Margin %						
SGA Expense						
Net Income						
Operating Cash Flow						
Capital Expenditure						
EBITDA						
Return on Assets %						
Return on Equity %						
Debt to Equity						

CONTACT INFORMATION:

Phone: 510-687-6100 Fax: 510-687-6101
Toll-Free:
Address: 3541 Gateway Blvd., Fremont, CA 94538 United States

STOCK TICKER/OTHER:

Stock Ticker: Subsidiary
Exchange:
Employees: 72
Fiscal Year Ends: 09/30
Parent Company: SPX Corporation

SALARIES/BONUSES:

Top Exec. Salary: $ Bonus: $
Second Exec. Salary: $ Bonus: $

OTHER THOUGHTS:

Estimated Female Officers or Directors:
Hot Spot for Advancement for Women/Minorities:

TDS Telecommunications LLC

NAIC Code: 517110

www.tdstelecom.com

TYPES OF BUSINESS:

Mobile Phone and Wireless Services
Local Telephone Service
Long-Distance Service
Internet Access

BRANDS/DIVISIONS/AFFILIATES:

Telephone and Data Systems Inc (TDS)
TDS Broadband Service LLC
BendBroadband

CONTACTS: *Note: Officers with more than one job title may be intentionally listed here more than once.*

Jim Butman, CEO
Michelle Brukwicki, CFO
Mike Pandow, Sr. VP-Admin.
Mark Barber, VP-Cable Oper.
Vicki L. Villacrez, VP-Finance
Phil LaForge, Pres., TDS Hosted & Managed Svcs.
Kevin Hess, Sr. VP-Gov't & Regulatory Affairs

GROWTH PLANS/SPECIAL FEATURES:

TDS Telecommunications, LLC (TDS Telecom), a wholly-owned subsidiary of Telephone and Data Systems, Inc., is a telecommunications service company that provides voice, internet and entertainment services to rural and suburban communities nationwide. TDS Telecom provides high-speed internet, phone and TV entertainment services to customers in nearly 1,000 rural, suburban and metropolitan communities. The company deploys up to 1Gig internet access, IPTV services, cable TV options and traditional wireline services. For businesses, TDS Telecom offers advanced communications solutions such as voice over internet protocol (VoIP), high-speed internet, fiber optics, data networking and hosted-managed services. Subsidiary TDS Broadband Service, LLC serves the cable industry within the U.S. states of Arizona, Colorado, Nevada, New Mexico, Utah and Texas. Its cable operations offer businesses metro Ethernet, passive optical network technology, hosted private branch exchange (PBX), carrier backhaul and transport solutions. Subsidiary BendBroadband offers internet, cable TV and telephone services in the state of Oregon.

TDS Telecom offers its employees medical, dental, vision and life insurance; a 401(k) plan; a pension plan; an employee stock purchase plan; flexible spending accounts; education assistance; telephone and Internet discounts; and training and development p

FINANCIAL DATA: *Note: Data for latest year may not have been available at press time.*

In U.S. $	2021	2020	2019	2018	2017	2016
Revenue	1,000,000,000	976,000,000	930,000,000	927,000,000	919,000,000	1,151,000,000
R&D Expense						
Operating Income						
Operating Margin %						
SGA Expense						
Net Income		100,000,000	92,000,000	89,000,000	138,000,000	42,000,000
Operating Cash Flow						
Capital Expenditure						
EBITDA						
Return on Assets %						
Return on Equity %						
Debt to Equity						

CONTACT INFORMATION:

Phone: 608-664-4000 Fax: 608-664-4035
Toll-Free: 866-571-6662
Address: 525 Junction Rd., Madison, WI 53717 United States

STOCK TICKER/OTHER:

Stock Ticker: Subsidiary Exchange:
Employees: 2,700 Fiscal Year Ends: 12/31
Parent Company: Telephone and Data Systems Inc (TDS)

SALARIES/BONUSES:

Top Exec. Salary: $ Bonus: $
Second Exec. Salary: $ Bonus: $

OTHER THOUGHTS:

Estimated Female Officers or Directors:
Hot Spot for Advancement for Women/Minorities:

TE Connectivity Ltd

www.te.com

NAIC Code: 334417

TYPES OF BUSINESS:

Electronic Components and Connectors
Network Infrastructure Components
Application Tooling Manufacturing
Internet of Things
Sensors Manufacturing
Wire & Cable Manufacturing

GROWTH PLANS/SPECIAL FEATURES:

TE Connectivity is the largest electrical connector supplier in the world, supplying interconnect and sensor solutions to the transportation, industrial, and communications markets. With operations in 150 countries and over 500,000 stock-keeping units, TE Connectivity has a broad portfolio that forms the electrical architecture of its end customers' cutting-edge innovations.

BRANDS/DIVISIONS/AFFILIATES:

CONTACTS: *Note: Officers with more than one job title may be intentionally listed here more than once.*

Terrence R. Curtin, CEO
Joel Dubs, Sr. VP-Operations
Health Mitts, CFO
Kari Janavitz, CMO
Tim Murphy, Sr. VP-Global Human Resources
Phil Gilchrist, VP
Rob Shaddock, CTO
John S. Jenkins, Jr., General Counsel
Brad Gambill, Sr. VP-Strategy & Bus. Dev.
Amy Shah, Sr. VP-Comm.
Keith Kolstrom, VP-Investor Rel.
Joan Wainwright, Pres., Channel & Customer Experience
Terrence Curtin, Pres., Industrial Solutions
James O'Toole, Pres., Consumer Solutions
Steven Merkt, Pres., Transportation Solutions
Tom. Lynch, Chmn.
Jenny Wang, Sr. VP-China

FINANCIAL DATA: *Note: Data for latest year may not have been available at press time.*

In U.S. $	2021	2020	2019	2018	2017	2016
Revenue	14,923,000,000	12,172,000,000	13,448,000,000	13,988,000,000	13,113,000,000	12,238,000,000
R&D Expense	677,000,000	613,000,000	644,000,000	680,000,000	658,000,000	644,000,000
Operating Income	2,698,000,000	1,730,000,000	2,260,000,000	2,471,000,000	2,201,000,000	1,926,000,000
Operating Margin %						
SGA Expense	1,512,000,000	1,392,000,000	1,490,000,000	1,594,000,000	1,591,000,000	1,463,000,000
Net Income	2,261,000,000	-241,000,000	1,844,000,000	2,565,000,000	1,683,000,000	2,009,000,000
Operating Cash Flow	2,676,000,000	1,992,000,000	2,422,000,000	2,451,000,000	2,321,000,000	1,922,000,000
Capital Expenditure	690,000,000	560,000,000	749,000,000	935,000,000	702,000,000	628,000,000
EBITDA	3,203,000,000	1,283,000,000	2,689,000,000	3,014,000,000	2,693,000,000	1,874,000,000
Return on Assets %						
Return on Equity %						
Debt to Equity						

CONTACT INFORMATION:

Phone: 41-52-633-6661 Fax:
Toll-Free:
Address: Muhlenstrasse 26, Schaffhausen, 8200 Switzerland

STOCK TICKER/OTHER:

Stock Ticker: TEL
Employees: 89,000
Parent Company:
Exchange: NYS
Fiscal Year Ends: 09/30

SALARIES/BONUSES:

Top Exec. Salary: $1,200,000 Bonus: $
Second Exec. Salary: $673,111 Bonus: $

OTHER THOUGHTS:

Estimated Female Officers or Directors: 5
Hot Spot for Advancement for Women/Minorities: Y

Tech Mahindra Limited

NAIC Code: 541512

www.techmahindra.com

TYPES OF BUSINESS:

IT Consulting
Information Technology
Consulting
Cloud
Data Analytics
Business Process
Customer Experience
Automation

BRANDS/DIVISIONS/AFFILIATES:

Information Technology Solutions and Services
Global Systems Integration
Consulting Services
Next-Generation Technologies
Cloud Solutions
Data Analytics
Artificial Intelligence
Blockchain

CONTACTS: *Note: Officers with more than one job title may be intentionally listed here more than once.*

C.P. Gurnani, Managing Dir.
Milind Kulkarni, CFO
Harshvendra Soin, Chief People Officer & Dir.-Mktg.
Manoj Chugh, Global Head-Bus. Dev.
Vineet Nayyar, Vice Chmn.
Rakesh Soni, COO-Enterprise Div.
Amitava Roy, COO-Telecom Div., Europe
L. Ravichandran, COO-Telecom Div., Americas

GROWTH PLANS/SPECIAL FEATURES:

Tech Mahindra Limited is an India-based firm that offers information technology (IT), global systems integration and related consulting services. The firm serves customers worldwide across a wide range of industries, including banking/financial services, insurance, communication, media/entertainment, energy, utilities, healthcare, life sciences, high-tech, manufacturing, public sector, government, retail, consumer goods, travel, transportation, logistics and professional services. Tech Mahindra's NXT.NOW offers next-generation technologies that power its solutions to meet client's current and future business goals, including cloud, data analytics, 5G, artificial intelligence (AI), blockchain and cybersecurity. Services by Tech Mahindra include infrastructure and cloud services, network services, integrated engineering services, SAP, data analytics, customer experience, experience design, testing services, performance engineering, Oracle, AI, digital supply chain, business process services, business, excellence services, telecommunications product engineering, intelligent automation and more.

Tech Mahindra offers its employees a range of insurance coverage, and financial and on-the-job support, which may differ by location.

FINANCIAL DATA: *Note: Data for latest year may not have been available at press time.*

In U.S. $	2021	2020	2019	2018	2017	2016
Revenue	5,266,680,000	5,058,680,000	4,682,390,000	4,438,145,024	4,202,759,168	3,821,059,840
R&D Expense						
Operating Income						
Operating Margin %						
SGA Expense						
Net Income	57,747,500	518,015,000	616,455,000	548,016,640	405,683,488	449,685,760
Operating Cash Flow						
Capital Expenditure						
EBITDA						
Return on Assets %						
Return on Equity %						
Debt to Equity						

CONTACT INFORMATION:

Phone: 9120-4225-0000 Fax: 9120-4225-2501
Toll-Free:
Address: Plot No. 1, Phase III, Rajiv Gandhi Infotech Park,, Pune, 411057 India

STOCK TICKER/OTHER:

Stock Ticker: 532755
Employees: 121,000
Parent Company: Mahindra Group
Exchange: Bombay
Fiscal Year Ends: 03/31

SALARIES/BONUSES:

Top Exec. Salary: $ Bonus: $
Second Exec. Salary: $ Bonus: $

OTHER THOUGHTS:

Estimated Female Officers or Directors: 1
Hot Spot for Advancement for Women/Minorities:

Telecom Italia SpA

www.gruppotim.it/en.html

NAIC Code: 517110

TYPES OF BUSINESS:

Local Telephone Service
Mobile Communications Services
Internet Access
Data Communications Services
IT Products & Services
Media & TV Broadcasting

GROWTH PLANS/SPECIAL FEATURES:

Telecom Italia is the incumbent telephone operator in Italy with more than 30% market share in the Italian mobile market and 45% market share in broadband. In the mobile market it competes with Vodafone, Wind Tre and Iliad. On the broadband side, its main competitor is Open Fiber, which operates a wholesale network giving equal access to several operators. TIM also has a 21% wireless market share in Brazil and has started building a broadband network in the country, although its reach is very small compared with its competitors Telefonica and America Movil.

BRANDS/DIVISIONS/AFFILIATES:

Vivendi SA
TIM SpA
Gruppo TIM
Telecom Italia Sparkle SpA
Olivetti
INWIT SpA

CONTACTS: *Note: Officers with more than one job title may be intentionally listed here more than once.*

Luigi Gubitosi, CEO
Piergiorgio Peluso, Head-Admin.
Antonino Cusimano, Head-Legal Affairs
Oscar Cicchetti, Head-Strategy
Franco Brescia, Head-Public & Regulatory Affairs
Piergiorgio Peluso, Head-Finance & Control
Simone Battiferri, Head-Bus.
Stefano De Angelis, CEO-Telecom Argentina
Alessandro Talotta, Head-National Wholesale Svcs.
Paolo Vantellini, Head-Bus. Support Office
Salvatore Rossi, Chmn.
Rodrigo Abreu, CEO-TIM Participacoes

FINANCIAL DATA: *Note: Data for latest year may not have been available at press time.*

In U.S. $	2021	2020	2019	2018	2017	2016
Revenue		17,849,280,000	20,298,820,000	21,389,770,000	22,392,630,000	21,485,760,000
R&D Expense						
Operating Income		3,067,298,000	4,335,551,000	4,189,865,000	4,963,466,000	4,768,090,000
Operating Margin %						
SGA Expense						
Net Income		8,158,379,000	1,034,479,000	-1,593,504,000	1,265,994,000	2,041,853,000
Operating Cash Flow		7,398,331,000	6,701,526,000	5,185,947,000	6,097,327,000	6,444,035,000
Capital Expenditure		5,304,527,000	4,120,975,000	5,117,057,000	6,001,333,000	5,260,483,000
EBITDA		8,191,131,000	9,123,968,000	5,382,452,000	8,710,628,000	9,729,296,000
Return on Assets %						
Return on Equity %						
Debt to Equity						

CONTACT INFORMATION:

Phone: 39-06-36-881 Fax:
Toll-Free:
Address: Corso D'Italia, 41, Rome, 00198 Italy

STOCK TICKER/OTHER:

Stock Ticker: TIIAY
Employees: 51,929
Parent Company:
Exchange: PINX
Fiscal Year Ends: 12/31

SALARIES/BONUSES:

Top Exec. Salary: $1,027,703 Bonus: $
Second Exec. Salary: $525,000 Bonus: $

OTHER THOUGHTS:

Estimated Female Officers or Directors: 1
Hot Spot for Advancement for Women/Minorities:

Telefonica SA

NAIC Code: 517110

www.telefonica.com

TYPES OF BUSINESS:

Fixed Line & Mobile Telecommunications
Internet Access Service
Data Service
Digital Media

GROWTH PLANS/SPECIAL FEATURES:

Telefonica operates mobile and fixed networks in Spain (where it is the incumbent telephone operator), U.K., Germany, Brazil, and other Latin American countries. The company derives approximately 30% of its revenue from Spain and 20%, 15%, and 15% from Germany, U.K., and Brazil, respectively. In Latin America, Telefonica also operates in Mexico, Argentina, Chile, Peru, and others.

BRANDS/DIVISIONS/AFFILIATES:

Telefonica Espana
Telefonica UK
Telefonica Deutschland
Telefonica Brasil
Telefonica HispanoAmerica
Telefonica
Movistar
O2

CONTACTS: *Note: Officers with more than one job title may be intentionally listed here more than once.*

Jose Maria Alvarez-Pallette, CEO
Angel Vila, COO
Laura Abasolo, CFO
Marta Machicot, Chief People Officer
Enrique Blanco, CTO
Ramiro Sanchez de Lerin Garcia-Ovies, General Counsel
Angel Vila Voix, Gen. Mgr.-Corp. Dev.
Angel Vila Voix, Gen. Mgr.-Finance
Guillermo Ansaldo Lutz, Gen. Mgr.-Global Resources
Matthew Key, Chmn.-Telefonica Digital
Eduardo Navarro, Gen. Mgr.-Strategy & Alliances
Eva Castillo, CEO-Telefonica Europe
Jose Maria Alvarez-Pallette, Chmn.
Santiago Fernandez Valbuena, Chmn.-Telefonica Latin America

FINANCIAL DATA: *Note: Data for latest year may not have been available at press time.*

In U.S. $	2021	2020	2019	2018	2017	2016
Revenue		48,647,610,000	54,685,080,000	54,991,130,000	58,734,910,000	58,766,530,000
R&D Expense						
Operating Income		5,342,925,000	4,111,941,000	7,504,489,000	7,516,912,000	6,095,069,000
Operating Margin %						
SGA Expense		6,063,447,000	10,255,570,000	9,522,627,000	10,324,460,000	11,779,060,000
Net Income		1,786,622,000	1,289,711,000	3,761,844,000	3,537,105,000	2,675,415,000
Operating Cash Flow						
Capital Expenditure		7,927,993,000	8,649,644,000	9,695,416,000	10,155,060,000	10,375,280,000
EBITDA		16,216,250,000	18,176,790,000	19,548,940,000	19,600,890,000	19,616,700,000
Return on Assets %						
Return on Equity %						
Debt to Equity						

CONTACT INFORMATION:

Phone: 34 914823734 Fax: 34 914823768
Toll-Free:
Address: Distrito C, Ronda de la Comunicacion, Madrid, 28050 Spain

STOCK TICKER/OTHER:

Stock Ticker: TEF
Employees: 112,797
Parent Company:
Exchange: NYS
Fiscal Year Ends: 12/31

SALARIES/BONUSES:

Top Exec. Salary: $2,171,841 Bonus: $3,514,473
Second Exec. Salary: $1,806,950 Bonus: $2,436,672

OTHER THOUGHTS:

Estimated Female Officers or Directors: 1
Hot Spot for Advancement for Women/Minorities:

Telenor ASA

NAIC Code: 517210

www.telenor.com

TYPES OF BUSINESS:

Mobile Telephone Services
Fixed-Line Telephone Services
Cable Services
Satellite Communications
Satellite Television Broadcasting
Internet of Things

BRANDS/DIVISIONS/AFFILIATES:

Telenor Norway
Telenor Sweden
Telenor Denmark
DNA
dtac
Digi
Grameenphone
Telenor Pakistan

CONTACTS: *Note: Officers with more than one job title may be intentionally listed here more than once.*

Sigve Brekke, CEO
Tone Hegland Bachke, CFO
Cecilie Blydt Heuch, Chief People Officer
Ruza Sabanovic, CTO
Morten Karlsen Sorby, Head-Strategy & Regulatory Affairs
Rolv-Erik Spilling, Exec. VP
Hilde M. Tonne, Exec. VP
Berit Svendsen, Exec. VP
Bjorn Magnus Kopperud, Acting Head-Central & Eastern European Oper.
Gunn Waersted, Chmn.
Sigve Brekke, Head-Asia Oper.

GROWTH PLANS/SPECIAL FEATURES:

Telenor is an international provider of telecom, data, and media communication services. It is the incumbent dominant telecom operator in Norway and the Norwegian government holds an almost 54% stake in the firm. Telenor also operates in other Nordic countries and is an established player in faster-growing emerging markets. Telenor owns both fixed-line and mobile networks, though fixed-line services (telephony, Internet, TV, data services) provide around 10% of service revenue. The firm's fixed-line operations are in Sweden, Norway, Finland and Denmark. In the rest of its markets, Telenor offers only mobile services.

FINANCIAL DATA: *Note: Data for latest year may not have been available at press time.*

In U.S. $	2021	2020	2019	2018	2017	2016
Revenue		13,628,860,000	12,613,890,000	12,247,340,000	13,844,810,000	14,585,010,000
R&D Expense						
Operating Income		2,829,954,000	2,806,760,000	2,475,391,000	2,950,139,000	2,855,589,000
Operating Margin %						
SGA Expense		834,748,200	864,378,400	1,069,237,000	1,252,344,000	1,515,464,000
Net Income		1,924,404,000	862,602,800	1,634,762,000	1,329,804,000	314,279,100
Operating Cash Flow		4,862,892,000	3,797,761,000	4,038,797,000	4,666,023,000	4,414,333,000
Capital Expenditure		2,108,511,000	2,439,880,000	2,321,581,000	2,037,598,000	2,633,086,000
EBITDA		6,511,303,000	5,565,802,000	4,641,498,000	5,185,161,000	4,705,530,000
Return on Assets %						
Return on Equity %						
Debt to Equity						

CONTACT INFORMATION:

Phone: 47 81077000 Fax: 47 67890000
Toll-Free:
Address: Snaroyveien 30, Fornebu, N-1360 Norway

STOCK TICKER/OTHER:

Stock Ticker: TELNY
Employees: 19,000
Parent Company:
Exchange: PINX
Fiscal Year Ends: 12/31

SALARIES/BONUSES:

Top Exec. Salary: $ Bonus: $
Second Exec. Salary: $ Bonus: $

OTHER THOUGHTS:

Estimated Female Officers or Directors: 6
Hot Spot for Advancement for Women/Minorities: Y

Telenor Connexion AB

www.telenorconnexion.com

NAIC Code: 511210B

TYPES OF BUSINESS:

Computer Software: Network Management (IT), System Testing & Storage
Internet of Things
IoT Solutions and Services
IoT Development
Mobile Network Connectivity Solutions
Technology Innovation
IoT Cloud Services
IoT Testing Services

BRANDS/DIVISIONS/AFFILIATES:

Telenor ASA

CONTACTS:

Note: Officers with more than one job title may be intentionally listed here more than once.

Mats Lundquist, CEO
Robert Bellwaldius, COO
Lisa Hultin, CFO
Cristoff Martin, CMO
Karin Stenklef, Chief Human Resources Officer
Martin Whitlock, CTO

GROWTH PLANS/SPECIAL FEATURES:

Telenor Connexion AB, a subsidiary of Telenor ASA, designs and provides Internet of Things (IoT) services, enabling businesses to connect their products and services on a global scale across every vertical. Telenor Connexion helps customers design, implement and operate IoT solutions that connect devices, machines, people and places. The firm's connectivity is based on more than 500 mobile networks throughout the world and on technology. Each customer is offered an agile, dedicated, global IoT specialist with power, reach and support. Customer support is available 24/7/365. Telenor Connexion manages more than 10 million connections and is experienced in building and operating large-scale IoT solutions. IoT solutions include IoT connectivity, IoT cloud, IoT services and IoT testing services. Solutions are provided for industries including automotive, industrial manufacturing, transport and logistics, utilities and smart cities. Headquartered in Sweden, Telenor Connexion has sales representation in the U.K., the U.K., Germany, Italy, South Africa, Japan, Korea, China, Singapore and Malaysia. Partners of Telenor Connexion include Ericsson, GSMA, Capgemini, AWS, Salesforce and IoT World Alliance.

FINANCIAL DATA:

Note: Data for latest year may not have been available at press time.

In U.S. $	2021	2020	2019	2018	2017	2016
Revenue						
R&D Expense						
Operating Income						
Operating Margin %						
SGA Expense						
Net Income						
Operating Cash Flow						
Capital Expenditure						
EBITDA						
Return on Assets %						
Return on Equity %						
Debt to Equity						

CONTACT INFORMATION:

Phone: 46-8-410-338-00 Fax:
Toll-Free:
Address: Garvis Carlssons gata 3, Solna, 169 51 Sweden

STOCK TICKER/OTHER:

Stock Ticker: Subsidiary
Employees:
Parent Company: Telenor ASA
Exchange:
Fiscal Year Ends:

SALARIES/BONUSES:

Top Exec. Salary: $ Bonus: $
Second Exec. Salary: $ Bonus: $

OTHER THOUGHTS:

Estimated Female Officers or Directors:
Hot Spot for Advancement for Women/Minorities:

Telesat Corporation

www.telesat.com

NAIC Code: 334220

TYPES OF BUSINESS:

Satellite Communications Equipment Manufacturing
Satellites
Telecommunication Services
Global Connectivity Services
Teleports
Low-Earth Orbit Network
Geostationary Satellite Fleet

BRANDS/DIVISIONS/AFFILIATES:

Loral Space & Communications

GROWTH PLANS/SPECIAL FEATURES:

Telesat Corp is a global satellite operator, providing its customers with mission-critical communications services. The firm offers a state of the art global geostationary satellite fleet called Telesat Lightspeed comprised of 298 highly advanced low Earth orbit satellites. Telesat serves customers in the telecom, government, maritime and aeronautical sectors.

Telesat offers its employees comprehensive health benefits, retirement and pension plans, performance-based compensation and bonuses and company perks.

CONTACTS: *Note: Officers with more than one job title may be intentionally listed here more than once.*

Daniel S. Goldberg, CEO
Andrew Browne, CFO
Glenn Katz, CCO
David Wendling, CTO

FINANCIAL DATA: *Note: Data for latest year may not have been available at press time.*

In U.S. $	2021	2020	2019	2018	2017	2016
Revenue						
R&D Expense						
Operating Income						
Operating Margin %						
SGA Expense						
Net Income						
Operating Cash Flow						
Capital Expenditure						
EBITDA						
Return on Assets %						
Return on Equity %						
Debt to Equity						

CONTACT INFORMATION:

Phone: 613 748 8700 Fax:
Toll-Free:
Address: 160 Elgin St., Ste. 2100, Ottawa, ON K2P 2P7 Canada

STOCK TICKER/OTHER:

Stock Ticker: TSAT
Employees: 471
Parent Company:
Exchange: NAS
Fiscal Year Ends: 12/31

SALARIES/BONUSES:

Top Exec. Salary: $ Bonus: $
Second Exec. Salary: $ Bonus: $

OTHER THOUGHTS:

Estimated Female Officers or Directors:
Hot Spot for Advancement for Women/Minorities:

Telit Communications PLC

www.telit.com

NAIC Code: 517911

TYPES OF BUSINESS:

Wireless Telecommunications Resellers
Internet of Things
IoT Modules
IoT Software

BRANDS/DIVISIONS/AFFILIATES:

Telit deviceWISE
Telit secureWISE
simWISE

GROWTH PLANS/SPECIAL FEATURES:

Telit Communications PLC operates in the field of the Internet of Things (IoT). It has a portfolio of IoT products and services including wireless connectivity modules, global navigation satellite system, short-range wireless modules, IoT platforms, virtual cellular IoT operators and professional services. Its business segments include IoT Products and Cloud & Connectivity. The group is organized on a worldwide basis in three geographical segments: EMEA, APAC, and Americas, of which it generates most of its revenue from the Americas region. It serves Automotive and Transport, Energy and Utilities, Healthcare, Retail, Agriculture, Security and Surveillance and other industries.

CONTACTS: *Note: Officers with more than one job title may be intentionally listed here more than once.*

Paolo Dal Pino, CEO
Itzik Molcho, COO
Yariv Dafna, Pres.
Manish Watwani, CMO
Sharon Arad-Tzuk, VP-Human Resources
Carlos Perez, Pres.-Sales
Antonio Sgroi, Head-Global R&D

FINANCIAL DATA: *Note: Data for latest year may not have been available at press time.*

In U.S. $	2021	2020	2019	2018	2017	2016
Revenue		343,621,000	392,537,000	427,483,000	374,531,000	370,264,000
R&D Expense		43,937,000	46,687,000	72,985,000	66,870,000	38,256,000
Operating Income		14,352,000	11,929,000	-18,738,000	-28,277,000	21,218,000
Operating Margin %						
SGA Expense		64,807,000	74,043,000	85,112,000	95,426,000	93,844,000
Net Income		6,220,000	47,400,000	-36,360,000	-52,216,000	16,615,000
Operating Cash Flow		41,649,000	13,973,000	25,766,000	-4,814,000	47,651,000
Capital Expenditure		20,652,000	22,755,000	34,465,000	45,262,000	41,956,000
EBITDA		34,502,000	85,828,000	-3,122,000	-11,675,000	46,805,000
Return on Assets %						
Return on Equity %						
Debt to Equity						

CONTACT INFORMATION:

Phone: 39 040 4192 111 Fax:
Toll-Free:
Address: 90 High Holborn, 7/Fl, London, WC1V 6XX United Kingdom

STOCK TICKER/OTHER:

Stock Ticker: TTCNF
Exchange: PINX
Employees: 820
Fiscal Year Ends: 12/31
Parent Company:

SALARIES/BONUSES:

Top Exec. Salary: $250,000 Bonus: $1,000,000
Second Exec. Salary: $377,000 Bonus: $513,000

OTHER THOUGHTS:

Estimated Female Officers or Directors:
Hot Spot for Advancement for Women/Minorities:

Tellabs Inc

www.tellabs.com

NAIC Code: 334210

TYPES OF BUSINESS:

Wireline & Wireless Products & Services
Wireline Products and Services
Wireless Voice Products
Data Products
Video Services
Broadband Solutions
Fiber-based Innovation

BRANDS/DIVISIONS/AFFILIATES:

Marlin Equity Partners LLC

CONTACTS: *Note: Officers with more than one job title may be intentionally listed here more than once.*

Rich Schroder, CEO
Norm Burke, CFO
Karen Leos, VP-Global Sales
Tom Dobozy, VP-Engineering
James M. Sheehan, Chief Admin. Officer
James M. Sheehan, General Counsel
John M. Brots, Exec. VP-Global Oper.
Kenneth G. Craft, Exec. VP-Product Dev.

GROWTH PLANS/SPECIAL FEATURES:

Tellabs, Inc. provides products and services that enable customers to deliver wireline and wireless voice, data and video services to business and residential customers. The firm operates in two segments: enterprise and broadband. The enterprise segment offers a passive optical local area network (LAN) infrastructure, which is secure, scalable and sustainable. This division serves the business enterprise, federal government, hospitality, higher education, K-12 education, healthcare and transportation industries. The broadband segment offers solutions to service providers that deliver stability and scalability while increasing flexibility. These broadband solutions help telecommunications companies grow HSI (high-speed internet) subscribers, extend service area coverage and offer faster internet service speeds. They also enable Ethernet business services while continuing to support time-division multiplexing (TDM) and automated teller machine (ATM) services. Tellabs offers services such as technical support, professional network services and training. The company is an innovation leader in fiber-based technologies, with many first-to-market accomplishments and investments in fiber optic research and development innovations. Tellabs is a subsidiary of Marlin Equity Partners, LLC.

FINANCIAL DATA: *Note: Data for latest year may not have been available at press time.*

In U.S. $	2021	2020	2019	2018	2017	2016
Revenue	1,640,000,000	1,610,256,375	1,533,577,500	1,460,550,000	1,391,000,000	1,372,000,000
R&D Expense						
Operating Income						
Operating Margin %						
SGA Expense						
Net Income						
Operating Cash Flow						
Capital Expenditure						
EBITDA						
Return on Assets %						
Return on Equity %						
Debt to Equity						

CONTACT INFORMATION:

Phone: 972-588-7000 Fax:
Toll-Free:
Address: 4240 International Pkwy, St. 105, Carrollton, TX 75007 United States

STOCK TICKER/OTHER:

Stock Ticker: Private
Exchange:
Employees: 9,400
Fiscal Year Ends: 12/31
Parent Company: Marlin Equity Partners LLC

SALARIES/BONUSES:

Top Exec. Salary: $ Bonus: $
Second Exec. Salary: $ Bonus: $

OTHER THOUGHTS:

Estimated Female Officers or Directors: 1
Hot Spot for Advancement for Women/Minorities: Y

Telstra Corporation Limited

www.telstra.com.au

NAIC Code: 517110

TYPES OF BUSINESS:

Wireless & Wireline Telephony Services
Telecommunications
Communications Technology
Mobile
Broadband
Contract Management
5G

BRANDS/DIVISIONS/AFFILIATES:

GROWTH PLANS/SPECIAL FEATURES:

Telstra is Australia's largest telecommunications entity, with material market shares in voice, mobile, data and Internet, spanning retail, corporate and wholesale segments. Its fixed-line copper network will gradually be wound down as the government-owned National Broadband Network rolls out to all Australian households, but the group will be compensated accordingly. Investments into network applications and services, media, technology and overseas are being made to replace the expected lost fixed-line earnings longer term, while continuing cost-cuts are also critical.

CONTACTS: *Note: Officers with more than one job title may be intentionally listed here more than once.*

Andrew Penn, CEO
Vicki Brady, CFO
Kate McKenzie, Managing Dir.-Prod. & Innovation
Carmel Mulhern, General Counsel
Will Irving, Managing Dir.-Telstra Bus.
Tony Warren, Managing Dir.-Corp. Affairs
Andrew Keys, Acting Dir.-Investor Rel.
Andrew Penn, Managing Dir.-Finance
Paul Geason, Group Managing Dir.-Enterprise & Govt
Damien Coleman, Sec.
Gordon Ballantyne, Chief Customer Officer
Stuart Lee, Managing Dir.-Telstra Wholesale
Timothy Y. Chen, Pres.

FINANCIAL DATA: *Note: Data for latest year may not have been available at press time.*

In U.S. $	2021	2020	2019	2018	2017	2016
Revenue	15,004,750,000	16,268,840,000	18,049,580,000	18,586,940,000	18,588,370,000	18,515,480,000
R&D Expense						
Operating Income	1,041,143,000	578,095,200	1,840,758,000	2,293,802,000	3,086,985,000	4,028,802,000
Operating Margin %						
SGA Expense	3,717,960,000	4,052,383,000	5,206,430,000	5,450,817,000	5,311,473,000	4,983,481,000
Net Income	1,326,975,000	1,299,821,000	1,539,205,000	2,546,049,000	2,780,431,000	4,130,272,000
Operating Cash Flow						
Capital Expenditure	2,243,781,000	2,459,584,000	3,122,715,000	3,524,308,000	3,802,280,000	2,996,948,000
EBITDA	5,472,253,000	6,481,241,000	5,875,277,000	7,290,860,000	7,729,612,000	7,539,534,000
Return on Assets %						
Return on Equity %						
Debt to Equity						

CONTACT INFORMATION:

Phone: 61 883081721 Fax: 61 396323215
Toll-Free:
Address: 242 Exhibition St., Level 41, Melbourne, VIC 3000 Australia

STOCK TICKER/OTHER:

Stock Ticker: TLSYY
Exchange: PINX
Employees: 27,015
Fiscal Year Ends: 06/30
Parent Company:

SALARIES/BONUSES:

Top Exec. Salary: $ Bonus: $
Second Exec. Salary: $ Bonus: $

OTHER THOUGHTS:

Estimated Female Officers or Directors: 6
Hot Spot for Advancement for Women/Minorities: Y

Telular Corporation

www.telular.com

NAIC Code: 334220

TYPES OF BUSINESS:

Fixed Wireless Terminals
Wireless Security Products
GPS Products

BRANDS/DIVISIONS/AFFILIATES:

AMETEK Inc
SkyBitz
Telguard

CONTACTS: *Note: Officers with more than one job title may be intentionally listed here more than once.*

Joseph A. Beatty, Pres.
Christopher Bear, VP-Prod. Dev.
George S. Brody, Sr. VP
Henry Popplewell, Sr. VP
Pat Barron, VP
David A. Zapico, Chmn.-AMETEK

GROWTH PLANS/SPECIAL FEATURES:

Telular Corporation designs, develops and distributes products and services that utilize wireless networks to provide data and voice connectivity among people and machines. The company's strategy consists of leveraging domain expertise to identify opportunities for Internet of Things (IoT) solutions to enterprise scale problems. Once identified, Telular utilizes hardware derived from internal designs that connect into the appropriate Telular analytics cloud via a wide range of connectivity options. The firm then rolls the solution out to targeted industries with the goal of delivering a one-year return on investment for customers. Examples for this strategy include trailer tracking, remote oilfield, intermodal asset tracking, local fleet telematics, petroleum logistics, industrial tank monitoring, residential security/home automation, commercial security, fire and personal emergency response systems. Connectivity partners include AT&T, Verizon, Telefonica, Iridium, Inmarsat, Globalstar and Rogers. Ecosystem partners include Sierra Wireless, Salesforce, CISCO Jasper, Windows Azure and Telit. Telular's own brands include: SkyBitz, offering asset tracking and information management services and solutions; and Telguard, offering home security and automation solutions. Telular is a subsidiary of AMETEK, Inc., a global manufacturer of electronic instruments and electromechanical devices.

FINANCIAL DATA: *Note: Data for latest year may not have been available at press time.*

In U.S. $	2021	2020	2019	2018	2017	2016
Revenue	167,310,000	160,875,000	165,000,000	152,500,000	150,000,000	145,000,000
R&D Expense						
Operating Income						
Operating Margin %						
SGA Expense						
Net Income						
Operating Cash Flow						
Capital Expenditure						
EBITDA						
Return on Assets %						
Return on Equity %						
Debt to Equity						

CONTACT INFORMATION:

Phone: 312 379-8397 Fax: 312 379-8310
Toll-Free: 800-835-8527
Address: 200 S. Wacker Dr., Ste. 1800, Chicago, IL 60606 United States

STOCK TICKER/OTHER:

Stock Ticker: Subsidiary
Employees: 155
Parent Company: AMETEK Inc
Exchange:
Fiscal Year Ends: 09/30

SALARIES/BONUSES:

Top Exec. Salary: $ Bonus: $
Second Exec. Salary: $ Bonus: $

OTHER THOUGHTS:

Estimated Female Officers or Directors:
Hot Spot for Advancement for Women/Minorities:

Tesla Inc

NAIC Code: 336111

www.teslamotors.com

TYPES OF BUSINESS:

Automobile Manufacturing, All-Electric
Battery Manufacturing
Lithium Ion Battery Storage Technologies
Energy Storage Systems
Automobile Manufacturing
Electric Vehicles

BRANDS/DIVISIONS/AFFILIATES:

Model S
Model X
Model 3
Model Y
Roadster
Tesla Semi
Tesla Cybertruck
Gigafactory

GROWTH PLANS/SPECIAL FEATURES:

Founded in 2003 and based in Palo Alto, California, Tesla is a vertically integrated sustainable energy company that also aims to transition the world to electric mobility by making electric vehicles. The company sells solar panels and solar roofs for energy generation plus batteries for stationary storage for residential and commercial properties including utilities. Tesla has multiple vehicles in its fleet, which include luxury and midsize sedans and crossover SUVs. The company also plans to begin selling more affordable sedans and small SUVs, a light truck, a semi truck, and a sports car. Global deliveries in 2020 were roughly 500,000 units.

CONTACTS: *Note: Officers with more than one job title may be intentionally listed here more than once.*

Elon Musk, CEO
Zachary Kirkhorn, CFO
Robyn Denholm, Chairman of the Board
Vaibhav Taneja, Chief Accounting Officer
Andrew Baglino, Senior VP, Divisional

FINANCIAL DATA: *Note: Data for latest year may not have been available at press time.*

In U.S. $	2021	2020	2019	2018	2017	2016
Revenue		31,536,000,000	24,578,000,000	21,461,270,000	11,758,750,000	7,000,132,000
R&D Expense		1,491,000,000	1,343,000,000	1,460,370,000	1,378,073,000	834,408,000
Operating Income		1,994,000,000	80,000,000	-252,840,000	-1,632,086,000	-667,340,000
Operating Margin %						
SGA Expense		3,145,000,000	2,646,000,000	2,834,491,000	2,476,500,000	1,432,189,000
Net Income		690,000,000	-862,000,000	-976,091,000	-1,961,400,000	-674,914,000
Operating Cash Flow		5,943,000,000	2,405,000,000	2,097,802,000	-60,654,000	-123,829,000
Capital Expenditure		3,242,000,000	1,437,000,000	2,319,516,000	4,081,354,000	1,440,471,000
EBITDA		4,224,000,000	2,174,000,000	1,559,376,000	-101,770,000	399,561,000
Return on Assets %						
Return on Equity %						
Debt to Equity						

CONTACT INFORMATION:

Phone: 650 681-5000 Fax:
Toll-Free:
Address: 3500 Deer Creek Rd., Palo Alto, CA 94304 United States

STOCK TICKER/OTHER:

Stock Ticker: TSLA
Employees: 70,757
Parent Company:
Exchange: NAS
Fiscal Year Ends: 12/31

SALARIES/BONUSES:

Top Exec. Salary: $301,154 Bonus: $
Second Exec. Salary: $301,154 Bonus: $

OTHER THOUGHTS:

Estimated Female Officers or Directors: 1
Hot Spot for Advancement for Women/Minorities:

TESSCO Technologies Incorporated

www.tessco.com

NAIC Code: 423430

TYPES OF BUSINESS:

Wireless Communications Products Distributor
Technology Distribution
Base Station Infrastructure
Network Systems
Installation
Testing

BRANDS/DIVISIONS/AFFILIATES:

GROWTH PLANS/SPECIAL FEATURES:

Tessco Technologies Inc is the United States-based value-added technology distributor, manufacturer, and solutions provider. The company supplies wireless communications products for network infrastructure, site support, fixed and mobile broadband networks. It offers products related to power systems, Wi-Fi Networks, Broadband, DAS((Distributed Antenna Systems) for In-Building Cellular and Public Safety Coverage, IoT (Internet of Things), Mobile Devices and Accessories, and others. The operating segments of the company are Commercial and Retail, of which the majority of the revenue is derived from the Commercial segment. The Commercial segment consists of the public carriers and value-added resellers and integrators. All the business activities are functioned through the United States.

TESSCO offers its employees health and retirement benefits, life and disability insurance, product discounts and other assistance plans and programs.

CONTACTS: *Note: Officers with more than one job title may be intentionally listed here more than once.*

Sandip Mukerjee, CEO
Aric Spitulnik, Chief Accounting Officer
Joseph Cawley, Chief Information Officer
Douglas Rein, Senior VP, Divisional

FINANCIAL DATA: *Note: Data for latest year may not have been available at press time.*

In U.S. $	2021	2020	2019	2018	2017	2016
Revenue	373,340,700	540,298,300	606,813,800	580,274,700	533,295,100	530,682,100
R&D Expense						
Operating Income	-17,791,500	-15,991,700	8,145,000	7,901,700	3,351,500	9,033,600
Operating Margin %						
SGA Expense	85,507,100	107,814,700	113,213,700	112,326,700	108,416,300	102,932,300
Net Income	-8,742,900	-21,568,900	5,545,800	5,195,400	1,445,100	5,340,500
Operating Cash Flow	-684,200	908,200	8,246,700	-9,247,100	3,051,270	20,141,110
Capital Expenditure	11,855,900	6,845,700	5,164,700	3,539,400	2,563,000	3,513,813
EBITDA	-14,047,000	-24,131,300	11,763,900	11,894,300	6,783,800	13,763,600
Return on Assets %						
Return on Equity %						
Debt to Equity						

CONTACT INFORMATION:

Phone: 410 229-1000 Fax: 410 527-0005
Toll-Free:
Address: 11126 McCormick Rd., Hunt Valley, MD 21031 United States

STOCK TICKER/OTHER:

Stock Ticker: TESS
Employees: 589
Parent Company:
Exchange: NAS
Fiscal Year Ends: 03/31

SALARIES/BONUSES:

Top Exec. Salary: $550,000 Bonus: $
Second Exec. Salary: $345,000 Bonus: $

OTHER THOUGHTS:

Estimated Female Officers or Directors:
Hot Spot for Advancement for Women/Minorities:

Texas Instruments Incorporated

www.ti.com

NAIC Code: 334413

TYPES OF BUSINESS:

Chips-Digital Signal Processors
Semiconductors
Calculators
Educational Software
Power Management Products
Broadband RF/IF & Digital Radio
MEMS
Microcontrollers (MCU)

BRANDS/DIVISIONS/AFFILIATES:

GROWTH PLANS/SPECIAL FEATURES:

Dallas-based Texas Instruments generates about 95% of its revenue from semiconductors and the remainder from its well-known calculators. Texas Instruments is the world's largest maker of analog chips, which are used to process real-world signals such as sound and power. Texas Instruments also has a leading market share position in digital signal processors, used in wireless communications, and microcontrollers used in a wide variety of electronics applications.

CONTACTS: *Note: Officers with more than one job title may be intentionally listed here more than once.*

Richard Templeton, CEO
Cynthia Trochu, Sr. VP
Rafael Lizardi, CFO
Julie Knecht, Chief Accounting Officer
Haviv Ilan, COO
Julie Van Haren, Senior VP
Ahmad Bahai, Senior VP
Darla Whitaker, Senior VP
Bing Xie, Senior VP
Hagop Kozanian, Senior VP
Kyle Flessner, Senior VP
Amichai Ron, Senior VP
Mark Gary, Senior VP
Ellen Barker, Senior VP

FINANCIAL DATA: *Note: Data for latest year may not have been available at press time.*

In U.S. $	2021	2020	2019	2018	2017	2016
Revenue		14,461,000,000	14,383,000,000	15,784,000,000	14,961,000,000	13,370,000,000
R&D Expense		1,530,000,000	1,544,000,000	1,559,000,000	1,508,000,000	1,370,000,000
Operating Income		6,116,000,000	5,975,000,000	7,034,000,000	6,531,000,000	5,103,000,000
Operating Margin %						
SGA Expense		1,623,000,000	1,645,000,000	1,684,000,000	1,694,000,000	1,767,000,000
Net Income		5,595,000,000	5,017,000,000	5,580,000,000	3,682,000,000	3,595,000,000
Operating Cash Flow		6,139,000,000	6,649,000,000	7,189,000,000	5,363,000,000	4,614,000,000
Capital Expenditure		649,000,000	847,000,000	1,131,000,000	695,000,000	531,000,000
EBITDA		7,199,000,000	6,948,000,000	7,765,000,000	7,062,000,000	5,965,000,000
Return on Assets %						
Return on Equity %						
Debt to Equity						

CONTACT INFORMATION:

Phone: 972 995-3773 Fax: 972 995-4360
Toll-Free: 800-336-5236
Address: 12500 TI Blvd., Dallas, TX 75266-0199 United States

STOCK TICKER/OTHER:

Stock Ticker: TXN
Employees: 30,000
Parent Company:
Exchange: NAS
Fiscal Year Ends: 12/31

SALARIES/BONUSES:

Top Exec. Salary: $1,336,667 Bonus: $
Second Exec. Salary: $779,167 Bonus: $

OTHER THOUGHTS:

Estimated Female Officers or Directors: 3
Hot Spot for Advancement for Women/Minorities: Y

Textron Inc

www.textron.com

NAIC Code: 336411

TYPES OF BUSINESS:

Helicopters & General Aviation Aircraft Manufacturing
Aerospace
Electrical Test & Measurement Equipment
Fiber Optic Equipment
Off-Road Vehicles
Financing

BRANDS/DIVISIONS/AFFILIATES:

Bell Helicopter Textron Inc
Textron Systems
Textron Aviation
TRU Simulation + Training Inc
Textron Specialized Vehicles Inc
Beechcraft
Cessna
Response Technologies LLC

GROWTH PLANS/SPECIAL FEATURES:

Textron is a conglomerate that designs, manufactures, and services specialty aircraft for various end markets, but it also has several unrelated businesses. The firm's aviation segment manufactures and services Cessna and Beechcraft business aircraft. Bell is a helicopter manufacturer and servicer for both the commercial and military end market. Textron Systems produces uncrewed aircraft and armored vehicles for the military market as well as aircraft simulators for the commercial and military end markets. Textron Industrial contains a Kautex business that manufactures plastic fuel tanks for conventional and hybrid motor vehicles and produces specialized vehicles such as golf carts, snowmobiles, all-terrain vehicles, and others.

Textron offers its employees comprehensive benefits.

CONTACTS: *Note: Officers with more than one job title may be intentionally listed here more than once.*

Scott Donnelly, CEO
Frank Connor, CFO
Mark Bamford, Chief Accounting Officer
E. Lupone, Chief Compliance Officer
Julie Duffy, Executive VP, Divisional

FINANCIAL DATA: *Note: Data for latest year may not have been available at press time.*

In U.S. $	2021	2020	2019	2018	2017	2016
Revenue		11,651,000,000	13,630,000,000	13,972,000,000	14,198,000,000	13,788,000,000
R&D Expense						
Operating Income		512,000,000	1,072,000,000	1,103,000,000	1,066,000,000	1,173,000,000
Operating Margin %						
SGA Expense		1,045,000,000	1,152,000,000	1,275,000,000	1,337,000,000	1,304,000,000
Net Income		309,000,000	815,000,000	1,222,000,000	307,000,000	962,000,000
Operating Cash Flow		768,000,000	1,014,000,000	1,107,000,000	953,000,000	1,012,000,000
Capital Expenditure		317,000,000	339,000,000	369,000,000	423,000,000	446,000,000
EBITDA		839,000,000	1,529,000,000	1,987,000,000	1,383,000,000	1,499,000,000
Return on Assets %						
Return on Equity %						
Debt to Equity						

CONTACT INFORMATION:

Phone: 401 421-2800 Fax: 401 421-2878
Toll-Free:
Address: 40 Westminster St., Providence, RI 02903 United States

STOCK TICKER/OTHER:

Stock Ticker: TXT
Employees: 33,000
Parent Company:
Exchange: NYS
Fiscal Year Ends: 12/31

SALARIES/BONUSES:

Top Exec. Salary: $1,093,385 Bonus: $
Second Exec. Salary: $942,308 Bonus: $

OTHER THOUGHTS:

Estimated Female Officers or Directors: 10
Hot Spot for Advancement for Women/Minorities: Y

T-Mobile US Inc

NAIC Code: 517210

www.t-mobile.com

TYPES OF BUSINESS:

Mobile Phone and Wireless Services
Wireless Services
Cellular
Mobile Devices
5G

BRANDS/DIVISIONS/AFFILIATES:

Deutsche Telekom AG
T-Mobile International AG
T-Mobile
Metro by T-Mobile
Sprint Corporation

GROWTH PLANS/SPECIAL FEATURES:

Deutsche Telekom merged its T-Mobile USA unit with prepaid specialist MetroPCS in 2013, creating T-Mobile US. Following the merger, the firm provided nationwide service in major markets but spottier coverage elsewhere. T-Mobile spent aggressively on low-frequency spectrum, well suited to broad coverage, and has substantially expanded its geographic footprint. This expansion, coupled with aggressive marketing and innovative offerings, produced rapid customer growth. With the Sprint acquisition, the firm's scale now roughly matches its larger rivals: T-Mobile now serves 68 million postpaid and 21 million prepaid phone customers, equal to nearly 30% of the U.S. retail wireless market. In addition, the firm provides wholesale service to resellers.

CONTACTS: *Note: Officers with more than one job title may be intentionally listed here more than once.*

G. Sievert, CEO
Peter Osvaldik, CFO
Timotheus Hottges, Chairman of the Board
Dara Bazzano, Chief Accounting Officer
Matthew Staneff, Chief Marketing Officer
Peter Ewens, Executive VP, Divisional
David Miller, Executive VP
Deeanne King, Executive VP
Neville Ray, President, Divisional

FINANCIAL DATA: *Note: Data for latest year may not have been available at press time.*

In U.S. $	2021	2020	2019	2018	2017	2016
Revenue		68,397,000,000	44,998,000,000	43,310,000,000	40,604,000,000	37,242,000,000
R&D Expense						
Operating Income		7,054,000,000	5,722,000,000	5,309,000,000	4,653,000,000	3,071,000,000
Operating Margin %						
SGA Expense		18,926,000,000	14,139,000,000	13,161,000,000	12,259,000,000	11,378,000,000
Net Income		3,064,000,000	3,468,000,000	2,888,000,000	4,536,000,000	1,460,000,000
Operating Cash Flow		8,640,000,000	6,824,000,000	3,899,000,000	7,962,000,000	6,135,000,000
Capital Expenditure		12,367,000,000	7,358,000,000	5,668,000,000	11,065,000,000	8,670,000,000
EBITDA		20,411,000,000	12,354,000,000	11,760,000,000	10,816,000,000	10,300,000,000
Return on Assets %						
Return on Equity %						
Debt to Equity						

CONTACT INFORMATION:

Phone: 425-378-4000 Fax: 425-378-4040
Toll-Free: 800-318-9270
Address: 12920 SE 38th St., Bellevue, WA 98006-1350 United States

STOCK TICKER/OTHER:

Stock Ticker: TMUS
Exchange: NAS
Employees: 50,000
Fiscal Year Ends: 12/31
Parent Company: Deutsche Telekom AG

SALARIES/BONUSES:

Top Exec. Salary: $1,446,154 Bonus: $3,500,000
Second Exec. Salary: $655,962 Bonus: $600,000

OTHER THOUGHTS:

Estimated Female Officers or Directors:
Hot Spot for Advancement for Women/Minorities:

TomTom International BV

www.tomtom.com

NAIC Code: 334511

TYPES OF BUSINESS:

Communications Equipment-GPS-Based
Navigation Services
Mapping Technology
PDA & Smartphone Software

GROWTH PLANS/SPECIAL FEATURES:

TomTom is a software company that specializes in maintaining a robust digital mapping database. Its mapping software serves business-to-business needs, like auto infotainment systems and third-party app integrations, as well as business-to-consumer needs, such as mobile mapping apps and portable navigation devices for functions such as navigation, traffic monitoring, and autonomous driving visualization.

BRANDS/DIVISIONS/AFFILIATES:

TomTom

CONTACTS: *Note: Officers with more than one job title may be intentionally listed here more than once.*

Harold Goddijn, CEO
Taco Titulaer, CFO
James Joy, General Counsel
Peter-Frans Pauwels, Mgr.-Online Strategy & e-commerce
Richard Piekaar, Mgr.-Investor Rel.
Taco Titulaer, Treas.
Corinne Vigreux, Managing Dir.-Consumer Bus. Unit
Giles Shrimpton, Managing Dir.-TomTom Automotive
Maarten van Gool, Managing Dir.-Licensing Bus. Unit
Lucien Groenhuijzen, Managing Dir.-Places Bus. Unit
Derk Haank, Chmn.
Kirvan Pierson, Head-Bus. Dev. China

FINANCIAL DATA: *Note: Data for latest year may not have been available at press time.*

In U.S. $	2021	2020	2019	2018	2017	2016
Revenue		596,502,400	791,397,800	775,631,000	1,020,240,000	1,115,034,000
R&D Expense		351,088,100	364,535,200	249,418,900	234,742,000	215,109,500
Operating Income		-324,923,500	-260,829,800	3,280,744	-35,188,090	10,044,380
Operating Margin %						
SGA Expense		162,299,100	183,157,000	161,912,900	310,633,900	310,947,900
Net Income		-290,963,000	714,746,900	50,658,970	-230,371,500	13,537,440
Operating Cash Flow		-22,790,160	105,795,800	258,589,200	195,175,400	162,983,500
Capital Expenditure		7,112,607	27,172,010	95,036,540	135,795,700	132,793,900
EBITDA		-8,415,870	67,627,360	187,501,600	163,576,400	159,020,600
Return on Assets %						
Return on Equity %						
Debt to Equity						

CONTACT INFORMATION:

Phone: 31-20-757-5000 Fax:
Toll-Free:
Address: De Ruyterlade 154, Amsterdam, 1011 AC Netherlands

STOCK TICKER/OTHER:

Stock Ticker: TMOAF
Employees: 4,575
Parent Company:
Exchange: PINX
Fiscal Year Ends: 12/31

SALARIES/BONUSES:

Top Exec. Salary: $ Bonus: $
Second Exec. Salary: $ Bonus: $

OTHER THOUGHTS:

Estimated Female Officers or Directors: 3
Hot Spot for Advancement for Women/Minorities: Y

Toshiba Corporate R&D Center

NAIC Code: 541712

www.toshiba.co.jp/rdc/index.htm

TYPES OF BUSINESS:

Research & Development
Semiconductor Processes
MEMS Applications
Biotechnology Tools
Electronic Devices
Software
Artificial Intelligence
Recognition Technologies

BRANDS/DIVISIONS/AFFILIATES:

Toshiba Corporation

GROWTH PLANS/SPECIAL FEATURES:

Toshiba Corporate R&D Center (CRDC) manages a global network of research laboratories, test facilities and planning groups that support the ongoing commercialization of products and technologies for Toshiba Corporation, its parent company. Toshiba is a global leader in the manufacture of consumer, industrial, medical and communications electronics. CRDC has focused the bulk of its short-term research and development initiatives on digital products and electronic devices, while its scientists and engineers continue to develop a range of platform technologies, including new nanometric semiconductor processes, innovative microelectromechanical systems (MEMS) applications and chip-based biotech tools. The firm has facilities in Japan, Europe and China. Its research and development areas include: information and communication, comprising the development of wireless real-time video transmission technology of whole-genome sequence data using quantum cryptography, and quantum encryption technology for large-capacity data transmission; intelligent systems, developing artificial intelligence (AI) with three-dimensional recognition that measures distance, utilizing AI solutions to enhance train time-tabling and to improve customer convenience, to develop machine learning algorithm for identifying failure factors from data, developing an algorithm that offers large-scale combinatorial optimization, developing an advanced service platform for rapid problem-solving in logistics, drug development and other social needs; nano materials, developing no-plug charging EV systems, photovoltaic modules, energy consumption reduction solutions, carbon recycling technology, magnetic material production, cancer detection test solutions, and microRNA detection technology; and electronic devices, which develops a Gate dielectric process technology, Gate insulation film process technology, and next-generation power device technology that reduces power consumption and carbon dioxide emissions.

CONTACTS: *Note: Officers with more than one job title may be intentionally listed here more than once.*

Yutaka Sata, Managing Dir.

FINANCIAL DATA: *Note: Data for latest year may not have been available at press time.*

In U.S. $	2021	2020	2019	2018	2017	2016
Revenue						
R&D Expense						
Operating Income						
Operating Margin %						
SGA Expense						
Net Income						
Operating Cash Flow						
Capital Expenditure						
EBITDA						
Return on Assets %						
Return on Equity %						
Debt to Equity						

CONTACT INFORMATION:

Phone: 81-44-549-2056 Fax:
Toll-Free:
Address: 1, Komukai Toshiba-cho, Saiwai-ku, Kawasaki-shi, 212-8582 Japan

STOCK TICKER/OTHER:

Stock Ticker: Subsidiary
Employees: 49
Parent Company: Toshiba Corporation
Exchange:
Fiscal Year Ends: 03/31

SALARIES/BONUSES:

Top Exec. Salary: $ Bonus: $
Second Exec. Salary: $ Bonus: $

OTHER THOUGHTS:

Estimated Female Officers or Directors:
Hot Spot for Advancement for Women/Minorities:

Toshiba Corporation

www.toshiba.co.jp

NAIC Code: 334413

TYPES OF BUSINESS:

Memory Chip Manufacturing
Infrastructure Systems
Digital Products
Electronic Devices
Power Systems
Retail
Identification
Semiconductor

BRANDS/DIVISIONS/AFFILIATES:

GROWTH PLANS/SPECIAL FEATURES:

Founded in 1875, Toshiba is Japan's largest semiconductor manufacturer and its second-largest diversified industrial conglomerate. After the accounting scandal in 2015, Toshiba reorganized into six major segments: energy systems and solutions; infrastructure systems and solutions; building solutions; retail and printing solutions; storage and electronic devices solutions; and digital solutions. Toshiba is the second-largest manufacturer of NAND flash memory with a market share of 16.5% in 2017, and it concentrates business resources in this area.

CONTACTS: *Note: Officers with more than one job title may be intentionally listed here more than once.*

Nobuaki Kurumatani, CEO
Norio Sasaki, Vice Chmn.
Hidejiro Shimomitsu, Sr. Exec. VP
Hideo Kitamura, Sr. Exec. VP
Makoto Kubo, Sr. Exec. VP
Satoshi Tsunakawa, Chmn.

FINANCIAL DATA: *Note: Data for latest year may not have been available at press time.*

In U.S. $	2021	2020	2019	2018	2017	2016
Revenue	26,838,900,000	29,786,920,000	32,455,260,000	34,687,670,000	42,799,660,000	49,810,970,000
R&D Expense						
Operating Income	917,384,300	1,146,357,000	397,921,000	562,985,500	2,528,048,000	-3,635,777,000
Operating Margin %						
SGA Expense	6,319,259,000	6,918,992,000	7,598,063,000	7,879,213,000	8,844,600,000	11,148,570,000
Net Income	1,001,555,000	-1,007,284,000	8,903,518,000	7,064,874,000	-8,485,317,000	-4,042,151,000
Operating Cash Flow	1,275,395,000	-1,249,060,000	1,097,106,000	365,901,000	1,178,895,000	-10,808,060
Capital Expenditure	1,222,743,000	1,187,726,000	1,214,694,000	1,756,599,000	1,588,125,000	2,561,114,000
EBITDA	2,137,429,000	329,382,100	878,615,900	2,019,367,000	3,557,731,000	-3,501,836,000
Return on Assets %						
Return on Equity %						
Debt to Equity						

CONTACT INFORMATION:

Phone: 81 334572096 Fax: 81 354449202
Toll-Free:
Address: 1-1, Shibaura 1-chome, Minato-ku, Tokyo, 105-8001 Japan

STOCK TICKER/OTHER:

Stock Ticker: TOSBF
Employees: 128,697
Parent Company:
Exchange: PINX
Fiscal Year Ends: 03/31

SALARIES/BONUSES:

Top Exec. Salary: $ Bonus: $
Second Exec. Salary: $ Bonus: $

OTHER THOUGHTS:

Estimated Female Officers or Directors:
Hot Spot for Advancement for Women/Minorities:

Toyota Industries Corporation

NAIC Code: 336111

www.toyota-industries.com

TYPES OF BUSINESS:

Automobile Manufacturing

BRANDS/DIVISIONS/AFFILIATES:

Toyota
BT
Cesab
Raymond
Toyota Material Handling Group
MIRAI

CONTACTS:

Note: Officers with more than one job title may be intentionally listed here more than once.

Akira Onishi, Pres.
Chiaki Yamaguchi, Exec. VP
Kazue Sasaki, Exec. VP
Hirotaka Morishita, Exec. VP
Shinya Furukawa, Sr. Managing Officer
Tetsuro Toyoda, Chmn.

GROWTH PLANS/SPECIAL FEATURES:

Toyota Industries Corp is primarily engaged in manufacturing and sale of automobiles, industrial vehicles, and textile machinery, as well as logistics business. The company manufactures and sells automobiles, engines, foundry pieces and electronic equipment. It also provides forklift trucks, warehouse equipment, automatic warehouse, vehicles for high-place work. In addition, it also engaged in the land transportation service, collection, and delivery service. The business of the group is primarily functioned through Japan and its amplifying internationally. Toyota derives most of the income through the sale of products and recycled waste products.

FINANCIAL DATA:

Note: Data for latest year may not have been available at press time.

In U.S. $	2021	2020	2019	2018	2017	2016
Revenue	18,613,600,000	19,079,780,000	19,462,810,000	17,608,980,000	14,719,590,000	19,585,810,000
R&D Expense						378,317,100
Operating Income	1,038,285,000	1,126,797,000	1,183,491,000	1,295,622,000	1,119,003,000	1,124,512,000
Operating Margin %						
SGA Expense	3,292,046,000	3,352,017,000	3,311,536,000	2,937,919,000	2,358,036,000	148,887,600
Net Income	1,201,188,000	1,281,862,000	1,342,202,000	1,477,804,000	1,154,599,000	1,608,344,000
Operating Cash Flow	3,360,040,000	2,752,091,000	2,375,189,000	2,359,908,000	2,100,928,000	2,064,576,000
Capital Expenditure	1,953,885,000	1,898,018,000	1,982,540,000	1,758,418,000	1,443,051,000	1,343,916,000
EBITDA	3,547,151,000	3,628,018,000	3,500,782,000	3,359,759,000	2,996,467,000	3,888,879,000
Return on Assets %						
Return on Equity %						
Debt to Equity						

CONTACT INFORMATION:

Phone: 81 566222511 Fax: 81 566275650
Toll-Free:
Address: 2-1, Toyoda-cho, Kariya-shi, Aichi, 448-8671 Japan

STOCK TICKER/OTHER:

Stock Ticker: TYIDY
Exchange: PINX
Employees: 66,947
Fiscal Year Ends: 03/31
Parent Company:

SALARIES/BONUSES:

Top Exec. Salary: $ Bonus: $
Second Exec. Salary: $ Bonus: $

OTHER THOUGHTS:

Estimated Female Officers or Directors:
Hot Spot for Advancement for Women/Minorities:

Toyota Motor Corporation

www.toyota.co.jp

NAIC Code: 336111

TYPES OF BUSINESS:

Automobile Manufacturing
Manufactured Housing
Advertising & e-Commerce Services
Financial Services
Telecommunications Services
Information Technology
Nanotechnology Research

BRANDS/DIVISIONS/AFFILIATES:

Daihatsu Motor Co Ltd
Hino Motors Ltd
Toyota Financial Services Corporation
Toyota Housing Corporation

GROWTH PLANS/SPECIAL FEATURES:

Founded in 1937, Toyota is one of the world's largest automakers with 9.92 million units sold at retail in fiscal 2021 across its light vehicle brands. Brands include Toyota, Lexus, Daihatsu, and truck maker Hino; market share in Japan is about 52%, while U.S. share is over 15%. The firm also owns large stake in Denso, a parts supplier, at least 16% of Subaru (with a deal to raise that to 20%), and holds investments in many other firms, including shares of Uber Technologies and about 5% in each of Mazda and Suzuki. Fiscal 2021 sales excluding financial services were JPY 25.1 trillion. Toyota also has a financing arm and manufactures homes and boats.

CONTACTS: *Note: Officers with more than one job title may be intentionally listed here more than once.*

Akio Toyoda, Pres.
Satoshi Ozawa, Exec. VP-Gen. Admin.
Mitsuhisa Kato, Exec. VP-Customer Service Oper.
Mamoru Furuhashi, CEO-Govt & Public Affairs
Satoshi Ozawa, Exec. VP-Acct.
Satoshi Ozawa, Exec VP-European Oper.

FINANCIAL DATA: *Note: Data for latest year may not have been available at press time.*

In U.S. $	2021	2020	2019	2018	2017	2016
Revenue	239,135,600,000	262,995,900,000	265,594,200,000	258,158,800,000	242,497,600,000	249,579,200,000
R&D Expense						
Operating Income	19,311,690,000	21,465,580,000	21,682,410,000	21,087,680,000	17,524,620,000	25,077,950,000
Operating Margin %						
SGA Expense	23,150,550,000	26,051,450,000	26,153,310,000	27,156,290,000	25,205,480,000	25,866,240,000
Net Income	19,729,190,000	18,243,500,000	16,544,870,000	21,914,720,000	16,090,020,000	20,321,730,000
Operating Cash Flow	23,963,670,000	31,551,110,000	33,097,230,000	36,993,500,000	30,001,030,000	39,197,720,000
Capital Expenditure	33,109,070,000	31,590,550,000	32,853,740,000	31,621,970,000	31,118,740,000	35,668,480,000
EBITDA	40,587,890,000	36,837,080,000	36,078,850,000	38,505,220,000	33,690,630,000	40,812,460,000
Return on Assets %						
Return on Equity %						
Debt to Equity						

CONTACT INFORMATION:

Phone: 81 565282121 Fax: 81 565235800
Toll-Free:
Address: 1 Toyota-Cho, Toyota City, Toyota, Aichi Prefecture 471-8571 Japan

STOCK TICKER/OTHER:

Stock Ticker: TM
Employees: 366,283
Parent Company:
Exchange: NYS
Fiscal Year Ends: 03/31

SALARIES/BONUSES:

Top Exec. Salary: $2,187,972 Bonus: $6,827,528
Second Exec. Salary: $869,917 Bonus: $2,460,370

OTHER THOUGHTS:

Estimated Female Officers or Directors:
Hot Spot for Advancement for Women/Minorities:

Toyota Motor Sales USA Inc (TMS)

www.toyota.com/usa/operations

NAIC Code: 336111

TYPES OF BUSINESS:

Automobile Manufacturing
Automobile Manufacture

BRANDS/DIVISIONS/AFFILIATES:

Toyota Motor Corporation
4Runner
Avalon
C-HR
Camry
Highlander
Safety Connect
Toyota Motor North Americz (TMNA)

CONTACTS:

Note: Officers with more than one job title may be intentionally listed here more than once.

Tetsuo Ogawa, CEO

GROWTH PLANS/SPECIAL FEATURES:

Toyota Motor Sales, USA, Inc. manufactures and sells vehicles. Through various subsidiaries, Toyota operates plants throughout the U.S., manufacturing vehicles such as sport utilities, trucks, cars, crossovers, electrified, hybrids and racing. Model brands include 4Runner, Avalon, C-HR, Camry, Corolla, GR, Highlander, Mirai, Prius, RAV, Sequoia, Sienna, Tacoma, Tundra and Venza. Toyota's vehicles are primarily leased or sold through dealers located throughout the U.S., from which used vehicles are also sold. The company exports most of its U.S. models to more than 30 countries. Connected vehicles are smart device compatible. Toyota Motor Sales' Safety Connect offering is a subscription-based service that provides help after an emergency. Drivers can be connected to Toyota's 24/7 response center at the touch of a button, and obtain emergency assistance, roadside assistance, automatic collision notification and the connected vehicle can be located more easily through the GPS system if stolen. In addition, Toyota Motor Sales has a carshare service in Honolulu that is operated through Servco Pacific, Inc., the company's vehicle distributor in Hawaii. The service utilizes Toyota's proprietary global mobility service platform and a consumer-facing app called Hui, which was developed by Toyota USA's connected division, and enables users to reserve a vehicle either by the hour or day. Hui vehicles are parked in marked, reserved stalls for easy pickup and drop-off. Toyota Motor Sales operates as a subsidiary of Toyota Motor Corporation. During 2021, TMS established another manufacturing facility as a joint venture with Mazda, and is based in Huntsville, Alabama and assembles Corolla crossover vehicles.

FINANCIAL DATA:

Note: Data for latest year may not have been available at press time.

In U.S. $	2021	2020	2019	2018	2017	2016
Revenue	99,411,343,200	95,587,830,000	98,038,800,000	95,578,770,000	91,027,400,000	98,245,124,503
R&D Expense						
Operating Income						
Operating Margin %						
SGA Expense						
Net Income						
Operating Cash Flow						
Capital Expenditure						
EBITDA						
Return on Assets %						
Return on Equity %						
Debt to Equity						

CONTACT INFORMATION:

Phone: 310 468-4000 Fax: 310 468-7814
Toll-Free: 800-331-4331
Address: P.O. Box 259001, Plano, TX 75025-9001 United States

STOCK TICKER/OTHER:

Stock Ticker: Subsidiary
Employees: 32,000
Parent Company: Toyota Motor Corporation
Exchange:
Fiscal Year Ends: 03/31

SALARIES/BONUSES:

Top Exec. Salary: $ Bonus: $
Second Exec. Salary: $ Bonus: $

OTHER THOUGHTS:

Estimated Female Officers or Directors:
Hot Spot for Advancement for Women/Minorities:

TP-Link Technologies Co Ltd

www.tp-link.com/en

NAIC Code: 511210B

TYPES OF BUSINESS:

Computer Software: Network Management (IT), System Testing & Storage
Wi-Fi Solutions
Computer Network System Manufacturer
Connectivity Innovation
Smartphones

BRANDS/DIVISIONS/AFFILIATES:

TP-Link
kasa smart
tapo
Neffos

CONTACTS: *Note: Officers with more than one job title may be intentionally listed here more than once.*

Jeffrey Chao, Chmn.

GROWTH PLANS/SPECIAL FEATURES:

TP-Link Technologies Co., Ltd. is a Chinese manufacturer and global provider of computer networking products. TP stands for the twisted pair concept of electromagnetic cabling (EMC), which corrects the effects of electromagnetic interference and enables seamless power supply. The firm's products and services include Wi-Fi, routers, modems, gateways, smart home cameras, smart electrical plugs, smart lighting, smart switches, range extenders, mobile Wi-Fi devices (MiFi) and adapters, as well as related accessories. TP-Link's devices and solutions are available for consumers and businesses. For service providers, the company offers technology innovation and products to help service providers serve their own customers worldwide. Products and solutions span Wi-Fi systems, routers, xDSL (digital subscriber line), GPON (gigabit passive optical network), G.Fast (a DSL for local loops), range extenders and LTE (long-term evolution). The firm's high-performance baseband chip and power amplifier, as well as EMC technology are adopted in every mobile phone to make the signal stronger, faster and more stable. In addition, TP-Link created Neffos, a brand that develops products and services with a focus on improving signal phones. Neffos smartphones use TP-Link's Wi-Fi antenna design and comprise WLAN extenders, smart connect technology and QR code Wi-Fi sharing technology, among other features and technologies. TP-Link's Wi-Fi devices and accessories are distributed to more than 170 countries. Brands of the firm include TP-Link, kasa smart, tapo and neffos.

FINANCIAL DATA: *Note: Data for latest year may not have been available at press time.*

In U.S. $	2021	2020	2019	2018	2017	2016
Revenue	2,500,000,000	2,400,000,000	2,535,750,000	2,415,000,000	2,205,000,000	2,100,000,000
R&D Expense						
Operating Income						
Operating Margin %						
SGA Expense						
Net Income						
Operating Cash Flow						
Capital Expenditure						
EBITDA						
Return on Assets %						
Return on Equity %						
Debt to Equity						

CONTACT INFORMATION:

Phone: 86755-2650-4400 Fax: 86755-2663-6921
Toll-Free:
Address: S. Bldg., #5 Keyuan Rd., Central Zone, Science & T, Shenzhen, 518057 China

STOCK TICKER/OTHER:

Stock Ticker: Private
Employees:
Parent Company:
Exchange:
Fiscal Year Ends:

SALARIES/BONUSES:

Top Exec. Salary: $ Bonus: $
Second Exec. Salary: $ Bonus: $

OTHER THOUGHTS:

Estimated Female Officers or Directors:
Hot Spot for Advancement for Women/Minorities:

Trend Micro Inc

NAIC Code: 511210E

www.trendmicro.com

TYPES OF BUSINESS:

Computer Software: Network Security, Managed Access, Digital ID, Cybersecurity & Anti-Virus
Antivirus Software

GROWTH PLANS/SPECIAL FEATURES:

Trend Micro provides antivirus and other security products that protect the flow of information on PCs, file servers, e-mail servers, and the Internet gateway. Sales have averaged 75% annual growth over the past decade. Customers include British Airways, Merrill Lynch, Microsoft, Pacific Bell, and governmental agencies in the United States and Japan.

BRANDS/DIVISIONS/AFFILIATES:

XGen

CONTACTS: *Note: Officers with more than one job title may be intentionally listed here more than once.*

Eva Chen, CEO
Kevin Simzer, COO
Mahendra Negi, CFO
Leah MacMillan, CMO
Max Cheng, CIO
Raimund Genes, CTO
Steve Quane, Chief Product Officer
Felix Sterling, General Counsel
Wael Mohamed, Exec. VP-Corporate Strategy & Global Field Oper.
Jenny Chang, Chief Cultural Officer
Mitchel Chang, Sr. VP-Global Tech. Support
Oscar Chang, Chief Dev. Officer
Steve Chang, Chmn.
Oscar Chang, Exec. VP-Greater China Sales
Akihiko Omikawa, Gen. Manager-Japan Region & Consumer Business Unit

FINANCIAL DATA: *Note: Data for latest year may not have been available at press time.*

In U.S. $	2021	2020	2019	2018	2017	2016
Revenue		1,529,480,000	1,451,575,000	1,409,529,000	1,307,608,000	1,159,326,000
R&D Expense						
Operating Income		346,771,600	331,148,300	314,901,100	320,208,400	301,922,600
Operating Margin %						
SGA Expense						
Net Income		236,406,400	245,562,500	248,796,200	225,747,800	216,609,200
Operating Cash Flow		477,224,000	396,374,400	438,991,600	412,243,800	294,453,600
Capital Expenditure		104,038,500	93,951,000	109,205,300	107,447,900	79,215,140
EBITDA		546,035,300	470,132,800	466,644,400	448,569,400	412,243,800
Return on Assets %						
Return on Equity %						
Debt to Equity						

CONTACT INFORMATION:

Phone: 81-3-5334-3618 Fax: 81-3-5334-4008
Toll-Free: 800-228-5651
Address: Shibuya-ku, 2-1-1 Shinjuku Maynds Tower, Tokyo, 151-0053 Japan

STOCK TICKER/OTHER:

Stock Ticker: TMICF
Employees: 6,562
Parent Company:
Exchange: PINX
Fiscal Year Ends: 12/31

SALARIES/BONUSES:

Top Exec. Salary: $ Bonus: $
Second Exec. Salary: $ Bonus: $

OTHER THOUGHTS:

Estimated Female Officers or Directors: 3
Hot Spot for Advancement for Women/Minorities: Y

Trilogy Inc

www.trilogy.com

NAIC Code: 511210K

TYPES OF BUSINESS:

Business-to-Business Software
Business Software
Software Engineering Services
Technical Product Management Services
Finance Reporting Solutions
Innovation Solutions
Research and Development
Training

BRANDS/DIVISIONS/AFFILIATES:

Trilogy University CNU Edition
Trilogy RemoteU for Individuals
Trilogy RemoteU for Managers

GROWTH PLANS/SPECIAL FEATURES:

Trilogy, Inc helps software companies to become more efficient and profitable by streamlining business functions, from development to product management and research and development. The firm's platform offers end-to-end solutions, with services spanning software engineering, technical product management, support, finance reporting, accounting, innovation solutions, research and development, software-as-a-service (SaaS) cloud migration, inside sales representation, remote staff recruitment and more. Trilogy also offers resources and education courses, including: Trilogy University CNU Edition (CNU stands for Code Nation University), a technical training program focused on teaching developers how to optimize the software development process and deliver cost-effective software products; Trilogy RemoteU for Individuals, which teaches leading-edge programming practices based on software factory theory within a 100% remote workplace; and Trilogy RemoteU for Managers, which develops technical team managers to effectively build and manage a remote software development team, launching virtual team projects, virtual communication, constructive conflict and collaboration and other capabilities.

CONTACTS: *Note: Officers with more than one job title may be intentionally listed here more than once.*

Joe Liemandt, CEO
Kim Irwin, Dir.-Customer Satisfaction
Greg Gunwall, VP-Prod. Mgmt.
Jie Du, VP-Analytics
Michael Richards, Pres., Global Automotive Business

FINANCIAL DATA: *Note: Data for latest year may not have been available at press time.*

In U.S. $	2021	2020	2019	2018	2017	2016
Revenue						
R&D Expense						
Operating Income						
Operating Margin %						
SGA Expense						
Net Income						
Operating Cash Flow						
Capital Expenditure						
EBITDA						
Return on Assets %						
Return on Equity %						
Debt to Equity						

CONTACT INFORMATION:

Phone: 512-874-3100 Fax: 512-874-8900
Toll-Free: 855-550-0085
Address: 401 Congress Ave., Ste 2650, Austin, TX 78701 United States

STOCK TICKER/OTHER:

Stock Ticker: Private
Employees:
Parent Company:
Exchange:
Fiscal Year Ends: 12/31

SALARIES/BONUSES:

Top Exec. Salary: $ Bonus: $
Second Exec. Salary: $ Bonus: $

OTHER THOUGHTS:

Estimated Female Officers or Directors: 1
Hot Spot for Advancement for Women/Minorities:

Trimble Inc

NAIC Code: 334511

www.trimble.com

TYPES OF BUSINESS:

GPS Technologies
Surveying & Mapping Equipment
Navigation Tools
Autopilot Systems
Data Collection Products
Fleet Management Systems
Outdoor Recreation Information Service
Telecommunications & Automotive Components

BRANDS/DIVISIONS/AFFILIATES:

Applanix
AXIO-NET GmbH
Beena Vision Systems Inc
e-Builder
HHK Datentechnik GmbH
Innovative Software Engineering
MyTopo
Viewpoint

GROWTH PLANS/SPECIAL FEATURES:

Trimble Inc provides location-based solutions that are used in global positioning system (GPS), laser, optical and inertial technologies. Its products portfolio includes 3D laser scanning, flow and application control systems, monitoring systems, water management, and navigation infrastructure. It also manufactures laser and optics-based products, and GPS products. The company serves various industries which include agriculture, architecture, civil engineering, survey and land administration, construction, geospatial among others. The company operates in four reportable segments namely, Buildings and Infrastructure, Geospatial, Resources and Utilities, and Transportation. It derives most of its revenues from the US and Europe with the rest coming from the Asia Pacific and other markets.

CONTACTS: *Note: Officers with more than one job title may be intentionally listed here more than once.*

Robert Painter, CEO
David Barnes, CFO
Steven Berglund, Chairman of the Board
Julie Shepard, Chief Accounting Officer
James Kirkland, General Counsel
Bryn Fosburgh, Senior VP, Divisional
Darryl Matthews, Senior VP, Divisional
Ronald Bisio, Senior VP, Divisional
James Langley, Senior VP, Divisional

FINANCIAL DATA: *Note: Data for latest year may not have been available at press time.*

In U.S. $	2021	2020	2019	2018	2017	2016
Revenue		3,147,700,000	3,264,300,000	3,108,400,000	2,654,200,000	2,362,200,000
R&D Expense		475,900,000	469,700,000	446,100,000	370,200,000	349,600,000
Operating Income		445,600,000	402,700,000	328,900,000	252,900,000	192,600,000
Operating Margin %						
SGA Expense		767,900,000	834,800,000	829,600,000	706,500,000	633,600,000
Net Income		389,900,000	514,300,000	282,800,000	121,100,000	132,400,000
Operating Cash Flow		672,000,000	585,000,000	486,700,000	411,900,000	407,100,000
Capital Expenditure		56,800,000	69,000,000	67,600,000	43,700,000	26,300,000
EBITDA		670,100,000	634,400,000	566,400,000	467,500,000	390,400,000
Return on Assets %						
Return on Equity %						
Debt to Equity						

CONTACT INFORMATION:

Phone: 408 481-8000 Fax: 408 481-2218
Toll-Free: 800-874-6253
Address: 935 Stewart Dr., Sunnyvale, CA 94085 United States

STOCK TICKER/OTHER:

Stock Ticker: TRMB
Employees: 11,402
Parent Company:
Exchange: NAS
Fiscal Year Ends: 12/31

SALARIES/BONUSES:

Top Exec. Salary: $870,950 Bonus: $
Second Exec. Salary: $839,808 Bonus: $

OTHER THOUGHTS:

Estimated Female Officers or Directors: 5
Hot Spot for Advancement for Women/Minorities: Y

Tyler Technologies Inc

www.tylertech.com

NAIC Code: 511210B

TYPES OF BUSINESS:

Computer Software: Network Management (IT), System Testing & Storage
Information Management
Local Governments
Property Appraisal

BRANDS/DIVISIONS/AFFILIATES:

MyCivic
MicroPact Inc
Courthouse Technologies

GROWTH PLANS/SPECIAL FEATURES:

Tyler Technologies provides a full suite of software solutions and services that address the needs of cities, counties, schools, courts and other local government entities. The company's three core products are Munis, which is the core ERP system, Odyssey, which is the court management system, or CMS, and payments. The company also provides a variety of add-on modules and offers outsourced property tax assessment services.

CONTACTS: *Note: Officers with more than one job title may be intentionally listed here more than once.*

Brian Miller, CFO
John Marr, Chairman of the Board
W. Smith, Chief Accounting Officer
H. Moore, President

FINANCIAL DATA: *Note: Data for latest year may not have been available at press time.*

In U.S. $	2021	2020	2019	2018	2017	2016
Revenue		1,116,663,000	1,086,427,000	935,282,000	840,662,000	756,043,000
R&D Expense		88,363,000	81,342,000	63,264,000	47,324,000	43,154,000
Operating Income		172,926,000	156,367,000	152,492,000	160,930,000	131,305,000
Operating Margin %						
SGA Expense		259,561,000	257,746,000	207,605,000	176,974,000	167,161,000
Net Income		194,820,000	146,527,000	147,462,000	163,945,000	109,857,000
Operating Cash Flow		355,089,000	254,720,000	250,203,000	195,755,000	191,859,000
Capital Expenditure		28,466,000	42,040,000	27,424,000	43,057,000	37,726,000
EBITDA		254,583,000	233,039,000	214,251,000	214,855,000	181,606,000
Return on Assets %						
Return on Equity %						
Debt to Equity						

CONTACT INFORMATION:

Phone: 972 713-3700 Fax: 972 713-3741
Toll-Free:
Address: 5101 Tennyson Pkwy., Plano, TX 75024 United States

STOCK TICKER/OTHER:

Stock Ticker: TYL
Employees: 5,368
Parent Company:
Exchange: NYS
Fiscal Year Ends: 12/31

SALARIES/BONUSES:

Top Exec. Salary: $525,000 Bonus: $
Second Exec. Salary: $400,000 Bonus: $

OTHER THOUGHTS:

Estimated Female Officers or Directors:
Hot Spot for Advancement for Women/Minorities:

Uber Technologies Inc

NAIC Code: 561599

uber.com

TYPES OF BUSINESS:

Car Ride Dispatch Service, Mobile App-Based
Freight Truck Dispatch Service
Restaurant Meal Delivery Service
Transportation Marketplace Technologies
Self-Driving Truck Technologies
Self-Driving Car Technologies

BRANDS/DIVISIONS/AFFILIATES:

UberEATS
Uber Freight
JUMP Bikes
Uber for Business
Postmates

CONTACTS: *Note: Officers with more than one job title may be intentionally listed here more than once.*

Dara Khosrowshahi, CEO
Nelson Chai, CFO
Ronald Sugar, Chairman of the Board
Glen Ceremony, Chief Accounting Officer
Tony West, Chief Legal Officer
Nikki Krishnamurthy, Other Executive Officer
Jill Hazelbaker, Senior VP, Divisional

GROWTH PLANS/SPECIAL FEATURES:

Uber Technologies is a technology provider that matches riders with drivers, hungry people with restaurants and food delivery service providers, and shippers with carriers. The firm's on-demand technology platform could eventually be used for additional products and services, such as autonomous vehicles, delivery via drones, and Uber Elevate, which, as the firm refers to it, provides "aerial ride-sharing." Uber Technologies is headquartered in San Francisco and operates in over 63 countries with over 110 million users that order rides or foods at least once a month. Approximately 76% of its gross revenue comes from ride-sharing and 22% from food delivery.

FINANCIAL DATA: *Note: Data for latest year may not have been available at press time.*

In U.S. $	2021	2020	2019	2018	2017	2016
Revenue		11,139,000,000	14,147,000,000	11,270,000,000	7,932,000,000	3,845,000,000
R&D Expense		2,205,000,000	4,836,000,000	1,505,000,000	1,201,000,000	864,000,000
Operating Income		-4,863,000,000	-8,596,000,000	-3,033,000,000	-4,080,000,000	-3,023,000,000
Operating Margin %						
SGA Expense		6,249,000,000	7,925,000,000	5,233,000,000	4,787,000,000	2,575,000,000
Net Income		-6,768,000,000	-8,506,000,000	997,000,000	-4,033,000,000	-370,000,000
Operating Cash Flow		-2,745,000,000	-4,321,000,000	-1,541,000,000	-1,418,000,000	-2,913,000,000
Capital Expenditure		616,000,000	588,000,000	558,000,000	829,000,000	1,635,000,000
EBITDA		-5,913,000,000	-7,402,000,000	2,386,000,000	-3,586,000,000	-2,537,000,000
Return on Assets %						
Return on Equity %						
Debt to Equity						

CONTACT INFORMATION:

Phone: 415-986-2715 Fax: 415-986-2104
Toll-Free:
Address: 1455 Market St., Ste. 400, San Francisco, CA 94103 United States

STOCK TICKER/OTHER:

Stock Ticker: UBER
Employees: 22,800
Parent Company:
Exchange: NYS
Fiscal Year Ends: 12/31

SALARIES/BONUSES:

Top Exec. Salary: $1,208,333 Bonus: $
Second Exec. Salary: $800,000 Bonus: $

OTHER THOUGHTS:

Estimated Female Officers or Directors: 1
Hot Spot for Advancement for Women/Minorities:

UIB Holdings Pte Ltd

uib.ai

NAIC Code: 511210B

TYPES OF BUSINESS:

Computer Software: Network Management (IT), System Testing & Storage
Internet of Things
Communications Technology
Artificial Intelligence
Natural-Language Technology
Human-to-Machine Communication
Human-to-Human Intelligence Communication

BRANDS/DIVISIONS/AFFILIATES:

UnificationEngine
SHOUT
Outbox Pro
Media Flow
UnificationEngine Chatbots
UE Messaging API
UE IoT API
UE AI API

CONTACTS: *Note: Officers with more than one job title may be intentionally listed here more than once.*

Toby Ruckert, CEO
Daisy Jiang, Dir.-Oper.
Ken Herron, CMO
Aby Varghese, CTO

GROWTH PLANS/SPECIAL FEATURES:

UIB Holdings Pte., Ltd. develops technology solutions that enable uninterrupted communication by solving the problem of information overload. The company integrates all communication channels such as email, voice mail, texts, social media, messaging, chat applications and push notifications into a single, unified inbox (hence, UIB). To power the unified inbox, UIB created an Internet of Things (IoT) messaging platform called UnificationEngine (UE), which solves the problems of interoperability, security and convenience, including app overload. Using natural language processing, UE allows users to remotely control and receive alerts and notifications from their devices on the communications channels they use most, eliminating the need for a separate app for each device. The UE platform encompasses end-to-end encryption by matching device ownership with user ID, offering enhanced security through IoT devices. Products built for UE include: SHOUT, a UE-powered emergency broadcast app for mission-critical communications; Outbox Pro, which offers social media publishing capabilities; and Media Flow, offering communications analytics. UnificationEngine Chatbots is a computer program designed to simulate a conversation/chat, enabling businesses, governments or other to monetize data with conversational customer service, conversational commerce and conversational analytics. UIB's natural-language-equipped chatbots instantly connect people to the information they want 24/7/365. The chatbots work with any device, any language and any platform for solutions such as smart home, smart enterprise and smart city. UIB's UE Messaging API (application program interface) enables developers to connect to over 20 global communication channels in 10 languages; UE IoT API enables developers to provide human-to-machine communications for smart devices and sensors in any industrial vertical; and UE AI (artificial intelligent) API enables the creation of customized, integrated cognitive chatbots for financial services, insurance, retail, entertainment, education, supply chain and other verticals.

FINANCIAL DATA: *Note: Data for latest year may not have been available at press time.*

In U.S. $	2021	2020	2019	2018	2017	2016
Revenue						
R&D Expense						
Operating Income						
Operating Margin %						
SGA Expense						
Net Income						
Operating Cash Flow						
Capital Expenditure						
EBITDA						
Return on Assets %						
Return on Equity %						
Debt to Equity						

CONTACT INFORMATION:

Phone: 65-6871-4035 Fax:
Toll-Free:
Address: 3 Temasek Ave., Fl. 18, Centennial Tower, Singapore, 039190 Singapore

STOCK TICKER/OTHER:

Stock Ticker: Private
Employees:
Parent Company:
Exchange:
Fiscal Year Ends:

SALARIES/BONUSES:

Top Exec. Salary: $ Bonus: $
Second Exec. Salary: $ Bonus: $

OTHER THOUGHTS:

Estimated Female Officers or Directors:
Hot Spot for Advancement for Women/Minorities:

UKG Inc (Ultimate Kronos Group)

NAIC Code: 511210H

www.ukg.com

TYPES OF BUSINESS:

Employee Management Software
Human Resource Services
Talent Management Solutions
Payroll Solutions
Benefits Administration Services
Attendance Solutions

BRANDS/DIVISIONS/AFFILIATES:

Hellman & Friedman
Ultimate Kronos Group
UKG Pro
UKG Dimensions
UKG Ready
UKG HR Service Delivery

CONTACTS: *Note: Officers with more than one job title may be intentionally listed here more than once.*

Aron Ain, CEO
Chris Todd, Pres.
John Butler, CFO
Jody Kaminsky, CMO
Dave Almeda, Chief People Officer
John Machado, CTO
Marc Scherr, Director
Vivian Maza, Other Executive Officer
Julie Dodd, Other Executive Officer
Chris Phenicie, Other Executive Officer
Greg Swick, Other Executive Officer
Jody Kaminsky, Senior VP, Divisional
Robert Manne, Senior VP
Jim Kizielewicz, COO

GROWTH PLANS/SPECIAL FEATURES:

UKG, Inc. (Ultimate Kronos Group) designs, markets, implements and supports human resources (HR), payroll and talent management solutions principally in the U.S. and Canada. The firm provides human capital management (HCM), payroll, HR service delivery and workforce management solutions. Products include UKG Pro, UKG Dimensions and UKG Ready. UKG Pro provides HR, payroll, benefits administration, open enrollment and life events, time, attendance, scheduling, payroll administration and tax management. UKG Dimensions is a platform that automates processes such as timekeeping, scheduling and leave management. UKG Ready offers human resources management, workforce management and payroll management in a single unified platform. The firm also offers UKG HR Service Delivery for HR digitization and process automation. In addition, UKG offers custom-designed solutions, industry-specific solutions, and automated staff scheduling and integrated communications. The company is headquartered in Weston, Florida, and has domestic offices in Massachusetts and New York, as well as offices in Canada, Mexico, the U.K., Netherlands, France, Germany, Spain, the United Arab Emirates, Australia, India and Singapore. UKG is owned by private equity firm Hellman & Friedman. During 2021, UKG acquired Great Place to Work Institute, Inc., which helps organizations become great workplaces.

UKG offers its employees medical and dental benefits, tuition reimbursement, life insurance, stock units, 401(k) retirement plan, an employee assistance program, family/medical leave and paid maternity/adoption leave.

FINANCIAL DATA: *Note: Data for latest year may not have been available at press time.*

In U.S. $	2021	2020	2019	2018	2017	2016
Revenue	3,150,000,000	3,000,000,000	1,197,571,200	1,140,544,000	940,729,024	781,291,008
R&D Expense						
Operating Income						
Operating Margin %						
SGA Expense						
Net Income		770,000,000	68,397,000	65,140,000	14,055,000	30,253,000
Operating Cash Flow						
Capital Expenditure						
EBITDA						
Return on Assets %						
Return on Equity %						
Debt to Equity						

CONTACT INFORMATION:

Phone: 954 266-1000 Fax:
Toll-Free: 800-432-1729
Address: 2000 Ultimate Way, Weston, FL 33326 United States

STOCK TICKER/OTHER:

Stock Ticker: Private
Employees: 12,500
Parent Company: Hellman & Friedman
Exchange:
Fiscal Year Ends: 09/30

SALARIES/BONUSES:

Top Exec. Salary: $ Bonus: $
Second Exec. Salary: $ Bonus: $

OTHER THOUGHTS:

Estimated Female Officers or Directors: 2
Hot Spot for Advancement for Women/Minorities:

UNICOM Engineering Inc

www.unicomengineering.com

NAIC Code: 511210B

TYPES OF BUSINESS:

Computer Software, Network Management (IT), System Testing & Storage
Storage & Security Software & Equipment
Supply Chain Services

BRANDS/DIVISIONS/AFFILIATES:

UNICOM Global Inc

CONTACTS:

Note: Officers with more than one job title may be intentionally listed here more than once.

Rusty Cone, Gen. Mgr.
Robert Sheriff, VP-Bus. Operations
Larry Yelsey, VP-Finance
Kevin Murphy, VP-Global Sales
Lisa Ryan, VP-Mktg.
Austin Hipes, CTO
Jeff Hudgins, VP-Prod. Mgmt. & Quality
Austin Hipes, VP-Eng.
William O'Connell, VP-Manufacturing Oper.
Tom Paquette, VP-Worldwide Sales
Brent Colombo, VP-IT Infrastructure
Keith Paul, VP-Global Supply Chain Systems

GROWTH PLANS/SPECIAL FEATURES:

UNICOM Engineering, Inc. is an international developer, manufacturer and distributor of storage equipment, network security devices and services to original equipment manufacturers (OEM) and independent software vendors. The firm offers a comprehensive suite of services, including development, manufacturing, fulfillment and post-sale support. This enables customers to accelerate the time to market for their products, to optimize their server appliance solutions and, in some cases, utilize the company's infrastructure for fulfillment of server appliance solutions. UNICOM can fulfill orders from its software partners to their end user base or to their channels. The company produces equipment branded for its customers, who in turn resell the products to their own customers. Its flexible services model enables customers to select from a comprehensive set of services designed to augment technology and deployment. This service model includes: solution design, featuring system design, custom designs, lifecycle management, compliance services and branding; system integration, featuring global manufacturing, track integration, control systems and revision controls; business analytics, featuring securing the OS (operating system), image creation, product lifecycle management and customer experience reporting; logistics and compliance, featuring global shipping, trade compliance, return merchandise authorization (RMA), evaluation, reverse logistics and freight systems logistics; and global support, featuring basic warranty, advance parts/server replacement and on-site response. UNICOM provides industry-specific solutions, including the security, storage, telecom, digital media and healthcare IT sectors. UNICOM Engineering is a division and subsidiary of UNICOM Global, Inc.

UNICOM offers employees medical, dental, vision, life and disability insurance; a 401(k); and tuition reimbursement.

FINANCIAL DATA:

Note: Data for latest year may not have been available at press time.

In U.S. $	2021	2020	2019	2018	2017	2016
Revenue	349,892,156	333,230,625	341,775,000	325,500,000	310,000,000	303,000,000
R&D Expense						
Operating Income						
Operating Margin %						
SGA Expense						
Net Income						
Operating Cash Flow						
Capital Expenditure						
EBITDA						
Return on Assets %						
Return on Equity %						
Debt to Equity						

CONTACT INFORMATION:

Phone: 781-332-1000 Fax: 781-770-2000
Toll-Free:
Address: 25 Dan Rd., Canton, MA 02021 United States

STOCK TICKER/OTHER:

Stock Ticker: Subsidiary
Employees: 237
Parent Company: UNICOM Global Inc
Exchange:
Fiscal Year Ends: 09/30

SALARIES/BONUSES:

Top Exec. Salary: $ Bonus: $
Second Exec. Salary: $ Bonus: $

OTHER THOUGHTS:

Estimated Female Officers or Directors: 1
Hot Spot for Advancement for Women/Minorities:

Uniden Holdings Corporation

NAIC Code: 334220

www.uniden.co.jp/english

TYPES OF BUSINESS:

Communications Equipment-Wireless Devices
Wireless Communications Devices
Electronics
Manufacture
Marine Electronics
Two-Way Radios
Digital Tuners
HD TV

BRANDS/DIVISIONS/AFFILIATES:

Uniden America Corporation
Uniden Australia Proprietary Limited
Uniden Vietnam Limited
Uniden Japan Corporation
Attowave Co Ltd

GROWTH PLANS/SPECIAL FEATURES:

Uniden Holdings Corporation, based in Japan, provides wireless communications devices through its global companies. The group manufactures and markets wireless communication equipment and consumer products such as CB radios, marine electronics, two-way radios, scanners, high-definition televisions, digital tuners for homes and cars and more. Group companies include Uniden America Corporation, Uniden Australia Proprietary Limited, Uniden Vietnam Limited, Uniden Japan Corporation, and Attowave Co. Ltd.

CONTACTS:

Note: Officers with more than one job title may be intentionally listed here more than once.

Hidero Fujimoto, Chmn.

FINANCIAL DATA:

Note: Data for latest year may not have been available at press time.

In U.S. $	2021	2020	2019	2018	2017	2016
Revenue	174,850,006	185,786,000	144,087,300	137,226,000	117,642,000	117,114,954
R&D Expense						
Operating Income						
Operating Margin %						
SGA Expense						
Net Income	33,191,558	-4,284,380	16,834,440	16,032,800	13,282,000	-42,439,908
Operating Cash Flow						
Capital Expenditure						
EBITDA						
Return on Assets %						
Return on Equity %						
Debt to Equity						

CONTACT INFORMATION:

Phone: 81-3-5543-2800 Fax: 81-3-5543-2921
Toll-Free:
Address: 2-12-7 Hatchobori, Chuo-ku, Tokyo, 104-8512 Japan

STOCK TICKER/OTHER:

Stock Ticker: 6815
Employees: 833
Parent Company:
Exchange: Tokyo
Fiscal Year Ends: 03/31

SALARIES/BONUSES:

Top Exec. Salary: $ Bonus: $
Second Exec. Salary: $ Bonus: $

OTHER THOUGHTS:

Estimated Female Officers or Directors:
Hot Spot for Advancement for Women/Minorities:

UNISOC Communications Inc

www.unisoc.com

NAIC Code: 334413

TYPES OF BUSINESS:

Chips & Semiconductors
Radio Frequency Transceivers
Multi-Mode & Multi-Band Technology
Internet of Things
Artificial Intelligence

BRANDS/DIVISIONS/AFFILIATES:

Tsinghua Holdings Co Ltd

CONTACTS: *Note: Officers with more than one job title may be intentionally listed here more than once.*

Qiwei Ren, Acting CEO
Leo Li, Pres.
Diana Jovin, VP-Strategy
Diana Jovin, VP-Investor Rel.
Shengwu Wu, Chmn.

GROWTH PLANS/SPECIAL FEATURES:

UNISOC Communications, Inc. is a China-based fabless semiconductor company primarily engaged in the research and development of core chipsets in mobile communications and Internet of Things (IoT). UNISOC's products cover chipset platforms supporting 2G, 3G, 4G and 5G communication standards. With research and development and customer support centers worldwide, the firm is among the Top 3 mobile baseband chipset suppliers in terms of global market share, a leading 5G company and one of the largest chipset providers in China for IoT and connectivity devices. UNISOC's artificial intelligence (AI) is composed of three parts: deep learning framework, a deep learning cloud computing platform and data management platform. UNISOC'S mobile chipsets include entry level S100, mid-end S300, high-end S500 and 5G. The firm's IoT solutions include radio frequency front-end (RFFE) solutions that deliver high performance and power efficiency through its integrated family of chipsets. The RFFE solutions are designed for products such as broadband power amplifiers with multi-frequency bandwidth, transmission modules, Wi-Fi front-end modules, IoT front-end modules that support CAT0, CATM1 and CATNB1, T/R switches. The modules are designed to deliver low-power, wide-area air interface that enables connection to IoT and machine-to-machine devices. The chipsets help to achieve premium data transmission between Bluetooth products, next-gen digital television devices and encompass power management architecture for extending battery life and delivering quality wireless audio experiences. UNISOC's range of IoT solutions can be utilized within the smart traffic, automation, smart industry, security & payment and special communication domains. UNISOC operates as a subsidiary of Tsinghua Holdings Co., Ltd. In early-2022, UNISOC jointly completed a 5G end-to-end module multi-slice solution. The collaboration included Ziguang Zhanrui, the Pan-Terminal Research Center of China Unicom Research Institute and the Guangdong Unicom Network Product Innovation Center.

FINANCIAL DATA: *Note: Data for latest year may not have been available at press time.*

In U.S. $	2021	2020	2019	2018	2017	2016
Revenue	1,610,000,000	1,595,261,850	1,519,297,000	1,061,760,000	1,696,690,000	1,650,000,000
R&D Expense						
Operating Income						
Operating Margin %						
SGA Expense						
Net Income			38,186,014	37,073,800		
Operating Cash Flow						
Capital Expenditure						
EBITDA						
Return on Assets %						
Return on Equity %						
Debt to Equity						

CONTACT INFORMATION:

Phone: 8621-20360600 Fax: 8621-20360700
Toll-Free:
Address: Zuchongzhi Rd., Ln. 2288, Bldg. 1, Zhangjiang, Shanghai, Shanghai 201203 China

STOCK TICKER/OTHER:

Stock Ticker: Subsidiary
Employees: 5,000
Parent Company: Tsinghua Holdings Co Ltd
Exchange:
Fiscal Year Ends: 12/31

SALARIES/BONUSES:

Top Exec. Salary: $ Bonus: $
Second Exec. Salary: $ Bonus: $

OTHER THOUGHTS:

Estimated Female Officers or Directors: 2
Hot Spot for Advancement for Women/Minorities:

Unisys Corporation

NAIC Code: 541512

www.unisys.com

TYPES OF BUSINESS:

IT Consulting
Enterprise Systems & Servers
Outsourcing Services
Infrastructure Services
Security Technology
Server Software & Middleware

BRANDS/DIVISIONS/AFFILIATES:

ClearPath
Unisys Stealth

GROWTH PLANS/SPECIAL FEATURES:

Unisys Corp is engaged in providing information technology outsourcing solutions and technology products. The company builds security-centric solutions for clients across the Government, Financial Services and Commercial markets. Its offerings include security software and services; digital transformation and workplace services; industry applications and services; and software operating environments for high-intensity enterprise computing. The organization operates in segments namely, Digital Workplace Services, Cloud & Infrastructure, ClearPath Forward, and Others.

The firm offers employees health services, recreational facilities and employee discounts.

CONTACTS: *Note: Officers with more than one job title may be intentionally listed here more than once.*

Peter Altabef, CEO
Michael Thomson, CFO
Ann Ruckstuhl, Chief Marketing Officer
Eric Hutto, COO
Mathew Newfield, Other Executive Officer
Katie Ebrahimi, Other Executive Officer
Lisa Madion, Senior VP, Divisional
Gerald Kenney, Senior VP
Shalabh Gupta, Treasurer

FINANCIAL DATA: *Note: Data for latest year may not have been available at press time.*

In U.S. $	2021	2020	2019	2018	2017	2016
Revenue		2,026,300,000	2,948,700,000	2,825,000,000	2,741,800,000	2,820,700,000
R&D Expense		26,600,000	31,300,000	31,900,000	47,200,000	55,400,000
Operating Income		87,000,000	238,200,000	284,100,000	4,600,000	47,600,000
Operating Margin %						
SGA Expense		369,400,000	396,900,000	370,300,000	426,500,000	455,600,000
Net Income		750,700,000	-17,200,000	75,500,000	-65,300,000	-47,700,000
Operating Cash Flow		-681,200,000	123,900,000	73,900,000	166,400,000	218,200,000
Capital Expenditure		100,000,000	111,300,000	116,300,000	90,200,000	95,800,000
EBITDA		-81,600,000	249,200,000	371,300,000	137,200,000	203,500,000
Return on Assets %						
Return on Equity %						
Debt to Equity						

CONTACT INFORMATION:

Phone: 215 986-4011 Fax: 215 986-6850
Toll-Free: 800-874-8647
Address: 801 Lakeview Dr., Ste. 100, Blue Bell, PA 19422 United States

STOCK TICKER/OTHER:

Stock Ticker: UIS
Employees: 17,200
Parent Company:
Exchange: NYS
Fiscal Year Ends: 12/31

SALARIES/BONUSES:

Top Exec. Salary: $861,408 Bonus: $
Second Exec. Salary: $499,750 Bonus: $225,000

OTHER THOUGHTS:

Estimated Female Officers or Directors: 2
Hot Spot for Advancement for Women/Minorities: Y

United Microelectronics Corporation

www.umc.com

NAIC Code: 334413

TYPES OF BUSINESS:

Chips/Semiconductors

BRANDS/DIVISIONS/AFFILIATES:

Mie Fujitsu Semiconductor Limited
United Semiconductor Japan Co Ltd

GROWTH PLANS/SPECIAL FEATURES:

Founded in 1980, UMC is the world's third-largest dedicated chip foundry, with 7% market share in 2020 according to Gartner after TSMC and GlobalFoundries. UMC's headquarters are in Hsinchu, Taiwan, and it operates 12 fabs in Taiwan, Mainland China, Japan and Singapore, with additional sales offices in Europe, the U.S. and South Korea. UMC features a diverse customer base including Texas Instruments, MediaTek, Qualcomm, Broadcom, Xilinx and Realtek, supplying a wide range of products applied in communications, display, memory, automotive and more. UMC employs about 20,000 people.

UMC offers its employees counseling services and the use of a recreation center at its Hsinchu headquarters, which features sports facilities, an art gallery, a performance venue and meeting spaces.

CONTACTS: *Note: Officers with more than one job title may be intentionally listed here more than once.*

Jason Wang, Pres.
Peter Courture, General Counsel
Stan Hung, Chmn.

FINANCIAL DATA: *Note: Data for latest year may not have been available at press time.*

In U.S. $	2021	2020	2019	2018	2017	2016
Revenue		6,372,935,000	5,341,447,000	5,451,407,000	5,380,482,000	5,329,498,000
R&D Expense		464,776,400	427,464,000	469,448,800	492,675,900	487,729,800
Operating Income		742,281,500	170,568,700	199,778,500	240,186,400	242,107,200
Operating Margin %						
SGA Expense		389,842,300	328,923,700	318,710,600	305,401,300	374,487,300
Net Income		823,941,200	293,924,000	276,719,000	348,765,100	310,721,200
Operating Cash Flow		2,369,572,000	1,978,842,000	1,835,786,000	1,891,269,000	1,674,157,000
Capital Expenditure		1,021,940,000	683,426,400	736,287,900	1,640,628,000	3,356,024,000
EBITDA		2,647,456,000	2,059,063,000	2,052,048,000	2,277,025,000	2,088,774,000
Return on Assets %						
Return on Equity %						
Debt to Equity						

CONTACT INFORMATION:

Phone: 886 35782258 Fax: 886 35779392
Toll-Free:
Address: No. 3 Li-Hsin 2nd Rd., Hsinchu Science Park, Hsinchu City, 30078 Taiwan

STOCK TICKER/OTHER:

Stock Ticker: UMC
Employees: 14,589
Parent Company:
Exchange: NYS
Fiscal Year Ends: 12/31

SALARIES/BONUSES:

Top Exec. Salary: $ Bonus: $
Second Exec. Salary: $ Bonus: $

OTHER THOUGHTS:

Estimated Female Officers or Directors:
Hot Spot for Advancement for Women/Minorities:

Universal Security Instruments Inc

www.universalsecurity.com

NAIC Code: 334290

TYPES OF BUSINESS:

Fire Detection and Alarm Systems Manufacturing
Security Alarm Manufacturer
Security Alarm Distributor
Carbon Monoxide Alarm Manufacturer
Carbon Monoxide Alarm Distributor
Import

BRANDS/DIVISIONS/AFFILIATES:

USI Electric Inc
UNIVERSAL
USI Electric

GROWTH PLANS/SPECIAL FEATURES:

Universal Security Instruments Inc is a U.S based manufacturer and distributor of safety and security devices. The company markets a line of residential smoke and carbon monoxide alarms under the trade names UNIVERSAL and USI Electric. It also markets products to the electrical distribution trade such as electrical and lighting distributors as well as manufactured housing companies. Its product portfolio consists of smoke and fire alarms, carbon monoxide alarms, multi-gas alarms, universal smoke sensing technology, and plug-in alarms.

CONTACTS:
Note: Officers with more than one job title may be intentionally listed here more than once.

Harvey Grossblatt, CEO
James Huff, CFO

FINANCIAL DATA:
Note: Data for latest year may not have been available at press time.

In U.S. $	2021	2020	2019	2018	2017	2016
Revenue	17,520,150	14,803,020	17,588,040	14,873,190	14,083,430	13,740,840
R&D Expense	471,545	691,886	502,845	653,899	682,508	665,278
Operating Income	133,784	-1,561,913	186,864	-726,235	-978,140	-1,366,178
Operating Margin %						
SGA Expense	5,034,380	4,628,881	4,864,522	4,616,391	4,444,230	4,480,330
Net Income	268,343	-5,813,891	-1,347,986	-2,262,310	-2,058,902	-2,137,792
Operating Cash Flow	1,388,172	9,248	5,874	534,883	-2,153,188	-822,957
Capital Expenditure				16,106		
EBITDA	521,455	-5,240,248	-842,975	-2,017,899	-1,965,916	-2,070,490
Return on Assets %						
Return on Equity %						
Debt to Equity						

CONTACT INFORMATION:

Phone: 410 363-3000 Fax: 410 363-2218
Toll-Free:
Address: 11407 Cronhill Dr., Ste. A, Owings Mills, MD 21117 United States

STOCK TICKER/OTHER:

Stock Ticker: UUU
Employees: 13
Parent Company:
Exchange: ASE
Fiscal Year Ends: 03/31

SALARIES/BONUSES:

Top Exec. Salary: $352,286 Bonus: $2,712
Second Exec. Salary: $162,395 Bonus: $

OTHER THOUGHTS:

Estimated Female Officers or Directors:
Hot Spot for Advancement for Women/Minorities:

VeriSign Inc

www.verisigninc.com

NAIC Code: 511210E

TYPES OF BUSINESS:

Computer Software: Network Security, Managed Access, Digital ID, Cybersecurity & Anti-Virus
Domain Name Registration

BRANDS/DIVISIONS/AFFILIATES:

Registry Services
Security Services

GROWTH PLANS/SPECIAL FEATURES:

Verisign is the sole authorized registry for several generic top-level domains, including the widely utilized .com and .net top-level domains. Additionally, the company operates two of the world's 13 root servers that are used to route Internet traffic. In 2018, the firm sold off its security services business, signaling a renewed focus on the core registry business. Verisign generates about 60% of its sales from the United States.

Employees of VeriSign receive a flexible benefits package that includes health, dental, vision, disability and life insurance; flexible spending accounts; a 401(k); an employee assistance program; a group legal plan; domestic partner coverage; tuition ass

CONTACTS: *Note: Officers with more than one job title may be intentionally listed here more than once.*

D. Bidzos, CEO
George Kilguss, CFO
Todd Strubbe, COO
Thomas Indelicarto, Executive VP

FINANCIAL DATA: *Note: Data for latest year may not have been available at press time.*

In U.S. $	2021	2020	2019	2018	2017	2016
Revenue		1,265,052,000	1,231,661,000	1,214,969,000	1,165,095,000	1,142,167,000
R&D Expense		74,671,000	60,805,000	57,884,000	52,342,000	59,100,000
Operating Income		824,201,000	806,127,000	767,392,000	707,722,000	686,572,000
Operating Margin %						
SGA Expense		186,003,000	184,262,000	197,559,000	211,705,000	198,253,000
Net Income		814,888,000	612,299,000	582,489,000	457,248,000	440,645,000
Operating Cash Flow		730,183,000	753,892,000	697,767,000	702,761,000	667,949,000
Capital Expenditure		43,395,000	40,316,000	37,007,000	49,499,000	169,574,000
EBITDA		883,659,000	895,717,000	892,728,000	785,226,000	754,904,000
Return on Assets %						
Return on Equity %						
Debt to Equity						

CONTACT INFORMATION:

Phone: 703 948-3200 Fax:
Toll-Free: 800-922-4917
Address: 12061 Bluemont Way, Reston, VA 20190 United States

STOCK TICKER/OTHER:

Stock Ticker: VRSN
Employees: 872
Parent Company:
Exchange: NAS
Fiscal Year Ends: 12/31

SALARIES/BONUSES:

Top Exec. Salary: $960,577 Bonus: $
Second Exec. Salary: $586,731 Bonus: $

OTHER THOUGHTS:

Estimated Female Officers or Directors:
Hot Spot for Advancement for Women/Minorities:

Sales, profits and employees may be estimates. Financial information, benefits and other data can change quickly and may vary from those stated here.

Verizon Communications Inc

NAIC Code: 517110

www.verizon.com

TYPES OF BUSINESS:

Mobile Phone and Wireless Services
Communications Services
Mobile Services
Home Services
Business Services
Network Technologies
Wireless
Wireline

BRANDS/DIVISIONS/AFFILIATES:

Verizon Consumer Group
Verizon Business Group
Verizon Fios

GROWTH PLANS/SPECIAL FEATURES:

Verizon is now primarily a wireless business (more than 70% of revenue and nearly all operating income). It serves about 91 million postpaid and 4 million prepaid phone customers and connects another 25 million data devices, like tablets, via its nationwide network, making it the largest U.S. wireless carrier. The firm has agreed to acquire Tracfone, a wireless reseller that serves about 20 million prepaid customers in the U.S., from America Movil. Fixed-line telecom operations include local networks (12% of revenue) in the Northeast, which reach about 25 million homes and businesses, and nationwide enterprise services (10%). Verizon Media Group, the online media and advertising firm formed with the acquisitions of AOL and Yahoo, provides the remainder of revenue.

Verizon offers comprehensive employee benefits.

CONTACTS: *Note: Officers with more than one job title may be intentionally listed here more than once.*

Ronan Dunne, CEO, Divisional
Tami Erwin, CEO, Divisional
Hans Vestberg, CEO
Matthew Ellis, CFO
Anthony Skiadas, Chief Accounting Officer
Craig Silliman, Chief Administrative Officer
Rima Qureshi, Chief Strategy Officer
Kyle Malady, Chief Technology Officer
Christine Pambianchi, Executive VP

FINANCIAL DATA: *Note: Data for latest year may not have been available at press time.*

In U.S. $	2021	2020	2019	2018	2017	2016
Revenue		128,292,000,000	131,868,000,000	130,863,000,000	126,034,000,000	125,980,000,000
R&D Expense						
Operating Income		28,798,000,000	30,470,000,000	26,869,000,000	29,188,000,000	27,059,000,000
Operating Margin %						
SGA Expense		31,573,000,000	29,990,000,000	31,083,000,000	28,336,000,000	31,569,000,000
Net Income		17,801,000,000	19,265,000,000	15,528,000,000	30,101,000,000	13,127,000,000
Operating Cash Flow		41,768,000,000	35,746,000,000	34,339,000,000	25,305,000,000	22,715,000,000
Capital Expenditure		20,318,000,000	18,837,000,000	18,087,000,000	17,830,000,000	17,593,000,000
EBITDA		44,934,000,000	44,145,000,000	41,859,000,000	42,281,000,000	41,290,000,000
Return on Assets %						
Return on Equity %						
Debt to Equity						

CONTACT INFORMATION:

Phone: 212 395-1000 Fax:
Toll-Free: 800-837-4966
Address: 1095 Avenue of the Americas, New York, NY 10036 United States

STOCK TICKER/OTHER:

Stock Ticker: VZ
Employees: 132,200
Parent Company:
Exchange: NYS
Fiscal Year Ends: 12/31

SALARIES/BONUSES:

Top Exec. Salary: $1,500,000 Bonus: $
Second Exec. Salary: $1,000,000 Bonus: $

OTHER THOUGHTS:

Estimated Female Officers or Directors: 5
Hot Spot for Advancement for Women/Minorities: Y

VIA Technologies Inc

www.via.com.tw

NAIC Code: 334413

TYPES OF BUSINESS:

Chips-PCs & Internet
Core Logic Chipsets
Microprocessors
Multimedia Chips
Audio Chips
Graphics Products
Networking Controllers
CDMA Chipsets

BRANDS/DIVISIONS/AFFILIATES:

Formosa Plastics Group

GROWTH PLANS/SPECIAL FEATURES:

VIA Technologies, Inc., part of the Formosa Plastics Group, designs, manufactures and markets highly-integrated embedded platform and system solutions for machine-to-machine, Internet of Things (IoT) and smart applications. These application solutions include personal computers, panels, power boards, modules, processors, chipsets, solid-state controllers and related accessories. VIA provides the hardware and software for creating innovative embedded systems and devices that enable connectivity and the IoT to deliver new connected experiences. The company's systems include Android signage, industrial PCs, panel PCs, rugged tablets, small form factor PCs and computer vision solutions, as well as related accessories. Headquartered in Taipei, Taiwan, VIA's global network links the high-tech centers of the U.S., Europe and Asia.

CONTACTS: *Note: Officers with more than one job title may be intentionally listed here more than once.*

Wen-Chi Chen, CEO
Wen-Chi Chen, Pres.
Tzu-Mu Lin, Sr. VP-R&D
Tzu-Mu Lin, Sr. VP-Eng.

FINANCIAL DATA: *Note: Data for latest year may not have been available at press time.*

In U.S. $	2021	2020	2019	2018	2017	2016
Revenue		231,269,059	183,796,000	156,651,000	151,844,000	163,123,845
R&D Expense						
Operating Income						
Operating Margin %						
SGA Expense						
Net Income		172,306,521	2,992,610	2,542,060	1,228,720	6,656,564
Operating Cash Flow						
Capital Expenditure						
EBITDA						
Return on Assets %						
Return on Equity %						
Debt to Equity						

CONTACT INFORMATION:

Phone: 886-2-2218-5452 Fax: 886-2-2218-5453
Toll-Free:
Address: Fl. 8, 533 Zhongzheng Rd., Xindian District, New Taipei City, 231 Taiwan

STOCK TICKER/OTHER:

Stock Ticker: 2388
Employees: 2,300
Parent Company: Formosa Plastics Group
Exchange: TWSE
Fiscal Year Ends: 12/31

SALARIES/BONUSES:

Top Exec. Salary: $ Bonus: $
Second Exec. Salary: $ Bonus: $

OTHER THOUGHTS:

Estimated Female Officers or Directors: 1
Hot Spot for Advancement for Women/Minorities:

ViaSat Inc

NAIC Code: 334220

www.viasat.com

TYPES OF BUSINESS:

Telecommunications Equipment-Digital Satellite
Networking & Wireless Signal Processing
Satellite Broadband Internet Service Provider

BRANDS/DIVISIONS/AFFILIATES:

GROWTH PLANS/SPECIAL FEATURES:

Viasat Inc provides bandwidth technologies and services in three segments: satellite services, which provides satellite-based high-speed broadband services to consumers, enterprises, and commercial airlines; commercial networks, which develops end-to-end communication and connectivity systems; and government systems, which produces network-centric Internet Protocol-based secure government communication systems. A large majority of the firm's revenue is generated in the United States, with the rest coming from the Americas, Europe, Middle East, Africa, and Asia-Pacific.

ViaSat offers employee benefits such as health, 401(k) and tuition reimbursement, depending on the location.

CONTACTS: *Note: Officers with more than one job title may be intentionally listed here more than once.*

Richard Baldridge, CEO
Mark Dankberg, Chairman of the Board
Shawn Duffy, Chief Accounting Officer
Keven Lippert, Chief Administrative Officer
Krishna Nathan, Chief Information Officer
Mark Miller, Chief Technology Officer
Girish Chandran, Chief Technology Officer
Kevin Harkenrider, COO
Robert Blair, General Counsel
Melinda Kimbro, Other Executive Officer
Evan Dixon, President, Divisional
Craig Miller, President, Divisional
James Dodd, President, Divisional
David Ryan, President, Divisional

FINANCIAL DATA: *Note: Data for latest year may not have been available at press time.*

In U.S. $	2021	2020	2019	2018	2017	2016
Revenue	2,256,107,000	2,309,238,000	2,068,258,000	1,594,625,000	1,559,337,000	1,417,431,000
R&D Expense	115,792,000	130,434,000	123,044,000	168,347,000	129,647,000	77,184,000
Operating Income	58,233,000	38,421,000	-60,620,000	-92,187,000	36,459,000	41,119,000
Operating Margin %						
SGA Expense	512,316,000	523,085,000	458,458,000	385,420,000	333,468,000	298,345,000
Net Income	3,691,000	-212,000	-67,623,000	-67,305,000	23,767,000	21,741,000
Operating Cash Flow	727,215,000	436,936,000	327,551,000	358,633,000	411,298,000	296,937,000
Capital Expenditure	885,271,000	761,078,000	686,820,000	584,487,000	585,658,000	450,625,000
EBITDA	455,775,000	382,247,000	258,142,000	154,208,000	283,389,000	285,421,000
Return on Assets %						
Return on Equity %						
Debt to Equity						

CONTACT INFORMATION:

Phone: 760 476-2200 Fax: 760 929-3941
Toll-Free:
Address: 6155 El Camino Real, Carlsbad, CA 92009 United States

STOCK TICKER/OTHER:

Stock Ticker: VSAT
Employees: 5,800
Parent Company:
Exchange: NAS
Fiscal Year Ends: 03/31

SALARIES/BONUSES:

Top Exec. Salary: $1,300,000 Bonus: $
Second Exec. Salary: $1,180,000 Bonus: $

OTHER THOUGHTS:

Estimated Female Officers or Directors:
Hot Spot for Advancement for Women/Minorities:

VironIT

vironit.com

NAIC Code: 511210M

TYPES OF BUSINESS:

Computer Software, e-Commerce, Web Analytics & Applications Management
Blockchain Development
Game Development
Internet of Things
Virtual Reality
Augmented Reality
Application Development
Web Development

BRANDS/DIVISIONS/AFFILIATES:

CONTACTS:

Note: Officers with more than one job title may be intentionally listed here more than once.

Maxim Osipau, Co-CEO
Alexey Grakov, Co-CEO

GROWTH PLANS/SPECIAL FEATURES:

VironIT is an international software development company established in 2004. The firm provides comprehensive services, including development of mobile applications, web development, enterprise software development, game development, virtual reality (VR) and augmented reality (AR) application development, blockchain development, Internet of Things (IoT) software development and robotic process automation. VironIT also offers a team extension to projects within 1-2 week's time, of up to 20-30 developers. VironIT's software development process is focused on meeting the specific requirements and wishes of the customer, and therefore begins with the planning stage, then the methodology, the reporting of progress and collaboration. Methodology is a choice of either agile for undefined requirements, rational unified process (RUP) for design/implementation/testing/deployment or waterfall/sequential approach. VironIT has expertise in technologies regarding Android, iOS, C++, Unity 3D, Angular js, Node.JS, PHP, .NET, Cocos 2d, Java and Python. Headquartered in the country of Georgia, VironIT has an international office in California, USA.

FINANCIAL DATA:

Note: Data for latest year may not have been available at press time.

In U.S. $	2021	2020	2019	2018	2017	2016
Revenue						
R&D Expense						
Operating Income						
Operating Margin %						
SGA Expense						
Net Income						
Operating Cash Flow						
Capital Expenditure						
EBITDA						
Return on Assets %						
Return on Equity %						
Debt to Equity						

CONTACT INFORMATION:

Phone: 375-445-852971 Fax:
Toll-Free:
Address: 8 Avlabari St., Tbilisi, 0131 Georgia

STOCK TICKER/OTHER:

Stock Ticker: Private
Employees:
Parent Company:
Exchange:
Fiscal Year Ends:

SALARIES/BONUSES:

Top Exec. Salary: $ Bonus: $
Second Exec. Salary: $ Bonus: $

OTHER THOUGHTS:

Estimated Female Officers or Directors:
Hot Spot for Advancement for Women/Minorities:

Vishay Precision Group Inc

vpgsensors.com

NAIC Code: 334513

TYPES OF BUSINESS:

Integrated Circuits
Sensor System Manufacturer
Weighing System Manufacturer
Foil Technology

BRANDS/DIVISIONS/AFFILIATES:

Vishay
Micro-Measurements
Pacific Instruments
VPG
BLH
KELK
Gleeble

GROWTH PLANS/SPECIAL FEATURES:

Vishay Precision Group Inc manufactures and markets sensors, and sensor-based measurement systems, as well as specialty resistors and strain gages based on proprietary technology. The company provides precision products and solutions, many of which are designed-in by customers, specializing in the growing markets of stress, force, weight, pressure, and current measurements. Its most products and solutions are primarily based upon proprietary foil technology and are produced as part of a vertically integrated structure. The product segments of the group are Foil Technology Products, Force Sensors and Weighing and Control Systems. It has a business presence in the United States and other countries.

CONTACTS: *Note: Officers with more than one job title may be intentionally listed here more than once.*

Ziv Shoshani, CEO
William Clancy, CFO
Marc Zandman, Chairman of the Board
Amir Tal, Chief Accounting Officer

FINANCIAL DATA: *Note: Data for latest year may not have been available at press time.*

In U.S. $	2021	2020	2019	2018	2017	2016
Revenue		269,812,000	283,958,000	299,794,000	254,350,000	224,929,000
R&D Expense						
Operating Income		26,015,000	31,995,000	40,332,000	23,669,000	13,871,000
Operating Margin %						
SGA Expense		78,256,000	79,622,000	80,935,000	74,614,000	68,938,000
Net Income		10,787,000	22,188,000	23,646,000	14,345,000	6,404,000
Operating Cash Flow		35,313,000	30,932,000	35,379,000	22,729,000	11,420,000
Capital Expenditure		22,949,000	11,196,000	14,521,000	6,960,000	10,425,000
EBITDA		32,182,000	39,742,000	46,358,000	33,031,000	22,242,000
Return on Assets %						
Return on Equity %						
Debt to Equity						

CONTACT INFORMATION:

Phone: 484 321-5300 Fax: 484 321-5301
Toll-Free:
Address: 3 Great Valley Pkwy., Ste. 150, Malvern, PA 19355 United States

STOCK TICKER/OTHER:

Stock Ticker: VPG
Employees: 2,600
Parent Company:
Exchange: NYS
Fiscal Year Ends: 12/31

SALARIES/BONUSES:

Top Exec. Salary: $646,709 Bonus: $
Second Exec. Salary: $367,744 Bonus: $

OTHER THOUGHTS:

Estimated Female Officers or Directors:
Hot Spot for Advancement for Women/Minorities:

Vivint Smart Home Inc

www.vivint.com

NAIC Code: 561621

TYPES OF BUSINESS:

Security Systems Services (except Locksmiths)
Smart Home Platform

BRANDS/DIVISIONS/AFFILIATES:

GROWTH PLANS/SPECIAL FEATURES:

Vivint Smart Home Inc is a smart home platform company. It provides a fully integrated solution for consumers with vertically integrated business model which includes hardware, software, sales, installation, support and professional monitoring. The company offers Home Security Systems, Wireless Security Cameras, Smart Security Devices such as Smart Locks and Garage Door Openers, Doorbell Video Cameras, and Burglary Sensor Detection, among others. The group operates in the United States and Canada, of which key revenue is derived from the United States.

CONTACTS: *Note: Officers with more than one job title may be intentionally listed here more than once.*

Todd R. Pedersen, CEO
Dale R. Gerard, CFO
JT Hwang, Chief Technology Officer
David F. D'Alessandro, Chmn.

FINANCIAL DATA: *Note: Data for latest year may not have been available at press time.*

In U.S. $	2021	2020	2019	2018	2017	2016
Revenue		1,260,730,000	1,155,981,000	1,050,441,000		
R&D Expense						
Operating Income		-232,363,000	-142,285,000	-242,097,000		
Operating Margin %						
SGA Expense		569,677,000	385,541,000	422,643,000		
Net Income		-484,240,000	-395,924,000	-472,635,000		
Operating Cash Flow		226,664,000	-221,592,000	-220,499,000		
Capital Expenditure		29,726,000	11,920,000	20,898,000		
EBITDA		309,131,000	408,843,000	285,050,000		
Return on Assets %						
Return on Equity %						
Debt to Equity						

CONTACT INFORMATION:

Phone: 801 377-9111 Fax: 801 377-4116
Toll-Free:
Address: 4931 North 300 West, Provo, UT 84604 United States

STOCK TICKER/OTHER:

Stock Ticker: VVNT
Employees:
Parent Company:
Exchange: NYS
Fiscal Year Ends: 12/31

SALARIES/BONUSES:

Top Exec. Salary: $650,495 Bonus: $1,112,634
Second Exec. Salary: $650,495 Bonus: $931,678

OTHER THOUGHTS:

Estimated Female Officers or Directors:
Hot Spot for Advancement for Women/Minorities:

vivo Mobile Communication Co Ltd

NAIC Code: 334220

www.vivo.com

TYPES OF BUSINESS:

Cellular Telephones Manufacturing
Technology Innovation
Smartphones Production
Artificial Intelligence

BRANDS/DIVISIONS/AFFILIATES:

BKK Electronics Corporation
V
Y
X
NEX
S

CONTACTS:

Note: Officers with more than one job title may be intentionally listed here more than once.

Shen Wei, CEO

GROWTH PLANS/SPECIAL FEATURES:

Vivo Mobile Communication Co., Ltd., a subsidiary of BKK Electronics Corporation, is a technology company that designs, develops and manufactures smartphones, smartphone accessories, software and online services. The firm's phone products are composed of a series of smartphones each targeted at middle to upper-income white collar professionals and students living in urban areas. The V, Y, X, NEX and S series offer a full-view display, a camera, long-lasting battery, fast-charging capabilities, enhanced gaming and audio capabilities, and fingerprint unlocking. The V series includes the V23, V21, V20, V19, V17, V15, V11, V9 and V7 phones. The Y series includes the Y31, Y50, Y3, Y01, Y11, Y95, Y21, Y91, Y20, Y19, Y30, Y33, Y53, Y15, Y75, Y93, Y17, Y51, Y76, Y72, Y1, Y12, Y85, Y81, Y83 and Y71 phones. The X series includes the X70, X60, X50 and X21. The NEX series includes the NEX 3, NEX Dual Display and NEX phones. The S series includes the S1 Pro and S1. vivo implements artificial intelligent (AI) technology into its smartphones, which offers: image recognition for automatically creating photo memory albums and videos; enhanced images and phone-reply options during gaming; scanning viruses via the cloud for real-time security; navigation gestures; augmented reality (AR) glass; 5G; and easy touch features, among others. Based in China, vivo has six research and development centers (Beijing, Nanjing, Hangzhou, Dongguan, Shenzhen and San Diego (USA)), and four global manufacturing bases in China, India and Indonesia.

FINANCIAL DATA:

Note: Data for latest year may not have been available at press time.

In U.S. $	2021	2020	2019	2018	2017	2016
Revenue						
R&D Expense						
Operating Income						
Operating Margin %						
SGA Expense						
Net Income						
Operating Cash Flow						
Capital Expenditure						
EBITDA						
Return on Assets %						
Return on Equity %						
Debt to Equity						

CONTACT INFORMATION:

Phone: 86-0769-85545555 Fax: 86-0769-85540007
Toll-Free:
Address: Fl. 5, BBK Bldg., #89 An'de St., Meilin Rd., Futian, Shenzhen, 518049 China

STOCK TICKER/OTHER:

Stock Ticker: Subsidiary
Exchange:
Employees:
Fiscal Year Ends:
Parent Company: BBK Electronics Corporation

SALARIES/BONUSES:

Top Exec. Salary: $ Bonus: $
Second Exec. Salary: $ Bonus: $

OTHER THOUGHTS:

Estimated Female Officers or Directors:
Hot Spot for Advancement for Women/Minorities:

VMware Inc

www.vmware.com

NAIC Code: 511210B

TYPES OF BUSINESS:

Computer Software: Network Management (IT), System Testing & Storage
Virtual Infrastructure Automation
Virtual Infrastructure Management

BRANDS/DIVISIONS/AFFILIATES:

vSphere
VMware Horizon
VMware AirWatch
Nyansa
Octarine
Lastline
Blue Medora TVS
Datrium

CONTACTS: *Note: Officers with more than one job title may be intentionally listed here more than once.*

Rangarajan Raghuram, CEO
Zane Rowe, CFO
Michael Dell, Chairman of the Board
Andrew Munk, Chief Accounting Officer
Jean Brulard, Executive VP, Divisional
Amy Olli, Executive VP
Sumit Dhawan, Other Executive Officer

GROWTH PLANS/SPECIAL FEATURES:

VMware is an industry leader in virtualizing IT infrastructure and became a stand-alone entity after spinning off from Dell Technologies in November 2021. The software provider operates in the three segments: licenses; subscriptions and software as a service; and services. VMware's solutions are used across IT infrastructure, application development, and cybersecurity teams, and the company takes a neutral approach to being the cohesion between cloud environments. The Palo Alto, California, firm operates and sells on a global scale, with about half its revenue from the United States, through direct sales, distributors, and partnerships.

FINANCIAL DATA: *Note: Data for latest year may not have been available at press time.*

In U.S. $	2021	2020	2019	2018	2017	2016
Revenue	11,767,000,000	10,811,000,000	8,974,000,000	7,922,000,000		7,093,000,000
R&D Expense	2,816,000,000	2,522,000,000	1,975,000,000	1,755,000,000		1,503,000,000
Operating Income	2,430,000,000	1,520,000,000	2,059,000,000	1,779,000,000		1,491,000,000
Operating Margin %						
SGA Expense	4,478,000,000	4,970,000,000	3,682,000,000	3,247,000,000		3,046,000,000
Net Income	2,058,000,000	6,412,000,000	2,422,000,000	570,000,000		1,186,000,000
Operating Cash Flow	4,409,000,000	3,872,000,000	3,663,000,000	3,211,000,000		2,381,000,000
Capital Expenditure	329,000,000	279,000,000	245,000,000	263,000,000		153,000,000
EBITDA	3,611,000,000	2,460,000,000	3,647,000,000	2,211,000,000		1,844,000,000
Return on Assets %						
Return on Equity %						
Debt to Equity						

CONTACT INFORMATION:

Phone: 650 427-5000 Fax: 650 475-5005
Toll-Free: 877-486-9273
Address: 3401 Hillview Ave., Palo Alto, CA 94304 United States

STOCK TICKER/OTHER:

Stock Ticker: VMW
Exchange: NYS
Employees: 34,000
Fiscal Year Ends: 12/31
Parent Company:

SALARIES/BONUSES:

Top Exec. Salary: $885,417 Bonus: $
Second Exec. Salary: $698,438 Bonus: $

OTHER THOUGHTS:

Estimated Female Officers or Directors: 3
Hot Spot for Advancement for Women/Minorities: Y

VMware Tanzu Labs

NAIC Code: 511210B

tanzu.vmware.com

TYPES OF BUSINESS:

Computer Software, Network Management (IT), System Testing & Storage
Application Development Tools
Software Development Tools
Microservice Platform
Cloud Migration Solutions
Multi-cloud Kubernetes Management Product
Connectivity Products
Consulting Services

BRANDS/DIVISIONS/AFFILIATES:

VMware Inc
Tanzu Application Platform
Tanzu Application Service
Tanzu Build Service
Tanzu Data Services
Tanzu Kubernetes Grid
Tanzu Mission Control
Tanzu Observability

CONTACTS: *Note: Officers with more than one job title may be intentionally listed here more than once.*

Rangarajan Raghuram, CEO-VMware Corporate
Andrew Cohen, General Counsel
Onsi Fakhouri, Senior VP, Divisional
Scott Yara, Senior VP, Divisional
Edward Hieatt, Senior VP, Divisional

GROWTH PLANS/SPECIAL FEATURES:

VMware Tanzu Labs, a subsidiary of VMware Inc., offers innovative products and services that help organizations build applications and modernize their software development practices. The company's Tanzu Application Platform provides a set of developer tools for building and deploying software swiftly and securely on any compliant public cloud or on-premises Kubernetes cluster. The Tanzu Application Service is a platform for enterprises that want to continuously deliver and run microservices across clouds. Tanzu Build Service automates container creation, management and governance at enterprise scale. Tanzu Data Services enables migration to the cloud through its portfolio of on-demand caching, messaging and database software for development teams building modern applications. The Tanzu Kubernetes Grid enables organizations to streamline operations across multi-cloud infrastructure. Tanzu Mission Control is a multi-cloud Kubernetes management platform that virtualizes the cloud that enables management, operation and distribution of applications at scale on any cloud. Tanzu Observability by Wavefront offers enterprise observability for multi-cloud environments, a future-proof system that scales with the enterprise. The Tanzu Service Mesh provides advanced, end-to-end connectivity, security and insights for modern applications, across application end-users, microservices, application programming interfaces (APIs) and data, enabling compliance with Service Level Objectives (SLOs), data protection and privacy regulations. VMware Tanzu offers consulting services as well as online resources. VMware Tanzu has headquarter locations in California, New York, London and Singapore, as well as offices in the Americas, Europe and Asia Pacific.

FINANCIAL DATA: *Note: Data for latest year may not have been available at press time.*

In U.S. $	2021	2020	2019	2018	2017	2016
Revenue	610,000,000	605,209,968	611,323,200	509,436,000	416,267,000	280,874,000
R&D Expense						
Operating Income						
Operating Margin %						
SGA Expense						
Net Income			-141,903,008	-163,514,000	-232,866,000	-282,672,000
Operating Cash Flow						
Capital Expenditure						
EBITDA						
Return on Assets %						
Return on Equity %						
Debt to Equity						

CONTACT INFORMATION:

Phone: 415-777-4868 Fax:
Toll-Free:
Address: 875 Howard St., Fl. 5, San Francisco, CA 94103 United States

STOCK TICKER/OTHER:

Stock Ticker: Subsidiary
Exchange:
Employees: 2,518
Fiscal Year Ends: 12/31
Parent Company: VMware Inc

SALARIES/BONUSES:

Top Exec. Salary: $ Bonus: $
Second Exec. Salary: $ Bonus: $

OTHER THOUGHTS:

Estimated Female Officers or Directors:
Hot Spot for Advancement for Women/Minorities:

Vodafone Group plc

www.vodafone.com

NAIC Code: 517210

TYPES OF BUSINESS:

Cell Phone Service
Mobile Communications
Fixed Communications
Unified Communications
Cloud Hosting
Internet of Things
Carrier Services

BRANDS/DIVISIONS/AFFILIATES:

TPG Telecom

GROWTH PLANS/SPECIAL FEATURES:

With about 270 million wireless customers, Vodafone is one of the largest wireless carriers in the world. More recently, the firm has acquired cable operations and gained access to additional fixed-line networks, either building its own or gaining wholesale access. Vodafone is increasingly pushing converged services of wireless and fixed-line telephone services. Europe accounts for about three fourths of reported service revenue, with major operations in Germany (about 30% of total service revenue), the U.K. (13%), Italy (12%), and Spain (10%). Outside of Europe, 65%-owned Vodacom, which serves sub-Saharan Africa, is Vodafone's largest controlled subsidiary (12% of total service revenue). The firm also owns stakes in operations in India, Australia, and the Netherlands.

CONTACTS: *Note: Officers with more than one job title may be intentionally listed here more than once.*

Nick Read, CEO
Margherita Della Valle, CFO
Ahmed Essam, Chief Commercial Operations Officer
Leanne Wood, Chief Human Resources Officer
Johan Wibergh, Group Technology Officer
Rosemary Martin, General Counsel
Warren Finegold, Dir.-Strategy & Bus. Dev.
Matthew Kirk, Dir.-External Affairs
Morten Lundal, Chief Commercial Officer
Philipp Humm, CEO-Northern & Central Europe
Paulo Bertoluzzo, CEO-Southern Europe
Nick Jeffery, Dir-Group Enterprises
Gerard Kleisterlee, Chmn.
Nick Read, CEO-Asia-Pacific, Africa & Middle East Region

FINANCIAL DATA: *Note: Data for latest year may not have been available at press time.*

In U.S. $	2021	2020	2019	2018	2017	2016
Revenue	49,475,420,000	50,791,100,000	49,313,930,000	52,594,670,000	53,791,770,000	58,675,140,000
R&D Expense						
Operating Income	6,119,913,000	10,106,500,000	4,581,748,000	4,921,680,000	4,153,726,000	2,553,334,000
Operating Margin %						
SGA Expense	10,019,540,000	10,868,800,000	10,504,030,000	10,903,810,000	11,777,930,000	12,430,140,000
Net Income	126,486,500	-1,038,996,000	-9,057,336,000	2,754,469,000	-7,111,478,000	-5,762,545,000
Operating Cash Flow	19,441,650,000	19,626,860,000	14,658,880,000	15,359,080,000	16,062,660,000	15,009,250,000
Capital Expenditure	9,757,530,000	8,588,659,000	9,205,281,000	9,218,832,000	10,007,110,000	16,975,450,000
EBITDA	23,783,980,000	20,074,080,000	10,258,960,000	17,479,980,000	17,603,080,000	15,036,460,000
Return on Assets %						
Return on Equity %						
Debt to Equity						

CONTACT INFORMATION:

Phone: 44 163533251 Fax: 44 1635238080
Toll-Free:
Address: Vodafone House, The Connection, Newbury, Berkshire RG14 2FN United Kingdom

STOCK TICKER/OTHER:

Stock Ticker: VOD
Employees: 105,000
Parent Company:
Exchange: NAS
Fiscal Year Ends: 03/31

SALARIES/BONUSES:

Top Exec. Salary: $1,398,080 Bonus: $1,732,288
Second Exec. Salary: $932,053 Bonus: $1,154,415

OTHER THOUGHTS:

Estimated Female Officers or Directors: 2
Hot Spot for Advancement for Women/Minorities: Y

Volkswagen AG (VW)

NAIC Code: 336111

www.volkswagenag.com

TYPES OF BUSINESS:

Automobile Manufacturing
Truck Manufacturing
Car Rental Services
Consumer Financing
Digital Services
Electric Cars

BRANDS/DIVISIONS/AFFILIATES:

Volkswagen
Audi
Bentley
Bugatti
Lamborghini
SEAT
Skoda
Ducati

GROWTH PLANS/SPECIAL FEATURES:

Volkswagen is one of the world's largest automotive manufacturers. Automotive brands include Volkswagen passenger cars, Audi, Bentley, Bugatti, Lamborghini, Porsche, SEAT, and Skoda. Commercial vehicle brands include MAN, Navistar, Scania, and Volkswagen. The company's financial services group provides dealer financing to support floor plans, consumer financing for vehicle purchases, vehicle leasing, banking, and other financial services.

CONTACTS: *Note: Officers with more than one job title may be intentionally listed here more than once.*

Herbert Diess, CEO
Frank Witter, Dir.-Finance & IT
Gunnar Kilian, Dir.-Human Resources
Michael Macht, Dir.-Group Production
Hans Dieter Potsch, Dir.-Finance
Leif Ostling, Dir.-Group Commercial Vehicles
Herbert Diess, Chmn.
Jochem Heizmann, Dir.-China
Francisco Javier Garcia Sanz, Dir.-Procurement

FINANCIAL DATA: *Note: Data for latest year may not have been available at press time.*

In U.S. $	2021	2020	2019	2018	2017	2016
Revenue		251,712,700,000	285,309,500,000	266,354,600,000	260,519,300,000	245,370,300,000
R&D Expense						
Operating Income		11,357,810,000	18,090,960,000	16,299,820,000	15,181,770,000	9,406,304,000
Operating Margin %						
SGA Expense		31,402,530,000	34,721,670,000	33,122,520,000	34,969,000,000	33,920,970,000
Net Income		10,013,890,000	15,682,070,000	13,705,710,000	13,132,010,000	6,063,447,000
Operating Cash Flow		28,121,790,000	20,308,990,000	8,212,588,000	-1,338,272,000	10,649,710,000
Capital Expenditure		20,041,330,000	21,910,400,000	21,415,750,000	20,680,540,000	21,346,850,000
EBITDA		45,796,020,000	50,835,150,000	44,700,550,000	42,793,100,000	34,469,830,000
Return on Assets %						
Return on Equity %						
Debt to Equity						

CONTACT INFORMATION:

Phone: 49 536190 Fax: 49 5361-928282
Toll-Free:
Address: Berliner Ring 2, Wolfsburg, 38440 Germany

STOCK TICKER/OTHER:

Stock Ticker: VLKPF
Exchange: PINX
Employees: 662,600
Fiscal Year Ends: 12/31
Parent Company:

SALARIES/BONUSES:

Top Exec. Salary: $ Bonus: $
Second Exec. Salary: $ Bonus: $

OTHER THOUGHTS:

Estimated Female Officers or Directors:
Hot Spot for Advancement for Women/Minorities:

Volvo AB

www.volvogroup.com

NAIC Code: 336120

TYPES OF BUSINESS:

Truck Manufacturer
Engines
Buses
Aerospace Products
Construction Equipment
Financial Services
Intelligent Transport Systems
Overhaul & Repair Services

BRANDS/DIVISIONS/AFFILIATES:

Volvo Group
Volvo
Volvo Penta
Rokbak
Renault Trucks
Revost
Nova Bus
Mack

GROWTH PLANS/SPECIAL FEATURES:

Volvo AB is the world's second- largest manufacturer of heavy-duty trucks and largest manufacturer of heavy diesel engines. Its Volvo brand sells medium- and heavy-duty trucks worldwide; the Renault brand sells various types of commercial trucks in Europe and Mack manufactures primarily vocational trucks for sale in North America. Volvo also sells buses, construction equipment, marine drive systems, aircraft engine components, and financial services.

CONTACTS: *Note: Officers with more than one job title may be intentionally listed here more than once.*

Martin Lundstedt, CEO
Jan Gurander, Deputy CEO
Jan Ytterberg, Exec. VP-Group Finance
Diana Niu, Exec. VP-Group Human Resources
Scott Rafkin, Chief Digital Officer\Exec. VP
Sofia Frandberg, General Counsel
Mikael Bratt, Exec. VP-Group Truck Oper.
Karin Falk, Exec. VP-Corp. Strategy
Marten Wikforss, Exec. VP-Corp. Comm.
Anders Osberg, Exec. VP-Corp. Finance & Control
Niklas Gustavsson, Exec. VP-Public & Environmental Affairs
Martin Weissburg, Exec. VP-Volvo Construction Equipment
Torbjorn Homstrom, Exec. VP-Group Trucks Tech.
Dennis Slagle, Exec. VP-Group Trucks Sales & Mktg., Americas
Carl-Henric Svanberg, Chmn.
Peter Karlsten, Exec. VP-Group Trucks Sales & Mktg., EMEA

FINANCIAL DATA: *Note: Data for latest year may not have been available at press time.*

In U.S. $	2021	2020	2019	2018	2017	2016
Revenue		37,350,540,000	47,672,970,000	43,132,030,000	36,942,430,000	33,318,910,000
R&D Expense		1,853,810,000	2,045,944,000	1,754,597,000	1,776,558,000	1,614,662,000
Operating Income		3,214,977,000	5,146,148,000	3,664,579,000	3,170,061,000	2,537,594,000
Operating Margin %						
SGA Expense		3,435,585,000	4,297,157,000	4,048,849,000	3,776,925,000	3,530,162,000
Net Income		2,131,914,000	3,957,582,000	2,747,607,000	2,315,441,000	1,450,889,000
Operating Cash Flow		3,378,087,000	4,309,186,000	3,441,764,000	4,149,386,000	1,937,793,000
Capital Expenditure		1,911,417,000	2,428,890,000	2,302,970,000	2,122,644,000	2,244,922,000
EBITDA		5,282,331,000	7,624,920,000	5,765,703,000	5,184,112,000	4,176,093,000
Return on Assets %						
Return on Equity %						
Debt to Equity						

CONTACT INFORMATION:

Phone: 46 31660000 Fax: 46 31665170
Toll-Free:
Address: Volvo Bergegardsvag 1, Torslanda, Gothenburg, SE-405 08 Sweden

STOCK TICKER/OTHER:

Stock Ticker: VLVLY
Employees: 95,850
Parent Company:
Exchange: PINX
Fiscal Year Ends: 12/31

SALARIES/BONUSES:

Top Exec. Salary: $ Bonus: $
Second Exec. Salary: $ Bonus: $

OTHER THOUGHTS:

Estimated Female Officers or Directors: 5
Hot Spot for Advancement for Women/Minorities: Y

WatchGuard Technologies Inc

NAIC Code: 511210E

www.watchguard.com

TYPES OF BUSINESS:

Computer Software: Network Security, Managed Access, Digital ID, Cybersecurity & Anti-Virus
Firewall & VPN Appliances
Training & Technical Support
Online Services
Network Security Services
Authentication Solutions
Endpoint Security Solutions

BRANDS/DIVISIONS/AFFILIATES:

Gladiator Corporation

CONTACTS:

Note: Officers with more than one job title may be intentionally listed here more than once.

Prakash Panjwani, CEO
Shari McLaren, Sr. VP-Operations
Andy Reinland, CFO
Michelle Welch, Sr. VP-Mktg.
Shane Watkins, VP-Global Human Resources
Wayson Vannatta, CIO
Sin-Yaw Wang, VP-Eng.
Dave R. Taylor, VP-Corp. Strategy
Jon Bickford, VP-Sales, U.S.
Shari McLaren, VP-Customer Svcs. & Support
Philippe Ortodoro, VP-Sales, EMEA
Corey Nachreiner, CTO
Scott Robertson, VP-Sales, Asia Pacific

GROWTH PLANS/SPECIAL FEATURES:

WatchGuard Technologies, Inc. develops and implements network security services designed to protect enterprises, small-to-medium-sized businesses and organizations that use the internet for ecommerce and secure communications. WatchGuard offers off-network security services, including trusted wireless environments, weak and stolen passwords, advanced malware, SD-WAN, managed security services, data loss, network blind spots and Ransomware; and regulatory compliance services such as KCSiE (keeping children safe in education), GDPR (general data protection regulation), PCI DSS (payment card industry data security standard) and HIPAA (Health Insurance Portability and Accountability Act). These solutions primarily serve the education, finance, healthcare, manufacturing, retail, hospitality and state and local government industries. WatchGuard's products and services are categorized into four groups: network security, offering solutions that combat security threats for organizations, small/midsize businesses and enterprises; multi-factor authentication on an easy-to-use cloud platform; secure Wi-Fi, from wireless-enabled Firebox appliances to cloud-ready access points; and endpoint security, providing always-on protection no matter where the endpoint is located. WatchGuard appliances conduct more than 1 billion security scans every hour. Based in Washington, USA, the firm has office locations throughout North America, Latin America, Europe, the Middle East, Africa and Asia Pacific. WatchGuard is privately-owned by Gladiator Corporation. In June 2020, WatchGuard completed the acquisition of Panda Security, an advanced endpoint protection provider.

FINANCIAL DATA:

Note: Data for latest year may not have been available at press time.

In U.S. $	2021	2020	2019	2018	2017	2016
Revenue						
R&D Expense						
Operating Income						
Operating Margin %						
SGA Expense						
Net Income						
Operating Cash Flow						
Capital Expenditure						
EBITDA						
Return on Assets %						
Return on Equity %						
Debt to Equity						

CONTACT INFORMATION:

Phone: 206-613-6600 Fax: 206-521-8342
Toll-Free: 800-734-9905
Address: 505 5th Ave. S., Ste. 500, Seattle, WA 98104 United States

STOCK TICKER/OTHER:

Stock Ticker: Private
Employees: 1,200
Parent Company: Gladiator Corporation
Exchange:
Fiscal Year Ends: 12/31

SALARIES/BONUSES:

Top Exec. Salary: $ Bonus: $
Second Exec. Salary: $ Bonus: $

OTHER THOUGHTS:

Estimated Female Officers or Directors: 1
Hot Spot for Advancement for Women/Minorities:

Waymo LLC

www.waymo.com

NAIC Code: 511210

TYPES OF BUSINESS:

Technology for Self-Driving Vehicles
Self-Driving Hardware
Self-Driving Software
Proprietary Sensors
Proprietary Technology
Autonomous Ride-Hailing Services

BRANDS/DIVISIONS/AFFILIATES:

Alphabet Inc
Google
Waymo Driver
Waymo One
Waymo Via

CONTACTS: *Note: Officers with more than one job title may be intentionally listed here more than once.*

Dmitri Dolgov, Co-CEO
Tekedra Mawakana, Co-CEO
Mauricio Pena, Chief Safety Officer
Becky Bucich, Chief People Officer
Dan Chu, Chief Product Officer

GROWTH PLANS/SPECIAL FEATURES:

Waymo, LLC is an autonomous car development company and subsidiary of Alphabet, Inc., the owner of Google. Waymo was enabled as a separate entity in order to commercialize and distribute the self-driving vehicle technology that Google developed. Waymo offers both software and hardware for self-driving vehicles called the World's Most Experienced Driver (Waymo Driver), which is a combination of light detection and ranging (lidar) technology, cameras and radar. The Waymo One driverless system's vehicles have sensors and software designed to detect pedestrians, cyclists, vehicles, road work and more from up to three football fields away in all 360 degrees. The sensors and software detect and predict the behavior of all road users within the range. The sensors can even observe when a cyclist has extended his/her arm as a traffic signal. This signals the Waymo vehicle to slow down and make room for the cyclist to pass safely. Waymo Via is a driverless system for large trucks which is under testing in various states. The Waymo app enables users to locate and hire a self-driving car. The vehicle comes to the confirmed rider, who is then able to follow the route through the app throughout the ride until the destination is reached. During 2021, Waymo began its autonomous ride-hailing service in San Francisco for everyday needs to an initial group of users who would provide feedback.

FINANCIAL DATA: *Note: Data for latest year may not have been available at press time.*

In U.S. $	2021	2020	2019	2018	2017	2016
Revenue						
R&D Expense						
Operating Income						
Operating Margin %						
SGA Expense						
Net Income						
Operating Cash Flow						
Capital Expenditure						
EBITDA						
Return on Assets %						
Return on Equity %						
Debt to Equity						

CONTACT INFORMATION:

Phone: 650-253-0000 Fax:
Toll-Free:
Address: 1600 Amphitheatre Pkwy., Mountain View, CA 94043 United States

STOCK TICKER/OTHER:

Stock Ticker: Subsidiary
Employees: 1,500
Parent Company: Alphabet Inc
Exchange:
Fiscal Year Ends: 12/31

SALARIES/BONUSES:

Top Exec. Salary: $ Bonus: $
Second Exec. Salary: $ Bonus: $

OTHER THOUGHTS:

Estimated Female Officers or Directors:
Hot Spot for Advancement for Women/Minorities:

Wieden+Kennedy

NAIC Code: 541810

www.wk.com

TYPES OF BUSINESS:

Advertising Agency
Entertainment Content Production
Viral Marketing
VR/AR
Internet of Things

BRANDS/DIVISIONS/AFFILIATES:

W+K Lodge

CONTACTS:

Note: Officers with more than one job title may be intentionally listed here more than once.

Colleen DeCourcy, Co-Exec. Dir.-Creative
Mark Fitzloff, Co-Exec. Dir.-Creative
Tom Blessington, Chmn.

GROWTH PLANS/SPECIAL FEATURES:

Wieden+Kennedy (W+K) is a global advertising agency. Key accounts have included Nike, KFC, Facebook, Samsung, McDonalds, Ford, Old Spice, P&G, Sprite, Coca-Cola Company and Converse, although Nike remains the agency's signature client. The company has two U.S. offices in Portland and New York, and six offices internationally in Sao Paulo, London, Amsterdam, Delhi, Shanghai and Tokyo. W+K works in broadcast, print and online media, while also utilizing unconventional marketing techniques such as its KFC: The Dating Simulator free dating simulator game, which follows the player's journey through cooking school, navigating relationships and social challenges to bring them closer to dating Colonel Sanders. W+K claims that its expertise lies in understanding cultural trends and in utilizing this understanding to make brands influence culture. W+K's Lodge division entirely focuses on creativity through emerging technology, using the firm's engineers, designers, strategists and producers to build creative solutions, from concept to execution. W+K Lodge specializes in mobile, machine learning, virtual reality (VR), augmented reality (AR), robotics and Internet of Things (IoT) platforms and technologies. Primary industries that W+K serves include automobile, beverages, consumer packaged goods, consumer products, financial, food, media, sports, sustainable energy, transportation and travel.

FINANCIAL DATA:

Note: Data for latest year may not have been available at press time.

In U.S. $	2021	2020	2019	2018	2017	2016
Revenue						
R&D Expense						
Operating Income						
Operating Margin %						
SGA Expense						
Net Income						
Operating Cash Flow						
Capital Expenditure						
EBITDA						
Return on Assets %						
Return on Equity %						
Debt to Equity						

CONTACT INFORMATION:

Phone: 503-937-7000 Fax: 503-937-8000
Toll-Free:
Address: 224 NW 13th Ave., Portland, OR 97209 United States

STOCK TICKER/OTHER:

Stock Ticker: Private
Employees: 1,400
Parent Company:
Exchange:
Fiscal Year Ends:

SALARIES/BONUSES:

Top Exec. Salary: $ Bonus: $
Second Exec. Salary: $ Bonus: $

OTHER THOUGHTS:

Estimated Female Officers or Directors: 10
Hot Spot for Advancement for Women/Minorities: Y

Wipro Limited

www.wipro.com

NAIC Code: 541512

TYPES OF BUSINESS:

IT Consulting
Computer Hardware & Software Design
Hydraulic Equipment
Medical Electronics
Lighting Equipment
Soaps & Toiletries

BRANDS/DIVISIONS/AFFILIATES:

Cloud Studios
METRO-NOM GMBH
METRO Systems Romania SRL

CONTACTS: *Note: Officers with more than one job title may be intentionally listed here more than once.*

Abidali Z. Neemuchwala, CEO
Bhanumurthy B. M., Pres.
Jatin Dalal, CFO
MIlan Rao, Pres.-Mktg., Innovation & Tech.
Saurabh Govil, Chief Human Resources Officer
Sangita Singh, Sr. VP- Health Care & Life Sciences
Nitin Parab, Sr. VP-Global Technology
N.S. Bala, Sr. VP-Mfg. & High Tech.
Inderpreet Sawhney, Sr. VP
Rishad Premji, Chief Strategy Officer
Ayan Mukerji, Sr. VP-Media & Telecom
Vineet Agrawal, Pres., Wipro Consumer Care & Lighting
Anurag Behar, Chief Sustainability Officer
Alexis Samuel, Chief Process Officer
Rajat Mathur Rajat Mathur Rajat Mathur, Chief Sales & Oper. Officer-Growth Markets
Rishad Premji, Chmn.
Ulrich Meister, Sr. VP-Continental Europe

GROWTH PLANS/SPECIAL FEATURES:

Wipro is a leading global IT services provider, with 175,000 employees. Based in Bengaluru, the Indian IT services firm leverages its offshore outsourcing model to derive over half of its revenue (57%) from North America. The company offers traditional IT services offerings: consulting, managed services, and cloud infrastructure services as well as business process outsourcing as a service.

FINANCIAL DATA: *Note: Data for latest year may not have been available at press time.*

In U.S. $	2021	2020	2019	2018	2017	2016
Revenue	8,253,025,000	8,130,474,000	7,805,553,000	7,259,632,000	7,333,325,000	6,827,535,000
R&D Expense						
Operating Income	1,599,602,000	1,366,480,000	1,288,324,000	1,103,272,000	1,200,481,000	1,241,145,000
Operating Margin %						
SGA Expense	1,013,738,000	921,871,800	1,009,248,000	959,044,600	855,094,000	785,824,800
Net Income	1,438,227,000	1,295,292,000	1,199,535,000	1,066,966,000	1,131,105,000	1,184,759,000
Operating Cash Flow	1,965,894,000	1,340,925,000	1,549,745,000	1,122,285,000	1,236,068,000	1,050,871,000
Capital Expenditure	260,835,700	313,064,200	303,524,500	291,386,700	277,836,600	185,877,300
EBITDA	2,277,812,000	1,978,685,000	1,872,030,000	1,692,748,000	1,803,733,000	1,746,668,000
Return on Assets %						
Return on Equity %						
Debt to Equity						

CONTACT INFORMATION:

Phone: 91 8028440055 Fax: 91 8028440256
Toll-Free:
Address: Doddakannelli, Sarjapur Rd., Bengaluru, Karnataka 560035 India

STOCK TICKER/OTHER:

Stock Ticker: WIT
Exchange: NYS
Employees: 175,000
Fiscal Year Ends: 03/31
Parent Company:

SALARIES/BONUSES:

Top Exec. Salary: $1,312,938 Bonus: $1,542,132
Second Exec. Salary: $796,178 Bonus: $761,311

OTHER THOUGHTS:

Estimated Female Officers or Directors: 3
Hot Spot for Advancement for Women/Minorities: Y

Wireless Telecom Group Inc

www.wirelesstelecomgroup.com

NAIC Code: 334220

TYPES OF BUSINESS:

Communications Equipment, Mobile and Microwave, Manufacturing
Radio Frequency Components
Microwave Components
Manufacture
Electronic Test Equipment

BRANDS/DIVISIONS/AFFILIATES:

Boonton
Microlab
Noisecom
CommAgility
Holzworth

GROWTH PLANS/SPECIAL FEATURES:

Wireless Telecom Group Inc designs and manufactures radio frequency (RF) and microwave-based products for wireless and advanced communications industries. It focuses on manufacturing a wide selection of RF passive components and integrated subsystems for signal conditioning and distribution in the wireless infrastructure markets, particularly the in-building wireless solutions industry, radio base-station market and medical equipment sector. It also designs and produces electronic test and measurement equipment including power meters, audio and modulation meters, intermodulation test equipment. The company markets its products under the Microlab, Boonton, Noisecom, CommAgility and Holzworth brands.

CONTACTS:

Note: Officers with more than one job title may be intentionally listed here more than once.

Timothy Whelan, CEO
Michael Kandell, CFO
Alan Bazaar, Chairman of the Board
Daniel Monopoli, Chief Technology Officer
Charles Gibson, Director
Alfred Rodriguez, Other Executive Officer

FINANCIAL DATA:

Note: Data for latest year may not have been available at press time.

In U.S. $	2021	2020	2019	2018	2017	2016
Revenue		41,748,000	48,921,000	52,788,000	46,078,000	31,326,730
R&D Expense		6,389,000	5,917,000	4,909,000	4,395,000	4,046,106
Operating Income		-2,284,000	-1,479,000	1,357,000	-3,198,000	-2,548,109
Operating Margin %						
SGA Expense		16,862,000	17,851,000	17,901,000	18,064,000	11,663,760
Net Income		-8,088,000	-414,000	35,000	-4,493,000	-1,832,024
Operating Cash Flow		2,980,000	80,000	3,990,000	1,403,000	623,779
Capital Expenditure		364,000	392,000	853,000	927,000	818,588
EBITDA		-5,674,000	670,000	2,963,000	-1,203,000	-2,045,049
Return on Assets %						
Return on Equity %						
Debt to Equity						

CONTACT INFORMATION:

Phone: 973 386-9696 Fax: 973 386-9191
Toll-Free:
Address: 25 Eastmans Rd., Parsippany, NJ 07054 United States

STOCK TICKER/OTHER:

Stock Ticker: WTT
Employees: 150
Parent Company:
Exchange: ASE
Fiscal Year Ends: 12/31

SALARIES/BONUSES:

Top Exec. Salary: $325,000 Bonus: $
Second Exec. Salary: $237,211 Bonus: $

OTHER THOUGHTS:

Estimated Female Officers or Directors:
Hot Spot for Advancement for Women/Minorities:

WM Motor Technology Co Ltd

www.wm-motor.com

NAIC Code: 336111

TYPES OF BUSINESS:

Automobile Manufacturing, All-Electric
Electric Vehicles
Smart Car Development
Smart Car Manufacturing
Technologies
Lithium Ceramic Batteries

BRANDS/DIVISIONS/AFFILIATES:

Weltmeister
E5
EX5
EX6
EX6 Plus

GROWTH PLANS/SPECIAL FEATURES:

WM Motor Technology Co., Ltd. designs, develops and manufactures intelligent electric motor automobiles. Based in Shanghai, China, WM Motor revealed its first car in December 2017 under the Weltmeister brand, the EX5 model, and began taking orders domestically the following year. Current makes include the Weltmeister E5 electric compact sedan, the EX5 electric compact sport utility vehicle (SUV), the EX6 electric mid-size SUV and the W6 electric compact SUV. The EX6 Plus is a smart large six-seater, a pure electric SUV. The company's vehicles feature its own next-generation lithium ceramic battery, full car interaction system, hidden door handles, light-emitting diode (LED) headlights, an intelligent interaction system that recognizes authorized users, among other features.

CONTACTS: *Note: Officers with more than one job title may be intentionally listed here more than once.*

Freeman Shen, CEO

FINANCIAL DATA: *Note: Data for latest year may not have been available at press time.*

In U.S. $	2021	2020	2019	2018	2017	2016
Revenue						
R&D Expense						
Operating Income						
Operating Margin %						
SGA Expense						
Net Income						
Operating Cash Flow						
Capital Expenditure						
EBITDA						
Return on Assets %						
Return on Equity %						
Debt to Equity						

CONTACT INFORMATION:

Phone: 4006 - 999 - 666 Fax:
Toll-Free:
Address: 333 SongZe Ave., 5/Fl, Twr. C, National Exhibition, Shanghai, Shanghai 201702 China

STOCK TICKER/OTHER:

Stock Ticker: Private
Employees:
Parent Company:
Exchange:
Fiscal Year Ends:

SALARIES/BONUSES:

Top Exec. Salary: $ Bonus: $
Second Exec. Salary: $ Bonus: $

OTHER THOUGHTS:

Estimated Female Officers or Directors:
Hot Spot for Advancement for Women/Minorities:

Wolfspeed Inc

NAIC Code: 334413

www.wolfspeed.com

TYPES OF BUSINESS:

Semiconductor and Related Device Manufacturing
Wide Bandgap Semiconductors
Manufacturing
Silicon Carbide Materials
Gallium Nitride Materials
Radio Frequency Applications
Power Products
Broadband

BRANDS/DIVISIONS/AFFILIATES:

Cree Inc
CreeLED Inc

GROWTH PLANS/SPECIAL FEATURES:

Wolfspeed Inc is involved in the manufacturing of wide bandgap semiconductors. It is focused on silicon carbide and gallium nitride (GaN) materials and devices for power and radio-frequency (RF) applications. The company serves applications such as transportation, power supplies, inverters, and wireless systems. Geographically, it derives a majority of revenue from Europe and also has a presence in the United States; China; Japan; South Korea, and other countries.

CONTACTS: *Note: Officers with more than one job title may be intentionally listed here more than once.*

Gregg Lowe, CEO
Neill Reynolds, CFO
Darren Jackson, Chairman of the Board

FINANCIAL DATA: *Note: Data for latest year may not have been available at press time.*

In U.S. $	2021	2020	2019	2018	2017	2016
Revenue	525,600,000	903,900,000	1,080,000,000	1,493,680,000	1,473,000,000	1,616,627,000
R&D Expense	177,800,000	184,200,000	157,900,000	164,321,000	158,549,000	168,848,000
Operating Income	-209,300,000	-161,800,000	-11,200,000	-70,940,000	-28,651,000	6,442,000
Operating Margin %						
SGA Expense	181,600,000	211,400,000	200,700,000	283,489,000	277,175,000	283,052,000
Net Income	-523,900,000	-191,700,000	-375,100,000	-279,968,000	-98,118,000	-21,536,000
Operating Cash Flow	-125,500,000	-29,000,000	202,300,000	167,358,000	215,900,000	203,316,000
Capital Expenditure	576,400,000	244,300,000	153,000,000	195,803,000	99,333,000	134,461,000
EBITDA	-173,900,000	-31,600,000	132,400,000	82,997,000	121,857,000	165,587,000
Return on Assets %						
Return on Equity %						
Debt to Equity						

CONTACT INFORMATION:

Phone: 919 313-5300 Fax: 919 361-5452
Toll-Free:
Address: 4600 Silicon Dr., Durham, NC 27703 United States

STOCK TICKER/OTHER:

Stock Ticker: WOLF Exchange: NYS
Employees: 5,130 Fiscal Year Ends: 06/27
Parent Company:

SALARIES/BONUSES:

Top Exec. Salary: $473,468 Bonus: $500,000
Second Exec. Salary: $873,072 Bonus: $

OTHER THOUGHTS:

Estimated Female Officers or Directors:
Hot Spot for Advancement for Women/Minorities:

Woodward Inc

www.woodward.com

NAIC Code: 334513

TYPES OF BUSINESS:

Industrial Controls
Energy Controls
Power System Equipment

BRANDS/DIVISIONS/AFFILIATES:

GROWTH PLANS/SPECIAL FEATURES:

Woodward Inc creates energy control and optimization solutions. The systems and solutions can help evaluate the performance, efficiencies, and emissions of its customers' products. Specifically, the control and optimization solutions are for aerospace, energy, and other industrial markets. Fluid and electrical energy, motions, or other outputs may be monitored or improved with the company's products. Also, Woodward provides aftermarket repair and replacements to enhance support. A majority of sales derive from the United States, but facilities in different regions of the world help assemble and promote its products through various locations.

CONTACTS: *Note: Officers with more than one job title may be intentionally listed here more than once.*

Thomas Gendron, CEO
Mark Hartman, CFO
A. Fawzy, Chief Compliance Officer
Thomas Cromwell, COO
Chad Preiss, President, Divisional
Sagar Patel, President, Divisional
Steven Meyer, Vice President
Paul Benson, Vice President, Divisional
John Tysver, Vice President, Divisional
Dan Bowman, Vice President, Divisional
Matteo Pisciotta, Vice President, Divisional

FINANCIAL DATA: *Note: Data for latest year may not have been available at press time.*

In U.S. $	2021	2020	2019	2018	2017	2016
Revenue	2,245,832,000	2,495,665,000	2,900,197,000	2,325,873,000	2,098,685,000	2,023,078,000
R&D Expense	117,091,000	133,134,000	159,107,000	148,279,000	126,519,000	126,170,000
Operating Income	247,101,000	289,399,000	337,231,000	265,162,000	269,407,000	238,931,000
Operating Margin %						
SGA Expense	186,866,000	217,710,000	211,205,000	192,757,000	176,633,000	154,951,000
Net Income	208,649,000	240,395,000	259,602,000	180,378,000	200,507,000	180,838,000
Operating Cash Flow	464,669,000	349,491,000	390,608,000	299,292,000	307,537,000	435,379,000
Capital Expenditure	37,689,000	47,087,000	99,066,000	127,140,000	92,336,000	175,692,000
EBITDA	409,605,000	448,850,000	506,617,000	367,479,000	361,094,000	322,298,000
Return on Assets %						
Return on Equity %						
Debt to Equity						

CONTACT INFORMATION:

Phone: 970 482-5811 Fax: 815 636-6033
Toll-Free:
Address: 1081 Woodward Way, Fort Collins, CO 80524 United States

STOCK TICKER/OTHER:

Stock Ticker: WWD
Employees: 7,200
Parent Company:
Exchange: NAS
Fiscal Year Ends: 09/30

SALARIES/BONUSES:

Top Exec. Salary: $849,231 Bonus: $
Second Exec. Salary: $560,100 Bonus: $

OTHER THOUGHTS:

Estimated Female Officers or Directors:
Hot Spot for Advancement for Women/Minorities:

Xiaomi Corporation

NAIC Code: 334220

www.mi.com/en

TYPES OF BUSINESS:

Cellular Telephones Manufacturing
Internet
Smartphone
Manufacture
Internet of Things
Artificial Intelligence
Laser Projector
Smart Devices

BRANDS/DIVISIONS/AFFILIATES:

Mi
Redmi
POCO

GROWTH PLANS/SPECIAL FEATURES:

Xiaomi is a technology product and services company founded in early 2010, focusing mainly on smartphones and Internet of Things products and related Internet services. An early adopter of online smartphone sales, Xiaomi uses Android as its operating system but has its own customized user interface called MIUI. As competition in its home Chinese smartphone market intensified and growth has slowed, it has expanded into other markets and has become the smartphone market leader in India and is gaining market share in Europe. In 2020, from a country perspective, 50% of its overall revenue was generated in mainland China, down from 94% in 2015. The company listed on the Hong Kong market at the beginning of July 2018.

CONTACTS: *Note: Officers with more than one job title may be intentionally listed here more than once.*

Lei Jun, CEO
Wang Xiang, Pres.
Lei Jun, Chmn.

FINANCIAL DATA: *Note: Data for latest year may not have been available at press time.*

In U.S. $	2021	2020	2019	2018	2017	2016
Revenue		38,494,700,000	32,227,750,000	27,386,160,000	17,946,570,000	10,714,600,000
R&D Expense		1,449,215,000	1,173,094,000	904,466,200	493,408,600	329,454,500
Operating Income		1,529,888,000	1,234,595,000	-519,797,400	889,313,100	240,326,900
Operating Margin %						
SGA Expense		2,862,979,000	2,110,846,000	3,145,788,000	660,927,900	391,765,100
Net Income		3,187,021,000	1,572,595,000	2,122,105,000	-6,861,753,000	86,621,260
Operating Cash Flow		3,425,473,000	3,727,940,000	-221,476,600	-155,889,900	709,451,000
Capital Expenditure		473,700,100	533,139,600	592,650,500	190,669,500	285,931,600
EBITDA		4,181,422,000	2,203,251,000	2,357,919,000	945,827,300	235,131,700
Return on Assets %						
Return on Equity %						
Debt to Equity						

CONTACT INFORMATION:

Phone: 86-400-100-5678 Fax: 86-10-6060-6666
Toll-Free:
Address: 68 Qinghe Middle St., Huarunwucai Bldg., Haidian D, Beijing, 100085 China

STOCK TICKER/OTHER:

Stock Ticker: XIACY
Exchange: PINX
Employees: 33,427
Fiscal Year Ends: 12/31
Parent Company:

SALARIES/BONUSES:

Top Exec. Salary: $ Bonus: $
Second Exec. Salary: $ Bonus: $

OTHER THOUGHTS:

Estimated Female Officers or Directors:
Hot Spot for Advancement for Women/Minorities:

Xilinx Inc

www.xilinx.com

NAIC Code: 334413

TYPES OF BUSINESS:

Integrated Circuits
Development System Software
Engineering & Technical Services
Design Services & Field Engineering
Customer Training & Tech. Support

GROWTH PLANS/SPECIAL FEATURES:

Founded in 1984, Xilinx is the leader in FPGAs by market share. Its chips are critical in the performance of various devices in the communications, data processing, industrial, consumer, and automotive markets. Xilinx designs and sells chips, but it outsources manufacturing to third-party chip foundries such as TSMC.

Xilinx offers comprehensive benefit programs.

BRANDS/DIVISIONS/AFFILIATES:

Virtex Ultrascale+
Kintex Ultrascale+
Zynq Ultrascale+
Spartan-7
Atrix-7
Alveo
Solarflare
Vitis

CONTACTS: *Note: Officers with more than one job title may be intentionally listed here more than once.*

Victor Peng, CEO
Brice Hill, CFO
Dennis Segers, Chairman of the Board
Sumeet Gagneja, Chief Accounting Officer
Vincent Tong, Executive VP, Divisional
William Madden, Executive VP
Salil Raje, Executive VP
Catia Hagopian, General Counsel
Vamsi Boppana, Senior VP, Divisional
Mark Wadlington, Senior VP, Divisional

FINANCIAL DATA: *Note: Data for latest year may not have been available at press time.*

In U.S. $	2021	2020	2019	2018	2017	2016
Revenue	3,147,599,000	3,162,666,000	3,059,040,000	2,539,004,000	2,349,330,000	2,213,881,000
R&D Expense	904,639,000	853,589,000	743,027,000	639,750,000	601,443,000	533,891,000
Operating Income	753,139,000	820,250,000	956,799,000	778,405,000	699,394,000	669,881,000
Operating Margin %						
SGA Expense	483,749,000	432,308,000	398,416,000	362,329,000	335,150,000	331,652,000
Net Income	646,508,000	792,721,000	889,750,000	512,381,000	622,512,000	550,867,000
Operating Cash Flow	1,093,221,000	1,190,836,000	1,091,215,000	820,027,000	934,131,000	730,102,000
Capital Expenditure	49,665,000	129,289,000	89,045,000	49,918,000	72,051,000	34,004,000
EBITDA	969,881,000	1,031,337,000	1,125,575,000	893,002,000	807,659,000	760,722,000
Return on Assets %						
Return on Equity %						
Debt to Equity						

CONTACT INFORMATION:

Phone: 408 559-7778 Fax: 408 559-7114
Toll-Free:
Address: 2100 Logic Dr., San Jose, CA 95124 United States

STOCK TICKER/OTHER:

Stock Ticker: XLNX
Employees: 4,890
Parent Company:
Exchange: NAS
Fiscal Year Ends: 02/28

SALARIES/BONUSES:

Top Exec. Salary: $950,000 Bonus: $
Second Exec. Salary: $537,660 Bonus: $350,000

OTHER THOUGHTS:

Estimated Female Officers or Directors: 1
Hot Spot for Advancement for Women/Minorities:

XIUS

www.xius.com

NAIC Code: 511210C

TYPES OF BUSINESS:

Computer Software, Telecom, Communications & VOIP
Payment Processing Solutions
Mobile Technology Innovation
Mobile Payments
Over-the-Top Solutions
Internet of Things Solutions

BRANDS/DIVISIONS/AFFILIATES:

Megasoft Limited
XIUS AMPLIO
XIUS Infinet
XIUS Inergy
XIUS PowerRoam
XIUS Payment Manager
XIUS Wireless Wallet
X-Connect

CONTACTS: *Note: Officers with more than one job title may be intentionally listed here more than once.*

G.V. Kumar, CEO
Shridhar Thathachary, CFO
Sridhar Lanka, VP-Eng.
Kevin Bresnahan, Exec. VP-Oper.
Derek Bowman, Dir.-Bus. Dev.
Umakanta Mansingh, Head-Quality
Sundaresan Nandyal, Head-Global Sales

GROWTH PLANS/SPECIAL FEATURES:

XIUS, a subsidiary of Indian company Megasoft Limited, is a mobile technology specialist focused on real-time transaction processing in mobile infrastructure, mobile payments and over-the-top (OTT) solutions. The company's mobile infrastructure solutions division provides mobile virtual network operator (VNO) services, a mobile services platform, 4G LTE services, Internet of Things (IoT) connectivity and control, solutions its XIUS AMPLIO mobile infrastructure solutions platform, real-time billing through its XIUS INfinet product, real-time mobile services through its XIUS INergy application, and steering of roaming services through its XIUS PowerRoam solution. The mobile commerce division provides domestic and international recharge services through XIUS Payment Manager, mobile payment technology via its XIUS Wireless Wallet application, mobile banking as well as mobile kiosks that offer mobile operator services via its Active Poster product; an end-to-end platform for payment banks to set up technology infrastructure and launch services, and a secure authentication online/mobile platform called eCognito. The mobile-enabled solutions division consists of business intelligence and geo-referencing, which allows the mining of data and creation of custom views, reports and dashboards, along with the capability of viewing key information data on a map; and retail consumer engagement, providing consumer mobile interaction and engagement data to brands and retailers. IoT solutions include X-Connect, X-Fleet, X-Care device management, X-Asset Tracking/Management, and X-Manufacturing. XIUS is headquartered in Massachusetts, with a global delivery center in Hyderabad, India, and operations in the U.S., Mexico, Malaysia and India.

FINANCIAL DATA: *Note: Data for latest year may not have been available at press time.*

In U.S. $	2021	2020	2019	2018	2017	2016
Revenue	468,231,000	507,385,000	480,600,000	480,612,000	385,400,000	354,955,000
R&D Expense						
Operating Income						
Operating Margin %						
SGA Expense						
Net Income	3,979,000	-3,782,000	33,419,000	86,900,000	26,000,000	21,856,000
Operating Cash Flow						
Capital Expenditure						
EBITDA						
Return on Assets %						
Return on Equity %						
Debt to Equity						

CONTACT INFORMATION:

Phone: 781-904-5000 Fax: 781-904-5601
Toll-Free:
Address: 15 Tyngsboro Rd., Unit 8C, North Chelmsford, MA 01863 United States

STOCK TICKER/OTHER:

Stock Ticker: Subsidiary
Employees:
Parent Company: Megasoft Limited
Exchange:
Fiscal Year Ends: 03/31

SALARIES/BONUSES:

Top Exec. Salary: $ Bonus: $
Second Exec. Salary: $ Bonus: $

OTHER THOUGHTS:

Estimated Female Officers or Directors:
Hot Spot for Advancement for Women/Minorities:

Xperi Holding Corporation

www.xperi.com

NAIC Code: 334413

TYPES OF BUSINESS:

Semiconductor and Related Device Manufacturing
Consumer Product Licensing
Entertainment Product Licensing
Intellectual Property Licensing
Media IP
Semiconductor IP
Technologies

BRANDS/DIVISIONS/AFFILIATES:

Perceive Corporation
DTS
HD Radio
IMAX Enhanced
Invensas
TiVo

GROWTH PLANS/SPECIAL FEATURES:

Xperi Holding Corp is a provider of semiconductor packaging and interconnects solutions and intellectual property products to original equipment manufacturers. The company has two reportable segments: Product Licensing segment and the Semiconductor and IP Licensing segment. It generates maximum revenue from the Product Licensing segment. The company has a presence in Korea, Japan, U.S., Europe and the Middle East, Taiwan and other countries of which it generates maximum revenue from Korea.

CONTACTS: *Note: Officers with more than one job title may be intentionally listed here more than once.*

Jon Kirchner, CEO
Robert Andersen, CFO
David Habiger, Chairman of the Board
Paul Davis, Chief Legal Officer
Matthew Milne, Other Executive Officer
Geir Skaaden, Other Executive Officer
Samir Armaly, President, Divisional
Murali Dharan, President, Subsidiary

FINANCIAL DATA: *Note: Data for latest year may not have been available at press time.*

In U.S. $	2021	2020	2019	2018	2017	2016
Revenue		892,020,000	280,067,000	406,133,000	373,732,000	259,565,000
R&D Expense		195,154,000	112,345,000	106,406,000	105,849,000	44,738,000
Operating Income		198,409,000	-63,581,000	50,079,000	4,996,000	110,341,000
Operating Margin %						
SGA Expense		245,356,000	122,897,000	127,907,000	144,649,000	72,065,000
Net Income		146,762,000	-62,530,000	-289,000	-56,558,000	56,089,000
Operating Cash Flow		427,603,000	169,253,000	135,133,000	147,265,000	145,632,000
Capital Expenditure		58,314,000	13,313,000	7,438,000	3,499,000	13,376,000
EBITDA		348,526,000	46,987,000	147,701,000	89,080,000	127,254,000
Return on Assets %						
Return on Equity %						
Debt to Equity						

CONTACT INFORMATION:

Phone: 408 321-6000 Fax: 408 321-8257
Toll-Free:
Address: 3025 Orchard Pkwy., San Jose, CA 95134 United States

STOCK TICKER/OTHER:

Stock Ticker: XPER
Employees: 1,850
Parent Company:
Exchange: NAS
Fiscal Year Ends: 12/31

SALARIES/BONUSES:

Top Exec. Salary: $629,167 Bonus: $
Second Exec. Salary: $506,250 Bonus: $

OTHER THOUGHTS:

Estimated Female Officers or Directors:
Hot Spot for Advancement for Women/Minorities:

YASKAWA Electric Corporation

www.yaskawa.co.jp

NAIC Code: 335312

TYPES OF BUSINESS:

Motor and Generator Manufacturing
Controls
Industrial Robotics

BRANDS/DIVISIONS/AFFILIATES:

GROWTH PLANS/SPECIAL FEATURES:

Yaskawa Electric Corporation engages in manufacturing mechatronics products, which combine electrical and mechanical systems, and has core technologies related to motion control, robotics, and power conversion. It operates mainly in Asia, the Americas, and Europe, as one of the leading players in the AC servo motor/controller, AC drives (inverter), and robotics markets. According to the company, it has the leading global share with AC Servo motors/controllers, where the company's cumulative AC servo motor shipments reached 20 million units in 2020, and it is also considered as one of the big four industrial robotics companies. The company was founded in 1915, and its head office is in Kitakyushu, Fukuoka Prefecture, Japan.

CONTACTS:

Note: Officers with more than one job title may be intentionally listed here more than once.

Hiroshi Ogasawara, Pres.
Junji Tsuda, Chmn.

FINANCIAL DATA:

Note: Data for latest year may not have been available at press time.

In U.S. $	2021	2020	2019	2018	2017	2016
Revenue	3,424,414,000	3,611,094,000	4,170,662,000	3,941,188,000	3,469,852,000	3,613,757,000
R&D Expense						
Operating Income	238,840,400	212,628,700	437,295,700	475,607,100	267,205,000	322,747,900
Operating Margin %						
SGA Expense	796,641,600	889,432,600				
Net Income	166,312,200	136,831,700	361,709,600	349,275,900	179,229,200	196,522,100
Operating Cash Flow	347,984,200	188,745,600	288,496,000	404,678,200	296,580,100	280,781,000
Capital Expenditure	75,647,610	196,170,600	202,602,700	155,978,700	133,158,800	181,408,400
EBITDA	392,077,600	380,636,900	615,347,400	597,052,800	384,186,800	442,005,500
Return on Assets %						
Return on Equity %						
Debt to Equity						

CONTACT INFORMATION:

Phone: 81 936458801 Fax: 81 936318837
Toll-Free:
Address: 2-1, Kurosaki-shiroishi, Kitakyushu, 806-0004 Japan

STOCK TICKER/OTHER:

Stock Ticker: YASKY Exchange: PINX
Employees: 14,892 Fiscal Year Ends: 02/28
Parent Company:

SALARIES/BONUSES:

Top Exec. Salary: $ Bonus: $
Second Exec. Salary: $ Bonus: $

OTHER THOUGHTS:

Estimated Female Officers or Directors:
Hot Spot for Advancement for Women/Minorities:

Yokogawa Electric Corporation

www.yokogawa.com

NAIC Code: 334513

TYPES OF BUSINESS:

Instruments and Related Products Manufacturing for Measuring, Displaying, and Controlling Industrial Process Variables

BRANDS/DIVISIONS/AFFILIATES:

OpreX
APB Corporation

GROWTH PLANS/SPECIAL FEATURES:

Yokogawa Electric Corporation offers systems and solutions for measurement, control, and information technologies. Software, data acquisition instruments, field instruments, and other components compose a diverse product portfolio and allow the company to reach various customers involved in different end-markets. Essentially, the company helps link plant operations and corporate management. It has three business segments: industrial automation (majority of total revenue), control, test and measurement, and aviation and other businesses. In addition to its product offerings, Yokogawa offers consulting and execution services to supply customers with resources to make timely operating decisions. The majority of sales derive from Asia, with Japan being a key region for the company.

CONTACTS: *Note: Officers with more than one job title may be intentionally listed here more than once.*

Hitoshi Nara, CEO
Takashi Nishijima, Pres.
Toshiaki Shirai, Sr. VP-Innovation Headquarters
Yoshitoshi Manabe, VP-Mfg.
Hiroshi Suzuki, Sr. VP-Corp. Admin.
Junichi Anabuki, VP-Acct. & Treasury Headquarters
Koichi Chujo, VP-Quality Assurance Headquarters
Chiaki Ito, VP-Industrial Automation Mktg. Headquarters
Shuhei Sakuno, Sr. VP-Audit and Compliance Headquarters
Nobuaki Konishi, VP-Systems Bus. Div.

FINANCIAL DATA: *Note: Data for latest year may not have been available at press time.*

In U.S. $	2021	2020	2019	2018	2017	2016
Revenue	3,288,162,000	3,553,759,000	3,547,423,000	3,572,721,000	3,439,536,000	3,635,479,000
R&D Expense						
Operating Income	277,670,400	312,721,900	303,987,600	287,309,800	277,749,400	348,344,500
Operating Margin %						
SGA Expense						
Net Income	168,878,000	129,046,400	249,956,000	188,473,200	226,345,300	265,025,800
Operating Cash Flow	288,583,900	273,558,000	188,130,500	281,009,400	344,847,300	280,578,900
Capital Expenditure	145,126,700	149,511,400	118,475,600	119,354,300	120,391,200	122,069,500
EBITDA	436,294,000	396,822,600	490,000,300	421,883,200	474,974,500	509,507,600
Return on Assets %						
Return on Equity %						
Debt to Equity						

CONTACT INFORMATION:

Phone: 81 488525555 Fax: 81 422550461
Toll-Free:
Address: 2-9-32 Nakacho, Tokyo, 180-8750 Japan

STOCK TICKER/OTHER:

Stock Ticker: YOKEY
Employees: 17,715
Parent Company:
Exchange: PINX
Fiscal Year Ends: 03/31

SALARIES/BONUSES:

Top Exec. Salary: $ Bonus: $
Second Exec. Salary: $ Bonus: $

OTHER THOUGHTS:

Estimated Female Officers or Directors:
Hot Spot for Advancement for Women/Minorities:

ZF Friedrichshafen AG (ZF)

NAIC Code: 336350

www.zf.com

TYPES OF BUSINESS:

Automotive Components
Automotive Technology
Industrial Technology
Next Generation Mobility Solutions
Active Safety Systems
Car Chassis Technology
Advanced Driver-Assistance Systems
Commercial Vehicle Control Systems

BRANDS/DIVISIONS/AFFILIATES:

Zeppelin Foundation
ZF Race Engineering
ZF Gastronomie Service GmbH
Apex.AI

CONTACTS:

Note: Officers with more than one job title may be intentionally listed here more than once.

Wolf-Henning Scheider, CEO
Konstantin Sauer, CFO
Stefan Sommer, Dir.-Corp. Dev
Stefan Sommer, Dir.-Corp. Comm.
Konstantin Sauer, Exec. VP-Finance & Controlling
Wilhelm Rehm, Exec. VP-Industrial Tech.
Gerhard Wagner, Exec. VP-Powertrain Tech. Div.
Reinhard Buhl, Exec. VP-Car Chassis Tech. Div.
Rolf Lutz, Exec. VP-Commercial Vehicles, South America
Peter Ottenbruch, Exec. VP-Tech., Asia Pacific

GROWTH PLANS/SPECIAL FEATURES:

ZF Friedrichshafen AG is a global technology company that supplies systems for passenger cars, commercial vehicles and industrial technology, enabling the next generation of mobility. Zeppelin Foundation, which is administered by the city of Friedrichsafen, holds a majority interest in the firm. ZF's business units mostly operate as jointly- or wholly-owned subsidiaries. The company has nine units: active safety systems, car chassis technology, electrified powertrain technology, electronics and advanced driver-assistance systems (ADAS), passive safety systems, commercial vehicle control systems, commercia vehicle technology, industrial technology and aftermarket. In addition, subsidiary ZF Race Engineering provides motorsports applications, small volume production applications, engineering, consultancy and testing for the automotive and related manufacturing markets. ZF Gastronomie Service GmbH provides food services at ZF sites and also provides catering, vending and party services to external customers. In December 2021, ZF Friedrichshafen acquired a stake in software company Apex.AI, which offers additional options for ZF middleware and supercomputers used in software-defined vehicles.

FINANCIAL DATA:

Note: Data for latest year may not have been available at press time.

In U.S. $	2021	2020	2019	2018	2017	2016
Revenue	41,343,565,000	40,054,300,000	39,627,840,000	42,236,100,000	43,654,900,000	37,230,900,000
R&D Expense						
Operating Income						
Operating Margin %						
SGA Expense						
Net Income	2,062,806,900	1,285,970,000	434,045,624	1,103,760,000	1,397,910,000	978,257,000
Operating Cash Flow						
Capital Expenditure						
EBITDA						
Return on Assets %						
Return on Equity %						
Debt to Equity						

CONTACT INFORMATION:

Phone: 49-7541-77-0 Fax: 49-7541-77-908000
Toll-Free:
Address: Lowentaler Strasse 20, Friedrichshafen, 88046 Germany

STOCK TICKER/OTHER:

Stock Ticker: Private
Employees: 153,522
Parent Company: Zeppelin Foundation
Exchange:
Fiscal Year Ends: 12/31

SALARIES/BONUSES:

Top Exec. Salary: $ Bonus: $
Second Exec. Salary: $ Bonus: $

OTHER THOUGHTS:

Estimated Female Officers or Directors:
Hot Spot for Advancement for Women/Minorities:

Zoom Telephonics Inc (dba Minim)

www.minim.com

NAIC Code: 334210A

TYPES OF BUSINESS:

Computer Networking & Related Equipment, Manufacturing
Internet Access
Wi-Fi
Mobile Application
Smart Home Security
Web Portal
Application Programming Interface
Cloud

BRANDS/DIVISIONS/AFFILIATES:

Minim
Motorola

GROWTH PLANS/SPECIAL FEATURES:

Minim Inc is the creator of innovative internet access products that dependably connect people to the information they need and the people they love. The company delivers smart software-driven communications products under the Motorola brand. Its products include Zoom ZM.1, Motorola WiFi.

CONTACTS: *Note: Officers with more than one job title may be intentionally listed here more than once.*

Graham Chynoweth, CEO
Sean Doherty, CFO
Jeremy Hitchcock, Chairman of the Board
Nicole Zheng, Chief Marketing Officer
John Lauten, COO

FINANCIAL DATA: *Note: Data for latest year may not have been available at press time.*

In U.S. $	2021	2020	2019	2018	2017	2016
Revenue		47,988,550	37,614,460	32,323,480	29,417,990	17,834,240
R&D Expense		3,828,223	2,237,416	1,771,887	1,944,690	1,522,510
Operating Income		-4,820,202	-3,221,226	52,679	-1,212,325	-2,884,451
Operating Margin %						
SGA Expense		14,598,210	11,889,610	9,819,800	8,678,013	6,729,098
Net Income		-3,858,415	-3,275,800	-74,277	-1,366,999	-2,933,140
Operating Cash Flow		-7,093,874	-1,536,821	-1,803,595	1,334,460	-4,205,121
Capital Expenditure		1,079,934	484,254	236,910	99,790	58,163
EBITDA		-3,410,972	-2,594,226	394,993	-753,504	-2,326,924
Return on Assets %						
Return on Equity %						
Debt to Equity						

CONTACT INFORMATION:

Phone: 617 423-1072 Fax:
Toll-Free:
Address: 848 Elm St., Manchester, NH 03101 United States

STOCK TICKER/OTHER:

Stock Ticker: MINM
Employees: 38
Parent Company:
Exchange: NAS
Fiscal Year Ends: 12/31

SALARIES/BONUSES:

Top Exec. Salary: $129,272 Bonus: $
Second Exec. Salary: $128,336 Bonus: $

OTHER THOUGHTS:

Estimated Female Officers or Directors: 1
Hot Spot for Advancement for Women/Minorities:

Zoox Inc

NAIC Code: 336111

zoox.com

TYPES OF BUSINESS:

Autonomous Automobile Technologies
Self-Driving Taxis
Software for Autonomous Vehicles

BRANDS/DIVISIONS/AFFILIATES:

Amazon.com Inc

GROWTH PLANS/SPECIAL FEATURES:

Zoox, Inc. is engaged in developing autonomous mobility. The firm is applying its technology to the automotive, robotics and renewable energy segments by designing a symmetrical, bi-directional, zero-emissions vehicle from the ground up to solve the unique challenges of autonomous mobility. Zoox tests its software and sensors on conventional vehicles with safety drivers. The company's plans are to operate a series of fully autonomous battery electric vehicles optimized for ride-sharing cities, creating a next-generation mobility society of riders as opposed to drivers. As a ride-hailing company, Zoox will handle the driving, charging, maintenance and upgrades for its fleet of vehicles, and riders only pay for the rides. Zoox is a subsidiary of Amazon.com, Inc.

CONTACTS: *Note: Officers with more than one job title may be intentionally listed here more than once.*

Aicha Evans, CEO
Ilan Hart, CFO
Feargal Moorhead, Chief People Officer
Jesse Levinson, CTO

FINANCIAL DATA: *Note: Data for latest year may not have been available at press time.*

In U.S. $	2021	2020	2019	2018	2017	2016
Revenue						
R&D Expense						
Operating Income						
Operating Margin %						
SGA Expense						
Net Income						
Operating Cash Flow						
Capital Expenditure						
EBITDA						
Return on Assets %						
Return on Equity %						
Debt to Equity						

CONTACT INFORMATION:

Phone: 650-539-9669 Fax:
Toll-Free:
Address: 1149 Chess Dr., Foster City, CA 94404 United States

STOCK TICKER/OTHER:

Stock Ticker: Subsidiary
Employees: 700
Parent Company: Amazon.com Inc
Exchange:
Fiscal Year Ends: 12/31

SALARIES/BONUSES:

Top Exec. Salary: $ Bonus: $
Second Exec. Salary: $ Bonus: $

OTHER THOUGHTS:

Estimated Female Officers or Directors:
Hot Spot for Advancement for Women/Minorities: Y

Zscaler Inc

www.zscaler.com

NAIC Code: 511210E

TYPES OF BUSINESS:

Computer Software, Network Security, Managed Access, Digital ID, Cybersecurity & Anti-Virus

BRANDS/DIVISIONS/AFFILIATES:

Zscaler Internet Access
Zscaler Private Access
Zscaler App
Edgewise Networks

GROWTH PLANS/SPECIAL FEATURES:

Zscaler is a security-as-a-service firm that offers its customers cloud-delivered solutions for protecting user devices and data. The firm leverages its position in 150 colocation data centers to deliver traditionally appliance-based security functionality, such as firewalls and sandboxes, as a completely cloud-native platform. The firm focuses on large enterprise customers and offers two primary product suites: Zscaler Internet Access, which securely connects users to externally managed application and websites (such as Salesforce and Google), and Zscaler Private Access, which securely connects users to internally managed applications. Both product suites encompass a broad gamut of capabilities situated across the traditional security stack.

CONTACTS: *Note: Officers with more than one job title may be intentionally listed here more than once.*

Eileen Naughton,
Jagtar Chaudhry, CEO
Remo Canessa, CFO
Robert Schlossman, Chief Legal Officer
Amit Sinha, Chief Technology Officer
Dalibor Rajic, Other Executive Officer

FINANCIAL DATA: *Note: Data for latest year may not have been available at press time.*

In U.S. $	2021	2020	2019	2018	2017	2016
Revenue	673,100,000	431,269,000	302,836,000	190,174,000	125,717,000	80,325,000
R&D Expense	174,653,000	97,879,000	61,969,000	39,379,000	33,561,000	20,940,000
Operating Income	-207,812,000	-113,956,000	-35,313,000	-34,624,000	-35,073,000	-26,843,000
Operating Margin %						
SGA Expense	555,942,000	351,613,000	216,511,000	147,544,000	99,757,000	66,101,000
Net Income	-262,029,000	-115,116,000	-28,655,000	-33,646,000	-35,460,000	-27,438,000
Operating Cash Flow	202,040,000	79,317,000	58,027,000	17,307,000	-6,019,000	-11,916,000
Capital Expenditure	58,297,000	51,809,000	30,162,000	15,170,000	8,174,000	6,247,000
EBITDA	-169,977,000	-86,585,000	-24,007,000	-26,636,000	-28,233,000	-21,971,000
Return on Assets %						
Return on Equity %						
Debt to Equity						

CONTACT INFORMATION:

Phone: 408-533-0288 Fax:
Toll-Free:
Address: 110 Rose Orchard Way, San Jose, CA 95134 United States

STOCK TICKER/OTHER:

Stock Ticker: ZS
Exchange: NAS
Employees: 3,153
Fiscal Year Ends: 07/31
Parent Company:

SALARIES/BONUSES:

Top Exec. Salary: $400,000 Bonus: $
Second Exec. Salary: $375,000 Bonus: $

OTHER THOUGHTS:

Estimated Female Officers or Directors:
Hot Spot for Advancement for Women/Minorities:

ZTE Corporation

NAIC Code: 334210

www.zte.com.cn

TYPES OF BUSINESS:

Telecommunications Equipment Manufacturing
Optical Networking Equipment
Intelligent & Next-Generation Network Systems
Mobile Phones

BRANDS/DIVISIONS/AFFILIATES:

GROWTH PLANS/SPECIAL FEATURES:

ZTE Corp offers a suite of telecommunications and information technology equipment to carriers, businesses, and the public sector. The firm's product portfolio covers wireless networks, core networks, fixed access, terminals, and other telecom verticals. ZTE generates a majority of its revenue from equipment supporting carriers' networks, but also provides handset terminals and telecom software systems. The Asia-Pacific region accounts for a majority of the firm's revenue, but ZTE also has a presence in Europe and the Americas.

CONTACTS:

Note: Officers with more than one job title may be intentionally listed here more than once.

Ziyang Xu, CEO
Junshi Xie, COO
Ying LI, CFO
Zixue Li, Chmn.

FINANCIAL DATA:

Note: Data for latest year may not have been available at press time.

In U.S. $	2021	2020	2019	2018	2017	2016
Revenue		15,883,930,000	14,206,450,000	13,388,620,000	17,036,990,000	15,849,880,000
R&D Expense		2,316,741,000	1,964,600,000	1,707,466,000	2,029,473,000	1,998,130,000
Operating Income		875,003,200	1,456,729,000	931,224,400	1,215,385,000	400,217,800
Operating Margin %						
SGA Expense		1,554,464,000	1,590,917,000	1,635,203,000	2,034,271,000	2,049,055,000
Net Income		666,940,900	805,992,900	-1,093,418,000	715,229,600	-369,096,300
Operating Cash Flow		1,602,106,000	1,165,892,000	-1,442,835,000	1,130,417,000	823,580,000
Capital Expenditure		1,013,254,000	1,025,618,000	764,345,000	936,903,800	626,657,200
EBITDA		1,648,837,000	1,951,885,000	-555,679,000	1,640,789,000	441,326,100
Return on Assets %						
Return on Equity %						
Debt to Equity						

CONTACT INFORMATION:

Phone: 86 75526770000 Fax: 86 75526770286
Toll-Free:
Address: Hi-tech Rd. S., No. 55, Shenzhen, Guangdong 518057 China

STOCK TICKER/OTHER:

Stock Ticker: ZTCOF
Employees: 73,700
Parent Company:
Exchange: PINX
Fiscal Year Ends: 12/31

SALARIES/BONUSES:

Top Exec. Salary: $ Bonus: $
Second Exec. Salary: $ Bonus: $

OTHER THOUGHTS:

Estimated Female Officers or Directors:
Hot Spot for Advancement for Women/Minorities:

Zygo Corporation

www.zygo.com

NAIC Code: 334513

TYPES OF BUSINESS:

Optical Instrument & Lens Manufacturing
Advanced Optical Metrology Systems
Optical Components
Product Development
Product Manufacturing
Sensors
Laser Interferometers

BRANDS/DIVISIONS/AFFILIATES:

AMETEK Inc
Ultra Precision Technologies

CONTACTS: *Note: Officers with more than one job title may be intentionally listed here more than once.*

Bruce Robinson, Chmn.

GROWTH PLANS/SPECIAL FEATURES:

Zygo Corporation, part of the Ultra Precision Technologies division of AMETEK, Inc., designs and manufactures advanced optical metrology systems and ultra-precise optical components and assemblies. The firm is comprised of the following product groups: 3D optical profilers, laser interferometers, nano position sensors and precision optical components & systems. 3D optical profiler instruments enable precise, quantitative, ISO-compliant, non-contact surface measurement and characterization of micro- and nano-scale surface features, capturing up to 2 million data points in mere seconds. Laser interferometers provide accurate production measurements of optical components and assemblies. Nano-position sensors are widely used in closed-loop motion control systems, primarily for lithography and inspection tool staging, as well as for deformable optical systems. Zygo's precision optical components & systems division specializes in producing complex electro-optical systems and high-precision optical components for the medial, life sciences, defense, aerospace, semiconductor and industrial original equipment manufacture (OEM) markets. Zygo has been awarded approximately 1,200 patents since its 1970 founding.

FINANCIAL DATA: *Note: Data for latest year may not have been available at press time.*

In U.S. $	2021	2020	2019	2018	2017	2016
Revenue						
R&D Expense						
Operating Income						
Operating Margin %						
SGA Expense						
Net Income						
Operating Cash Flow						
Capital Expenditure						
EBITDA						
Return on Assets %						
Return on Equity %						
Debt to Equity						

CONTACT INFORMATION:

Phone: 860 347-8506 Fax: 860 347-8372
Toll-Free:
Address: Laurel Brook Rd., Middlefield, CT 06455-0448 United States

STOCK TICKER/OTHER:

Stock Ticker: Subsidiary
Employees: 500
Parent Company: AMETEK Inc
Exchange:
Fiscal Year Ends: 09/30

SALARIES/BONUSES:

Top Exec. Salary: $ Bonus: $
Second Exec. Salary: $ Bonus: $

OTHER THOUGHTS:

Estimated Female Officers or Directors:
Hot Spot for Advancement for Women/Minorities:

ADDITIONAL INDEXES

CONTENTS:

INDEX OF FIRMS NOTED AS HOT SPOTS FOR ADVANCEMENT FOR WOMEN & MINORITIES

3M Company
ABB Ltd
Accenture plc
Adobe Inc
Advanced Micro Devices Inc (AMD)
Agero Inc
Agilent Technologies Inc
Akamai Technologies Inc
Allscripts Healthcare Solutions Inc
Alphabet Inc (Google)
Amazon.com Inc
Analog Devices Inc
Arm Holdings plc
ASE Technology Holding Co Ltd
Aspen Technology Inc
AT&T Inc
Atos SE
BAE Systems plc
Bayerische Motoren Werke AG (BMW Group)
BCE Inc (Bell Canada Enterprises)
Bharti Airtel Limited
BlackBerry Limited
Boeing Company (The)
Bombardier Inc
Broadcom Inc
BT Group plc
CACI International Inc
Capgemini SE
Cerner Corporation
Check Point Software Technologies Ltd
China Mobile Limited
China Telecom Corporation Limited
Cirrus Logic Inc
Cisco Systems Inc
CYREN Ltd
Dell Technologies Inc
Deutsche Telekom AG
Emerson Electric Co
Extreme Networks Inc
F5 Networks Inc
Flex Ltd
Forcepoint LLC
Ford Motor Company
Forrester Research Inc
Fortinet Inc
Garmin Ltd
Gartner Inc
GE Aviation
General Dynamics Corporation
General Motors Company (GM)
Getronics NV
Gilat Satellite Networks Ltd
Hewlett Packard Laboratories (HP Labs)
Honeywell International Inc
HP Inc
Huawei Technologies Co Ltd
IBM Research
Infosys Limited
Inmarsat Global Limited
Intel Corporation
International Business Machines Corporation (IBM)
Itron Inc
Jabil Inc
Johnson Controls International plc
Juniper Networks Inc
Koninklijke Philips NV (Royal Philips)
L3Harris Technologies Inc
LiveRamp Holdings Inc
LM Ericsson Telephone Company (Ericsson)
Lockheed Martin Corporation
Mandiant Inc
Marketo
McAfee Corp
Medical Information Technology Inc (MEDITECH)
Mercedes-Benz Group AG
Microchip Technology Incorporated
Microsoft Corporation
Motorola Solutions Inc
NETGEAR Inc
Nokia Corporation
Northrop Grumman Corporation
NortonLifeLock Inc
NVIDIA Corporation
Oracle Corporation
Oracle NetSuite
Orange
Progress Software Corporation
Qualcomm Incorporated
Radware Ltd
Raytheon Technologies Corporation
Renault SA
Robert Bosch GmbH
Rolls-Royce plc
salesforce.com inc
SAP SE
SAS Institute Inc
Science Applications International Corporation (SAIC)
Siemens AG
Skyworks Solutions Inc
Stellantis North America (FCA US LLC)
Stellantis NV
STMicroelectronics NV
Swisscom AG
Taiwan Semiconductor Manufacturing Co Ltd (TSMC)
TE Connectivity Ltd
Telenor ASA
Tellabs Inc
Telstra Corporation Limited
Texas Instruments Incorporated
Textron Inc
TomTom International BV

Trend Micro Inc
Trimble Inc
Unisys Corporation
Verizon Communications Inc
VMware Inc
Vodafone Group plc
Volvo AB
Wieden+Kennedy
Wipro Limited
Zoox Inc

INDEX OF SUBSIDIARIES, BRAND NAMES AND AFFILIATIONS

INDEX OF SUBSIDIARIES, BRAND NAMES AND AFFILIATIONS, CONT.

INDEX OF SUBSIDIARIES, BRAND NAMES AND AFFILIATIONS, CONT.

INDEX OF SUBSIDIARIES, BRAND NAMES AND AFFILIATIONS, CONT.

INDEX OF SUBSIDIARIES, BRAND NAMES AND AFFILIATIONS, CONT.

INDEX OF SUBSIDIARIES, BRAND NAMES AND AFFILIATIONS, CONT.

INDEX OF SUBSIDIARIES, BRAND NAMES AND AFFILIATIONS, CONT.

INDEX OF SUBSIDIARIES, BRAND NAMES AND AFFILIATIONS, CONT.

INDEX OF SUBSIDIARIES, BRAND NAMES AND AFFILIATIONS, CONT.

INDEX OF SUBSIDIARIES, BRAND NAMES AND AFFILIATIONS, CONT.

INDEX OF SUBSIDIARIES, BRAND NAMES AND AFFILIATIONS, CONT.

INDEX OF SUBSIDIARIES, BRAND NAMES AND AFFILIATIONS, CONT.

INDEX OF SUBSIDIARIES, BRAND NAMES AND AFFILIATIONS, CONT.

INDEX OF SUBSIDIARIES, BRAND NAMES AND AFFILIATIONS, CONT.

INDEX OF SUBSIDIARIES, BRAND NAMES AND AFFILIATIONS, CONT.

A Short Internet of Things (IoT) & Machine-to-Machine (M2M) Industry Glossary

3G Cellular: Short for third-generation, this term refers to high speed enhancements to mobile telephone service. 3G enables wireless e-mail, Internet browsing and data transfer. 3G will be largely replaced by advanced 4G and 5G technologies.

3GPP: Third Generation Partnership Project. It is an organization set up to create and monitor advanced 3G wireless standards.

4G Cellular: An advancement in speed and capabilities over 3G wireless networks. 4G not only features high data transfer speeds, it also has an enhanced ability to support interactive multimedia, internet access, mobile video and other vital tasks. It will eventually be surpassed by 5G and higher networks, with 5G beginning to rollout on a major basis in the 2020s.

5G Cellular: A wireless technology that is expected to produce blinding download speeds of one gigabyte per second (Gbps), and perhaps as high as 10 Gbps. The first specifications for 5G were agreed to by the global wireless industry from 2017 to 2019. Significant rollout was expected to begin in the early 2020s. While certain 5G features can be used to boost speeds of earlier 4G networks, a true rollout requires major investment in new cellular infrastructure and systems.

802.11: See "Wi-Fi."

802.11n (MIMO): Multiple Input Multiple Output. MIMO is a standard in the series of 802.11 Wi-Fi specifications for wireless networks. It can provide very high speed network access. 802.11n also boasts better operating distances than many networks. MIMO uses spectrum more efficiently without any loss of reliability. The technology is based on several different antennas all tuned to the same channel, each transmitting a different signal. Advancements include MU-MIMO (Multi-User MIMO) and OFDMA (Orthogonal Frequency-Division Multiple Access), each of which improves network throughput.

802.15: See "Ultrawideband (UWB)." For 802.15.1, see "Bluetooth."

802.15.1: See "Bluetooth."

802.16: See "WiMAX."

Access Network: The network that connects a user's telephone equipment to the telephone exchange.

ADM: The application, development and maintenance of software.

AI: See "Artificial Intelligence (AI)."

Algorithm: In mathematics and computer science (software), an algorithm is a set of instructions designed to perform a specific task. These tasks include data processing, the performance of calculations and automated reasoning tasks, amongst others.

Ambient Backscatter: Ambient Backscatter converts wireless signals into both a source of power and a communication medium. It enables battery-free devices to communicate by backscattering existing wireless signals. Backscatter communication is vastly more power-efficient than traditional radio communication. Since it leverages the ambient RF signals that are already around us, it does not require a dedicated power source.

Analytics: Generally refers to the deep examination of massive amounts of data, often on a continual or real-time basis. The goal is to discover deeper insights, make recommendations or generate predictions. Advanced analytics includes such techniques as big data, predictive analytics, text analytics, data mining, forecasting, optimization and simulation.

Analytics of Things (AoT): The term used to describe the analysis of Internet of Things (IoT) data. IoT data is the data generated by sensors and devices connected to the IoT. It is through AoT that connected things make intelligent decisions.

ANSI: American National Standards Institute. Founded in 1918, ANSI is a private, non-profit organization that administers and coordinates the U.S. voluntary standardization and conformity assessment system. Its mission is to enhance both the global competitiveness of U.S. business and the quality of U.S. life by promoting and facilitating voluntary consensus standards and conformity assessment systems, and safeguarding their integrity. See www.ansi.org.

Applications: Computer programs and systems that allow users to interface with a computer and that collect, manipulate, summarize and report data and information. Also, see "Apps."

Applied Research: The application of compounds, processes, materials or other items discovered during basic research to practical uses. The goal is to move discoveries along to the final development phase.

Artificial Intelligence (AI): The use of computer technology to perform functions somewhat like those normally associated with human intelligence, such as reasoning, learning and self-improvement.

ASCII: American Standard Code for Information Exchange. There are 128 standard ASCII codes that represent all Latin letters, numbers and punctuation. Each ASCII code is represented by a seven-digit binary number, such as 0000000 or 0000111. This code is accepted as a standard throughout the world.

ASEAN: Association of Southeast Asian Nations. A regional economic development association established in 1967 by five original member countries: Indonesia, Malaysia, Philippines, Singapore, and Thailand. Brunei joined on 8 January 1984, Vietnam on 28 July 1995, Laos and Myanmar on 23 July 1997, and Cambodia on 30 April 1999.

Asia Pacific Economic Cooperation (APEC): An organization established to promote investment and trade in the Pacific basin.

Automation: In business, automation is the application of systems, process or technology with the end goal of achieving recurring tasks automatically. Typical uses of automation include artificial intelligence and software algorithms in computers, and robotics on the factory floor and in warehouses.

B2B: See "Business-to-Business."

B2C: See "Business-to-Consumer."

B2E: See "Business-to-Employee."

B2G: See "Business-to-Government."

Bandwidth: The data transmission capacity of a network, measured in the amount of data (in bits and bauds) it can transport in one second. A full page of text is about 15,000 to 20,000 bits. Full-motion, full-screen video requires about 10 million bits per second, depending on compression.

Base Station: The fixed receiver/transmitter in a wireless network.

Basic Research: Attempts to discover compounds, materials, processes or other items that may be largely or entirely new and/or unique. Basic research may start with a theoretical concept that has yet to be proven. The goal is to create discoveries that can be moved along to applied research. Basic research is sometimes referred to as "blue sky" research.

Baud: Refers to how many times the carrier signal in a modem switches value per second or how many bits a modem can send and receive in a second.

Beam: The coverage and geographic service area offered by a satellite transponder. A global beam effectively covers one-third of the earth's surface. A spot beam provides a very specific high-powered downlink pattern that is limited to a particular geographical area to which it may be steered or pointed.

Benchmarking: The procedure of measuring a process or practice against those of a group of other companies in the same industry. For example, it is common to compare the operating profit margin of a firm against a benchmark that is the average of the profit margin of a group of other firms in the same industry.

Big Data: The massive sets of data that are generated and captured to a growing extent by a wide variety of enterprises. For example, the digitization of health care records is creating big data sets. Likewise, consumer activities on an extremely popular website like Facebook create big data sets. A growing trend will be the generation of big data sets by remote wireless sensors. The challenges created by big data include the steps of data capture, storage, visualization and analysis. The opportunities include targeted online advertising: greater efficiency in health care, energy, business and industry, as well as intelligent transportation systems and better outcomes in health care.

Big Data Analytics: A subset of advanced analytics, big data analytics allows one to examine massive volumes of data to uncover information such as hidden patterns, unknown correlations, market trends, customer preferences and other insights that can help an organization answer business questions and make informed business decisions.

Bit: A single digit number, either a one or a zero, which is the smallest unit of computerized data.

Bits Per Second (Bps): An indicator of the speed of data movement.

Blockchain: A technology that utilizes distributed computer networks to record transactions, records or documents, such as Bitcoin.

Bluetooth: An industry standard for a technology that enables wireless, short-distance infrared connections between devices such as cell phone headsets, Palm Pilots or PDAs, laptops, printers and Internet appliances.

Business Process Reengineering: The process of reviewing a company's business practices to eliminate wasteful methods and create more efficient practices.

Business-to-Business: An organization focused on selling products, services or data to commercial customers rather than individual consumers. Also known as B2B.

Business-to-Consumer: An organization focused on selling products, services or data to individual consumers rather than commercial customers. Also known as B2C.

Business-to-Employee: A corporate communications system, such as an intranet, aimed at conveying information from a company to its employees. Also known as B2E.

Business-to-Government: An organization focused on selling products, services or data to government units rather than commercial businesses or consumers. Also known as B2G.

Byte: A set of eight bits that represent a single character.

CAE: See “Computer-Aided Engineering (CAE).”

CAM: See “Computer-Aided Manufacturing (CAM).”

Capex: Capital expenditures.

CASE: See “Computer-Assisted Software Engineering (CASE).”

Case Team: The team working on a specific project in consulting or business process engineering.

CEM: Contract electronic manufacturing. See “Contract Manufacturing.”

Changeover: The refitting of equipment to either neutralize the effects of the just completed model production or to prepare equipment for production of the next scheduled model, or both. This term is frequently used in connection with automotive manufacturing.

Chat Bot: Like a voice assistant, chatbots are services accessed through a digital chat interface. A chatbot is intended to enable a website to interface in a non-human manner to provide instant service to customers and visitors. Chat bots can be connected to artificial intelligence in order to provide reasonable answers to common customer questions or needs. ChatterBot is a dialog engine for creating chatbots.

Climate Change (Greenhouse Effect): A theory that assumes an increasing mean global surface temperature of the Earth caused by gases (sometimes referred to as greenhouse gases) in the atmosphere (including carbon dioxide, methane, nitrous oxide, ozone and chlorofluorocarbons). The greenhouse effect allows solar radiation to penetrate the Earth's atmosphere but absorbs the infrared radiation returning to space.

Cloud: Refers to the use of outsourced servers to store and access data, as opposed to computers owned or managed by one organization. Firms that offer cloud services for a fee run clusters of servers networked together, often based on open standards. Such cloud networks can consist of hundreds or even thousands of computers. Cloud services enable a client company to immediately increase computing capability without any investment in physical infrastructure. (The word “cloud” is also broadly used to describe any data or application that runs via the Internet.) The concept of cloud is also increasingly linked with software as a service.

Cognitive Computing: Technology platforms that simulate the human cognition process, i.e. artificial intelligence, to solve complex questions. This technology utilizes a computerized, self-learning algorithm that focuses on language processing, pattern recognition and data mining to mimic human thought.

Commoditization: The process whereby a good or service is deemed essentially the same by consumers, leading to price being almost the exclusive competitive factor.

Computer-Aided Design (CAD): A tool used to provide three-dimensional, on-screen design for everything from buildings to automobiles to clothing. It generally runs on workstations.

Computer-Aided Engineering (CAE): The use of computers to assist with a broad spectrum of engineering design work, including conceptual and analytical design.

Computer-Aided Manufacturing (CAM): The use of computers to assist with manufacturing processes, thereby increasing efficiency and productivity.

Computer-Assisted Software Engineering (CASE): The application of computer technology to systems development activities, techniques and methodologies. Sometimes referred to as "computer-aided systems engineering."

Connected Factory: A factory that utilizes the Industrial Internet of Things (IIoT) to effectively consolidate and manage real-time data from a range of physical systems and interacting devices within the factory. This is done in order for operations to achieve peak performance and to maximize efficiency and profits.

Consumer Telematics: In-vehicle consumer devices including GPS and advanced entertainment and information systems. Ford's Sync is an example of consumer telematics. See "Telematics."

Contract Manufacturing: A business arrangement whereby a company manufactures products that will be sold under the brand names of its client companies. For example, a large number of consumer electronics, such as laptop computers, are manufactured by contract manufacturers for leading brand-name computer companies such as Dell and Apple. Many other types of products, such as shoes and apparel, are made under contract manufacturing. Also see "Original Equipment Manufacturer (OEM)" and "Original Design Manufacturer (ODM)."

Contract Research Organization (CRO): An independent organization that contracts with a client to conduct part of the work on a study or research project. For example, drug and medical device makers frequently outsource clinical trials and other research work to CROs.

Core Competencies: A business's main area of capability.

Core Task: A task that does not represent a competitive advantage, such as human resources operations.

Cost Plus Contract: A contract that sets the contractor's compensation as a percentage of the total cost of labor and materials.

Critical Path Management: A critical path represents the series of tasks that must be completed in order to finish an entire project. Critical path management attempts to determine which tasks must be completed, in order of completion, by which dates so that a project may be completed on time.

Critical Task: A task that represents a competitive advantage, such as research and development.

CRO: See "Contract Research Organization (CRO)."

Cycle Time Reduction (CTR): The process of reducing cycle time with the intention of lowering costs or improving customer service.

Data Lake: A storage system or repository of structured and unstructured data, at any scale, in its natural format. This is usually a single set of all enterprise data, including raw copies of source system data and transformed data. It can be used for tasks such as reporting, visualization, analytics and machine learning.

Data Mining: Analyzing large sets of data in order to find patterns. Machine learning is often utilized.

Data Scientist: A professional responsible for collecting, analyzing and interpreting large amounts of data to identify ways to help a business improve operations or marketing, and gain a competitive edge.

Data Streaming: Processing data as it becomes available, in real time, instead of processing it after it has been stored in an database.

DDOS: See "Distributed Denial-of-Service (DDOS)."

Deep Learning: A subset of machine learning, deep learning helps automate predictive analytics by taking unstructured, unlabeled data and creating accurate predictive models. Often found in applications used in speech and image recognition.

Demand Chain: A similar concept to a supply chain, but with an emphasis on the end user.

Descriptive Analytics: The simplest form of data analytics. It transforms stored, historical data into summaries of insightful information. It answers, "What has happened in the past?"

Design Patent: A patent that may be granted by the U.S. Patent and Trademark Office to anyone who invents a new, original, and ornamental design for an article of manufacture.

Development: The phase of research and development (R&D) in which researchers attempt to create new products from the results of discoveries and applications created during basic and applied research.

Digital: The transmission of a signal by reducing all of its information to ones and zeros and then regrouping them at the reception end. Digital transmission vastly improves the carrying capacity of the spectrum while reducing noise and distortion of the transmission.

Digital Signal Processing (DSP): Technology that enables instruments and computers to understand a stream of data coming from a sensor, such as an accelerometer, digital camera, heat probe or seismic monitor.

Digital Transformation (DX): The implementation of digital technologies into as many areas of a business as reasonably possible Goals may include: to fundamentally change how the enterprise operates: how data is gathered and tracked: how innovation is launched: and how value is delivered to customers. The hoped-for result is to create new operating efficiencies and develop new revenue or profit opportunities, while better positioning the enterprise for the future. Also abbreviated as DX or DT.

Direct Broadcast Satellite (DBS): A high-powered satellite authorized to broadcast television programming directly to homes. Home subscribers use a dish and a converter to receive and translate the TV signal. An example is the DirecTV service. DBS operates in the 11.70- to 12.40-GHz range.

Disaster Recovery: A set of rules and procedures that allow a computer site to be put back in operation after a disaster has occurred. Moving backups off-site constitutes the minimum basic precaution for disaster recovery. The remote copy is used to recover data if the local storage is inaccessible after a disaster.

Disintermediate: A business or distribution model that bypasses the middleman in marketing or retailing. For example, a web site that enables end-consumers to purchase apparel direct from a designer or manufacturer, bypassing retail stores and traditional catalogs, is attempting to disintermediate the supply chain.

Disruptive: A new technology or business model that unexpectedly threatens to displace existing products or services. For example, the manner in which email has disrupted standard postal service. By some estimates, in order to be disruptive, a new service or product must provide most of the value of existing methods, and ideally even enhanced value, while reducing costs and/or speeding delivery.

Distributed Ledger Technology (DLT): A blockchain-enabled database of transactions. It can be shared across multiple sites or nodes. Any changes to the ledger are instantly copied to all participating sites. Also, see "Blockchain".

Distributed-Denial-of-Service (DDOS): An attack on computer systems, usually web servers. Hackers and cyber-criminals launch such attacks to bring down an organization's ability to serve its customers and employees through its online systems and web sites. (Also known as DDoS.)

DLT: See "Distributed Ledger Technology (DLT)."

DoF: See "Degree of Freedom."

DSP: See "Digital Signal Processing (DSP)."

DX: See "Digital Transformation (DX)."

Earnings Before Interest and Taxes (EBIT): An indicator of a company's financial performance calculated as revenue minus expenses excluding tax and interest. Also see "Net Income," "Net Operating Income" and "Earnings Before Interest, Taxes, Depreciations and Amortization (EBITDA)."

Earnings Before Interest, Taxes, Depreciation & Amortization (EBITDA): An indicator of a company's financial performance calculated as revenue minus expenses excluding taxes, interest, depreciation and amortization. It is a prime indicator of a company's potential to earn profits. Also, see "Net Income," "Net Operating Income" and "Earnings Before Interest and Taxes (EBIT)."

EBIT: See "Earnings Before Interest and Taxes (EBIT)."

EBITDA: See "Earnings Before Interest, Taxes, Depreciation & Amortization (EBITDA)."

Echo Boomers: See "Generation Y."

EDI: See "Electronic Data Interchange (EDI)."

Electronic Data Interchange (EDI): An accepted standard format for the exchange of data between various companies' networks. EDI allows for the transfer of e-mail as well as orders, invoices and other files from one company to another.

EMEA: The region comprised of Europe, the Middle East and Africa.

EMS: Electronics Manufacturing Services. See "Contract Manufacturing."

Engineer-to-Order (ETO): A term used to describe a product that requires unique design or significant customization, which is only designed and produced when a confirmed order or contract exists.

Enterprise Application: A major software tool intended to manage data over an extremely large corporate or government user base (e.g., SAP, Oracle).

Enterprise Resource Planning (ERP): An integrated information system that helps manage all aspects of a business, including accounting, ordering and human resources, typically across all locations of a major corporation or organization. ERP is considered to be a critical tool for management of large organizations. Suppliers of ERP tools include SAP and Oracle.

Environmental Audit: An independent assessment of a facility's compliance procedures, policies and controls. Many pollution prevention initiatives require an audit to determine where wastes may be reduced or eliminated or energy conserved.

ERP: See "Enterprise Resource Planning (ERP)."

EU: See "European Union (EU)."

EU Competence: The jurisdiction in which the European Union (EU) can take legal action.

European Community (EC): See "European Union (EU)."

European Union (EU): A consolidation of European countries (member states) functioning as one body to facilitate trade. Previously known as the European Community (EC). The EU has a unified currency, the Euro. See europa.eu.int.

Experience Curve: The idea that the more experienced a company is, the less it costs to design a project or product. The goal is generally considered to be a 25% cost reduction per doubling in production.

Expert Systems: A practical development of AI that requires creation of a knowledge base of facts and rules furnished by human experts and uses a defined set of rules to access this information in order to suggest solutions to problems. See "Artificial Intelligence (AI)."

Facilities Management: The management of a company's physical buildings and/or information systems on an outsourced basis.

Factory Automation: The use of systems, controls, computers and robotics to increase production while decreasing human action on the factory floor and in the warehouse. Also, see "Automation."

FASB: See "Financial Accounting Standards Board (FASB)."

FCC: See "Federal Communications Commission (FCC)."

FDA: See "Food and Drug Administration (FDA)."

Federal Communications Commission (FCC): The U.S. Government agency that regulates broadcast television and radio, as well as satellite transmission, telephony and all uses of radio spectrum.

Femtocell: A device used to boost performance of cell phones on a local basis, such as in a consumer's home or office. It utilizes nearby licensed wireless spectrum. The femtocell, in the form of a small box, routes wireless phone calls from a cell phone handset to the central office of a cellular service provider via a consumer's high speed Internet line.

Financial Accounting Standards Board (FASB): An independent organization that establishes the Generally Accepted Accounting Principles (GAAP).

Fixed Expenses: Costs that do not fluctuate in response to sales or inventory changes over time. Examples include rent fees and depreciation.

Fixed Wireless: Refers to the use of Wi-Fi, WiMAX or other wireless receivers that remain fixed in a stationary place, to provide Internet service.

Food and Drug Administration (FDA): The U.S. government agency responsible for the enforcement of the Federal Food, Drug and Cosmetic Act, ensuring industry compliance with laws regulating products in commerce. The FDA's mission is to protect the public from harm and encourage technological advances that hold the promise of benefiting society. www.fda.gov

Free Space Optics (FSO): A cost-effective alternative to fiber-optic broadband access, FSO uses lasers, or light pulses, to send packetized data in the terahertz spectrum range. Air, rather than fiber, is the transport medium.

GAAP: See "Generally Accepted Accounting Principles (GAAP)."

Gainsharing: A contract structure where both the customer and the service provider share financially in the value created through the relationship. One example is when a service provider receives a share of the savings it generates for its client.

Generally Accepted Accounting Principles (GAAP): A set of accounting standards administered by the Financial Accounting Standards Board (FASB) and enforced by the U.S. Security and Exchange Commission (SEC). GAAP is primarily used in the U.S.

Geofencing: The practice of setting virtual boundaries around a physical location and targeting mobile device users within those areas for a variety of purposes including search and rescue, advertising and social interaction.

Geostationary: A geosynchronous satellite angle with zero inclination, making a satellite appear to hover over one spot on the earth's equator.

Gigabyte: 1,024 megabytes.

Global Positioning System (GPS): A satellite system, originally designed by the U.S. Department of Defense for navigation purposes. Today, GPS is in wide use for consumer and business purposes, such as navigation for drivers, boaters and hikers. It utilizes satellites orbiting the earth at 10,900 miles to enable users to pinpoint precise locations using small, electronic wireless receivers.

Global Warming: An increase in the near-surface temperature of the Earth. Global warming has occurred in the distant past as the result of natural influences, but the term is most often used to refer to a theory that warming occurs as a result of increased use of hydrocarbon fuels by man. See "Climate Change (Greenhouse Effect)."

Globalization: The increased mobility of goods, services, labor, technology and capital throughout the world. Although globalization is not a new development, its pace has increased with the advent of new technologies.

GLP: See "Good Laboratory Practices (GLP)."

GMP: See "Good Manufacturing Practices (GMP)."

Good Laboratory Practices (GLP): A collection of regulations and guidelines to be used in laboratories where research is conducted on drugs, biologics or devices that are intended for submission to the FDA.

Good Manufacturing Practices (GMP): A collection of regulations and guidelines to be used in manufacturing drugs, biologics and medical devices.

Granularity: The description of the fine details of a business problem.

Grid Computing: A computer network where each computer's resources are shared with every other computer in the system. Processing power, memory and data storage are all community resources that can be can tapped into and leveraged for specific tasks.

Gross Domestic Product (GDP): The total value of a nation's output, income and expenditures produced with a nation's physical borders.

Gross National Product (GNP): A country's total output of goods and services from all forms of economic activity measured at market prices for one calendar year. It differs from Gross Domestic Product (GDP) in that GNP includes income from investments made in foreign nations.

Group of Eight (G8): The eight major industrial countries, including the United States, Japan, Germany, France, the United Kingdom, Italy, Russia and Canada, whose leaders meet at annual economic summits to coordinate economic policies. The group was formerly known as the G7, before Russia was admitted in June 2002.

H-1B Visa: In the United States, the H-1B is a nonimmigrant classification used by an alien of distinguished merit and ability who will be employed temporarily in a specialty occupation that requires theoretical and practical application of a body of specialized knowledge, along with at least a bachelor's degree or its equivalent.

Haptics: A technology in which a user of electronics, wireless devices and electronic games experiences unique sensations from a video game interface or a touchscreen, such as one might find on a smartphone. Advanced touchscreens using haptics can enable the user to feel the sensation of clicks on an icon, vibrations and other types of touch sensations.

Hot Spot: A location where access to the Internet is available via Wi-Fi.

Hybrid Cloud: A data strategy where some applications and data are moved to cloud-based systems, while highly sensitive data or certain functions are kept on client-owned systems.

I2OT: Industrial Internet of Things.

ICT: See "Information and Communication Technologies (ICT)."

IEEE: See "Institute of Electrical and Electronic Engineers (IEEE)."

IFRS: See "International Financials Reporting Standards (IFRS)."

Industrial IoT (IIoT): The use of Internet of Things (IoT) in manufacturing or industrial processes. Part of the Industry 4.0 trend, it incorporates machine learning and big data to harness sensor data, machine-to-machine (M2M) communication and automation technologies.

Industry Code: A descriptive code assigned to any company in order to group it with firms that operate in similar businesses. Common industry codes include the NAICS (North American Industrial Classification System) and the SIC (Standard Industrial Classification), both of which are standards widely used in America, as well as the International Standard Industrial Classification of all Economic Activities (ISIC), the Standard International Trade Classification established by the United Nations (SITC) and the General Industrial Classification of Economic Activities within the European Communities (NACE).

Information and Communication Technologies (ICT): A term used to describe the relationship between the myriad types of goods, services and networks that make up the global information and communications system. Sectors involved in ICT include landlines, data networks, the Internet, wireless communications, (including cellular and remote wireless sensors) and satellites.

Information Technology (IT): The systems, including hardware and software, that move and store voice, video and data via computers and telecommunications.

Infrastructure: 1) The equipment that comprises a system. 2) Public-use assets such as roads, bridges, water systems, sewers and other assets necessary for public accommodation and utilities. 3) The underlying base of a system or network. 4) Transportation and shipping support systems such as ports, airports and railways.

Infrastructure (Telecommunications): The entity made up of all the cable and equipment installed in the worldwide telecommunications market. Most of today's telecommunications infrastructure is connected by copper and fiber-optic cable, which represents a huge capital investment that telephone companies would like to continue to utilize in as many ways as possible.

Initial Public Offering (IPO): A company's first effort to sell its stock to investors (the public). Investors in an up-trending market eagerly seek stocks offered in many IPOs because the stocks of newly public companies that seem to have great promise may appreciate very rapidly in price, reaping great profits for those who were able to get the stock at the first offering. In the United States, IPOs are regulated by the SEC (U.S. Securities Exchange Commission) and by the state-level regulatory agencies of the states in which the IPO shares are offered.

Institute of Electrical and Electronic Engineers (IEEE): An organization that sets global technical standards and acts as an authority in technical areas including computer engineering, biomedical technology, telecommunications, electric power, aerospace and consumer electronics, among others. www.ieee.org.

Intellectual Property (IP): The exclusive ownership of original concepts, ideas, designs, engineering plans or other assets that are protected by law. Examples include items covered by trademarks, copyrights and patents. Items such as software, engineering plans, fashion designs and architectural designs, as well as games, books, songs and other entertainment items are among the many things that may be considered to be intellectual property. (Also, see "Patent.")

INTELSAT: The International Telecommunications Satellite Organization. INTELSAT operates a network of 20 satellites, primarily for international transmissions, and provides domestic services to some 40 countries.

Interconnectivity: The state or quality of being connected to other devices on a network.

International Financials Reporting Standards (IFRS): A set of accounting standards established by the International Accounting Standards Board (IASB) for the preparation of public financial statements. IFRS has been adopted by much of the world, including the European Union, Russia and Singapore.

International Telecommunications Union (ITU): The international body responsible for telephone and computer communications standards describing interface techniques and practices. These standards include those that define how a nation's telephone and data systems connect to the worldwide communications network.

Internet of Everything (IoE): A concept that extends the Internet of Things (IoT) emphasis on machine-to-machine (M2) communications. IoE describes a more complex system that also encompasses people and processes.

Internet of Things (IoT): A concept whereby individual objects, such as kitchen appliances, automobiles, manufacturing equipment, environmental sensors or air conditioners, are connected to the Internet. The objects must be able to identify themselves to other devices or to databases. The ultimate goals may include the collection and processing of data, the control of instruments and machinery, and eventually, a new level of synergies, artificial intelligence and operating efficiencies among the objects. The Internet of Things is often referred to as IoT. Related technologies and topics include RFID, remote wireless sensors, telecommunications and nanotechnology.

Internet Protocol Version 6 (IPv6): The next-generation of IP standard. IPv6 is intended to first work with, and eventually replace, IPv4. Version 6 will enable a vastly larger number of devices to each utilize one internet address (an IP address) at one time. Specifically, it will allow for 340 trillion, trillion, trillion addresses.

IoT: See "Internet of Things (IoT)."

IP: See "Intellectual Property (IP)."

IP Number/IP Address: A number or address with four parts that are separated by dots. Each machine on the Internet has its own IP (Internet protocol) number, which serves as an identifier.

IPv6: See "Internet Protocol Version 6 (IPv6)."

ISO 9000, 9001, 9002, 9003: Standards set by the International Organization for Standardization. ISO 9000, 9001, 9002 and 9003 are the highest quality certifications awarded to organizations that meet exacting standards in their operating practices and procedures.

IT: See "Information Technology (IT)."

Kaizen: A Japanese manufacturing process concept that is widely studied by the global automotive industry. It is a philosophy based on continuous improvement of the manufacturing and business process. Facets of Kaizen may include just-in-time delivery of components, zero defects, productivity enhancement and a customer-oriented mindset.

Kanban: From the Japanese word for "visual record," a just-in-time methodology, initially attributed to Toyota, whereby sub-assemblies are delivered to a product line at the time required in the appropriate number. Kanban has also come to refer to tag-like cards used to track flow along the product line.

Kbps: One thousand bits per second.

Kilobyte: One thousand (or 1,024) bytes.

Kinematics: A kind of mechanics focused on the motion of objects with no reference to what caused that motion such as force or mass.

LAC: An acronym for Latin America and the Caribbean.

Large-Scale Integration (LSI): The placement of thousands of electronic gates on a single chip. This makes the manufacture of powerful computers possible.

LDCs: See "Least Developed Countries (LDCs)."

Lean Manufacturing: See "Lean Production."

Lean Production: An enhancement of the mass production concept. Lean production, also known as lean manufacturing, involves optimizing the factory floor, design team, supply chain and other areas in order to manufacture a higher-quality product in less time, with less labor at less cost.

Least Developed Countries (LDCs): Nations determined by the U.N. Economic and Social Council to be the poorest and weakest members of the international community. There are currently 50 LDCs, of which 34 are in Africa, 15 are in Asia Pacific and the remaining one (Haiti) is in Latin America. The top 10 on the LDC list, in descending order from top to 10th, are Afghanistan, Angola, Bangladesh, Benin, Bhutan, Burkina Faso, Burundi, Cambodia, Cape Verde and the Central African Republic. Sixteen of the LDCs are also Landlocked Least Developed Countries (LLDCs) which present them with additional difficulties often due to the high cost of transporting trade goods. Eleven of the LDCs are Small Island Developing States (SIDS), which are often at risk of extreme weather phenomenon (hurricanes, typhoons, Tsunami): have fragile ecosystems: are often dependent on foreign energy sources: can have high disease rates for HIV/AIDS and malaria: and can have poor market access and trade terms.

Light Emitting Diode (LED): A small tube containing material that emits light when exposed to electricity. The color of the light depends upon the type of material. The LED was first developed in 1962 at the University of Illinois at Urbana-Champaign. LEDs are important to a wide variety of industries, from wireless telephone handsets to signage to displays for medical equipment, because they provide a very high quality of light with very low power requirements. They also have a very long useful life and produce very low heat output when. All of these characteristics are great improvements over a conventional incandescent bulb. Several advancements have been made in LED technology. See "Organic LED (OLED)," "Polymer Light Emitting Diode (PLED)," "Small Molecule Organic Light Emitting Diode (SMOLED)" and "Dendrimer."

LINUX: An open, free operating system that is shared readily with millions of users worldwide. These users continuously improve and add to the software's code. It can be used to operate computer networks and Internet appliances as well as servers and PCs.

Lithography: In the manufacture of semiconductors and MEMS (microelectromechanical systems), lithography refers to the transfer of a pattern of photosensitive material by exposing it to light or radiation. The photosensitive material changes physical properties when exposed to a source of radiation. Typically, a mask is employed that creates a desired pattern by blocking out light to some areas. Using this process to deposit materials on a substrate, integrated circuits can be manufactured.

LoRa: A long range, low power, wide-area wireless platform (such as NB-IoT and LTE Cat M1) utilized to build Internet of Things (IoT) networks in smart cities.

M2M: See "Machine-to-Machine (M2M)."

Machine Learning: The ability of a computer or computerized device to learn based on the results of previous actions or the analysis of a stream of related data. It is a vital branch of Artificial Intelligence that uses advanced software in order to identify patterns and make decisions or predictions.

Machine-to-Machine (M2M): Refers to communications from one device to another (or to a collection of devices). It is typically through wireless means such as Wi-Fi or cellular. Wireless sensor networks (WSNs) will be a major growth factor in M2M communications, in everything from factory automation to agriculture and transportation. In logistics and retailing, M2M can refer to the advanced use of RFID tags. See "Radio Frequency Identification (RFID)." The Internet of Things is based on the principle of M2M communications. Also, see "Internet of Things (IoT")."

MAN: See "Metropolitan Area Network (MAN)."

Mbps (Megabits per second): One million bits transmitted per second.

Megabytes: One million bytes, or 1,024 kilobytes.

Megahertz (MHz): A measure of frequency equal to 1 million Hertz.

MEMS: See "Microelectromechanical Systems (MEMS)."

Mesh Network: A network that uses multiple Wi-Fi repeaters or "nodes" to deploy a wireless Internet access network. Typically, a mesh network is operated by the users themselves. Each user installs a node at his or her locale, and plugs the node into his/her local Internet access, whether DSL, cable or satellite. Other users within the mesh can access all other nodes as needed, or as they travel about. A mesh network can provide access to an apartment complex, an office building, a campus or an entire city. Meraki is a leading node brand in this sector.

Metropolitan Area Network (MAN): A data and communications network that operates over metropolitan areas and recently has been expanded to nationwide and even worldwide connectivity of high-speed data networks. A MAN can carry video and data.

Microelectromechanical Systems (MEMS): Micron scale structures that transduce signals between electronic and mechanical forms. MEMS sometimes combine electronic sensors or switches with mechanical features such as gears, pumps or motors. A common use is the accelerometer found in electronic game playing machines and automobile airbags.

Microwave: Line-of sight, point-to-point transmission of signals at high frequency. Microwaves are used in data, voice and all other types of information transmission. The growth of fiber-optic networks has tended to curtail the growth and use of microwave relays.

MIMO: See "802.11n (MIMO)."

ML: Machine Learning. See "Machine Learning".

MU-MIMO: Mulit-User, Mutiple-Inut, Multiple-Output. See "802.11n (MIMO)."

NAICS: North American Industrial Classification System. See "Industry Code."

Nanotechnology: The science of designing, building or utilizing unique structures that are smaller than 100 nanometers (a nanometer is one billionth of a meter). This involves microscopic structures that are no larger than the width of some cell membranes.

National Telecommunications and Information Administration (NTIA): A unit of the Department of Commerce that addresses U.S. government telecommunications policy, standards setting and radio spectrum allocation. www.ntia.doc.gov.

NC: See "Numerical Control."

Net Operating Income: Net profit from operations, before allowances for payments due for income taxes and interest. Also see "Earnings Before Interest and Taxes (EBIT)" and "Earnings Before Interest, Taxes, Depreciation and Amortization (EBITDA)."

Node: Any single computer connected to a network or a junction of communications paths in a network.

Non-Durable Goods: Manufactured goods that have a relatively short life. Examples include food, chemicals, apparel and petroleum products. Also see "Durable Goods."

Numerical Control: Technology that automates machine tools through the use of computer generated operating commands, as opposed to manually controlled operation.

ODM: See "Original Design Manufacturer (ODM)."

OECD: See "Organisation for Economic Co-operation and Development (OECD)."

OEM: See "Original Equipment Manufacturer (OEM)."

OFDMA: Orthogonal Frequency-Division Multiple Access. See "802.11n (MIMO)."

OLED: See "Organic LED (OLED)."

Open Source (Open Standards): A software program for which the source code is openly available for modification and enhancement as various users and developers see fit. Open software is typically developed as a public collaboration and grows in usefulness over time. See "LINUX."

Optimum Lean Production: See "Lean Production."

Organic LED (OLED): A type of electronic display based on the use of organic materials that produce light when stimulated by electricity. Also see "Polymer," "Polymer Light Emitting Diode (PLED)," "Small Molecule Organic Light Emitting Diode (SMOLED)" and "Dendrimer."

Organisation for Economic Co-operation and Development (OECD): A group of more than 30 nations that are strongly committed to the market economy and democracy. Some of the OECD members include Japan, the U.S., Spain, Germany, Australia, Korea, the U.K., Canada and Mexico. Although not members, Estonia, Israel and Russia are invited to member talks: and Brazil, China, India, Indonesia and South Africa have enhanced engagement policies with the OECD. The Organisation provides statistics, as well as social and economic data: and researches social changes, including patterns in evolving fiscal policy, agriculture, technology, trade, the environment and other areas. It publishes over 250 titles annually: publishes a corporate magazine, the OECD Observer: has radio and TV studios: and has centers in Tokyo, Washington, D.C., Berlin and Mexico City that distributed the Organisation's work and organizes events.

Original Design Manufacturer (ODM): A contract manufacturer that offers complete, end-to-end design, engineering and manufacturing services. ODMs design and build products, such as consumer electronics, that client companies can then brand and sell as their own. For example, a large percentage of laptop computers, cell phones and PDAs are made by ODMs. Also see "Original Equipment Manufacturer (OEM)" and "Contract Manufacturing."

Original Equipment Manufacturer (OEM): 1) A company that manufactures a component (or a completed product) for sale to a customer that will integrate the component into a final product. The OEM's customer will put its own brand name on the end product and distribute or resell it to end users. 2) A firm that buys a component and then incorporates it into a final product, or buys a completed product and then resells it under the firm's own brand name. This usage is most often found in the computer industry, where OEM is sometimes used as a verb. Also see "Original Design Manufacturer (ODM)" and "Contract Manufacturing."

Passive Wi-Fi: An 802.11 wireless technology that requires dramatically less electric power than traditional Wi-Fi requires. This makes passive Wi-Fi ideal for widespread use in remote wireless sensor networks and other high-volume applications. This technology has wide applications in the Internet of Things where multitudes of remote data sensors needs the ability to gather and transmit information, independent of outside power supplies. Various methods are being developed for this technology, including the use of central power sources that can transmit electricity wirelessly to nearby sensors, as well as devices that can generate tiny amounts of power through changes in local temperature. Also see "Ambient Backscatter".

Patent: An intellectual property right granted by a national government to an inventor to exclude others from making, using, offering for sale, or selling the invention throughout that nation or importing the invention into the nation for a limited time in exchange for public disclosure of the invention when the patent is granted. In addition to national patenting agencies, such as the United States Patent and Trademark Office, and regional organizations such as the European Patent Office, there is a cooperative international patent organization, the World Intellectual Property Organization, or WIPO, established by the United Nations.

Peer-to-Peer Network: Refers to a connection between computers that creates equal status between the computers. P2P can be used in an office or home to create a simple computer network. However, P2P more commonly refers to networks of computers that share information online. For example, peer-to-peer music sharing networks enable one member to search the hard drives of other members to locate music files and then download those files.

Predictive Analytics: See “Analytics.”

Prescriptive Analysis: As a step taken after "predictive" analysis, Prescriptive Analysis answers the question, “What should we do?” It can recommend multiple course of action as well as the likely outcome of each course. (Also, see "Predictive Analysis".)

Proximity Network: Allows devices in close proximity to communicate with each other wirelessly. This is also called a near-me network (NAN).

Quality of Service (QoS): The improvement of the flow of broadband information on the Internet and other networks by raising the data flow level of certain routes and restricting it on others. QoS levels are supported on robust, high-bandwidth technologies such as 4G.

R&D: Research and development. Also see “Applied Research” and “Basic Research.”

Radio Frequency Identification (RFID): A technology that applies a special microchip-enabled tag to an individual item or piece of merchandise or inventory. RFID technology enables wireless, computerized tracking of that inventory item as it moves through the supply chain from factory to transport to warehouse to retail store or end user. Also known as radio tags.

Real Time: A system or software product specially designed to acquire, process, store and display large amounts of rapidly changing information almost instantaneously, with microsecond responses as changes occur.

Reengineering: The redesign of an object or process. This phrase is typically used to describe the complete reworking of a company's manufacturing, services or management structures.

Return on Investment (ROI): A measure used to determine the efficiency of an investment. It is calculated as (total gain from an investment, minus the cost of that investment), divided by (cost of the investment). ROI may be adjusted to reflect the average yearly return on an investment.

RFID: See “Radio Frequency Identification (RFID).”

Robotic Process Automation (RPA): A category of software that operates in a "robotic" manner to repeatedly complete basic tasks that might otherwise have been done by human workers. Examples include editing electronic files or forms and checking them for completeness or accuracy. This technology is being widely applied to back-office tasks in such departments as human resources, insurance claims and expense reimbursement. RPA has very broad implications for many types of office work.

Robotics: The use of machines (robots) operated by control systems and computers for the performance of repetitive, dangerous or highly-exacting tasks. Also, see “Automation.” Robots may be combined with artificial intelligence or other software features that enable the machine to learn through experience. Robots may work side-by-side with human workers.

Router: An electronic device that enables networks to communicate with each other. For example, the local area network (LAN) in an office connects to a router to give the LAN access to an Internet connection such as a T1 or DSL. Routers can be bundled with several added features, such as firewalls.

RPA: See "Robotic Process Automation (RPA)."

SaaS: See “Software as a Service (SaaS).”

Satellite Broadcasting: The use of Earth-orbiting satellites to transmit, over a wide area, TV, radio, telephony, video and other data in digitized format.

Scope Creep: The expansion of a project far beyond its initial bounds.

Sensor Fusion: A method of utilizing data from multiple unique sources (which may include digital sensors) to better understand the given state of an object or condition. The goal is to combine information from various sensors in order to increase the accuracy of the calculated outcome and improve performance of a system. For example, fusing data from GPS, LIDAR and cameras can provide a better understanding of the status of a self-driving vehicle. Sensor fusion is sometimes referred to as "data fusion" or "information fusion."

Sensornet: A wireless sensor network. See "Mesh Network."

Service Level Agreement (SLA): A detail in a contract between a service provider and the client. The agreement specifies the level of service that is expected during the service contract term. For example, computer or Internet service contracts generally stipulate a maximum amount of time that a system may be unusable.

Shared Services Center: Created when common business processes from several business units are combined in one location. Such services may include purchasing, human resources, accounting or other common day-to-day business needs.

SIC: Standard Industrial Classification. See "Industry Code."

Six Sigma: A quality enhancement strategy designed to reduce the number of products coming from a manufacturing plant that do not conform to specifications. Six Sigma states that no more than 3.4 defects per million parts is the goal of high-quality output. Motorola invented the system in the 1980s in order to enhance its competitive position against Japanese electronics manufacturers.

SLA: See "Service Level Agreement (SLA)."

Smart Dust: The use of vast quantities of self-powered, remote wireless sensors to gather local data and transmit it to a central database for predictive analytics purposes, and for monitoring of environmental, structural stress and other local conditions.

Smart Home: A home whose devices and systems have been connected to the Internet of Things (IoT) for control of systems such as lightning, air conditioning, locks and safety. Often controlled via mobile apps.

Software as a Service (SaaS): Refers to the practice of providing users with software applications that are hosted on remote servers and accessed via the Internet. Excellent examples include the CRM (Customer Relationship Management) software provided in SaaS format by Salesforce. An earlier technology that operated in a similar, but less sophisticated, manner was called ASP or Application Service Provider.

Subsidiary, Wholly-Owned: A company that is wholly controlled by another company through stock ownership.

Supply Chain: The complete set of suppliers of goods and services required for a company to operate its business. For example, a manufacturer's supply chain may include providers of raw materials, components, custom-made parts and packaging materials.

Supply Chain Management: The coordination of all supply chain activities. Also referred to as "SCM."

Supply Chain Operations Reference (SCOR): A model developed by the Supply-Chain Council that specifies top-level supply chain processes in five key steps.

SWOT: A popular acronym for Strengths, Weaknesses, Opportunities and Threats. It is a process used to analyze corporations, organizations and industries for strategic planning and risk analysis.

Technical Barriers to Trade (TBT): Instances when technical regulations and industrial standards differ from country to country, making free trade of goods difficult if not impossible.

Telecommunications: Systems and networks of hardware and software used to carry voice, video and/or data within buildings and between locations around the world. This includes telephone wires, satellite signals, wireless networks, fiber networks, Internet networks and related devices.

Telematics: The use of cellular or radio transmission to exchange information between an automobile or truck and a base data center or customer service center. In the trucking industry, telematics is used to provide a headquarters with information about the location and routing of a truck. Telematics can also be used to alert a central service office about the temperature, oil pressure and other vital statistics of a gas or diesel engine. In passenger automobiles, telematics may be used to provide emergency response during accidents or breakdowns. Such emergency response may occur automatically, for example, when an air bag inflates. GM's OnStar service is a well-known example of telematics services for passenger car owners. Consumer telematics may provide advanced information, location-based services and entertainment to passenger vehicles.

Total Quality Management (TQM): The management of an operation with the goal of producing a product with zero defects.

Trade Secrets: Proprietary formulas, research, manuals, methods of operation and concepts owned by a business. Generally trade secrets are carefully guarded by the owner and are shared only on a need-to-know basis.

Trademark (Trade Mark): A name or phrase that has been registered by a company or organization for its exclusive use. A "TM" indicates that a trademark has been applied for (or that the owner intends to protect the trademark) but is still pending, while ® indicates it has been processed and is legally upheld. A trademark may or may not include an accompanying, distinctive design or font for the word or phrase. Trademarks must be renewed on a regular basis with the appropriate regulatory authorities. In America, trademarks are registered with the U.S. Patent and Trademark Office. There are also cooperative, international trademark agreements and agencies.

UDDI: See "Universal Description, Discovery and Integration (UDDI)."

Ultrawideband (UWB): A means of low-power, limited-range wireless data transmission that takes advantage of bandwidth set aside by the FCC in 2002. UWB encodes signals in a dramatically different way, sending digital pulses in a relatively secure manner that will not interfere with other wireless systems that may be operating nearby. It has the potential to deliver very large amounts of data to a distance of about 230 feet, even through doors and other obstacles, and requires very little power. Speeds are scalable from approximately 100 Mbps to 2Gbps. UWB works on the 802.15.3 IEEE specification.

Universal Description, Discovery and Integration (UDDI): A vital protocol used in web services. UDDI enables businesses to create a standard description of their activities so that they can be searched for appropriately by automatic software tools.

Utility Patent: A utility patent may be granted by the U.S. Patent and Trademark Office to anyone who invents or discovers any new, useful, and non-obvious process, machine, article of manufacture, or composition of matter, or any new and useful improvement thereof.

V2X: See "Vehicle-to-Everything (V2X)."

Value Added Tax (VAT): A tax that imposes a levy on businesses at every stage of manufacturing based on the value it adds to a product. Each business in the supply chain pays its own VAT and is subsequently repaid by the next link down the chain: hence, a VAT is ultimately paid by the consumer, being the last link in the supply chain, making it comparable to a sales tax. Generally, VAT only applies to goods bought for consumption within a given country: export goods are exempt from VAT, and purchasers from other countries taking goods back home may apply for a VAT refund.

Vehicle-to-Everything (V2X): The digital connection of data between vehicles and other entities such as infrastructure systems, other vehicles, networks, pedestrians, devices or grids. V2X are WLAN-based or cellular-based, and can be used to increase road safety and traffic and energy efficiency.

Vertical Integration: A business model in which one company owns many (or all) of the means of production of the many goods that comprise its product line. For example, founder Henry Ford designed Ford Motor Company's early River Rogue plant so that coal, iron ore and other needed raw materials arrived at one end of the plant and were processed into steel, which was then converted on-site into finished components. At the final stage of the plant, completed automobiles were assembled.

Water Footprint: A measurement of the fresh water usage of a given activity (such as manufacturing or agriculture), organization or country. It is often used to describe the total annual usage of fresh water by all activities and all people in a nation.

Web 3.0: See “Semantic Web" and "Web3."

Web of Things: See “Internet of Things (IoT).”

Web3: Not to be confused with the Semantic Web (which has, from time-to-time in the past, been called Web 3.0), an attempt to restrain the overwhelming market share of internet activities held by a few giant platforms, such as Google and Facebook, and create a more distributed or decentralized internet. For example, consumers' personal data and identities might be held in blockchain format, directly controlled by each consumer, and readily reusable on-the-fly across any Web3 site or service. One goal would be greatly increased security of data. Also known as Web 3.0.

WFH: Work from home.

WiFi: See “Wi-Fi.”

Wi-Fi: Wireless Fidelity. Refers to 802.11 wireless network specifications. The 802.XX standards are set by the IEEE (Institute of Electrical and Electronics Engineers). Wi-Fi enables very high speed local networks in homes, businesses, factories, industrial and transportation infrastructure, public spaces and vehicles. Wi-Fi networks enable computing devices of all types to connect to each other and to the internet, including smartphones, laptops, desktops and tablet computers. In addition, Wi-Fi enables machine-to-machine (M2M) communication between devices, providing a backbone for the Internet of Things. These networks can be made reasonably secure when strong passwords are required and additional cybersecurity measures are in place. (Also, see 'Internet of Things".)

WiMAX: An advanced wireless standard with significant speed and distance capabilities, WiMAX is officially known as the 802.16 standard. Using microwave technologies, it has the theoretical potential to broadcast at distances up to 30 miles and speeds of up to 70 Mbps. The 802.XX standards are set by the IEEE (Institute of Electrical and Electronics Engineers).

Wireless: Transmission of voice, video or data by a cellular telephone or other wireless device, as opposed to landline, fiber or cable. It includes Bluetooth, Cellular, Wi-Fi, WiMAX and other local or long-distance wireless methods.

Wireless Access Protocol (WAP): A technology that enables the delivery of internet pages in a smaller format readable by screens on smartphones.

Wireless LAN (WLAN): A wireless local area network. WLANs frequently operate on 802.11-enabled equipment (Wi-Fi).

Wireless Sensor Network (WSN): Consists of a grouping of remote sensors that transmit data wirelessly to a receiver that is collecting data into a database. Special controls may alert the network's manager to changes in the environment, traffic or hazardous conditions. Long-term collection of data from remote sensors can be used to establish patterns and make predictions. The use of WSNs is growing rapidly, in such applications as environmental monitoring, agriculture, military intelligence, surveillance, factory automation, home automation and traffic control. (Also, see "Internet of Things".)

World Trade Organization (WTO): One of the only globally active international organizations dealing with the trade rules between nations. Its goal is to assist the free flow of trade goods, ensuring a smooth, predictable supply of goods to help raise the quality of life of member citizens. Members form consensus decisions that are then ratified by their respective parliaments. The WTO’s conflict resolution process generally emphasizes interpreting existing commitments and agreements, and discovers how to ensure trade policies to conform to those agreements, with the ultimate aim of avoiding military or political conflict.

WoT: Web of Things. See “Internet of Things.”

WPA: Wireless Protected Access. A basic security standard for wireless networking, including Wi-Fi.

WTO: See “World Trade Organization (WTO).”

Yottabyte: Unit of measure equal to one septillion, 10^24, bytes.

Z-Wave: A wireless mesh networking protocol popular in home automation. It competes with Zigbee.

CPSIA information can be obtained
at www.ICGtesting.com
Printed in the USA
LVHW060025060522
717194LV00006B/11